Critical Thinking in
Clinical Practice

Critical Thinking in Clinical Practice

Improving the Quality of Judgments and Decisions

Third Edition

Eileen Gambrill

John Wiley & Sons, Inc.

Published by John Wiley & Sons, Inc., Hoboken, New Jersey.
Published simultaneously in Canada.

This publication is designed to provide accurate and authoritative information in regard to the subject matter covered. It is sold with the understanding that the publisher is not engaged in rendering professional services. If legal, accounting, medical, psychological or any other expert assistance is required, the services of a competent professional person should be sought.

For general information on our other products and services please contact our Customer Care Department within the United States at (800) 762-2974, outside the United States at (317) 572-3993 or fax (317) 572-4002.

Wiley publishes in a variety of print and electronic formats and by print-on-demand. Some material included with standard print versions of this book may not be included in e-books or in print-on-demand. If this book refers to media such as a CD or DVD that is not included in the version you purchased, you may download this material at http://booksupport.wiley.com. For more information about Wiley products, visit www.wiley.com.

Library of Congress Cataloging-in-Publication Data:

Gambrill, Eileen D., 1934–
    Critical thinking in clinical practice: improving the quality of judgments and decisions / Eileen Gambrill. — 3rd ed.
p. ; cm.
    Includes bibliographical references and indexes.
    ISBN 978-0-470-90438-1 (pbk.: alk. paper)
    ISBN 978-1-118-21701-6 (ebk)
    ISBN 978-1-118-21703-0 (ebk)
    ISBN 978-1-118-21699-6 (ebk)
    I. Title.
    [DNLM: 1. Psychology, Clinical. 2. Counseling. 3. Decision Making. WM 105]
    616.89—dc23
                                                                                    2011

037264
Printed in the United States of America

10 9 8 7 6 5 4 3 2 1

In memory of all the Daisy Andersons

Contents

Preface

Critical Thinking in Clinical Practice is for clinicians who want to think more clearly about the decisions they make and the context in which they make them. This third edition describes related developments in evidence-based practice (EBP) and policy, and updates content throughout while maintaining classic and still-relevant past contributions that illustrate the continuity of clinical concerns and research threads. This book will be of value to all professionals who offer services to clients, including psychologists, psychiatrists, social workers, nurses, and counselors. The emphasis is on offering readers tools that can improve the accuracy of clinical judgments and related decisions. Surprisingly little attention is devoted in professional training programs to many sources of error that can lead clinicians astray. For example, little attention is given to informal fallacies that may result in questionable decisions, such as relying on tradition or what is popular to select practices and policies.

Readers are encouraged to learn about and recognize errors and to acquire strategies for minimizing avoidable ones. Clinical decision making is approached as a challenging process that can be improved by acquiring skills integral to evidence-based practice, such as posing well-formed questions that guide an efficient, effective search for practice- and policy-related research. Beliefs, attitudes, and interpersonal skills that influence the effectiveness with which available knowledge is used are reviewed. Some clinicians view clinical practice as an art, rejecting as irrelevant related research. However, research findings are available in many areas that can be put to good use, both at the individual level of practice and when making policy decisions. Critical thinking and evidence-informed practice are closely related; both reject authority as a guide (such as someone's status), both emphasize the importance of honoring ethical obligations such as informed consent, and both involve a spirit of inquiry.

DEVELOPMENT OF THIS BOOK

A number of influences led to the writing of the first edition of this book and remain pertinent today. One was the prevalence of common errors in thinking among clinicians.

Examples include making decisions based on small biased samples, not recognizing pseudo-explanations, and having a false sense of accuracy in predicting future events. Another was puzzlement about the success of colleagues who used weak rather than strong strategies when trying to influence others: Examples include using straw person arguments, misrepresenting positions, and begging the question. A third was the discovery of books such as *Straight and Crooked Thinking* (Thouless, 1974)—an engaging book describing a range of common errors as well as remedies. A fourth influence was research concerning problem solving, judgment, and decision making, including material describing decision making in case conferences as well as research and theory in the area of learning to be a critical thinker rather than a true believer.

What's New and What's Not Over the Past Years

Clinical practice remains an uncertain enterprise. Much remains unknown about what works best with which client toward what aim. Wide variations continue in how clinicians carry out their practice. The criteria that should be used to evaluate outcomes are in dispute. Mistakes are inevitable, even in the best of circumstances. However, even in uncertain areas such as clinical practice, some decisions are better than others. The percentage of those that are better can be increased by avoiding common sources of error. This is one area in which research has blossomed, and this third edition illustrates the variety and frequency of errors as well as related factors and strategies for minimizing them. The years since the publication of the second edition are a mix of progress and challenges. The Internet is a source of both accurate information as well as bogus claims and quackery. Progress includes continuing growth of the Cochrane and Campbell databases of systematic reviews, development of user-friendly tools to facilitate critical appraisal of different kinds of research, and increasing research regarding the relative contributions of particular interventions compared to nonspecific factors as these are related to outcome. There has been greater attention to pseudoscience and fads in the helping professions, as well as to harming in the name of helping and to flaws in traditional sources of knowledge dissemination such as peer-reviewed publications. Increasing attention has been given to ethical obligations of professionals—for example, involving clients as informed participants. All of these developments promise to enhance the quality of services provided to clients.

What Is New in This Edition

Additional attention is given in this new edition to developments over the past few years that highlight the importance of taking a broad view to understanding the helping professions and what can go wrong, and what remedies may contribute to enhancing quality of care. Increased attention is given to propaganda in the helping professions and related venues and the role of the biomedical-industrial complex in distributing this, including conflicts of interest between academic researchers and Big Pharma. Propaganda has grown by leaps and bounds, including its distribution via advertisements on the Internet and on our television screens. Disease mongering continues to grow—the creation of bogus risks and alleged health problems that are indeed in the normal range of variability of bodies, behaviors, and/or thoughts. Attention to these saps life of its joy, creates needless worry, encourages unnecessary treatment, and gets in the way of attending to real concerns. It is perhaps the very growth and the absurdity of some of the claims, along with the revelations of fraud and the play of special interests, that have resulted in a vigorous counterreaction in terms of greater attention to propaganda, harm, and fraud in the helping professions and to related conflicts of interest—including the creation of ways to decrease them. When parents are threatened with being reported to child protection services because they refuse to place their child on Ritalin, counterpressure is bound to occur, including formation of advocacy groups. Readers are encouraged to become familiar with the players in the biomedical-industrial complex who forward disease mongering, including public relations agencies employed by pharmaceutical companies. This creation of bogus problems renders the need for critical thinking ever more important both on the part of helping professionals and on the part of clients. Toward this end, this new edition also devotes more attention to development of decisions aids that can be used by professionals as well as by clients.

Attention to ignorance as well as knowledge is highlighted in this new edition. Those who write in the field of agnotology argue that it is just as important to study ignorance (e.g., kinds and uses) as it is to study knowledge. Content regarding evidence-based practice has been updated, including the greater ease of searching for answers via Google. Recent research concerning the relative contribution of specific interventions compared to nonspecific factors in helping (e.g., empathy) is included in this new edition as well as recent research findings concerning influences on the effectiveness of decisions made in team meetings. This new edition also includes valuable new websites such as DUETS—database of uncertainties regarding the effectiveness of interventions. Also included are websites that provide an alternative view to mainstream framing of personal problems as psychiatric in nature, such as the Alliance for Human Research Protection (http://www.ahrp.org). Douglas Walton's pragmatic theory of fallacies has been integrated into the discussion of fallacies, allowing us to see the relationship between different contexts and the use of fallacies. Additional attention has been devoted to reliance on authority as a basis for making decisions, including "the authority of the citation." New developments regarding intuitive and analytic reasoning are described in more detail (e.g., fast and frugal decision making). Greater attention is devoted to the influence of language on decisions in the helping professions—not only the labels we use, but what is not said.

OVERVIEW OF THE CHAPTERS

Chapter 1 describes the vital role of decision making in clinical practice, kinds of errors that may occur and their sources, as well as the importance of thinking critically about decisions. Hallmarks of critical thinking are reviewed, including related values, attitudes, and styles, and its integral association with evidence-based practice is emphasized. Barriers to making sound decisions are discussed, including social, economic, and political influences on the helping professions. Finally, the costs and benefits of critical thinking are reviewed.

Chapter 2 describes sources of influence on clinical decisions. Readers are encouraged to take a broad view of such influences—to consider the influence of political, social, and economic factors on what is defined as a personal or social problem, and what are considered suitable intervention options in relation to different kinds of problems. The influence of agency variables is highlighted; many clinicians either work in an agency or have contacts with agencies—perhaps through services that are contracted out. In addition, the helper-client relationship is discussed, as this may influence decisions, as well as psychological factors such as confirmation biases that may result in misleading clients because of premature acceptance of faulty assumptions.

Reasoning is at the heart of clinical decision making—forming hypotheses about presenting concerns, gathering data to evaluate the accuracy of different views, offering arguments for assumptions, and evaluating the quality of these arguments. Chapter 3 provides an overview of different kinds of reasons (for example, hot and cold); suggests helpful distinctions (for example, between facts and beliefs); and describes different kinds of arguments and explanations.

Chapter 4 discusses different views of knowledge and how to get it. Questionable criteria on which to base decisions, such as testimonials and popularity, are reviewed and contrasted with scientific criteria. The difference between pseudoscience and science is discussed. Readers are invited to review their personal epistemology. If we rely on questionable criteria to accept knowledge claims, clients may be harmed rather than helped. Thus, it is vital to review personal beliefs about knowledge and how to get it.

Chapter 5 discusses the influence of language and social-psychological persuasion strategies. The interview is the context in which most helping efforts are carried out, and language plays a crucial part in what transpires there. Sources of error related to language are described in this chapter, including bafflegab, use of emotional words, and conviction through repetition.

Rarely are clinicians trained in the various kinds of formal and informal fallacies that may occur in clinical practice and may compromise the quality of decisions. Informal and formal fallacies may involve overlooking, evading, or distorting facts. Although most clinicians may be familiar with some fallacies described in Chapter 6, they may not be familiar with others that may result in avoidable errors, such as inappropriate use of analogies and circular reasoning. Chapter 6 suggests how learning to identify and remedy fallacies can improve the quality of decisions.

Chapter 7 discusses the topics of classification, authority, and a pathological focus. Classification is inevitable in clinical practice. This chapter describes sources of error that may result from it, such as an incorrect classification of clients and incorrect intervention methods. Authority is singled out for special focus, including the authority of the citation, because it represents a key source of potential error in clinical practice. For example, clinicians may accept knowledge based on appeals to consensus or tradition. A pathological set also is singled out for attention, because of tendencies to focus on pathology and to ignore positive attributes of clients.

Chapter 8 highlights the importance of content and procedural knowledge (data that decrease uncertainty). Differences between experts and novices are reviewed, and the importance of active learning is emphasized. Different approaches to reviewing competencies are discussed, and the kind of problem-based learning emphasized in evidence-based practice is described.

Chapter 9 provides an overview of research in the areas of judgment, problem solving, and decision making of value to clinicians, including developments in naturalistic decision making. Structuring problems is a critical phase. Research highlights the importance of situation awareness and development of expertise based on corrective feedback. The uncertainty of problem solving is emphasized, and tools of value are suggested for decreasing common biases based on research on judgment and decision making.

Chapter 10 describes the origins of and process and philosophy of evidence-based practice. Evidence-based practice and policy are designed to facilitate well-informed, ethical decisions in a context of transparency and accountability. They suggest a way to handle the uncertainty in making decisions in an informed, ethical manner. Attention is devoted to developing tools required to do so, such as high-quality systematic reviews of practice-related research related to specific life-affecting decisions. Controversies regarding "What is evidence?" are discussed.

Chapter 11, "Posing Questions and Searching for Answers," offers detailed guidelines for preparing well-structured questions that guide an effective, efficient search for practice- and policy-related research findings. Questions that often arise, such as "What if the experts disagree?" and "Do research findings apply to my client?" are discussed, and common errors in each phase of the process of EBP are noted.

Chapter 12 offers guidelines for critically appraising different kinds of research, including qualitative reports. Common myths that hinder critical appraisal are discussed, such as "It is too difficult for me to learn" and "All research is equally sound." Sources of bias are reviewed, and questions to raise about all research are suggested. Guidelines are offered for critically appraising research related to different kinds of questions, including effectiveness questions as well as those related to description and identification of causes. Readers are referred to additional sources for further reading.

Chapter 13 describes options for collecting data. Sources of assessment data are described, as well as their advantages and disadvantages. Kinds of reliability and validity of concern in evaluating assessment measures are reviewed. Decisions in this stage influence those in later phases of working with clients. This chapter also discusses factors that influence what clinicians see and report, such as vividness, motivation, and insensitivity to sample size.

Clinicians make decisions about causal factors related to clients' concerns and desired outcomes. Chapter 14 reviews factors that influence selection of causes, such as similarity between effects and presumed causes and preferred practice theories, and offers guidelines to enhance the accuracy of causal assumptions. These include helpful rules of thumb, such as paying attention to sources of uncertainty and examining all four cells of a contingency table.

Clinical practice also involves making choices and predictions. Predictions are made about how clients will behave in the future and about the effectiveness of interventions. Chapter 15 reviews sources of error that may compromise accuracy of predictions and describes tools to increase accuracy, such as using natural frequencies rather than probabilities.

Interdisciplinary team meetings are another context in which life-affecting decisions are made. Tendencies that decrease the quality of decisions (such as the belief that all contributions are equally good, and confusion between the consistency and differential weight of signs) are noted in Chapter 16, and guidelines are provided for enhancing the quality of discussions. Reaching sound decisions in team meetings requires use of effective interpersonal skills for diplomatically raising vital questions.

Chapter 17 discusses personal obstacles that may get in the way of developing and using critical thinking skills. Examples include a disinterest in critical thinking, a preference for mystery over mastery, unrealistic expectations of success, failure to reflect on excuses used for lack of quality services, and a fear of discovering errors. Social anxiety may interfere with raising questions about dubious claims.

Guidelines for maintaining critical thinking skills and becoming a lifelong learner are suggested in Chapter 18. As in other areas, having a skill does not mean that it will be used; many influences may erode critical thinking skills.

PURPOSE OF THE BOOK

This book is not meant to be read at one sitting but is designed to be sampled over many readings. This will provide the reader with leisurely opportunities to catch errors that I no doubt have made in my thinking. Writing a book about critical thinking is a daunting prospect, given the inevitability of revealing crooked thinking. However, this book is written in the spirit that we all make errors and that the task is to recognize and correct them. It is important to note what this book attempts to do as well as what it does not do. This book does attempt to draw on a range of areas that are pertinent to critical thinking and evidence-based practice and to draw these together in a format that makes sense to clinicians and that can be used to enhance the quality of practice. It does not attempt to offer incisive reviews of the many fields that are touched on here as they relate to clinical decision making. The teaching of thinking is as old as philosophy itself, and entire domains of inquiry have been concerned with this subject. Material related to the area of clinical decision making lies in sociology, anthropology, psychology, medicine, rhetoric, philosophy, education, and popularized presentations of formal and informal fallacies, such as *Straight and Crooked Thinking* (Thouless, 1974). The potential arenas of relevant sources have been a challenge of manageability. Entire books could be (and have been) written on most of the topics discussed in this book. References are provided throughout the book to sources that offer more detail.

Strong differences of opinion exist about many of the topics discussed in this book, such as statistical versus clinical prediction and the most useful way to pursue knowledge, or even whether it can be gained. The sources of error described here, especially those resulting in confirmation of favored views, will encourage biased misreadings of some of the content. There has been a historical reluctance to make clinical assumptions explicit so that their accuracy can be carefully examined. Efforts in this direction, even though described with the utmost tentativeness, often have been greeted with negative reactions based on misreadings of content. Consider, for example, the ongoing discussion concerning the use of actuarial methods for making clinical decisions. Even though the advantages of such methods may be described in measured terms, positions may be distorted.

ACKNOWLEDGMENTS

I am indebted to the many authors of the excellent material from which I have drawn liberally. I thank Oxford University Press for its generosity in allowing me to reproduce material from my book *Social Work Practice: A Critical Thinker's Guide* (2006) that appears in Chapters 4, 10, 11, and 12. I wish to thank the participants of my workshops on making clinical decisions in the United States, Canada, Taiwan, and Great Britain who greeted this material with such enthusiasm and inspired me to continue work in this area. These workshops supported my impression over the years that most clinicians are open to examining their reasoning processes in an atmosphere of constructive inquiry linked to concerns about helping clients. I extend my thanks to reviewers of drafts of the first edition of this book, including William E. Henry and Gracia A. Alkema of Jossey-Bass, who were supportive yet critical in nudging the manuscript toward clarity and in considering the topic important. Warm thanks also to Tracey Belmont and Isabel Pratt for their enthusiastic support and encouragement regarding the second edition. I also thank Lisa Gebo and Rachel Livsey for their support for this third edition. I would like to extend my gratitude to two colleagues who reviewed this book and provided valuable feedback: Elizabeth K. Anthony, an assistant professor at Arizona State University, and Professor Bruce A. Thyer of Florida State University.

I thank the University of California at Berkeley for past research grants that facilitated preparation of this book, as well as the funders of the Hutto Patterson Chair in Child and Family Studies. I extend a special note of appreciation to Sharon Ikami for her word-processing support and consistent warmth and goodwill. And warm thanks to Gail Bigelow for her support and encouragement.

PART

I

Lay of the Land

1

The Need for Critical Thinking in Clinical Practice

Decision making is at the heart of clinical practice. You may have to decide how to assess a client's depression. What sources of information will you draw on and what criteria will you use to evaluate their accuracy? Will you rely on your intuition? Will you ask your client to complete the Beck Depression Inventory? Will you talk to family members and take a careful history? Will it help you to understand your client's depression if you provide a psychiatric diagnosis? Or you may have to decide how to help parents increase positive behaviors of their four-year-old child. What sources of information will you use? How can you locate valuable guidelines regarding the most effective methods? What criteria will you use to review the evidentiary status of a claim such as: "Attention-deficit/ hyperactivity disorder is due to a biochemical imbalance"? Think back to a client with whom you have worked. Which of the following 10 criteria did you use to make decisions (Gambrill & Gibbs, 2009)?

1. Your intuition (gut feeling) about what will be effective.
2. What you have heard from other professionals in informal exchanges.
3. Your experience with a few cases.
4. Your demonstrated track record of success based on data you have gathered systematically and regularly.
5. What fits your personal style.
6. What is usually offered at your agency.
7. Self-reports of other clients about what is helpful.
8. Results of controlled experimental studies (data that show that a method is helpful).
9. What you are most familiar with.
10. What you know by critically reading the professional literature.

In addition to complex decisions that involve collecting and integrating diverse sources of data, scores of smaller decisions are made in the course of each interview, including moment-to-moment decisions about how to respond. Options include questions, advice, reflections, interpretations, self-disclosures, and silence. Decisions are made about what outcomes to focus on, what information to gather, what intervention methods to use, and how to evaluate progress. The risks of different options must be evaluated, and probabilities must be estimated. Judgmental tasks include deciding on causes and making predictions. You may have to decide whether a child's injuries are a result of parental abuse or were caused by a fall (as reported by the mother). You will have to decide what criteria to use to make this decision and when you have enough material at hand. If a decision is made that the injuries were caused by the parent, a prediction must be made as to whether the parent is likely to abuse the child again. Errors that may occur include:

- Errors in description. (Example: Mrs. V. was abused as a child when she was not.)
- Errors in detecting the extent of covariation. (Example: All people who are abused as children abuse their own children.)
- Errors in assuming causal relationships. (Example: Being abused as a child always leads to abuse of one's own children.)
- Errors in prediction. (Example: Insight therapy will prevent this woman from abusing her child again when this is not true.)

The events of the past few years continue to illustrate the need for critical thinking in clinical practice. During these years there has been a continuing parade of revelations, including hiding of negative trials, hiding adverse effects of medications, creating bogus categories of illness, overmedicating young children and the elderly with antipsychotics, and related conflicts of interest. (See Gambrill, 2012a.) Academic researchers, including some heads of psychiatry departments at prestigious universities, have been shown to be in the pay of pharmaceutical companies while underreporting this income to their universities, sometimes by millions of dollars. Ioannidis (2005) argues that most research findings reported in the biomedical literature are false. Hiding alternative views is common, such as failure to describe a view of anxiety in social situations as a learned reaction created by a unique learning history and/or arousal threshold (Gambrill & Reiman, 2011). Anxiety in social situations is typically proclaimed to be a psychiatric disorder. Did you know that this "disorder" was created by Cohn and Wolfe, a public relations firm hired by a pharmaceutical company (Moynihan & Cassels, 2005)?

THE IMPORTANCE OF THINKING CRITICALLY ABOUT DECISIONS

Clinical practice allows a wide range of individual discretion: how to frame problems, what outcomes to pursue, when to stop collecting information, what risks to take, what criteria to use to select practice methods, and how to evaluate progress. The privacy of clinical practice (rarely is it observed by other clinicians) allows unique styles, which may or may not enhance the accuracy of decisions. Use of vague evaluation procedures may maintain styles that are not optimal. Clients may be harmed rather than helped if we do not think critically about the decisions we make. Are they well-reasoned? Are they informed by related research? Have we avoided being bamboozled into accepting bogus claims about the effectiveness of a method? As Karl Popper (1994) points out, "There are always many different opinions and conventions concerning any one problem or subject-matter. . . . This shows that they are not all true. For if they conflict, then at best only one of them can be true" (p. 39). The following 13 findings suggest that clinical decisions can be improved:

1. There are wide variations in practices (e.g., see Goodman, Brownlee, Chang, & Fisher, 2010).
2. Most services provided are of unknown effectiveness. There has been little rigorous critical appraisal of most variations in practices and policies in relation to their outcomes (e.g., do they do more good than harm?).
3. Clients are harmed as well as helped. Consider, for example, the death of a child in "rebirthing therapy" (Janofsky, 2001; see also Diaz & de Leon, 2002; Goulding, 2004; Moncrieff & Leo, 2010; Ofshe & Watters, 1994; Sharpe & Faden, 1998; Whitaker, 2010).
4. Intervention methods found to be harmful continue to be used (e.g., Petrosino, Turpin-Petrosino, & Buehler, 2003).
5. Assessment methods shown to be invalid continue to be used (e.g., Hunsley, Lee, & Wood, 2003; Thyer & Pignotti, in press).
6. Methods that have been found to be effective are often not offered to clients (e.g., Jacobson, Foxx, & Mulick, 2005).
7. There are large gaps between claims of effectiveness and evidence for such claims (Greenberg, 2009; Ioannidis, 2005).
8. Good intentions are relied on as indicators of good outcomes.
9. Journalists' exposés of avoidable harms are common.
10. Avoidable errors are common (e.g., DePanfilis, 2003; Kaufman, 2006).
11. Licensing and accreditation bodies such as the National Association of Social Workers (NASW) and the Council on Social Work Education rely on surrogates

of competence and quality of professional education, such as the diversity of faculty and size of faculty, their degrees, and their experience (Gambrill, 2002; Stoetz, Karger, & Carrilio, 2010).

12. Clients are typically not informed regarding the evidentiary status of recommended services (e.g., that there is no evidence that these are effective or do more good than harm; Braddock, Edwards, Hasenberg, Laidley, & Levinson, 1999; Cohen & Jacobs, 1998; Gottlieb, 2003).

13. There seems to be an inverse correlation between growth of the helping professions and problems solved.

The history of the helping professions shows that decisions made may do more harm than good. Consider the blinding of 10,000 babies by the standard practice of giving them oxygen at birth (Silverman, 1980). Scared Straight programs designed to decrease delinquency have been found to increase it (Petrosino, Turpin-Petrosino, & Buehler, 2003). Many clinicians carry out their practice with little or no effort to take advantage of practice-related research describing the evidentiary status of different interventions. Gaps between knowledge available and what was used were a key reason for the development of evidence-based practice and care (Gray, 2001a). The histories of the mental health industry, psychiatry, psychology, and social work are replete with the identification of false causes for personal troubles and social problems. Complex classification systems with no empirical status such as those based on physiognomy (facial type) and phrenology (skull formation) were popular, including the creation of metal phrenological hats to aid in diagnosis (Gamwell & Tomes, 1995; McCoy, 2000). (See Exhibit 1.1.)

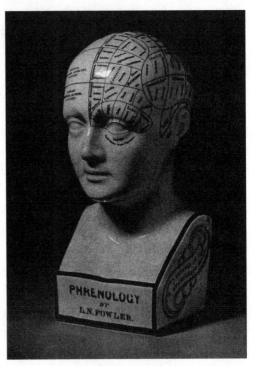

Exhibit 1.1 Phrenological head, by L. N. Fowler, mid-19th century, porcelain, 11 in. high. Courtesy Mrs. Erick T. Carlson. Reprinted from *Madness in America* (p. 86), by L. Gamwell and N. Tomes, 1995, Ithaca, NY: Cornell University Press.

Reviews of the history of psychiatry reveal a long list of intrusive interventions that can best be described as torture (e.g., Scull, 2005; Valenstein, 1986). Consider Darwin's chair, in which a patient was spun until bleeding from his or her nose. Water-based interventions were a popular strategy (see Exhibit 1.2). A former patient, Ebenezer

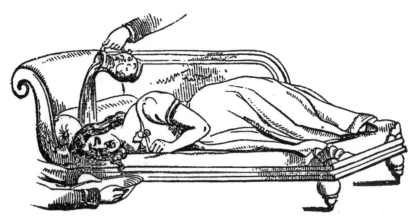

TREATMENT OF HYSTERIA

Exhibit 1.2 "Treatment of Hysteria." In Russell T. Trall, *Hydropathic Encyclopedia* (New York, NY: 1868). New York Academy of Medicine Library. Reprinted from *Madness in America* (p. 157), by L. Gamwell and N. Tomes, 1995, Ithaca, NY: Cornell University Press.

Haskell, said he witnessed the spread-eagle method while in Pennsylvania Hospital for the Insane. "A disorderly patient is stripped naked and thrown on his back, four men take hold of the limbs and stretch them out at right angles, then the doctor or some one of the attendants stands up on a chair or table and pours a number of buckets full of cold water on his face until life is nearly extinct, then the patient is removed to his dungeon cured of all diseases" (cited in Gamwell & Tomes, 1995, p. 63). The remedy of

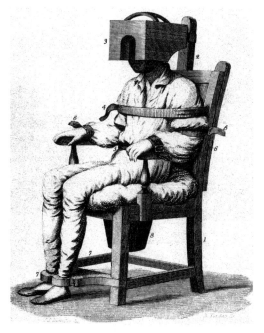

Exhibit 1.3 "The Tranquilizing Chair," in Benjamin Rush, "Observations on the Tranquilizer," The Philadelphia Medical Museum (1811). Archives of Pennsylvania Hospital, Philadelphia. Reprinted from *Madness in America* (p. 33), by L. Gamwell and N. Tomes, 1995, Ithaca, NY: Cornell University Press.

the tranquilizing chair is shown in Exhibit 1.3. Epidemiologists bring to our attention different rates of use of certain kinds of interventions, such as the higher number of hysterectomies in the United States as compared with Great Britain. Such differences may reflect actual need, or they may result from influences that conflict with client interests (such as an overabundance of surgeons or a tendency to think for clients rather than inform them fully and let them make their own decisions). Variations in services provided for the same concern were another reason for the development of evidence-based medicine and health care (Gray, 2001b; Wennberg, 2002).

The exposure of avoidable errors and harming in the name of helping is a topic of concern to journalists as well as investigators in a variety of fields, as illustrated by reports of children maltreated by their foster parents (e.g., DePanfilis, 2003; Pear, 2004); abuse of patients in facilities that purport to help them, such as group homes for the so-called mentally ill (e.g., Levy, 2003); and neglectful practices in hospitals and nursing homes (e.g., Delamothe, 2011; Mooney, 2011). Preventable medical error is responsible for 98,000 deaths per year and 99,000 deaths result from hospital-acquired infections per year. Exhibit 1.4 illustrates types of errors. What would be considered an error today might have been considered common (and good practice) years ago. For example, many people who entered a mental hospital in the 1950s and spent the rest of their lives there should not have been hospitalized in the first place. Many errors reflect a confirmatory bias (seeking only data that support favored views; Nickerson, 1998). Imagine that you are a community organizer in a low-income neighborhood and believe that new immigrants moving into the neighborhood are the least likely to

Exhibit 1.4 Examples of Errors in Medicine

Diagnostic
   Error or delay in diagnosis
   Failure to use indicated tests (e.g., use of outmoded tests)
   Failure to act on results of monitoring or testing

Treatment
   Error in the performance of a procedure or test
   Error in the dose or administration of a drug
   Avoidable delay in treatment or in taking action in relation to an abnormal test
   Inappropriate (not indicated) care

Preventive
   Failure to provide preventative treatment
   Inadequate monitoring or follow-up

Other
   Failure of communication (e.g. with team members)
   Equipment failure (e.g., not calibrated adequately)
   Other system failure (e.g., in training)

Source: From "Preventing Medical Injury," by L. Leape, A. G. Lawthers, T. A. Brennan, et al., 1993, *Qualitative Review Bulletin, 19*(5), pp. 144–149. Reprinted with permission.

become active in community advocacy efforts. Because of this belief, you may concentrate your attention on long-term residents. As a result, new resident immigrants are ignored, with the consequence that they are unlikely to become involved. This will strengthen your original belief.

The very nature of clinical practice leaves room for many sources of error. Decisions must be made in a context of uncertainty; the criteria on which decisions should be made are in dispute, and empirical data about the effectiveness of different intervention options are often lacking. Clients seek relief from suffering, and professionals hope to offer it; there is a pressure from both sides to view proposed options in a rosy light. Some errors result from a lack of information about how to help clients. Empirical knowledge related to clinical practice is fragmentary, and theory must be used to fill in the gaps. Other errors result from ignorance on the part of individual clinicians—that is, knowledge (defined here as information and procedural know-how that reduce or reveal uncertainty) is available but is not used. This lack of knowledge and skill may be due to inexperience or inadequate training. Errors also result from lack of familiarity with political, economic, and social influences on professions such as psychiatry, psychology, and social work (e.g., Cohen & Timimi, 2008). The interpersonal context within which counseling occurs offers many potential opportunities for mutual influence that may have beneficial or dysfunctional effects, as described in Chapter 2. Errors may occur because of personal characteristics of the clinician, such as excessive need for approval.

Avoidable errors may result in (1) failing to offer help that could be provided and is desired by clients, (2) forcing clients to accept practices they do not want, (3) offering help that is not needed, or (4) using procedures that aggravate rather than alleviate client concerns (that is, procedures that result in iatrogenic effects; e.g., Sharpe & Faden, 1998). Such errors may occur in all phases of clinical practice: assessment, intervention, and evaluation. Errors may occur during assessment by overlooking important data, using invalid measures, or attending to irrelevant data; during intervention by using ineffective methods; and during evaluation by using inaccurate indicators of progress. Reliance on irrelevant or inaccurate sources of data during assessment may result in incorrect and irrelevant accounts of client concerns and recommendation of ineffective or harmful methods. Important factors may not be noticed. For example, a clinician may overlook the role of physiological factors in depression. Depression is a common side effect of birth control pills and is also related to hormonal changes among middle-aged women. Failure to consider physical causes may result in inappropriate decisions. Failure to seek information about the evidentiary status of methods may result in use of an ineffective method. We may fail to recognize important cues or attend to irrelevant content. Errors may result from reliance on questionable criteria such as anecdotal experience to evaluate the accuracy of claims, as discussed in Chapter 4.

Given the role of decision making in clinical practice and the variety of factors that influence the quality of decisions, it is surprising that more attention is not devoted to this content in professional training. Meehl's book *Clinical Versus Statistical Prediction* appeared in 1954. The classic "Why I Do Not Attend Case Conferences" (Meehl, 1973) identifies errors and tendencies in groups that dilute the quality of decisions. The influence of illusory correlations on clinical observation was explored in the late 1960s (e.g., see Chapman, 1967; Chapman & Chapman, 1967, 1969). The tendency of clinicians to attribute problems to the person and overlook the role of environmental factors has been a topic of interest for some time (Rosenhan, 1973). Although students in professional education programs learn to attend to some sources of error (such as factors that influence reliability and validity) and are cautioned to avoid mistaking correlation for causation, they are not exposed to the range of formal and informal fallacies described in this book. Nor are they given information about conditions that encourage these fallacies and that increase the likelihood that their influence will slip by unnoticed. Students may not be exposed to the influential role of the biomedical industrial complex, including biological psychiatry, in framing problems and remedies (e.g., see Boyle, 2002; Brody, 2007; Carlat, 2010; Clarke, Mamo, Fosket, Fishman, & Shim, 2010; Szasz, 1994) or to critiques of psychological models (Illouz, 2008). Related literature shows that labeling attributes or actions as symptoms of psychopathology (deviations from the normal) is intimately associated with political and economic concerns and social conventions; therapists function as "moral managers" (Sedgwick, 1982, pp. 141, 147). They may not be exposed to critiques of prevalence rates such as the assertion that 46% of adults met criteria of the American Psychiatric Association (APA) for having had at least one mental illness in their lives.

Although the strategies we use to make decisions may often result in sound judgments, the task here is to identify ways in which they are not correctly used, so that errors can be minimized. Judgmental strategies are not necessarily used consciously, which is another reason it is helpful to be familiar with them. Indeed, two of the three routes to information lie outside of our awareness: perception and automatic associations. However, familiarity with sources of error is not enough. If this were true, certain kinds of errors would not recur in clinical practice. For example, many writers, both past and present, have argued that mental health professionals are too focused on pathology, that stereotypes interfere with making balanced decisions that reflect what a client can do as well as what the client cannot do (e.g., see Hobbs, 1975). However, some clinicians continue to focus on individual pathology, neglect client assets, and overlook environmental causes of personal troubles. Decreasing such errors requires a systemic approach, including attention to agency culture and climate as discussed in Chapter 9.

HALLMARKS OF CRITICAL THINKING

The term *reflection* is popular. But as Steven Brookfield notes, "Reflection is not by definition critical" (1995, p. 8). Critical thinking is a unique kind of purposeful thinking in which we use standards such as clarity and fairness. It involves the careful examination and evaluation of beliefs and actions in order to arrive at well-reasoned decisions. It is:

- Clear versus unclear.
- Precise versus imprecise.
- Specific versus vague.
- Accurate versus inaccurate.
- Relevant versus irrelevant.
- Consistent versus inconsistent.
- Logical versus illogical.
- Deep versus shallow.
- Complete versus incomplete.
- Significant versus trivial.
- Adequate (for purpose) versus inadequate.
- Fair versus biased or one-sided. (Paul, 1993, p. 63)

Both critical thinking and evidence-based practice encourage asking questions designed to make the invisible visible. Problems may remain unsolved because we rely on questionable criteria to evaluate claims about what is accurate, such as tradition, popularity, or authority. Consider a claim that recovered memory therapy works. Too often, the questions that should be asked to reveal the evidentiary status of a claim are not asked, such as: "What is the source?" "The method works for what?" "What kind of research was conducted to test this claim?" "Could such research rigorously test the claim?" "Has anyone been harmed by this method?" This illustrates the difference between propaganda and critical thinking. In the former, strategies such as censoring (not mentioning) alternative well-argued views and contradictory evidence are used.

Critical thinking involves clearly describing and carefully evaluating claims and arguments, no matter how cherished, and considering alternative views. This means paying attention to the process of reasoning (how we think), not just the product. Critical thinking encourages us to examine the context in which personal and social problems occur (to connect private troubles with public issues; Mills, 1959; Prilleltensky, Prilleltensky, & Voorhees, 2008); to view questions from different points of view; to identify and question our assumptions; and to consider the possible consequences of different beliefs or actions. It requires clarity rather than vagueness. "One cannot tell truth from falsity, one cannot tell an adequate answer to a problem from an irrelevant one,

one cannot tell good ideas from trite ones—unless they are presented with sufficient clarity" (Popper, 1994, p. 71).

Critical Thinking Is Integral to Evidence-Based Practice

Critical thinking knowledge, skills, and values are integral to evidence-based practice (EBP). Critical thinking, evidence-based practice, and scientific reasoning are closely related. All use reasoning for a purpose (i.e., to solve problems), relying on standards such as clarity, relevance, and accuracy. All regard criticism (self-correction) as essential to forward understanding; all encourage us to challenge our assumptions, consider well-argued opposing views, and check our reasoning for errors. All are antiauthoritarian. Critical appraisal skills are needed to accurately describe the extent to which a given research method can rigorously test a given practice or policy question, and many tools have been developed to facilitate this task, as described in Chapter 12. Critical thinking can protect us from being bamboozled and misled by deceptive descriptions of research and advertisements, for example for drugs. Consider the examples that follow. Each makes a claim concerning the effectiveness of a practice method. Are they true? What questions would you ask to evaluate the accuracy of these claims? How would you search for related research findings? Is there a high-quality review of research related to each claim?

- Eye movement desensitization is effective in decreasing anxiety. (Is it?)
- "Four hours a month can keep a kid off drugs forever. Be a mentor" (*New York Times*, December 31, 2002, p. A15; Partnership for a Drug-Free America, www. drugfreedomamerica.org). (Can it?)
- Anatomically detailed dolls can be used to accurately identify children who have been sexually abused. (Can they?)

Both critical thinking and EBP value clarity over obscurity, accuracy over inaccuracy, deep over superficial analysis, and fair-minded over deceptive practices. Both value transparency (honesty) concerning what is done to what effect, including candid description of lack of knowledge (uncertainty and ignorance). Consider the statement by the editor of *BMJ* (formerly the *British Medical Journal*):

The history of medicine is mostly a history of ineffective and often dangerous treatments. . . . Unfortunately there is still no evidence to support most diagnostic methods and treatments. Either the research hasn't been done or it is of too poor a quality to be useful. (Smith, 2003, p. 1307)

Material referred to as "evidence-based" reflects critical thinking values, knowledge, and skills to different degrees, ranging from a close relationship to little overlap, as illustrated by use of the term *evidence-based* without the substance (e.g., misrepresenting the philosophy and evolving technology of EBP, inflated claims of effectiveness, and not involving clients as informed participants; Gambrill, 2011).

Related Values, Attitudes, and Styles

Critical thinking is independent thinking—thinking for yourself. Critical thinkers question what others view as self-evident. They ask:

- Is this claim accurate? Have critical tests been performed? If so, were they relatively free of bias? Have the results been replicated? How representative were the samples used?
- Who presented it as true? How reliable are these sources?
- Are vested interests involved?
- Are the facts presented correct?
- Have any facts been omitted?
- Are there alternative well-argued points of view?

Critical thinkers are skeptics rather than believers. That is, they are neither gullible (believing anything people say, especially if it agrees with their own views) or cynical (believing nothing and having a negative outlook on life). This was illustrated by Susan Blackmore in a keynote address at the 1991 annual meeting of the Committee for the Scientific Investigation of Claims of the Paranormal (CSICOP) when she presented what she described as her favorite slide (a question mark) between slides of a sheep (illustrating gullibility) and a goat (illustrating cynicism). Cynics look only for faults. They have a contemptuous distrust of all knowledge. Skeptics (critical thinkers) value truth and seek approximations to it through critical discussion and the testing of theories. Criticism is viewed as essential to forward understanding.

Intellectual traits integral to critical thinking, suggested by Richard Paul, are shown in Exhibit 1.5. Critical thinking involves using related knowledge and skills in everyday life and acting on the results (Paul, 1993). It requires flexibility and a keen interest in discovering mistakes in our thinking. Truth (accuracy) is valued over winning or social approval. Values and attitudes related to critical thinking include open-mindedness, an interest in and respect for the opinion of others, a desire to be well informed, a tendency to think before acting, and curiosity. It means being fair-minded, that is, accurately describing opposing views and critiquing both preferred and disliked

Exhibit 1.5 Examples of Valuable Intellectual Traits

Intellectual autonomy: Analyzing and evaluating beliefs on the basis of reason and evidence.

Intellectual civility: Taking others seriously as thinkers, treating them as intellectual equals, attending to their views.

Intellectual confidence in reason: Confidence that in the long run our own higher interests and those of humankind will best be served by giving the freest play to reason—by encouraging people to come to their conclusions through a process of developing their own reasoning skills; to form rational viewpoints, draw reasonable conclusions, persuade each other by reason, and become reasonable people despite the many obstacles to doing so. Confidence in reason is developed through solving problems though reason, using reason to persuade, and being persuaded by reason. It is undermined when we are expected to perform tasks without understanding why, or to accept beliefs on the sole basis of authority or social pressure.

Intellectual courage: Critically assessing viewpoints regardless of negative reactions. It takes courage to tolerate ambiguity and to face ignorance and prejudice in our own thinking. The penalties for nonconformity are often severe.

Intellectual curiosity: An interest in deeply understanding, figuring things out, and learning.

Intellectual discipline: Thinking guided by intellectual standards (e.g., clarity and relevance). Undisciplined thinkers neither known or care when they come to unwarranted conclusions, confuse distinct ideas, or ignore pertinent evidence. It takes discipline to keep focused on the intellectual task at hand; to locate and carefully assess evidence; to systematically analyze and address questions and problems; and to honor standards of clarity, precision, completeness, and consistency.

Intellectual empathy: Putting ourselves in the place of others to genuinely understand them and recognize our egocentric tendency to identify truth with our views. Indicators include accurately presenting the viewpoints and reasoning from assumptions other than our own.

Intellectual humility: Awareness of the limits of our knowledge; sensitivity to bias, prejudice, and limitations of one's viewpoint. No one should claim more than he or she actually knows. Lack of pretentiousness and conceit, combined with insight into the strengths and weaknesses of the logical foundations of one's views.

Intellectual integrity: Honoring the same standards of evidence to which we hold others, practicing what we advocate, and admitting discrepancies and inconsistencies in our own thought and action.

Intellectual perseverance: The pursuit of accuracy despite difficulties, obstacles, and frustration; adherence to rational principles despite irrational opposition of others: recognizing the need to struggle with confusion and unsettled questions to pursue understanding. This trait is undermined when others provide the answers or do our thinking for us.

Source: Adapted from *Critical Thinking: What Every Person Needs to Survive in a Rapidly Changing World* (Rev. 3rd ed., pp. 470–472), by R. Paul, 1993; Foundation for Critical Thinking. www.criticalthinking.org. Reprinted with permission.

views using the same rigorous standards. Critical thinking discourages arrogance, the assumption that we know better than others or that our beliefs should not be subject to critical evaluation. As Popper emphasized, ". . . in our infinite ignorance we are all equal" (Popper, 1992, p. 50). These attitudes reflect a belief in and respect for the intrinsic worth of all human beings, for valuing learning and truth without self-interest, and a respect for opinions that differ from one's own (Nickerson, 1988–1989, p. 507). They also highlight the role of affective components, such as empathy for others and a tolerance for ambiguity and differences of opinion. Critical reflection stresses the value of self-criticism. It prompts questions such as: "Could I be wrong?"

"Have I considered alternative views?" "Do I have sound reasons to believe that this plan will help this client?" (See also Paul & Elder, 2004.)

Related Skills and Knowledge

Similar kinds of knowledge and skills are of value in problem solving and decision making, including accurately weighing the quality of evidence and arguments, identifying assumptions, and recognizing contradictions. Examples of critical thinking skills are (e.g., see Ennis, 1987; Paul, 1993):

- Clarify problems.
- Identify significant similarities and differences.
- Recognize contradictions and inconsistencies.
- Refine generalizations and avoid oversimplifications.
- Analyze or evaluate arguments, interpretations, beliefs, or theories.
- Identify unstated assumptions.
- Clarify and analyze the meaning of words or phrases.
- Use sound criteria for evaluation.
- Clarify values and standards.
- Detect bias.
- Distinguish relevant from irrelevant questions, data, claims, or reasons.
- Evaluate the accuracy of different sources of information.
- Compare analogous situations; transfer insights to new contexts.
- Make well-reasoned inferences and predictions.
- Compare and contrast ideals with actual practice.
- Discover and accurately evaluate the implications and consequences of a proposed action.
- Evaluate one's own reasoning process (metacognitive skills).
- Raise and pursue significant questions.
- Make interdisciplinary connections.
- Analyze and evaluate actions or policies.

We often fail to solve problems not because we lack intelligence, but because we fall into intelligence traps such as jumping to conclusions. This highlights the value of acquiring strategies that avoid these pitfalls in thinking. In addition to content knowledge, we need performance skills. For example, being aware of common errors in observing interaction between clients and significant others (e.g., students and teachers) will not be useful without the skills to avoid them (see Chapter 13). Critical thinking skills are not a substitute for problem-related knowledge. For example, you may need specialized knowledge to evaluate the plausibility of premises related to an argument. Consider the following example:

- Depression always has a psychological cause.
- Mr. Draper is depressed.
- Therefore the cause of Mr. Draper's depression is psychological in origin.

Even though the logic of this argument is sound, the conclusion may be false; the cause of Mr. Draper's depression could be physiological. The more information that is available about a subject that can decrease or reveal uncertainty about what decision is best, the more important it is to be familiar with this knowledge. Taking advantage of practice-related research findings is a hallmark of evidence-based practice.

Nickerson (1986b) suggests that self-knowledge is one of the three forms of knowledge central to critical thinking, in addition to knowledge of content related to a topic and critical thinking skills. Self-knowledge includes awareness of our style of thinking (e.g., the strategies we use) and its flaws, such as stereotypes that bias what we see and inaccurate (inflated) assessment of our competencies (Dunning, Heath, & Suls, 2004). Without self-knowledge, content and performance knowledge may remain unused. Three of the nine basic building blocks of reasoning suggested by Paul (1993) concern background beliefs that influence how we approach problems (ideas and concepts drawn on, whatever is taken for granted, and the point of view in which one's thinking is embedded).

BARRIERS TO MAKING SOUND JUDGMENTS

Judgments and decisions must be made in the face of uncertainty; even if all could be known, typically not enough time would be available to know all, nor may knowing all be needed to solve problems. The judgments that must be made are difficult ones, requiring distinctions between causes and secondary effects, problems and the results of attempted solutions, personal and environmental contributions to presenting complaints, and findings and evidence (links between clinical assumptions and findings). Problems that confront clients (e.g., lack of housing or day care) are often difficult ones that challenge the most skilled of helpers. Rarely is all relevant information available, and it is difficult to integrate different kinds of data. Knowledge may be available but not used. Physicians usually work in a state of uncertainty about the true state of the patient. They can only estimate the probability that a client has a certain illness. Uncertainty may concern: (1) the nature of the problem, (2) the outcomes desired, (3) what is needed to attain valued outcomes, (4) the likelihood of attaining outcomes, and (5) measures that will best reflect degree of success. Information about options may be missing or unreliable, and accurate estimates of the probability that different alternatives will result in desired outcomes may be unknown. It may be assumed that because there is uncertainty, there is no difference between the different degrees to which a claim has been critically appraised.

Even when empirical information is available, this knowledge is usually in the form of general principles that do not allow specific predictions about individuals (Dawes, 1994a). For example, many convicted rapists rape again when released from prison; however, this does not allow you to accurately predict whether a particular person will rape again if released. You can only appeal to the general information (see discussion of expert testimony in Chapter 13). Problems may have a variety of causes and potential solutions. The criteria on which decisions should be based are in dispute, and empirical data about the effectiveness of different options are often lacking. A desire to avoid uncertainty is a source of error. Yet another barrier is the effort required to make sound judgments. There are many pressures on clinicians to act more certain than they are, including the rhetoric of professional organizations that oversells the feats of clinicians, clients who seek more certainty than is possible, colleagues who make exaggerated claims of certainty, and journal articles that misrepresent findings (Doust & Del Mar, 2004). Such pressures encourage our tendency to be overconfident in the accuracy of our views (Baron, 2000). A reluctance to consider errors as inevitable may result in overlooking uncertainty. We work under environmental constraints such as time pressures. Preferences may change in the very process of being asked about them.

Some barriers, such as selective perception, are common to all judgmental tasks. Others, such as the lack of agreed-on criteria for evaluating the accuracy of decisions, are more problematic in clinical contexts than in the hard sciences or in activities such as car repair. Our perception is selective; we do not necessarily see what is there to be seen (see Chapter 9). Errors may occur during perception and when thinking about what we see. The former type of errors may be more difficult to alter because of their automatic nature. We may process data in a sequential manner, although a network or web approach to associations between variables will result in more accurate judgments. Although "fast and frugal" heuristics used to simplify judgmental tasks and decrease effort may often work well in making accurate judgments, at other times they may not. (See Chapter 9.) Our memories may not be accurate. Data that may decrease uncertainty may not be available. Because our beliefs are often implicit rather than explicit, it is often difficult to discover whether beliefs are compatible with one another. Lack of knowledge and interfering attitudes such as fear of failure and inflated self-assessments (for example, an unjustified belief in one's background knowledge) may limit success (see Chapter 17). We are often "unskilled and unaware of it" (Dunning, Heath, & Suls, 2004; Kruger & Dunning, 1999).

Unlike in medical practice in which there are signs (e.g., temperature reading) as well as symptoms (feeling hot), there are often no agreed-on criteria against which to check the accuracy of assumptions in clinical practice in psychology, social work, and psychiatry. The reports of a pathologist may verify clinical assumptions, although here, too, there is more disagreement than we recognize (Welch, 2004). Clients may not and probably do not know when an avoidable error occurs, since they usually are not informed about the potential risks and benefits of different assessment, intervention, and evaluation options (Braddock, et al., 1999). They may not be aware that methods suggested are not those that have been found to be most effective and offer little potential for attaining outcomes they value.

Economic and political interests influence decisions in the helping professions. Clinicians may not be aware of the influence of the biomedical-industrial complex in creating bogus problems and selling methods that do more harm than good (Angell, 2004; Clarke et al., 2010). The context in which decisions are made influences their soundness. (See Chapter 2.) These differ in how conducive they are to learning and critical thinking. Hogarth (2001) uses the term *wicked* to refer to environments that impede learning from experience. Critical questions regarding a view may result in ad hominem attacks rather than reasoned discussion (e.g., Gresham & MacMillan, 1997). Because many clinical tasks involve the same kinds of judgments made in everyday life, replacement of research-informed views by unsupported hunches is especially easy. For most clinicians, "practice theory" is probably a mix of common knowledge, hunches, and scientific knowledge (Bromley, 1986, p. 219). There are many application challenges, such as gaining timely access to research findings related to important questions. Indeed, a key aim of evidence-based practice is addressing these application challenges.

Lack of understanding of and misrepresentation of science may result in rejection of critical appraisal of claims of knowledge. Some confuse this with scientism, "the belief that science knows or will soon know all the answers, and it has the corrupting smugness of any system of opinions which contains its own antidote to disbelief" (Medawar, 1984, p. 60). Clinicians are not immune from this educational deficit, which is common in our culture and which accounts in large part for the ready acceptance of proposed causal factors without any evidence that they are relevant (Science and Engineering Indicators, 2010). Consider, for example, the uncritical acceptance of phenomena such as past lives, spirit guides, auras, and the occult (Shermer, 1997). Even quite elementary knowledge of scientific ways of weighing the value of evidence would call such claims into question. Hallmarks of a scientific approach toward clinical practice include looking for disconfirming evidence for favored views and considering the evidentiary status of practices and policies. It is assumed that nothing is ever proven, but rather that some claims have passed critical tests of their accuracy. Thus, a scientific approach is quite the opposite of the characteristics often attributed to it, such as "rigid," "dogmatic," "closed," or "trivial" (see Chapter 4).

Clinicians tend to form impressions of clients quickly; these first impressions influence their expectations about outcomes, which in turn may affect how they respond to clients and so confirm their original impressions. Different therapists may form quite different impressions of the same client. Initial beliefs may be resistant to new evidence as well as to challenges of the evidence that led to those beliefs. The generation of data, as well as the retrieval of material, is influenced by our assumptions. Premature commitment to a position and insufficient revision of beliefs as well as a tendency to believe (often falsely) in the consistency of behavior contribute to unsound decisions. Clinicians have a tendency not to search for evidence against their views; this tendency may result in errors. Different standards are used to criticize opposing evidence than to evaluate supporting evidence. Moreover, data that provide some support for and some evidence against preferred views increase the confidence of holders of both views (Lord, Ross, & Lepper, 1979).

Expectations tend to be self-fulfilling. A clinician may have read a report describing a client as schizophrenic. This may result in a selective search for evidence in support of this assumption and a selective ignoring of counterevidence. This justification focus (searching for data that confirm initial views rather than seeking to disconfirm preferred views) is at the heart of many sources of error. The unrepresentativeness of samples may be ignored (see Chapter 15). The tendency to attribute problems to dispositional (personal) characteristics of clients and to ignore environmental factors is common—the fundamental attribution error (see Chapter 14). The tendencies described may influence decision making in all phases of helping (for example, describing clients and their concerns, making inferences about causal factors, and making predictions about the effectiveness of different kinds of services). The more familiar we are with sources of error, the more likely we may be to avoid them. Some of these biases result in too little thinking, in contrast to too much thinking—a "premature cessation of search" (Baron, 1985b, p. 208).

CLINICAL REASONING AS A TEACHABLE SKILL

A rich literature is available describing efforts to enhance problem solving and decision making, including the tools and process of evidence-based practice designed to decrease gaps between a clinician's current knowledge and possibilities for resolution. Critical thinking skills can be enhanced and helpful strategies for improving accuracy can be acquired, such as using natural frequencies to estimate risk (see Chapter 15). Evidence-based practice offers an evolving process for integrating evidentiary, ethical, and application issues. Checklists are available to help us pay attention to important characteristics when critically appraising practice-related research (e.g., Greenhalgh, 2010). Debiasing strategies can be acquired, as described in later chapters. We can learn how to allocate scarce resources, such as time, wisely and become more aware of our reasoning process, as described in Chapter 3. We can become familiar with barriers to problem solving, including inflated self-assessments, and develop skills for avoiding them. We can acquire critical thinking values, knowledge, and skills that contribute to problem solving and decision making that are described throughout this book (e.g., see Croskerry & Nimmo, 2011; Janicek & Hitchcock, 2005). The term *metacognitive* refers to awareness of and influence on our reasoning processes (e.g., monitoring our thinking by asking questions such as: "How am I doing?" "Is this correct?" "How do I know this is true?" "What are my biases?" "Is there another way to approach this problem?" "Do I understand this point?"). These questions highlight the importance of self-correction in problem solving. Related behaviors can be thought of as self-governing processes (strategies we use to guide our thinking).

As skill is acquired in an area, knowledge tends to be stored in larger chunks, and these chunks are run off in a more automatic fashion. Components of practical intelligence tend to be learned on the job. The goal of practical intelligence is to accomplish tasks in real-life settings. Different kinds include managing emotions, developing and using interpersonal skills, responding to setbacks and failures, and dealing with procrastination. Successful managers seek concrete information when faced with ambiguity, obtain information from a range of sources, and identify useful analogies to explain a situation (Klemp & McClelland, 1986).

COSTS AND BENEFITS OF CRITICAL THINKING

Like anything else, critical thinking has advantages and disadvantages; there may be long-term benefits for short-term investments. A tendency to overemphasize immediate costs in relation to future gains may be an obstacle to critical thinking. The benefits depend on our goals and values. An interest in enhancing clinical competence, curiosity, and a desire to make ethical decisions encourage critical thinking (for example, searching for and critically appraising practice-related research).

Benefits of Critical Thinking

There are many benefits of thinking critically about clinical decisions, all of which contribute to helping clients and avoiding harming them:

- Discover problem-related resources and constraints.
- See the connection between private troubles and public issues; think contextually.
- Avoid cognitive biases.
- Avoid being bamboozled by others (avoid influence by human service propaganda).
- Recognize errors and mistakes as learning opportunities.
- Recognize pseudoscience, quackery, and fraud.
- Minimize avoidable harm to clients.
- Accurately assess the likelihood of attaining hoped-for outcomes.
- Make valuable contributions at case conferences (e.g., identify flawed arguments, suggest well-argued alternative views).
- Select effective programs and policies.
- Make accurate predictions.
- Accurately assess the effects of policies, programs, and plans.
- Make timely changes in plans, programs, and policies.
- Use resources (e.g., time) wisely and justly.
- Continue to enhance knowledge and skills.
- Increase self-awareness; for example, note contradictions between what you say ("I care about clients") and what you do (fail to keep up-to-date with research findings about clients' concerns).

Thinking critically about practice beliefs and judgments will increase the accuracy of decisions. Informal fallacies and weak rhetorical appeals used in human service propaganda will be less likely to be influential, and you may be more aware of cognitive biases that influence your judgments. Enhancing the quality of reasoning should provide useful problem-solving skills, such as deciding what questions to ask, what data to gather, and what factors to relate to problems. Selection of weak or ineffective practice methods may be avoided by a search for alternative views of problems and by consulting high-quality research reviews related to specific practice methods, such as those in the Cochrane and Campbell databases. Critical thinking skills and practice in their use can be used to avoid errors, such as the fundamental attribution error, in which environmental influences are overlooked, such as the role of significant others (those who interact with clients and influence their behavior). Clarifying vague terms such as *addiction, abuse, dementia,* and *self-determination* may prevent misunderstandings between clinicians and their clients, as well as among clinicians, and help to avoid the "patient uniformity myth," in which clients and their problems are incorrectly assumed to be identical (Kiesler, 1966). Only when desired outcomes are clearly described may it be obvious that, given available resources, some are unattainable or conflict with other valued outcomes. Clarifying values and preferences is another benefit of critical thinking.

Thinking carefully about decisions will minimize regret. Enhancing decision-making skills may help us to recapture a sense of discovery and curiosity in confronting the challenges of clinical work and in encouraging an attitude of "constructive discontent" (Koberg & Bagnall, 1976). Some clinicians may lose the sense of positive challenge over their careers as they labor in environments in which there is a poor match between resources available and tasks required. A sense of curiosity and discovery may be replaced by a mindless approach to work that is dull and dulling (Maslach, Schaufeli, & Leiter, 2001).

Familiarity with persuasion strategies and informal fallacies should upgrade the quality of decisions in all contexts: interviews with clients, case conferences, and discussions with colleagues. I was quite mystified when low-level appeals such as straw person arguments were often successful in swaying colleagues. After becoming familiar with persuasive tactics and the variety of fallacies that may occur, as well as reasons for their effectiveness, I understood their popularity and was better prepared to handle them. Argument-analysis skills are valuable in focusing on key assumptions and identifying problems with a position (see Chapter 3). An emphasis on helping clients and avoiding harming them will encourage a collaborative, critical approach to decision making and decrease the frequency of weak appeals and adversarial tactics. You and your clients will be in a better position to assess whether an outcome can be pursued successfully. It is disturbing to hear clinicians say "nothing can be done" when, in fact, if they were familiar with available knowledge, they could do something. Saying "nothing can be done" when this is not true leaves you helpless, and leaves clients without the benefit of the best chance of obtaining hoped-for outcomes.

Some clinicians view helping people as an art rather than a science—they believe that there is little if any empirical knowledge of value that will increase the accuracy of decisions and, therefore, taking the time to become familiar with and to draw on this not only is a waste of time, but will diminish the quality of service because it interferes with the creative, spontaneous flow that is the heart of effective helping. This is not an either-or question. Both art and science are involved (see Chapter 2). There is evidence in many areas that certain decisions are better than others in helping clients. Perhaps you should ask yourself, "In what areas would I want my dentist and doctor to base their recommendations on what feels best, without finding out whether what feels best is compatible with related research findings?" Do you base decisions you make about your clients on the same criteria you would like your doctor to use when making recommendations about a serious health problem of your own? (See criteria listed earlier in this chapter.) If not, why not? Comparison of criteria used when making decisions that affect one's own health with those relied on with clients shows that what's good for the goose (ourselves) may not be good for the gander (our clients). For example, 92% of respondents wanted physicians to base recommendations about treatment of a health problem on results of randomized controlled trials, but relied on criteria such as intuition with their clients. Exhibit 1.6 shows results from 86 master's degree students in social work (Gambrill & Gibbs, 2002). Personal preferences do have a role in selecting a method from among several different ones when all methods may be equally effective—especially if the client makes the choice. And such preferences may be acted on if many methods are equally effective or all are of unknown effectiveness.

Knowledge about different kinds of decision-making strategies and the situations in which they can be used to good effect will contribute to timely, well-reasoned decisions. It is often not necessary to optimize (choose the best of all possible alternatives) to achieve desired outcomes. Rather, we "satisfice" (seek a satisfactory option). For example, if any one of several methods can be used with equal effectiveness to enhance client participation, trying to select the optimal one is a waste of time. A more systematic approach to problem solving will be required at other times.

Exhibit 1.6 Percentage Endorsement of Criteria Over Three Situations (n = 86)

	Ideally With Client (%)	Physician (%)	Client (%)
1. Your intuition (gut feeling) about what will be effective.	77 (66)	22 (19)	38 (33)
2. What you have heard from other professionals in informal exchanges.	64 (55)	20 (17)	27 (23)
3. Your experience with a few cases.	73 (67)	26 (22)	26 (22)
4. Your demonstrated track record of success based on data you have gathered systematically and regularly.	39 (34)	92 (79)	91 (78)
5. What fits your personal style.	62 (53)	3.6 (3)	27 (22)
6. What was usually offered at your agency.	59 (51)	3.6 (3)	8 (7)
7. Self-reports of other clients about what was helpful.	65 (56)	52 (45)	64 (55)
8. Results of controlled experimental studies.	37 (32)	92 (79)	86 (74)
9. What you are most familiar with.	53 (45)	19 (16)	14 (12)
10. What you know by critically reading professional literature.	67 (58)	88 (76)	86 (74)

Source: From "Making Practice Decisions: Is What's Good for the Goose Good for the Gander?" by E. Gambrill and L. Gibbs, 2002, *Ethical Human Sciences and Services, 4*(1), p. 39. Reprinted with permission.

Costs of Thinking Critically About Decisions

A review of the costs of thinking suggests why so many people do not think carefully about their beliefs and the tasks they confront. There are social, psychological, and practical costs. You even may be sued (Sweet, 2011). You may falsely believe that only experts can understand what is going on in a field, and that it will take too much time to understand views related to a decision you must make. The media as well as professional publications encourage this belief by lack of clear description of facts and figures related to claims (e.g., see Schwartz, Woloshin, & Welch, 2007, for an exception). Scientists do too little to make their views accessible to those outside their field (Burnham, 1987). In fact, many of the basic principles vital to examining the evidentiary status of a claim or theory are quite straightforward and easy to understand, even though these are not generally taught. Consider our tendency to search our memories for one or two supporting examples when asked about the accuracy of an assumption, and to believe that these examples provide satisfactory evidence for our beliefs. It takes little training to realize that the case is far from settled. An overestimate of the costs of thinking may be combined with an underestimate of the value of further thinking and an overconfidence in the thinking already done. These tendencies result in impulsive decision making (Baron, 1985b). Reliance on a "makes-sense epistemology" (Perkins, Allen, & Hafner, 1983) encourages impulsive decisions (see discussion of empathic explanations in Chapter 3).

Making well-reasoned decisions may require additional time and effort in questioning initial hypotheses; consulting practice-related research; gathering data in real-life contexts to explore assumptions (for example, concerning the nature of parent-child exchanges); and encouraging colleagues to consider alternatives in case conferences. It often takes longer to refute an argument than it does to state a position. The benefits of thinking may be in the future, whereas the costs in time, effort, and lost opportunities may be immediate (Baron, 1985b). Learning to question inferences requires the cultivation of compatible values and goals—a commitment to helping clients and avoiding harming them. Effort will be required to learn how to critically appraise different kinds of research relevant to different kinds of questions. However, the time and effort devoted to critical thinking should be saved many times over in increased accuracy of decisions; errors are more likely to be avoided.

An interest in protecting self-worth is a key factor in avoiding information that is not self-serving. Questioning our views requires recognizing the uncertainty inherent in helping clients. It requires us to abandon attitudes of smug paternalism and related justifications used to impose services on clients. It requires a tolerance of ambiguity and doubt. Critically appraising views entails the possibility of discovering that "we were wrong." Suggesting positions and questioning the views of others carries the risk of negative reactions from colleagues. Critical thinkers may be viewed as acting unsociably by questioning assumptions others take for granted. Even though critical thinking skills are used with consummate diplomacy, negative reactions may result. Creating an environment that encourages critical thinking will decrease the probability of negative reactions. Cultural differences should also be considered regarding when and how questions are raised (see Tweed & Lehman, 2002).

Careful consideration of options and assumptions may reveal ignorance and uncertainty. The complexity of some tasks clinicians confront may challenge the clearest thinker. Dilemmas include (1) the tension between the need to act despite uncertainty and the desire for certainty, and (2) the attempt to not impose personal biases while increasing client options (Lenrow, 1978). Estimating the probability that a practice method will be effective may reveal that it is relatively low. Being aware of the slim probability of effectiveness should be helpful in preventing clinicians from blaming themselves for lack of success, given that they have offered the best services possible. Inadequate resources should be viewed as an occasion to work together with others to increase access to needed services.

Most decisions involve costs as well as benefits. Thinking about a decision may reveal trade-offs that have been ignored. As the need for defense against disturbing information gets stronger, curiosity gets weaker. Yet another cost is the time needed to critically review claims of what is true and what is not. Not asking questions saves time and effort. Also, if we do not have goals, tools, and beliefs that encourage such questions, we are less likely to raise questions and seek answers. Use of critical thinking skills increases responsibility for providing the help that can be offered to clients and decreases tendencies to blame clients for resistance. Responsibility in the absence of skills and other resources to act effectively is unpleasant. The flip side of responsibility is freedom; giving up responsibility entails giving up freedom (Fromm, 1963). Thinking critically increases freedom from the unwanted influence of other people, including researchers who misrepresent the evidentiary status of practices and policies. You will move beyond acceptance of arguments simply because they make sense, realizing that what makes sense is not necessarily true; uncritical acceptance of claims leaves you at the mercy of what others think, as well as at the mercy of flaws in self-assessment of your own competence. One of the basic choices in life is whether to look or not look. Critical thinking values and skills increase a willingness to look. (Dare to know.)

HOW SKEPTICAL SHOULD CLINICIANS BE?

A thoughtful approach to decision making requires a skeptical attitude. How skeptical should clinicians be? They should be as skeptical as they have to be to maximize opportunities to help clients and avoid harm. Decisions must be made in spite of uncertainties. "Practitioners are asked to solve problems every day that philosophers have argued about for the last two thousand years and will probably debate for the next two thousand. Inevitably, arbitrary lines have to be drawn and hard cases decided" (Dingwall, Eekelaar, & Murray, 1983, p. 244). As Thouless (1974, p. 166) points out, "What we do is more important than what we think. . . . So important is action that we can reasonably condemn as crooked thinking any device in thought which has as its purpose the evasion of useful or necessary action" (p. 166). We could not get through a day if we questioned every judgment. We cannot offer evidence for every belief we hold. We must trust the experts for many beliefs—that is, we cannot offer sound evidence for many of the everyday decisions we make. The case is different for clinicians in relation to their work: they should be able to offer cogent reasons for decisions they make regarding choice of assessment, intervention, and evaluation methods. We should be as skeptical as we need to be to avoid influence by propaganda in the helping professions, which is rife.

SUMMARY

Decision making is at the heart of clinical practice. Decisions include classifying clients into categories, making causal assumptions, and making predictions about the effectiveness of different kinds of interventions and future behavior of clients. Unless we critically reflect on our decisions, clients may be harmed rather than helped; we may be bamboozled by slick advertising and deceptive research reports. We may uncritically accept bogus claims in professional publications. Tendencies that decrease accuracy include discounting conflicting evidence, failing to search for disconfirming evidence, relying on experts, and a bias for dispositional explanations. Clinicians who are psycho-analytically oriented tend to search for and attend to different factors than those who are behaviorally oriented; these selective searches influence decisions. Clinical practice requires the integration of information from diverse sources, which places a strain on memory and on capacities to combine different kinds of data. Challenges include disagreements about criteria to use to assess the accuracy of decisions, cultural difference in views of personal troubles and social problems, and gaps in knowledge about how to achieve given outcomes.

Enhancing critical thinking skills and knowledge should yield long-term benefits for short-term investments. Benefits include doing more good than harm, recapturing a sense of discovery, and learning from mistakes how to enhance success in the future. Costs include the discovery of faulty beliefs, ignorance, and uncertainty. Using critical thinking skills may result in negative reactions from colleagues and increases personal responsibility because more accurate distinctions are possible between artificial and real constraints on helping clients. Critically evaluating the accuracy of practice- and policy-related claims requires time, effort, and skill. The process of evidence-based practice is designed to facilitate the integration of practice- and policy-related research in a user-friendly manner attentive to daily time pressures of clinicians and managers. The costs of forgoing critical thinking in clinical practice are substantial. "In exchange for the time saved, clinicians must preserve and encourage unwarranted complacency, unverified dogma, and self-perpetuating error" (Feinstein, 1967, p. 310). Increasing critical thinking knowledge, values, and skills may result in a change of preferred practice theory. Most importantly, it should enhance the quality of services offered to clients.

2

Sources of Influence on Clinical Decisions

Either a broad or a narrow view can be taken of factors that influence clinical decisions. A narrow view focuses only on the interaction between clients and clinicians—how they influence each other within the interview. An understanding of the variables that affect clinical decisions requires a much broader exploration of environments, past, present, and future. One of the purposes of this book is to enhance awareness of social, political, and economic influences on clinical decisions. Where do practice theories come from? What particular views of reality do they promote? Who are the promoters? Which views do they obscure or actively suppress? Who benefits from a given view? What claims have been critically tested, and if so, to what effect? To what extent does the biomedical-industrial complex influence the very framing of problems such as anxiety in social situations, blood pressure, and depression? Asking such questions is vital for awareness of the links between the personal and the political (Mills, 1959). As Mills (1959) suggests, freedom is not just choosing among the alternatives; it is having a say about what alternatives are considered. Confining attention to the clinical interview when attempting to understand sources of influence on clinical decisions is like trying to understand the circulatory system from the perspective of a single red blood cell.

Many players influence what is viewed as a problem and promoted as a remedy. Consider Exhibit 2.1, illustrating the multiple sources of influence on use of medical technology. Physicians may prescribe a drug based on information provided by a drug rep the day before. Are benefits accurately described? Are side effects noted? There has been an explosion of material describing the influence of pharmaceutical and biotech companies and academic researchers on their payrolls on what is considered a problem and how it should be addressed (see Angell, 2011; Brody, 2007; Carlat, 2010; Gambrill, 2012; Moncrieff, 2008; Whittaker, 2010). Hope for relief from suffering on the part of

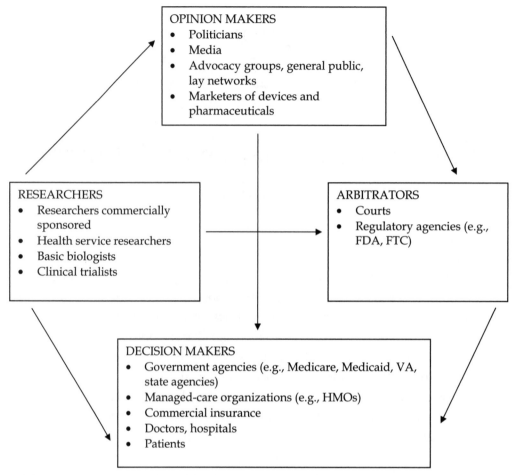

Exhibit 2.1 Influential Parties in the Adoption of New Medical Technology.

Source: From "Cascade effects of medical technology," by R. A. Deyo, 2002, *Annual Review of Public Health, 23,* p. 38.

clients and a mandate to help on the part of professionals contribute to overestimation of potential positive effects. Whittaker (2010) suggests that the growth of the pharmaceutical industry's influence in promoting the idea that troubled and troubling behaviors are caused by a brain disease with medication as the remedy has been forwarded through four avenues: (1) pharmaceutical companies offered the money, (2) the American Psychiatric Association and psychiatrists at top medical schools conferred intellectual legitimacy, (3) the National Institute of Mental Health offered governmental approval, and (4) the National Alliance for the Mentally Ill (NAMI) offered the moral authority (NAMI is heavily funded by Big Pharma). Not considering the big picture leaves you open to influence by concepts and perspectives that you might reject if you considered their consequences. Clinicians as well as clients are influenced by the historical period in which they live and work and by the current definitions of personal troubles, social problems, and proposed solutions. We can better understand why certain decisions are made and more accurately assess barriers and potential for change if we understand the context in which the health systems developed and are maintained.

Decisions are influenced by past environments (such as professional education programs and the historical circumstances within which practice theories and service-delivery systems emerge); current environments (such as the organizations in which clinicians work and the current political, economic, and social circumstances in which personal and social problems are defined and service systems provided); and future environments (hoped-for outcomes). Practice is carried out in the context of policies and related legislation that given patterns of behavior are problems, and certain remedies are appropriate. Current policies reflect different approaches to troubled and troubling behaviors, including paternalistic reactions in which professionals feel free, or obligated, to force unwanted help on others "for their own good." The particular settings in which clinicians work influence the kinds of clients and concerns they encounter, including the number of sessions permitted and payment policies. Only by understanding how these environments influence practice can the nature of clinical decisions be understood. Consider the examples given in Chapter 1. How could these happen? Why do harmful methods continue to be used? Why are methods we know to be effective not used? What external influences contributed to the death of a child from "rebirthing therapy" (Janofsky, 2001)?

Clarifying and critically examining basic assumptions is a key component of critical thinking. Recognizing underlying goals and points of view is not easy; they are often implicit rather than explicit. They may be part of the basic social fabric and related belief systems in which we live, perhaps unquestioned or even unrecognized, such as our competitive consumer-oriented society (Illouz, 2008). Related facts and figures such as lack of positive benefit and adverse effects of medication may be hidden. Even physicians may not be accurately informed; critical information is often missing in promotional material (Woloshin & Schwartz, 2011). Consider the antipsychotic drug Abilify, used to decrease depression and widely advertised to the public. Claims of effectiveness are based on a three-point difference on a 60-point scale and for only 10% of patients. Side effects are often omitted. To be informed, we would also have to know that 21% of patients developed akathisia (severe restlessness) and 4% had a substantial weight gain. So do the benefits outweigh the risks?

Conflicts of interest, including on the part of those who propose guidelines for the American Psychiatric Association, may be hidden until forced into the public realm (Cosgrove, Bursztajn, Krimsky, Anaya, & Walker, 2009; Lo & Field, 2009). Rarely are conflicts of interest reported in trials of drugs (Roseman et al., 2011). Many scholars argue that professionals are involved not so much in problem solving as in problem setting (e.g., Schon, 1990). Gusfield (2003) suggests, "The development of professions dedicated to benevolence, the so-called 'helping professions,' depend upon and accentuate the definition of problem populations as 'sick,' as objects of medical and quasi-medical attention" (p. 9). Indeed, the biomedicalization of life continues to advance (Conrad, 2007). This includes broadening the boundaries of what is viewed as abnormal and requiring the help of experts offering psychological and/or medical interventions (e.g., Moynihan, Heath, Henry, & Gotzsche, 2002; Moynihan & Mintzes, 2010; Summerfield, 2001; Welch, Schwartz, & Woloshin, 2011). (See Exhibit 2.2.) Assumptions underlying different views of personal and social problems are based on different beliefs about human nature—why people do what they do, how they change, and whether they can change. For example, social reform efforts emphasize the influence of political, economic, and social conditions, such as inequality of educational opportunities (e.g., Cohen & Timini, 2008).

Lack of understanding of the role of environmental factors may result in poor decisions; decisions to intervene may be made when there is no justifiable reason to do so. A decision may be made not to intervene when intervention would help clients to enhance the quality of their lives, or ineffective practices or policies may be chosen. Without a contextual understanding, you may accept views that limit opportunities to help clients. Without this, it is easy to fall into blaming clients and focusing on changing them or giving them rationales for their plights rather than addressing environmental circumstances related to their problems. Thinking critically about what is defined as a problem and proposed remedies requires effort as well as courage to question popular

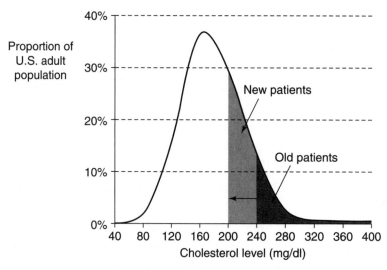

Exhibit 2.2 Distribution of Cholesterol Levels in Adult Americans and the Effect on Changing the Cutoff from 240 to 200.

Source: From *Overdiagnosed: Making People Sick in the Pursuit of Health* (p. 23), by H. G. Welch, L. Schwartz, and S. Woloshin, 2011, Boston, MA: Beacon Press.

assumptions and examine underlying points of view. But the rewards are well worth it. Clinicians informed about the economic, social, and political factors that influence practice are less likely to ignore environmental factors related to personal troubles and social problems. An important contribution of critical school analysis has been greater sensitivity to the value implications of psychiatric and psychological theory (Basaglia, 1987; Cohen & Timimi, 2008; Gergen, 1987). Sampson (1977) argues that psychological theory supports individualism and discourages recognition of our interdependency.

CHANGING VIEWS OF PROBLEMS AND THEIR PREVALENCE

In the most general view, deviance refers to variations in behavior; some are viewed as good, others as bad. Many behaviors once condemned as sinful were later considered crimes and are now viewed as mental illnesses (Scheff, 1984a, 1984b; Szasz, 1987). The view of "heretical actions" as sinful is still alive, as illustrated by Bishop Michael J. Sheridan of Colorado Springs, "who said in a pastoral letter that Catholics who vote for candidates who support gay marriage, euthanasia, or abortion rights must confess their sin before receiving communion" (Woodward, 2004, p. A23). The changing ways in which certain behaviors have been viewed supports a contextual view of deviance. For instance, only when women gained more political and economic independence was greater attention given to battered women. Throughout history, poverty has been variously viewed as a crime, a personal limitation, or a reflection of discrimination and oppression (social injustice). Technological advances such as meta-analysis enable new ways to examine problems. Using meta-analytic techniques, Galea et al. (2011) argue that in the United States, 176,000 deaths a year are due to racial discrimination and 133,000 deaths are due to individual poverty. (This compares to 400,000 deaths a year from smoking, 119,000 from accidents, and 156,000 from lung cancer.) Advances in knowledge often force changes in how people view a problem. It had been assumed that tuberculosis was inherited, because people who lived together tended to contract it. When the bacillus responsible for tuberculosis was isolated, people were no longer blamed for developing it. It has been argued that the modern concept of the self is relatively recent in origin, being dependent on reliance on the clock (Verhave & Van Hoorn, 1984).

Changing ideas about what is and what is not mental illness illustrate the consensual nature of psychiatric diagnoses. Homosexuality was defined as a mental illness until 1973, when the American Psychiatric Association, under pressure from gay and lesbian advocacy groups and bitter infighting, decided that it was not. History reveals change in policies that influence both clinicians and those in their gaze. Immediately prior to World War II, psychiatrists began developing screening procedures specifically designed to "discover and disqualify" homosexuals (Bérubé, 1992). In *Perfectly Normal: The*

Pursuit of Normality in Post War America, Anna Creadick (2010) notes that never before had homosexuals been systematically excluded from military service (p. 92). This focus resulted in development of "an expanding administrative apparatus for managing homosexual personnel that relied on diagnosis, hospitalization, surveillance, interrogation, discharge, administrative appeal, and mass indoctrination." Psychiatrists lead discussions on "normality," and increasingly do so together with the pharmaceutical industry (Angell, 2011). Carol Tavris, as well as many other scholars, describes the changing views of women's alleged mental illnesses. In *The Mismeasure of Women* (1992), she suggests that labels such as dependent personality disorder, which are most often given to women, punish women for fulfilling expected roles. She contends that we should examine the conditions in society that result in so many women showing these characteristics, and alter those conditions.

Badinter (1980) proposes that the notion of mother love arose only recently, when it became necessary to convince mothers that care of their children was critical in order to provide needed human resources to maintain the state, and that the modern-day concept of mother love stemmed from idealization sponsored by the state. In the past, housewives who wanted to work were often regarded as pathological (Oakley, 1976). Problems have careers. You could take any pattern of behavior (e.g., drug use, delinquency) and explore the different ways it has been viewed. Consider masturbation. At one time it was thought to be responsible for an enormous range of problems, including mental retardation (see Szasz, 1970). A variety of devices was created to decrease "self-abuse," as it was called. Now masturbation is considered healthy. Cultural values, common metaphors, as well as political and economic pressures influence decisions. Changing metaphors used to describe problems influence how we view them and what solutions we propose. A good example is the "war on drugs." This metaphor encourages use of force against those who sell and use drugs, as well as feelings of "us against them." (For critiques of current drug policies in the United States, see, for example, Balko, 2006; Greenwald, 2009; Szasz, 2001.)

Flawed People and/or Flawed Environments?

A historical understanding of the different ways in which deviance has been defined reveals the value-laden basis of definitions of individual troubles and social problems. Policies and practices may be based on beliefs about the moral character of clients rather than on objective accounts guided by empirically grounded theories of behavior. Should the focus of drug programs be on users rather than on environmental conditions that encourage substance abuse? Who would lose and who would benefit from decriminalizing the use of all controlled substances, including cocaine and opiates, as done in Portugal since 2001? Lack of attention to the larger picture encourages blaming problems on individuals and deflects attention from related political, economic, and social factors. Are parents who mistreat their children bad people who should be imprisoned or overburdened people who should be helped? Are they themselves victims of the inequitable distribution of employment, housing, and education opportunities? What are the costs and benefits to different involved parties of certain views and proposed remedies? Ascriptions of mental illness may excuse people from being responsible for their actions, including those which harm others. The advantages of the "sick role" have long been noted. Consider acceptance of the "Twinkie defense"—the man who killed Mayor George Moscone of San Francisco and Supervisor Harvey Milk was considered to have diminished capacity due to depression, a symptom of which was his consumption of junk food. Szasz (1987) has long argued that we live in a therapeutic culture in which we escape responsibility for the results of our actions.

There is a close relationship between explanation and evaluation (see discussion of empathic explanations in Chapter 3). The relation between judgments of moral character and ascriptions of deviance is emphasized by sociologists and often neglected by clinicians. One of the ongoing debates concerns whether to locate the source of problems in the people who have them and to focus on changing individuals and families, and/or to examine related environmental causes and pursue environmental reform. If someone drinks too much, is homeless, and is unemployed, is this his or her fault? Do environmental conditions such as high unemployment, poor-quality education, and lack of low-cost housing contribute to these problems? Moral definitions of problems emphasize individual responsibility. A concern about whether applicants for services are worthy of receiving aid has a long history in the helping professions (Leiby, 1978). The freedom to choose is a foundation requirement of moral behavior. A moralistic definition of problems encourages the belief that people with these problems are bad people who deserve whatever ill fate awaits them, including "justified" punishment or enforced "treatment." We make decisions concerning the intentionality of an act. The question of intention highlights the moral aspect of decisions—that is, the client knowingly selected one way to act from a variety of options. We assume that the choice characterizes the kind of person the client is; that is, it is a reflection of moral character. The allegation of a certain kind of character may rest on a retrospective analysis of past behavior and predictions of future behavior, as well as descriptions of current behavior.

Problems as Socially Constructed

Some scholars argue that some state of affairs becomes a social problem when an objective condition exists. Others believe that social problems are socially constructed. They argue that although certain needs of the sick, poor, elderly, and very young have been recognized throughout the centuries, they have been defined differently at different times and receive more or less attention at different times. Gusfield (2003) suggests that the very notion of a social problem is unique to certain times.

> The idea of "social problems" is unique to modern societies . . . modern societies, including the United States, display a culture of public problems. It is a part of how we think and how we interpret the world about us, that we perceive many conditions as not only deplorable but as capable of being relieved by and as requiring public action, most often by the state. The concept of "social problems" is a category of thought, a way of seeing certain conditions as providing a claim to change through public actions. (Gusfield, 2003, p. 7)

As Gusfield (2003) notes, there are many human problems that are not considered to be public problems, such as disappointed friendships and unrequited love.

> Again and again sociologists have pointed out how the conditions said to define the social problem are socially constructed, are only one of several possible "realities." The attempt to pose as the arbiters of standards is less and less taken for granted and more and more seen as an accompaniment to social control, to the quest for hegemony. (Gusfield, 2003, p. 15)

Feminist scholars and advocates have been in the vanguard in emphasizing the relationship between personal problems and social issues ("the personal is political"). The ascribed nature of deviance is shown by changing definitions of deviance and different perspectives concerning society's responsibility in relation to the homeless, the poor, the sick, the abused, and the neglected. If deviance is an ascribed rather than an inherent status, then there is room to build a case for or against ascriptions. The manner in which a case can be built is illustrated in the example given in Chapter 16.

Ethical and political concerns such as freedom from unwanted control are reframed into personal ones over which the state has power. What is a political issue is transformed into a social problem (see Mills's [1959] discussion of the relationship between the personal and political, as well as related writings by Foucault [1981]; Illich [1976]; Illich, Zola, McNight, Caplan, & Shaiken [1977]; and Szasz [2003]). "If, however, the difficulties are understood to be those of moral diversity, of contested meanings, then the problem is a political issue, and no system of training can provide help" (Gusfield, 2003). Consider again views of homosexuals. "If the condition is perceived as that of individual illness or deficiency, then there can be a social technology, a form of knowledge and skill that can be effectively learned. That knowledge is the mandate for professions licensed to 'own' their social problems" (p. 9). Some groups successfully resist an unwanted view.

The gay rights movement is perhaps the most salient example of how the ability to mobilize has enabled a subject group to transform its status. During this century, homosexuals have been thought of as sinful and as sick, objects of condemnation or of medical benevolence. What the gay rights movement did was to resist the public designation of deviance, of abnormality, by attacking the presumed norms and denying that homosexuality constituted a social problem. In the process, the phenomena of homosexuality lost its status as a "social problem" and became a matter of political and cultural conflict over the recognition of alternative sexual styles. What had been an uncontested meaning has been transformed into a political contest. (Gusfield, 2003, p. 15)

POLITICAL, ECONOMIC, AND SOCIAL INFLUENCES ON PROBLEM FRAMING AND PROPOSED REMEDIES

Psychotherapy as well as medicine and other helping enterprises are highly political. Consider individuals who are encouraged to seek treatment for their alcoholism. Environmental factors that contribute to drinking (such as poverty, unemployment, and the multimillion-dollar advertising of alcoholic beverages) are ignored in biomedical views of alcohol abuse (Barbour, Clark, Jones, Norton, & Veitch, 2011). Such a view is actively promoted by research-funding agencies such as the National Institute on Alcohol Abuse and Alcoholism (NIAAA) (Midanik, 2006). Who benefits and who loses from acceptance of a biomedical model of alcoholism, in which attention is focused on the individual? Indeed, is such a view accurate? (See Heyman, 2009.) What is the impact of such a view on the way resources are distributed, including research funding?

As we become immersed in the everyday world of practice, it is easy to forget about the economic, political, and social context in which problems are defined and reacted to. We may forget that problems are defined in accord with popular grand narratives of the times; we may forget to ask: "Who benefits and who loses from a particular view?" People have different opinions about what a problem is, who and what is responsible for it, and how it can be resolved. Consider dysfunctional gambling. Is it a learned behavior maintained by a complex reinforcement schedule? Is it a moral failing? The American Psychiatric Association (2000) views this as a mental disorder. Is this a disease? Is there a known etiology, a worsening without treatment, and a predictable course?

Companies involved in the biomedical-industrial complex spend millions on public relations agencies hired to promote views that encourage consumption of their products (Appelbaum, 2009a & b; Moynihan & Cassels, 2005). "Problem crusaders" (those with an interest in a particular view of a problem) forward certain definitions and may exaggerate potential risks and prevalence (e.g., MacCoun & Reuter, 2001). Economic interests influence views of problems and proposed remedies. "Just as the tobacco companies polluted the literature on smoking, and polluting industries try to distort the science of climate change, the pharmaceutical giants and the doctors on their payrolls are poisoning too much of the medical science with overly positive findings" (Moynihan, 2011). Concerns about funding and the need to respond to and consider reactions of outside pressure groups influence agency practice. Profit making is the key aim of for-profit and many (supposedly) not-for-profit organizations. Residential psychiatric facilities for youth and nursing homes are multimillion-dollar businesses. The concern for profit rather than service is reflected in the mistreatment (e.g., unneeded treatment) of clients in order to make money and in gross lapses in quality of care (e.g., Delamothe, 2011; Kmietowicz, 2011).Views of anxiety in social situations and depression as "brain diseases" requiring medication benefit the pharmaceutical industry, which has more lobbyists in Washington, D.C., than all senators and representatives combined. These lobbyists actively promote biomedical views of problems in living. Those favoring such views have been very successful, as illustrated by the ever-lengthening list of behaviors viewed as signs of mental illness requiring medication (Angell, 2011; Clarke, Mamo, Fosket, Fishman, & Shim, 2010; Conrad, 2007). Over the past decades a biomedical grand narrative has come to prevail in which problems in living are assumed to be biochemical in origin and medication is presumed to be the remedy (Moynihan, Heath, Henry, & Gøtzsche, 2002). The recent strategic plan of the National Institute of Mental Health emphasizes biomedical causes (downloaded June 30, 2011). Successful alternative policies are often hidden (Hughes & Stevens, 2010).

Ivan Illich (1976) described the medicalization of problems in *Medical Nemesis*. Indeed, he used the term *the medicalization of life*. (See also *Disease Mongers* by Lynn Payer [1992].) Illich (1976) argued that hospitals and drugs harm more people than they cure. Sources of human misery that are related to environmental factors and that create deviant behavior are falsely attributed to individual characteristics ("mental illness") and thus encapsulated. Special service-delivery systems can then be created for these individuals, and these systems become a source of jobs for professionals (Foucault, 1973; Loeske, 1999). Describing slight variations in weight as a disease increases sales of certain foods and medication (see discussion of "nondisease" in Skrabanek & McCormick, 1998). In his article "The Invention of Post-Traumatic Stress Disorder and the Social Usefulness of a Psychiatric Category," Summerfield (2001) suggests that "a psychiatric diagnosis is not necessarily a disease, distress or suffering is not psychopathology, post-traumatic stress disorder is an entity constructed as much from sociopolitical ideas as from psychiatric ones and that the increase in [this] diagnosis . . . is linked to changes in the relation between individual personhood and modern life" (p. 95). Thomas Szasz has been emphasizing such points for decades (e.g., 1961, 1987, 2001). Increased attention has been given to the concerning influence of the pharmaceutical industry forwarding biased research, including the censorship of negative results (e.g., see Angell, 2004; Beckelman, Li, & Gross, 2003).

The development of a discipline or profession occurs in a context of competition among professions (Abbott, 1988). Social work has long been concerned with its second-class image in relation to psychiatry and has been influenced by this concern by buying into a psychiatric view of human behavior—for example, using diagnostic criteria in the *Diagnostic and Statistical Manual of Mental Disorders* (DSM; American Psychiatric Association, 2000). Psychology has been occupied with establishing and defending its scientific credibility and gaining access to rights, such as prescription privileges, once confined to psychiatrists. Mental health services expanded during the community mental health movement, and the number of mental health professionals increased greatly. Critics argue that this expansion was not in the interests of the clients served but, on the contrary, was in the interests of expanding boundaries of attempted imposition of normative values and containment of unproductive deviance.

Professional organizations influence clinical decisions in a variety of ways, in terms of both what they do and what they do not do; for example, they may not blow the whistle on pseudoscience—bogus claims of effectiveness regarding approved continuing education courses—and they may not support those who publish controversial literature reviews, as illustrated by the Rind affair (Lilienfeld, 2002). Rind and his colleagues published a review concerning the effects of child abuse. It was denounced in Congress and even though a sound review, the American Psychological Association declined to come to the authors' support. Professional organizations influence both private and agency-based practices by setting standards for licensing—influencing who is allowed to practice. They influence practice by engaging in political activities to protect and expand their turf. Consider the intense struggles between psychologists and psychiatrists about who should have control over diagnosis and treatment of clients, including medication privileges (e.g., see Buie, 1987, 1989). Problem definition is influenced by professionals' interest in maintaining and gaining power, status, and economic resources, as well as by differences of opinion about what makes one explanation better than another. As the number of common concerns claimed to be in need of treatment has expanded, so, too, has the number of clinicians (e.g., social workers). Entries in the DSM (American Psychiatric Association, 2000) expanded from 265 in 1980 to 365 in 2000 and will expand further in DSM-5. Precursors of disorders will be added, such as "psychosis risk syndrome." Francis (2010b) argues that this will result in an epidemic of false positives.

Some have argued that the prime function of mental health professionals is to encourage values compatible with a capitalistic culture (Ehrenreich & Ehrenreich, 1977). Many scholars note the advantage of a focus on the psychological to corporations in our capitalistic society—to create dependable workers (e.g., Illouz, 2008). Clinicians are viewed as conscious or unconscious functionaries involved in imposing an ideology

of health care and treatment on clients; social scientists are viewed as offering legitima-
tion and justification for such practices that, although they seem to be universal for all
citizens, meet the needs of the dominant group and control or restrain the needs of the
dominated groups (Basaglia, 1987, p. 155); "collective social problems are redefined as
smaller, localized community problems, giving people a false perspective about where
the problems originate and how they might be resolved. When superficial changes are
made on the community level, the larger social and political issues that are at the root of
the oppression and the deviance of marginal groups are depoliticized and atomized" to
protect the interests of dominant vested interests (p. 99; Berger & Luckman, 1966; see
also Illich et al., 1977; Manning, 1985). Webster (1997) suggests that our focus on racial
and ethnic differences obscures our shared humanness and problems common across
groups, such as poverty and lack of access to health services.

Assumptions made by Western clinicians may be inappropriate when applied to
non-Western clients (e.g., see Weisz, Sunwanlert, Chaiyasit, & Walter, 1987; Ying,
2002). Differences include the greater role of physical complaints among Asian clients,
differences in how children are raised and differences in the relative importance of the
individual and the group (Lock, 1982; Sue & Sue, 2002). A focus on the individual
in what Beit-Hallahmi (1987) calls the "non-symptomatic psychotherapy subculture,"
which consists of those who seek counseling not to alleviate symptoms but to facilitate
self-understanding and self-improvement, may not be of interest in some groups (p. 481).
Clients who have trouble getting to work on time or arriving at clinical interviews
on time may have different views of time compared to employers and counselors. An
interest in psychological factors is more prominent in rights-based cultures, such as the
United States, than in duty-based cultures, such as Hindu groups in India (Shweder &
Miller, 1985). In rights-based cultures, emphasis is placed on personal decision making;
in duty-based cultures, moral actions are defined as those that are compatible with the
natural order. Overlooking such differences may result in inappropriate decisions concerning non-Western clients.

Seeking help from a mental health center is more likely to be viewed as a stigma
in Asian cultures, whereas experience in therapy is the norm in some Western communities. Problems such as agoraphobia are rarely seen in non-Western countries, and
problems such as *koro* (panic reactions due to fear that one's penis or nipples will retract
into the body and cause death) that occur among the Chinese are unknown in the West.

The Language of Problem Definition

The words we use influence how we think about problems and behaviors. "To give a
name to a problem is to recognize or suggest a structure developed to deal with it. Child
abuse, juvenile delinquency, mental illness, alcoholism all have developed occupations

and facilities that specialize in treatment, prevention, and reform" (Gusfield, 2003, p. 8). The role of language (rhetoric) in claims making has been noted by many scholars (e.g., Szasz, 1987). Indeed, Thomas Szasz views the very notion of "mental illness" as a rhetorical device that obscures the real differences between physical illness and problems in living, such as anxiety in social situations and depression. Illouz (2008) argues that the language of clinical psychology serves our capitalistic economy by harnessing emotions—learning to manage our emotions in a manner required on the job. The term *spectrum* used in the *DSM-5* broadens diagnostic boundaries. The metaphor of war, as in the "war against drugs" makes it easier to use violent means against "them" (e.g., seizing property; arresting drug abusers) (MacCoun & Reuter, 2001; Wacquant, 2009). Here, too, societal factors related to use of drugs are obscured. Labels and classifications (e.g., black, white, race, ethnicity) have policy implications and thus warrant critical review.

The widespread use of medical language—healthy/unhealthy, wellness/sickness, health/disease—directs attention toward medical remedies. The word *health* has been applied to an ever-widening range of behaviors, feelings, and thoughts. Language and the ideology it reflects play a key role in obscuring economic differences. Both working-class and middle-class people may be labeled as middle-class, creating the illusion that most people belong to the middle class. The term *middle-class* splits working-class people with stable jobs away from identifying with working-class people with lower-paying, unstable, or no jobs. Many problems created in part by inequities in housing, job opportunities, education, health care, and the court system are treated as separate from one another, which makes it difficult to detect shared causes. DeMott (1990) suggests that differences in economic circumstances are daily translated into other terms, including moral differences. Many authors have noted the increased use of the languages of managerial approaches, consumerism, and risk management in the helping professions.

Different Problem Framings Have Different Consequences

Different ways of framing problems have different consequences. There are great stakes in how problems are framed, and people with vested interests devote considerable time, money, and effort to influence what others believe and do. Costs to society of a particular view and involved individuals may not be apparent until later developmental stages, as illustrated in follow-up studies of antisocial children (e.g., Scott, Knapp, Henderson, & Maughan, 2001). Singh (2002, 2004) argues that the medicalization of deviant child behavior as a brain disease (e.g., ADHD) allows parents to transfer blame from themselves to their child's brain. He suggests that mothers accept such a view as a relief from the expectations to produce ideal, high-achieving children. (See also Timimi, 2008.) Thomas Szasz (1987, 1994) argues that many people who injure others and are labeled mentally ill have committed criminal offenses and should be treated accordingly. Others believe that many criminals are mentally ill and should receive psychiatric care. Views about problems and their causes affect who receives aid and who does not, as well as what is offered and the spirit in which it is offered. Defining behaviors as indicators of mental illness results in quite different consequences than does defining them as criminal.

Understanding the context in which troubled or troubling behaviors occur, including their functions, provides opportunities to destigmatize clients, for example by revealing related political and economic factors such as discriminatory policies and practices (e.g., Wacquant, 2009). In a behavioral perspective, behavior always makes sense, but often at a high cost. Only if we take the time to understand the functions of unusual reactions, including hallucinations, may we understand these functions (Layng, 2009). Tavris (1992, 2003) argues that there has been a turning away from the environmental context of personal problems in the current focus on individual characteristics such as past history of abuse and low self-esteem. This is not to say that individual histories are not important. It is to say that contextual factors such as gender role expectations comprise a part of individual histories. Service models that focus on altering the behavior of battered women so that their partners will stop abusing them encourage the view that women can control the behavior of their abusive partners if they change their own behavior. Focusing on the victim discounts the social roots of domestic violence (e.g., norms that support male dominance over women; see Gilbert, 1994). A study of 6,000 sheltered women revealed that access to resources permitting independent living (e.g., transportation, child care, and a source of income after leaving the shelter) was the best predictor of whether a woman would remain away from her abusive partner (Gondolf & Fisher, 1988). Responses to abuse of children have been quite different from responses to abuse of an intimate partner (Messing, 2011).

Professional education programs may not provide students with an understanding of historical and structural factors that influence the helping professions (Abbott, 1988; Friedson, 1994; Larson, 1977). The attention of clinicians on a day-to-day basis is on individual clients and families; it is easy to forget to step back to view the larger picture within which clinical practice takes place. It takes an effort to step outside our usual way of viewing the world and consider different perspectives. New ideas may diverge considerably from current views, making it a challenge to accurately understand them so that we can make informed decisions about them. Consider the different views of and reactions to evidence-based practice (e.g., Gambrill, 2006). Many authors define this as using effective interventions, a much narrower view than the philosophy and process of evidence-based practice described in original sources (see Chapter 10). The day-to-day concerns of practice may lull even informed clinicians into complacent acceptance of societal definitions of personal troubles, social problems, and proposed solutions, overlooking their social construction (Loeske, 1999)—forgetting the relativity of these definitions and proposed remedies and changes over time.

INFLUENCE OF AGENCY AND SERVICE SYSTEM VARIABLES

The nature of the practice setting, private or agency-based, influences options for increasing the quality of decisions. Nugus and his colleagues (2010) found that case conferences were more collaborative in community-based health settings than in hospitals. Problems and approaches to them are institutionalized in organizational structures, service systems, and related mission statements. Personal beliefs, as well as generally accepted views in an organization or profession, influence the perceived importance of different tasks. Staff may be overburdened, allowing little time for sound decision making. Commitment hearings and decisions made by child protection staff may be hurried, resulting in misguided (and unfair) actions. For example, public defenders are grossly overburdened; they often each have over 100 cases. Pressures to act quickly may result in avoidable errors. Such pressure may help to explain why professionals may fail to view situations of abuse from the child's perspective. Preferred views of clients, technology used, status and power difference, and beliefs about the importance of different kinds of tasks all influence decisions made. Staff turnover may compromise the quality of decisions. In agency-based practice, a family may have many different workers during one year. Rather than building on what has gone before, new staff members may approach a case as a tabula rasa, with little regard for prior data or recommendations.

Managed-care practices and policies influence duration and kinds of services offered. Services of many kinds have become more privatized as a business, and all services have been influenced by expanding managerialism (regulation of professional practices by administrators, e.g., see Charlton, 2010). Some related changes improve service and some do not, as reflected in dysfunctional documentation requirements, squeezing out time for clients (e.g., Munro, 2011; Rogowski, 2010). Practice is carried out in the context of currently accepted social and public policies and legislation that certain patterns of behavior are problems and certain remedies are appropriate. Many practitioners work in some kind of organization, such as a community mental health center or hospital. These settings differ in the degree to which critical thinking skills and questioning of current practices and policies are encouraged.

Although there is an overlap in the factors that influence decisions in private and agency-based practice, there are differences as well. An understanding on the part of private practitioners about factors that influence agency-based practice will be helpful in identifying constraints on decisions and resources. Professionals in private practice can filter out clients with whom they do not want to work. In agency-based practice, clinicians have much less control over whom they see and what they offer under managed care; clients here may be more challenging because they themselves face greater challenges such as poverty and past histories of victimization (Meichenbaum, 2008). Many professionals work as "double agents"—agents of the state, as in child protection, criminal justice, and psychiatric services in which staff can enforce hospitalization of patients against their will or require outpatient commitment. Policies and legislation and the compromises they reflect because of value differences influence agency constraints and options. Sources of influence on decisions made in agencies include the following:

- Nonvoluntary aspects of the context (for example, criminal justice and child welfare settings).
- Different kinds of professionals involved.
- Clients who use the agency.
- Decision-making style—for example, shared or top-down.
- Clarity of agency policy.
- Criteria used to select services (e.g., scientific, popularity).
- Views about error (recognized as learning opportunities, encouraged to hide, or blamed on individuals).
- Learning opportunities provided (e.g., via corrective feedback regarding the outcomes of decisions).
- Preferred-practice theories.
- Funding sources and related policies and legislation.
- Procedures used to evaluate services and how and with whom results are shared.
- Vulnerability to scandal (newspaper stories).
- Continuing education opportunities available for staff.
- Degree to which critical discussion of differences is sought and valued.
- Degree of integration among different service providers.

Status and Power Differences

Power differences between agency staff and clients favor staff, especially in nonvoluntary settings. This difference allows staff and their representatives (such as attorneys) to have an influential role in the negotiation of decisions, such as whether to return a child to a parent's care. Jacobs (1985), for example, presents a case in which parental and agency reports of what would be in "the best interests of the child" differed greatly. The court had to decide who had the authoritative version. The mother wanted her daughter returned to her care. Jacobs argues that the agency's power and status were used to create credibility for its version that was greater than the credibility of the mother's version, and that this was accomplished through "strategic written maneuvers in constructing the official court report." Identical factual evidence was given quite different interpretations consistent with the goal of the person presenting the view. Those with power in an agency are often interested in retaining it and may view attempts to share power as threatening. This is a key obstacle in moving to evidence-informed practice and social care—a reluctance, for example, to honestly share ignorance and uncertainty about the effectiveness of practice methods. Power relations in an agency may be concealed or denied; this is one way in which a given ideology is maintained (Thompson, 1987). For example, there may be an "old boys group" or an "old girls group" that makes all the important decisions. However, this may be denied by members of the in group.

The history of psychiatric care is replete with examples of the unwarranted exercise of power to deprive people of their freedom, including hospitalization (e.g., of women who wished to pursue a career). (See Scull, 2005; Valenstein, 1986.) Exposing (and decreasing) abuses of psychiatric power is the key aim of organizations such as MindFreedom (www.mindfreedom.org), Alliance for Human Research Protection (www.ahrp.org), Citizens Commission on Human Rights (CCHR) (www.cchr.org).

Available Resources

Decisions about who should receive services and what services should be provided are influenced by both actual and perceived resources which, in turn, are influenced by policies and legislation and their reflection in agency practices. These include access to technological innovations that facilitate informed decisions, such as electronic databases (e.g., the Cochrane and Campbell Libraries). Public policies and related legislation affect what resources are available. Three options are possible when resources are scarce. One is to widen the definition of a resource. Widening the definition may work for or against clients; it works against them if the resources selected are not effective. The second option is to increase the threshold of suffering and harm required before deciding that help should be provided. One of the major conclusions made by Dingwall and his colleagues (1983) following their observation of work in British child protection agencies was the reluctance of staff to identify child maltreatment; professionals tailored their decisions to the resources available. These authors highlighted the relativistic nature of clinical decisions, noting that social workers are continually admonished to consider the individual needs and norms of different groups: that what may constitute child abuse in one group may not in another, and that this relativistic view prevents the system from being overwhelmed by new cases. Often, neglectful circumstances were excused even when clients did have some control over them. Swings in policy in the opposite direction are often made after a high-profile death of a child in care—that is, too many children may be taken into care following a death as a result of media attention.

A third option when resources are scarce is to focus on problems for which resources are plentiful. Clinicians often do not have the resources to alleviate material deprivation and so may focus instead on problems they can resolve, such as psychological and/or interpersonal concerns. A large gap between what can be done and what is needed (whether due to lack of skills on the part of clinicians or lack of other resources) may encourage negative reactions toward clients (if their presence is a reminder of a limited ability to be of help); problems of secondary interest to clients may be focused on. Sedgwick (1982) suggests that too often a request for greater resources "amounts to a request for some form of tardy and individualized intervention in a problem that should be met in preventative terms implicating the wider social and political system" (p. 195).

Access to Information

Although some factors that limit access to information are insurmountable, others are discretionary or self-imposed. For example, a clinician may decide not to collect observational data in real-life settings regarding parent-child exchanges, even though clients are willing, there is time to do so, and such data would be helpful in understanding interaction patterns and in identifying specific changes needed to help the clients. Access to some environments is at the discretion of those who inhabit them, as in the case of those who can enter clients' homes only with the permission of residents. Clumsy efforts to do so may result in lack of access to the premises. Based on a review of case records, Margolin (1997) argues that the major achievement of social workers was gaining access to the privacy of clients' homes. Different kinds of professionals have access to different kinds of information. A physician in an emergency room, especially one who is not familiar with the local community in which a client resides, may ignore or not have information about a family's social situation that may be helpful in identifying the cause of a child's injuries (Dingwall et al., 1983). The physician may have access to medical evidence of child abuse but no data about social evidence or moral evidence (e.g., data about the moral character of clients).

Agency policy concerning record keeping and evaluation influences the quality of information available. Vagueness rather than clarity may be preferred. Clinicians may find it difficult to continue careful evaluation in a climate that favors sloppy evaluation. Clients may not have access to their records and so are unable to correct content they believe to be inaccurate. Staff may not have access to information needed to make informed decisions, such as high-speed computers with relevant databases.

Preferred Views of Clients

Settings differ in the views of clients that are encouraged. Imputations of moral character (as distinguished from objective descriptions) may be conveyed in the way clients and their actions are described as well as in the services selected. Clinicians prefer clients who are manageable and treatable. Past studies of workers in welfare offices found that clients were often viewed as liars and manipulators (Blau, 1960). Wills (1978) suggests that this may occur because workers make dispositional attributions about the cause of client behaviors; they overlook the influence of the situation. Behavior always makes sense to an applied behavior analyst, including delusions and hallucinations; the functions of such behavior are sought (e.g., see Layng, 2009).

Agency Culture and Climate

Clinical settings differ in the contingencies in effect—in what behaviors are reinforced, ignored, or punished. They differ in the extent to which conditions contribute to informed decisions and provide a learning culture (e.g., Gray, 2001a). Rather than being welcomed, raising questions about popular views of a profession, organization, supervisor, professor, or agency may be met with attempts to evade questions or discredit (or cajole) the questioner. Reason (1997) refers to organizational cultures in which "we don't want to know," whistle-blowers are punished, responsibility is skirted, and failure is hidden as pathological cultures. We are less likely to learn how to make better decisions in such cultures. The philosophy of evidence-based practice emphasizes the importance of involving clients as informed participants in decisions and considering their values and preferences. This differs from authoritarian approaches in which paternalism reigns ("We know what is best for you").

Little positive feedback may be offered for competencies that enhance the quality of decisions. Helpful behaviors may be punished. Administrators and supervisors may focus on catching staff doing something wrong rather than catching them performing competently. Supervisors may ignore approximations to desired outcomes. Settings differ in pressure to conform to the majority view. For example, alternative views concerning clients' concerns may be dismissed rather than explored by weighing the evidence for different views. Negative labels may be applied to people who raise questions. Whistle-blowers may be ostracized or fired. Staff may avoid the troublemaker, not wanting to be guilty by association. Attempts to present divergent accounts may gradually wane. It is no wonder that decisions are not optimal in noisy offices with ringing phones, constant interruptions, and heavy documentation demands—the environment in which many practitioners carry out their daily work. Child welfare workers spend considerable time on the computer documenting their activities, leaving little room for face-to-face contact with families (Munro, 2011).

Administrators differ in the kinds of appeals and political maneuvers they favor or tolerate. Such preferences influence the quality of decisions. Just as there are a variety of methods that can be used to encourage change, there are many that can be used to decrease its likelihood, including the manipulation of information. Only some alternatives may be presented. Data can be presented in a way that obscures rather than clarifies what is actually happening (e.g., see Best, 2008; Huff, 1954; Tufte, 1990; 2006). Doubts about a disliked position can be created by spreading rumors. "Once suspicions, apprehensions, or misgivings are created, people will be misled by the old adage 'where there is smoke there is fire.' However, both the smoke and the fire may be illusory" (Michalos, 1971, pp. 100–101). Stonewalling can be used to block change; verbal statements in favor of a decision may be made without doing anything to implement it. Administrators may reaffirm their agreement with an idea by setting a specific date to accomplish a certain task but take no steps to put it into effect. The maneuver of stonewalling occurs anytime someone grants a request but fails to deliver. One of the oldest ways to dilute competitive power is to divide and conquer—to create divisiveness among groups. As long as they are busy arguing with each other, they will not pose a threat.

Staff reorganization is another stratagem. New management systems may be implemented—success being their implementation, as suggested in *Technology as Magic* (Stivers, 2001). This deflects attention from other matters and may juggle responsibilities so that people with opposing views are in less advantageous positions. An administrator may request a study to gain more data relevant to a decision, which precludes action for weeks or months. In an appeal to no precedent it is assumed that if something has not been done by now, there is no good reason it should be done; the idea is that we (or you) would have discovered and corrected it by now if the disputed practice is a poor one. No evidence for or against the wisdom of the proposed change is offered. Tokenism refers to making minimal, unsatisfactory efforts and acting as if they are adequate. Impossible deadlines may be insisted on, restricting time for careful consideration of alternatives. Agreement on a small decision may be sought that can then be appealed to make subsequent larger decisions. It is often argued that the end justifies the means, that even though there are disadvantages to the route suggested, it provides a way to achieve valued outcomes and is therefore justified. It may be argued that because an idea is new, it is ipso facto good. This tactic is the opposite of the no-precedent fallacy. People who use this tactic may attempt to portray an advocate of other positions, especially those that have been or are being used, as a stick-in-the-mud who is not au courant. Developing and facilitating administrative and management arrangements is vital to encouraging evidence-informed practice and policy (Gray, 2001a). This includes a culture of thoughtfulness in which asking questions about practices and policies and their effects is encouraged, and clinicians have access to the tools they need to make informed decisions and to involve clients as informed participants, such as computers with access to relevant databases.

TECHNOLOGY DEVELOPMENT

Decisions are influenced by available technology (see Snyder, Wu, Miller, Jensen, Bantug, & Wolff, 2011). The case record, case conference, and the "medical gaze" are technologies. Each can (and should) be appraised as to whether it does more good than harm. A new app seems to be added every day to smart phones to facilitate informed decisions in clinical contexts. We live in a technological society pervaded by propaganda (Ellul, 1965). Propaganda is defined here as encouraging beliefs and actions with the least thought possible (Ellul, 1965). In *Technology as Magic* (2001), Stivers argues that technology has become so revered that simply making a change (e.g., in management practices) is viewed as an indicator of success. Gray (2001b) suggests that the origins of evidence-based practice and policy include the Internet revolution and the invention of the systematic review. Now clinicians, administrators, and policy makers can gain access to high-quality reviews of research related to many specific practice and policy questions—for example, from the Cochrane and Campbell Collaboration databases of reviews.

The influence of technology is illustrated in the following example. A young man got frostbite while hiking in the Andes, and the local surgeon advised amputation of his big toe. The young man had a digital camera and took pictures of his big toe; he sent these via the Internet to the British Mountaineering Council, which forwarded them to a vascular surgeon, who examined them and advised him not to have his toe amputated but to immediately return to the United Kingdom. There, a vascular surgeon operated— the toe was saved, and three months later the young man ran the London Marathon in just over four hours, dressed as a fairy (Hillebrandt & Imray, 2004). The example of our mountain climber illustrates one of the most robust findings in the literature on decision making—the role of specialized knowledge. It also illustrates the role of technology and access to it (such as the Internet). Without the digital camera and Internet access and without knowledge on the part of the climber about the British Mountaineering Council, the young man would have lost his big toe. Without access to a vascular surgeon with special knowledge and perhaps special equipment, his toe might have been lost. Technology may be oversold, as suggested by reviews of health information systems (Karsh, Weinger, Abbott, & Wears, 2010) and exposés of lack of effective oversight by the Food and Drug Administration (Wilmshurst, 2011). On the other hand, it may be neglected, forgoing opportunities to help clients.

THE INTERACTION BETWEEN CLIENTS AND CLINICIANS

If we want to understand the helping process, we must explore the interactions between helpers and clients and the contexts in which they occur (e.g., see Duncan, Miller,

Wampold, & Hubble, 2010). Studies of helping highlight social influences, even in nondirective approaches (Truax, 1966). Statements that match the therapist's views are reinforced; this may increase the congruence between therapist and client views. Helpers reinforce some behaviors, ignore others, and punish still others. In turn, clients influence the helpers' behavior. Clients may even report content from their dreams that is consistent with the counselor's conceptualizations (Whitman, Kramer, & Baldridge, 1963). The subtlety of these social influence processes (they may not be obvious) does not remove the fact that they occur. Margolin (1997) argues that this subtlety allows helpers to misuse their power to the detriment of their clients.

Professionals may selectively scan for negative information. Views based on a negatively biased sample will result in more pessimistic predictions concerning outcomes. Wills (1978) found that the focus on negative qualities grows with increasing experience. "Experience produces an increased emphasis on negative characterological aspects, particularly increased perception of maladjustment, and a less generous view of clients' motivation for change" (p. 981; see discussion of focusing on pathology in Chapter 7). Are professionals more accurate than others? Wills (1978) suggests they are not; "in general, there is no difference in judgmental accuracy between professionals and lay persons" (p. 981). More recent research suggests that professionals are more accurate than are laypeople in identifying pathology. But is what is identified really pathological? (See earlier discussion of the social construction of problems.) Clinicians like clients who participate in the helping process, and who offer counselors success: clients who get better (Wills, 1978). However, many clients are not like this. They have multiple concerns and may be very challenging to engage.

The match between helpers and clients influences outcomes. Houts (1984) found that "psychodynamic clinicians" were less pessimistic in their prognosis about a client when the client's view of their problem was consistent with a psychodynamic orientation. Negative events are more likely to be attributed to environmental factors when clients and clinicians are similar than they are when they are different (Jordan, Harvey, & Weary, 1988). The possibility of mismatches between helpers and clients has led some investigators to describe helper-client interactions as problematic social situations (Stone, 1979, p. 46). (See also Katz, 2002.) Waitzkin (1991) describes exchanges between physicians and patients as "micropolitical situations" in which the control of information reinforces the power relations that parallel those in the broader society, especially those concerning social class, gender, race, and age (p. 54). Studies of interaction between physicians and patients in establishing diagnoses (Fiks, Hughes, Gafen, Guevara, & Barg, 2011) show that although patients may view the exchange as reciprocal, physicians actively pursue their particular view. Research illustrates the social influence efforts of physicians to encourage patients to engage in certain behaviors, for example to get a test (Heritage & Clayman, 2010; Nugus et al., 2010). Power imbalances highlight the importance of ethical components of evidence-informed practice, such as transparency regarding what is done with what results and involving clients as informed participants in decisions.

Both clients and professionals arrive at the first interview with preconceptions. Clinicians differ in their beliefs about degree of personal responsibility for problems and solutions (McGovern, Newman, & Kopta, 1986). Personal barriers to communication include a lack of respect for others and a lack of relationship skills and knowledge of when to use them (Katz, 2002). Countertransference effects may result in being underprotective of clients or assuming too much responsibility for their lives. Cultural differences between clients and helpers may increase the likelihood of miscommunication and other avoidable errors. If clinicians believe that poor, relatively nonverbal clients are not good candidates for counseling, they may not try as hard to engage such clients, and, as a consequence, clients may drop out. This may confirm original beliefs. Client characteristics such as severity of concerns and motivation influence outcome (Clarkin & Levy, 2004). Class, race, and ethnicity influence diagnosis and services offered (Garb, 1998). Poor people and people of color receive more severe diagnoses and are more likely to be placed on medication (e.g., Kuno & Rothbard, 2002; Segal, Bola, & Watson, 1996). Socioeconomic status is related to dropout rate (Lambert & Ogles, 2004). African American clients are less likely to be referred for individual psychotherapy and are more likely to drop out of treatment than are white people (Abramovitz & Murray, 1983). (For additional discussion of race, gender, and class as they influence practice, see Bartholet, 2009; Gray-Little & Kaplan, 2000.)

Effective relationship skills increase the likelihood of establishing rapport with clients, gaining their participation, and avoiding dropout (see Duncan, Miller, Wampold, & Hubble, 2010; Norcross, 2011). Goldstein (1980) suggests that relationship enhancers such as empathy, warmth, and credibility increase liking, respect, and trust, which in turn increase openness and communication and strengthen the helping alliance. Strupp (1976) suggests that all forms of helping involve a relationship "characterized by respect, interest, understanding, tact, maturity, . . . a firm belief in [one's] ability to help," influence through suggestions, encouragement of open communication, self-scrutiny, honesty, interpretations of material that people are not aware of (such as self-defeating strategies in interpersonal relations), offering examples of "maturity," and "capacity and willingness to profit from the experience" (p. 97). Jerome Frank notes that research has not altered his earlier view of helping as an interpersonal process in which the helper's beliefs, values, and optimism overcome the client's demoralization and offer hope (Frank & Frank, 1991). Clinicians' views of clients are formed relatively swiftly and may remain stable over a long period. How clinicians structure problems affects what they inquire about, which in turn affects what clients report. The type of information focused on differs among therapists of differing theoretical preferences. Once they arrive at a point of view of what the problem is and what factors are related to it, they may search selectively for information to confirm this view in the client's history, current situation, and behavior. Clinicians typically sample only a small portion of a client's repertoires (behavior in the interview). This decreases the likelihood of discovering behavior that is not consistent with expectations. Environmental barriers clinicians may confront include being overworked, high noise levels, and frequent interruptions.

The extensive literature in psychology concerning the helping process and outcome continues to be characterized by controversy regarding contributors to outcome. All would argue that the quality of the relationship is vital and that the particular methods used are important sometimes. (See, for example, the common elements approach of Chorpita and his colleagues [Chorpita, Becker, & Daleiden, 2007].) Placebo effects exert a powerful influence in all helping venues (Benedetti, 2009). Indeed, given the questionable effectiveness of many medications, reports of positive effects may be mainly (or only) due to placebo effects (e.g., see Kirsch, 2010). In their summary of the research regarding the therapeutic relationship and psychotherapy outcome, Lambert and Barley (2002) describe the percentage of outcome variance as a function of different therapeutic factors: expectancy, 15%; common factors, 30%; techniques, 15%; and extratherapeutic change, 40%. Techniques refer to the specific methods used. Nonspecific factors refer to "variables found in most therapies regardless of the therapist's theoretical orientation such as empathy, warmth, acceptance, encouragement of risk taking, client and therapist characteristics, confidentiality of the client-therapist relationship, the therapeutic alliance or process factors" (Lambert & Barley, 2002, pp. 17–18). Another way of looking at this area of research is in terms of *unexplained* variance in outcome. This highlights the unexplained variance (40%) compared to patient contribution (30%), therapy relationship (12%), treatment method (8%), individual therapist (7%), and other factors (3%) (Norcross & Lambert, 2011). Lambert and Barley (2002) conclude that "Measures of therapeutic relationship variables consistently correlate more highly with client outcome than specialized therapy techniques. Associations between the therapeutic relationship and client outcome are strongest when measured by client ratings of both constructs." It is estimated that two thirds of the observed small differences between psychotherapies in relation to outcome can be attributed to allegiance (preferences of helpers for a particular method; Lambert & Barley, 2002, p. 20; Luborsky et al., 1999).

Based on his review of the literature, Wampold (2006) sums up his views as follows: ". . . in clinical trials, the variability of outcomes due to therapists (8%–9%) is larger than the variability among treatments (0%–1%), the alliance (5%), and the superiority of an EST [empirically established treatment] to a placebo treatment (0%–4%), making it the most robust predictor of outcomes of any factor studied, with the exception of the initial level of severity" (p. 204). (See also Imel, Wampold, Miller, & Flemming, 2008;

Wampold, 2010; Wampold, Imel, & Miller, 2009.) Therapist variables related to positive outcome include helper credibility, empathic understanding, affirmation of the client, skill in engaging clients, a focus on the client's problems, and skill in directing the client's attention to the client's affect or experience (Norcross, 2011). "Some therapists are better than others at contributing to positive client outcome. Clients characterize such therapists as more understanding and accepting, empathic, warm, and supportive. They engage in fewer negative behaviors such as blaming, ignoring, or rejecting" (Lambert & Barley, 2002, p. 26). Wampold (2006) concludes that "The relatively large proportion of variability in outcomes due to therapists infers that some psychotherapists consistently produce better outcomes than others" (p. 205). The quality of the relationship is related to sharing information needed to arrive at well-reasoned decisions and encouraging clients to participate in other ways. Relationship skills are a critical ingredient of evidence-based practice. Helpers who are cold, closed down, or judgmental are not as likely to involve clients as collaborators as are those who are warm, supportive, and empathic.

PSYCHOLOGICAL FACTORS THAT INFLUENCE JUDGMENTS

Clinicians' goals and affect influence interaction with clients, as do the information-processing strategies they use (see Chapter 9). How physicians feel influences their approach to patient safety (Croskerry, Abbass, & Wu, 2010). People differ in how they approach problems and in the way they handle uncertainty and risk. Evidence-informed practice emphasizes the importance of seeking information about the degree of uncertainty related to decisions and sharing what is found with clients. We must go beyond the information at hand in making decisions, because rarely (if ever) do we have all relevant data. Tools we use include practice theories. Preferred practice theories and the availability of information influence what we see. A psychoanalytically oriented clinician may attend to different factors than one who is behaviorally oriented. Our attention is drawn to data that are vivid such as bizarre symptoms, ignoring data that are less vivid such as the environmental functions of such behavior. Observers tend to attribute behavior to characteristics of the person rather than to situational factors (the fundamental attribution error); the actor's behavior is more noticeable (available) compared to more static situational events. In addition, our self-assessments are often flawed. Such incorrect beliefs may interfere with sound decisions. Based on a review of related literature, Dunning, Heath, and Suls (2004) concluded that ". . . people's capacity to evaluate themselves and predict their behavior is usually quite modest and often much more meager than common intuition would lead us to believe" (p. 70).

A number of authors describe what they term our "innumeracy," referring to our difficulties in reasoning correctly about uncertainty (Best, 2008; Paulos, 1988). Gigerenzer

(2002a) highlights four sources of uncertainty: (1) the illusion of certainty, (2) ignorance of risk, (3) miscommunication of risk, and (4) clouded thinking. The first point
is addressed in Chapter 4—that is, a justification approach to knowledge in which it is
assumed that we can arrive at certain truth, for example, by piling up examples. Ignorance of risk refers to being uninformed about the risks associated with different decisions, such as having a mammogram or attending an anxiety screening day. The third
point, miscommunication of risk, refers to not knowing how to communicate risk in
an understandable way. For example, a physician may know the risks associated with
a certain test but not be able to clearly communicate this knowledge to a patient so
that the patient can make an informed decision (Paling, 2006). The fourth kind of
innumeracy, clouded thinking, refers to knowing the risks but not knowing how to draw
correct inferences from them. "For instance, physicians often know the error rates of a
clinical test and the base rate of a disease, but not know how to infer from this information the chances that a patient with a positive test actually has the disease" (Gigerenzer,
2002a, p. 25). This potent foursome illustrates the many opportunities for others to
bamboozle us (intentionally or not). Professionals may be as ignorant of risks and how
to calculate, communicate, and draw inferences from them as may clients. Gigerenzer
as well as others illustrate the negative consequences that may occur from these sources
of innumeracy, such as being misinformed about the diagnostic accuracy of a test (such
as a mammogram) and as a result having invasive, unnecessary interventions, such as
biopsies or prophalactic mastectomies. Thus, as he suggests, the motto that applies is
"Dare to know." The rules of thumb we use also influence our judgments, as described in
Chapter 9. (See also discussion of barriers in Chapter 1.)

SUMMARY

Many environments affect the quality of clinical decisions in both private and agency-
based practice, including past (political, economic, and social influences on the development of the helping professions), present (interactions during interviews and current
service-delivery systems), and future (anticipated changes in policies). What is viewed
as deviant and what is not and what resources are provided to address problems are
related to larger structural variables. What is viewed as a problem differs at different
times and in different groups. Not considering the larger picture leaves you prey to influences you may reject if you understand them, including their consequences. Practice
theories and professions develop in a particular historical context. The setting in which
decisions are made also influences decisions. In agency-based practice, the quality of
decisions may be compromised by large caseloads, lack of clear policy concerning priorities, and contradictory demands from diverse sources. In both private and agency-based

practice, preferred views of clients, available resources, and social and time pressures affect decisions. Other influences include competing goals, access to different kinds of information, and agency culture. Cultures may be blame focused rather than learning focused in which errors are viewed as opportunities to learn how to avoid them in the future.

Clinical practice requires integrating information from diverse sources, often a challenging task. Motivational and emotional reactions may bias judgments. We are reluctant to acknowledge uncertainty and prone to various kinds of innumeracy when reasoning about it. We tend to discount conflicting evidence, fail to search for disconfirming evidence, and are biased toward dispositional explanations (searching for causes in the individual). The match between a client and a clinician and the quality of the helping relationship also affect decisions. All these influences on decisions highlight the importance of critical thinking to minimize influences that detract from making sound decisions. Ignorance is not bliss in relation to understanding how our environments influence decisions. It may result in misattributions for lack of success, which may be an obstacle to improving decisions. Clinicians may blame themselves for consequences that have little or nothing to do with the quality of their clinical skills but everything to do with the agency in which they practice and the agency's environment; or clients may be blamed. As a consequence of not identifying the true obstacles, we are less likely to take effective action. Attention to and critique of practices and policies that diminish client agency and ignore environmental contributions to avoidable suffering, and indeed contribute to it by pathologizing such suffering, have grown—fueled in part by revelations of the pursuit of profit by creation of ever more alleged illnesses in need of marketable products and conflicts of interest among the many players.

CHAPTER

3

Reasons and Reasoning: The Heart of Making Decisions

Clinical reasoning involves making and evaluating arguments, making judgments, and drawing conclusions. Considerable attention has been devoted to the description of reasoning fallacies on the part of clients, and this is a major emphasis in cognitive behavioral and rational-emotive therapy. Attention has also been devoted to describing biases and fallacies that occur in clinical reasoning. Consider the following claims: What do you think?

- We know that mental illnesses are brain diseases, because people get better after taking medication.
- Since most people labeled schizophrenic have taken medication, changes found in their brains are due to medication effects.
- The benefits of taking Abilify outweigh the side effects.

Colorful titles such as *Follies and Fallacies in Medicine* (Skrabanek & McCormick, 1998) and *Biomedical Bestiary* (Michael, Boyce, & Wilcox, 1984) suggest a concerning variety of fallacies that may affect the well-being of clients. Consider the following from *Biomedical Bestiary*:

Nerd of Nonsignificance—Assumes there is no real relationship between two or more variables because none was found in a study.

Diagnostic Zealot—Overzealous peddler of the latest diagnostic test. He has fooled himself (and may fool you, too) into untested belief in the benefits of a diagnostic test.

Examples from *Follies and Fallacies in Medicine*:

- *The ecological fallacy*: Assuming that relationships in populations occur in an individual.
- *The fallacy of obfuscation*: Use of language to mystify rather than clarify.

- *The "hush hush" fallacy:* Ignoring the fact that mistakes are inevitable.
- *The fallacy of the golden mean:* Assuming that the consensus of a group indicates the truth.

Gigerenzer (2002a) describes concerning lapses in reasoning on the part of physicians and social workers that have life-affecting consequences for clients such as overestimating the accuracy of tests. (See Chapter 15.)

Reasoning is "largely the conversion of unconscious judgments, feelings, and knowledge into something more explicit" (Scriven, 1976, p. 180). It is concerned with exploring assumptions related to premises; that is, a tentative conclusion is drawn and then assumptions related to the conclusion are reviewed to determine whether the conclusion is warranted. In evidence-based practice (EBP), a key part of this review involves considering research related to information needs. Clinical reasoning involves debating with ourselves and checking our assumptions. The terms *reasoning, problem solving, decision making,* and *thinking* are closely related, and the tasks they involve overlap. We make decisions to address problems. Reasoning involves an interaction between ourselves and the situations we encounter. (See discussion of the importance of the tasks we confront in Chapter 9.)

Far from being a dull, uncreative activity, arriving at well-reasoned inferences requires skill, flexibility, and sensitivity to the different kinds of evidence relevant to different kinds of questions—for example, about the effectiveness of an intervention such as cognitive-behavioral therapy for depression, or the accuracy of an assessment measure such as the Beck Depression Inventory. This does not mean that we go through Dewey's (1933) steps: (1) clarifying the problem, (2) identifying alternatives, (3) reviewing the advantages and disadvantages of each, and (4) selecting the best option and trying it out. Indeed, as we develop expertise in an area, we rapidly size up a situation based on past experiences that provided corrective feedback: that is, we move on to pattern recognition. We often "satisfice" rather than maximize, as described in Chapter 15. Experts pay attention to anomalies that may reflect that something is amiss. (See discussion of differences between experts and novices in Chapters 8 and 9.) Being reasonable "takes courage, because it seldom corresponds to being popular" (Scriven, 1976, p. 5).

VIEWS OF INTELLECTUAL COMPETENCE

Discussions about what makes a good thinker are as old as philosophy itself. Let's take a look at what one author views as knowledge, abilities, attitudes, and ways of behaving that are characteristic of a good thinker (Nickerson, 1987, pp. 29–30). These characteristics are integral to evidence-based practice and illustrate the close relationship between critical thinking and EBP. A good thinker:

- Uses evidence skillfully and impartially.
- Organizes thoughts and describes them concisely and coherently.
- Distinguishes between logically valid and invalid inferences.
- Understands the difference between reasoning and rationalizing.
- Tries to anticipate consequences of alternative options before choosing one.
- Understands the idea of degrees of belief.
- Has a sense of the value and cost of information, and knows how to seek information when needed.
- Detects similarities and analogies that are not obvious.
- Can learn independently and has an interest in doing so.
- Appropriately generalizes problem-solving techniques to different areas.
- Can structure informally presented problems so that formal techniques (e.g., mathematics) can be used to solve them.
- Listens carefully to other people's ideas.
- Understands the difference between winning an argument and being right.
- Recognizes that most real-world problems have more than one possible solution and that those solutions may differ in many ways and may be difficult to compare in terms of a single criterion of merit.
- Looks for unusual approaches to complex problems.
- Can represent differing viewpoints without distortion, exaggeration, or caricaturization.
- Is aware that understanding is always limited.
- Recognizes the fallibility of one's opinions and the probability of bias in them and the danger of differentially weighing evidence according to personal preferences.
- Can strip a verbal argument of irrelevancies and phrase it in terms of its essentials.
- Understands the differences among conclusions, assumptions, and hypotheses.
- Habitually questions one's own views and attempts to understand related assumptions and implications.
- Is sensitive to the difference between the validity of a belief and the intensity with which it is held.

There is a lively literature regarding the distinction between unskilled and skilled thinkers. A skill analogy suggests certain distinctions and concepts, such as the difference between general and specific skills. Whether there are general skills is a topic of controversy. Metacognitive skills include planning, monitoring, and evaluating knowledge and performance, as well as recognizing the utility of a skill; we reason about our reasoning (Schraw & Dennison, 1994). Research showing that the value of a strategy is often context bound (related to a particular kind of problem) is a strike against the economy hypothesis, in which it is proposed that great benefit can be derived from learning a few general strategies. (See other sources for discussion of transfer; Halpern, 2003; Haskell, 2001.) The importance of domain-specific knowledge, including both content knowledge (knowing what) as well as procedural knowledge (knowing how to carry out certain procedures), is supported by research that shows that physicians who made accurate clinical decisions in their areas of expertise were not as likely to do so when they were considering problems in another specialty (Elstein et al., 1978; see also Chapter 8).

A skill approach to critical thinking suggests use of strategies. For example, physicians who make accurate medical assessments pay attention to information that contradicts a diagnosis (Elstein et al., 1978). They question initial assumptions when confronted with anomalies. Analyses of lapses in reasoning in arguments given by 300 subjects about social issues showed that the most common ones involved failures to evaluate or elaborate the model offered—for example, counterexamples were overlooked (Perkins, Allen, & Hafner, 1983)—an illustration of the negative consequences of a justification approach to knowledge (searching only for data that support preferred views). So, both rules and pattern recognition may be important—serving as useful for different kinds of problems. Decision aids such as Palm Pilots and algorithms may be used as reminders (e.g., Larrick, 2005).

Thinking ability and intelligence are only partially related; either can be modified independently of the other; that is, how people use their intelligence can be altered. For example, high intelligence is no guarantee of creativity (Weisberg, 1986). Simply knowing about a strategy is not enough. Other requirements include knowing (1) how to apply it (necessary background knowledge and specific means of putting the strategy to work are needed), (2) when to apply it, and (3) fluidity of use (strategies become automatic; Perkins, 1985, p. 352). In addition, our values must encourage its use. Our view of strategies (for example, their plausibility), as well as factors such as forgetting, influence their use.

REASONS

Many kinds of reasons are used in clinical decision making, and different theories emphasize different ones. These differences affect how problems are framed and what information is gathered. Consider the following four examples:

1. Bill drinks because he is an alcoholic; he has a disease.
2. Mary's hallucinations are caused by a mental disorder—schizophrenia.
3. Joe's antisocial behavior at school is related to the teacher's ineffective curriculum planning and classroom management skills, as well as few recreational activities.

4. HIV risk behaviors are due to a variety of causes, all of which contribute to their frequency and all of which must be addressed.

In the first two examples we see appeals to underlying mental disorder, to biomedical causes. In the third, a social learning view is emphasized and the fourth takes a multi-attribute view. Different people appeal to different sources of evidence as reasons for using a method or policy. Clinicians often reason from analogy; that is, they look to what has happened before to discover what to do in novel situations; they seek and draw conclusions from a comparison of experiences. The analogy of psychological problems to illness is perhaps the best-known analogy in clinical practice and one that is widely accepted, as can be seen by the popularity of psychiatric diagnoses implying a "mental disorder." Spirited, well-argued critiques of this analogy, often presented as a fact, are available to those who wish to critically appraise it (e.g., Boyle, 2002; Moncreiff, 2008; Szasz, 1994). Troubling behaviors, feelings, and thoughts are often attributed to many different causes as in the fourth in the preceding list. This is an example of a multicausal view. Tesh (1988) argues that such a view allows planners to focus on only one, ignoring the rest, misleading the public that a problem has been addressed.

Arguments based on analogy depend on the similarity of the cases compared. Questions of concern (Terry, 1973, p. 99) include: How many respects are similar? How many respects are dissimilar? Are the bases of comparison relevant to the issue? Is there agreement on the major points? For example, those who do not accept the disease view of alcoholism argue that problematic drinking does not have the characteristic of a disease; for example, drinking does not necessarily become worse without treatment and, for some, one drink does not lead to many (e.g., Fingarette, 1988). (See also Heyman, 2009.) Analogies may be literal or figurative. Literal analogies involve comparison between classes, cases, or objects of the same kind. Figurative analogies involve comparison between unlike categories.

Clinicians generalize from samples to populations. A psychiatrist may interview three Vietnamese families and make assumptions about all Vietnamese families. The accuracy of a generalization depends on the size and representativeness of the sample and the degree of variability in a population. If there is no variability, a sample of one is sufficient. Questions of concern include: Do the examples accurately reflect characteristics of the population? What variations occur?

Making clinical decisions requires reasoning from signs and symptoms. Observed signs (such as slumped shoulders, downcast eyes, and tears) may be used to infer emotional states such as depression. That is, the signs are used as signifiers of a state. Signs may be used as indicative of a certain history. An example is the use of the (invalid) reflex anal dilatation test to evaluate whether children had been abused sexually by their parents (Hobbs & Wynne, 1989). A key question here concerns validity—whether the signs are really indicators of the state assumed. In medicine there are signs as well as symptoms. For example, if you feel hot (a symptom), your physician can take your temperature (a sign). Do we have signs in other helping professions? Some argue that magnetic resonance imaging (MRI) has revealed brain differences between those viewed as having a mental disorder and those not so labeled. Others argue that such research is flawed (e.g., see Leo & Cohen, 2003; Vul, Harris, Winkielman, & Pashler, 2009).

Clinicians also reason by cause; that is, they have assumptions about the causes of particular concerns such as homelessness, poverty, anxiety, substance abuse, obsessions, or marital disharmony. (See Chapter 15.) The study of attributions and factors that influence them is an active area of research. Publications such as *Skeptic* and *The Skeptical Inquirer* explore the evidentiary status of proposed causes of behavior, such as spirits from past lives. However, lack of evidence for a claim does not mean that it is incorrect. Nor does lack of evidence discourage people from believing a claim. Indeed, some clinicians believe in theories that have no supporting evidence. See, for example, *Science and Pseudoscience in Clinical Psychology* (Lilienfeld, Lynn, & Lohr, 2003); *Controversial Therapies for Developmental Disabilities: Fad, Fashion, and Science in Professional Practice* (Jacobson, Foxx, & Mulick, 2005). Beutler (2000) concludes that most of the theories and approaches that are used by practitioners are unsupported by empirical evidence of effects. Is the picture more positive in medicine? It depends on whom you ask. Some, such as Richard Smith (2003), past editor of the *British Medical Journal*, do not think so.

Another form of reasoning is by exclusion. Alternative accounts for an event or behavior are identified, and the adequacy of each is examined. This involves a search for rival explanations. For example, if a client is referred to a community mental health agency because of intractable depression, one hypothesis may be that this is an unsolvable problem, given modern-day knowledge. A rival hypothesis may be that this client did not receive state-of-the-art intervention and that improvement would follow such intervention. The book *Rival Hypotheses* (Huck & Sandler, 1979) presents 100 different claims and invites readers to evaluate these in order to sharpen their skills in identifying alternative hypotheses. A search for alternative explanations is a key strategy we can use to avoid premature acceptance of a claim or explanation that may be inaccurate (see Chapter 4).

Hot and cold reasons correspond to two major routes to persuasion—by affective association (hot) or by reasoned argument (cold) (e.g., MacCoun, 1998). Many people try to persuade others by offering reasons that play on our emotions and appeal to accepted beliefs and values (Walton, 1992). Simon (1983) uses the example of Hitler's *Mein Kampf*: "Hitler was an effective rhetorician for Germans precisely because his passion and incentives resonated with beliefs and values already present in many German hearts. The heat of his rhetoric rendered his readers incapable of applying the rules of reason and evidence to his arguments. Nor was it only Germans who resonated to the facts and values he proclaimed. The latent anti-Semitism and overt anti-Communism of many Western statesmen made a number of his arguments plausible to them" (pp. 98–99). Appealing to our emotions is a key strategy used in human service advertisements. Propaganda in the helping professions takes advantage of emotional reasoning, as discussed in Chapter 4.

HELPFUL DISTINCTIONS

Some people confuse the use of logical principles and reasoning. Logic is concerned with the form or validity of deductive arguments. "It provides methods and rules for restating information so as to make what is implicit explicit. It has little to do with the determination of truth or falsity" (Nickerson, 1986b, p. 7). Effective clinical reasoning requires much more than logic; it requires skill in developing arguments and hypotheses, establishing the relevance of information to an argument, and evaluating the plausibility of assertions. It requires inventiveness and a willingness to change beliefs on the basis of evidence gathered. Johnson-Laird (1985) offered this example concerning who committed a murder. The victim was stabbed to death in a movie theater. The suspect was traveling on a train to London when the murder took place. Logically it seems that this suspect must be innocent: One person cannot be in two places at once. However, the only way to guarantee the truth of a conclusion is to eliminate all possible counterexamples. "Logic cannot ensure that one has considered all the different ways in which the murder might have been accomplished. Like most everyday problems that call for reasoning, the explicit premises leave most of the relevant information unstated. Indeed, the real business of reasoning in these cases is to determine the relevant factors and possibilities, and it therefore depends on a knowledge of the specific domain. Hence, the construction of putative counter examples calls for an active exercise of memory and imagination rather than a formal derivation of one expression from others" (p. 45). Similarly, logic will not be of value in deciding that a client who complains of fatigue and headaches should be seen by a physician to determine if there is a physical cause of these complaints; knowledge as well as logic is required. Specialized knowledge may be required to evaluate the plausibility of premises related to an argument. Creativity and reasoning go hand in hand, especially in areas such as clinical decision making, which involves unstructured situations in which needed information is often hard to get or missing. Strategies suggested by Halpern (2003) to encourage creativity include defining a problem in different ways, working with people from different backgrounds, and combining attributes in different ways (p. 426).

Reasoning Compared to Rationalizing

Reasoning involves the review of evidence against as well as evidence in favor of a position. Rationalizing entails a selective search for evidence in support of a belief or action that may or may not be deliberate. "[It is] easy after having made some choice that is significant in our lives to fall into the trap of convincing ourselves of the reasonableness of that choice. It is also easy to forget, with the passage of time, what the real determinants of the choice were and to substitute for them 'reasons' that make the choice seem like a good one, and perhaps a better one than it actually was" (Nickerson, 1986b, p. 14). The research of Elizabeth Loftus and others shows that memory is a reconstructive process. False memories can be implanted (Loftus, 2004). Our views of an event, such as the reasons for a divorce, may change over time. When we rationalize arguments, we are interested in building a case rather than weighing evidence for and against an argument. (See also discussion of excuses in Chapter 17.) This is not to say that there is no interest in persuasion when arguments are presented; the difference lies in a search for evidence against as well as in support of a view and an openness to changing our mind when a better argument is offered.

Propaganda/Bias/Point of View

It is helpful to distinguish among propaganda, bias, and points of view (MacLean, 1981). *Bias* refers to an emotional leaning to one side (see also Chapter 12). Biased people try to persuade others but may not be aware that they are doing so. They may use propaganda tactics and faulty reasoning and may offer statements in a manner designed to gain uncritical acceptance of a biased position. Personal biases may make if difficult to identify biases. "*Propagandists* are aware of their interests and usually intentionally disguise these." Here, too, messages are couched in a way to encourage uncritical acceptance (see Chapter 4). Those with a *point of view* are also aware of their interests, but sources are described and propaganda ploys are avoided; statements are made in a manner that invites critical review. Views can be examined because they are clearly stated. People with a point of view are open to clarifying their statements when asked.

Reasoning and the Truth

Reasoning does not necessarily yield the truth. "People who are considered by many of their peers to be reasonable people often do take, and are able to defend quite convincingly, diametrically opposing positions on controversial matters" (Nickerson, 1986b, p. 12). However, effective reasoners are more likely to generate assertions that are closer to the truth than ineffective reasoners. The accuracy of a conclusion does not necessarily indicate that the reasoning used to reach it was sound; errors in the opposite direction may have canceled each other out.

Logical Reasoning and Creativity

A number of terms reflect the difference between rigorous logical reasoning and exploratory thinking, between the generation of hypothesis and the testing of hypotheses. Examples include divergent versus convergent thinking, and problem finding versus problem solving. However, a sharp distinction between the two kinds of thinking does not hold. Assigning appropriate weight to evidence for or against a claim is a key part of what it means to be reasonable. The term *evidence-based practice* draws attention to the kinds of evidence (reasons) relied on to make practice and policy decisions.

Consistency/Corroboration and Critical Testing

Distinguishing among consistency, corroboration, and proof is important in assigning proper weight. We often use consistency in support of an assumption; for example, we search for consistent evidence when exploring a depressed client's history of depression. An assertion should be consistent with other beliefs that are held; that is, self-contradictory views should not knowingly be entertained. Of the three criteria (proof, falsifiability, and consistency), consistency is the weakest for offering evidence. Two or more assertions may be consistent with each other but yield little or no insight into the soundness of an argument. Saying that A (a history of mental illness) is consistent with B (alleged current mental illness) is to say only that it is possible to believe B given A. (See discussion of use of the word proof in Chapter 4.)

Critically Appraising Claims Compared to Seeking Support

The accuracy of assumptions may be assessed using quite different criteria, including authority (e.g., status, credentials) and mysticism. Some assertions are not falsifiable; there is no way to determine if they are false. Psychoanalytic theory is often criticized on the grounds that it is not falsifiable—that contradictory hypotheses can be drawn from the theory (Popper, 1963/1972). However, a theory can be shown to be false given that it is falsifiable. Falsifiability is a vital characteristic of assertions.

- It is easy to obtain confirmations, or verifications, for nearly every theory—if we look for confirmations.
- Confirmations should count only if they are the result of risky predictions; that is to say, if, unenlightened by the theory in question, we should have expected an event that was incompatible with the theory—an event that would have refuted the theory.

- Every good scientific theory is a prohibition; it forbids certain things to happen. The more a theory forbids, the better it is.
- A theory that is not refutable by any conceivable event is nonscientific. Irrefutability is not a virtue of a theory (as people often think), but a vice.
- Every genuine test of a theory is an attempt to falsify it or to refute it. Testability is falsifiability, but there are degrees of testability; some theories are more testable, more exposed to refutation, than others; they take, as it were, greater risks.
- Confirming evidence should not count except when it is the result of a genuine test of the theory; and this means that it can be presented as a serious but unsuccessful attempt to falsify the theory. (Popper, 1959, p. 36)

If nothing can ever be proven, as Popper argues, the least we can do is construct falsifiable theories: theories that generate specific hypotheses that can be tested. (See Chapter 4 for further discussion.) In an evidence-based approach to practice, it is assumed that the evidentiary status of a claim is related to the rigor with which it has been critically tested; for example, does a risk-assessment measure accurately predict future behavior?

Facts, Beliefs, and Preferences

It is helpful to distinguish between facts, beliefs, and preferences. A belief can be defined as "confidence that a particular thing is true, as evidenced by a willingness to act as though it were" (Nickerson, 1986b, p. 2). Beliefs vary widely in their evidentiary status. Most clinicians would believe the statement that "childhood experiences influence adult development." There would be less agreement on the accuracy of the assertion that "childhood experiences determine adult development." Facts are capable of being critically appraised; beliefs may not be. Sound reasons consist of those for which sound arguments can be offered. Some beliefs are matters of definition (for example, 3 + 3 = 6). Another helpful distinction is between beliefs and preferences. Beliefs are statements that, in principle, can be shown to be true or false, whereas with preferences, it does not make sense to consider them as true or false because people differ in their preferences. An example of a preference statement is "I prefer insight-oriented treatment." An example of a belief is "Play therapy can help children to overcome anxiety." Here, evidence can be gathered to determine if this is indeed the case. Additional examples of opinions and beliefs follow. The first one is a preference and the last two are beliefs.

- "I like to collect payment for each session at the end of the session."
- "Insight therapy is more effective than cognitive behavioral treatment of depression."

- "My pet Rottweiler helps people with their problems" (quote from a psychologist on a morning talk show, April 6, 1988).

The woman who offered the last statement also described the value of her Rottweiler in offering support to her clients during interviews: The dog would sit by the wife when she spoke and move over to the husband and offer support to him when he spoke. We often allow our preferences to influence our beliefs, even though preferences and beliefs should be independent. Another common distinction is between mindful action, in which an active effort is made to understand something, and automatic functioning, in which tasks are carried out fairly automatically. The effectiveness of different styles depends on whether use of fast and frugal heuristics matches what is needed to solve problems. (See Chapter 9.)

ARGUMENTS

There are many products of reasoning: Arguments are one. The term *argumentation* refers to the process of making claims, challenging them, backing them with reasons, criticizing these reasons, and responding to the criticism offered (Toulmin, Rieke, & Janik, 1979, p. 13). In clinical practice, this process is often implicit, as different possible causes of client concerns are considered. An argument in this sense refers to the claims and reasons offered for these—that is, "a set of assertions that is used to support a belief" (Nickerson, 1986b, p. 2). This term has a different meaning in everyday use, in which it refers to disagreements between two or more people (for example, "They had an argument about who would go to the store"). Arguments involve a set of assertions, one of which is a conclusion, and the rest of which are intended to support that conclusion. For example, a clinician may argue that because a client has a history of being hospitalized for anxiety and compulsive hand-washing, current complaints about anxiety and obsessive thoughts indicate that another severe episode of compulsive hand-washing is imminent. This conclusion is based on the premise that there is a history of hospitalization for what seem to be similar problems. The purpose of arguments is often to convince someone (or oneself) that something is true, or to convince someone to act in a certain way. Another purpose is to explore the accuracy of an assumption—for example, about the effectiveness of a practice method.

Arguments consist of parts; they can be taken apart as well as put together. They may be strong (convincing) or weak (unconvincing), simple or complex. A complex argument usually involves several assertions in support of one or more conclusions. Assertions may involve statements of fact ("a belief for which there is enough evidence to justify a high degree of confidence"; Nickerson, 1986b, p. 36), assumptions, or hypotheses. For example, there may be no doubt that a client was hospitalized. The term assumption refers to "an assertion that we either believe to be true in spite of being unable to produce compelling evidence of its truth, or are willing to accept as true for purposes of debate or discussion." A hypothesis is an assertion that we do not know to be true but that we believe to be testable (pp. 36–37). Assumptions, hypotheses, or statements of fact may be used as premises in an argument—or, they may serve as conclusions; that is, an assertion may be a conclusion that is drawn from what precedes it and can also be a premise with respect to what follows it. "The credibility of a conclusion can be no greater than the least credible of the premises from which it is drawn, so a conclusion cannot be considered a statement of fact unless all of the premises are statements of fact. If the conclusion follows from two premises one of which is considered to be a fact and the other an assumption, the conclusion should not be considered a statement of fact" (p. 37). Universal assertions that contain words such as all or none are much more difficult to defend than are particular assertions that contain qualifiers such as some. The statement that all children of alcoholic parents have problems as adults would be more difficult to support than the more modest claim that some children of alcoholic parents have problems later.

A key part of an argument is the claim, conclusion, or position that is put forward (see Exhibit 3.1). In the statement "Mary Walsh is the person who is responsible for the abuse of this child; she had the greatest opportunity," the claim or conclusion is clear. Often, excessive wordiness makes the premises and/or conclusion difficult to identify; that is, "an eloquent speaker or writer can dress up his arguments in all kinds of ways so as to conceal their deficits and make them attractive to his audience" (Toulmin et al., 1979, p. 106). The claim here is that Mary Walsh is guilty of the abuse of the child. Claims or conclusions are often qualified; that is, some probability is expressed (for example, "I think there is a 90 percent probability that Mary Walsh abused this child"). Conclusions can be further qualified by describing the conditions under which they do, or do not, hold. A clinician may believe that she would only abuse the child "if she were under extreme stress."

A second critical feature of an argument consists of the reasons or premises offered to support the claim made. Premises can be divided into two parts—grounds and warrants. The grounds (data or evidence) must be relevant to the claim as well as sufficient to support the claim; that is where warrants come in. Warrants concern the justification for making the connection between the grounds and the claim. The question is: Do the grounds provide support for the claim made? Warrants may involve appeals to common knowledge, empirical evidence, practice theory, and so on. Let's return to the claim that Mary Walsh is responsible for the abuse of a child. The grounds are that

Exhibit 3.1 Toulmin's Six Types of Statements in a Rational Argument

Label	Name	Logical Function
C	Claim or conclusion	States a claim or a conclusion.
D	Data, evidence, or foundation	Offers data or foundations (i.e., relevant evidence) for the claim.
W	Inference warrant	Warrants or justifies the connection between data (D) and claim (C) by appealing to a rule of inference, such as an operational definition, a practical standard, or an analogy.
Q	Modal qualifier	Qualifies a claim or conclusion (C) by expressing degrees of confidence and likelihood.
R	Rebuttal or reservation	Rebuts a claim or conclusion (C) by stating the conditions under which it does not hold; or introduces reservations showing the limits within which the claim (C) is made.
B	Backing	Backs up, justifies, or otherwise supports an inference warrant (W) by appealing to further evidence (empirical data, common knowledge, professional practice, scientific theory, and so on).

Colloquially speaking:

C		Answers the questions "What are you saying?" "What is it you are claiming?" "What is your conclusion?"
D		Answers the questions "What have you to go on?" "Where is your evidence?" "What data do you have?"
W		Answers the questions "How do you make that out?" "What is the connection?" "Why are you entitled to draw that conclusion?"
Q		Answers the questions "How sure are you?" "What confidence do you have in your claim?" "How likely is it that what you say is correct?"
R		Answers the questions "What are you assuming?" "Under what conditions would your argument break down?" "What reservations would you make?"
B		Answers the questions "What proof have you?" "What is the justification for your line of reasoning?" "Is there any support for the connection you are making?"

Source: From *The Case-Study Method in Psychology and Related Disciplines* (p. 195), by D.B. Bromley, 1986, New York: Wiley. Copyright 1986 by John Wiley & Sons. Reprinted by permission.

she had the opportunity to abuse the child. The warrant is probably something of the nature that opportunity is sufficient to yield abuse, clearly an inaccurate assumption. There is no firm backing for the warrant; opportunity does not an abuser make. So warrants purport to offer evidence for making the step from the grounds to the claim, and the strength of the support offered should be evaluated. How reliably does the warrant offer such evidence? Are the grounds necessary or sufficient? For example, opportunity is necessary but not sufficient. (See also the discussion of clues to causality in Chapter 14.) The possible combinations of false or true premises and conclusions are shown in Exhibit 3.2.

Exhibit 3.2 The Four Combinations of True or False Premises and Conclusions in a Valid Logical Argument

		Conclusion	
		True	**False**
Premises	True	Necessary (Conclusion must be true if premises are true.)	Impossible (Conclusion cannot be false if premises are true.)
	False	Possible (Conclusion may be true even if premises are false.)	Possible (Conclusion may be false if premises are false.)

Note: Entries in the table indicate how the truth or falsity of the conclusion depends on the truth or falsity of the premises.

Source: From Reflections on Reasoning (p. 90), by R. S. Nickerson, 1986, Hillsdale, NJ: Erlbaum. Copyright 1986 by Lawrence Erlbaum Associates. Reprinted by permission.

An argument may be unsound for one of three reasons. There may be something wrong with its logical structure: (1) all mental patients are people; (2) John is a person; (3) therefore, John is a mental patient. It may contain false premises: (1) all battering men were abused as children; (2) Mr. Smith batters his wife; (3) therefore, Mr. Smith was abused as a child. It may be irrelevant or circular: (1) kicking other children is a sign of aggression; (2) Johnny kicks other children; (3) therefore, Johnny is aggressive. The last two arguments contain informal fallacies; they have a correct logical form but are still incorrect. Informal fallacies are related to the content of arguments rather than to their form. There are many varieties of informal fallacies (see Chapters 5 and 6). Arguments often contain unfounded premises. They may give the impression that they are valid arguments, but because relevant facts have not been presented correctly (they may have been left out, evaded, or distorted), they are not valid. An example of the logical error of affirming the consequence is: (1) if he has measles, he should have red spots; (2) he has spots; (3) therefore, he has measles. Denying the antecedent also involves a logical error: (1) if we don't conserve clinical resources, the supply will run out; (2) we will not waste clinical resources; (3) therefore, our supply should not run out. In none of the preceding cases does the conclusion follow from the premises. These errors involve a confusion between one-way and bidirectional implication (Nickerson, 1986b, p. 82). Contradictions are a type of implication. For example, to say that X contradicts Z is to say that if X is true, Z must be false. A premise implies another premise when the second premise must be true if the first is true. Contradictions involve a bidirectional relationship: if X contradicts Y, then Y contradicts X. However, this is not necessarily the case with implication; although X may imply Y, Y may not imply X. The premise conversion error occurs when the assertion "all X are Y" (all clinicians are human) is assumed to be the same as "all Y are X" (all humans are clinicians). (See other sources for a description of logical fallacies.)

Both deductive and inductive reasoning play a critical role in clinical decision making. Deductive arguments involve a sequence of premises and a conclusion; if the reasoning is logically valid, the conclusion necessarily follows (although it may not be true, because one or more of the premises may be false). Deductive arguments can produce false conclusions, either when one of the premises is false or when one of the rules of deductive inference is violated, as in the preceding example, illustrating the logical fallacy of affirming the consequent. The conclusion may be true but it is invalid, because it is arrived at by an illogical inference. Seldom are the major premises as well as the conclusion clearly stated in deductive arguments; more typically, at least one premise is missing.

Logical (deductive) arguments use deductive inferences; there are objective criteria that can be used to evaluate such arguments. With plausible (inductive) arguments, there are no objective criteria; what is convincing may differ from person to person. Key assertions can be identified in plausible arguments, as well as other assertions that are assumed to support the main one. Inductive reasoning involves generalizing from the particular to the general. It is assumed that what is true of the sample is true of all possible cases. For example, if a psychologist sees three young, successful professional men who use cocaine and who complain of stress in their work lives, the psychologist may conclude that all young professional men who use cocaine experience stress. Thus, in inductive reasoning, we go beyond the data at hand in drawing a conclusion that we cannot affirm with certainty (see Popper's 1963/1972 critique of induction).

ANALYZING ARGUMENTS

Skill in analyzing arguments will increase the quality of clinical decisions, whether considering those presented by others or your own—the latter is more challenging: "Playing prosecutor, judge, and jury when one is oneself the defendant requires an unusual degree of objectivity and commitment to the truth" (Nickerson, 1986b, p. 88). There are many excellent descriptions of how to analyze arguments (e.g., Nickerson, 1986b; Scriven, 1976; Toulmin et al., 1979; Walton, 2008a). Arguments are often incomplete. Key premises or conclusions may be missing, and an important part of examining an argument is filling in these parts. Vague language hampers appraisal. Consider the following statements. What are key premises? "Sexualization for purposes of stimulation of a dead self is frequent and addictive. In general, so-called masochistic behaviors of all types are probably more often the result of the desire and need to stimulate, even through pain, affects which will counter deadness and nothingness. They can be seen as the outgrowth of a motivation to be alive (self-cohesion enhancing) rather than a desire to be dead (self-destructive). Behaviors such as promiscuity, exhibitionism, or voyeurism seem to be sexualized attempts to fulfill nonsexual stimulating and calming self-needs, that is, mirroring, twinship, and idealization, which are necessary to help maintain a cohesive sense of self" (Chelton & Bonney, 1987, p. 41). The following steps can be used to analyze incomplete logical arguments.

- Identify the conclusion or key assertion.
- List all the other explicit assertions that make up the argument as given.
- Add any unstated assertions that are necessary to make the argument complete. (Put them in parentheses to distinguish them from assertions that are explicit in the argument as given.)
- Order the premises (or supporting assertions) and conclusion (or key assertion) so as to show the structure of the argument (Nickerson, 1986b, p. 87).

Since induction is based on facts, "all the principles and lines of arguments on facts apply to induction. Whenever we talk in terms of percentages, ratios, indices, the majority of cases, and the minority, we are referring to terms statistical in nature" (Huber, 1963, p. 123). These statistics are usually gathered by sampling (an inductive process). Statistics may be misleading in a number of ways that relate to the size and representativeness of the samples on which they are based. The most common meaning of the term *representative sample* refers to an absence of selective factors, which would render the sample unrepresentative of the population from which it is drawn. The importance of asking for precise figures is illustrated by the varied meanings for words referring to frequency expressions, such as *sometimes*, *often*, or *rarely*. For example, the meaning of the term *sometimes* has been found to range from 20% to 46% (Pepper, 1981).

Figures, charts, and graphs may mislead rather than inform (Tufte, 2006). Only relative risk may be given (see Chapter 15). Proponents of a new suicide prevention center may say that there has been a 200% increase in the number of suicides over the past year. The total increase may be two additional cases. Thus, misleading percentages may be offered. The total number of occurrences of a given event may be cited when a percentage would be more informative. A drug company may claim that more people have improved using drug X than any other drug. However, the best drug on the market may be effective only 5% of the time. Drug X may be effective 6% of the time—usually not much to write home about. Groups with a special interest in a problem may deliberately inflate the number of people claimed to be affected by a problem. They engage in advocacy scholarship. Consider, for example, Joel Best's (2004) critiques of the prevalence of stranger abduction. He argues that it is greatly exaggerated. (See also MacCoun & Reuter, 2001.) Questions to raise when evaluating inductive arguments include the following (Huber, 1963, p. 140):

- Are the facts accurate?
- Do the examples consist of universal (not isolated) instances?
- Do the examples used cover a significant time period?
- Are the examples given typical (not atypical)?
- Is the conclusion correctly stated?
- Is the argument really of concern (the "so what" and "what harm" questions)?

Our tendency to be influenced by vivid material makes us vulnerable to distortions created by visual material such as photographs, charts, and graphs. Consider the study by McCabe and Castel (2008), which found that subjects who read an article that included an image of a brain were more convinced of the accuracy of claims than those who read the same material without the picture. Graphic displays may lie by omission—by what is left out—leaving unanswered the question "compared with what?" Only a portion of a graph may be shown, resulting in a distorted version of data. Visual representation should be consistent with numerical representation. Often it is not. Principles of graphical excellence suggested by Tufte (1983) include the following: (1) complex ideas are communicated with clarity, precision, and efficiency; (2) the viewer receives the greatest number of ideas in the shortest time with the least ink in the smallest space; and (3) the truth about the data is depicted (p. 51).

Since plausible (inductive) arguments do not have to fit any particular form, objective evaluation is more difficult than it is with deductive arguments. As with logical arguments, the truth of the premises is important to assess. (See list of Socratic questions in Exhibit 3.3.) However, even if these are assumed to be true, we may disagree as to whether they provide evidence for a conclusion. Questions of concern in evaluating a logical argument include: Is it complete? Is its meaning clear? Is it valid (does the conclusion follow from the premises)? Do I believe the premises? (Nickerson, 1986b, p. 88). An argument may be worthy of consideration even though it has defects. We should consider the context when attempting to understand the intended meaning of a claim; however, we should interpret words as they generally would be defined. And, as Scriven (1976) points out, arguments should not be dismissed simply because they are presented emotionally or because a conclusion is disliked; the emotion with which a position is presented is not necessarily related to the soundness of an argument. (See also Walton, 1992.)

Counterarguments should be considered. Are there arguments on the same issue that point to the opposite conclusion or to a somewhat different conclusion? For example, an analogy may be used to support the opposite conclusion. Are there other arguments that support the same conclusion? Consider the following claims made by astrologers to support their belief in astrology (Kelly, Culver, & Loptson, 1989). What are possible counterarguments? (1) Astrology has great antiquity and durability; (2) astrology is found in many cultures; (3) many great scholars have believed in it; (4) astrology is

Exhibit 3.3 A Taxonomy of Socratic Questions

Questions of Clarification

- What do you mean by _____?
- What is your main point?
- How does _____ relate to _____?
- Could you put that another way?
- Let me see if I understand you; do you mean _____ or _____?

- Could you give me an example?
- Would this be an example: _____?
- Could you explain that further?

Questions That Probe Assumptions

- What are you assuming?
- What could we assume instead?
- You seem to be assuming _____. Do I understand you correctly?

Questions That Probe Reasons and Evidence

- What would be an example?
- Why do you think that is true?
- Do you have evidence for that?
- What other information do we need?
- Is there reason to doubt that evidence?
- Who is in a position to know if that is so?
- How could we find out whether that is true?

- Are these reasons adequate?
- How does that apply to this case?
- What difference does that make?
- What would change your mind?

Questions About Viewpoints or Perspectives

- What might someone who believed _____ think?
- Can/did anyone see this another way?
- What would someone who disagrees say?
- What is an alternative?

Questions That Probe Implications and Consequences

- What are you implying by that?
- What effect would that have?
- What is an alternative?

Questions About the Question

- How can we find out?
- What does this question assume?
- How could someone settle this question?
- Can we break this question down at all?
- Do we all agree that this is the question?
- To answer this question, what questions would we have to answer first?

- Is this the same issue as _____?
- Why is this question important?

Source: Adapted from *Critical Thinking: What Every Person Needs to Survive in a Rapidly Changing World* (Rev. 2nd ed., pp.367–368), by R. Paul, 1992, Foundation for Critical Thinking. Reprinted with permission. www.criticalthinking.org

based on observation; (5) extraterrestrial influences exist; (6) astrology has been proved by research; (7) nonastrologers are not qualified to judge; (8) astrology works. Many statements, written or spoken, are opinions or points of view; "they frequently don't pass the test of providing reasons for a conclusion, reasons that can be separated from a conclusion" (Scriven, 1976, p. 67). The question is: Can the premises be established independently of the conclusion? Is the argument convincing? Required characteristics Damer (1995) suggests for effective rational discussion include the following:

The Fallibility Principle: A willingness to admit you could be wrong.

The Truth-Seeking Principle: A commitment to search for the truth or the most defensible position on the issue—examination of alternative positions and a welcoming of raising objections to your view.

The Burden of Proof Principle: This rests on the person who presents it.

The Principle of Charity: Arguments are presented in their strongest version.

The Clarity Principle: Positions, defenses, and challenges are clear.

The Relevance Principle: Only reasons or questions that are directly related to the merit of the position at issue are given.

The Acceptability Principle: Premises or reasons relied on meet standard criteria of acceptability.

The Sufficient Grounds Principle: Those who present an argument for or challenge a position should attempt to provide reasons sufficient in number, kind, and weight to support the conclusion.

The Rebuttal Principle: The person who presents an argument for or challenges a position should attempt to provide effective responses to all serious challenges or rebuttals.

The Resolution Principle: An issue should be considered resolved if the proponent for a position presents an argument that uses relevant and acceptable premises that are sufficient in number, kind, and weight to support the premises and the conclusion and provides an effective rebuttal to all serious challenges.

The Suspension of Judgment Principle: If no position can be successfully defended, or if two or more positions can be defended with equal strength, you should suspend judgment, or if practical considerations require a decision, proceed based on preferences.

The Reconsideration Principle: Participants are obligated to reconsider the issue if subsequent flaws are found in an argument. (pp. 173–186)

KINDS OF ARGUMENTS: THE IMPORTANCE OF CONTEXT

Aristotle distinguished three kinds of arguments: didactic, dialectical, and contentious. The hallmark of dialectical arguments is a spirit of inquiry. The aim of people involved in teaching and learning was considered to differ from the aim of those involved in competition. ". . . for a learner should always state what he thinks; for no one is even trying to teach him what is false; whereas in a competition the business of a questioner is to appear by all means to produce an effect upon the other, while that of the answerer is to appear unaffected by him" (see Barnes, 1984). Aims of the questioner in contentious arguments include (1) to refute the opponent—that is, to prove the point contradictory to his or her thesis; (2) to show that the opponent has committed a fallacy; (3) to lead the opponent into paradox; (4) to make the opponent use an ungrammatical expression; and (5) to reduce the opponent to babbling (Aristotle cited in Hamblin, 1970, p. 63). Adversarial arguments are competitive in nature; that is, each party concentrates on defending one line of reasoning and attacking other lines presented. In arbitrational arguments, the focus is on arriving at a compromise resolution that is satisfactory to both parties. Neither party may be fully satisfied by the conclusion reached, but agree to abide by it.

The kinds of arguments that typically occur in clinical contexts can be contrasted to arguments in scientific contexts by the time frame involved; that is, judgments in clinical contexts must be made under time pressures and without all needed information. In both professional and scientific contexts, value is (or should be) placed on a "willingness and ability to be self-critical, to deal sensibly with justifiable objections and queries from others" (Bromley, 1986, p. 233). That such appraisal is not the norm can be seen in the case example in Chapter 16. Consideration of clashing viewpoints regarding an issue or question is vital to exploring the cogency of different assumptions. Popper (1994) attributes the invention of criticism to Xenophenes, who traveled outside of Greece and discovered that not everyone accepted the gods revered in his country. Grappling with different perspectives, for example, between our current beliefs and new ideas, is vital to learning—to expanding our knowledge.

Walton (2008) views argument as a pragmatic notion in which reasoning is used in a context of dialogue. (See Exhibit 3.4.) Arguments occur in different contexts, including articles in professional journals, courts of law, and case conferences. These different contexts influence the manner in which a topic is discussed in terms of different norms, values, procedures, and requirements for and types of evidence that are acceptable or unacceptable (Bromley, 1986, p. 223). The focus in this book is on reasoning processes that influence clinical decisions, including those found in the professional literature, meetings, and case conferences. The most elaborate and detailed set of rules related to the presentation and rebuttal of arguments can be found in the field of law. For example, specific grounds are described for objecting to the introduction of certain kinds of questions. Courts of law favor an adversarial (competitive) format in which each party tries to settle a dispute in its favor. In clinical settings, a concern such as child abuse must be considered from many different perspectives (for example, medical, legal, psychological, and educational), each of which has a unique framework for viewing problems and resolutions. In both professional and scientific contexts, there should be "willingness and ability to be self-critical [self-reflexive], to deal sensibly with justifiable objections and queries from others" (Bromley, 1986, p. 233). Misunderstandings and bad feelings may result when participants in a discussion do not recognize that different kinds of arguments are being used. Lawyers may view clinicians as fuzzy thinkers, and clinicians may view lawyers as inhumane and legalistic in questioning the accuracy of alleged evidence. Walton (2008a) identifies six types of dialogue:

1. *Persuasion (critical discussion)*. Here, the goal is to persuade the other party of a conclusion or point of view. There is an obligation to "co-operate with the other participant's attempts to prove his thesis also" (Walton, 2008a, p. 5). "What is distinctive about persuasion dialogue is that in order to prove something successfully, we must derive it by acceptable arguments from premises that the other party is committed to. In other words, argumentation in a critical discussion is, by its nature, directed toward the other party and is based on that other party's commitments. We must always ask: what will successfully persuade this particular person [or audience]?" (Walton, 1995, p. 100).

2. *Inquiry*. "The goal of inquiry is to [determine] whether a particular [claim] is true [or false] or, alternatively, to show that, despite an exhaustive search uncovering all the available evidence, it cannot be determined that a proposition is true [or false]" (Walton, 1995, p. 106). The goal is an increase

Exhibit 3.4 Types of Dialogue

Type of Dialogue	Initial Situation	Participant's Goal	Goal of Dialogue
Persuasion	Conflict of opinions	Persuade other party	Resolve or clarify issue
Inquiry	Need to have proof	Find and verify evidence	Prove (disprove) hypothesis
Negotiation	Conflict of interest	Get what you most want	Reasonable settlement both can live with
Information-seeking	Need information	Acquire or give information	Exchange information
Deliberation	Dilemma or practical choice	Coordinate goals and actions	Decide best available course of action
Quarrel	Personal conflict	Verbally hit out at opponent	Reveal deeper basis of conflict

Source: From *Informal Logic: A Pragmatic Approach* (2nd ed., p. 8), by D. Walton, 2008a, New York, NY: Cambridge University Press.

in knowledge (Walton, 2008a, p. 6). Such discussions are cumulative "in the sense that the line of reasoning always moves forward from well-established premises to conclusions that are derived from very careful [ideally, deductively valid] inferences, so that the conclusions are solidly established" (Walton, 1995, p. 106). Phases include collecting relevant data, discussing what conclusion can be drawn, and presenting what has been decided, perhaps in a report. Evidential priority (the premises are better established or are more reliable as evidence than the conclusion they were used to prove) is a key concern in inquiry (p. 108). Different types of inquiry have different standards of proof (e.g., legal, governmental). As Walton (1995) notes, a debate differs from inquiry because the judges or audience can be won over using fallacious arguments in an adversarial context.

3. *Negotiation*. Here "the primary goal is self interest, and the method is to bargain" (Walton, 2008a, p. 6). At stake here is not truth but goods or economic resources. Argumentation may occur, but the goal may not be to discover the truth.

4. *Information-seeking*. Here one party has some information that another party wants to find out about. This kind of discussion is asymmetrical. The role of the one party is to give information and the role of the other is to receive or gain access to it. This kind of dialogue differs from the inquiry in which all parties are "more or less equally knowledgeable or ignorant and their collective goal is to prove something" (Walton, 1995, pp. 113–114).

5. *Deliberation*. In this type of discussion there is a dilemma or practical choice that must be made. Questions may be "How do I do this?" or "Which of two possibilities is better?"

6. *The quarrel*. This kind of dialogue involves personal conflict. The goal is to share, acknowledge, and deal with "hidden grievances," often to facilitate continuation of a personal relationship.

Quarrelsome dialogue is that type of dialogue where the participants try to blame the other party for some wrong allegedly committed in the past. The aim is to humiliate or cast blame on the other party through a personal attack. In sophistical dialogue, the aim is to impress an audience [or third party] by showing how clever you are in attacking your opponent in a verbal exchange and showing how foolish her views are. Both subtypes are classified as eristic dialogues because the goal is to defeat the other party at all costs. The eristic dialogue is unique as a type of dialogue, of all the types of dialogue studied here, because it is a zero-sum game, in the sense of being completely adversarial—one party wins if and only if the other party loses.

All the other types of dialogues are based upon the Gricean cooperativeness principle (Grice, 1975; Walton, 1995, p. 112). Grice's conversational maxims can be used as a guide for productive conversations. We can draw on these to avoid self-propaganda as well as to avoid propagandazing others. These maxims include the following:

Maxim of Quantity

1.   Make your contribution to the conversation as informative as necessary.
2.   Do not make your contribution to the conversation more informative than necessary.

Maxim of Quality

1.   Do not say what you believe to be false.
2.   Do not say that for which you lack adequate evidence.

Maxim of Relevance

1.   Be relevant (i.e., say things related to the current topic of the conversation).

Maxim of Manner

1.   Avoid obscurity of expression.
2.   Avoid ambiguity.
3.   Be brief (avoid unnecessary wordiness).
4.   Be orderly.

Shifts from one type of dialogue to another may or may not reflect deception. For example, a shift from an inquiry discussion to an information-seeking one may not reflect deception. Shifts become a problem in inquiry dialogues where there is deception or misunderstanding. One participant may not be aware of a shift and the other party may conceal it "and take advantage of the first party's confusion" (Walton, 1995, p. 120). Walton gives the example of infomercials that have the format and appearance of a talk show, but are in fact commercials. He argues that infomercials "exploit the viewer's initial expectation that he is watching a news or talk show that is presenting information in a reporting or interviewing format. Not until the viewer watches the program for a while does it become clear that the program is really an advertisement for a product" (p. 121). He views this as a calculated deception.

There is nothing wrong per se with a sales pitch, a commercial advertisement for a product. But if the producers are trying to disguise the sales pitch by putting it in another format [such as an allegedly objective news report], this is quite a different matter. The argumentation in the sales pitch is not fallacious or open to critical condemnation per se, just because it is a sales pitch. We all know and expect that a sales pitch is taking a one-sided approach of promoting a product, making no pretense of being unbiased reporting of the assets as well as the defects or shortcomings of the product [in the way we would expect, for example, of Consumer Reports]. (Walton, 1995, pp. 121–122)

There may be a mutual misunderstanding in which both participants wrongly assume that the other party is engaged in one type of dialogue. One person may view the exchange as a critical discussion; the other may assume the first party is engaged in a quarrel (Walton, 1995, p. 123). Different types of dialogue may be mixed together in the same discussion. This pragmatic, contextual view highlights that what is viewed as a fallacy in one context may not be in another. (See Chapter 6.) Misunderstandings and bad feelings may result when participants in a discussion do not recognize that different kinds of arguments are being used. Lawyers and social workers often have negative views of each other because of their different frameworks for argument analysis.

EXPLANATIONS

Many different kinds of explanations are used in clinical practice, including biological, genetic, psychological, and sociological. Explaining is closely connected with judging whether something is good or bad. Different explanations suggest different reasons that may be offered for beliefs:

- Preferred kind of explanation → reasons → evidence sought/appealed to.
- Example: biomedical → brain differences → different levels of dopamine in those diagnosed with a mental illness and those not so labeled.

William James (1975) suggested that temperamental differences (tender versus tough-minded) account for preference for different kinds of explanations. Optimists are more likely to prefer explanations that allow appreciable room for change, whereas pessimists are more likely to be drawn to explanations that allow little room for change. People differ in the kinds of explanations that satisfy their curiosity. Explanations are often given by defining a word in terms of other words (for example, synonyms) as in dictionary definitions. Other kinds of explanations by definition include classifying (for example, social work is a profession), offering examples, or describing operations.

Exhibit 3.5 Hallmarks of Different Kinds of Explanations

A. *Ideological Explanations*

1. Provide few answers for many questions (a few principles cover a wide territory).

2. Seek to clarify the true meaning of scriptures.

3. Contain a high proportion of nonfactual sentences included as declarations ("nonfactual means ambiguous and improvable or without empirical warrant," p. 186). Values disguised as facts.

4. Contain "high ratio of hortatory-presumptive to declarative" sentences.

5. Contain many failures of logic.

6. Deny the possibility of objectivity (critical appraisal of claims); "all explanations of social behavior are considered to be distorted (cues include 'stating one's own motives ... locating the 'social position' from which the competing thesis allegedly originates," p. 186).

7. Favor ad hominem arguments, which are viewed as tools, not as errors; identification of "who said it" as an important test of a statement's validity.

8. Resort to reliance on authority.

9. Seek converts; respond to criticism with emotional defenses; attack critic's motives and develop cults (practices that a believing group develops as its distinctive mode of "meeting the world," p. 186); may seek to force theories on others.

10. Prescribe action; have an interest in persuading rather than explaining.

11. Are action oriented.

B. *Scientific Explanations*

1. Reject ad hominem arguments as persuasive.

2. Encourage dispute of key ideas.

3. Do not encourage unexamined commitment to one side.

4. Value critical appraisal and observation.

5. Question everything.

6. Seek to reduce influence of moral judgments on observation and inference.

7. Reflect an interest in improving accuracy of judgments.

C. *Empathic Explanations*

1. Do not require proof; consider the test of empathy to be empathy (p. 49); common sense is sufficient.

2. Use vague indicators; hard "to know when one has understanding"; do not use independent tests of interpretations.

3. Accept ad hominem arguments.

4. Entangle moral judgments with understanding.

5. Have a cognitive bias; an attempt to explain behavior "as if it arose from thought alone" (p. 56); an equation of awareness with verbal reports; knowledge of others limited by excessive attention to what they say.

6. Are vulnerable to tautology; infer inner states from behaviors, and explain behaviors by reference to inner states; prove motives from acts.

7. Confuse understanding and predictive capability; consider propositions to be nonpredictive.

8. Assume that understanding of individuals can offer knowledge of groups.

Source: Adapted from *Explanations* (pp. 49, 56, 186), by G. Nettler, 1970, New York: McGraw-Hill.

Some clinicians prefer empathic explanations. (These may or may not assume a causal connection.) Techniques of empathy building include telling a story; describing circumstances; labeling character; presuming drives, instincts, and needs; and describing intentions and feelings (motives). (See Exhibit 3.5.) "The heart of empathy is imagined possibility" (Nettler, 1970, p. 34).

The empathizer thinks, "Under these circumstances I, too, might have behaved similarly." An example of an empathic explanation is: "The reason he did it is because he hated her." Empathic explanations often involve concepts that are only variant definitions of the behavior to be explained, as shown in the following examples (Nettler, 1970, p. 71).

Case One

Probation: Why, doctor, does our client continue to steal?
Psychiatry: He is suffering from antisocial reaction.
Probation: What are the marks of antisocial reaction?
Psychiatry: Persistent thievery is one symptom.

Case Two

Defense: Whether one calls him insane or psychotic, he's a sick man. That's obvious.
Psychiatry: I should think that's largely a matter of terminology.
Defense: Do you mean to suggest that a man could do what that boy has done and not be sick?

A preference for empathic explanations reflects a search for explanations in terms of underlying essences—essential properties. Explanations that offer less are considered useless. Popper (1957/1983) refers to this position as essentialism. Essentialists seek empathic explanations and argue about the meaning of words rather than exploring meaning through empirical inquiry.

In scientific explanations, critical appraisal of claims is emphasized—there is an active effort to seek out errors in assumptions through this appraisal (see Chapter 4). Scientific explanations are not essentialist accounts—quite the opposite. The scientific process is designed to eliminate errors, not to claim final accounts. Ultimate claims stifle inquiry; they function as prisons that limit our vision (Popper, 1994). Nor do scientific explanations assume that objective accounts can be offered—accounts that are not influenced by diverse meanings associated with how events are interpreted. To the contrary, in no approach is objectivity so suspect as illustrated by the variety of methods devised to attempt to avoid biases (see discussion of falsifiability in Chapter 4).

Ideological explanations are distinguished from scientific ones by their rejection of objectivity, their ready acceptance of sound and unsound premises, and their reliance on ethical judgments. "Ideological explanations, then, became operative as they are believed, rather than as they are verified" (Nettler, 1970, p. 179). They are theory driven and discount empirical findings (e.g., see Gorman, 1998). It is difficult to find a term that has a more speckled history than the term *ideology*. Depending on who is talking and what they are talking about, ideology is a virtue or a sin. Criticisms of "let's drop the ideology" are used often in attempts to quiet critics. "The term 'ideology' is someone else's thought, seldom our own" (McLellan, 1986, p. 1). On the other hand, "ideology tells the point of it all. Life is no longer absurd. It describes the forces of light and darkness and names the innocent to be saved" (Nettler, 1970, p. 179).

Thompson (1987) distinguishes between two uses of the term *ideology*. One is as a purely descriptive term. For example, the beliefs of a particular clinical approach, such as psychoanalysis, can be described. In the second use, the term is "linked to the process of sustaining asymmetrical relations of power—that is, to maintaining domination" (p. 518). It is this use of ideology that has negative connotations, and it is in this sense that language is used as a medium of influence. "The difference between the scientific orientation and the empathetic and ideological outlooks, however, lies in the criteria of conceptual utility. In the latter explain ways, terms are maintained as they serve the explicators' purposes of building empathy or justifying ethical-political causes. In the scientific schema, any concept or construct is, in principle, dispensable regardless of these empathetic or ideological effects" (Nettler, 1970). Ideological explanations are used to account for "collective" behavior as empathetic ones do in the clarification of individual actions—they fill the needs of "curiosity left by the gaps in knowledge" (Nettler, 1970, p. 187). In professional contexts, scientific explanations may be preferred over ideological ones—but not always, as the most casual perusal of related discourse demonstrates.

Explanations do not necessarily involve arguments. For example, empathic and ideological explanations may not involve arguments. A client may say, "I hit her because I was annoyed," or a person with a drinking problem may say, "I saw the bar and couldn't stop myself from going in and having a drink." Offering an explanation for taking some action (indicating a cause) does not necessarily offer a justification (reason) for the action taken. If, for example, a clinician claims that he or she did not obtain assessment data that is generally considered desirable to gather, and, as a result, selected an ineffective intervention method, the excuse that he or she did not have time does not provide a moral justification for inaction. The latter refers to offering reasons that "are morally adequate to support a certain conclusion or action" (Scriven, 1976, p. 219). People tend to feel that they should be able to justify (have sound reasons for) their beliefs. An inability to explain why a certain view is held may create feelings of anger or embarrass-ment. It's not odd that cogent reasons for a belief may not be at hand, since many of our beliefs result from automatic processes that lie outside of our awareness (see Chapter 9). Most beliefs are not examined in terms of providing explanations or justifications for them.

Prediction refers to forecasting what will happen in the future. An example is to say that "attending Alcoholics Anonymous will help this client to remain abstinent." Explanations involve offering reasons for certain behaviors or events. Thus, the expla-nation here may be that if this client attains peer support, she or he will be able to use self-management skills to avoid alcoholic beverages. Practice theories suggest pos-sible explanations and predictions. The question is: "How much real understanding, as opposed to feeling of understanding, do these approaches provide? How much better are the predictions that they yield than those of an intelligent observer not using these theories but using all the other background knowledge that we have about psychological or socioeconomic events?" (Scriven, 1976, p. 219). Explanations may be psychologically compelling but be quite weak from an evidentiary standpoint. For example, astrological explanations may give many people the feeling of understanding; this does not mean that these explanations are accurate.

INDIVIDUAL AND CULTURAL DIFFERENCES

Thinking styles and skills are related to educational and socialization experiences. Stanovich and West (2002) have studied individual differences in reasoning. Thinking and the development of thinking styles occur in a particular context, involving an interaction between an individual and a particular physical and social situation. The results of differences in educational and socialization opportunities may be attributed inaccurately to an inherent style difference; for example, that women are naturally more subjective and intuitive in their approach to problems in contrast to men, who are more objective. Barnett and Rivers (2004) argue that similarities between men and women have been downplayed and differences exaggerated, with negative effects on both men and women. (For counterarguments, see Rhoads, 2004.) Poor people, com-pared to economically privileged individuals, often receive less training in the skills of rationality and objectivity and less cultivation of related beliefs, such as the belief that knowledge is individually and socially constructed. The superordinate position of class to gender is often overlooked; that is, what is attributed to gender differences may be a matter of class differences in access to educational opportunities that nourish effective problem-solving skills. Thus, a preference for subjectivity that is attributed to personal choice may be the result of socialization experiences that discourage critical thinking and reflective thought. The question is: what is gained and lost by such a preference? Encouraging intuitivism, depriving people of critical thinking skills, helps to maintain current power imbalances. It is to the advantage of those with economic resources to encourage individuals in less advantaged positions to embrace an intuitive approach to the exclusion of a rational approach. (See discussion of propaganda in Chapter 4.) Extreme subjectivism as a reaction against disliked "male styles of thinking" forgoes the option of reaping the benefits of critical appraisal. We can be critical thinkers as well as caring individuals.

Cultural differences include norms regarding questioning authority figures (Tweed & Lehman, 2002). If this is not permitted or is frowned on, a staff member may be reluctant to raise questions about agency policies that affect clients' well-being. If important questions are not raised, how can groupthink be avoided in which there is premature closure on an option (see Chapter 16). What are the options here? A shared focus on helping clients (rather than protecting the esteem of authority figures) should contribute to a culture in which asking questions is valued. Still, this may be an uphill battle, in contexts in which authority-based decision making is preferred.

SUMMARY

Clinical decision making involves reasoning-forming hypotheses about clients' concerns, offering arguments for case formulations and evaluating these assumptions. Reasons may be hot or cold—that is, developed by emotive associations or by reasoned argument. Reasoning does not necessarily yield the truth, nor does the accuracy of a conclusion necessarily indicate that the reasoning used to reach it was sound. Plausible reasons are more likely to be offered if distinctions are made among assumptions that have been critically tested, beliefs based only on confidence that they are true, and preferences that cannot be shown to be true or false. Effective reasoning requires much more than logic in developing and evaluating arguments to arrive at those that are well-reasoned. Domain-specific knowledge is also needed. Being familiar with the steps in argument analysis is useful in examining the quality of arguments. Different criteria are used to assess the quality of arguments in different settings. Effective reasoning requires a certain kind of attitude toward the truth—a questioning attitude and an openness to altering beliefs in light of evidence offered—a willingness to say, "I don't know." Clinicians differ in the kinds of explanations they prefer, which influences the plausibility of arguments offered. Some clinicians prefer empathic and ideological explanations rather than scientific ones. The kinds of explanations that we find satisfying depend in part on the subject or question at hand. Creativity, including flexibility, and reasoning are closely related, especially in areas such as clinical decision making, in which helpful information is often missing.

4

Different Views of Knowledge and How to Get It: Exploring Your Personal Epistemology

Professionals are assumed to have unique knowledge as a result of special education, experience, and training. This implies that there is some knowledge to master, that some decisions are better reasoned than others. Claimed special knowledge supposedly makes those with certain degrees, training, or experience more effective in achieving certain outcomes than those without such credentials. That is, the former are supposed to be experts in solving certain kinds of problems. Larson (1977) suggests:

> The main instrument of professional advancement, more than the profession of altruism, is the capacity to claim esoteric and identifiable skills—that is, to create and control a cognitive and technical basis. The claim of expertise aims at gaining social recognition and collective prestige which, in turn, are implicitly used by the individual to assert his authority and demand respect in the context of everyday transactions within specific role-sets. (p. 180)

Studies in medicine show that specialized content knowledge is vital to making sound decisions in many instances (see Chapter 3). Professional codes of ethics call on practitioners to draw on practice-related research. This obligates professionals to be informed about knowledge, ignorance, and uncertainty associated with decisions they make that affect clients' well-being. Our concern for helping and not harming clients obliges us to critically examine the criteria we use to evaluate knowledge claims. Evidence-based practitioners consider research findings related to decisions that affect clients' lives. But what is evidence? What is knowledge and what are underlying assumptions in different views of how to get it? How much evidence is needed to say that an intervention is appropriate, that it should be used, and how it should be paid for?

What criteria should we use to decide whether a service method is ineffective? This chapter describes different criteria for evaluating knowledge claims, and you are invited to explore your views on this important topic—to explore your personal epistemology. The connection between evidentiary and ethical issues is highlighted, including the importance of recognizing uncertainty and fallibility in making decisions.

Evidence-based practice (EBP) arose in part because of flaws in published reports of research findings, including peer-reviewed journals—for example, inflated claims of effectiveness. But what is a flaw? When is it so significant that we should dismiss a claim? Traditional and current criteria include what is standard or accepted or what a helper believes to be in a client's best interests. However, as Eddy notes, "the credibility of clinical judgement, whether examined individually or collectively, has been severely challenged by observations of wide variations in practices, inappropriate care, and practitioner uncertainty" (Eddy, 1993, p. 521; see also discussion of clinical and actuarial judgment in Chapter 15). The smaller the gap between the knowledge you have and the knowledge available to help clients, or to correctly determine that you cannot, the more likely you are to honor ethical obligations to help clients and avoid harm and to involve clients as informed participants in decisions made. Evidence-based practice is a process designed to reveal or decrease these gaps, as described in Chapter 10.

DIFFERENT VIEWS OF KNOWLEDGE AND HOW (OR IF) IT CAN BE GAINED

The question "What is knowledge?" has been of concern to philosophers throughout the ages. People differ in their beliefs about knowledge and how it can be gained (e.g., see Hofer & Pintrich, 2002). Many criteria are relied on in making claims of knowledge, including folklore, practice wisdom, common sense, superstition, pseudoscience, and the results of well-designed research studies. Cultural differences influence these beliefs (Nisbett, 2003). Given that we are all philosophers in making scores of decisions each day about how to act and how to solve problems, we, too should consider this question. Different ways of knowing differ in the extent to which they recognize uncertainty and are designed to weed out biases and distortions that may influence assumptions. Knowledge serves different functions, only one of which is to encourage the growth of knowledge. For example, Munz (1985) suggests that the function of *false knowledge* is to maintain social bonds among people by protecting shared beliefs from criticism (the growth of knowledge). This may be necessary to encourage cooperation in a group. Peter Munz (1985) defines *false knowledge* as beliefs that are not true and that are not questioned. This refers to "pieces of knowledge held consciously which have little direct bearing on physical survival" (p. 74). Such beliefs "can be held or discarded regardless of the environment in which people who hold them are living. Nevertheless, they enable cooperation and division of labor. In this kind of society, membership "depends on being able to give the correct answers to a catechism," beliefs "are not available for criticism and therefore cannot be examined. They are held dogmatically" (p. 74). Cultures often thrive because of false knowledge. Such cultures "are doubly effective in promoting social behavior because, not being exposed to rational criticism, they enshrine emotionally comforting and solidarity-producing attitudes" (pp. 283–284). This view suggests that the growth of knowledge can take place only in certain circumstances (i.e., cultures)—those in which alternative views are entertained and all views are subject to criticism (see the glossary at the end of this chapter). Only in this way do beliefs confront the environment.

Certain ways of knowing, compared to others, are designed to rigorously test guesses (e.g., about effectiveness). Frazer (1925) suggested that there is a closer connection between magic and science than between science and religion. Both magic and science attempt to predict certain events by taking certain actions, such as conducting a rain dance, hoping to make it rain. The very purpose of experimental studies and experimental single-case designs is to avoid unwarranted assumptions about effects. (Whether they offer information about the role of methods used in the reported effects depends on the particular design used.) Karl Popper (1994) suggests that we do not know more today than we did thousands of years ago, because solving some problems only creates new ones. For example, medical advances have created new problems, such as overpopulation. Some people believe that nothing can be known "for sure." This is assumed in science. But does that mean we don't know anything? Others argue that because we know nothing for sure, we really know nothing. We should follow out the logic of each position. If we know nothing, then what is the rationale for professional education? The success of scientific methods in distinguishing between correct and incorrect assumptions in hundreds of areas shows that all methods are not equally effective in testing knowledge claims.

Raymond Nickerson (1986b) defines knowledge as information that decreases uncertainty about how to achieve a certain outcome (I would add "or reveals uncertainty"). We can ask: "What knowledge will help us to solve problems clients confront (e.g., elder abuse, a need for reliable respite care)?" Studies of the development of assumptions about knowledge (e.g., what can be known and what cannot, how we can know, and how certain we can be in knowing), suggest a scale ranging from the belief that we can know reality with certainty by direct observation, to the view that there is never certainty and that we must critically appraise and synthesize information from multiple sources (King & Kitchener, 2002). Karl Popper (1992) defines knowledge as problematic and tentative guesses about what may be true. It results from selective pressures from the real world, in which our guesses come into contact with the environment through a process of trial and error (Munz, 1985).

EVALUATING KNOWLEDGE CLAIMS

You will encounter many different theories and claims. How will you choose among them? How will you select those most likely to be of value in helping clients? The criteria you rely on influence your selection of assessment, intervention, and evaluation methods. Consider the following statements:

- Mentoring programs for youth are effective. (Are they?)
- National depression screening days do more good than harm. (Do they?)
- If you have to urinate eight or more times a day, you have a condition called "irritable bladder" and should ask your doctor for medication. (Should you?)

Your beliefs about these claims will influence decisions you make.

AVOIDING HARMING IN THE NAME OF HELPING

Relying on false claims or theories may result in harming rather than helping clients; false hope may be created and opportunities to use effective methods missed. Consider Emma Eckstein, one of Sigmund Freud's patients (Masson, 1984). He attributed her complaints of stomach ailments and menstrual problems to masturbation. Freud's colleague Fleiss recommended a nose operation, based on his belief that the sexual organs and the nose were connected. Eckstein's subsequent pain and suffering then were attributed to her psychological deficiencies. The real cause was a large wad of dressing left in her nose by mistake. Consider claims of effectiveness regarding intervention based on anecdotal case reports that were later shown to be false in controlled research. For example, the findings of controlled—in contrast to uncontrolled—studies of the effects of facilitated communication (FC—a method alleged to help nonverbal people communicate) "have been consistently negative indicating that FC is neither reliably replicable nor valid when produced" (Jacobson, Mulick, & Schwartz, 1995, p. 754). These controlled studies showed that the communication alleged to be from previously nonverbal people was actually determined by the facilitators.

QUESTIONABLE CRITERIA

Decisions that get in the way of helping clients may be made because of lack of knowledge about the limitations of commonly accepted criteria for evaluating the accuracy of claims. Criteria such as popularity, testimonials, newness, or tradition do not provide sound grounds on which to accept claims, often because they consider only part of the picture (e.g., only examples that support a belief). The *post hoc ergo propter hoc* fallacy is common; the false belief that if an event (dream therapy) precedes an event (an increase in well-being), the preceding event caused the second one. Other examples include influence based on manner of presentation and reliance on anecdotal experience.

Authority

The source of the fallacy of authority is the mistaken assumption that status is correlated with accuracy. An example of appeal to cognitive authority is the assertion of a claim such as "Play therapy is the best method to use with acting-out children," based solely on someone's status or position, with no reference to empirical studies that provide evidence. Let us say that Ms. Sommers, a case manager for the elderly, tells her supervisor that she referred Mr. Rivers to the Montview Nursing Home because Dr. Lancaster told her that this home provides excellent services—even though Dr. Lancaster offered no evidence that it does. Appeals to authority are a common social persuasion strategy. Cereal companies often use famous baseball players to tout the many benefits of their cereals. Appeals to unfounded authority are common in the professional literature, such as citing a famous person to support a claim when in fact he or she has not conducted any critical tests of the claim. Citations are a kind of authority and are misused as shown by investigations of their (in)accuracy (Greenberg, 2009). Evidence-based practice arose as an alternative to authority-based practice (Gambrill, 1999; Sackett, Richardson, Rosenberg, & Haynes, 1997). Appeals to popularity and tradition are forms of appeals to authority. (For further discussion, see Chapter 7.)

Popularity/Consensus

Popularity refers to the acceptance of claims simply because many people accept them. For instance, an agency may decide to adopt psychoanalytic methods because many other agencies use these methods. Here, too, the question is whether there is any evidence that popular methods are effective:

> How much is spent in the USA every year on magnetic devices to treat pain? $500 million, with a total worldwide market to date above $4 billion. To put that into some sort of perspective, that $500 million is just half the annual sales that the pharmaceutical industry defines as a "blockbuster." And what do you think is the evidence for magnets affecting pain? You guessed it. None. There is a trial in a Cochrane review of interventions for plantar heel pain, and that

was negative, and poor. A new, well-conducted, randomised trial provides a powerful negative, and a great example of trial design. (Bandolier, 2003b, www. medicine.ox.ac.uk/bandolier)

In today's world of corporate science, consensus may reflect a successful struggle based on political and economic rather than evidentiary grounds. Resort to voting on an issue as with the American Psychiatric Association referendum on homosexuality in 1973 to remove or keep homosexuality in the *Diagnostic and Statistical Manual of Mental Disorders* reflects appeal to consensus. The vote was 5,854 in favor of removing this category and 3,810 opposing removal. Abstentions were 367 (Bayer, 1987, p. 395). Appeals to consensus are reflected in terms such as "Researchers agree . . ." "Experts agree . . ." "Everybody knows . . . ." (See discussion of weasel words in Chapter 5.)

Tradition

Tradition (what has been done in the past) may be appealed to support claims. For example, when asked why he or she was using genograms, a social worker may answer, "That's what our agency has used for years." Advertisers often note how long their product has been sold, suggesting that this establishes its effectiveness. Because a method has been used for many years does not mean it is effective. In fact, it may be harmful. Testing as well as guessing is needed (systematic exploration) to determine the accuracy of these beliefs.

Newness

Newness (the latest practice or policy) is often appealed to, as in "We use the new co-addiction model with all clients" or "Our new social policies for privatization will help all residents" (when they will not). Simply because something is new or innovative does not mean it is effective. After all, everything was new at some time. New technologies may be worse than old ones or simply doing nothing (Meier, 2011).

Manner of Presentation

We are often persuaded that a claim is correct by the confident manner in which it is presented. This fallacy occurs when (1) a speaker or writer claims that something is true of people or that a method is effective; (2) persuasive interpersonal skills are used (e.g., building the self-esteem of audience members, joking); and (3) data describing the effectiveness of the method are not reviewed (Gibbs, 1991). Being swayed by the style of presentation underlies persuasion by the material's entertainment value. How interesting is a view? Does it sound profound? Does it claim to empower clients? Here, too, the question is whether there is any evidence for the claims made. (See also Chapter 5.)

Good Intentions

We may accept claims of effectiveness because we believe that those who make them have good intentions, that they want to help clients. But, as the history of the helping professions shows, good intentions and services that help clients and avoid harm do not necessarily go together (Scull, 2005; Sharpe & Faden, 1998; Valenstein, 1986). Consider the following:

- People have died as a result of a "rebirthing."
- Babies were blinded as a result of being given oxygen at birth.
- Creating false memories resulted in innocent people being accused of sexual abuse.

Clients have been killed as a result of using methods assumed to be helpful. Programs that have been critically tested and found to be ineffective or harmful continue to be used (e.g., Petrosino, Turpin-Petrosino, & Beuhler, 2003).

Of all tyrannies, a tyranny sincerely exercised for the good of its victims may be the most oppressive.

It may be better to live under robber barons than under the omnipotent moral busybodies.

The robber baron's cruelty may sometimes sleep, his cupidity may at some point be satiated;

but those who torment us for our own good will torment us without end, for they do so with the approval of their own conscience.

—C. S. Lewis, The Humanitarian Theory of Punishment:
Issues in Religion and Psychotherapy

What Makes Sense: Plausibility

You may have read that expressing anger in frustrating situations is helpful in getting rid of your anger. This may make sense. But is it true? In fact, research on anger suggests that it does not have this happy effect (see Averill, 1982; Tavris, 1989). Explanations always make sense to the person who accepts them. People's thinking is logical if seen on its own premises (Renstrom, Andersson, & Marton, 1990, p. 556). Whether these premises are accurate is another question. What about common sense? This may refer to cultural maxims and shared beliefs or shared fundamental assumptions about the social and physical world (Furnham, 1988). One problem here is that different maxims often give contradictory advice.

Entertainment Value

Some claims are accepted simply because they sound interesting, even though interest value does not indicate accuracy. We live in an era in which alternative therapies have expanded enormously, in which therapy as entertainment or as spectacle is common. Hundreds may attend a lecture by a famous clinician.

Emotional Influences

When evaluating claims, we are easily swayed by our emotions, and politicians and advertisers take advantage of this. They may appeal to our self-pity, self-esteem, fears, and self-interest (e.g., Slovic, Finucane, Peters, & MacGregor, 2002). Vivid testimonials and case examples play on our emotions. For example, a TV commercial for an alcohol treatment center may show an unkempt, depressed man with a drinking problem, and describe the downward spiral allegedly caused by drinking, including the loss of job and family. We may then see him in the detoxification treatment center, which is clean and whose staff seem caring and concerned. Next we see our client shaved, well-dressed, employed, and looking happy and healthy. Words, music, and pictures may contribute to the emotive effect. Because of the commercial's emotional appeal, we may overlook the absence of evidence for the effectiveness of the detox treatment center.

Testimonials

Testimonials are reports by people who have used a product or service that that product or service is effective. For example, someone who has attended Alcoholics Anonymous may say, "I tried it and it works." The testimonial is a variant of the case example fallacy and is subject to the limitations of case examples in offering evidence for a claim; neither case examples nor testimonials provide comparative information needed to evaluate whether an assumption is true or false. Testimonials may include detailed, vivid descriptions of the method used, the distressing state of affairs prior to its use, and the positive results. Testimonials are widely used in advertising. The problem with testimonials is not that the report about an individual's personal experience with a given method is inaccurate, but the further step of making a claim that a method is effective. Rival explanations are not considered. These include placebo effects and misdiagnosing the natural history of a problem (it got better by itself). Perhaps the problem is cyclic in nature.

Case Examples

Professionals often appeal to their anecdotal experience to support claims of effectiveness. (Relying on a carefully documented track record of success is quite different, as this offers a systematic record.) A counselor may state, "I know cognitive behavioral methods are most effective with depressed clients because they are effective with my clients." In the case example fallacy, conclusions about many clients are made based on a few unrepresentative examples (Loftus & Guyer, 2002). There is a faulty generalization. What may be true in a few cases may not be at all true of other cases. Experience in everyday practice and beliefs based on this are the key source of what is known as practice wisdom. Although anecdotal experience (practice wisdom) does provide an important source of guesses about what is effective, it is not a sound basis for evaluating claims of effectiveness; it cannot critically test the accuracy of a claim. Gibbs (1991) suggests three reasons why case examples snare the unwary: (1) the detailed description of case examples has emotional appeal, especially compared to dull data from large representative samples; (2) we become immersed in the details of a case and forget that what may be true of this one may not be true of others; and (3) cases that supposedly prove the point can always be found. Case examples are easy to remember because they have a storylike quality. Often, extreme examples are selected, making them vivid and easy to remember, even though they are unrepresentative of other cases. We tend to overestimate the probability of detailed examples. Aronson (2003) notes that anecdotal case reports may be a valuable source of promising hypotheses, for example, regarding adverse events and possible causes, and may provide telling counterexamples that disprove a hypothesis. Anecdotes may be used to demonstrate diagnostic methods, to explain how to handle challenging clinical situations, or to remind or educate us about important clinical possibilities.

Problems With Learning From Experience

Experience does not necessarily result in improved performance. In fact, it may have the opposite effect (see also Chapter 9). Experience may decrease rather than enhance identification of creative options, as shown in a study by Johnson (1972) in which people who did not work in a spark plug factory identified more alternative uses for spark plugs than personnel who worked in the factory. Thus, learning may become context bound. Expertise is not necessarily a monotonic function of experience. For example, third- and fourth-year residents did not perform as well as either first- or second-year students or experts in interpreting X-rays (Lesgold et al., 1988). Possible reasons for such findings include vacillation between old (but inaccurate) representations of problems and new (perhaps untrusted) views about what is accurate. Experience alone may not offer the tactical guidance and necessary representation of problems that is required for practice to be beneficial (Dawes, 1994a; Perkins, 1987). Practice may occur in what Hogarth (2001) refers to as a "wicked" environment that does not offer corrective feedback. Even if some improvement does occur without tactical coaching, it may not match the potential gains of what would be possible with guidance.

The key problem with relying on experience as a guide to the evidentiary status of a claim (e.g., is it true?) is the lack of comparison (Dawes, 1988). An interest in comparison is a hallmark of scientific thinking. Our experience is not a sound guide because it is often restricted and biased. For example, a child welfare worker may assume that few child abusers stop abusing their children because she sees those who do not stop abusing their children more than those who do stop. Her experience with this biased sample results in incorrect inferences about the recurrence of child abuse (i.e., an overestimate). When relying on experience we may not recognize that conditions have changed; that what worked in the past may no longer work in the present. Western-style mental health services may not be appropriate for many clients. Another problem with relying on experience to test the accuracy of claims concerns the biased nature of our memory of what happened. We tend to recall our successes and forget our failures. That is, we tend to selectively focus on our hits. Unless we have kept track of both our hits and our misses, we may arrive at incorrect conclusions. We tend to be overconfident in the accuracy of our beliefs, perhaps because of our interest in predicting what happens in our world (Baron, 2000). This interest can encourage an illusion of control in which we overestimate how much control we really have. Also, as Dawes (1988) points out, we tend to create our own experience. If we are friendly, others are likely to be friendly in return. If we are hostile, others are likely to be hostile. Dawes refers to this as "self-imposed bias in our own experience" (p. 106).

We alter views about the past to conform to current moods or views. We don't know what might have happened if a different sequence of events had occurred. Overlooking this, we may unfairly praise or blame ourselves (or someone else). A psychologist might say, "If only I had focused more on the teenager, Mario and his mother would have returned for a second interview." But maybe if he had concentrated more on the teen-ager, Mario would have walked out in the first interview. Where is the comparison? Relying on experience opens us to accepting irrelevant causes. We may assume that mental illness results in homelessness because many homeless people are mentally ill. But does it? So experience, while honing skills in many ways, especially in environments in which we gain corrective feedback (see Chapter 9), may have negative effects, such as a reluctance to consider new ideas and an unwarranted overconfidence in the extent to which we can help clients. Indeed, one advantage of being a novice may be a greater willingness to question beliefs. King (1981) suggests that "severely critically handling of experience was an important part of scientific method, applicable to clinical practice as well as to research investigation" (pp. 303–304). These concerns call for caution about generalizing from the past and present to the future.

Intuition

Intuition is another criterion used to evaluate the accuracy of claims. *Webster's New World Dictionary, third edition* (1988) defines intuition as "the direct knowing or learning of something without the conscious use of reasoning." Intuition is a quick judgment, often based on a "rule of thumb" developed in particular situations (see discussion of fast and frugal heuristics in Chapter 9). Such quick reactions may or may not be well informed—that is, lead to sound decisions. Intuitions (inferences) may refer to looking back in time (interpreting experience) or forward in time (predictions). For example, we may make a diagnosis of a client or we may predict that he or she will act in a certain manner in the future. Beliefs based on intuition may be either sound or unsound. They may reflect experience providing corrective feedback (informed intuition). Or they may be based on experience that does not provide such feedback, or on pure speculation (uninformed intuition). Basing beliefs on uninformed intuition may result in harm that could have been prevented. Intuition, in contrast to analytical thinking, cannot be defined by a description of steps used in the process (Hammond, 1996, p. 60). This does not mean that intuition is wrong. As Hogarth (2001) suggests, it means "that non-intuitive processes are deliberative and can be specified after [or before] the fact. Logic and analysis can be made transparent. Intuition cannot without effort." (See discussion of cognitive task analyses of expert decision makers in Chapter 9.) Someone may ask, "How did you know that this method would be effective?" The answer may be: "My intuition." The view that intuition involves a responsiveness to information that, although not consciously represented, yields productive insights, is compatible with the differences found between experts and novices. Experts rely on pattern recognition that they no longer may be able to describe. No longer remembering where we learned something encourages attributing solutions to intuition. When asked what made you think that "Y" service would be effective, your answer may be: "Intuition." When asked to elaborate, you may offer sound reasons reflecting knowledge of related research and appropriate inference rules. That is, you used far more than uninformed hunches.

   Intuition cannot show which method is most effective in helping clients; a different kind of evidence is required for this. It, too, like anecdotal experience, lacks a comparison. Relying on intuition or what feels right is ethically questionable when other grounds, including a critical examination of intuitive beliefs, will result in better-informed decisions.

Decisions based on intuition may be inconsistent; this inconsistency may not be evident, because no one keeps track of the decisions made, the grounds for making them, and their outcomes. The greater the number of factors that must be considered in arriving at a well-reasoned decision and the more that is known about the relevance of considering them, the less likely is intuition to offer the best guide for decisions. (See discussion of actuarial compared to consensus-based methods in Chapter 15.) Attributing judgments to intuition decreases the opportunities to teach practice skills; one has it but doesn't know how or why it works. If you ask your supervisor, "How did you know to do that at that time?" and she says, "My intuition," this will not help you learn what to do.

Hogarth (2001) suggests that we can develop our intuition most effectively by using a scientific approach in which we make maximal use of feedback. Science offers a particular way of learning about our world, a particular way of trying to solve problems (Popper, 1963/1972). It is a method in which we learn from our errors—that is, corrective feedback. A key step is becoming aware of the limitations of experiential (intuitive) learning: "1) people discover for themselves that it is to their benefit to 'take greater control of their processes,' and, 2) they must understand at an intellectual level why learning from experience has limitations" (Hogarth, 2001, p. 224). In making the scientific method intuitive, he suggests that we seek feedback, explore connections, and accept conflict when making choices. Thus, "even though intuitive learning takes place largely tacitly, only by being aware of the process can we manage it (by being aware of whether an environment is 'kind'—provides valuable feedback or 'wicked'—provides misleading or no feedback). Otherwise, we leave what we learn to chance" (p. 215). The terms *kind* and *wicked* refer to different types of feedback environments, a kind one being one that provides helpful feedback, and a wicked one being one that does not. In the latter, we can be misled if we rely on intuition. "Wicked" learning structures are those that do not contribute to learning. Thus, the accuracy of intuition is related to the kind of feedback we get from our environments.

Hogarth (2001) urges us to learn to observe better, to speculate more intelligently about what we see, to think carefully about how we can generalize from experience, and to always be willing to test our ideas. He suggests that "each of these requires different skills to counteract and compete with our normal, tacit, automatic way of learning." Questions that need to be asked about the connections observed include: "Are these significant or due to chance? What do they mean relative to what we already know?" (p. 227). Ideally, as Hogarth notes, these habits of learning would become second nature; they would occur without effort. They themselves would become tacit. Examples include strategies discussed in later chapters, such as asking, "Could I be wrong?" "Is there another way to look at this?" "Have I left anything out?" Different questions may be of value in different stages of problem solving to avoid common errors.

Thus, the environments in which we grow up and spend our time influence how we reason. If we change our environments, we can change how we think. A key question is: "How can I make the kind of feedback I acquire in my everyday work more helpful in educating my intuition?" One of the obstacles to use of evidence-based practices and policies is the quality of feedback we get about our decisions. Often, the kind of feedback provided is exactly opposite to what is needed to "educate our intuition." For example, those who work in intake units in child welfare agencies typically do not find out what happens to their cases; they get no feedback regarding the accuracy of their decisions—for example, to remove a child from his or her home. Hogarth (2001) notes that rarely do emergency room personnel see the outcomes of their decisions. He calls this a classic case of the wicked learning environment. It is also true of interviewing job candidates. We typically do not know what would have happened if we had hired those whom we rejected. The value of learning from feedback emphasizes the importance of avoiding confirmation biases that do not allow us to test whether our intuition is correct. In contrast, in a falsification approach to learning, we question ourselves; we ask "Could I be wrong?" (See later discussion.)

Uncritical Documentation

Simply because something appears in print does not mean that it is true. Indeed, Ioannides (2005) argues that most biomedical research findings are false. Similarly, just because a claim is accompanied by a reference is not a good reason for assuming that it is accurate. Unless the report describes the evidence for this statement, it is uncritical documentation. For all we know, this statement could be someone's uninformed opinion.

SCIENCE AND SCIENTIFIC CRITERIA

Our concern for helping and not harming clients obliges us to critically evaluate claims about what is true. Some of the results of not doing so are described in our daily newspapers. Consider the withdrawal of the arthritis drug Vioxx because of side effects such as strokes.

Misunderstandings and Misrepresentations

Surveys show that most people do not understand the basic characteristics of science (*Science and Engineering Indicators*, 2010). Misconceptions include the following:

- There is a search for final answers.
- Intuitive thinking has no role.

- It is assumed that science knows, or will soon know, all the answers.
- Objectivity is assumed.
- Chance occurrences are not considered.
- Scientific knowledge is equivalent to scientific thinking.
- The accumulation of facts is the primary goal.
- Linear thinking is required.
- Passion and caring have no role.
- There is one kind of scientific method.
- Unobservable events are not considered.

Bell and Linn (2002) note: "When textbooks attempt to synthesize historical accounts of discovery, they often omit controversy and personality" (p. 324). These accounts may give an incorrect view of a logical progression of uncomplex discovery when the history is quite different: "serendipitous, personality-filled, conjectural, and controversial" (p. 324). "Scientific journal articles often erase controversy from the record, leaving the disputes and discussions behind the closed doors of the scientific laboratory" (p. 324). Lack of understanding of science is responsible for the "sterile study fallacy" in which a study is disregarded because it focuses on a narrow aspect of some subject. This criticism reflects a lack of appreciation for the developmental nature of knowledge; one study represents but one step among many that may be required to understand a problem. Removing a study from its programmatic context may misrepresent its role in the overall picture. Critics may selectively pick out studies that do not contribute much, if anything, to knowledge development, and ignore those that do.

Misunderstandings of science may result in ignoring this problem-solving method and the knowledge it has generated. Misunderstandings and misrepresentations of science are so common that D. C. Phillips entitled one of his books *The Social Scientist's Bestiary: A Guide to Fabled Threats to, and Defenses of, Naturalistic Social Studies* (1992). (See also Phillips, 1990.) Even academics confuse logical positivism (discarded by scientists long ago) and science as we know it today. Logical positivism emphasizes direct observation by the senses. It is assumed that observation can be theory free. It is justification focused, contending that greater verification yields closer approximations to the truth. This approach to knowledge was discarded decades ago because of the induction problem (see later discussion of justification/falsification), the theory-laden nature of observation, and the utility of unobservable constructs. Theories are conjectures about what may be true. We always have theories. "There is no pure, disinterested, theory-free observation" (Popper, 1994, p. 8). Science is often misrepresented as a collection of facts or as referring only to controlled experimental studies. Many people confuse science with pseudoscience, bogus science, and scientism (see the glossary at the end of this chapter).

Some people protest that science is misused. Saying that a method is bad because it has been or may be misused is not a cogent argument. Anything can be misused. Some people believe that critical reflection is incompatible with passionate caring. Reading the writings of any number of scientists, including Loren Eiseley, Carl Sagan, Karl Popper, and Albert Einstein, would quickly put this false belief to rest. Consider a quote from Karl Popper: "I assert that the scientific way of life involves a burning interest in objective scientific theories—in the theories in themselves, and in the problem of their truth, or their nearness to truth. And this interest is a *critical* interest, an *argumentative* interest" (1994, p. 56).

A scientific approach may be criticized on the grounds that it cannot capture the full meaning of psychological experiences—that scientific accounts are trivial, unrepresentative accounts. A trivial account, by definition, cannot account for events of interest. A scientific approach to practice requires use of a broad range of methods that faithfully represent significant aspects of the phenomena under investigation, including our subjectivities (Biehl, Good, & Kleinman, 2007). There is no doubt that social science and professional journals are replete with research reports with dubious claims. As noted before, Ioannidis (2005) argues that most biomedical research is false. This does not mean that such an approach is not useful. Indeed, history shows that critical tests of common practices have prevented further harms such as the blinding of babies (Silverman, 1980). It does indicate that, like anything else, it can be appropriately or inappropriately applied. (See later discussion of scientism.) The bogus presentation of research findings was a key reason for the development of evidence-based practice. Statistics are often used inappropriately (Best, 2004; Holmes, 2004; Huff, 1954; Penston, 2010).

Far from reinforcing myths about reality, as some claim (e.g., Karger, 1983, p. 204), science is likely to question them. All sorts of questions that people may not want raised may be raised, such as: "Does this residential center really help residents? Would another method be more effective? Does what I'm doing really help clients? How accurate is my belief about _____?" Many scientific discoveries, such as Charles Darwin's theory of evolution, clashed with some religious views of the world (and still do). Consider the church's reactions to the discovery that the earth was not the center of the universe. Only after 350 years did the Catholic Church agree that Galileo was correct in stating that the earth revolves around the sun. Objections to teaching evolutionary theory remain common (see reports published by the National Center for Science Education). An accurate understanding of science will help you distinguish among helpful, trivializing, and bogus uses. Bogus uses may create and maintain views of problems and proposed solutions that leave unchanged or decrease the quality of life for clients (Basaglia, 1987; Cohen & Timimi, 2008).

What Is Science?

Science is a way of thinking about and investigating the accuracy of assumptions about the world. It is a process for solving problems in which we learn from our mistakes. Science rejects a reliance on authority (e.g., pronouncements by highly placed officials or professors) as a route to knowledge. Authority and science are clashing views of how knowledge can be gained. The history of science and medicine shows that the results of experimental research involving systematic investigation often frees us from false beliefs that harm rather than help and decrease our susceptibility to fraudulent claims. There are many ways to do science and many philosophies of science. The terms *science* and *scientific* are sometimes used to refer to any systematic effort—including case studies, correlational studies, and naturalistic studies—to acquire information about a subject. All methods are vulnerable to error, which must be considered when evaluating the data they generate. Nonexperimental approaches to understanding include natural observation, as in ethology (the study of animal behavior in real-life settings), and correlational methods that use statistical analysis to investigate the degree to which events are associated. These methods are of value in suggesting promising experiments as well as when events of interest cannot be experimentally altered, or if doing so would destroy what is under investigation. Where does magic fit in? Magic has been defined by anthropologists "as an intervention designed to reduce anxiety at times of uncertainty" (Frazer, 1925, p. 364)—for example, doing a rain dance. As mentioned earlier, Frazer (1925) suggested that there is a much closer relationship between magic and science than between science and religion. In both magic and science there is an interest in predicting the environment, for example.

The view of science presented here, critical rationalism, is one in which the theory-laden nature of observation is assumed (i.e., our assumptions influence what we observe) and rational criticism is viewed as the essence of science (Miller, 1994; Phillips, 1987, 1992; Popper, 1963/1972). (See Exhibit 4.1.) Concepts are assumed to have meaning and value even though they are unobservable. Popper's view of science can be summed up in four steps: (1) we select a problem; (2) we try to solve it by proposing a theory as a guess about what may be true; (3) we critically discuss and test our theory; and (4) this always reveals new problems ($P_1 \rightarrow Th \rightarrow Test \rightarrow Error \rightarrow P_2$). This view of science emphasizes the elimination of errors by means of criticism: "Knowledge grows by the elimination of some of our errors, and in this way we learn to understand our problems, and our theories, and the need for new solutions" (Popper, 1994, p. 159). The growth of knowledge is not in accuracy of depiction or certainty but in an increase in universality and abstraction (Munz, 1985). That is, a better theory can account for a wider range of events. By testing our guesses, we eliminate false theories and learn a bit more about our problems. Corrective feedback from the physical world allows us to test our guesses about what is true or false. We learn which of our guesses are false. Evolutionary epistemologists highlight the two different histories of science: the creation of theories (e.g., through random variation) and their selection (by testing; Munz, 1985).

Testable Theories and Criticism as the Essence of Science

The scientific tradition is the tradition of criticism (Popper, 1994, p. 42). The essence of science is creative, bold guessing and rigorous testing in a way that offers accurate information about whether a guess (conjecture or theory) is accurate (Asimov, 1989). Popper argues that "The growth of knowledge, and especially of scientific knowledge, consists of learning from our mistakes" (1994, p. 93). It is assumed that we can discover approximations to the truth by means of rational argument and critical testing of theories and that the soundness of an assertion is related to the uniqueness and rigor of the relevant critical tests. Karl Popper considers the critical method to be one of the great Greek inventions. Scientific statements are those that can be tested (they can be refuted). Consider the question: How many teeth are in a horse's mouth? You could speculate about this, or you could open a horse's mouth and look inside. If an agency for the homeless claims that it succeeds in finding homes for applicants within 10 days, you could accept this claim at face value or systematically gather data to see whether this claim is true. Bunge (2003) suggests the following possibilities:

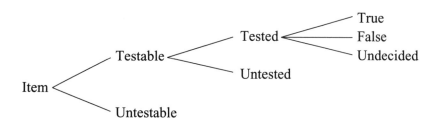

Some tests are more rigorous than others (they control for more biases) and so offer more information about what may be true or false. Theories differ in the extent to which they have been tested and in the rigor of the tests used. The question raised will suggest the research method required to explore it (see Chapter 12). Every research method is limited in the kinds of questions it can address successfully. Purpose will suggest the kinds of evidence needed to test different kinds of claims. Thus, if our purpose is to communicate the emotional complexity of a certain kind of experience (e.g., the death of an infant), then qualitative methods are needed (e.g., detailed case examples, thematic analyses of journal entries, open-ended interviews at different times).

A theory should describe what cannot occur as well as what can occur. If you can make contradictory predictions based on a theory, it cannot be tested. If you cannot discover a way to test a theory, it is not falsifiable. Testing may involve examining the past, as in Darwin's theory of evolution. Some theories are not testable (falsifiable). There is no way to test them to find out if they are correct. Psychoanalytic theory is often criticized on the grounds that it cannot be falsified, that contradictory hypotheses can be drawn from the theory. As Karl Popper points out, irrefutability is not a virtue of a theory, but a vice. Theories can be falsified only if specific predictions are made about what can happen and also about what cannot happen.

Many people accept a justificationist approach to knowledge development, focusing on gathering support for (justifying, confirming) claims and theories (see Exhibit 4.1). Let's say that you see 3,000 swans, all of which are white. Does this mean that all swans are white? Can we generalize from the particular (seeing 3,000 swans, all of which are white) to the general, that all swans are white? Karl Popper and others contend that we cannot discover what is true by means of induction (making generalizations based on particular instances), because we may later discover exceptions (swans that are not white). (In fact, black swans are found in New Zealand.) Popper maintains that falsification (attempts to falsify, to discover the errors in our beliefs) by means of critical discussion and testing is the only sound way to develop knowledge (Popper, 1992, 1994). (For critiques of Popper's view of knowledge, see, for example, Kuhn, 1996.)

Exhibit 4.1 Contrasts Between Two Philosophies of Science—The Verificationist Philosophy and the Refutationist Approach Propounded by Popper

Verificationist	**Refutationist**
Certainty is possible.	Certainty is impossible.
Science is based on proof.	Science is based on disproof.
Observation reveals truth.	Observation involves interpretation.
Recognition of facts precedes formulation of theories.	Formulation of theories precedes recognition of facts.
A good theory predicts many things.	A good theory forbids many things.
A good theory is probable: it has been repeatedly confirmed.	A good theory is improbable yet it has repeatedly failed to be refuted.
A prediction is more informative the more it conforms to experience.	A prediction is more informative the more it is risky or deviant from expectations.
Induction is the logical foundation of science.	Deduction is the logical foundation of science.
Inductive inference is logical.	Induction is illogical.
A theory can be validated independently and absolutely.	A theory can be corroborated only relative to other theories.
Among competing theories, the preferable is the one that has been more often verified.	Among competing theories of equal refutability, the preferable is the one that has withstood more diverse tests.
Theories become more scientific the more they have been proven true by objective observations.	Theories become more scientific as they are made more refutable through both reformulations and technological advances in methods.

Source: From "Popperian Refutation in Epidemiology," by M. Maclure, 1985, *American Journal of Epidemiology, 121*(3), pp. 343–350. Reprinted with permission.

Confirmations of a theory can readily be found if one looks for them. Popper uses the criterion of falsifiability to demarcate what is or could be scientific knowledge from what is not or could not be. For example, there is no way to refute the claim that "there is a God," but there is a way to refute the claim that "assertive community outreach services for the severely mentally ill reduce substance abuse." We could, for example, randomly distribute clients to a group providing such services and compare outcomes with those of clients receiving no services or other services. Although we can justify the selection of a theory by its having survived more risky tests concerning a wider variety of hypotheses (it has not been falsified), compared with other theories that have not been tested or that have been falsified, we can never accurately claim that this theory is the truth. We can only eliminate false beliefs.

A Search for Patterns and Regularities

It is assumed that the universe has some degree of order and consistency. This does not mean that unexplained phenomena or chance variations do not occur or are not considered. For example, chance variations contribute to evolutionary changes (e.g., see Lewontin, 1995; Strohman, 2003). And uncertainty is assumed. Since a future test may show an assumption to be incorrect, even one that is strongly corroborated (has survived many critical tests), no assertion can ever be proved. This does not mean that all beliefs are equally sound; some have survived more rigorous tests than have others.

Parsimony

An explanation is parsimonious if all or most of its components are necessary to explain most of its related phenomena. Unnecessarily complex explanations may get in the way of detecting relationships between behaviors and related events. Consider the following two accounts:

1. Mrs. Lancer punishes her child because of her own unresolved superego issues related to early childhood trauma. This creates a negative disposition to dislike her oldest child.
2. Mrs. Lancer hits her child because this temporarily removes his annoying behaviors (he stops yelling) and because she does not have positive parenting skills (e.g., she does not know how to identify and reinforce acceptable behaviors).

The second account suggests specific behaviors that could be altered. Unless clarified, concepts such as "unresolved superego issues" and "negative disposition" may not yield guidelines for discovering the potential to help clients.

Scientists Strive for Objectivity

Basic to objectivity is the critical discussion and testing of theories (eliminating errors through criticism). "What we call scientific objectivity is nothing else than the fact that no scientific theory is accepted as dogma, and that all theories are tentative and are open all the time to severe criticism—to a rational, critical discussion aiming at the elimination of errors" (Popper, 1994, p. 160). The theory-laden nature of observation is assumed; observation is always selective (influenced by our theories and related concepts). We are influenced by our evolutionary history in how we see and react to the world as well as by the culture in which we have grown up. We see what we expect to see. Scientists are often wrong and find out that they are wrong by testing their predictions. In this way, better theories (those that can account for more findings) replace earlier ones.

Science is conservative in insisting that a new theory account for previous findings. Science is revolutionary in its calling for the overthrow of previous theories shown to be false, but this does not mean that the new theory has been established as true. (For critiques of the view that advancing knowledge means abandoning prior knowledge, see Phillips, 1987.) Although the purpose of science is to seek true answers to problems (statements that correspond to facts), this does not mean that we can have certain knowledge. Rather, we may say that certain beliefs (theories) have (so far) survived critical tests or have not yet been exposed to them. And some theories have been found to be false. An error "consists essentially of our regarding as true a theory that is not true" (Popper, 1992, p. 4). We can avoid error or discover it by doing all that we can to discover and eliminate falsehoods (p. 4). The study of errors when making decisions has received much greater attention in recent years (see Chapter 9).

A Skeptical Attitude

Scientists are skeptics. They question what others view as fact or common sense. They ask for arguments and evidence. They do not have sacred cows.

> Science . . . is a way of thinking. . . . [It] invites us to let the facts in, even when they don't conform to our preconceptions. It counsels us to consider hypotheses in our heads and see which ones best match the facts. It urges on us a fine balance between no-holds-barred openness to new ideas, however heretical, and the most rigorous skeptical scrutiny of everything—new ideas and established wisdom. (Sagan, 1990, p. 265)

Scientists and skeptics seek criticism of their views and change their beliefs when they have good reason to do so. Skeptics are more interested in arriving at accurate answers than in not ruffling the feathers of supervisors or administrators.

Other Characteristics

Science deals with specific problems/questions that may be solvable. For example, is intensive in-home care for parents of abused children more effective than the usual agency services? Is the use of medication to decrease depression in elderly people more (or less) effective than cognitive-behavioral methods? Examples of unsolvable questions are: "Should punishment ever be used in raising children?" "Are people inherently good or evil?" Saying that science deals with problems that can be solved does not mean, however, that other kinds of questions are unimportant or that a problem will remain unsolvable. New methods may be developed that yield answers to questions previously unapproachable in a systematic way. Science is collective. Scientific knowledge is publicly reviewed by a community. Scientists communicate with one another, and the results of one study inform the efforts of other scientists.

The Rise of Big Science

As "big science" becomes more common (research institutes jockeying for limited research funds) and collaboration between industry and universities increases, resistance to new ideas becomes more likely. (See description of "research cartels" in Bauer, 2004.) Researchers with certain kinds of laboratories have a big stake in maintaining certain views of reality, those that call for the kind of methods used in their laboratories. "Skepticism toward research claims is absolutely necessary to safeguard reliability. In corporate settings, where results are expected to meet corporate goals, criticism may be brushed off as disloyalty and skepticism is thereby suppressed" (Bauer, 2004, p. 649).

THE DIFFERENCE BETWEEN SCIENCE AND PSEUDOSCIENCE

The term *pseudoscience* refers to material that makes sciencelike claims but provides no evidence for them (see Exhibit 4.2; e.g., see Lilienfeld, Lynn, & Lohr, 2003; Sarnoff, 2001). Surveys of college students reveal a variety of pseudoscientific beliefs (e.g., see Wilson, 2001). (See also *Science and Engineering Indicators*, 2010.) Pseudoscience is characterized by a casual approach to evidence (weak evidence is accepted as readily as strong evidence). Hallmarks include the following:

- Discourages critical examination of claims/arguments.
- Uses the trappings of science without the substance.
- Relies on anecdotal evidence.
- Is not self-correcting.
- Is not skeptical.

Exhibit 4.2 Comparison of Attitudes and Activities of Scientists and Pseudoscientists

Typical Attitudes and Activities	Scientist			Pseudoscientist		
	Yes	No	Optional	Yes	No	Optional
Admits own ignorance, hence need for more research.	X				X	
Finds own field difficult and full of holes.	X				X	
Advances by posing and solving new problems.	X				X	
Welcomes new hypotheses and methods.	X				X	
Proposes and tries out new hypotheses.	X					X
Attempts to find or apply laws.	X				X	
Cherishes the unity of science.	X				X	
Relies on logic.	X					X
Uses mathematics.	X					X
Gathers or uses data, particularly quantitative data.	X					X
Looks for counterexamples.	X				X	
Invents or applies objective checking procedures.	X				X	
Settles disputes by experiment or computation.	X				X	
Falls back consistently on authority.		X		X		
Suppresses or distorts unfavorable data.		X		X		
Updates own information.	X				X	
Seeks critical comments from others.	X				X	
Writes papers that can be understood by anyone.		X		X		
Is likely to achieve instant celebrity.		X		X		

Source: From "What Is Pseudoscience?" by M. Bunge, 1984, *The Skeptical Inquirer,* 9, p. 41. Copyright 1984 by Committee for the Scientific Investigation of Claims of the Paranormal. Reprinted with permission.

- Equates an open mind with an uncritical one.
- Ignores or explains away falsifying data.
- Relies on vague language.
- Is not empirical.
- Produces beliefs and faith but not knowledge.
- Is often not testable.
- Does not require repeatability (e.g., see Bunge, 1984; Gray, 1991; Jarvis, 1990).

A critical attitude, which Karl Popper (1963/1972) defines as a willingness and commitment to open up favored views to severe scrutiny—is basic to science, distinguishing it from pseudoscience. Indicators of pseudoscience include irrefutable hypotheses and a reluctance to revise beliefs even when confronted with relevant criticism. It makes excessive (untested) claims of contributions to knowledge. Results of a study may be referred to in many different sources until they achieve the status of a law without any additional data being gathered. Richard Gelles calls this the "Woozle Effect" (1982, p. 13). Pseudoscience is a billion-dollar industry (Dawes, 2001). Products include self-help books, subliminal tapes, and call-in advice from "authentic psychics" who have no evidence that they accomplish what they promise (Beyerstein, 1990; Druckman & Bjork, 1991). Pseudoscience can be found in all fields, including multiculturalism (e.g., Ortiz de Montellano, 1992) and clinical psychology (Lilienfeld, Lynn, & Lohr, 2003; see also later discussion of propaganda).

A good part of the prestige of the helping professions rests on their alleged scientific base. This does not represent the practice of many clinicians and researchers who, knowingly or not, embrace a pseudoscientific perspective. They use the trappings of science without the substance (Bunge, 1984). Examples include use of invalid assessment measures and ineffective or harmful services (e.g., see Jacobson, Foxx, & Mulick, 2005; Lilienfeld et al., 2003). The picture presented both to professionals and to the public in terms of "what is known" often far exceeds reality. Inflated claims about "what is known" abound throughout the history of the helping professions (e.g., Colman, 1987; Gardner, 1957; Kohn, 1988; Leo & Cohen, 2003; Medawar, 1979). Such misrepresentations are not benign. They result in intrusive, unnecessary services and encourage paternalistic coercion in the name of helping. Basaglia (1987) suggests that the ideology and trappings of science are used to pull the wool over people's eyes in suggesting a credibility of claims that does not exist.

Clinicians are not immune from the influence of bogus claims in the media, as well as in professional sources such as newsletters, books, the Internet, and journals. The battle for acceptance of critical appraisal of claims as being of value in assessing their accuracy that has been won in the physical sciences and in many areas of medicine has not yet been won in the interpersonal helping professions. Medawar (1984, p. 58) argues that quasi-scientific psychologies "are getting away with a concept of truthfulness which belongs essentially to imaginative literature" and that this represents "a style of thought that will impede the growth of our understanding of mental illness." He describes this approach as "poetism," which "stands for the belief that imaginative insight and a mysteriously privileged sensibility can tell us all the answers that are truly worthy of being sought or being known" (p. 60). A sound grounding in the differences between science and pseudoscience is vital to avoid influence by bogus claims. The terms *science* and *scientific* are often used to increase the credibility of a view or approach, even though no evidence is provided to support it. The term *science* has been applied to many activities that in reality have nothing to do with science. Examples are *scientific charity* and *scientific philanthropy*. The term *evidence-based* is often applied to material that shares none of the characteristics of the philosophy and process of EBP as described in Chapter 10. Proseletizers of many sorts cast their advice as based on science. Classification of clients into psychiatric categories lends an aura of scientific credibility to this practice, regardless of whether there is any evidence that it is warranted or that it is helpful to clients (e.g., see Houts, 2002; Kirk, 2010; Kirk & Kutchins, 1992b; Kutchins & Kirk, 1997). For example, is it really true that half of Americans develop a mental disorder sometime during their lives (see "New Report Opens," 2005, p. 23)? The misuse of appeals to science to sell products or encourage certain beliefs is a form of propaganda.

Scienticism

The term *scienticism* refers to the assumption that science should have authority over all other views of life—the tendency to "ape the methods in the natural sciences" (Hayek, 1967). "Scienticism dogmatically asserts the authority of scientific knowledge" (Popper, 1992, p. 6). It reflects a "dogmatic belief in the authority of the method of the natural sciences and its results" (1992, p. 41). Serge Lang (1998) critiqued favoring quantitative methods simply because they are quantitative and gives examples. Because of our tendency to be impressed with authority (e.g., of science and scientists), scientistic material can easily fool us.

Antiscience

Antiscience refers to rejection of science. For example, some people believe that there is no such thing as privileged knowledge, i.e., that some is more sound than others. Typically, such views are not related to real-life problems and to a candid appraisal of the results of different ways of solving a problem. That is, they are not problem-focused, allowing a critical appraisal of competing views. Antiscience is common in academic settings (Gross & Levitt, 1994; Patai & Koertge, 2003) as well as in popular culture (e.g., John Burnham, *How Superstition Won and Science Lost*, 1987). Many people confuse science, scienticism, and pseudoscience, resulting in an antiscience stance (see the glossary at the end of this chapter).

Relativism

Relativists argue that all methods are equally valid in testing claims (e.g., anecdotal reports and experimental studies). It is assumed that knowledge and morality are inherently bounded by or rooted in culture; Gellner, 1992, p. 68). "Knowledge or morality outside culture is, it claims, a chimera. . . . Meanings are incommensurate, meanings are culturally constructed, and so all cultures are equal" (p. 73). Postmodernism is a current form of relativism. Gellner suggests that in the void created, some voices predominate, throwing us back on authority, not a criterion that will protect clients' rights and allow clinicians to be faithful to their code of ethics. If there is no means by which to tell what is accurate and what is not, if all methods are equally effective, the vacuum is filled by an elite who are powerful enough to say what is and what is not (Gellner, 1992). Gellner suggests that the sole focus on cognitive meaning in postmodernism ignores political and economic influences. He argues that postmodernism "denies or obscures tremendous differences in cognition and technical power" (pp. 71–72). He points out that there are real constraints in society that are obscured within this recent form of relativism (postmodernism) and suggests that such cognitive nihilism constitutes a "travesty of the real role of serious knowledge in our lives" (p. 95). Gellner argues that this view undervalues coercive and economic constraints in society and overvalues conceptual ones. "If we live in a world of meanings, and meanings exhaust the world, where is there any room for coercion through the whip, gun, or hunger?" (p. 63).

Gellner (1992) argues that postmodernism is an affectation: "Those who propound it or defend it against its critics, continue, whenever facing any serious issue in which their real interests are engaged, to act on the non-relativistic assumption that one particular vision is cognitively much more effective than others" (p. 70). Consider, for example, the different criteria social workers want their physicians to rely on when confronted with a serious medical problem compared to criteria they say they rely on to select service methods offered to clients. They say they rely on criteria such as intuition and experience with a few cases when making decisions about their clients, but want their physicians to rely on the results of controlled experimental studies and a demonstrated track record of success based on data collected systematically and regularly when making decisions about a serious medical problem of their own (Gambrill & Gibbs, 2002).

Quackery

Quackery refers to the promotion and marketing, for a profit, of untested, often worthless, and sometimes dangerous health products and procedures by either professionals or others (Jarvis, 1990; Young, 1992).

> People generally like to feel that they are in control of their life. Quacks take advantage of this fact by giving their clients things to do—such as taking vitamin pills, preparing special foods, meditating, and the like. The activity may provide a temporary psychological lift, but believing in false things can have serious consequences. The loss may be financial, psychological (when disillusionment sets in), physical (when the method is harmful or the person abandons effective care), or social (diversion from more constructive activities). (Barrett, Jarvis, Kroger, & London, 2002, p. 7)

Reasons Jarvis (1990) suggests as to why some people become quacks are shown in Exhibit 4.3.

Barrett and his colleagues (2002) suggest that victims of quackery usually have one or more of the following vulnerabilities: (1) lack of suspicion; (2) desperation; (3) alienation (e.g., from the medical profession); (4) belief in magic; or (5) overconfidence in discerning whether a method works. Advertisers, both past and present, use the trappings of science (without the substance) to encourage consumers to buy products (Pepper, 1984). Indicators of quackery include the promise of quick cures, the use of anecdotes and testimonials to support claims, privileged power (only the great Dr. _____ knows how to _____), and secrecy (claims are not open to objective scrutiny). Natale (1988) estimates that in 1987 Americans spent $50 million on subliminal tapes, even though there was no evidence that they provided what they promised (Druckman & Bjork, 1991). For every claim supported by sound evidence, there are scores of bogus claims in advertisements, newscasts, films, TV, newspapers, and professional sources, making it a considerable challenge to resist their lures. McCoy (2000) describes a cornucopia of questionable medical devices. Reasons suggested by William Jarvis (1990) as to why some professionals become quacks include the profit motive (making money) and the prophet motive (enjoying adulation and discipleship resulting from a pretense of superiority).

Exhibit 4.3 Why Professionals Become Quacks

- *Boredom.* "Daily practice can become humdrum. Pseudoscientific ideas can be exciting" (p. 5).
- *Low self-esteem.* Some professions such as social work are not the most highly regarded. Dissatisfaction with a limited scope of practice may encourage pursuit of grandiose goals and unwarranted claims of effectiveness.
- *Reality shock.* Professionals regularly see troubling situations. This may require psychological adjustments that some helpers are not up to.
- *Belief encroachment.* Science is limited in its methodology to dealing with problems that are possible to solve. This constraint may become burdensome, and additional aims, and embraced such as helping people with religious questions.
- *The profit motive.* Quackery can be lucrative.
- *The prophet motive.* "Some clients experience uncertainty, doubt, and fear about the meaning and purpose of life. Others confront situations that may seem hopeless. The power over people provided by the prophet role is seductive. Egomania is commonly found among quacks. They enjoy the adulation and discipleship their pretense of superiority evokes. By promoting themselves, they project superiority not only to their clinical colleagues, but often to the entire scientific community" (p. 6).
- *Psychopathic traits.* "Psychopaths exhibit glibness and superficial charm, grandiose sense of self-worth, pathological lying, conning/manipulative behavior, lack of guilt, proneness to boredom, and lack of empathy often seen in quacks" (p. 7).
- *The conversion phenomenon.* Many professionals who become quacks have gone through emotionally difficult experiences such as a practice failure, midlife crisis, divorce, or life-threatening illness.

Note: Quackery refers to promoting services known to be ineffective, or which are untested, for a profit.

Source: Based on *Dubious Dentistry* (Part 4, pp. 1–29), by William Jarvis, 1990, Loma Linda, CA: Loma Linda University.

The history of quackery is quite fascinating (Porter, 2002). Quacks probably have existed as long as people have. They may award themselves degrees or obtain degrees from bogus institutions. They use a creative variety of ploys to woo people, including propaganda methods designed to encourage beliefs and actions with the least thought possible.

Propaganda

Quackery and pseudoscience make use of propaganda strategies (see Exhibit 4.4). Jacques Ellul (1965) views propaganda as principally interested in shaping action and behavior with little thought. A major function of propaganda is to squelch and censor dissenting points of view (e.g., see Rank, 1984). Its purpose is not to inform but to persuade. Interrelated kinds of propaganda in the helping professions include deep propaganda that obscures political, economic, and social contingencies that influence problem-related behaviors claimed by a profession (e.g., alcohol use, depression) and the questionable accuracy of basic assumptions, (for example, relabeling problems in living as mental disorders that require the help of experts) (Gambrill, 2012a). It also includes inflated claims of effectiveness regarding assessment, intervention, and evaluation methods that woo clients to professionals and professionals to professions, perhaps because of profit and/or prophet motives (Jarvis, 1990). There are troubling gaps between the obligations of researchers to report limitations of research, prepare systematic reviews, and accurately describe well-argued alternative views and what we find in published literature. Common propaganda methods include glittering generalizations, emotional reasoning, creation of fear, appeals to self-interest, and censorship of alternative views and contradictory evidence (see prior discussion of questionable criteria). Key propaganda methods include confusion, distortion, censorship, and fabrication.

Exhibit 4.4 Mental Illness Model and Rank's (1984) Fourfold Classification of Propaganda

Overemphasize the positive aspects of preferred model:
Inflated claims of success in removing complaints (puffery).
Inflated claims of success in preventing problems (puffery).

Hide and minimize negative aspects of preferred model:
Harmful effects of neuroleptic drugs.
Questionable reliability and validity of psychiatric classification systems.

Overemphasize negative aspects of opposing views:
Associate alternative approaches with negative terms (mechanistic, dehumanizing).
Allege that positive effects of alternative approaches are only temporary.

Hide and minimize positive aspects of opposing views:
Ignore research showing that nonprofessionals are as effective as professionals with many problems (e.g., see Dawes, 1994).
Ignore positive results achieved by alternative approaches.

Censoring of competing views and counterevidence is common (e.g., Angell, 2004; Gambrill & Reiman, 2011; Kondro & Sibbald, 2004; Moran, 1998). Internet sources, including those of government agencies such as the National Institutes of Health, may censor well-argued competing views; they claim that anxiety in social situations and attention-deficit/hyperactivity disorder (ADHD) are "brain diseases," not mentioning alternative well-argued views (e.g., WebMDHealth). Consider, for example, the propagandistic nature of the International Consensus Statement on ADHD (Barkley et al., 2002). Rather than addressing cogent criticisms of the diagnosis of ADHD and related recommended interventions, Barkley et al. (2002) dismiss criticisms as dangerous myths. Instead of arguing ad rem (addressing critics' concerns), they direct ad hominem arguments toward critics. Indeed, this brief statement (most pages contain a series of signers and references) is replete with propaganda strategies such as begging the question and omitting well-argued critiques and alternative views. For example, many view the labeling of thousands of little boys (mostly) as having ADHD as a cultural phenomenon encouraged by our consumer-oriented society and by vigorous promotion of biomedical framing and medication as a remedy by Big Pharma and the American Psychiatric Association, not a biomedical one (e.g., Angell, 2011; Singh, 2002; Timimi, 2008; Timimi & Taylor, 2004). Censorship thrives at all levels of education (e.g., Gambrill, 1997; Ravitch, 2003). Here too, as with fraud, websites and organizations have been developed to counter material viewed as propaganda (e.g., National Coalition Against Censorship).

The inflation of knowledge claims (puffery) is a key propaganda strategy (Rank, 1984). The resultant harms of professional propaganda are varied and may ripple out to others for decades. Those who market ideas attempt to forward a view, not through a balanced and accurate presentation of related evidence and alternative views, but through reliance on strategies such as vague, emotional, distorted presentations of disliked positions, presentation of only data that support a favored position, and question begging. Skrabanek and McCormick (1998) illustrate the many false promises made in the name of prevention: that is, if we avoid certain risky behaviors, we will live longer, have a higher quality of life, and so on. They view the inflated claims and promises in the prevention area as a crusade and suggest that the self-righteous intolerance of some wellness zealots borders on health fascism. "Historically, humans have been at greatest risk while being improved in the best image of their possibilities as seen by somebody else" (p. 113) (see also Edgley & Brissett, 1999). Although many public health experts would have us believe that taking certain steps to improve our health will prolong or enhance the quality of our life, typically, this is far from known; it is far from certain (see also Nettleton & Bunton, 1995).

Treatment programs may misrepresent the nature of their services and their outcomes (e.g., O'Hagan, 2003). The interpersonal helping industry is a huge one, consuming billions of dollars a year in direct and third-party payments. Cost per child at the Oswald D. Heck Development Center is $1.4 million annually. Hakim (2011) recently exposed abuse of children at this center, including being sat on and asphyxiated. Those who have products to sell, including residential centers, pharmaceutical companies, and professional organizations promoting their training programs, take advantage of sophisticated marketing strategies to encourage purchase of their products. Strategies range from the obvious, such as advertisements in professional journals, to the subtle, such as offering workshops or conferences without identifying the funding source of these conferences. It is estimated that pharmaceutical companies spend between $8,000 and $11,000 per medical student per year to market their products to these individuals. A review of advertising on marketing brochures distributed by drug companies to physicians in Germany revealed that 94% of the content in these had no basis in scientific evidence (reported in Tuffs, 2004).

Drug companies promote the creation of new "diseases" such as "social anxiety disorder" and "premenstrual dysphoric disorder" to increase markets for their medications (Parry, 2003). Economic interests of pharmaceutical companies encourage promotion of a biomedical view of problems such as framing common concerns, such as anxiety in social situations, as "mental illnesses" via use of a variety of propaganda methods, including question begging—simply asserting that anxiety in social situations is a mental illness requiring medication (Antonuccio, Burns, & Danton, 2002; Bekelman, Li, & Gross, 2003; Moncrieff, 2008; Starcevic, 2002). Websites sponsored by this industry contain material such as the following:

> If you think you are suffering from depression, panic disorder, obsessive compulsive disorder (OCD), posttraumatic stress disorder (PTSD), or Premenstrual Dysphoric Disorder (PMDD) know that you're not alone. In the United States, millions of people have these disorders. It is important to know these medical conditions are treatable. Read some of the articles and brochures below to learn about options for improving your mental health. (December 8, 2003, www.pfizerforwomen.com)

Biomedical views ignore context. This may be the most insidious effect of promoting pharmaceuticals directly to consumers. The message is that problems such as anxiety and depression are brain diseases that are biomedical in origin and that can be treated with medication. This ignores and hides contributors to stress such as lack of employment and health care, high-cost housing, discrimination, poverty, and poor schools. It ignores the social context of human experience and the unique causes of and ways distress is experienced and the resulting differences in how it should be approached (e.g., see Biehl et al., 2007). Presenting pitches for a product in an article form (advertorials) may lull readers into uncritical acceptance of promotional material (Prounis, 2004). Recently, more attention has been given in professional education programs to helping students understand marketing strategies used and how to avoid unwanted influences (Wilkes & Hoffman, 2001). Related courses encourage clinicians to critically appraise claims, including advertisements in journals (see also Gambrill & Gibbs, 2009). Much of continuing education in psychiatry has been funded by the pharmaceutical industry (Angell, 2004). Screening days for anxiety and depression are often funded by this industry. Organizations such as the National Alliance for the Mentally Ill (NAMI) and Children and Adults with Attention-Deficit/Hyperactivity Disorder (CHADD) are heavily funded by Big Pharma.

Fraud

Fraud is an intentional misrepresentation made for personal (or corporate) gain, such as promoting the effectiveness of a drug known to be ineffective or harmful. There is deception drawing on a variety of ploys, such as hiding harmful side effects (Charatan, 2011; Limb, 2011; Sackett & Oxman, 2003; Smith, 2005; Sparrow, 2000). Fraudulent claims (often appealing to the trappings of science) may result in overlooking effective methods or being harmed by remedies that are supposed to help (e.g., Jacobson, Foxx, & Mulick, 2005). Gould (cited in Jensen, 1989) included fraud (manufacture of evidence, presenting fiction as fact) as one of four pathologies of science. The three others were propaganda (selective presentations of evidence), prejudice, and finagle. The last refers to minor hoaxes and intentional errors in data description or recording that result in a misrepresentation of findings. Scientific prejudice involves use of different standards of evidence for preferred and disliked views; that is, less rigorous standards are used for preferred views. Fraud is so extensive in some areas that special organizations have been formed, newsletters written, and Internet sites created to help consumers evaluate claims (e.g., *Health Letter* published by the Public Citizens Research Group; see also the Center for Media Education [CME]). (See also Exhibit 4.5.)

The attorney general of the State of New York, Eliot Spitzer, filed a civil suit accusing the drug giant GlaxoSmithKline of committing fraud by concealing negative information about Paxil, a drug used to treat depression.

> The suit says that the company conducted five clinical trials of Paxil in adolescents and children, yet published only one study whose mixed results it deemed positive. The company sat on two major studies for up to four years, although the results of one were divulged by a whistle-blower at a medical conference in 1999 and all of the studies were submitted to the Food and Drug Administration in 2002 when the

Exhibit 4.5 Internet Resources Regarding Fraud and Quackery

- American Council on Science and Health: "founded in 1978 by scientists who became concerned that many important public policies related to health and the environment did not have a sound scientific basis. . . ."
- Anti-Quackery Ring: "This ring is for sites that combat & debunk health-related frauds, myths, fads, and fallacies, and are more interested in real, objective, scientific proof, than in the speculative, subjective, and unproven theories and anecdotes of so-called Alternative Medicine. If you are sympathetic to the aims of the National Council Against Health Fraud, and you consider QuackWatch to be a reliable source of anti-quackery information, then this ring may be just what you're looking for. . . ."
- *Chirobase: A Skeptical Guide to Chiropractic History, Theories, and Current Practices*, by Stephen Barrett, M.D., William T. Jarvis, Ph.D., Charles E. DuVall Jr., D.C.
- Commission for Scientific Medicine and Mental Health
  - *Scientific Review of Alternative Medicine and Aberrant Medical Practices* "is the only peer-reviewed journal devoted exclusively to objectively analyzing the claims of 'alternative medicine.'"
  - The *Scientific Review of Mental Health Practice* "is the only peer-reviewed journal devoted exclusively to distinguishing scientifically-supported claims from scientifically-unsupported claims in clinical psychology, psychiatry, social work, and allied disciplines."
- Dietfraud.com DietFraud HQ: Home of the best diet and weight loss scams and dubious treatments.
- Federal Trade Commission for the Consumer
- Health Watcher: Canada's Best Consumer Health Watchdog.
- Internet Healthcare Coalition: Mission is quality health care resources on the Internet.
- National Association of Attorneys General
- National Council Against Health Fraud: "Enhancing freedom of choice through reliable information."
- National Fraud Information Center: The National Consumers League tracks complaints of inappropriate health care practices; works in conjunction with the Federal Trade Commission, and National Association of Attorneys General.
- National Library of Medicine, Medlineplus Health Fraud
- National Patient Safety Foundation, American Medical Association
- QuackWatch: *Guide to Health Fraud, Quackery, and Intelligent Decisions*, by Stephen Barrett, M.D.
- *Skeptic's Dictionary: Alternative Medicine*, by Robert T. Carroll.
- State Attorney General Offices: Addresses and phone numbers of every State Attorney's office in the United States from the National Association of Attorneys General.
- United States Food and Drug Administration, Center for Food Safety and Applied Nutrition, Protecting Yourself Against Health Fraud: Collection of links to government agency resources.

company sought approval for new uses of Paxil. At that time it became apparent that Paxil was no more effective than a placebo in treating adolescent depression and might even provoke suicidal thoughts. ("When Drug Companies Hide Data," *New York Times*, June 6, 2004)

In another report it was noted that Pfizer Inc. "agreed to pay $430 million in fines and plead guilty to charges that a company it acquired four years ago promoted a drug for non-approved uses, in part by plying doctors with favors to get them to talk up the medication" (Harris, 2004). Pennsylvania's attorney general sued 13 pharmaceutical companies for alleged deceptive pricing and sales practices. In June 2004, the editors of leading medical journals and the American Medical Association called on drug companies to register all their clinical trials on a website. Fraud awards against pharmaceutical companies have now edged out such awards to defense contractors (Tanne, 2010). However, the money paid is a pittance compared to the billions of dollars gained in overall sales of one prescribed drug.

KNOWLEDGE VALUED IN EVIDENCE-INFORMED PRACTICE

Many kinds of knowledge are valued in evidence-informed practice and policy. Pawson and his colleagues (Pawson, Boaz, Grayson, Long, & Barnes, 2003) suggest a hierarchy of knowledge from a practice perspective. (See Exhibit 4.6.)

User and Service Provider Knowledge

Clients have unique knowledge, including the acceptability of different methods and related obstacles and resources. Clinical expertise is needed to identify and integrate

Exhibit 4.6   Hierarchy of Knowledge From a Practice Perspective

---

Service User and Care Provider Knowledge
Service users possess knowledge gained from the use of and reflection on interventions. Care providers (foster parents, home health assistants, volunteers, etc.) also have knowledge gained from the provision of interventions.

Practitioners'[*] Knowledge
Line staff: Practitioners possess tacit knowledge based on their experiences. This may be shared informally with colleagues. Practitioners also have knowledge about how organizations facilitate or impede service delivery, how policies affect service delivery, and how community and neighborhood factors influence service.
Management staff: Supervisors, middle managers, and senior managers have knowledge about client populations, staff experiences, internal organizational dynamics, and external interagency dynamics.

Organizational Knowledge
This may be reflected in written policies and procedural manuals. It includes administrative data gathered regarding number and characteristics of clients served, outcomes of service, and costs of service provision. Data is described in quarterly or annual reports to funding sources (government, foundations, and donors) and to the community.

Policy Knowledge
This may be in the form of legislative reports, concept papers, grand jury investigations, court decisions, technical reports, and monographs from research institutes. This may inform policy development or administrative practices.

Research Knowledge
Often derived from empirical studies using quantitative and/or qualitative methods. This may be in research reports, service evaluations, and service instrumentation. Research knowledge may focus on one or more of the categories above (user/care provider, practitioners, organizational, and policy).

---

[*]Adapted from *Types and Quality of Knowledge in Social Care*, by R. Pawson, A. Boaz, L. Grayson, A. Long, and C. Barnes, 2003, London, UK: Care Institute for Excellence.

information about the unique circumstances and characteristics of a client, including his or her preferences, values, and expectations as well as information about local circumstances in making decisions. Practitioners have knowledge about client concerns, information needs related to decisions, services available, local community resources, organizational obstacles, and the effects of policies and legislation on availability of local resources.

Research Related to Information Needs

Clinical practice often requires searching for information needed to answer questions that arise, such as, "Is this client suicidal?" "Should I prescribe medication for blood pressure for this client?" (See Chapters 10 and 11.) The importance of specialized content knowledge and skills is one of the major findings from research in problem solving and decision making, including professional decision making (see Chapter 8). Both content and performance knowledge are important.

Kinds of Research Needed to Critically Appraise Different Kinds of Claims

The phrase *evidence-based practice* (EPB) draws attention to the kind of evidence needed to rigorously test different kinds of practice-related claims (see Chapter 10). What is needed depends on the question; for example, does it concern the effectiveness of an intervention or predictive accuracy of a risk measure? Knowledge valued in evidence-informed practice includes how to critically test claims related to important practice and policy questions, such as, "Is this assessment measure valid?" "Does this parent training program help clients to enhance positive parenting skills?" Such knowledge can help us to avoid biases that may provide misleading conclusions and to avoid fooling ourselves that we have knowledge when we do not. Have claims been critically examined in relation to their consequences for clients? It can help us to avoid being fooled by misleading claims in the media as well as in the professional literature (e.g., see *Harlot Pie* by Sackett & Oxman, 2003).

Mistakes and Errors

Mistakes (what kind occur, when they occur, what contributes to them, and how we can minimize them) are viewed as a vital kind of knowledge, as is knowledge about application obstacles and how we can overcome them, such as creating technological innovations, enhancing communication skills, and increasing self-knowledge that forwards integration of practice and research. Knowledge about rival explanations for a claim of effectiveness is helpful for avoiding inflated claims.

Kinds and Degrees of Uncertainty

Clinicians work under uncertainty. Yet they must act. Awareness of the degree of uncertainty associated with a decision is another kind of valued knowledge—so valuable that an entire enterprise has been created to harvest it: the UK Database of Uncertainties About the Effects of Treatments (DUETs).

"For the purposes of UK DUETs, treatment uncertainties are defined as 'uncertainties that cannot currently be answered by referring to reliable, up-to-date systematic reviews of existing research evidence.' Eligible uncertainties—'known unknowns'—thus meet at least one of the following criteria, with implications for action noted in italics.

- No relevant systematic reviews are identified—*implication: prepare systematic review(s)*.
- Relevant, reliable, up-to-date systematic reviews do not address continuing uncertainties about treatment effects—*implication: extend existing systematic review(s)*.
- Existing relevant systematic reviews are not up-to-date—*implication: update existing systematic review(s)*.
- Reliable, up-to-date systematic reviews have revealed important continuing uncertainties about treatment effects—*implication: conduct additional primary research*." (Fenton, Brice, & Chalmers, 2009, p. 168)

Knowledge that decreases or reveals the degree of uncertainty about how to attain outcomes that clients value is emphasized in evidence-based practice: guesses (theories) that have survived critical tests of their efficacy in resolving problems. Attempts to locate research findings regarding information needs will suggest the degree of uncertainty related to specific decisions. Thinking carefully about claims will keep uncertainty in view. We are less likely to promote bogus claims that may harm clients if acted on (Oreskes & Conway, 2010).

Ignorance as Knowledge

Kerwin and Witte (1983) suggest the following kinds of ignorance:

- *Known unknowns:* All the things you know you don't know.
- *Unknown unknowns:* All the things you don't know you don't know.
- *Errors:* All the things you think you know but don't.
- *Unknown knowns:* All the things you don't know you know.
- *Taboos:* Dangerous, polluting, or forbidden knowledge.
- *Denials:* All the things too painful to know, so you don't. (Kerwin & Witte, 1983)

There is ignorance that has harmful consequences and ignorance that has positive consequences. There is avoidable and unavoidable ignorance. There is ignorance that may be decreased someday and ignorance that will probably never lessen. Different types of ignorance may be visible at different times to different parties who are involved in or affected by outcome evaluation, including politicians, funding agencies, legislators, agency administrators, clients, staff, and the general public. What ignorance is revealed and what is not?

Proctor and Schriebinger (2008) suggest three kinds of ignorance: (1) native (a challenge to be overcome); (2) ignorance as a lost realm (selective choice; we always make choices in what to study, for example); and (3) ignorance as a strategic ploy. Questions arise, such as, "Who did not know, what did they not know, when, who was affected, and in what ways? Who at what time deliberately created ignorance that could never be recaptured?" Ignorance as lost knowledge may be deliberate—a choice of what to study and how to do so, leaving out other possibilities or not. The concept of ignorance is closely related to doubt and uncertainty. The creation of doubt concerning research linking smoking and health consequences was a key strategy used by the tobacco companies (Oreskes & Conway, 2010).

Other Kinds of Knowledge

Administrators have knowledge regarding organizational characteristics that influence quality of service, data regarding services offered and their effects, and the service system. Like direct line staff, they have knowledge about how policies affect services offered (Pawson, Boaz, Grayson, Ling, & Barnes, 2003). Knowledge of common biases that may lead us astray is another kind of valued knowledge, as is knowledge about tools, such as decision aids that help clients make informed decisions. Knowledge concerning ethical obligations is also vital in EBP. Criteria used to select knowledge in authority-based practice are quite different: popularity, tradition, status, degrees, or credentials.

CRITICAL APPRAISAL OF PRACTICES AND POLICIES AS AN ETHICAL OBLIGATION

Ethical obligations require clinicians to draw on practice-related research, to be competent, and to accurately inform clients about the risks and benefits of recommended services and alternatives. The intellectual attitudes of empathy, courage, curiosity, open-mindedness, and reliance on standards such as clarity (Paul, 1993) contribute to making ethical decisions. Karl Popper (1994) argues that relying on unexamined claims about what is true reflects an arrogance that is at odds with a compassion for others. Popper

(1994) argues that we must value "truth, the search for truth, the approximation to truth through the critical elimination of error, and clarity" in order to overcome the influence of other values such as trying to appear profound by using obscure words or jargon (p. 70). If criticism is the route to knowledge, we must value truth over certainty, ignorance, and prejudice, and clarity over obscurity; we must value getting closer to the truth more than winning arguments and maintaining status (p. 44). The philosophy of evidence-based practice emphasizes the close relationship between evidentiary and ethical obligations. It is a way to handle uncertainty constructively for the client's benefit—to deal "with inadequate information in ways that can help to identify really important uncertainties, uncertainties that are often reflected in dramatic variations in clinical practices and which cry out for coordinated efforts to improve knowledge" (Chalmers, 2004).

Popper (1992) suggests that we are all equal in our vast ignorance. "It is important never to forget our ignorance. We should therefore never pretend to know anything, and we should never use big words. What I call the cardinal sin . . . is simply talking hot air, professing a wisdom we do not possess" (p. 86). We have "the obligation never to pose as a prophet" (p. 206). Valuing truth over prejudice and ignorance requires critical testing of claims and conclusions. Only through criticism can we discover our errors and perhaps learn how to do better in the future. A candid recognition of and active search for mistakes keeps the inevitable uncertainty involved in trying to help clients clearly in view, and encourages us to keep track of our mistakes as a way to improve services (McIntyre & Popper, 1983). Valuing truth calls for making well-reasoned decisions—you can make a sound argument for them. For example, claims have survived risky predictions and are compatible with and informed by research findings. Critical discussion with oneself as well as with others is necessary for making well-informed decisions. Three principles that Karl Popper highlights as the basis of every rational discussion are:

1. *The principle of fallibility*: Perhaps I am wrong and perhaps you are right. But we could easily both be wrong.
2. *The principle of rational discussion*: We want to try, as impersonally as possible, to weigh up our reasons for and against a theory: a theory that is definite and criticizable.
3. *The principle of approximation to the truth*: We can nearly always come closer to the truth in a discussion that avoids personal attacks. It can help us to achieve a better understanding, even in those cases where we do not reach an agreement. (Popper, 1992, p. 199)

Valuing truth requires basing decisions on data as well as theory when necessary to solve problems. Guesses about the causes of problems should be checked against data gathered in real life. Only by collecting observational data in problem-related circumstances, such as the classroom or residential setting, may informed guesses be made about the causes of complaints and related circumstances. Collecting systematic data concerning outcomes provides a guide for decisions and allows us to discover whether we are helping, harming, or having no effect. It allows clients to find out whether the quality of their lives has improved, remained the same, or diminished. Anthony Flew (1985) contends that the sincerity of our interest in helping clients is reflected in the efforts we make to find out whether we do help them.

THE BURDEN OF KNOWLEDGE

One topic that seems to have been slighted in the literature on the integration of practice and research concerns the burden of knowledge—for example, the negative consequences of information that all is not as it should be regarding the quality of services provided to clients (e.g., see Sagan, 1987). We are exposed to reports showing harming in the name of helping—for example, adverse events that a professional knew about but did not say or do anything about. My students routinely report concerning lapses in agency practices—often ongoing events in their agency—about which nothing is being done and that are not being discussed. Examples include the following:

- A medical social worker who knows that a client who is dying is not receiving proper pain medication and the medical director will not alter the pain medication schedule.
- A social worker who works in a legal advocates office who knows that a client has been required to attend a drug treatment program, even though it is known that the client has no drug problem—a mistake was made by the person who prepared the report for the court. This parent will not regain custody of her children until she attends this drug treatment program for her alleged drug use.

Even among beginning master's students there is a surprising acceptance of troubling practices and policies based on the assumption that nothing can be done. Such descriptions would often be accompanied by embarrassed laughter and a shrugging off of the possibility that anything could be done. Rarely was the description of the practice, policy, or mistake accompanied by statements such as the following:

- I am going to do something about this.
- We must do something about this.
- I am going to bring this up to my agency team.
- We must work together to change this.

If recognizing unnecessary burdens and harms to clients creates negative feelings (stress, anxiety, sadness for the plights of others, perhaps shame that nothing is being done), then forgetting provides relief. When we cannot act in the face of avoidable suffering, is not forgetting an adaptive reaction?

SUMMARY

There are many views of knowledge, what it is, and how to get it. Some, compared to others, are more likely to result in sound decisions. Thus, thinking about knowledge and how to get it, reviewing your personal epistemology, is vital to being a professional. If we rely on questionable criteria for evaluating practice- and policy-related claims, clients may be harmed rather than helped, false hope may be created, harmful effects may be experienced, and effective methods may be forgone. Some clinicians rely on authority as a guide—for example, what high-status people say, what is popular (how many people use a method), or tradition (what's usually done). These criteria do not provide sound guides. Avoiding confirmation biases (searching only for data that confirm our views and ignoring data that do not) requires seeking evidence against favored views and considering well-argued alternative views. Critical appraisal will help you to identify flaws in your thinking, such as referring clients to agencies that use ineffective practices and programs. You are more likely to acquire knowledge and skills that help you to help your clients if you take an active role in critically appraising what you read, hear, and believe. Sound criteria for making decisions include well-reasoned arguments and critical tests that suggest that one option is more likely than another to result in outcomes that clients value.

Glossary

antiscience   Rejection of science as a way to pursue answers.

critical discussion   "Essentially a comparison of the merits and demerits of two or more theories (usually more than two). The merits discussed are mainly the explanatory power of the theories . . . the way in which they are able to solve our problems of explaining things, the way in which the theories cohere with certain other heavily valued theories, their power to shed new light on old problems and to suggest new problems. The chief demerit is inconsistency, including inconsistency with the results of experiments that a competing theory can explain" (Popper, 1994, pp. 160–161).

cynicism   A negative view of the world and what can be learned about it.

eclecticism   The view that we should adopt whatever theories or methodologies are useful in inquiry, no matter what their source and without undue worry about their consistency.

empiricism   The position that all knowledge (usually excluding that which is logical or mathematical) is in some way based on experience. Adherents of empiricism differ markedly over what the "based on" amounts to—"starts from" and "warranted in terms of" are, roughly, at the two ends of the spectrum of opinion (Phillips, 1987, p. 203).

evidence   "Ground for belief, testimony or facts tending to prove or disprove any conclusions" (*Oxford English Dictionary*, 1994).

false knowledge   Beliefs that are not true and that are not questioned (Munz, 1985).

falsification approach to knowledge   The view that we can discover only what is false, not what is true.

hermeneutics   "The discipline of interpretation of textual or literary material, or of meaningful human actions" (Phillips, 1987, p. 203).

justification approach to knowledge   The view that we can discover the truth by seeking support for our theories.

knowledge   Problematic and tentative guesses about what may be true (Popper, 1992, 1994); "guesswork disciplined by rational criticism" (1992, p. 40). Criticism is "the crucial quality of knowledge" (Munz, 1985, p. 49).

logical positivism   The main tenet of logical positivism is the verifiability principle of meaning: "Something is meaningful only if it is verifiable empirically (i.e., directly, or indirectly, via sense experiences) or if it is a truth of logic or mathematics" (Phillips, 1987, p. 204). The reality of theoretical entities is denied.

nonjustificationist epistemology   The view that knowledge is not certain. It is assumed that although some claims of knowledge may be warranted, no warrant is so firm that it is not open to question (see Karl Popper's writings).

paradigm   "A theoretical framework that influences the problems that are regarded as crucial, the ways these problems are conceptualized, the appropriate methods of inquiry, the relevant standards of judgment, etc." (Phillips, 1987, p. 205).

phenomenology   "The study, in depth, of how things appear in human experience" (Phillips, 1987, p. 205).

postmodernism   An approach that disputes assumptions of science and its products. All grounds for knowledge claims are considered equally questionable (see, for example, Rosenau, 1992; Munz, 1992).

postpositivism   The approach to science that replaced logical positivism decades ago (see, for example, Phillips, 1987, 1992).

pseudoscience   Material that makes sciencelike claims but provides no evidence for them.

quackery   The promotion of products and procedures known to be false or that are untested, for a profit (Pepper, 1984).

rationality   An openness to criticism. "A limitless invitation to criticism is the essence of rationality" (Munz, 1985, p. 50). Rationality consists of making mistakes and eliminating error by natural selection (p. 16).

relativism   Relativists "insist that judgments of truth are always relative to a particular framework or point of view" (Phillips, 1987, p. 206). This point of view prevents criticism from outside a closed circle of believers.

science   A process designed to develop knowledge by critically discussing and testing theories.

scientific objectivity   Scientific objectivity is solely the critical approach (Popper, 1994, p. 93). It is based on mutual rational criticism in which high standards of clarity and rational criticism are valued (Popper, 1994, p. 70). *See also* critical discussion.

scientism   A term used "to indicate slavish adherence to the methods of science even in a context where they are inappropriate" and "to indicate a false or mistaken claim to be scientific" (Phillips, 1987, p. 206). Scientism refers to the view that "authority should be conferred upon knowledge and the knower, upon science and the scientists, upon wisdom and the wise man, and upon learning and the learned" (Popper, 1992, p. 33).

skepticism   A provisional approach to claims; the careful examination of all claims.

theory   Myths, expectations, guesses, and conjectures about what may be true. A theory always remains hypothetical or conjectural. "It always remains guesswork. And there is no theory that is not beset with problems" (Popper, 1994, p. 157).

theory ladenness (of perception)   "The thesis that the process of perception is theory-laden in that the observer's background knowledge (including theories, factual information, hypotheses, and so forth) acts as a 'lens' helping to 'shape' the nature of what is observed" (Phillips, 1987, p. 206).

truth   "An assertion is true if it corresponds to, or agrees with, the facts" (Popper, 1994, p. 174). We can never be sure that our guesses are true. "Though we can never justify the claim to have reached truth, we can often give some very good reasons, or justification, why one theory should be judged as nearer to it than another" (Popper, 1994, p. 161).

Common Sources of Error

The Influence of Language and Persuasion Strategies

Although considerable attention has been devoted to problematic use of language on the part of clients, less attention has been devoted to exploration of how common sources of error influence clinicians in their daily practice. Clinicians use words to describe people and events, to describe relationships between behavior and events, and to express evaluations. Language is used in posing and thinking about clinical questions and in processing material read. The words clinicians use shape their own experiences and actions as well as those of their clients. Here, too, as with other sources of error described in this book, having a name for a fallacy highlights its uniqueness, and may help us to recognize and plan how to avoid it. Ethical limits on how far a writer or speaker may go in being persuasive are suggested by Grice's maxims of conversation, such as: "Do not say what you believe to be false" and "Do not say that for which you lack sufficient evidence" (Grice, 1975, p. 46). The latter rule is routinely broken in professional discourse. That is, claims are made for which there is little or no evidence.

THE INFLUENCE OF LANGUAGE

Many critical thinking skills involve recognition of the ways in which language affects decisions (Halpern, 2003; Walton, 2008a). Discussions between clients and practitioners are a key component in most practice frameworks. Use of language is integral to decisions made during case conferences and in court presentations, as well as in interpretations of clinical records. All writing in the professions and the social sciences can be viewed as rhetorical in that a position is advanced and a point of view is presented that is then reviewed for its soundness (Edmondson, 1984). Increasing attention has been paid to the prevalence of inflated claims of knowledge in the peer-reviewed literature (e.g., Ioannides, 2008; Rubin & Parrish, 2007). Claims are made and arguments for them offered. The term *rhetoric* has varied definitions: (1) "the art of using words effectively in speaking or writing; now, the art of prose composition (2) artificial eloquence; language that is showy and elaborate but largely empty of clear ideas or sincere emotion" (*Webster's New World Dictionary*, 1988). It is in the latter sense that the term is in ill repute. It is not unusual to hear someone say, "We need less rhetoric and more straight facts." When rhetoric is defined in its broader sense, as in the first definition, it is an important area of study and skill, especially in helping professions that rely heavily on the spoken and written word.

Carelessness, lack of skill in writing and thinking, and deliberate intent on the part of a speaker may compromise the quality of decisions. The varied functions language serves complicate understanding of spoken or written statements. One function is description. Description of clients, procedures used, and progress achieved is an integral part of clinical records. The aim of descriptive statements is to inform (for example, "Mr. Larkin has been hospitalized three times"). We can find out whether they are true or false. Another function is to persuade others to believe or act differently. Clinicians attempt to persuade clients to act, think, or feel differently in problem-related situations by talking to them. A third function of language is expressive—to express some emotion or feeling or to create such a feeling without trying to influence future behavior. Other statements direct or guide us, as in "Call the parental stress hotline." A given statement may serve several functions; not only may a speaker or writer have more than one purpose in mind when making a statement, but the listener or reader also may have more than one in mind, which may or may not match those of the speaker. The context is used to interpret the speaker's or writer's purpose. Language also has presymbolic functions, such as affirming social cohesion (as in "Isn't it a nice day?"). Lack of understanding of this function may result in naive assumptions about the triviality of conversation, as Hayakawa (1978) notes in his "Advice to the Literal-Minded" (p. 85). Only if we correctly understand the motive behind a sentence may we translate it correctly.

Words differ in their level of abstraction. At the lowest level are definitions in extensional terms. The extensional meaning of a word refers to what it points to in the physical world; it is what the word stands for. A psychiatrist could point to the disheveled clothes of a person admitted to an emergency psychiatry unit. A client advocate may observe a failure of nurses to respond to a hospitalized client's call for help (Delamothe, 2011). Many words have no extensional meaning—that is, there is nothing we can point to. In operational definitions, a rigorous attempt is made to exclude nonextensional meaning, as in the definition of length in terms of the operations by which it is measured. The intentional meaning of a word refers to what is connoted or suggested. Clinicians may act toward people, objects, or events in accord with the intentional (affective) connotations associated with a name. For example, reactions to terms such as *sociopath* or *welfare recipient* may go far beyond the extensional meaning of these terms without recognizing that this is happening. Definitions describe our linguistic habits; they are statements about how language is used. The higher the level of abstraction, the less the utility of referring to a dictionary definition to capture meaning, especially intentional meaning.

FALLACIES RELATED TO LANGUAGE

Problems related to use of language that influence the quality of clinical decisions are described next, together with suggested remedies. The list in Exhibit 5.1 is by no means exhaustive, and readers are referred to other sources for greater detail (e.g., Halpern, 2003; Hayakawa, 1978; Thouless, 1974). Carelessness is often responsible for foggy writing and speaking—not taking the time and thought to clearly state inferences and reasons for them. Words may suggest differences that do not exist.

Exhibit 5.1 Sources of Errors Related to Use of Language

---

1. Assumption of one word, one meaning.
2. Misleading use of scientific terms.
3. Misleading metaphors.
4. Use of vague terms.
5. Shifting definitions of terms.
6. Reification (acting as if an abstract concept actually exists).
7. Influence by semantic linkages and cuing effects.
8. Predigested thinking.
9. Confusing verbal and factual propositions.
10. Use of pseudotechnical jargon.
11. Misuse of speculation (assuming what is can be discovered by merely thinking about a topic).
12. Conviction through repetition.
13. Insistence on a specific definition that oversimplifies a situation.
14. Influence through emotional words.
15. Use of a confident manner and bold assertions.
16. Judgments based on primacy effects.
17. Newsspeak.
18. Excess wordiness.
19. Misuse of labels.
20. Confusion of different levels of abstraction.
21. Careless use of language.
22. Eloquence without clarity.
23. Misleading metaphors.

Predigested Thinking: Oversimplifications

The term *predigested thinking* refers to the tendency to oversimplify complex topics, issues, or perspectives into simple formulas that distort content, such as describing Freudian theory as reducing everything to sex or describing behavioral theory as favoring mechanistic stimulus-response connections. Stereotyping is a form of predigested (oversimplified) thinking. A striking example of oversimplification is the assertion that a wide variety of problems are caused by a "chemical imbalance in the brain." Critics argue that there is no evidence for this bold assertion. The brain is very complex. Compared with what there is to know, we know little about it, contrary to claims such as: "We have found . . ." "This shows that . . ." "We now know . . ." What is a "chemical imbalance"? (See Lacasse & Leo, 2005; Moncrieff, 2008.) Are changes seen in the brain a result of prescribed medication (Whittaker, 2010)? Oversimplifications may result in clinical errors and impede further research. Oversimplifications include use of words that obscure differences between entities and words that suggest that some phenomenon is unchanging when it does change.

Metaphors and analogues used to simplify material may obscure the complexity of concerns; for example, of hallucinations or anxiety. Consider a diagnosis of "social anxiety disorder" based on reports of a client that she is fearful in social situations and avoids them. Describing this as a "mental disorder" (assuming such concerns are caused by brain diseases) and prescribing medication ignores the environmental context in which such reactions develop and are maintained that, if changed, may decrease distressing reactions (e.g., see Gilbert, 1989). Such questionable claims may create "a false sense of understanding and inhibit pursuit of contextual understanding" (Woods & Cook, 1999, p. 152). Referring to hundreds of different behaviors, feelings, and thoughts as "mental disorders" (diseases) is an oversimplification; for example, it ignores the continuous nature of the vast majority of related behaviors, such as drinking alcohol or anxiety.

Another example of an oversimplification is reflected in the following answer of a doctoral student during a discussion of twin studies: "We know the environment was the same because the twins were raised in the same home." Is it the same home for each of these individuals? Research suggests that it is not, that even twins have different environments (see Plomin, 2011). As Lewontin (1991, 1995) suggests, we each construct (not adapt to) our environments. Clinicians are sometimes guilty of reducing an answer to a simple formula, such as "rapists will rape again." A practitioner who does not believe that evaluation of client progress can be done in a way that is meaningful may say that "evaluation is mechanistic," or "it trivializes concerns," or "it does not represent the true complexity of human problems." Such views overlook the fact that evaluation can be carried out in either an irrelevant or a relevant manner.

Another example is the statement that "a scientific approach to clinical questions offers trivial answers." What is the meaning of "a scientific approach" here? What is a "trivial answer"? Synecdoches refer to the representation of large amounts of information in a short representational bit. A part is selected to represent the whole. Predigested thinking in the form of slogans, such as "Support community care," are used to encourage actions. Slogans are easy to remember and so are readily available to influence us on an emotional level. Consider the following: "Stay healthy," "Maximize your potential," "Proven effective," "Find your true self." The use of predigested thinking obscures complexities and so may encourage inaccurate inferences. This kind of thinking is common because of indifference, lack of information, and idleness, and the fact that it often offers a practical guide for life. The tendency to simplify complex matters may help to account for ignoring the undistributed middle (substituting all for some) and the readiness to accept an extension of a position.

We can guard against predigested thinking by avoiding mental idleness, which encourages us "to accept mental food well below the limits of our digestion" (Thouless, 1974, p. 164). The remedy is to consider the actual complexity of the issue at hand as needed to arrive at accurate accounts. The emotional appeal of predigested thinking and the fact that it often provides a practical guide for daily life make it difficult to challenge. For example, a clinician may object to the oversimplistic presentation of Freudian theory that "everything is related to sex." The other person may protest that the objections raised are too "learned," that "nothing will convince him that art, romantic love, and religion are just sex, which is generally agreed by everybody to be the teaching of Freud" (Thouless, 1974, p. 161). Note the reaffirmation of the original position (begging the question) and the appeal to consensus. As Thouless notes, if this is a discussion with other people, the user of predigested thinking can usually rely on "having their sympathy, for his opponent will seem to be a person trying to make himself out to be too clever and who makes serious argument impossible by throwing doubt on what everyone knows to be true" (pp. 161–162). The only recourse here may be to state an argument so clearly that the inadequacies of a position are quite obvious. Negative reactions can be avoided by posing inquiries in a tactful manner and by emphasizing common interests, such as helping clients achieve outcomes they value.

Missing Language (Censorship)

Missing language is the most deceptive language ruse. We are less likely to make sound decisions if we do not have access to relevant information. Hundreds of terms for alleged negative states (e.g., "disorders") are in use compared to few terms for positive states of being. This is a prime example of missing language. Physicians often fail to communicate vital information about new medications to patients (Tarn et al., 2006). Advertisements deceive by bold assertions and what is not clearly described.

Pseudotechnical Jargon/Bafflegab

Jargon can be useful in communicating in an efficient manner if listeners (or readers) share the same meaning of technical terms. However, jargon may be used to conceal ignorance and "impress the innocent" (Rycroft, 1973, p. xi; see also Tavris, 2001). Consider the earlier discussion of claims that problems are due to "chemical imbalances in the brain." An economic incentive may perpetuate obscure writing; for example, highly specialized jargon in the legal profession increases the need to hire lawyers who can understand it. We tend to be impressed with things we cannot understand. Professors tend to rate journals that are hard to read as more prestigious than journals that are easier to read (Armstrong, 1980). Of course, it is possible that the more prestigious journals discuss more complex subjects that require more difficult language. This possibility was tested by Armstrong. Portions of management journals were rewritten to increase readability without changing the content; unnecessary words were eliminated, easy words were substituted for difficult ones, and sentences were broken into shorter ones. A sample of 32 management professors were asked to rate as easy or difficult versions of four such passages and also rate them on a scale of "competence" ranging from 1 to 7. They knew neither the name of the journal nor the name of the author. Versions that were easier to read were considered to reflect less competent research than were the more difficult passages.

Obscurity may be desirable in some circumstances, such as when exploring new possibilities. However, in most situations that arise in clinical practice, obscurity is not an advantage; it is often a cloak for ignorance. Examples of pseudotechnical jargon include *psychic deficiencies*, *structural frame of reference*, and *generational dysfunctions*. The proliferation of terms adds to jargon in psychotherapy. Consider, for example, terms that Firestone and Seiden (1987) present as similar to *microsuicide*.

- indirect suicide
- masked suicide
- partial suicide
- hidden suicide
- installment plan suicide
- parasuicide
- slow suicide
- chronic suicide
- embryonic suicide

Who has not suffered from bureaucratese—turgid, unnecessarily complex descriptions that yield only to the most persistent of readers (or listeners)? Examples include *mumblistic* (planned mumbling) and *profundicating* (translating simple concepts into obscure jargon; Boren, 1972). Management-speak has become an epidemic (Watson, 2008). The remedy is to simplify and clarify. Examples of rules suggested by Orwell (1946/1958) include the following:

- Never use a metaphor, simile, or other figure of speech that you are used to seeing in print.
- Never use a long word when a short one will do.
- If it is possible to cut a word out, always cut it out.
- Never use the passive when you can use the active.
- Never use a foreign phrase, a scientific word, or a jargon word if you can think of an everyday English equivalent.
- Break any of these rules sooner than say anything outright barbarous. (Orwell, 1946/1958, p. 143)

The potential for obscure terms to become clear can be explored by asking questions such as "What do you mean by that?" or "Can you give me an example?" Asking such questions when reading case records and practice-related literature is a valuable rule of thumb (see list of Socratic questions in Exhibit 3.3).

Obscure language often remains unquestioned because of worries that the questioner will look ignorant or stupid. The risks of lack of clarification should be considered, as well as the risks of revealing a lack of knowledge. Writers and speakers should clarify their terms, bearing in mind appropriate levels of abstraction. If they don't, it may be because they cannot. They should be thankful that someone cares enough to want to understand their position and that lack of clarity is discovered. Not all people will be open to questions, especially those who use vague language to hide aims or lack of knowledge they would rather not reveal. "The great enemy of clear language is insincerity. When there is a gap between one's real and one's declared aims, one turns as it were instinctively to long words and exhausted idioms like a cuttlefish squirting out ink" (Orwell, 1958, p. 142). Some people will become defensive and try to put others down for asking questions, perhaps using their prestige to do so. They may share Humpty Dumpty's attitude:

"When I use a word," Humpty Dumpty said, in a rather scornful tone, "it means just what I choose it to mean, neither more nor less."

"The question is," said Alice, "whether you can make words mean so many different things."

"The question is," said Humpty Dumpty, "who is to be master, that's all." (Lewis Carroll, 1946, *Through the Looking Glass*, p. 229)

A question could be asked in such a straightforward manner that if the person still cannot understand it, his own lack of astuteness is revealed (Thouless, 1974).

Misleading Use of Medical and Scientific Discourse

In *Schizophrenia: A Scientific Delusion?* Boyle (2002) gives many examples of how the discourse of science is used to create a false impression of objectivity and rigor—for example, by using specialized terminology that is often unfamiliar to lay readers as well as to many in the mental health profession. She notes that terms are often misused (e.g., base rate) in a manner that favors the assumption that schizophrenia exists as a unique entity, that it is a mental disorder, and that it is biochemical in origin. Questionable appeals to the language of neuroscience are rife. She, as well as others, suggests that narratives of scientific progress are used to imply that advances are being made when they are not. For example, even though biochemical correlates have not yet been discovered, claims are made that they soon will be. She points out that the language of medicine is also appealed to and that this combines with the language of science in a potent rhetorical mix to give illusions of objectivity, knowledge, and progress.

Use of Emotional Buzzwords or Images

Professionals, as well as advertisers and politicians, make use of emotional words and images, as illustrated in this letter to the editor, National Association of Social Workers' *NASW News*:

Example	*Comments*
The conspiracy of silence continues to state implicitly that social workers, because of their training and clinical expertise, cannot possibly be impaired by alcohol and drug abuse. As long as this conspiracy exists, impaired social workers will be afraid to seek help and to come out into the open about their addiction, just as I am. ("Letter to the Editor," 1986, p. 15)	The term "conspiracy" is highly pejorative, as is "impaired." No evidence is offered that there is a "conspiracy of silence," or for the assumption that the "conspiracy" stops social workers from disclosing their "addiction." No evidence is offered for the assumption that people assume that social workers cannot have a substance abuse problem "because of their training and expertise." It is assumed that substance abuse is an "addiction."

Emotional terms are rife in the turf battles between psychologists and psychiatrists. Consider the opening sentence in an article in the *Psychiatric Times*: "Clinical psychology is in a war for survival against American psychiatry" (Buie, 1987, p. 25). The use of emotionally toned words is not always dysfunctional; however, in the context of trying to make correct inferences, such words may interfere with clear thinking (for example, they may interfere with identifying useful options). Feelings and biases that may influence decisions can be coaxed out by exploring reactions to terms such as *nursing home resident* and *developmentally disabled youth*. Being aware of the possible biasing effects of emotional terms and using more neutral ones may increase the quality of decisions in all venues, including case conferences and discussions with oneself.

Metaphors

Proverbs, similes, or metaphors that have emotional effects may be used to describe or support a position. On one hand, they may be of value in developing new ideas about how to solve problems. On the other hand, they may obscure rather than clarify a problem or issue; they may create a feeling of understanding without an accompanying increase in real understanding. Points against a disliked (and perhaps misunderstood) position may be referred to as ammunition. Clinicians who do not believe that clinical practice can be evaluated may refer to such efforts as treating people like cars—mechanistically, simplistically. (For further discussion of the influence of metaphors, see Lakoff and Dean, 2004, and Sontag, 1991.) Examples of the use of emotionally toned words can be seen in the excerpts from a case conference in Chapter 16.

Naming/Labeling

Who has power to name often wins the day. Labels are one kind of good/bad words we use to persuade others via transfer effects and emotional reasoning. Consider words such as *prostitute* and *racist*. Such extensions may result in weighty consequences such as coerced intervention. Labels that have few if any implications for selection of effective interventions but are stigmatizing are often applied to clients (Watson & Eack, 2011). Naming hundreds of everyday behaviors or feelings (or their lack) as mental illnesses in need of treatment influences our feelings and attitudes toward the people so labeled. Calling these "mental illnesses" transfers our associations with physical illness onto behaviors, thoughts, and feelings now labeled "mental illnesses," as Szasz (1961, 1987) has argued in his rhetorical analysis of this concept. Use of psychiatric labels has increasingly entered the public domain (e.g., referring to a difficult supervisor as bipolar or labeling oneself as having "social anxiety disorder"). Such labels are used as explanations for life's travails (Herzberg, 2009). The costs of such accounts in terms of loss of agency (taking charge of one's own life) may not be recognized.

Labels often are applied incorrectly. The term *evidence-based practice* is often used to describe practices that do not reflect the philosophy of evidence-based decision making as described in original sources (see Chapter 10 as well as the list of distortions of evidence-based practice in Exhibit 6.3 in Chapter 6). A label such as behavior modification may be used inaccurately to describe a program that is just the opposite of what a behavioral program would be like (see discussion of faulty classification in Chapter 7). Pseudoexplanations are one result of unexamined use of labels. Labels are often used in ad hominem arguments—attacking or praising the person rather than addressing his or her argument. Labels may be deliberately misused to forward a view, hiding the fact that a term is misused. Practices described as "best" may not be best (e.g., Gandhi, Murphy-Graham, Petrosino, Chrismer, & Weiss, 2007; Gorman & Huber, 2009). (See also Chapter 7.)

The Assumption of One Word, One Meaning

Words have different meanings in different contexts. As Hayakawa (1978) has bluntly put it, "Ignoring of contexts in any act of interpretation is at best a stupid practice. At its worst, it can be a vicious practice" (p. 56), as when a sentence is taken out of context. Differences that exist in the world may not be reflected in different uses of words, or differences in language may not correspond to variations in the world. Misunderstandings arise when different uses of a word are mistaken for different opinions about a topic of discussion. "Unless people mean the same thing when they talk to each other, accurate communication is impossible" (Feinstein, 1967, p. 313). Two people discussing "addiction" may not have the same definition of this term, and a muddled discussion may result. One way to avoid this is to define key terms. The following dialogue illustrates how the same word may have different meanings.

> *Counselor:* I think you have an addiction to alcohol.
> *Client:* I don't think so.
> *Counselor:* You drink every day.
> *Client:* But it doesn't interfere with my life. I'm happily married and like my job. Just because I drink every day doesn't mean I'm addicted.
> *Counselor:* I think it does.

Results of assessment are often presented in vague terms, such as *probable* or *cannot be excluded*, which have a wide range of meaning to different clinicians (Bryant & Norman, 1980). Definition of terms such as *panic reaction* or *dementia* may be shared initially but diverge as discussion proceeds. Clinicians may differ in how they define certain intervention methods. Confusion can be avoided by checking definitions of key concepts.

Use of Vague Terms

Vague terms are common in clinical contexts: *uncommunicative, aggressive, immature, drug dependency, dependent patient, dysfunction, family therapy, social work intervention, family-oriented modality, psychic deficiencies, dysfunctional alignments,* and *proper boundary lines.* Examples of vague and ambivalent words and phrases, called weasel words/phrases, include "some researchers believe," "some sources claim," and "critics agree." Such vague phrases and words allow you to say anything without placing yourself in danger of being contradicted (www.changingminds.org, accessed May 9, 2009). Such words are designed to influence without informing. Examples given on this website include:

- *Helps, supports, is useful* (friendly, but no real value added).
- *Better, improved, gains* (does not say how much).
- *Act, works, effective, efficient* (no quantity described).
- *Seems, appears, looks, is like* (gives only vague impression).
- *Many, most, virtually, almost all* (no quantity described).
- *Up to, from, at least, as many as* (vague).

Weasel words/phrases are rife in advertising (Schrank, 2011). If terms are not clarified, different meanings may be used, none of which may reflect the real world. Fashionable phrases or terms often become vague phrases in time. Examples include *supportive therapy* and *case management.* Two individuals with different meanings of the term *evidence-based practice* may make little progress in discussing related advantages and disadvantages because of different views of this term. Clichés and "unoriginal remarks do have their uses in terms of highlighting similarity between people; that those present are on the 'right-side' so to speak" (Hayakawa, 1978). (For a general discussion of vagueness, see Keefe, 2000.)

Reification, Word Magic

Here it is mistakenly assumed that a word corresponds to something real; in fact, "the existence of a word does not guarantee the existence of any corresponding entity" (Fearnside & Holther, 1959, p. 68). (See also discussion of labeling.) The term *aggressive,* used as a summary term for specific actions, may also be used to refer to an aggressive disposition, which is believed to be responsible for these actions. This disposition then comes to be thought of as an attribute of the person (Bromley, 1977). Staats and Staats (1963) refer to this as the use of pseudoexplanations. Noting the circularity of such terms reveals that no new information is offered and that no evidence other than the behavioral referents described support the influence of this higher-order concept.

Perhaps the most common example of word magic in clinical psychology, psychiatry, and social work is the term *mental illness*. Because we use the word, we assume the associated entity exists when it may not. I do not mean to say that troubling behaviors, thoughts, or feelings are not real. They are. But the alleged mental illness may not be. (See also Didi-Huberman, 1982/2003.) In *Schizophrenia: A Scientific Delusion?* Mary Boyle (2002) describes how language used (such as repeated use of the word *clinical*), kinds of arguments presented, and benefits, both touted and actual, intersect to maintain an illusion that a coherent entity called schizophrenia exists, and that the methods used to identify it are unproblematic. As Boyle notes, it is easy to believe that what is referred to by a word actually exists—particularly if authority figures such as psychiatrists use the term and act as if it is unproblematic. She illustrates the problematic nature of terms such as *mental illness* and *mental disorder* on both methodological and conceptual grounds. (See also earlier discussion of misleading use of scientific discourse.) Our tendency to rely on experts and to believe that if there is a word, it refers to some coherent entity in the real world (reification), combines with other factors, such as lack of time, a disinterest in digging deeper, laziness, and an interest in avoiding responsibility for behavior or troubles by attributing them to a brain disease. This is a powerful mix.

Confusing Verbal and Factual Propositions

Questions (such as "What is a borderline personality?") often involve disputes about use of words, as if they were questions of facts. (See also discussion of reification.) Discussions of the meaning of mental illness are often conducted as if there were an independent, objective reality to be discovered, rather than with the realization that what will be accepted as referents for this term are at issue—a constructed reality, not a discovered reality. What must be established by critical inquiry is presumed as fact, as in the fallacy of begging the question (see Chapter 6). Questions of fact cannot be settled by arguments over the use of words. The problem of how to use a word is different from the problem of what is a fact. Pointing out the lack of objective criteria is helpful when there is confusion between verbal and factual propositions.

Influence of Semantic Linkages and Cuing Effects

Examples range from the subtle to the obvious. Words and concepts are linked as a result of language use. (See, for example, discussions of stimulus equivalence.) A familiar example is the tendency to think in terms of opposites, such as *good/bad* or *addicted/nonaddicted*. Such thinking obscures the situational variability of behavior as well as individual differences in behavior, feelings, or thoughts that may occur in a given context. For example, consider the term *addiction*. Patterns of substance use and abuse vary widely; the description of a client as addicted is not very informative. This does not indicate what substances are used, with what frequency, or in what situations, nor offer any information about the functions served by ingestion of such substances (although within some practice perspectives all clients who are "addicted" are assumed to have similar personality dynamics, which purport to account for the addiction, and a description of the exact nature of the addiction may not be considered important). Manufacturers of drugs select names for drugs, such as chemotherapies, to encourage sales. Abel and Glinert (2008) conducted an analysis of the sound symbolism of 60 frequently used cancer-related medications. Their results showed that the names of chemotherapy medications contained a high frequency of sounds associated with lightness, smallness, and quickness. The authors suggest that such associations may influence decisions made by patients regarding use of chemotherapy. Decisions concerning degree of responsibility for an action differ depending on whether a person is in the subject of the sentence, as in "Ellen's car hit the fireplug," compared to "The fireplug was hit by Ellen's car" (Loftus, 1980, 1996). (See also Loftus, 1997, 2004.) Familiarity with the influence of semantic linkages and cuing effects may help us to avoid related errors. Statements can be rearranged to see if this yields different causal assumptions.

Misuse of Verbal Speculation

This refers to the use of "speculative thinking to solve problems which can only be solved by the observation and interpretation of facts" (Thouless, 1974, p. 78). Speculation is valuable in discovering new possibilities, but it does not offer information about whether these insights are correct; that is, what is cannot be deduced from what ought to be, nor can vague terms referring to client behavior or situational contexts of interest be clarified simply by thinking about them. For example, if a client is described as a drug abuser and no information is provided about what this means, speculation will not be helpful. Facts gathered from some reliable and valid source are needed. Misuse of speculation occurs often in clinical practice and is not without its effects, since assumptions influence what we attend to. Thus, a little unchecked speculation can be a dangerous thing. The process of evidence-based practice encourages critical appraisal of speculation that may influence the quality of clients' lives.

Conviction Through Repetition

Simply hearing, seeing, or thinking about a statement many times may increase belief in the statement. As Thouless (1974) notes, we tend to think that what goes through our minds must be important. A willingness to challenge even cherished beliefs helps to combat this source of error. Popper (1992) suggests, "We are all equal in our vast ignorance." Recognizing this may help us to question our beliefs. Valid inferences cannot be made on the basis of repeated affirmation, conviction, or the manner in which something is said. "If our examination of the facts leads to a conclusion which we find to be inconceivable, this need not be regarded as telling us anything about the facts, but only about the limits of our powers of conceiving" (Thouless, 1974, p. 80). Conviction through repetition may be attempted in case conferences to influence group members. For example, a client may be continually referred to as mentally incompetent, when in fact no evidence has been offered. Pointing out the danger of repeating unsupported assertions may be helpful in discouraging such descriptions.

Simply repeating a position increases the likelihood of its acceptance, especially if the statement is offered in a confident manner by a person of prestige and has a slogan quality that plays on our emotions. Repetitions of a statement are more effective if they are varied; we are less likely to discover that no reasons are provided as to why we should believe or act in a certain manner (Thouless, 1974). Consider the repetition in the media, professional journals, books, conferences, human services advertisements, and websites of the chemical imbalance theory of mental illness. This biomedical view of problems flourishes in the United States. The billions spent on promotion of biomedical accounts of client concerns by Big Pharma daily expose the public to a medical view of human behavior and influence the funding of research (Angell, 2004; Kassirer, 2005). I do not mean to say that biomedical causes are not implicated in some behaviors, thoughts, or feelings. No doubt they are. But as Szasz (1994) suggests, if that is discovered, would not related disorders pass over into the field of neurology (as in certain kinds of dementia)? And changes in behavior may alter biomedical characteristics.

Bold Assertions

People often act as if they have a conclusive argument when they do not. They may simply assert a position with no attempt to provide any evidence for it. A clinician may protest, "Mr. Greenwood is obviously a psychopath who is untreatable." A confident manner and bold assertions often accomplish what should be achieved only by offering sound reasons for a position. Words that are cues for this tactic include *unquestionable*, *indisputably*, *the fact is*, and *the truth is*. Bold assertions are a form of begging the question; the truth or falsity of the point is assumed (Walton, 2008a). This informal fallacy, like many others, takes advantage of our tendency to be lulled into accepting a position because of the confidence with which it is described. Evidence should be requested for the position asserted. An example of a bold assertion is: "We know that social work is effective. More than any other single profession, we see the youth in the settings where we work. We know what is needed and what works" ("From the President" [NASW], 1986, p. 2). In fact, some research suggests the opposite (harming in the name of helping;

e.g., McCord, 2003). Indeed, concerns about the gap between practice- and policy-related research and what practitioners draw on was a key reason for the development of evidence-based practice and health care.

Primacy Effects

We are influenced by what we see or hear first. This is referred to as the primacy or anchoring effect (Nisbett & Ross, 1980). Although this influence may often work for us, as illustrated by use of fast and frugal heuristics (see Chapter 9), it may not always do so. What we hear or see first influences what we attend to, and thus influences our causal attributions. It narrows the range of data that is attended to. The influence of initial suggestions is shown by an experiment in which four groups of clinicians diagnosed a client under different conditions (Temerlin, 1968). One group was informed that the person was sane, one group was told that they were selecting scientists to work in research, one group (the control group) received no suggestions, and one group (the experimental group) was informed that the interviewee was mentally ill. Diagnoses were made by psychiatrists and clinical psychologists, who listened to a tape-recorded interview. The diagnoses differed greatly. All 25 psychiatrists and most of the clinical psychologists (22 of 25) in the experimental group made a diagnosis of mental illness. The majority of clinicians in the control group stated that the interviewee was mentally healthy. These results illustrate not only the influence of primacy effects on presumptions of illness but also concerns regarding psychiatric diagnoses. (See discussion of labels in Chapter 7.)

Newspeak

Newspeak refers to "language that distorts, confuses, or hides reality" (MacLean, 1981, p. 43). Examples from the media include *neutralized* (meaning killed), *misspoke* (meaning lied), and *air support* (meaning bombing and strafing). *Newspeak* refers to the intentional abuse of language to obscure the truth. Orwell (1958) wrote, "In our time, political speech and writing are largely in defense of the indefensible . . . political language has to consist of euphemisms, question begging, and sheer cloudy vagueness" (p. 136). Newspeak occurs in the mental health industry as well, as illustrated in the following examples:

Statement or Term	*Translation*
Fiscal constraints call for retrenchment.	Some people are going to be fired; clinics will be closed.
New policies have been put in place to ensure better services for clients.	All services will be provided by psychiatrists.

Improve your practice tenfold.	Attend Dr. X's workshop.
Pregnancy crisis center.	Pro-life centers, which are anti-abortion.
Community care in place of warehousing.	Patients will be discharged from mental hospitals even though no adequate community care is available.

The goal of protecting professional interests requires presenting one's own profession in a uniquely favorable light in comparison with other professions (Friedson, 1973). Political and economic aims increase the likelihood that stratagems will be used that distort material presented. Misleading or unfair headlines may be used; editors and publishers are aware that many more people read the headlines than read the material under the headlines. Thus, even if the small print presents an accurate view, the headlines may be misleading. Readers, unless they are experts in an area, rarely are aware of what is not discussed in a report, such as alternative well-argued views (see discussion of suppressed evidence in Chapter 4). Too seldom are the pros and cons concerning an issue reviewed, even though readers would benefit from this. Other sources of hidden bias include unacknowledged conflicts of interests (Lo & Field, 2009), cherry-picking of research reports (Tufte, 2006), bias in placement of words and selection of photographs, and hidden editorials (content presented as disinterested descriptions that give a biased account—they advocate for one particular position) (Cirino, 1971). Use of these devices may or may not be deliberate. Whether deliberate or accidental, they may have biasing effects. Familiarity with commonly used strategies and ways to avoid or counter these should be helpful in avoiding distorting influences (see also Chapter 6).

Manner of Presentation

The eloquence with which an argument is presented, whether in writing or in speech, is not necessarily related to its cogency; words that move and charm may not inform. To the contrary, eloquence may lull our critical powers into abeyance. Consider the Dr. Fox lecture. An actor who could convincingly present a professional manner was hired to give a lecture to psychiatrists, psychologists, social worker educators, psychiatric social workers, and other educators and administrators on the application of mathematics to human behavior (Naftulin, Ware, & Donnelly, 1973). Dr. Fox was introduced with an impressive list of qualifications and gave an eloquent lecture. Indeed, he knew nothing about the subject, but no one detected the ruse. Thus, a confident manner may accompany nonsense. Some clinicians are excellent orators and engaging writers. However, efforts to use methods they describe may prove frustrating because of a lack of clarity. A focus on the eloquence of a presentation may decrease motivation to examine arguments because one tends to focus on the words alone. Given the scarcity of eloquence, it is hard to resist a desire for more. Best of all is the combination of eloquence and clarity.

Euphemisms

The term *euphemism* refers to use of words that are supposed to be less distasteful or offensive than others, often in order to hide what is actually going on (see also the earlier discussion on Newspeak). Consider this example from the National Coalition of Mental Health Professionals and Consumers (www.thenationalcoalition.org, December 20, 2009, p. 2).

> Professional ethics emphasize giving patients accurate and straightforward information. Managed care on the other hand uses misleading language at every level. Companies which intentionally restrict choice call themselves names like "Choice Health" or "Options Health." Companies who are hired to restrict access to treatment call themselves a name like "Access Health." Cost cutting programs are called "quality improvement programs." Gatekeepers, hired to divert patients from treatment, are called "patient advocates." Such misleading language does not belong in health care.

Perhaps the most common euphemism in the helping profession is calling enforced incarceration "treatment" for the benefit of the client. In *Social Work: The Rise and Fall of a Profession?* Rogowski (2010) suggests that "phrases like the 'mixed economy of care' and 'empowerment of service users and carers' as well as the 'independent sector' were deliberately obscure and misleading" (p. 156). The latter term includes both for-profit and voluntary organizations—"cloaking the profit motive with the use of the private sector in social services/care provision" (p. 156).

Failure to Recognize Palaver

The term *palaver* refers to extended often confusing messages designed to create desires and establish credibility rather than to explore what is true and what is false (Combs & Nimmo, 1993). Some people may not be interested in whether claims are false or true; they simply want to get through the situation. Frankfurt (2005) argues that this is the essence of "bullshit." Combs and Nimmo (1993) suggest that palaver characterizes political discussions. Is it also prevalent in professional venues?

Other Sources of Fallacy Related to Language

Insisting on a specific definition of a term is inappropriate if this obscures the complexity of a situation. Vagueness of terms may be an advantage in the early stages of thinking about a topic, for the purpose of discovering approaches that otherwise may not be considered. Not recognizing that words differ in level of abstraction may create confusion and needless arguments. Both the one word, one meaning fallacy and the assumption that definitions represent realities reflect a confusion among (or ignorance of) different levels of abstraction. Metaphors may lead to faulty attributions and thus contribute to incorrect selection of intervention. Ferreting out the nature of an argument is often difficult because of excessive wordiness. Confusing factual and emotional uses of words can result in errors. Offering descriptions is but one of the many functions of language. Persuading people to act is a common aim in many kinds of discourse, including professional contexts, and this is often accomplished through emotive use of language. For example, if a physician wants to discourage a patient from taking a blood thinner, he or she may describe the drug as "rat poison." Distinguishing between the emotive and informative uses of language should be helpful in avoiding influence by emotional terms.

MAKING EFFECTIVE USE OF LANGUAGE

Tips for making effective use of language include the following:

- Be alert for special interest. Is someone trying to sell you something?
- Recognize use of emotional language and vagueness.
- Clearly describe arguments.
- Be on the lookout for reification and palaver.
- Be wary of analogies and metaphors; examine their similarity and claimed relationships to conclusions.
- Keep the context of a dialogue in mind (e.g., is the goal to discover what is true or false?)
- Use different examples when thinking about members of a category in order to avoid stereotypes.
- Use analogies appropriately (examine similarity and its relationship to a conclusion).
- Recognize when an anchor may bias your judgments about a quantity or cost, and consider alternative anchors.
- Use active questioning and explaining as a skill for comprehension.
- Use graphic organizers (linear arrays, hierarchies, networks, matrices, flowcharts). (Halpern, 2003, p. 133)

Ploys related to language as well as social psychological persuasion strategies (discussed next) are so common and so effective that some professional education programs are now paying attention to this source of persuasion. Guides for "Talking with a Drug Rep" have been developed (e.g., see ProvenEffective.org). Drug reps are carefully trained in scripts for dealing with particular kinds of physicians in order to encourage them to promote the drug reps' products. Physician categories include "Aloof and Skeptical," "Thought Leaders," and "Prescribing a Competitive Drug" (Fugh-Berman & Ahari, 2007).

THE INFLUENCE OF SOCIAL-PSYCHOLOGICAL PERSUASION STRATEGIES

Persuasive attempts are common in clinical contexts. They are integral to motivational interviewing (Norcross, Krebs, & Prochaska, 2011). Clinicians try to persuade clients to carry out agreed-on tasks and try to convince other professionals to offer needed resources. Conversely, clinicians are the target of persuasive attempts by clients, colleagues, friends, and family members, as well as by professional organizations, the pharmaceutical industry, and the mass media (e.g., Angell, 2004; Ewen, 1976). The essence of persuasion is influencing someone to think or act in a certain manner. There is an extensive literature on persuasion (Brock & Green, 2005; Dillard & Pfau, 2002; Wosinka, Cialdini, Barrett, & Reykowski, 2001). Persuasion may occur intentionally or unconsciously, as a part of the interpersonal context in which exchanges take place. Both beliefs and actions are influenced by persuasion efforts, which may be masked in terms of their intent to influence. Knowledge about social-psychological persuasion strategies is important for clinicians, both in resisting unwanted effects that dilute the quality of decisions and in effectively using persuasive appeals toward clinically desired ends. Competence in the use of influence is a key component of practical intelligence. One route to persuasion is based on thoughtful consideration of arguments related to a topic. The other major route is through emotional associations or inferences based on peripheral cues in the persuasion context, such as our mood or the status of the person offering a pitch (Petty & Cacioppo, 1986, p. 191). In the first route, there is an elaboration process; we are motivated to think about arguments for and against a position.

Persuasion by affect (the affect heuristic) comes into play when we do not engage in elaboration and are influenced not so much by what people say but by extraneous variables, such as how attractive they are or how confidently they present their views (e.g., Slovic, Finucane, Peters, & MacGregor, 2002). Persuasion strategies based on liking and authority attain their impact largely because of affective associations. The elaboration likelihood model suggests that we must be both motivated and able to engage in the cognitive effort to critique information regarding a topic, person, or idea (see Petty, Cacioppo, Strathman, & Priester, 2005). Within this model it is suggested that a given variable may serve as a cue as to what to believe by influencing the amount of elaboration we engage in, or it may bias the direction of elaboration (Fabrigar, Smith, & Brannon, 1999). Here we have yet another example of different ways to reach a decision—quickly based on emotions or in a more deliberative, thoughtful manner. What we use is the subject of considerable research and is of great interest to advertisers of products.

Becoming familiar with persuasion strategies and decreasing automatic influence by these tactics should upgrade the quality of clinical decisions. Compliance-induction strategies will be more readily identified, and thus you will be in a better position to decide if going along with the strategies will diminish or enhance the quality of decisions. (See Cialdini, 2008, for an entertaining, well-written, and empirically based description of persuasion strategies.) In everyday life, the principles on which these strategies are based provide convenient shortcuts that often work for us. We don't have time to fully consider the merits of each action we take or pitch we hear—we take shortcuts that often work for us (see Chapter 9). These compliance-induction strategies thus take advantage of our natural human tendencies. However, others can exploit them for their own purposes; our automatic reactions work in their favor. "All the exploiters need do is to trigger the great stores of influence that exist in a situation and direct them toward the intended target. . . . Even the victims themselves tend to see their compliance as due to the actions of natural forces rather than to the designs of the person who profits from that compliance" (Cialdini, 1984, p. 24). Thus, these strategies offer others the ability to manipulate without the appearance of manipulation. (See also Cialdini & Sagarin, 2005.)

The principle of liking is one of the most frequently used persuasive strategies. We like to please people we know and like; we like to comply with their requests. Clinicians prefer clients who are likable (see Chapter 2). The liking rule is often used by people we do not know, to gain our compliance. Factors that encourage liking include physical attractiveness, similarity, compliments, familiarity, and cooperation (see discussion of the influence of client characteristics in Chapter 2). "Compliance professionals are forever attempting to establish that we and they are working for the same goals, that we must 'pull together' for mutual benefit, that they are, in essence, teammates" (1984, p. 182). The good guy/bad guy routine takes advantage of the liking rule—we like the good guy (in contrast to the bad guy), so we comply with what he wants. The rule of liking also works through conditioning and association. Workshops that advertisers wish clinicians to attend are associated with positive qualities such as big names (for example, Albert Ellis). Clinicians will be more receptive to new material if they like the person presenting it. Associating pitches with food, as in the luncheon technique, is a well-known strategy designed to create liking/loyalty (Razran, described in Cialdini, 2001, p. 167). Big Pharma wines and dines opinion leaders to gain their loyalty to a product (Brody, 2007). Concerns about disapproval are often responsible for a reluctance to offer counterarguments to popular views in case conferences.

Another persuasion strategy is based on a desire to be (and appear) consistent with what we have already done. (This is not a trait of creative people.) A colleague may argue that because insight therapy was used to help a client with her depression, it should also be used to help her with her substance-abuse problem. A clinician may be reluctant to alter a service plan even though such a change will help to achieve client-desired outcomes, because of a fear of appearing inconsistent to a client. Being consistent usually works for us. "But because it is so typically in our best interests to be consistent, we easily fall into the habit of being automatically so, even in situations where it is not the sensible way to be" (Cialdini, 1984, pp. 68–69). Consistency can protect us from troubling realizations we would rather not think about. Since automatic consistency "functions as a shield against thought" (p. 72), it can be exploited by people who want us to comply with their requests. Gaining commitment sets the consistency rule into effect. "Commitment strategies are . . . intended to get us to take some action or make some statement that will trap us into later compliance through consistency pressures" (p. 75). An advertisement for a clinical workshop on a new intervention method may urge readers to reserve a space now—to ensure a place (scarcity principle)—and send a refundable deposit of $10.00 (commitment). A clinician may encourage a reluctant spouse to come in for "just one interview," hoping to persuade him to enter a course of relationship counseling.

Obtaining an initial concession or offering a favor may be used to gain compliance through the influence of the reciprocity rule; we feel obliged to return favors. A colleague who is eager to receive referrals may refer some clients to other clinicians. Offering concrete help at an early point may be used to encourage clients to participate in a counseling program. It may be difficult to counter or neutralize the influence of reciprocation, since we often do not know whether an offer is an honest one or the first step in an exploitation attempt. The rule of reciprocity "entitles a person who has acted in a certain way to a dose of the same thing" (Cialdini, 1984, p. 65). Thus, if an action is viewed as a compliance device instead of a favor, this rule will not work as an ally. The reciprocity rule lies behind the success of the rejection-then-retreat technique, in which a small request follows a large request—the small request is viewed as a concession, and is likely to be reciprocated by a concession from the other person. For example, when college students were asked to serve as chaperones for a group of juvenile delinquents on a day trip to the zoo, 83% of those requested refused. However, when this was first preceded by a larger request—which they refused (to spend two hours a week for two years as a counselor to the delinquent), three times as many students agreed to the smaller request (Cialdini, 1984, pp. 50–51). The contrast effect is also at work here (see later discussion).

Informal fallacies appealing to pseudoauthority take advantage of our tendency to go along with authorities (see examples in Chapter 6). Many appeals to authority are symbolic, such as certain kinds of titles; they connote rather than offer any content supporting the credibility of the authority. Some appeals to authority attempt to influence through fear, as in the advertisement for professional liability insurance in Exhibit 5.2. The test format is designed to convey a sense of authority. Notice that no facts and figures are presented in relation to what percentage of social workers are sued for what reasons. Types of strategies used are noted on Exhibit 5.2. Understanding the basis for the effectiveness of informal fallacies that appeal to pseudoauthority should be helpful in resisting appeals that compromise the quality of decisions.

The scarcity principle rests on the fact that opportunities seem more valuable when their availability is limited (Cialdini, 1984, p. 230). A prospective client who is informed that a clinician has no time to take on any new clients for two months may value the chance to work with this clinician even more. A nursing home intake worker may say, "If you don't decide now, space may not be available" (which may not be true). Here too, as with the impulse to use other shortcuts, it is accurate in its basic thrust; things that are scarce are usually more valuable; also, freedom is lost as opportunities become less available. Cialdini (1984) provides a good example of the influence of the scarcity principle:

Exhibit 5.2 Self-Test Advertisement for Professional Liability Insurance.

Test Yourself

Answer the following questions to find out whether you need malpractice coverage.

	Yes	No		Type of Strategy
1.	☐	☐	I am a practicing social worker.	(Setting the stage)
2.	☐	☐	I don't have my own coverage if I'm sued for malpractice.	(Fear induction)
3.	☐	☐	I let my malpractice coverage drop.	(Fear induction)
4.	☐	☐	I've heard about other social workers being sued.	(Fear induction)
5.	☐	☐	I know I need my own liability insurance, even though my employer provides it.	(Neutralization of counterarguments)
6.	☐	☐	I'm aware that malpractice suits against social workers have considerably increased over the past few years.	(Fear induction)
7.	☐	☐	I don't want to worry about being sued.	(Fear induction)

Source: From 1987, NASW News, 32(4), p.17. Copyright 1987 by National Association of Social Workers. Reprinted with permission.

One set of customers heard a standard sales presentation before being asked for their orders. Another set of customers heard the standard sales presentation plus information that the supply of imported beef was likely to be scarce in the upcoming months. A third group received the standard sales presentation and the information about a scarce supply of beef, too; however, they also learned that the scarce supply news was not generally available information. It had come, they were told, from certain exclusive contacts that the company had. Thus the customers who received this last sales presentation learned that not only was the availability of the product limited, so also was the news concerning it—the scarcity double whammy. . . . Compared to customers who got only the standard sales appeal, those who were told about the future scarcity of beef bought more than twice as much. But the real boost in sales occurred among the customers who heard of the impending scarcity via "exclusive" information. They purchased six times the amount that the customers who received only the standard sales pitch did. (Cialdini, 1984, p. 239; based on Knishinsky, 1982)

Actions are often guided by the principle of social proof—that is, finding out what other people think is correct. (Creative people are not as likely to follow this principle.) This principle provides a convenient shortcut that often works well; however, if it is accepted automatically, it can result in errors. A clinician may decide that since most clinicians refer clients to Alcoholics Anonymous, he or she will do so as well. The danger in appealing to the principle of social proof is the "pluralistic ignorance phenomenon" (Cialdini, 1984, p. 129): The majority view may be (and often is) incorrect. As with other social-psychological sources of influence, this one is more effective under some conditions than under others. Uncertainty increases the effects of this principle; we are more likely to go along with what other people do in ambiguous situations. Similarity also influences the impact of social proof; this principle operates most powerfully when we observe the behavior of people who are similar to ourselves. Observation of the behavior of people who are similar offers insight into what is viewed as correct behavior (Cialdini, 1984, p. 140). (See also Gigerenzer & Brighton, 2011.) False evidence may be provided to influence people through the principle of social proof, such as claiming (without evidence) that hundreds have benefited from use of a new therapy.

We are also influenced by the contrast effect. A client who is fairly cooperative may be viewed as extremely cooperative following an interview with a very resistant person. A study found that men assigned more negative ratings of pictures of potential blind dates when they were watching *Charlie's Angels* on TV than when they were watching some other program (Kenrick & Gutierres, 1980).

SUMMARY

Misuse of language contributes to inaccurate clinical decisions. Careless use of language is perhaps the greatest source of error. Confusion about the different functions of language may result in muddled discussions, as may confusion among different levels of abstraction. If terms are not clarified, confused discussions (or thinking) may occur, due to the assumption of one word, one meaning. Reification of terms (using a descriptive term as an explanatory term) offers an illusion of understanding without providing any real understanding. Technical terms may be carelessly used, resulting in bafflegab or psychobabble—words that sound informative but are empty and not helpful for making sound decisions. We are often unaware of the influence of emotional terms. Labels, for example, have emotional connotations that influence us in ways that do not necessarily enhance the accuracy of decisions. We are influenced by primacy effects (by what we hear first) and are often guilty of the misuse of verbal speculation (assuming that what is can be discovered by merely thinking about it). Knowledge of fallacies related to use of language and care in using language while thinking, listening, writing, or reading should improve the quality of decisions.

Clinicians both use and are influenced by social-psychological persuasion appeals in their everyday practice. A thorough knowledge of these strategies can be of value in avoiding sources of influence that decrease the accuracy of decisions. Learning how to recognize and counter persuasion strategies (such as attempted influence based on liking and appeals to consistency, authority, or scarcity) should increase well-reasoned decisions.

6

Formal and Informal Fallacies: Mistakes in Thinking and How to Avoid Them

Fallacies that may dilute the quality of decisions are described in this chapter as well as in Chapter 5. A fallacy can be defined as "an argument that not only does not contribute to the goal of a dialogue (e.g., arriving at the truth) but actually blocks or impedes the realization of that purpose" (Walton, 1995, p. 255). Thus a fallacy "is not just any error, lapse, or blunder in an argument. It is a serious error or trick tactic to get the best of one's speech partner illicitly" (p. 15). (See also discussion of appeal to authority in Chapter 7.) Walton's (1995, 2008a) pragmatic view of fallacies highlights their role in blocking critical appraisal.

> The one party tries to move ahead too fast by making an important move that is not yet proper in the sequence. Or, the one party tries to shut the other party up by closing off the dialogue prematurely or by shifting to a different type of dialogue.
>
> Or, key moves are left out of a sequence that should have been properly in. The result is that the sequence is not in the right order required for that type of dialogue and at that particular stage of the dialogue. This is where a fallacy occurs, where the resulting disorder is a type of sequence that blocks the dialogue or impedes it seriously. (Walton, 1995, p. 301)

Fallacies are techniques of argumentation that have been used in a counter-productive way to steer a discussion away from its proper goals or even in an aggressive attempt to close off the effective possibilities of an adversary's critical questioning in the dialogue. But identifying the pragmatic context of dialogue is the key to fixing the claim that an argument is fallacious. An aggressive personal attack that could be perfectly appropriate for an outright quarrel . . . could be highly destructive to the balance required for fair and constructive persuasion dialogue [critical discussion]. . . . In a scientific inquiry, yet another context of dialogue, the same use of the technique of personal attack could be even more outrageous and clearly out of place. . . . (Walton, 1995, p. 258)

The focus of attention concerning fallacies typically has been on clients: assessing their thinking patterns and identifying how distortions in their thinking are related to problems they experience (e.g., see Beck, 1976; Burns, 1999; Ellis & Grieger, 1977). The focus here is on clinicians, educators, researchers, and peer reviewers—on how formal and informal fallacies may compromise the quality of decisions. Errors that may result include assuming that pathology exists when it does not, missing pathology that is present, and choosing ineffective or harmful practice methods. Practice- and policy-related research findings may be ignored because they are associated with a disliked view, resulting in harming in the name of helping. The terms *trick* and *stratagem* refer to foul ploys often used deliberately as persuasion strategies, although they also may occur because of sloppy thinking or lack of critical thinking skills. (See Exhibit 6.1.) Fallacies may be intentional or unintentional. Intentional fallacies could be called deceptions. Does it make a difference? It may in terms of what must be done to avoid their influence.

Becoming familiar with fallacies and acquiring effective ways to avoid them will enhance the quality of decisions. Familiarity with the names of fallacies can be helpful in identifying and pointing them out to others. A catalog of flaws in thinking discussed here and in other chapters that may interfere with making sound decisions is included at the end of this chapter. Examples of fallacies encountered in my own experience are illustrated in Exhibit 6.2. Gambrill and Gibbs (2009) include reasoning-in-practice games designed to increase awareness of fallacies in reasoning when making clinical decisions. Gibbs (2003) includes interactive videos that offer practice in spotting such fallacies. (Other sources include Damer, 1995; Engel, 1994; Kahane & Cavender, 1998; Thouless, 1974.) The Skeptic's Dictionary (www.skepdic.com) and Fallacy Files (www.fallacyfiles.org) are valuable sources that describe a wide array of fallacies, including the *divine fallacy* (the assumption that if you can't understand some phenomenon, God must have created it) and the *pragmatic fallacy* (arguing that something is true because it works; e.g., "therapeutic touch"). But does it work? What does *work* mean?

FALSE EVEN THOUGH VALID

Some arguments are false even though they are valid. A valid argument is one whose premises, if true, offer good or sufficient grounds for accepting a conclusion.

Exhibit 6.1 Examples of Foul Ways to Win an Argument

- Accuse your opponent of doing what he accuses you of or worse ("You also …").
- Assume a posture of righteousness.
- Call for perfection (the impossible).
- Use vivid analogies and metaphors to support your view even when they are misleading.
- Create misgivings (dirty the water).
- Use double standards (for evidence, for example).
- Deny or defend inconsistencies.
- Focus on inconsistencies in your opponent's argument.
- Attack only evidence that undermines your case.
- Demonize his side and sanitize yours (a la Rank, 1982, 1984).
- Evade questions.
- Flatter your audience.
- Hedge what you say.
- Ignore the evidence.
- Ignore the main point.
- Focus on a minor point.
- Say "It is a cruel world" to justify the unethical.
- Use glittering generalizations.
- Make an opponent look ridiculous.
- Raise only objections.
- Shift the ground.
- Introduce distracting jokes.
- Focus on a vivid case example.
- Shift the burden of proof.
- Use double-talk.
- Tell lies.
- Reify concepts (treat abstract words as if they are real).
- Use red herrings.
- Use bogus statistics.
- Claim the point is "old hat."
- Use faint praise.

Source: Adapted from *Critical Thinking: Tools for Taking Charge of Your Professional and Personal Life*, by R. W. Paul and L. Elder, 2004, Upper Saddle River, NJ: Prentice Hall; "Factifuging," by N. Kline, 1962, *The Lancet*, pp. 1396–1399.

Doubtful Evidence

In one kind of "false even though valid" argument, the conclusions are accepted even though the premises are questionable. For example, it may be assumed that problems have a biochemical cause based on findings described in flawed studies of neuroimaging (Leo & Cohen, 2003; Vul et al., 2009). That is, someone may insist that the form of an argument is valid while ignoring the possible (or probable) inaccuracy of the premises. Clinicians often refer clients to other practitioners; they make decisions about the competence of colleagues. It may be assumed that "All psychologists are competent. Max is a psychologist. Therefore, Max is competent." If the premises are true, the conclusion is true. However, the truth of the first premise is debatable, and because one of the premises is doubtful, the argument is unsound, and a client may be referred to a

Exhibit 6.2 Examples of Exchanges From My Experience That Illustrate Informal Fallacies

---

1. *Situation:* Continuing education course through the University of California Extension given by Dr. Presti on alcohol abuse.
   Me: You use the term *alcohol disorder* often. Can you tell me what this means?
   Dr. Presti: A lack of order.

2. *Situation:* A faculty meeting in a school of social work.

   Faculty member A: We have made great strides in creating a list of empirically derived competencies for child welfare staff. We are delighted with our progress and will use this list to provide training programs.
   Me: Could you describe what is "empirical" about these competencies?
   Faculty member A. (looking annoyed—frowning): We asked people in focus groups of child welfare staff what they believed to be key competencies. We went to those who could provide the information. (*No information was provided about how many focus groups there were, how many people were in each, how these people were selected, whether those selected provided a representative sample of all staff, let alone whether what they reported bears any relationship to skills needed to provide high-quality services to clients.*)

3. *Situation:* Conference symposium

   Me: Could you please give me an example of what you mean by "working at the integration level"?
   Dr. X: You know what I am talking about.
   Me: No, I do not understand what you mean, but if we take a specific example related to social work practice this may help.
   Dr. X: I will not give you a specific example. You know what I mean.

---

clinician who is not competent to offer needed services. (An argument must be both valid and have accurate premises for it to be sound.) Because the argument stands or falls on whether a false premise is accepted, those who use doubtful evidence often try to distract readers or listeners from examining the premises; they may even try to use a below-the-belt technique such as ridicule.

Many facts are unknowable by anyone (for example, the exact number of gay/lesbian people who live in the United States). Some facts are potentially knowable or are known by someone, but are not known by the person who is using doubtful evidence. *Doubtful evaluation* refers to the insertion of an "unsupported controversial value judgment into an argument as a premise" (Kahane, 1971, p. 9). This may be confused with simple opinion statements, which are not really arguments (see Chapter 3). Examples of such statements are: "Behavioral methods are superficial" and "Psychoanalytic methods are overly complex in their view of causative factors." Some arguments contain premises that are contradictory, so even if the form of the argument is accurate, the conclusions cannot be true. The contradictory nature of the premises may not be obvious because of vagueness.

Suppressed Evidence

The suppression of evidence is one of the most widely and successfully used strategies. (See also discussion of propaganda in Chapter 4.) These errors of omission allow people to create false impressions and mislead others without actually lying. For example, in a recent newspaper article, a pharmaceutical representative claimed that the company's drug was responsible for decreasing surgery for stomach ulcers. No mention was made that the decreased need for surgery was mainly due to the discovery that ulcers were caused by a bacterium. A drug company may run 10 trials to examine the effectiveness of a drug, only two of which are positive, and send only these two to the Food and Drug Administration (FDA) for approval. It may test many people on a placebo and drop all placebo reactors before randomly distributing remaining subjects to a placebo and drug condition (Antonuccio, Burns, & Danton, 2002). It may not share information that use of an antidepressant results in a significant risk of suicide (Healy, 2003). Information about the evidentiary status (costs and benefits) of recommended intervention methods in relation to other options is often not shared with clients (Braddock et al., 1999). A clinician may suggest to the client that "X" intervention is best without informing the client that other options are available that have greater empirical support concerning their effectiveness. In such situations, clients are involved as uninformed participants, in violation of professional codes of ethics that call for informed consent.

An advertisement for a drug may not inform people that use of the drug results in only a three-point change on a 60-item scale or inform readers of adverse side effects (e.g., Woloshin & Schwartz, 2011). Clients are often unaware of what is not offered to them and so are in a disadvantaged position to request alternative methods. One remedy here is for the client to ask whether there are alternative methods and, if the answer is yes, to seek information about their evidentiary status. Information concerning the false-positive and false-negative rates regarding a diagnostic measure may not be reported. Without these data, clinicians may make incorrect decisions because of overestimating the accuracy of a measure. Reviews of websites regarding screening for breast cancer found that the negative effects of overdiagnosis and overtreatment are often not mentioned (Jørgensen & Gøtzsche, 2004; Thornton, Edwards, & Baum, 2003). Only relative risk may be given, omitting information about absolute risk (see Chapter 15).

Presenting only facts that serve one's own purpose while ignoring other relevant data is especially insidious, because readers or listeners are often unaware of information left out (MacLean, 1981, p. 37). It is a form of propaganda (see Chapter 4). There may be a conscious effort to suppress evidence. For example, someone may not just have a point of view that he or she is open to examining, but be interested in persuading us of the truth of a conclusion by appealing to our emotions. However, not considering important evidence related to a claim may be unintentional; it may occur because of unrecognized biases and preconceptions (see discussion of partiality in use of evidence in Chapter 14). The more educated the readers or listeners are, the more likely it may be that a tactic such as suppressed evidence is used rather than an obvious ploy such as use of emotional language.

Published sources contribute to influence by suppressed evidence, by failing to discuss well-argued alternative views of issues and by not including corrections of inaccurate reports (e.g., Gambrill & Reiman, 2011). Boyle (2002) identifies many examples of suppression of contradictory data in her book *Schizophrenia: A Scientific Delusion?* Many books, articles, and media reports attest to censorship of negative results regarding the effects of certain drugs on the part of pharmaceutical companies (e.g., see Angell, 2004). A sophisticated campaign may be mounted to suppress data contradictory to a preferred position, as illustrated in the following excerpts from an article describing court proceedings concerning the death of a smoker:

> "Evidence presented by the plaintiff," Judge Sarokin said, "particularly that contained in documents of the defendants themselves, indicates the development of a public relations strategy aimed at combating the mounting adverse scientific reports regarding the dangers of smoking.
>
> "The evidence indicates further that the industry of which these defendants were and are a part entered into a sophisticated conspiracy. The conspiracy was organized to refute, undermine and neutralize information coming from the scientific and medical community and, at the same time, to confuse and mislead the consuming public in an effort to encourage existing smokers to continue and new persons to commence smoking."
>
> Judge Sarokin noted that evidence had been introduced showing that results of industry-sponsored research adverse to the industry's goals had been "suppressed and concealed."
>
> "At least one scientist testified as to threats made to him if he published his findings, and there was other evidence of attempts to suppress or coerce others," he said. (Janson, 1988, p. A13)

The remedy to the use of suppressed evidence depends partly on whether the suppression is intentional or unintentional. The goal is to identify unmentioned information that bears on the accuracy of a claim. Possible options include (1) seeking information from alternative sources, such as talking to people holding other views or reviewing information on various web sites, especially those with a reputation for rigorous appraisal, such as the Cochrane and Campbell databases; (2) exploring negative as well as positive effects of a decision; and (3) asking speakers if there is anything else we should know before making a decision, such as important consequences of a proposed view that have not been mentioned, or alternative options; speakers may not be willing to lie and so share suppressed views and relevant evidence, or they may be unwilling to appear uninformed at a later date by having failed to do so under direct questioning. (See also discussion of missing language in Chapter 5.)

IRRELEVANT APPEALS

Irrelevant appeals include fallacies in which the wrong point is supported or when a conclusion established by premises is not relevant to the issues being discussed. These are informal fallacies; that is, none involve a formal mistake. Many such fallacies achieve their effect by taking advantage of one or more of our natural tendencies, such as wanting to please others or going along with what others think (the principle of social proof).

Emotional Appeals

Emotional appeals include appeal to pity, force or threat, flattery, guilt, and shame. Propaganda appeals to our deepest motivations—to avoid danger (fear), to be one of the boys/girls (acceptance and emotional support), and to be free to hate our enemies (Ellul, 1965). However, the emotion with which a position is offered does not mean that the argument is poor. Good arguments can be (and often are) offered with emotion. And appeal to emotions such as pity and sympathy may be reasonable in some kinds of arguments (Walton, 2008a).

Ad Hominem Arguments

Here, the background, habits, associates, or personality of an individual are attacked or appealed to, rather than his or her argument. Rather than arguing ad rem (to the argument), someone argues ad hominem (to the person proposing it). There are many forms of this genetic fallacy—the view that the source of an idea indicates its soundness. The appeal or attack may be subtle or obvious. You may suggest that an advocacy group should be made up of community residents because they have had experience with advocacy and are eager to work together. Another staff member may respond, "But how can you say this? You haven't completed your clinical training program yet." Rather than addressing your argument, he is commenting on your education. This example illustrates that ad hominem appeals may function as diversions—an attempt to sidetrack people. The theories of Jung may be rejected because of his alleged racism and anti-Semitism; this rejection is made on an ad hominem basis: these alleged characteristics do not necessarily bear on the cogency of his theory. Improper appeals to authority to support a position are a kind of ad hominem argument. The effectiveness of ad hominem arguments depends partially on the principle of liking (disliking), as well as the principle of authority (see Chapter 5).

Is an ad hominem attack or appeal ever relevant? (For a detailed discussion, see relevant readings in Hansen & Pinto, 1995.) If an attack on the presenter of the argument is related to the issue at hand, then in some cases it may be relevant. For example, someone could be shown to offer unreliable accounts on most occasions. However, this person may be offering a correct account this time. Thus, the credibility of the person presenting an argument is important to consider. Ad hominem arguments are surprisingly effective for a variety of reasons, only one of which is failure to identify the fallacious nature of the argument. Others include the following:

- Implicit agreement with the implications about the individual.
- Agreement with the conclusion of the argument with little concern for its correctness.
- Unwillingness to raise questions, cause a fuss, or challenge authorities who may counterattack.
- Social pressures in group settings—not wanting to embarrass others.

The remedy in relation to ad hominem arguments is to point out that the appeal made provides no evidence for or against a claim.

Guilt (or credit) by association is a variation of an ad hominem argument—judging people by the company they keep. A youth accused of theft may associate with a gang known to engage in criminal activities. Such association offers indirect, circumstantial evidence—it does not offer direct support for the argument that he is guilty. The best use of circumstantial or indirect evidence is as a cue for further exploration. There may be a grain of truth in assessing an argument by considering the associates of the person proposing it. However, not all of an individual's friends may be disreputable or uninformed (or reputable or informed, in the case of assumptions of credit). And, even if they all are (either one or the other), the individual may still speak the truth. An attempt to discredit a position may be made by associating it with a disliked institution, value, or philosophy, as in the statement that behavioral methods are antihumanistic or psychoanalytic methods are antifeminist. "Imposter terms" or euphemisms may be used to make an unpopular view or method acceptable. For example, use of long-term lockups in a prison may be referred to as behavior modification. Dumping patients into the community from mental hospitals may be called community care. As Nickerson (1986b) points out, we are more likely to agree with institutions and philosophies we favor; however, it is unlikely that we will agree with every facet, and similarly, it is unlikely that we would disagree with every aspect of a disliked view. So, "Credit or discredit by association becomes a fallacy when it is applied in a blind and uncritical way. Whether or not a particular view is one that is held by a specific individual, institution, or philosophy that we generally support (or oppose) is very meager evidence as to the tenability of that view" (Nickerson, 1986b, p. 116).

In the bad seed fallacy, it is assumed that a person's character or habits are passed on to his descendants (Michalos, 1971, p. 54); that because a client's parents acted in a certain way, that is why the client acts in this manner. The bad seed fallacy is common in clinical contexts. A striking example of guilt by association is shown in the excerpts from a case conference given in Chapter 16. Genetic factors do play a role in influencing behavior; however, the correlations presented are typically far from perfect and, in any case, may not support a causal connection (Lewontin, 2009; Strohman, 2003). An argument may be made that a position is not acceptable because the person's motives for supporting the issue are questionable. For example, a proposal that a new suicide prevention center be created may be denied on the grounds that those who propose this are "interested parties"—that they will profit from such a center by gaining needed jobs. In fact, the accuracy or inaccuracy of the view proposed cannot be determined from an examination of the motives of those who proposed it, but only from an examination of the evidence presented in its favor. It may be argued that because our intentions or motives are good, a claim is true. A psychologist may wish to place a child on Ritalin even though there is little evidence that this is indicated. He may protest that his intent is to help this child. Appeals to good intentions are the opposite of the assumption of suspect motives. In both cases, evidence is needed that the claim is correct; motives, whether altruistic or otherwise, are not evidence.

Claims of inconsistency may be made to distract us from considering evidentiary issues. A discrepancy between a person's behavior and his principles may be invalidly used against him. For example, an argument may be dismissed on the grounds that the person's behavior is not consistent with his argument. A clinician who is not sympathetic to behavioral methods may say to his behavioral friend, "If behaviorists know so much about how to change behavior, why are you still smoking when you want to stop?" Another kind of false claim of inconsistency is when a charge is made that a person's behavior is not consistent with his principles when his principles have changed. It may be argued that because a clinician held a certain view many years ago, he holds the same view today. Altering a position does not necessarily entail inconsistency. It depends on whether a person states that his position has changed and explains the reasons for these changes. Not recognizing that people often have rational grounds for changing their opinions results in a false charge of inconsistency. This fallacy takes advantage of our desire to be consistent and to expect others to be consistent as well. (See discussion of persuasion in Chapter 5.)

You Would Do It, Too

Objections to a position or action may be countered with "You'd do it, too, if you had an opportunity," as in "You would refer difficult clients to someone else if you could." This argument does not provide evidence for (or against) a position.

Vacuous Guarantees

A warrant may be offered for a claim that is without substance. Self-help books have long been criticized for offering unsupported, vacuous guarantees of effectiveness (Rosen, 1982). For example, an advertisement in a professional journal directed to mental health facilities and substance abuse centers assures potential customers interested in consultation, training, and supervision that "it works," that they "custom-design safe programs," that "I can, you can, together we can." No criteria are described as to what is meant by "it works" or what "safe programs" consist of. No evidence is offered in support of claims made.

Appeal to Common Practice

It may be argued that because other people do something, it is all right to do the same. *Common practice* is a variety of this fallacy. It may be argued that because few clinicians keep up with practice-related literature, this is okay. Objections may be countered with "You'd do it, too, if you had an opportunity." This argument does not provide evidence for (or against) a position. Standard practice may be (and often is) of poor quality.

Fallacy of Ignorance

The fallacy of ignorance involves the assumption that an absence of evidence against a claim must be counted as evidence for it (Michalos, 1971, p. 52). A clinician may argue that because there is no evidence showing that "directed aggression" (hitting objects such as pillows) does not work, it should be used. The fact that no one can think of a course of action that is better than one proposed may be used as an argument that the proposed course is a good one. In fact, they could all be bad. It is hard to believe that this fallacy would ever work (that is, influence people), but it does, as do some other weak appeals—such as simply asserting that a position is true.

Fallacy of Special Pleading

The fallacy of special pleading involves favoring our own interests by using different standards for different people, as in "I am firm, thou art obstinate, he is pigheaded" (Thouless, 1974, p. 11). A clinician may claim that she does not have to evaluate her work as carefully as other clinicians because of her lengthy experience.

Appeal to Will

An example of the fallacy of appeals to will is to say that "if he really wanted to . . . he would." It would be hoped that clinicians, with their more sophisticated understanding of motivation, would not use appeals to will. However, I have heard clinicians say, "If she was interested in getting better, she'd come in for counseling." Appeals to willpower offer no information about how to create desired changes.

Attacking the Example

Attacking the example is a relatively transparent strategy—the example given of a position is attacked rather than the position itself. The example offered might not be an apt one. A remedy here is to point out that a successful attack on the example does not take away from the possible soundness of a position, and to offer a better example. This fallacy is the opposite of the use of a suspect particular case as proof for a generalization (see later discussion). It may be argued that two wrongs make a right—that because other people do something, it is all right to do the same. Common practice is a variety of this fallacy. It may be argued that it is all right not to keep up with practice-related empirical literature because other clinicians do not do so.

EVADING THE FACTS

Fallacies that evade the facts, such as begging the question, appear to address the facts but do not: "Such arguments deceive by inviting us to presume that the facts are as they have been stated in the argument, when the facts are quite otherwise" (Engel, 1994, p. 144).

Begging the Question

This refers to assuming the truth or falsity of what is at issue; that is, trying to settle a question by simply reasserting a position. This tactic is surprisingly effective often because it is accompanied by appeals to authority. Such appeals take advantage of persuasive bases, such as liking (we are less likely to question poor arguments of people we like), authority (we accept what experts say), and social proof (we are influenced by what other people do). Consider the statement, "The inappropriate releasing of mentally ill patients must be ended." The speaker assumes that releasing mentally ill patients is inappropriate, instead of offering evidence to show that it is. Presenting opinions as facts is a common variant of this fallacy. Michalos (1971) has identified seven ways to beg the question, some of which overlap with improper appeals to authority (see Chapter 7). Use question begging as a clue that relevant facts are being evaded.

Bold assertions are a common form of question begging. Alleged certainty is used to encourage readers or listeners to accept a claim without any evidence that the claim is accurate. The claim is presented as if it were obvious, in the hope that our critical senses will be neutralized. Examples are: (1) "No one doubts the number of alcoholics in the United States today." (2) "It is well accepted that therapy works." Appeals to consensus may be made with no evidence provided that there is a consensus concerning a position, as in "Everyone knows it's in the genes." This appeal, as well as the appeal of alleged certainty, takes advantage of the principle of social proof (our tendency to believe that what most other people think or do is correct). A clinician may say that "use of play therapy with autistic children is the accepted method of choice." Even if evidence for a consensus is offered, that does not mean that the position is correct. Consensus is a notoriously unreliable ground on which to believe a claim.

Wishful thinking involves the assumption that because some condition ought to be, it is the case—without providing any support for the position. Statements made about declassification (hiring staff without advanced clinical degrees) are often of this variety. That is, it is assumed that declassification is bad; no evidence is presented to support the position by showing, for example, that hiring staff without graduate degrees results in lower quality services for clients. "We continue to hear about professional caregivers coming into conflict with case managers who lack the requisite training to perform the complicated tasks involved in assessment and evaluation" ("From the President," 1987, p. 2). No evidence is provided that case managers without professional training lack the requisite skills to perform the tasks described, and the conflict alluded to is assumed to reflect negatively on the case managers rather than on "professional caregivers."

Speakers or writers are guilty of using question-begging epithets when they add evaluative terms to neutral descriptive terms—the aim is to influence through emotional reactions. For example, "Fairview Hospital opened today" is a simple declarative statement. "The long-needed Fairview Hospital opened its doors today" includes evaluative epithets. Variations of this fallacy include the use of emotive language (see Chapter 5), loaded words, and verbal suggestion. Emotional terms may be used to attempt to prejudice the facts by using evaluative language that supports what we want to demonstrate but have not shown. Overstatement, ridicule, flattery, and abuse are used to evade the facts.

Circular arguments are a form of question begging, as in the following example (Engel, 1994, p. 146).

> People can't help what they do.
> Why not?
> Because they always follow the strongest motive.
> But what is the strongest motive?
> It is, of course, the one that people follow.

This argument is circular in saying that A is so because of B, and B is true because of A. The conclusion that a speaker or writer is trying to establish is used as a premise or presupposed as a premise. Such circular arguments may seem so transparent that they would never be a problem in clinical practice. However, they occur in clinical practice. Consider the following dialogue.

> Mr. Levine can't control his outbursts.
> Why is that?
> Because he is developmentally disabled.
> Why do you say that he is developmentally disabled?
> Well, because he has outbursts when he is frustrated.

Attributing the cause of outbursts to the developmental disability offers no information about how to alter the frequency of the outbursts.

A clinician may alter a definition or question a diagnosis rather than admit that a counterexample to a position has been identified. Believers in the disease view of alcoholism contend that drinkers who can return to limited nonproblem drinking were never "true alcoholics." "In its extreme, this argument maintains that even individuals who have suffered distinct alcohol withdrawal symptoms must have been misclassified as alcoholics" (Sobell & Sobell, 1982, p. 156). As Michalos (1971) points out, "facts cannot shake the generalization because the truth is guaranteed by definitions."

Apriorism is a form of question begging in which a position is claimed as true (prior to any investigation) because it is necessary according to a particular view of the world (or of clinical practice). Consider the assertion of psychiatrists that they should supervise treatment of patients (implying that psychologists and other kinds of mental health professionals, such as social workers, would work under their supervision) and that to arrange services otherwise (to allow other kinds of professionals to work autonomously) would lower the quality of service offered to clients. The view of practice that is assumed is that training as a psychiatrist is superior to other kinds of professional training. This is not necessarily true. What is needed is a description of evidence for and against the position advanced.

Unfounded generalizations may be used to support a conclusion. For example, someone may say, "Offering positive incentives for desired behaviors is dehumanizing because it is behavioral." The assumptions are that behavioral methods are dehumanizing and that offering positive incentives for desired behaviors is behavioral. Since the truth of the wider generalizations is questionable, the particular example is questionable. A supervisor could beg the question of whether practice should be evaluated on the grounds that this violates client confidentiality. When a more general claim is assumed, the accuracy of this claim should be examined. Complex, leading, or trick questions with indirect assumptions may be used. A question may be asked in such a way that any answer will incriminate the speaker (for example, "Do you still beat your wife?" or "Where do you keep your cocaine?"). This is the interrogative form of the fallacy of begging the question; the conclusion at issue is assumed rather than supported. "Complex questions accomplish this by leading one to believe that a particular answer to a prior question has been answered in a certain way when this may not be the case" (Engel, 1994, p. 152). These questions bring with them assumptions that influence how they will be answered. The remedy is to question the question. Because of their leading nature, some questions would be ruled out in a court of law, given that lawyers were on their toes. Such questions are also fallacious "because they assume that one and the same answer must apply to both the unasked and the asked question as in the example of 'Isn't Dr. Green an unthinking feminist?'" (p. 124). If the question is divided into its parts, different answers may apply: Is Dr. Green a feminist? Is she unthinking? Thus, the remedy is to divide the original question into its implied components and answer each one at a time.

Complex questions are often used to encourage clients to comply with a request, as in the example of a staff member who is having trouble getting a patient to take a bath. Rather than asking him if he wants to take a bath tonight, she might say, "Do you want to take a bath now or at seven?" Another variation of complex questions is requesting explanations for supposed facts that have not been supported, as in "How do you account for extrasensory perception (ESP)?" Since there is controversy about whether ESP exists, and many people believe that research exploring such phenomena has yielded negative results, there may be no extraordinary effects to explain, perhaps just fallacies or questionable experimental designs to be uncovered.

Simply ignoring a question is a common tactic. This tactic can be successful if no one is present who will object, perhaps because everyone agrees with the original position. One form of ignoring the issue is to claim there is no issue. The question may be swept aside as irrelevant, trivial, or offensive.

OVERLOOKING THE FACTS

Relevant facts are often neglected, as in the *fallacy of the sweeping generalization*, in which a rule or assumption that is valid in general is applied to a specific example to which it is not valid (Engel, 1994). It might be argued that since expressing feelings is healthy, Susan should do it more, because it will increase her self-esteem and make her happier. However, if expressing feelings will result in negative consequences from significant others (such as work supervisors and her husband), the general rule may not apply here. This kind of fallacy can be exposed by identifying the rule involved and showing that it cannot be applied accurately to the case at hand. In the *fallacy of hasty generalization*, an example is used as the basis for a general conclusion that is not warranted. For example, if a psychologist has an unpleasant conversation with a social worker and says, "Social workers are difficult to work with," the generalization to all social workers might be inaccurate. This fallacy is also known as the *fallacy of hasty conclusion* (Kahane, 1971), and it has many variants. All have in common making unwarranted generalizations from small or biased samples. This fallacy entails a disregard for the law of large numbers. (See Chapter 13 and prior discussion of suppressed evidence and of either-or thinking.)

In the *fallacy of composition*, it is assumed that what is true of a part is also true of the whole. An example is the assumption that because each staff member in a psychiatric hospital is skilled, the hospital as a whole is an effective treatment center. A clinician may assume that because a young man has been caught stealing money at home he also engages in other criminal activities. The more vivid the particular behavior or person singled out for attention (that is, the more vivid the part), the more likely it is that generalizations will be made from the part to the entire person. In the *fallacy of division*, it is assumed that what is true of the whole is true of all the parts. A client may assume that because a clinic has a good reputation, every counselor on the staff is competent, but this is not necessarily true.

DISTORTING FACTS/POSITIONS

A number of informal fallacies distort positions. Famous people may be misquoted or views misrepresented (see discussion of incorrect classification of procedures in Chapter 7).

Straw Person Arguments

In straw person arguments, a position similar to but different from the one presented is attacked; an argument is distorted and the distorted version is then attacked. Such arguments are often seen in the discussion of disliked practice theories. Examples of distortions of the philosophy of evidence-based decision making, as described in original sources, can be seen in Exhibit 6.3. Distorted presentations of Skinner's views are common, such as the incorrect view that he believes in stimulus-response Watsonian behaviorism (e.g., Thyer, 2005). Incorrect assertions may then be criticized. Inaccurate descriptions may be used to give a misleading view of what indeed occurred, as in the statement that "there is an epidemic of drug use" when in fact there has been a modest increase or no increase at all (Best, 2004; MacCoun, 2001). Advocacy in place of accurate presentation of data is common (Best, 2004).

Exhibit 6.3 Fallacies in Misrepresentation of Evidence-Based Practice (EBP)

Distortion	Reply
1. EBP stems from behaviorism and positivism.	1. It does not stem from either.
2. EBP ignores client values.	2. Attending to client values and preferences is a hallmark of EBP.
3. EBP ignores clinical expertise.	3. Clinical expertise is used to integrate information from diverse sources.
4. EBP simply substitutes another from of authority.	4. This indeed could happen by distorting EBP and is illustrated by use of the term evidence-based without the substance; EBP is an alternative to authority-based practices and policies.
5. EBP is a cookbook approach.	5. EBP involves the use of clinical expertise to consider unique client characteristics and circumstances and available resources.
6. EBP is simply a cost-cutting tool.	6. A review of the evidence related to a concern may result in more money being spent.
7. Only randomized controlled trials are drawn on.	7. A wide variety of research is drawn on to match the question raised.
8. Research shows it cannot be done.	8. Research suggests that it can be done (e.g., see Chapter 10).
9. EBP results in therapeutic nihilism.	9. If no evidence is found, this is shared with clients and practice theory is drawn on to guide decisions.
10. There is nothing new about EBP.	10. Not true—see Chapter 10.
11. We are already doing it.	11. Not true—see Chapter 10.
12. No evidence is available that can guide practice.	12. Many questions have been critically examined. See, for example, Cochrane and Campbell databases.
13. EBP assumes that professionals are rational agents.	13. One of the reasons EBP originated was because clinicians often do not draw on practice-related research.

Note: Based on Gibbs and Gambrill (2002); Straus and McAlister (2000). See Chapter 10 for a description of evidence-based practice and care as described in original sources.

Forcing an Extension

Forcing an extension may be intentionally used by someone aware of the fact that it is usually impossible to defend extreme positions; that is, most positions have some degree of uncertainty attached to them, like the statement that insight therapy is useful with many (not all) clients. The original position may be misstated in an extreme version ("insight therapy is effective with all clients"), and this extreme version is then criticized. The original, less extreme position should be reaffirmed.

The Fallacy of False Cause

The fallacy of false cause involves arguments that suggest that two events are causally related when no such connection has been demonstrated. It may be argued that because one event followed another, it was caused by that event. A client may state that she made a bad mistake because she had a bad dream the night before (see Chapter 14).

Irrelevant Conclusion

An argument may be made for a conclusion that is not the one under discussion. While seeming to counter an argument, irrelevant statements advance a conclusion that is different from the one at issue. Other names for this fallacy include *red herring*, *ignoring the issue*, and *diversion*. This fallacy can be quite deceptive because the irrelevant argument advanced often does support a conclusion and so gives an impression of credibility to the person offering it, and the illusion of a lack of cogency for the original argument, but the argument does not address the conclusion at issue (Engel, 1994). An example is: "The advocates of reality therapy contend that if we adopt their practice methods, clients will be better off. They are mistaken, for it is easy to show that reality therapy will not cure the ills of the world." There are two different points here: (1) whether reality therapy is effective and (2) whether it will "cure the ills of the world." Showing that the latter is not true may persuade people that the first point has also been shown to be untrue. The fallacy of irrelevant thesis is a version of forcing an extension. Notice that distortion of a position can make it look ridiculous and so easily overthrown. If the presenter of the original, more modest view is duped into defending an extreme version, he or she will likely fail.

Inappropriate Use of Analogies

Analogies can be helpful in understanding clinical problems and in selecting treatment methods. Analogies often are used in daily life to decide what to do in novel situations;

that is, we try to identify a familiar experience and use it to make decisions in new contexts. Analogies often are used to clarify meanings. For example, the Freudian theory of motivation is sometimes likened to a hydraulic system, in which repressed forces are kept in check by defenses, and if these are removed, repressed content will emerge. Analogies can be helpful if they compare two phenomena that are indeed similar in significant ways; the more familiar event can be helpful in highlighting aspects of the less familiar event that should be considered. However, if the two events differ in important ways, then the analogy can interfere with understanding. Two things may bear a superficial resemblance to each other but be quite unlike in important ways. Consider the question "Should couples have sex before marriage?" A response might be "You wouldn't buy a car without taking it out for a test drive, would you?" (Bransford & Stein, 1984, p. 88). Some people who hear this argument simply say, "Oh, yes, you have a point there." Others will see that the analogy is inappropriate; marriage is significantly different from buying a car. The soundness of the analogy must always be explored. It is only a guide; it becomes dangerous "when the conclusions to which it points are regarded as certain" (Thouless, 1974, p. 171). Does "mental illness" (disease/disorder) match the characteristics of a disease? Does it have a known etiology, a predictable course, and get worse without treatment? Peele (1999) and Fingarette (1988) argue that alcohol abuse is not a disease; that is, it does not have these characteristics. Consider also schizophrenia. Its etiology is unknown (contrary to bold assertions by some to the contrary, and candidly acknowledged by others, including the surgeon general of the United States in 1999). It does not have a predictable course, and it does not necessarily get worse without treatment.

Argument by mere analogy refers to the use of an analogy "to create conviction of the truth of whatever it illustrates, or when it implies that truth in order to deduce some new conclusion" (Thouless, 1974, p. 169). When an argument from analogy is reduced to its bare outline, it "has the form that because some thing or event N has the properties a and b which belong to M, it must have the property c which also belongs to M" (p. 171). Arguments from analogy may sometimes be difficult to recognize; that is, the analogy may be implied rather than clearly stated. The mind of a child may be likened to a container that must be filled with information. This analogy carries implications that may be untrue, such as that we have sharply limited capacities. So "the use of analogy becomes crooked argumentation when an analogy is used not as a guide to expectations, but as proof of a conclusion" (p. 176). Analogies create vivid images that are then readily available. They may oversimplify concerns in a misleading manner. Their vividness may crowd out less vivid but more accurate analogies and discourage a review of possible limitations of the analogy. There is thus an emotional impact; analogies play upon our emotions. We forget that, although they may be a useful guide to what to look for, "They are never final evidence as to what the facts are" (p. 175). They are one of many devices for creating conviction, even though there are no rational grounds for the conviction. Arguments from mere analogy can be dealt with by noting at what point the analogy breaks down.

In *argument from forced analogy*, an analogy is used to advance an argument when there is not enough resemblance between the things compared to ever expect that they would resemble each other in relation to the main point under discussion. One example is "Delusional processes are like a machine run amok." Those who use such analogies are often aware of their influence in creating beliefs, despite the absence of rational grounds for such beliefs. Forced analogies are often used in public speeches where their deficiencies cannot be readily pointed out. The remedy consists of examining just how closely the analogy really fits the matter at hand. Thouless (1974) recommends trying out other analogies and noting whether these carry as much force as the original one.

DIVERSIONS

Many informal fallacies succeed by diverting attention from the main points of an argument. Some of the informal fallacies already discussed could be so classified, such as red herring and ad hominem arguments in which attention is focused on the person making the argument rather than the argument itself. Trivial points or irrelevant objections may be focused on. "If you find that you are being worsted, you can make a diversion—that is, you can suddenly begin to talk of something else, as though it had a bearing on the matter in dispute" (Schopenhauer, 1942, p. 29). Here the diversion is not to a new question (as in the fallacy of irrelevant thesis), but to a question related to the prime question under consideration. In any discussion, a number of points may be raised, one or more of which may not be true. In this fallacy, some trivial point is addressed and shown to be incorrect and it is assumed that the main question has been disposed of. Showing the inaccuracy of a fact that is not relevant to a position can create the impression that the entire argument is incorrect. Witty comments and jokes can be used to divert attention from the main point of an argument or from the fact that little evidence is provided for a position. A joke can be made that makes a valid position appear ridiculous or poorly conceived. Attempts to defend a position in the face of such a response may seem pedantic. The remedy is to point out that, although what has been said may be true (or humorous), it is irrelevant.

Answering a Question With a Question

In an appeal to ignorance, a "why?" is met with a "why not?" (Michalos, 1971, p. 81). In the fallacy of answering questions with questions, hypothetical questions are introduced that provide a distraction from important points. Questions cannot be true or false, so continued questioning is not informative. Certainly, some questions are vital to evaluation of arguments. However, in arguments they are never an end in themselves. In other contexts, such as an exchange between Buddhist monks, another end may be sought (see Engel, 1994, p. 82).

Appeal to Emotion

Creating anger is another way to distract people. Emotional language can be used to create anger, anxiety, or blind adherence to a position, and to distract us from noticing flaws in an argument. Anger may be created by inflammatory statements about a position or by ad hominem attacks. The focus may shift to insults rather than the issues under discussion. Anger may be distracting also if others become angry. Appeals to anxiety and fear are widely used to distract listeners and readers from the main issues. Many authors highlight the hyping of risks and fears in our society. Furedi (2006) argues that we live in a culture of fear. In "Marketing: A Lifeline for Private Practice," readers are told that "as more social workers go into private practice, and as competition between them and other mental health professionals heats up, marketing becomes a necessary survival tool" (*NASW News*, October 1987, p. 5). Notice the term *survival*, appealing to fear. The principle of social proof is one of the bases of appeals to anxiety—"You will be out of step with everyone else if you don't agree with an accepted position." Appeals to anxiety and fear may draw on any one of the sources of persuasion, as illustrated in Exhibit 6.4 (see also Chapter 5). Appeals to fear were used by psychiatrists in their battle against psychologists to retain and expand their turf. For example, they predicted that the quality of services would decrease if psychologists received hospital admission privileges (Buie, 1989). Appeals to pity or friendship may also direct attention away from careful examination of evidence for a claim.

Exhibit 6.4 Use of Persuasion Tactics to Create Fear and Anxiety

Social-Psychological Principle	Anxiety-Arousing Appeal
Liking	You don't like me if you don't go along with my position (and therefore I won't like you as much).
Consistency	You're inconsistent with your beliefs if you don't agree with me.
Reciprocity	I helped you out in the past; now you're not fulfilling your obligation to return the favor if you don't support my position.
Authority	Other people (namely me) know what is best.
Scarcity	We won't have this opportunity for long; it's now or never.
Social proof	Everyone (but you) accepts this position; what's the matter with you?

Red Herring

Here someone tries to distract you from the main point of an argument by introducing irrelevant content. The point is to divert others from the central issue.

THE USE OF CONFUSION

Some fallacies work by confusion: "If you can't convince them (or if you don't know what you're talking about), confuse them." Raising doubt was a key strategy used by the tobacco industry regarding the link between smoking and health consequences (Oreskes & Conway, 2010). People may attempt to create confusion by citing a counterexample to a position, saying that "the exception proves the rule." It does no such thing. Finding an example that does not fit a rule may be informative about the boundaries within which a rule is applicable, but may say nothing about the truth or falsity of the rule in question. (See discussion of the fallacy of the sweeping generalization earlier in this chapter.) Excessive verbiage is a common means of creating confusion as described by Orwell (1946/1958)—someone may talk about many different things and then state a conclusion that supposedly stems from all of them. Excessive wordiness, whether written or spoken, makes the task of argument analysis difficult. We tend to assume that if someone is talking (or writing), he or she must be making sense. We may think we have missed the point and are limited in our ability to understand an issue; we "tend to put the burden of comprehension on ourselves" (Michalos, 1971, p. 79). If excessive verbiage is complemented by prestige, the use of pseudoarguments is even more likely to confuse and mislead. We are misled by our tendency to go along with what authorities say. Another persuasive influence at work here may include liking—if we like someone, we are more prone to agree with what they say and to think they are saying something of value.

Equivocation involves playing on the double meaning of a word in a misleading or inaccurate manner (see Hamblin, 1970). "If someone informs you that Simon Butcher is independent, exactly what has he told you? Is he politically, religiously, economically, or socially independent? Is he a free thinker or a free lover? Is he a lover of free thinking or does he just think about loving freely? The fallacy of equivocation would be committed if someone began with a premise attributing independence in one sense to Butcher and concluded from that that Butcher possessed independence in an entirely different sense" (Michalos, 1971, p. 71).

People may claim a lack of understanding to avoid coming to grips with an issue, or try to confuse issues by repeatedly asking for alternative statements of a position (Michalos, 1971, p. 75). This tactic, like some others, such as arousing anger, may be used to gain time to consider a position better in terms of what to do next in order to prevail. Feigned lack of understanding is often combined with use of power, as when an instructor tells a student that he does not understand the point being made. Often there is an implication that the other person's point of view is irrelevant or silly, anyway. A possible remedy here may be to ask the person exactly what aspect of the argument is confusing.

SUMMARY

Both formal and informal fallacies may dilute the quality of clinical decisions. Some arguments are false even though they are valid. A valid argument is one whose premises, if true, offer good or sufficient grounds for accepting a conclusion. The incorrectness of premises may be overlooked, resulting in poor decisions. Most fallacies are informal ones; that is, they do not involve a formal mistake. There are many different kinds of informal fallacies. Ad hominem arguments may be used, in which the background, habits, associates, or personality of the person (rather than the arguments) are criticized or appealed to. Variants of ad hominem arguments include guilt (or credit) by association, the bad seed fallacy, appeals to faulty motives or good intentions, special pleading, and false claims of inconsistency. Vacuous guarantees may be offered, as when someone assumes that because a condition ought to be, it is the case, without providing support for the position.

Fallacies that evade the facts (such as begging the question) appear to address the facts, but do not. Variants of question begging include use of alleged certainty; circular reasoning; use of unfounded generalizations to support a conclusion; complex, trick, or leading questions; and ignoring the issue. Some informal fallacies overlook the facts, as in the fallacy of the sweeping generalization, in which a rule or assumption that is valid in general is applied to a specific example for which it is not valid. Other informal fallacies distort facts or positions; in straw person arguments, a position similar to (but significantly different from) the one presented is described and attacked. The informal fallacies of false cause, forcing an extension, and the inappropriate use of analogies also involve the distortion of facts or positions. Diversions may be used to direct attention away from a main point of an argument. Trivial points, irrelevant objections, or emotional appeals may be made. Some fallacies work by creating confusion, such as feigned lack of understanding and excessive talk that obscures arguments. Knowledge of formal and informal fallacies decreases the likelihood that decisions will be influenced by these sources of error.

EXAMPLES OF QUESTIONABLE APPEALS AND FAULTY INFERENCES

1. *Relying on similarity (representativeness)*. Assuming that two or more things or events are related simply because they resemble each other.
   "Foxes have remarkable lungs. Therefore the lungs of a fox will remedy asthma."

2. *Irrelevant conclusion*. A conclusion is irrelevant to the reasoning that led to it.
   "I don't think Mr. Jones abused his child. He acts like a normal father; he even spends time on the weekend repairing his car."

3. *Emotional reasoning*. Using our emotions or feelings as evidence of a truth.
   "This is true because I feel it is true."

4. *Fallacy of labeling*. Faulty assumptions that a label explains something when it does not.
   "Mr. Young says he hears voices. Clearly he is psychotic."

5. *Hasty generalization*. Considering only exceptional cases and generalizing from those cases to a rule that fits only those exceptions.
   Bill and a friend are discussing the director of their agency. Bill says, "He is a total failure because he has not increased funding for our agency."

6. *Overlooking the role of chance*. Assuming that an outcome due to chance is related to past occurrences.
   "My next baby must be a boy. We've had five girls."

7. *Fallacy of composition*. Assuming that what is true of parts of a whole is true of the whole.
   "Jane is behaviorally oriented. Therefore, staff at her agency are behaviorally oriented."

8. *Fallacy of division*. Assuming what is true of the whole is true of each individual part of the whole.
   "Mercer Center's Cancer Center has a good reputation. Dr. A, who works there, is a good surgeon."

9. *False cause*. Relying on the mere fact of coincidence of temporal succession to identify a cause.
   John works in a large office. He applied for a promotion, but a woman received it. He says to himself, "It's clear that the woman was promoted and not me because she is a woman."

10. *Invalid disjunction (either/or-ing)*. Considering only two options when more than two should be considered.
    "We must either hospitalize him or leave him to wander the streets."

11. *Fallacies related to the availability of material*. Accepting the first explanation for an event that occurs to you without considering other, less obvious explanations.

"I can see he is an angry man by how he acts in the office. I think he is guilty of abusing his wife."

12. *Argument from ignorance.* Assuming that something is true simply because it has not been shown to be false, or that it is false simply because it has not been shown to be true.

"You don't have any proof that your method works. Therefore, I don't think it does."

13. *Appeal to authority.* Arguing that a claim is true based purely on an authority's status with no reference to evidence.

"Dr. Monston said . . ."

14. *Argumentation ad populum.* Assuming that "if everyone else thinks this way, it must be right." Appeal to popularity.

"Everyone is using this new method. I think we should use it, too."

15. *Argumentum ad hominem.* Attacking or praising some aspects of a person's character, lifestyle, race, religion, sex, and so on, as evidence for (or against) a conclusion, even when these circumstances are irrelevant to the situation being examined.

"He has a point. But look at how he is dressed."

16. *Inference by manner of presentation.* How believable is this person?

"She gave a convincing talk. I'm going to use her methods."

17. *Appeal to experience.*

"I've seen 5 clients and used X successfully with all of them. It works!"

18. *Appeal to tradition.*

"That's the way we have always done it. We should continue to use these methods."

19. *Influence by testimonials.*

"I believe it works because Mrs. Rivera said she tried it and it helped."

20. *Appeal to newness.*

"It's the latest thing. We should try it, too."

21. *Assume hard-headed—therefore, hard-hearted.*

"She can't really care about her clients if she spends that much time questioning our agency's methods."

22. *Assume that good intentions result in good services* (e.g., protect clients from harm).

In response to a question from a client about an agency's effectiveness, you say: "We really care about our clients."

23. *Weak documentation.*

Accepting a claim based on vague, undocumented evidence.

24. *"Should" statements* (e.g., "I must do this," "I should feel that," "They should do this") are fallacies when they are used as the sole reason for behavior.
    A supervisor tells her staff: "You should evaluate your practice."

25. *Personalization.* Assuming you are the cause of some event for which you were not primarily responsible, or taking personally a statement that is not directed toward you.
    A client failed to keep an agreement that you believe he could have kept. You say to yourself, "It's my fault."

26. *Magnification/minimization.* Magnifying our negative characteristics or mistakes or minimizing positive characteristics or accomplishments.
    Mrs. Silvers (a supervisor) congratulates Max on his success with his client. He says, "Oh, it's really not a big thing."

27. *Mental filter.* Picking out some small aspect of a situation (often a negative one) and focusing on this so that the bigger picture is ignored. All events are viewed through the filter of one aspect of the situation.
    "I just don't like the way my director dresses."

Source: See, for example, *Intelligence Applied: Understanding and Increasing Your Intellectual Skills,* by R. J. Sternberg and J. Kagan (1986), San Diego, CA: Harcourt Brace Jovanovich; *Straight and Crooked Thinking: Thirty-Eight Dishonest Tricks of Debate,* by R. H. Thouless (1974), London, UK: Pan Books.

7

Classification, Authority, and Focusing on Pathology

Additional sources of fallacy that have special relevance to clinical decision making are discussed in this chapter. These include fallacies related to classification, appeals to authority, a pathological set, and the rule of optimism.

CONCERNS AND FALLACIES RELATED TO CLASSIFICATION

Classification (sorting objects, events, or people into different categories and giving different names to these categories) is necessary in everyday life as well as in clinical practice. Possible classifications can be illustrated by diagrams (see Exhibit 7.1). Classification is of great interest in the helping professions (e.g., see Taylor & Rutter, 2002). An enormous literature is devoted to developing measures that will permit the reliable and valid classification of clients into different categories. Among the potential benefits of classification are selection of effective interventions and standard usage of terms. Predictions or new discoveries may result from classification. Dmitri Mendeleev's classification of the elements according to their atomic weights and chemical properties enabled the prediction of the discovery of unknown elements. Labels that point to effective interventions are helpful. Meehl (1973) suggests that not applying the correct label may prevent clients from receiving appropriate help. Labels can normalize client concerns. For example, parents who have been struggling to understand why their child is developmentally slow may view themselves as failures. Recognition that this slowness is a result of a specific kind of disability can be a great relief. Too often, however, labels, although they may sound sophisticated, offer little or no information about what to do to help a client. In addition, labels often have iatrogenic effects; they medicalize, stigmatize, and pathologize clients (Morgan, 1983; Watson & Eack, 2011).

Exhibit 7.1 Venn Diagrams Illustrating Relationships Between A's and B's for Different Premises

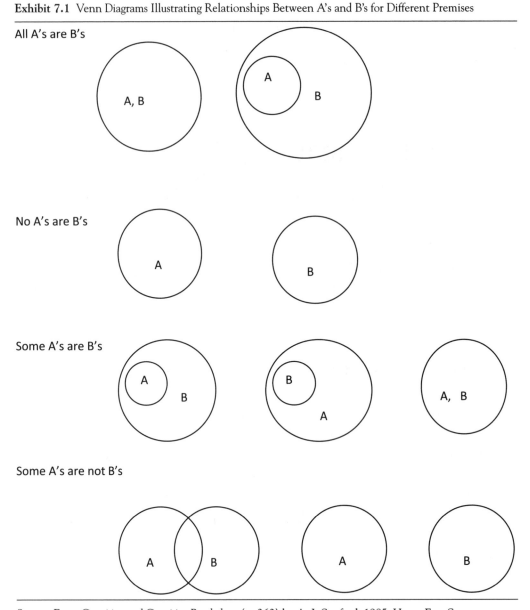

Source: From *Cognition and Cognitive Psychology* (p. 360) by A. J. Sanford, 1985, Hove, East Sussex, England: Erlbaum. Copyright 1985 by Lawrence Erlbaum. Reprinted by permission.

Classification requires overlooking differences among objects, people, or events and focusing on similarities. Faulty classification may occur when the classification is not exhaustive or exclusive, is not adequate to the purpose for which it was created, or does not permit precise divisions, resulting in serious marginal cases (e.g., Shorter & Tyrer, 2003). A belief that classification systems accurately reflect the world can lead clinicians astray. "Science and common sense inquiry alike do not discover the ways in which events are grouped in the world; they invent ways of grouping" (Abercrombie, 1960, p. 113). Attention may be directed toward what is observable, which may not reflect relevant factors. (See Exhibit 7.2.) At lower levels of abstraction, difficulties may not be great in making correct classifications. It is at the higher levels of abstraction that problems often occur. Even at lower levels, sloppy thinking may lead to inaccurate generalizations, such as "a rose is a rose"; in the context of a competition among rose growers for the most beautiful rose of the year, a rose is certainly not a rose. Even the same rose may differ from day to day. The context influences the features attended to in categorizing an event, object, or behavior; these may differ from person to person and from time to time. For example, Rosenhan's (1973) research suggests that once a normal person enters a psychiatric hospital he or she will continue to be viewed as mentally ill. Overlooking cultural differences may result in misdiagnosis, neglect of problems, or overestimation or underestimation of pathology (Sue & Sue, 2002; Westermeyer, 1987).

Exhibit 7.2 Lymphatic, Sanguine, Bilious, Nervous

LYMPHATIC.   SANGUINE.

BILIOUS.   NERVOUS.

Source: In George Combe, *Outlines of Phrenology* (Boston, MA, 1838). General Research Division, New York Public Library, Astor, Lenox, and Tilden Foundations. Reprinted in *Madness in America* (p. 71), by L. Gamwell and N. Tomes, 1995, Ithaca, NY: Cornell University Press.

Classification as a Method of Control

Many writers, past and present, have argued that psychiatric classification serves the interests of the ruling majority (Sedgwick, 1982; Szasz, 1994). "Categories and labels are powerful instruments for social regulation and control and they are often employed for obscure, covert, or hurtful purposes: to degrade people, to deny them access to opportunity, to exclude 'undesirables' whose presence in some way offends, disturbs familiar custom, or demands extraordinary effort" (Hobbs, 1975, p. 11). Those who receive psychiatric or criminal labels are often those who are observed in deviant acts, sometimes because they are poor and so have little access to privacy. The fact that assignment of a deviant status and subsequent actions partially depend on social class supports the social control function of labels. New labels are created to identify and document behavior that deviates from the norm. "Whoever is exuberant is labeled overly emotional. . . . Whoever stands up for himself suffers from a combativeness that could turn into protest and contentiousness" (p. 112). "Confronted with new forms of deviance and abusive behavior, which might be symptoms of an unbearable, abnormal life, lists and technical terms are found to categorize them. This may be brought up to date with a vague reference to a hypothetical 'social' factor, which supposedly guarantees that the problem will be confronted in contemporary modern terms. In the meantime, prisons and asylums continue to preserve their marginal, class character" (p. 218).

Szasz (2003) suggests that those who try to resist involuntary commitment as mental patients are then labeled "paranoid." Critics of the mental health industry argue that, rather than fulfilling promises of alleviating human suffering, professions such as psychiatry, psychology, and social work have helped to create institutions and practices that classify, define, and control behavior (including coercive efforts) and fulfill the interest of dominant groups (Basaglia, 1987, p. 151; Cohen & Timimi, 2008). There is, however, a symbiotic relationship between those applying labels and those who are labeled; for example, the latter escape responsibility for their behavior and the former have a reason for lack of success (e.g., labeling a difficult client as having a "borderline personality").

Use of Classification to Expand Turf

Expanding the boundaries of what is normal and what is not, what is healthy and what is not is a key way used to expand potential users (and alleged needers) of services and medications. Stretching the boundaries of what is viewed as high blood pressure brings in thousands of new individuals now urged to take medication that may do more harm than good. Those newly labeled as "not normal" now need help. This *disease mongering* (e.g., overdiagnosis and overtreatment) is rampant (e.g., Payer, 1992; Welch, Schwartz, & Woloshin, 2011).

Classification as Stigmatizing

Labels that limit exploration do not have to be fancy ones like *hyperactive* or *paranoid*; they can be everyday terms like *old lady*. Someone who carries a negative label such as *schizophrenic* often is regarded as if he possesses only the characteristics of this category (Rosenhan, 1973). Classification magnifies and strengthens differences between people, perpetuating the isolation of those labeled from others. Psychiatric classification systems have been criticized for blaming the victim for his plight rather than examining the social, economic, and political circumstances related to concerns (e.g., Cohen & Timimi, 2008). Although Axis IV (psychosocial and environmental problems) is included in the *Diagnostic and Statistical Manual of Mental Disorders*, in everyday practice, little attention may be given to this. Critics of the *DSM* raise concerns about the growing number of behaviors classified as mental disorders. For example, McReynolds (1989) suggests that it seems inappropriate to view children's problems in reading, spelling, and arithmetic as psychiatric disorders. Is enuresis really a mental disorder? It is included in the *DSM*. Such labels may result in the neglect of environmental conditions that require attention. They do not reflect changes that take place; that is, even though changes occur, the same label (such as *retarded*) may be retained. Acceptance of a label may prematurely close off consideration of options.

Misleading Assumption of Understanding

Causal relationships are not necessarily implied by classification. Indeed, the Introduction to the *Diagnostic and Statistical Manual of Mental Disorders* (American Psychiatric Association, 2000) states that the psychiatric labels described suggest neither etiology nor service guidelines. One way labels are used is as shorthand terms to refer to specific behaviors. A teacher may use the term *attention-deficit/hyperactivity disorder* (ADHD) to refer to the fact that a student often gets out of his seat at school and talks out of turn in class. She may use this label as a summary term to refer to these behaviors. A second way labels are used is as a diagnostic category that has causal implications. Where a label connotes more than a cluster of behaviors, it involves additional assumptions about the person labeled, which supposedly will be of value in altering the situation. Slips may be made form using a label as a description to using it as an explanation. Even though psychiatric labels are said *not* to carry treatment implications in everyday practice, they often *do* have this use. For example, a counselor, after verifying that a student does engage in certain behaviors, may agree that he has ADHD, meaning that he has a mental disorder, and therefore should be placed on medication. That is, inferences are based on observed behavior that a condition of ADHD exists, and intervention recommendations stem from these inferences. In fact, the label is based simply on the observed behaviors. This is an example of the use of a descriptive term as a pseudoexplanatory term (see also

Chapter 13). Even if criteria described in the *DSM* are accurately used (unlikely because of reliability problems), inferences about causation based on these occurrences may be inaccurate. For example, rather than being caused by a brain disorder, related behaviors may be a result of environmental contingencies (e.g., Timimi, 2002).

> Intervention programs cannot be based solely on a diagnostic or classification category such as "depression" or "attention-deficit disorder" because such topographically based [description of form] diagnoses do not identify which of many possible determinants are operational for a particular client. Diagnoses typically provide only an array of possible causal factors. The generalizability of the suggested variables and weights to a particular client cannot be presumed.
>
> Diagnosis can facilitate the design of intervention programs only if any of three conditions are met: (1) specific causal paths are invariably associated with specific diagnostic categories, (2) a hierarchy of the most probable paths or their weights is associated with specific diagnostic categories, and/ or (3) effective interventions are available for specific diagnostic categories regardless of within-category variance in causality. These conditions are seldom met. (Haynes, 1992, p. 109)

Classification Based on Consensus Rather Than Empirical Data

The consensual nature of diagnostic categories is reflected in controversies about adding the terms *self-defeating personality disorder, sadistic personality disorder,* and *premenstrual syndrome* (later changed to *late luteal phase dysphoric disorder*) to the DSM and reliance on voting to make decisions. The consensus base on which diagnoses are identified is often downplayed or obscured by the scientific narrative within which diagnoses are framed. Houts (2002) suggests that "the field of modern psychopathology has garnered authority and legitimacy, both professional and civic, by casting its knowledge claims within a master narrative of scientific discovery and progress" (p. 23). (See also Boyle, 2002.) Critics of the brain disease view of troubled, troubling, and dependent behaviors note that basic questions are often ignored such as "What is a disease?" "Are behaviors diseases?" (Szasz, 1994). Items listed in the *DSM* have grown by leaps and bounds. Hundreds of alleged disorders are described in the *Diagnostic and Statistical Manual of Mental Disorders,* and spirited discussions take place about adding or removing entries. Such psychiatric labels must be applied to clients as a requirement for third-party payments. Cantor (1982) suggests that psychiatric diagnostic knowledge conforms better to a fuzzy prototype description, in which categories are described by a set of correlated features, than it does to a small set of necessary and sufficient defining features, as in the normative descriptions in the *DSM*. According to the classical model, categorization is simply a matter of presence or absence of all of the defining features of a category. By contrast, the prototype model views categorization as a probabilistic process of assessing degree of similarity of a particular target to each of the prototypes for a set of relevant categories—categorization is a matter of degree (Cantor, 1982, p. 33).

Debates concerning other labels illustrate the consensual nature of diagnosis. For example, the term *learning disability* included different referents at different times on the list of skills a learning-disabled person may have difficulty acquiring. Former definitions included listening, speaking, reading, writing, reasoning, and mathematics and more recently social skills. The U.S. Department of Education, concerned with the increase in the number of students identified as learning disabled, warned that inclusion of social skills deficiencies would increase the number of children classified as learning disabled and eligible for special education services (Landers, 1987, p. 350). (See also Merrell & Walker, 2004.) This category has been further expanded over recent years.

Labeling theorists stress the relativity with which labels are used in accord with changing societal views about what is proper and improper behavior (Lemert, 1951; Scheff, 1984a, 1984b). It is argued that labels reflect moral judgments based on societal definitions of what is normal and abnormal. The relationship between judgments of moral character and ascriptions of deviance is emphasized by sociologists as well as by those who have been critical of accepted psychiatric practices (see Chapter 2). In the labeling theory of mental illness, "symptoms of mental illness" are conceptualized as a kind of "nonconformity: the violation of residual rules" (Scheff, 1984a, p. 188). The term *residual rules* refers to all of those situations in which a conventional label of deviance, such as drunkenness, cannot readily be found. Scheff (1984a) suggests that it is here, in this residual category, that the label "mental illness" is applied. Rule breaking may occur for a variety of different reasons, only some of which (a small percentage according to labeling theorists) are a true result of disease.

A question of concern to labeling theorists is: "From whatever cause, why are some [symptoms] short-lived or self-limited and others stable?" (Scheff, 1984b, p. 189). They suggest that societal reactions to residual rule breaking stabilize the symptoms and result in a career of deviance. Thus, within labeling theory, the label itself is considered to be partly responsible for the continuation of and increase in deviant acts. Labeling is viewed as a behavior that varies from culture to culture, from person to person, and from time to time, and which has social functions in relation to regulating the boundaries between accepted and unaccepted behavior. This stance is very different from a psychiatric one, in which there is a search for an objective diagnostic label for a client that justifies certain consequent actions, such as reimbursement for services (see *DSM-IV-R*,

American Psychiatric Association, 2000). In the former instance there is a concern that labeling stigmatizes clients and encourages deviant behavior, and diverts attention from client strengths and related environmental factors; also, that it results in "blaming the victim" and deflects attention away from social, economic, and political conditions that encourage deviant behavior.

Classification as Offering an Illusion of Objectivity

Classification often offers an illusion of objectivity. What is normal? What is the "divine" average? (Creadick, 2010). In *Perfectly Average*, Anna Creadick (2010) describes the obsession with "what is normal" in the post–World War II era in the United States.

> Much of the rhetoric and imagery of postwar culture was coercive—telling Americans how to be men, how to be women, how to be parents, how to be sexual, how to be political, how to dress, what to buy, where to live, how to seem: normal. The chorus of "experts" spoke in new ways during the postwar decades, and at greater volume. Advice literature, produced by churches, schools, the government, and the media, was ubiquitous. *Dr. Spock's Baby and Child Care*, for example, had sold twice as many copies by 1965 as had the all-time fiction best seller, *Peyton Place*. (Creadick, 2010, p. 5)

The view of "normal" as the condition of the average man or woman acquires the meaning of the healthy condition. But is it? Acceptance of the statistically normal condition as equivalent to the psychologically healthy one results in pathologizing people who vary from the statistical norm and even imposing intervention on such individuals. The vagueness of the word *normal* and the tendency of professionals to link the term with *healthy* are discussed by Abercrombie (1960) in her work with medical students. (See also the discussion of reification in Chapter 5.) Photography played a key role in the invention of the label of hysteria. Patients in the Salpetriere were bribed with promises of special status to assume poses depicting "hysterical attacks" (Didi-Huberman, 1982/2003).

Incorrect Classification of People

Incorrect classification may result in inappropriate selection of interventions. Classification may result in false positives or false negatives. The consequences of a false positive (for example, saying someone is a danger to society when he or she is not) or a false negative (that is, deciding someone is not a danger to others when he or she is) depend on the situation. The less reliable and valid a measure, the greater the likelihood of incorrect classification. Concerns about the reliability and validity of *DSM* categories have been described by many critics (e.g., Houts, 2002; Kirk, 2010; Kirk & Kutchins, 1992b; Kutchins & Kirk, 1997). Overestimating the accuracy of measures and ignoring base-rate data (the frequency with which a sign or symptom occurs in a population) increase the possibility of inaccurate classification (see Chapter 15).

Blurring the Difference Between Degrees of Avoidable Suffering

Consider *post-traumatic stress disorder*, a term originally developed to refer to shell-shocked Vietnam War veterans. This is now applied also to relatively minor stresses (Summerfield, 2001). Donovan (2004) refers to this as "the erasure of degrees of suffering and fear" (p. 153). Summerfield (2001) argues that there has been a medicalization of trauma (viewing this as a health concern) when indeed much trauma is a direct result of stress induced by events such as wars and power imbalances in society resulting in rape, torture, and mutilation and constant fear and lack of basic necessities such as food and water. (See also Eagle, 2002.) Who benefits and who loses from this expansion of a psychiatric framing and obscuring of environmental causes?

Use of Vague Terms

Diagnostic labels are typically imprecise. They say little about positive attributes, potential for change, and change that does occur, and say too much about presumed negative characteristics of individuals and limits to change. Symptom lists are often quite vague, as illustrated by the following example of symptoms used to diagnose ADHD.

A. Either (1) or (2):

    (1) six (or more) of the following symptoms of inattention have persisted for at least 6 months to a degree that is maladaptive and inconsistent with developmental level: *Inattention*

        (a) often fails to give close attention to details or makes careless mistakes in schoolwork, work, or other activities.

        (b) often has difficulty sustaining attention to tasks or play activities.

        (c) often does not seem to listen when spoken to directly.

        (d) often does not follow through on instructions and fails to finish schoolwork, chores, or duties in the workplace (not due to oppositional behavior or failure to understand instruction).

        (e) often has difficulty organizing tasks and activities.

        (f) often avoids, dislikes, or is reluctant to engage in tasks that require sustained mental effort (such as schoolwork or homework).

(g) often loses things necessary for tasks or activities (e.g., toys, school assignments, pencils, books, or tools).

(h) is often easily distracted by extraneous stimuli.

(i) is often forgetful in daily activities. (American Psychiatric Association, 2000, pp. 92–93).

What is a "careless mistake"? What exactly does "fails to give close attention to details" mean? A distinction can be made between vague and ambiguous terms; ambiguous terms can be clarified by describing the context in which the term is used. Vague terms remain imprecise even when the context is clear (Michalos, 1971, p. 89). Examples of vague clinical terms include *supportive therapy, family systems theory, resistance,* and *sociopath.* Although some terms may have more precise meanings, this does not mean they are used precisely; that is, they may mean different things to different people, resulting in different classifications and decisions (see discussion of the one word, one meaning fallacy in Chapter 5).

False Dilemma (Either/Or-ing)

It may be proposed that there are just two possibilities in relation to a question when there are many. A clinician may argue that either a client is mentally disturbed or he is not. Such accounts get in the way of discovering individual variations. This fallacy often occurs in conjunction with other fallacies, such as the straw person argument, which offers a distorted view of a position (Kahane, 1995). A continuum may be involved rather than a binary representation, as in family *or* individual therapy, drug dependent *or* not, dysfunctional *or* functional, and sick *or* well. The tendency to use a binary classification system, in which people are labeled as either having or not having something (for example, as being an alcoholic or not), obscures the continuous nature of behaviors; a continuous distribution is transformed into a binary one. Chauncey (1995) describes the strict heterosexual/homosexual binary as a "stunningly recent creation" (p. 94).

Contrary statements may be presented as if they were contradictory statements (Engel, 1994). Contrary statements are two statements that cannot both be true but may both be false. Contradictory statements are those that cannot both be true nor can they both be false (for example, "either today is New Year's Day or it is not"). The fallacy of the false dilemma presents two contraries as two contradictory statements. Engel (1994) classified this under fallacies of presumption, since facts are overlooked—namely, the fact that choices are not limited to only two alternatives. This fallacy is known also as the either/or fallacy and black-and-white fallacy. A remedy is to point out other possibilities that have been ignored.

Confusing Inclusion and Exclusion Tests

Some characteristics may indicate that a client is not an X (an exclusion test) whereas others may indicate that if the client has certain characteristics he is an X (an inclusion test). These two kinds of criteria are confused when it is argued that because Mr. A does not have a certain characteristic, he is not an X when, in fact, this characteristic may not be associated with a particular diagnosis (it is not critical to the diagnosis). Meehl (1973) uses the example of a trainee who argues that a patient is not schizophrenic because he does not have "delusions or hallucinations with clear sensorium" (p. 230). Meehl argues that not all schizophrenics have these accessory symptoms.

Incorrect or Misleading Classification of Procedures

Use of punitive lock-downs and other punishment-based programs may be inaccurately described as behavioral when indeed the conditions described are quite the opposite of characteristics of a behavioral approach. Hallmarks of the latter include an emphasis on the use of positive reinforcement. There is a constructional approach to change (e.g., Alberto & Troutman, 2009; Goldiamond, 1984; Layng, 2009; McGimsey, Greene, & Lutzker, 1995; Pryor, 1984). If incorrect classification of procedures results in clients being deprived of helpful methods, those effects are worrisome. The history of psychiatry is replete with euphemisms for cruel and unusual punishment of psychiatric patients (Valenstein, 1986). The pleasant-sounding term *community care* often means that the patient is released from an institution to fend for himself.

Fallacy of Stereotyping

Stereotyping is an incorrect assessment of variability, "a set of people who are labeled as belonging to a given group is presumed to be more homogeneous than is in fact the case" (Holland, Holyoak, Nisbett, & Thagard, 1986, p. 245). It is a false estimate of the complexity of a group. Clinicians often represent people as examples of categories and, on the basis of this classification, entertain certain feelings toward and expectations about them that influence how they respond to these individuals. The fallacy of stereotyping refers to treating a description as if it represents all the individuals in a group of which it may (or may not) be a fairly typical example (Scriven, 1976, p. 209). The past and present clinical literature offers a rich source of stereotypes such as the *schizophrenagenic mother* (now dismissed by most clinicians). Stereotypes are often based on visible characteristics such as gender and race. Stereotypes may be cultural—that is, shared by many people in a society. Other stereotypes are unique to certain individuals, based on their past experiences. Stereotypes are often inaccurate in that they reflect only one of many characteristics of an individual. Consider the homeless. There are many different kinds of homeless people who may need different kinds of services. Similarly, there are many patterns of substance abuse, ranging from once-a-week cocaine use by a middle-class white-collar worker to daily use by a teenager.

Stereotypes influence what we see since we tend to seek information that supports them. Consider a study by Duncan (1976). Subjects watched a videotape of a discussion between two men during which one of the men shoved the other. The race of the actors was varied in different versions. Subjects were asked to classify a behavior whenever they received a signal from the experimenter. More subjects classified the black protagonist's behavior as violent than so classified the white protagonist's behavior, especially if the person shoved was white. Brian Nosek and his colleagues (Nosek, Banaji, & Greenwald, 2002) developed the Implicit Association Test (a computer-based test of implicit attitudes). Data collected on 600,000 test takers indicated that both white and black participants had an implicit preference for white faces and names. Preferences shown on the test were greater than those verbally described, revealing implicit biases to test takers, which is a key purpose of the test—to reveal that we have thoughts, feelings, and behaviors that are not compatible with what we think, feel, and do. The influence of labels on stereotyping is also illustrated by a study in which information about socioeconomic background was varied. One group of subjects was informed that a child was from a high socioeconomic background, and another group of subjects was informed that the child was from a low socioeconomic background (Darley & Gross, 1983). Both groups watched a videotaped performance of the child taking an academic test. Subjects who had received information that the child was from a high socioeconomic background rated her capabilities well above grade level; subjects in the other group rated the child's abilities as below grade level. In both groups, subjects indicated that the ability test was used as evidence to support their ratings.

There is an extensive literature exploring the influence of stereotypes, including those related to race, ethnicity, gender, and class (e.g., Nelson, 2009). Greater attention is given to class-based stereotypes in the United Kingdom compared to the United States. The extent to which class-based stereotypes are ignored in the United States can be seen in the 704-page book *The Psychology of Stereotyping* (Schneider, 2004), where we do not find class mentioned in the index, although we do find some attention to socioeconomic status in the book (e.g., p. 525). We find gender, race, and ethnicity in the index, but no listing for class. (For sources that do attend to class difference, see, for example, Nelson, 2009.) The danger of stereotyping is that the ways in which an individual does not fit a stereotype may be overlooked and incorrect decisions may be made as a result, such as selecting an ineffective intervention or deciding to intervene when there is no good reason to do so. For example, a behavior, thought, or feeling may be normative. This is not to say that intervention is not called for if a behavior pattern is normative. Clearly, this is not true. Consider, for example, the low level of positive feedback and the high level of negative feedback that secondary school teachers may offer their students. This pattern is normative but certainly not desirable, and a school psychologist may strive to reverse it.

Other Sources of Fallacy

In the fallacy of the continuum, it is argued that because there is a continuous distribution of gradations between two extremes, there is no real difference. Staff members in a residential treatment center for adolescents may argue that hitting residents is really no different from yelling at them. A common argument attempting to justify the use of torture makes use of this fallacy, saying that all governments take steps to protect the integrity of their countries and sometimes encroach on the rights of citizens. There is a refusal to recognize a shift from a quantitative to a qualitative difference. In the *slippery-slope* fallacy, a position is opposed on the grounds that, if it is acted on, it will result in a series of inevitable negative consequences, which indeed are not inevitable. A familiar example is the domino theory: If Vietnam falls, all of Southeast Asia will fall into Communist hands. (For further discussion of this fallacy, see Walton, 1992.) A clinician may argue (incorrectly) that if a client's overidentification with her father is focused on, a series of negative effects will follow, such as increased anxiety and depression. A decision may be made not to offer services to one needy group of clients on the basis that this would require provision of services to all other needy groups.

APPEALS TO AUTHORITY

As emphasized throughout this book, propaganda ploys take advantage of common human tendencies. We grow up learning to respect authority, and those who use appeals to illegitimate authority take advantage of this tendency. Appeals to authority also take advantage of the principle of social proof; decisions are based on what other people think is correct (as in appeals to traditional wisdom and to consensus). Administrative authority (e.g., via a position of legal or administrative authority) should be distinguished from cognitive authority, "a relationship between two individuals where what one says carries weight or plausibility, within a certain domain or field of expertise, for the other individual" (Walton, 2008a, p. 211). The fallacy *ad verecundiam* (appeal to respect or reverence) refers to fallacious appeals to authority in argument—that is, to the abuse of appeals to alleged authority or expert opinion in order to prevent a respondent in an argument from asking critical questions in further dialogue on an issue

(Walton, 1995, pp. 278–279). These fallacious instances should be "distinguished from instances of critically weak, faulty or incomplete appeals to authority in argument where the proponent has failed to back up one or more of the required steps of documentation . . ." (p. 279). Those who use unfounded authority try to prevail unfairly. There is an effort to suppress critical questions. As Walton (2008a) notes, "appeal to authority is an inherently weak type of plausible argumentation that can go badly wrong. It can be [and often is] weak and undocumented" (p. 244).

Appeals to unfounded authority are common in the professional literature, such as citing a famous person to support a claim when in fact he or she has not conducted any critical tests of the claim and including citations that do not provide empirical support for related claims. Lists of programs distributed by governmental agencies alleged to be "evidence-based" have been found to be based on research that has significant methodological flaws (Gorman, Conde, & Huber, 2007; Gorman & Huber, 2009). And just because a claim is accompanied by a reference is not a good reason for assuming it is accurate. We would have to know what is in the reference cited. For all we know, the reference refers to someone's uninformed opinion. Misleading citations are a key form of propaganda in the professional literature. They give an illusion of credibility (Greenberg, 2009). Any appeal to authority such as "expertise" is a kind of plausible argument and should be "treated as fallible" (Walton, 2008a, p. 211). Experts may be biased or prejudiced. They may misunderstand material. They may be paid for their testimony and thus have something to gain. People contacted for "expert" opinion by journalists may not be those most knowledgeable in a subject. Thus, questioning "cognitive authority" is wise.

What about credentials? Do they reflect special knowledge? The possession of a credential or degree in an area may indicate some level of knowledge in a subject. But is the appeal to a credential a substitute for offering cogent reasons for a claim? Appeals to expert status are often buttressed by use of pseudotechnical jargon geared to impress unwary listeners. In some cases ("Doctors report that," "Studies show that"), we may not even be informed about who is responsible for the statement (Michalos, 1971). Proper appeals to authority should be distinguished from improper ones. (See also discussion of quackery in Chapter 4.) The following rules of thumb can be used to distinguish proper from improper appeals.

- Remember that an authority in one area is not necessarily an authority in other areas.
- Do not accept the opinions of authorities when experts disagree or there is little known in a field. For example, experts often disagree about the sanity of a defendant; therefore, it would be unwise to accept the opinion offered by any one person.

- Examine the evidence, reasons, and arguments when experts disagree. If psychiatrists claim that a client is psychotic, find out why they believe this and evaluate the reasons given.
- Review the track record of the expert. (Kahane, 1995)

Inappropriate appeals to authority can take quite subtle forms in the area of clinical decision making, and occur during clinical interviews as well as in case conferences, in discussions among colleagues, and during moments of self-reflection. Data supporting a position may be described in detail, whereas data counter to it may be mentioned only in passing or not at all. The remedy to appeals to authority is to point out that no evidence is offered in support of the appeal or to request or seek such evidence. Appeals to authority are another kind of informal fallacy—that is, they may occur without any formal error. Michalos (1971) identifies 16 varieties of pseudoauthority. A number that occur in clinical situations are reviewed in the sections that follow. Some of the informal fallacies discussed under the influence of language in Chapter 5 could be included here as well, such as the use of pseudotechnical jargon. Appeals to authority are often used to present preferred positions with a false aura of credibility.

Popular Sentiments

The feelings and attitudes of a group may be appealed to in order to gain acceptance for a position. In the statement "As members of the American Psychological Association, we know that," the appeal is to a respected professional group. Stereotyped descriptions of an out-group (as in the statement "Sophisticated diagnostics are eschewed in narrow behavioristic approaches") appeal to the sentiments of an in-group. Although appeals to popular sentiment may make people feel better, superior, or complacent, they do little to advance the quality of arguments. Such appeals are particularly insidious in a clinical setting, where they may bolster personal beliefs about what is normal and what is deviant without the clinician recognizing this connection (see later section on fallacies related to a pathological set). The remedy for appeals to popular sentiments is to point out that no evidence is offered for the position stated.

Misleading Aura of Authority

Most of the material in the media consists of secondary information: "Most news is given to reporters, not discovered by them" (Kahane, 1971, p. 153). However, the material is often presented in a way that makes it seem as if it were based on firsthand experiences. Opinions may be presented as facts, as in the statements that "reality therapy works" or "codependents need help." Here we should ask, "What evidence is provided for the statement?" The kind of evidence that is relevant depends on the kind of claim made (see Chapter 12). References cited in support of a comment in an article may in fact provide none (Greenberg, 2009). For example, a claim may be made that feminist counseling has been shown to be effective, followed by a series of references that, in fact, contain no data supporting the claim. Gambrill and Gibbs (2009) refer to this as "uncritical documentation." Reliance on secondary sources amplifies such errors. A misleading aura of authority may be given by using impressive-sounding but vague terms and by obtuse descriptions of data analysis methods or clinical procedures in place of clear accounts (which may reveal lack of evidence for a claim). The call for transparency in evidence-based practice, including clear descriptions of limitations of research studies, discourages hiding of research flaws that may result in inaccurate conclusions that, in turn, result in ill-advised decisions, such as use of ineffective or harmful interventions.

Popular People and Irrelevant Authority

The authority of popular people may be appealed to in order to support a claim. A writer may cite Freud far more often than is necessary in a manuscript submitted to a psychoanalytic journal, hoping that such name-dropping will lend an aura of credibility to the work. This tactic is often used in advertising. For example, a famous baseball player may be shown talking about the positive attributes of a cereal. Gullible viewers may not realize that an outstanding baseball player is not necessarily an expert in evaluating cereal. This appeal (as well as the next one) is a type of ad hominem argument (see Chapter 6).

Titles and Supposed Experts

In some variants of this use of pseudoauthority ("Doctors report that," "Studies show that"), we may not even be informed which particular person is responsible for the statement (Michalos, 1971). The studies cited were supposedly conducted by scrupulous, well-trained researchers. The possession of a credential or degree in an area may indicate some level of knowledge in a subject. The question is, does this background by itself substantiate the claim made by the bearer of these credentials? Appeals to authority can be buttressed by use of pseudotechnical jargon geared to impress listeners with the speaker's erudition. (See discussion of pseudoscience in Chapter 4.) The remedy is to ask the person to explain points more simply.

Traditional Wisdom

It is often assumed that what is old is best, with no evidence offered in support of the view other than that people used that method in the past. An example is: "That's the way I've always done it." Reluctance to question such appeals in case conferences may be related to not wishing to accept an unpopular view or to appear contrary or difficult. Appeal to traditional wisdom may be combined with other kinds of appeals to authority, as in the statement "Historians have found that this has been the custom for many centuries" (reference to supposed experts). Or it may be combined with question-begging definitions. A clinician may say, "The traditional role of women is the proper role because it is the traditional role" (Michalos, 1971, p. 40). One antidote to persuasion by appeals to traditional wisdom is being informed about the history of science or medicine, which offers countless examples of times when the majority view or traditional wisdom was incorrect, often resulting in harm to people.

Appeals to Consensus (Authority of the Many)

This variant is also referred to as the appeal to large numbers (Michalos, 1971) and the fallacy of popularity (MacLean, 1981). It refers to attempted support of a claim by saying that many people agree with a position (see discussion of social proof in Chapter 5). "We view a behavior as more correct to the degree that we see others performing it" (Cialdini, 1984, p. 117). Alcoholics Anonymous may claim that its success is demonstrated by the thousands of people who have taken part in the program. But what percentage of those who participate in such programs stop drinking, and for how long? Appeals to consensus and traditional wisdom may block the acceptance of new methods for years or decades. Consider the neglect of Semmelweiss's discovery that puerperal fever could be eliminated "by having doctors wash their hands in a chlorine solution before examining the mother" (Broad & Wade, 1982, p. 137). His work was ignored for years, resulting in thousands of unnecessary deaths. The authority of the psychiatric profession is often appealed to in an effort to bolster claims, as in "Most psychiatrists believe that psychotropic medication is of benefit for clients."

Provincialism

Provincialism is a variety of the use of traditional wisdom and popular sentiment. It appeals to the tendency to identify with an in-group and to assume that the familiar is better or more important, when it may not be. Imposition of Western views of psychological problems and proposed remedies on non-Western clients is a form of provincialism in clinical practice. Provincialism is carried to an extreme in cases in which beliefs are based on loyalty to a position rather than on evidence. This appeal, as well as plain folks and bandwagon appeals that are variants on it, exerts influence through the principle of social proof (see Chapter 5). The plain folks appeal is at the opposite end of the spectrum from snob appeal and the appeal of pseudojargon (MacLean, 1981,

p. 39). This tactic works (if it works) by associating the appearance of simplicity and straightforwardness with a particular view of reality. In fact, there may be little relationship between reality and this appearance.

Bandwagon Appeal

In the bandwagon appeal, it is assumed that everybody is behind something: What is implied is that everybody who "knows what's best" supports a position. An article about a topic that is controversial may start with "We all know that." This tactic takes advantage of our tendency to be influenced by what other people do: If other people do it, it must be good or right (the principle of social proof). This kind of pitch partly accounts for the fads and fashions in psychotherapy. There are a number of questions that should be raised, such as, "Is everybody doing it?" Probably not. Even if many people do act in a certain way or accept a certain belief, that does not mean they are correct. History is replete with infamous examples of the acceptance by many of incorrect ideas. Consider the hundreds of papers by scientists and doctors in the early twentieth century concerning N-rays—these were "discovered" in many places, including the human brain (Nye, 1980). Popular clinical approaches are not necessarily those that help clients achieve valued outcomes (e.g., Jacobson, Foxx, & Mulick, 2005).

Imaginary Authority

Reference may be made to imaginary evidence; that is, a speaker or writer may refer to evidence that does not exist. A psychologist may report that he has seen many clients with anorexia so he can speak with authority about this disorder, when in fact he has seen one such client. An infamous example of the use of imaginary authority is the extraordinary case of Sir Cyril Burt. This is perhaps the best-known and most flagrant example of "the failure of psychologists to spot dogma masquerading as objective truth" (Broad & Wade, 1982, p. 203). Burt invented data to support his views. "He used his mastery of statistics and gift of lucid exposition to bamboozle alike his bitterest detractors and those who claimed his greatness as a psychologist" (p. 204). He submitted articles in favor of his views under an assumed name and published them in the *British Journal of Statistical Psychology*, of which he was editor for 16 years. He not only made up data, he invented coauthors "from the vast deep of his tormented imagination and clothed them so well in the semblance of scientific argument that the illusion fooled all his fellow scientists for as much as thirty years" (p. 204). Some argue that the fabrication of data is becoming more common as pressures mount to publish and as competition for funding becomes keener. For a spirited (and concerning) discussion, see, for example, Sackett and Oxman (2003). (For discussions of fraud and error in science, see Judson,

2004; Miller & Hersen, 1992.) Each year brings some retraction of published articles on the grounds that data were fabricated (e.g., see Limb, 2011). Claims may be attributed to a famous person who never said or wrote such a thing. Inflated claims of knowledge abound (Ioannidis, 2008). Indeed, this was one of the key reasons for the development of evidence-based practice.

Other Kinds of Appeals to Authority

Some writers and speakers refer to the authority of a proverb, maxim, cliché, or aphorism (a concise statement of a principle, truth, or sentiment), instead of offering evidence related to their position. These sayings have a ring of truth that encourages their acceptance (see discussion of empathic explanations in Chapter 3). They can usually be interpreted in a variety of ways and thus may seem psychologically compelling. When asked why he does not carefully evaluate his work with clients, a clinician may say that "capturing human experience is like trying to describe a beautiful aroma; it is not possible." Metaphors and similes may be helpful in suggesting solutions to problems, as well as in offering clients a view of concerns that encourages maintenance of gains—as in the metaphor of a journey used by Marlatt and Gordon (1985) in their relapse prevention program (see also Lakoff & Dean, 2004; Lakoff & Johnson, 1980).

Views may be presented as those of a vague or mysterious and generally respected group or ideal (Michalos, 1971). A clinical supervisor may argue that to challenge her views is to challenge the very authority required to maintain high-quality professional programs. A clinician may support his use of an unfocused approach to therapy by saying that this reflects a humanistic approach to counseling, in which client values are respected and nourished. Snob appeal (authority of a select few) takes advantage of our feeling that we are special—one of a select few. In the past, psychologists were not permitted entry into psychoanalytic training programs: Acceptance required a medical degree, a restriction that ensured privileged entry to psychiatrists. Historians of social work have noted the tendency of social workers to identify with psychiatrists in order to bolster their image. People can sometimes be seduced into going along with a position in an uncritical way (without examining the soundness of the position) by the allure of association with an elite group. Persuasive strategies based on elitism may be combined with strategies based on the principle of liking—for example, friendly overtures may be made toward typically ignored or disliked colleagues to win their support.

In an appeal to faith, we are asked to accept a position based on faith alone—when evidence for or against the claim should be produced. A counselor may tell a client who questions her selection of intervention, "Trust me—I have your interests at heart." This may be combined with an appeal to expertise or longevity: "I've been a psychiatrist for twenty years."

A FOCUS ON PATHOLOGY

Clinicians tend to emphasize client pathology (e.g., Ganzach, 2000). Vague metaphorical descriptions of exotic pathology may appear profound; clear descriptions of complaints and related factors may appear simpleminded. Describing vague, exotic inferences about the presumed causes of a problem may offer an illusion of astuteness and gain the attention of listeners. Whether they are accurate and helpful in minimizing problems is another question. Although there is a great deal of talk and writing about empowerment of clients and focusing on client strengths, everyday practice may not reflect this focus. The psychiatric classification system (DSM) describes hundreds of behaviors viewed as pathological based on consensus. A focus on pathology encourages attention to what is wrong with people. Lack of participation on the part of clients may be attributed to their deficiencies. A search for personal causes obscures environmental obstacles, such as lack of transportation or day care for children; it reflects lack of appreciation for the difficulty of change; resistance is a natural part of any effort to change.

Many writers, both past and present, have noted the recycling of sickness ideology under new euphemisms (such as the term *clinical population*, which is considered to be qualitatively different from nonclinical populations; Bandura, 1978). The terms *healthy* and *unhealthy* have been extended to an ever-wider range of physiological reactions, behaviors, thoughts, and feelings (McCormick, 1996). Such terms select out as unique people with a given behavioral pattern who seek or are sent for help from the much larger group of people with the same pattern (such as excessive use of alcohol) who do *not* seek help. More and more behaviors and related risk factors are referred to as "sicknesses" requiring the help of experts (e.g., see Moynihan, Heath, Henry, & Gøtzsche, 2002). Risks are transformed into diseases (e.g., osteoporosis). Meehl (1973) referred to the tendency to focus on pathology as the "sick-sick" fallacy. Wills (1978) found that professional training increases this tendency.

It is important to accurately identify pathology, especially if there are intervention implications. However, this should be balanced by a search for client assets and potential for change. Undue attention to pathology creates unnecessary fear, results in a neglect of client assets, creates undue pessimism about the possibility of positive outcomes, and may stigmatize clients if negative views are conveyed to clients, significant others, and authorities. For example, a negative label may make it more likely that a client will be involuntarily hospitalized (or imprisoned) and less likely that helpful services will be offered. Negative impressions may be difficult to alter. Negative events have been found to carry more weight than do positive events in a number of areas, including social interaction (e.g., Rook, 1984).

Factors That Encourage an Overemphasis on Pathology

Theories emphasized during graduate education, such as an interest in protecting oneself from failure (you can blame lack of success on the client's brain diseases), reliance on metaphors such as adjustment (connoting maladjustment), lack of awareness of the influence of the biomedical-industrial complex on the creation of alleged illnesses, and an interest in appearing erudite, all may encourage a focus on pathology. Clinicians in many settings encounter a biased sample of individuals—those with rare patterns of behavior, such as severe depression. Inferences of pathology may occur because of lack of familiarity with normative data concerning behaviors, thoughts, or feelings—that is, from a lack of knowledge regarding base rates and the range of individual variability of a behavior. In our increasingly diverse society ignorance concerning cultural differences may result in the imposition of biased views of what is healthy and what is not on clients. To the extent to which clinicians are unaware of cultural differences or ignore them, clients may suffer from arbitrarily imposed views. Defining pathology as deviation from "normal" provides a bonanza of potential pathologies, while at the same time ignoring problems in describing what is normal and who decides this (Creadick, 2010). This is especially true when what is viewed as normal can be changed arbitrarily. Imposition of a clinical label on clients further removes them from individuals considered normal.

Clinical case studies reported in the professional literature focus on pathology and neglect positive attributes of individuals and families. Information about people who do well despite challenges, such as caring for a developmentally disabled child, may be absent. Professional training may bias students toward pathology, not only by what it includes but also by what it excludes such as discussion of the political functions of varying definitions of deviance, a working knowledge of basic behavioral principles describing relationships between behavior and the environment (e.g. see Reid, Patterson, & Snyder, 2002), and information regarding base rates and individual differences. Theories may focus on discovering pathology in both the client's history and current functioning. Students may not be exposed to critiques of the DSM, lending an indoctrination quality to the discussion of related material. A review of 71 courses on psychopathology from 58 different schools of social work showed that such courses typically present a biomedical view of behavior, ignoring alternative viewpoints (Lacasse & Gomory, 2003). Labels for describing behavior at the opposite pole are usually tepid (such as *well-adjusted, normal*). Some more lively labels are suggested in Exhibit 7.3.

Exhibit 7.3 Negative Labels and Positive Counterparts

Negative Label	Positive Counterparts
Paranoia	Perspicacity (sensitivity to the motives and feelings of others); perceptive identification and neutralization of hostile intentions
Depression	Elan vital
Substance abuse	Creative substance use
Obsessive-compulsive disorder	Effective attention to detail; good attention span
Exhibitionism	Freedom from undue modesty
Multiple personality	A creative mixture of personas

An emphasis on dispositional attributions for problems and a tendency to ignore environmental causes (the fundamental attribution error) encourages a pathological view of clients; people rather than their environments are blamed for problems (see discussion of dispositional bias in Chapter 14). The common occurrences of negative experiences in the history of both individuals who do not seek counseling and those who do make it easy to discover pathogenic experiences that are assumed to be responsible for clients' complaints and render the causative character of these symptoms questionable. Renaud and Estess (1961) interviewed 100 men who were selected because there was no indication that they had any problems. They had no history of either mental or psychological conflict and did not complain of any problems. The men were functioning as normal or superior on all objective indices. They were in good health, had attained superior educational and occupational status, and had positive relationships with others, in both their personal and work lives. The interviews held with these 100 men were similar to clinical intake interviews. These interviews revealed all kinds of traumatic events and experiences that could well be considered pathogenic and were at least as serious as experiences in the histories of psychiatric patients.

Clinicians are influenced by the values of the society in which they live. Some have not been exposed to a political and social perspective on deviance—to the fact that what is considered to be a social or personal problem is consensual and relative (ascribed), rather than inherent (fixed). What is considered pathological changes with the times and differs in different cultures. Lack of knowledge about historical differences in how a certain pattern of behavior has been viewed over time encourages pathologizing clients. Consider anxiety in social situations (now dubbed "social anxiety disorder"). In *Shrinking Violets and Casper Milquetoasts*, McDaniel (2003) describes the changing views of reticent, shy behavior. (See also Cottle, 1999.) Ignoring information about base rates and individual difference in environmental challenges increases the likelihood of pathologizing clients and making inaccurate clinical judgments. Most people are shy in some social situations. The fact that a professional organization decides what is and what is not a mental illness illustrates the consensual basis of psychiatric labels. Without knowledge about social, economic, and political factors related to behaviors viewed as deviant, including crimes and psychiatric disorders, associated structural factors such as poverty and related heightened surveillance (of the poor) may be ignored, as described in *Punishing the Poor* by Wacquant (2009). (See also Reiman, 2004.) Without effective skills for handling the inevitable uncertainty and lack of success involved in clinical practice. It is easy to fall into a pathological focus as a protection against failure (Houts, 2002). Negative pronouncements offer a reason for lack of success in remedying or preventing problems.

Personal beliefs about what is normal may encourage a focus on pathology. For example, some psychiatrists continue to believe that homosexuality is an illness despite the decision of the American Psychiatric Association that it is not. How many practitioners carefully review their personal biases in relation to given behaviors? How many accept a view of deviance as ascribed rather than inherent? Many biases are implicit, and it is thus easy to unknowingly impose beliefs about what is normal, what is healthy, and what is good on clients. Since their beliefs usually mirror commonly accepted norms regarding behavior, little in the way of contradiction may challenge personal beliefs. For example, a heterosexual counselor may be consulted by a lesbian couple who want to have a child by artificial insemination. A counselor with a traditional view of family life may respond differently to this request than may a counselor with a broader view of healthy family life. Meehl (1973) suggests that family psychiatrists often harbor a stereo type of what a healthy family should be; and if a family differs from this, it is viewed as a sign of pathology. This tendency is increased by the fact that practitioners tend to be from the middle class and many of their clients are poor or working-class. Meehl notes that clinicians will say, "Yes, we know about that." Knowing about something is not enough—both related skills and values and contingencies that encourage their use are also needed.

THE RULE OF OPTIMISM

In some contexts, such as criminal justice settings, services for the severely and chronically "mentally ill," and child welfare agencies, overattention to pathology may be replaced by the *well-well fallacy* to protect the service system from being overwhelmed. Increasing budget cuts encourage this fallacy; services are ever more residual rather than preventative, especially in the social services. The constraints imposed by managed care may encourage lack of attention to dysfunctional behaviors that should be addressed, as may the rule of optimism. The opposite of the *sick-sick fallacy*, the well-well fallacy refers to the tendency not to see pathology or behavior that harms others when it is actually there. Dingwall, Eekelaar, & Murray (1983) argue that this rule is used in child protection agencies because the resources of the system would be depleted if all families that needed state intervention were taken into the system. This rule states that the least discrediting interpretations of observed conduct will be used (p. 218). These authors suggest cultural relativism as one vehicle through which the rule of optimism is carried out—the view that "any style of child rearing may be justified as a valid cultural statement which should not be illiberally suppressed" (p. 218). The following dialogue illustrates cultural relativism (Dingwall et al., 1983, p. 84).

> *Social Worker:* Her father was very annoyed and beat her with a strap.
> *Senior SW:* With a strap?
> *Social Worker:* Oh, this sort of thing happens in this community.
> *Senior SW:* This violence is very difficult to prove, and we have to accept that it is
> just part of the West Indian culture.

Dingwall and his colleagues found that the more familiar a professional was with a particular area in which a family lived, the more likely such reactions were. Appeals may be made to natural love; the parent–child relationship is viewed as a natural rather than as a social phenomenon, with the implication that a charge of mistreatment is equivalent to an allegation that the parents involved do not share in our common humanity. As with cultural relativism, behaviors are recognized as deviant but there is no allegation of moral liability. These two views "combine to produce an attitude of acceptance towards parental accounts and a sense that an accusation of parental failure is a matter of almost inconceivable gravity" (p. 218). They combine to eliminate the majority of potential cases by "allowing front-line workers to prefer an optimistic reading of client behavior" (p. 82). These authors offer an example in which a child was clearly made a scapegoat. Because her parents demonstrated a capacity for loving relationships with their other children, the agency did not intervene. Just as clinicians may misinterpret the significance of signs that are there, they may misinterpret the importance of signs that are absent (see discussion of nonoccurrences in Chapter 14).

Dingwall and his colleagues highlight the elasticity of the rules of cultural relativism and natural love. "What may seem like eccentricities or perversions are elevated into valid cultural statements" (1983, p. 88). Reliance on these rules encourages acceptance of clients' accounts or conclusions. These authors point out that use of these principles helps to solve the problems faced by helpers. That is, cultural relativism and natural love can be invoked to bridge the gap between ideals and the realities of practice. At a higher level, they serve to maintain current imbalances in resources between those who are poor and those who are not. The rule of optimism may be used to rationalize insufficient services to clients insured by managed care systems. This rule may be balanced against concern to protect clients from serious harm, such as restoring a child who has been abused to parents who again abuse him or her. The fallacy of prevention is another form of the rule of optimism. That is, potential benefits of behaviors alleged to decrease risk of certain diseases are greatly inflated, obscuring the uncertainty of achieving such outcomes.

SUMMARY

Many kinds of classifications are made in clinical practice. Factors that may compromise the accuracy of classification are often ignored, resulting in errors such as inappropriate stereotyping and false dilemmas. Pathological labels may be accepted as describing reality with little understanding of the ascribed nature of these labels and the political, economic, and social functions they serve, for example, to control and regulate undesired behaviors. Clinicians base their selection of practice knowledge on various kinds of authority, some of which are sound (relevant evidence is offered for the claim) and many of which appeal to pseudoauthority (such as popular sentiment, traditional wisdom, and consensus). Clinicians often have a pathological set; they search for deficiencies and neglect client assets. This creates undue pessimism about the possibility of change and may stigmatize clients. Factors that contribute to this tendency include practice theories that emphasize pathology and ignore the role of environmental contingencies; lack of familiarity with the political, social, and economic functions of psychiatric labels; ignorance of norms and the range of individual differences; and protection against failure. An opposite rule, the rule of optimism, may come into play when resources would be overwhelmed by recognizing all the problems and needs that are present. This also serves a function in saving funds that would be required to address the social and economic conditions related to many social and personal problems, such as child maltreatment, depression, and substance abuse.

Decision Aids

8

Content and Procedural Knowledge

Critical thinking skills are not enough to make well-reasoned decisions—specialized knowledge may also be needed. This may concern the following:

- Developmental norms related to given age groups.
- Indicators of physical illness.
- Evidentiary status of assessment measures related to given concerns.
- Propaganda methods used by the biomedical industrial complex to promote sales of products.
- Strategies for enhancing client participation.
- The difference between absolute and relative risk.
- Evidentiary status of intervention methods.
- Risk indicators for suicide attempts.
- Accuracy of different measures of progress.
- Procedures for encouraging generalization and maintenance.

Fox and Swazey (1974) suggest that there are three major causes of failure: (1) lack of available information about the problem, (2) failure to get it, and (3) failure to recognize one's own ignorance. Gaps between practice-related knowledge and what is used by clinicians was a key reason for the development of evidence-based practice. "Reasoning does not occur in a vacuum. Although logic has to do with the forms of argument as distinct from their content, the arguments we encounter in real life have content as well as form, and being able to judge the truth or falsity of that content, clearly a knowledge-based ability, is essential to effective reasoning in any but the most abstract sense" (Nickerson, 1985, p. 359; see also discussion of naturalistic decision making in Chapter 9). Clinicians as well as clients may be bamboozled into accepting bogus claims about practice methods by the emotive persuasiveness of human services advertisements and rhetorical presentations in professional contexts, such as conferences—often because they do not raise questions such as, "What's missing?" Claims may be draped in the trappings of science to increase credibility. Consider appeals to the scientific status of psychiatric classification systems and claims of effectiveness of interventions that do not match empirical findings (e.g., see Houts, 2002; Ioannidis, 2005; Kutchins & Kirk, 1997). Our tendency to have inflated self-assessments of our knowledge contributes to not raising vital questions (Dunning, Heath, & Suls, 2004). Critical thinking skills can be used to increase the percentage of accurate information acquired relative to unsupported or incorrect information.

The term *knowledge* refers to information that decreases or reveals uncertainty about how to attain a certain outcome (Nickerson, 1986b). The importance of knowledge of content was one of the major findings of the study of diagnostic decision making among physicians (Elstein et al., 1978). As Nickerson (1988–1989) points out, "To think effectively in any domain one must know something about the domain and, in general, the more one knows the better" (p. 13). Specialists who make accurate decisions in their area of expertise may not display expertise when making decisions outside of their field. There are different kinds of problems; different aspects of decision making differ in their importance in relation to the kind of problem. For example, in some medical problems, if you diagnose the problem, all else falls in place. In other cases, diagnosis offers little guidance. Empirical literature related to clinical decisions has increased, as have tools to get access to useful information, such as the Cochrane and Campbell databases of systematic reviews and the UK Database of Uncertainties About the Effects of Treatments (DUETs). Practice guidelines, including assessment protocols and treatment manuals, have been developed in many areas. A key challenge concerns gaining timely access to research findings related to life-affecting decisions.

Knowledge that is helpful in making accurate inferences includes content or topical knowledge (facts related to a domain and concepts that contribute to understanding clients and their characteristics and circumstances), procedural knowledge (how-to), and self-knowledge (such as awareness of personal assets and limitations in decision making). For example, being informed regarding dysfunctional and constructive communication patterns in families offers a framework for translating concerns such as poor communication into a picture that may clarify concerns. Practice-related claims and beliefs differ along many dimensions, including their evidentiary status and the intensity with which they are believed. They differ in how easy it is to critically appraise their accuracy. There may be uncertainty about something that can be determined, such as the existence of Freud, or personal uncertainty about the exact indeterminacy of an event that is determinate, such as the probability of a coin that is unbiased coming up heads. Proctor and Schriebinger (2008) suggest ignorance as a kind of knowledge, as discussed in Chapter 4.

IS KNOWLEDGE IMPORTANT IN THE HELPING PROFESSIONS?

Research exploring decision making in medicine highlights the importance of specialized knowledge (e.g., Elstein et al., 1978). Information gaps (differences between knowledge available and what is used in making decisions) are common, and many are avoidable. Such gaps are related to errors such as making the wrong diagnosis, giving the wrong medication, or cutting off the wrong limb. Failure to communicate information is a key source of avoidable error, as discussed in Chapter 9. Examples of errors are illustrated in Exhibit 8.1. Both conceptual and procedural errors may occur because of miscommunications (e.g., between a nurse and a physician) or failure to communicate in the first place. Consequences of errors include delayed or extended care, costs in terms of money and time, and health consequences including death of patient. (For a taxonomy of patient errors, see Buetow et al., 2009.) The development of treatment manuals and practice guidelines assumes that specialized knowledge contributes to successful outcomes. (See related discussion in Chapter 2.) However, studies comparing the relative effectiveness of lay helpers (people with no specialized training in interpersonal helping) with trained practitioners show that nonprofessionals are as effective as professionals in attaining a variety of outcomes valued by clients (Christensen & Jacobson, 1994; Dawes, 1994a).

Exhibit 8.1 Taxonomy of Errors Recognized in Family Medicine

Description	N
Errors in a process of health care delivery system	284
• Errors in the process of conducting an administrative task:	102
• Information filed in wrong place or wrong time.	41
• Unavailability of information that should have been in patients' charts:	27
• Entire chart or part of chart could not be accessed when needed.	9
• Care provided was not documented.	10
• Item(s) of information missing from chart.	8
• Errors in patients' movement through the health care delivery system.	7
• Errors in the taking and distributing of messages.	14
• Errors in managing appointments for health care.	10
• Errors in the process of investigating a patient's condition:	82
• Errors in the process of laboratory investigations:	65
• Wrong test ordered or test not ordered when appropriate.	3
• Errors in the process of obtaining or processing a laboratory specimen.	33
• Error in the process of physician receiving accurate laboratory results in a timely fashion.	16
• Inappropriate response to an abnormal laboratory result.	13

(Continued)

Exhibit 8.1 (*continued*)

• Errors in the process of diagnostic imaging investigations:	11
• Wrong test ordered or test not ordered when appropriate.	1
• Errors in the process of obtaining or processing of a diagnostic image.	4
• Error in the process of physician receiving accurate results of a diagnostic image in a timely fashion.	5
• Inappropriate response to an abnormal diagnostic image.	1
• Errors in the process of other investigations:	6
• Wrong test ordered or test not ordered when appropriate.	0
• Errors in the process of obtaining or processing of other diagnostic investigation.	2
• Errors in the process of physician receiving accurate test results of other investigation in a timely fashion.	3
• Inappropriate response to an abnormal result of other investigations.	1
• Errors in the process of treating a patient's condition:	76
• Errors in the process of treating with medications.	57
• Wrong medication or wrong dose of medication ordered or medication not ordered by physician when appropriate.	35
• Errors in the process of delivering a medication order or inappropriate medication order by a provider working under physician supervision.	13
• Error in the process of dispensing medication as ordered.	9
• Errors in the process of treating other than by medication:	20
• Wrong treatment ordered or treatment not ordered when appropriate.	9
• Error in the process of providing treatment other than medication.	10
• Errors in the process of communication:	19
• Errors in communication between physicians and patients:	10
• Errors in the process of obtaining informed consent.	1
• Errors in communication between physicians and nonphysician health care providers.	3
• Errors in communication with physicians outside the practice.	6
• Errors in the process of health care payment systems.	4
Errors arising from lack of clinical knowledge or skills	46
• Errors arising during the performance of a clinical task due to a lack of clinical knowledge or skills.	19
• Wrong or missed diagnosis.	13
• Wrong treatment decision arising from a lack of clinical knowledge or skills.	14

Source: "A Preliminary Taxonomy of Medical Errors in Family Practice," by S. M. Dovey et al., 2002, *Quality and Safety in Health Care, 11*, pp. 233–238.

Strupp and Hadley (1979) found that a college professor of English who was friendly and supportive but had no specialized training in working with clients was more effective than trained professionals in helping clients. Garb (1998) concludes that "Overall, results on presumed expertise, experience, training, and validity are disappointing" (p. 17). Lack of differences between professionals and untrained individuals in many situations may be related to common nonspecific factors shared by many helping efforts, such as warmth and empathy (Norcross, 2011; Wampold, 2001). Both trained clinicians and naive subjects display biases, such as incorrect assumptions regarding associations between certain signs and symptoms. For example, reports of undergraduate students about covariations of symptoms with signs in clinical data that contained no systematic relationship duplicated those of experienced clinicians (Chapman & Chapman, 1969). Both naive subjects and clinicians reported that patients who were suspicious of others tended to distort drawings of the eyes, that dependent clients tended to make feminine or childlike drawings, and that impotent clients drew figures with broad shoulders. Gigerenzer (2002a) describes various sources of innumeracy on the part of professionals, such as the illusion of certainty and miscommunication of risk.

If little is known in an area, there might not be much difference in effectiveness between trained and untrained helpers; so-called nonspecific factors and characteristics of particular practitioners may assume preeminence and eliminate differences in effectiveness between professionals and nonprofessionals. If graduate education encourages excessive focus on pathology, untrained helpers may have a more positive approach. However, when specialized knowledge is needed and available, its use, combined with nonspecific helping skills, will give the edge to professionals who are familiar with this knowledge and who also possess high levels of communication skills. The more empirically based domain-specific knowledge is available, the more important it is to consider this in making decisions. And, no matter what the current state of knowledge, ignorance, and uncertainty is regarding decisions, ethical obligations call on professionals to share this with clients to fulfill informed consent requirements.

DIFFERENCES BETWEEN NOVICES AND EXPERTS

Experts differ from novices both in quality of outcomes achieved (experts are superior) and in the processes used. Experts pay more attention to problem definition and structure problems at a deeper (more abstract) level compared to novices, who tend to accept problems as given. For example, experts in physics tend to sort problems in relation to abstract laws and principles, whereas novices sort problems in relation to surface structure (i.e., concepts directly stated in the problem); experts categorize problems by using essential information required to discover a solution, whereas novices attend to the superficial aspects of problems (Chi, Feltovich, & Glaser, 1980). Skill in solving unstructured problems seems to require a great deal of experience with the domain; this experience permits the building of an extensive library of distinguishable situations. Chase and Simon (1973) estimate that a chess master can recognize 50,000 types of positions. Expertise is closely related to pattern recognition, based on extensive experience offering corrective feedback concerning what is the best course of action. This experience allows experts, compared to novices, to see different things, such as opportunities for problem solution. Thus, experienced decision makers do not follow a rational model of decision making, in which we define a problem, identify options, evaluate them, and then make a decision. Rather, experts quickly size up a situation based on past experience and decide on an option.

Novices may fail to note relevant features such as unexpected anomalies or may attend to irrelevant ones. Based on interviews with experienced firefighters, nurses, and paramedics, Klein (1998) argues that expert decision makers quickly size up a situation based on informed intuition; they identify important cues relying on the similarity of the new situation to others previously experienced. Klein calls this "primed decision making." Interviews with experts show that it is difficult for them to identify the cues they use. For example, an experienced pediatric nurse looked at a baby and said, "This baby is in trouble" (which was true). When asked why, she said, "I just knew it." It took a while for her to identify specific characteristics of the baby's features she used as cues. Such research highlights the importance of situation awareness—accurate understanding of what is occurring in a situation from moment to moment as circumstances change. (See Chapter 9.)

Experts learn about possible causes associated with a given behavior, sign, or syndrome; this has been referred to as the "logical competitor set" (Feltovich, Johnson, Moller, & Swanson, 1984). They develop skill in planning as well as carrying out tasks. This may include considering competing hypotheses, asking questions that reveal helpful data, and reviewing assumptions in terms of their consistency with the evidence at hand. Such metacognitive skills are an important component of clinical reasoning (e.g., see Dunphy et al., 2009). Expert problem solving takes advantage of new possibilities as they arise; it is opportunistic (Lesgold et al., 1988). Being aware of knowledge gaps (what we know and what we do not know) is an ingredient of expertise. The role of self-knowledge and self-reflection has been emphasized by scholars in the area of critical thinking and decision making (e.g., Nickerson, 1986a, 1986b; Paul, 1993; Schon, 1990). Socrates was the preeminent advocate of self-knowledge—particularly in relation to one's own vast ignorance. Experts compared to novices possess domain-specific knowledge in an area and can more rapidly identify what information is needed to solve a problem. Differences between experts and novices include the following:

- They know more (what, how, and when to do what).
- They demonstrate superior performance, mainly in their own areas of expertise.

- They are motivated to do well.
- They know better how to use what they know (procedural knowledge); they are faster than novices at solving problems.
- What they know is better organized, enabling speedy recognition of patterns.
- They represent problems at a deeper level compared to novices.
- What they know is more accessible; they have superior short- and long-term memory.
- They have better learning skills.
- They are more likely to carry out an executive review of their reasoning process—to assume simultaneously the roles of doer and observer—if there is time to do so (e.g., see Salas & Klein, 2001).

Skills and knowledge suggested in Phillips, Klein, and Sieck (2005), include the following:

- Perception skills (making fine discriminations).
- Mental models: representations of the world that reflect broader and deeper knowledge compared to novices—"they know how tasks and subtasks are supposed to perform, how equipment is supposed to function, and how teams are supposed to coordinate" (p. 300).
- Sense of typicality and association: Experts have a "repertoire of patterns" (p. 30); they can quickly recognize and accurately interpret information. This repertoire allows experts to recognize situations as typical, and helps them to spot information that is expected but missing and to detect anomalies (p. 301).
- Routines.
- Declarative knowledge.
- Running mental simulations: imagining different patterns of events "by combining what they know to be true with what might be based on what they see in the new situation" (p. 301).
- Spotting anomalies and detecting problems: Experts spend more time analyzing situations.
- Finding leverage points.
- Managing uncertainty.
- Taking one's own strengths and limitations into account.

Useful strategies include dividing a problem into subproblems and recognizing that a problem is similar to certain kinds of past problems—there is a similar story. What is visible to experts that is not visible to others includes:

- Patterns that novices do not notice.
- Anomalies—events that did not happen and other violations of expectancies.

- The big picture (situational awareness).
- The way things work.
- Opportunities and improvisations.
- Events that either already happened (the past) or are going to happen (the future).
- Differences that are too small for novices to detect.
- Their own limitations. (Klein, 1998, pp. 148–149)

Klein (1998) argues that these characteristics are related to pattern matching and mental simulation. Pattern matching refers to the ability of the expert to detect typicality and to notice events that did not happen and other anomalies that violate the pattern. Mental simulation refers to quickly running things through one's mind as to what could happen in real time, in real-life situations. By recognizing typicality (a certain kind of pattern), experts identify when this pattern is violated—that is, when there is an anomaly that should be attended to. Indeed, failure to recognize anomalies is related to escalation toward a major mistake. Based on his study of decision makers in real-life situations, he argues that:

- Experience counts.
- Expertise depends on perceptual skills: "Learning takes many cases to develop."
- The computer metaphor of thinking is incomplete.
- Skilled problem solvers and decision makers are themselves scientists and experimenters. They are actively searching for and using stories and analogues to learn about important causal factors.
- Skilled problem solvers and decision makers are chameleons. They can simulate all types of events and processes in their heads.
- Sources of power such as situation awareness and pattern recognition operate in ways that are not analytical. They are generative, channeling decision making from opportunity to opportunity rather than exhaustively filtering through all the permutations. They enable the decision maker to redefine goals and also to search for ways to achieve existing goals. They trade accuracy for speed, and therefore allow errors (p. 287). (See also discussion of less is more in Chapter 9.)

"Sources of power" include the following:

1. Intuition (pattern recognition, having the big picture, achieving situation awareness).
2. Mental simulation (seeing the past and the future).

3. Using leverage points to solve ill-defined problems.
4. Seeing the invisible (perceptual discriminations and expectancies).
5. Storytelling.
6. Analogical and metaphorical reasoning.
7. Reading people's minds (communicating intent).
8. Rational analysis.
9. Team learning (drawing on the experience base of a team). (Klein, 1998, p. 288)

Other kinds of judgments and abilities include the following:

1. Judging the typicality of the situation.
2. Judging typical goals.
3. Recognizing typical courses of action.
4. Judging the solvability of a problem.
5. Detecting anomalies.
6. Judging the urgency of a problem.
7. Detecting opportunities.
8. Making fine discriminations.
9. Detecting gaps in a plan of action.
10. Detecting barriers that are responsible for gaps in a plan of action. (p. 288)

Experts draw on both the past and the future in making decisions in the present. "The ability to see the past and the future rests on an understanding of the primary causes in a domain and the ability to apply these causes to run mental simulations. This is one way to distinguish true experts from people who pretend to be experts. The pretenders have mastered many procedures and tricks of the trade; their actions are smooth. . . . However, if they are pushed outside of the standard pattern, they cannot improvise. They lack a sense of the dynamics of the situation. They have trouble explaining how the current state of affairs came about and how it will play out" (Klein, 1998, p. 156). Different decision tasks require different time horizons (how long we should look into the future to make a decision). Experts prepare themselves for changing situations. Klein offers the example of the term *flying behind the plane* in aviation that is used to describe people who are so wrapped up in what they are doing that they are insensitive to what lies ahead (p. 155). "It describes people who are either so novice or so overworked or have such poor situation awareness that they are not generating expectancies; they are not preparing themselves properly" (p. 155). Klein suggests that experts are better at seeing both outside and inside. Experts are better at critiquing themselves when things are slipping away. Because their content knowledge is better organized, they have more free time compared to a novice who is still struggling to integrate different bits of knowledge, and who therefore lacks time to look ahead and backward in ways that facilitate decision making in the present.

Research regarding naturalistic decision making suggests that the best way to become an expert is to have repeated practice opportunities with corrective feedback. In this view, we will not acquire expertise by reading books. We must practice in real-life situations and receive corrective feedback regarding the consequences of our decisions. This focus is reflected in problem-based learning, in which students are repeatedly confronted with problems of real-life concern to clients in real time. (See later discussion.) Thus, as Klein (1998) suggests, we can "learn like experts, rather than trying to teach [people] to think like experts" (p. 169). This view of expertise highlights the close connection between a scientific approach and developing expertise, such as testing assumptions. It is compatible with what has been found about the causes of error (see Chapter 9). Decisions can be improved by use of simple empirically based rules. An example is use of a fast and frugal decision tree to make predictions about heart disease patients (Gigerenzer, 2007). Building blocks in such a tree include: (1) a search rule (look up factors in order of importance), (2) a stopping rule (stop the search if a factor allows it), and (3) a decision rule (classify the object according to this factor) (p. 176). Here transparent, diagnostic rules are used to make timely, effective decisions. Gigerenzer (2007) suspects that professionals already use simple rules of thumb but because of lawsuits do not always admit this. Or they may not be aware of their use. (See the discussion of naturalistic decision making in Chapter 9.)

Challenges in developing expertise include the following: (1) situations are dynamic (changing), (2) human behavior is often unpredictable, (3) we often lack opportunities for corrective feedback, and (4) a task may not have enough repetition to build a sense of typicality (Shanteau, 1992, p. 282). This characterizes situations professionals encounter. Experts do not necessarily perform better than novices in unstructured problem areas such as psychology and psychiatry (Johnson, 1988). For example, Goldberg (1959) compared the ability of psychiatrists with that of their secretaries in diagnosing brain damage by using the Bender-Gestalt test. There was no difference between these two groups. And no relationship was found between individual diagnostic accuracy and degree of confidence. (See also Hinds, 1999.) Experts as well as novices are prey to a variety of illusions, such as the illusion that one can have control over an outcome when this is not possible. Whether familiar with a domain or not, integrating varied kinds of information is challenging, and we tend to make certain kinds of errors (such as being influenced by redundant data). Clinicians as well as laypeople often have incorrect views about probability and are unaware of their statistical innumeracy. Health illiteracy is encouraged by biased reports in the media and in the professional literature, as well as in health pamphlets (Gigerenzer & Gray, 2011).

WHAT COMPETENCIES CONTRIBUTE TO SUCCESS?

Barrows (1994) suggests that if we concentrate on producing students who provide effective, efficient, ethical services to clients, all else would follow. This is an outcome-focused approach to identification of competencies. Agreement based on consensus is often used to identify competencies. Lists of competencies based on consensus give an illusion of knowledge. Indeed, they get in the way of identifying what knowledge, skills, and values are critical in offering high-quality services and attaining hoped-for outcomes via systematic investigation. Many competencies start with "knows," "understands," or "is able to." But what do these terms mean? What would someone who "knows family system theories" or "understands family system theories" do compared to someone who did not "know" or "understand" these theories? What criteria would we use to tell the difference? What would someone who knows accomplish compared to someone who did not know? I may know how to define positive reinforcement but be unable to help a parent to increase the frequency with which she reinforces her child's desirable behaviors. That is, I may have *inert knowledge*—content knowledge unaccompanied by performance knowledge. Identifying competencies required to achieve a valued outcome (involving clients as active participants) may require a task analysis, in which those who are successful are observed and specific behaviors and thoughts are identified, including their sequence and contexts. It may require talking to experts to find out what they are thinking when making certain decisions—a cognitive task analysis, as described earlier in this chapter. Here, goal attainment in real-life situations is the criterion of competent performance. Base rates of success by experts are important to consider, because some outcomes are difficult to attain, even by highly competent individuals.

HOW SHOULD WE ASSESS PROFESSIONAL COMPETENCE?

Methods for assessing competencies differ in how specific and detailed they are, ranging from global assessments to lists of specific clusters of competencies in a variety of areas (Erault, 1994). The former have been found by some investigators to be more valid (Regehr, Freeman, Robb, Missiha, & Heisey, 1999). The repeated finding that self-report does not correlate highly with actual performance should encourage us to move beyond measures such as self-report, reported self-efficacy, views of supervisors, and grades (Ward, Gruppen, & Regehr, 2002). Facilitators tend to overestimate the skills of their students (Whitfield & Xie, 2002). Medicine has taken the lead in using standardized patients. These are individuals who are trained to display certain behaviors, such as presenting certain symptoms to a physician and responding in certain ways depending on the physician's questions and actions. Standardized clients can be trained to a very high level of reliability—that is, to perform in the same way over different practitioners. Such clients offer advantages of assessing quality of services while controlling for variation and case mix (Luck & Peabody, 2002). Use of standardized clients offers the possibility of discovering different ways to achieve the same outcome—that is, to discover the varied ways in which a given outcome can be attained, allowing for individual styles. Given that communication skills are so vital in making sound decisions, such repertories should be evaluated. Some applicants to medical school are now being required to respond in brief interviews as a part of their admission requirements (Harris, 2011, p. 260).

You could review your content and procedural knowledge in an area to discover gaps. Can you fluidly carry out valuable assessment or intervention methods? Is your understanding of a theory accurate? You may be familiar with only a small percentage of knowledge available concerning a topic, not because of any inherent limitations on your part, but because of the kinds of learning environments you have encountered, including graduate education. Each may have offered only some percentage of helpful knowledge and probably also offered a certain amount of misinformation.

TO KEEP UP-TO-DATE OR NOT

Sheldon and Chilvers (2000) found that only 18% of social services staff had consulted practice-related literature in the past 6 months. This neglect has also been found among other professionals. Plausible but surmountable excuses for neglecting valuable sources include: It takes too much time, I cannot find good articles or books, I do not remember what I read, and I do not know how to acquire procedural knowledge to complement knowledge of content. Evidence-based practice suggests methods to decrease the costs of searching and increase the payoffs, for example, by posing well-structured questions that facilitate an effective, efficient search for related research findings, taking advantage of the work of others (e.g., Cochrane and Campbell reviews) and learning how to critically appraise different kinds of research. Poor excuses for not keeping up-to-date may be based on overgeneralizations, such as: all research is fatally flawed (some is and some is not), the writing is bad (often but not always true), non-clinical samples are used (findings are often relevant for clinical samples as well), and some research is fabricated (most is not). Is reading (or listening or thinking) always a good idea? On the basis of decision-making research, one might conclude that sometimes not reading is better, since we tend to select material that supports our biases, and we are influenced by irrelevant material. So reading is not necessarily a help. It depends on what we read and how.

DECIDING WHAT INFORMATION TO SEEK AND WHERE TO SEEK IT

Learning can be planned or unplanned (as in incidental learning). In planned learning, we make decisions about what to read, see, and hear, and where to seek it. We make decisions about websites to consult, what journals (if any) to read, how to read, what to discuss with colleagues, what workshops to take, and what lectures to attend. We make decisions about whether to critically appraise what we read. Our decisions influence what we offer to clients. Thus, our choices are more than a personal matter; they influence the quality of services we provide to clients. We select material that reflects our preferred practice framework. Behaviorists tend to read articles written by behaviorists. Psychoanalysts read articles in psychoanalytical journals, attend psychoanalytical conventions, and speak to other psychoanalysts. These preferences, if acted on, protect us from contact with well-argued alternative views—not always a happy outcome for clients. Confirmation biases and an interest in saving time and effort encourage us to search for and read material with which we already agree—unless we use debiasing strategies to avoid such one-sided approaches. You could review your knowledge related to important practice questions by talking to people who are knowledgeable in an area or by seeking related research. The quality of your search skills influences what you discover (see Chapter 11).

Credibility as a Guide

Selection of what to read is influenced by judgments of credibility. However, as Phillips (1992) suggests, almost anything can be credible, that is, possible to believe. People differ in the criteria they use to assess credibility (the accuracy of claims). Degree of conviction is not necessarily correlated with the accuracy of a statement. Indeed quacks, fraudsters, and advertisers take advantage of manner of presentation (illusion of confidence) to create an illusion of knowledge. Criteria that may be appealed to include the following:

- *Authority:* believed because of who said it (for example, Freud, Skinner, your supervisor).
- *Liking:* believed because your friends believe it.
- *Consensus:* believed because it is the dominant view in a field.
- *Fear:* believed because of fear of being different or left out.
- *Empathy:* believed because it feels right. (See discussion of empathic explanations in Chapter 3.)
- *Scientific:* critical appraisal (accepted tentatively until disconfirmed) because an assumption or claim has survived critical tests (see Chapter 4).

Mysticism

Claims may be accepted on the basis of divine revelation, altered states of consciousness, or inspiration. Beliefs based on mysticism lack "a high degree of intra- and inter-judge reliability" (Thorngate & Plouffe, 1987, p. 67). However, there may be consensus within a group because of conformity and habit rather than common mystical experience. (See discussion of Munz's view of false knowledge in Chapter 4.) Reliance on variations of mysticism is common, as illustrated in publications such as *The Skeptical Inquirer* and *The Skeptic*. Stivers (2001) argues that our reverance for technology has become so great that simply using a new method such as a new management system is viewed as an indicator of success. Burnham (1987) suggests that the popularization of science by journalists in fragmented bits and pieces is one of the major reasons for the widespread acceptance of superstitious beliefs.

Science/Critical Rationalism

Here, premises are assessed through critical testing and systematic observation (see Chapter 4). Premises may or may not be intuitively obvious or testable by observation and/or measurement.

Anecdotal Empiricism

Some clinicians favor anecdotal empiricism: "a claim to knowledge is assessed as credible if it is similar to, or congruent with, recalled anecdotes from personal experience; otherwise it is deemed incredible" (Thorngate & Plouffe, 1987, p. 69). Anecdotal empiricism requires little effort or time. However, beliefs based on such anecdotes may not be correct.

Analogy

Accuracy may be assessed in terms of how well the structure or form of the claim, rather than its content, agrees or is compatible with views judged to be accurate. We tend to anthropomorphize what we see. Different kinds of analogies include metaphors, similes, and models. Advantages of analogies include their value in understanding new events, thoughts, or ideas. Disadvantages include being led astray by superficial similarities.

Authority

Most knowledge is secondhand, and thus the source should be considered in estimating accuracy. We may evaluate the credibility of an authority by use of one or more of the other criteria discussed in this section. Authority may be ascribed on the basis of irrelevant variables, such as gender and number of academic degrees. (See discussion of authority in Chapter 7.)

Clarity

The importance of clarity depends on our goals and what is needed to attain them. As Popper (1994) suggests, we should never be more precise than we have to be. Some people value what they cannot understand, perhaps assuming that because of the imminence of the author, it has a profundity they cannot grasp. Sokal (1998) took advantage of this in his bogus manuscript that was published. That is, we may believe that if we cannot understand something, it is profound—that what is clear is simple-minded. (See also discussion of the Dr. Fox effect in Chapter 5.) We can use obscure knowledge to impress our colleagues. Both the media and professional sources contain descriptions that appear informative but are not. Social problems may be attributed to obscure social conditions with no description of these conditions or the factors responsible for maintaining them. Tesh (1988) suggests that complex multivariate models of causality allow different advocacy or research groups to focus on only one factor, ignoring the rest.

Is It Important? Will It Help Us to Help Clients?

If material is not considered useful, it probably is not sought. Psychological importance must be considered. "Knowledge can also be important because it promotes understanding, provides a sense of order, continuity, elation or peace, establishes a locus for the expression of emotion, inflates or guards the ego, develops or maintains a favored (usually positive) self-image" (Thorngate & Plouffe, 1987, p. 79).

Knowledge as Entertainment

We are more likely to read material if we find it interesting. Thorngate and Plouffe (1987) suggest that valuable knowledge should be digestible (comprehensible), edible (credible), and nutritious (important) (p. 85). Content in professional sources, such as journals, may not reflect these characteristics. Rather it "is by tradition, if not by necessity, stripped of its wonder, ground to an emotional pulp, and distributed in plain brown envelopes. It is food for the cortex not the soul. It is meant to bypass the senses and the passions. It has the subtlety and all the excitement of weak tea" (Thorngate & Plouffe, 1987, p. 88). This does not have to be. Scientific reports can and should be written in an engaging yet informative manner.

ACTIVE VERSUS PASSIVE LEARNING

People differ in their preferred learning style, in the effectiveness of their learning skills, and in their beliefs about how (or if) knowledge can be gained. Reading or listening can be active or passive. Our learning style affects the ease of acquiring knowledge. Personal, social, and cultural views of knowledge, thinking, and learning influence what knowledge we acquire. We each have a "personal epistemology" (beliefs about what knowledge is and how or if it can be gained) that influences whether we seek information, what we seek, and how we evaluate it (e.g., Hofer & Pintrich, 2002; see also Chapter 4). We may have an *illusion of knowledge*. Gullibility serves important functions, such as preserving a sense of optimism about people, preserving social bonds with other believers, and avoiding time spent on checking claims. Jarvis (1990) argues that a key hallmark of objectivity is being willing to say, "I don't know." A willingness to examine beliefs encourages an openness to new knowledge. Biases such as the tendency to interpret what is read (or heard) in accord with preferred views emphasize the value of active reading in which we question assumptions. Clinicians are no less immune to the influence of confirmation biases than any other group.

It is not only others who create avoidable ignorance. We ourselves are a source of suppressed information via decisions about what to read and whom to listen to. We ourselves arrange a large part of our knowledge and gaps in it. We may not realize how little we actually understand about material, accepting empathic explanations (does it feel right?) and not testing its utility by applying it to real-life problems and seeking corrective feedback. The introduction of new material may be followed by the statement "It doesn't feel right." Feelings about what is true are not necessarily good guides to what *is* true. Some clinicians believe that they learn best through experience—just getting in and working with clients. To result in knowledge, this experience must be complemented by corrective feedback. (See discussion of experience in Chapter 4 and intuition in Chapter 9.) Faulty beliefs about how we learn will get in the way of keeping up with new information and putting this to use.

We learn and remember more if we use an active process in which relationships between our previous views (our background knowledge) and new information are explored. Conditions of learning include the following:

- Clear identification of objectives (what is to be learned).
- Clear description of content and procedural knowledge already available.
- Sequential steps that match available skill levels.
- Clear, relevant means of monitoring progress.
- Model presentation accompanied by instruction concerning skills to be learned, the reasons for using these, and the conditions under which they are useful.

- Multiple practice opportunities with corrective feedback.

The prevalence of confirmation biases (the tendency to accept beliefs that match preferred views) highlights the value of active learning (a deep approach to learning) versus passive learning (a surface approach). Differences between these approaches are shown here (Entwistle, 1987, p. 16).

The deep approach involves:

- Intention to understand.
- Vigorous interaction with content.
- Relation of concepts to everyday experience.
- Relation of new ideas to previous knowledge.
- Relation of evidence to conclusion.
- Examination of the logic of the argument.

The surface approach involves:

- Intention to complete task assignments.
- Memorization of information.
- Failure to distinguish principles from examples.
- Treatment of the task as an external imposition.
- Focus on discrete elements without integration.
- Nonreflectiveness about purpose or situation.

Surface approaches encourage assimilation of new material; new concepts are integrated into existing frameworks, with relatively small changes in overall views. Deep approaches are needed to create large changes in conceptual views. Conflicts between current background and new knowledge are more likely to occur in deep approaches; they are important in the development of new ideas.

Passive learning often results in *inert knowledge* (Whitehead, 1929). There are two kinds of inert knowledge. One kind is conceptual knowledge unaccompanied by procedural knowledge. This has been referred to as the "parroting problem" (Bereiter & Scardamalia, 1985, p. 65); a principle may be recited but not applied correctly. For example, the correct definition of insight may be given, but examination of clinical work may reveal a lack of understanding of this concept. Only when we are asked to apply knowledge can our procedural understanding be assessed. The second kind of inert knowledge is information that is available but not used. Knowing when to apply relevant knowledge is one of the characteristics that distinguishes experts from novices. The two kinds of inert knowledge represent the difference between a behavior deficit (lack of a competency) and a prompting or motivational deficit (a skill is available but not used). The problem of inert knowledge highlights the importance of seeking learning opportunities that enhance procedural as well as content knowledge. Confusion between the entertainment value of information and its value in helping clients and avoiding harm (how useful is it in clinical contexts) encourages the development of inert knowledge. Active reading differs from passive reading in a number of ways. In the former we pose and answer questions about what we read:

- What kind of claim is made?
- What evidence is needed and offered for this claim? (See Exhibit 8.2.)
- Is this true for all people, including my clients? Is it important?
- Can I use this information to help clients?
- Is there anything missing in this argument?
- What is the main point of this section?
- How does this relate to other well-argued views and related evidence about this topic?

Examples of helpful learning strategies are described in the following sections. Using these should enhance learning as well as enjoyment of the process. (See also later discussion of problem-based learning.)

Comprehension Monitoring

Comprehension monitoring includes asking questions about content, paraphrasing, noting progress, identifying troublesome content, summarizing information, and reviewing the adequacy of explanations. A common error is reacting to difficulties in learning by skipping material rather than trying to understand it. Effective learners "identify and define problems with their ability to understand the significance of new information . . . they actively apply particular strategies and look at the effects" (Bransford & Stein, 1984, p. 68). Questions of value when reviewing practice-related research include the following (see also Chapter 12):

- Are concepts clearly defined?
- Are measures valid and reliable and is related data clearly described?
- Is it clear how concepts are derived from a theory? Is the derivation appropriate?
- Are data collection methods clearly described?
- Is the study design clearly described?
- Are sampling procedures clearly described? Are they adequate?

Exhibit 8.2 Examples of Questions Regarding Different Kinds of Claims

1. **About a problem**
   - Exactly how is it defined? Give specific examples.
   - Who says X is a problem? Do they have any special interests? If so, what are they?
   - What is the base rate?
   - What kind of problem is it?
   - What controversies exist regarding this problem?
   - Is there a remedy?

2. **About prevalence**
   - Exactly what is it?
   - Who or what organization presented this figure? Are special interests involved?
   - How was this figure obtained? Do methods used enable an accurate estimate?
   - Do other sources make different estimates?

3. **About risk**
   - What is the absolute risk reduction? (See Chapter 15.)
   - What is the number needed to harm (NNH)? (See Chapter 12.)
   - What is the false positive rate?
   - What is the false negative rate?
   - Is risk associated with greater mortality?

4. **About assessment and diagnostic measures**
   - Is a measure reliable? What kind of reliability was checked? What were the results? Is this the most important kind of reliability to check? (See Chapter 13.)
   - Is a measure valid? Does it measure what it is designed to measure? What kind of validity was investigated? What were the specific results (e.g., correlations of scores with a certain measure)? Is this the most important kind of validity for clients? (See Chapter 13.)

5. **About effectiveness**
   - Were critical tests of claims carried out? What were the results?
   - How rigorous were the tests?
   - Are reviews of related research of high quality (e.g., rigorous, comprehensive in search, and transparent in description of methods and findings)? (See Chapter 12.)
   - Was the possibility of harmful effects investigated?

6. **About causes**
   - Is correlation confused with causation?
   - Could associations found be coincidental?
   - Could a third factor be responsible?
   - Are boundaries or necessary conditions clearly described (circumstances where relationships do not hold)?
   - Are well-argued alternative views accurately presented?
   - How strong are associations?
   - Are interventions based on presumed causes effective?
   - Is the post hoc ergo propter hoc fallacy made?
   - Are vague multifactorial claims made that do not permit critical tests?

7. **About predictions**
   - Are key valued end states accurately predicted (rather than surrogates)?
   - What percentage of predictions are accurate?
   - What is the variance in accuracy? (See Chapter 15.)

Source: From *Critical Thinking for Helping Professionals: A Skills-Based Workbook* (3rd ed.), (pp. 219–220), by E. Gambrill and L. Gibbs, 2009, New York: Oxford.

- Is the study design appropriate to the question pursued?
- Are appropriate control or comparison groups included?
- Are data-collection methods free of bias?
- Are the data-analysis methods appropriate?
- Are follow-up data available? If so, for how long?
- Were changes clinically impressive?
- Are conclusions warranted?
- Are well-argued alternative explanations for results likely?
- Can findings be generalized to other situations?

Asking "What's missing?" and "Is there evidence that this claim is true?" decreases acceptance of bogus claims that limit the quality of services offered to clients. Checklists are available for reviewing the quality of different kinds of research pertinent to a clinical question. (See Chapter 12.)

Elaboration Strategies

We construct our own interpretation of a text, which might be quite different from that intended by an author (Hagert & Waern, 1986). Elaboration strategies include "adding mental imagery, reading to answer questions, noticing categories, attending to hierarchical structure, and finding examples to illustrate principles" (Nickerson, Perkins, & Smith, 1985, p. 304). There is an active search for relationships, and new content is related to old information. Current views (background knowledge) may be discarded as no longer accurate. "Effective learners attend to factual content, but they also try to understand the significance or relevance of facts" (Bransford & Stein, 1984, p. 56). Counterexamples are sought. Such strategies increase interconnections among material and so increase options for recall. Klein (1998) emphasizes the value of stories and metaphors that capture effective decisions in the past. You may draw a concept map, a graph describing assumed relationships between variables, or prepare a flow chart. The clearer we are about our assumptions, the more clearly we can compare different views.

Avoiding Confirmation Biases

Deliberately searching for theories and research findings that may disconfirm your assumptions will help you to avoid confirmation biases (searching only for views and data that support your view) and related negative consequences such as offering clients ineffective or harmful services. Data undermining a preferred belief may even be misinterpreted as supporting the belief. Too much credit is given to data that support preferred views. Consider the study by Lord, Ross, & Lepper (1979), in which two studies concerning the deterrent effects of capital punishment (one offering supportive evidence and the other offering negative evidence) were read by Stanford University students who had previously indicated whether they believed in capital punishment as a deterrent to potential murderers. The studies involved two different designs. Regardless of the design used, students found the study supporting their own position to be more convincing and better conducted than the study opposing their position. (Conditions were counterbalanced across direction and belief.) Furthermore, after reading both studies, students were more certain of the accuracy of their original position than they were before they read either of the studies. Reading only material that matches our assumptions is unlikely to create discrepancies—one of the triggers for learning (Hayes-Roth, Klahr, & Mostow, 1981).

Be Charitable

"The principle of charity requires that we look for the best, rather than the worst, possible interpretation of material" (Scriven, 1976, p. 71). This approach increases the likelihood you will discover useful applications of material. People often respond to differences in a defensive or rejecting way rather than viewing differences as opportunities to explore new ideas and discover new options. Material may be rejected because of the label attached to it. A clinician who is behaviorally oriented might pass by an article with the term *psychoanalytic* in its title; those who are psychoanalytically oriented may feel a cold chill when seeing the word *behavioral*. Look beyond labels to the quality of information offered. The advantages of looking for applications rather than limitations are illustrated by a study in which two groups of engineers were given different instructions in viewing new material. Engineers who were asked to focus on how content could be used came up with more creative ideas than did those who were asked to identify its limitations (Hyman, 1961). A charitable approach is especially important when reading material regarding disliked (but potentially valuable) practice theories. As Popper (1994) suggests, the clash of cultures is essential to knowledge development.

Other Helpful Habits

Identifying goals when reading or listening encourages a focus on material of interest and is helpful in avoiding distraction by irrelevant details. You may have a specific question in mind related to a particular client (see Chapter 10). Effective readers attend to how content can be organized in terms of multiple linkages. Related strategies involve deep processing (in contrast to superficial descriptions), in which key principles are used to structure content. Tree diagrams may be useful to illustrate the relationship among hierarchically ordered events. Can you explain a concept or data to another person? If you cannot, perhaps you do not understand it. You could try to communicate your understanding in writing. "The experienced writer sees writing as a technique for learning and discovery, whereas the novice tends to view it as a chore analogous to 'tidying up' [fixing sentence structure and words]" (Bransford & Stein, 1984, p. 104). It is an opportunity to review evidence related to a position, avoid unwarranted generalizations, and provide illustrative examples (Paul, Elder, & Bartell, 1997). The environment in which reading (and listening) takes place influences how much is learned. Concentration (and thus comprehension) may be compromised by interruptions, noise, and fatigue.

REMEMBERING WHAT WE READ

Active reading using elaboration and comprehensive monitoring strategies increases the likelihood that we will remember material. Rehearsal of information and use of different modes of representation during rehearsal increase recall. Problems attributed to memory difficulties may be due to lapses of attention as well as decisions about how to distribute attention. The manner in which information is arranged in our memory also influences recall; the more associations we have with certain content, the easier it is to remember. Some strategies for enhancing memory, such as rehearsal and elaboration, can be used when information is first encountered. Others are helpful when trying to recall material. The nature of a task influences the effects of stress; if a habit is well learned, it is less susceptible to disruption by stress or fatigue. Deliberately attending to certain features enhances memory for those features. Important information can be entered into a user-friendly referencing or notation system to be referred to later. (See other sources for more detail, e.g., Baddeley, Conway, & Aggleton, 2002; Cowan, 2005; Halpern, 2003.)

PROBLEM-BASED LEARNING

The importance of developing professionals who are lifelong learners is highlighted by research that shows that the typical professional program produces graduates who do not keep up with the literature; this results in knowledge becoming rapidly out of date, with all the implications of this for clients. Content knowledge is emphasized in many clinical courses: learning *what* rather than *how*. Traditional approaches to professional education reflect a certain theory of education and the assessment of its quality and success. It reflects a theory in which we assume that we can pour knowledge into students—the bucket theory of education. In the traditional format of education, students are given the *products* of the process of investigation rather than being involved in the process of creating the products themselves, so that they can not only understand this process, but also experience the excitement and the challenges of wrestling with problems that make a difference in the lives of their clients. Many have criticized this bucket theory, including Dewey (1933), Lipman (2003), Perkins (1992), and Perkinson (1993). Such criticisms are compatible with research findings in related areas such as professional education, human judgment, and decision making (see Chapter 9).

A key problem with the bucket theory is that what is poured in may not be poured out when needed in the form necessary to solve problems. Perkinson (1993) argues that knowledge does not come to us from without: "We are not buckets into which knowledge can be dumped." He suggests that such attempts result in knowledge becoming true beliefs—knowledge that will not grow. Content knowledge is of limited value if it is not complemented by procedural knowledge—how and when to use it in practice and how to automatize procedures so they can be used efficiently. Research suggests that educational meetings alone are not likely to be effective in changing complex behavior (Forsetlund et al., 2009). Learning-how-to-learn skills are critical for clinicians but are often not taught in clinical programs. King and Kitchener (2002) emphasize the value of offering opportunities to discuss and analyze ill-structured problems, teaching students how to gather and evaluate data, encouraging students to discuss controversial issues, and helping them to explore their assumptions about knowledge and how it is gained.

Problem-based learning (PBL) was initiated at McMaster University in Canada. Students are placed in small groups of five or seven, together with a tutor trained in group process as well as in skills involved in evidence-based practice, such as posing well-structured questions and searching effectively and efficiently for related literature (see Exhibit 8.3). Barrows (1994) identifies six characteristics of problem-based learning.

Exhibit 8.3 Paradigms in Learning

Old	New
Knowledge-based.	Problem-based.
Knowing what one should know.	Knowing what one does not know.
Intuition very powerful.	Ability to generate and define a question and to search for, appraise, and act on the evidence to solve it.
Learning for received wisdom.	Ability to question received wisdom.
Learning almost complete at end of formal training—only a finite amount of knowledge to be absorbed.	Lifelong learning—there is always new knowledge to be absorbed.
Learning dominated by knowledge from experience.	Learning involves complementing experience with knowledge to be absorbed.

Source: From *Evidence-Based Healthcare: How to Make Health Policy and Management Decisions* (2nd ed., p. 328), by J. A. M. Gray (2001), New York, NY: Churchill Livingstone. Reprinted with permission.

1. Learning is student-centered.
2. Client concerns are the focus and stimulus for learning.
3. Learning takes place in groups of about five to eight students.
4. Teachers are facilitators or guides.
5. Problems are a vehicle for the development of problem-solving skills.
6. New information is acquired through self-directed learning.

This kind of problem-based learning has spread throughout the world. Those who initiated the program were concerned that medical students were inundated by vast amounts of information and that traditional modes of professional education eroded rather than facilitated clinical reasoning ability (Barrows, 1994).

Problem-based learning emphasizes the *process* of problem solving and decision making, the need to help practitioners to integrate practice and external research findings (if any) with the unique circumstances and characteristics of clients, including clients' values and preferences, and to develop the tools to help them to do so. This focus suggests different professional competencies and different professional practice and educational formats—evidence-based practice and problem-based learning, as described by Sackett and his colleagues (Sackett, Straus, Richardson, Rosenberg, & Haynes, 2000). They were influenced by the fact that traditional education methods such as workshops, texts, and peer-reviewed journals were not effective (e.g., Thomson O'Brien et al., 2003). This process reflects an educational theory in which it is assumed that we learn by actively engaging with problems we confront—by offering repeated opportunities to integrate knowledge from diverse areas that bear on a hoped-for outcome and in which we continually confront our information needs (our ignorance) and learn how to address them. This model focuses on making decisions about real clients, in real time, in real circumstances. The focus is on the process of decision making.

A problem focus grounds content squarely on practice concerns, highlights key decisions and related questions and options, and links curriculum areas such as research and practice, policy and practice, and knowledge about human behavior and the environment in a manner that reflects the needs of everyday practice decisions. It highlights common errors in different decision phases as well as biases common to all phases, such as confirmation biases. It emphasizes the unstructured and uncertain nature of problem solving. Repeated practice opportunities are provided to learn how to handle uncertainty in a constructive and ethical manner. Focusing on problems of concern to clients and/or significant others in no way implies that client strengths are overlooked. It would be a poor problem solver indeed who did not take advantage of both personal and environmental resources. For reviews of the effectiveness of PBL, see Newman, Van den Bossche, Gijbels, McKendree, Roberts,

Rolfe, et al. (2003). Wood (2003) suggests that problem-based learning provides a more stimulating and challenging educational environment. Only if we confront real-life problems can we see whether our approach is effective. In *Teachers Without Goals, Students Without Purposes*, Perkinson (1993) suggests that learning or growth is up to the student: "it is the student who must modify, or refine, his or her existing knowledge when he or she recognizes its inadequacies" (p. 16). In problem-based learning these inadequacies are repeatedly confronted. Teachers and tutors serve as facilitators in this process.

BECOMING A LIFELONG LEARNER

Professional development requires lifelong learning. Perkinson (1993) notes that many teachers, including Socrates, emphasized that "all education is self-education; the student educates himself or herself. The teacher's task is simply to facilitate this self-education" (p. 20) by providing an educational environment that is free, critical, and supportive. "Students must become critical of their own performances and their own understandings—while remaining confident in their ability to do better—if they are to continue growing" (pp. 40–41). The need for such an approach is emphasized by research showing how flawed our self-assessments are (Dunning, Heath, & Suls, 2004). This philosophy of education is reflected in problem-based learning and its goal: to develop lifelong learners. Knowledge and skills in critically appraising the evidentiary status of practice and policy-related literature are vital. In place of accurate descriptions of research limitations and findings, we often find opinions masquerading as facts, straw man arguments, question begging, suppression of evidence against favored views, and methodological flaws.

Many obstacles to critical thinking (such as lack of motivation, impulsive decisions, and procrastination) are related to a lack of self-management skills (see Chapter 17). Research concerning the differences between effective and ineffective problem solvers highlights the critical role of self-regulatory skills, such as monitoring performance and seeking feedback. Self-management, as well as contingency management skills, will be required to maintain and enhance critical thinking skills in work environments that do not support or are actively hostile to the use of such skills. To prevent knowledge from becoming inert, use it, train others, use prompts, arrange effective incentives for its use, and place clients front and center in terms of attending to helping and avoiding harming them. Prompts, such as checklists, decision aids, and incentives, may foster use of valuable knowledge and skills. Agency policies and practices concerning continuing education programs influence the quality of learning opportunities. Gains in knowledge and on-the-job use are more likely if such programs include ingredients that facilitate learning, retention, and generalization of new skills on the job.

The Problem of Belief Perseverance

A key challenge is replacing old beliefs with new ones when new information contradicts old beliefs. We tend to cling to old beliefs and do so for reasons that seem and often are good: they have worked for us, they are familiar, and they give us a sense of control over the environment. Beliefs can survive significant logical and empirical challenges. Consider the failure of debriefing. Subjects continued to believe in initial estimates that affected their judgments even after they were informed that these initial estimates were wrong in an experiment in which subjects were asked to distinguish real from fictitious suicide notes and were provided with false feedback in relation to their performance (Ross, Lepper, & Hubbard, 1975). All participants were debriefed following this phase of the study; they were informed that the feedback they had received was false and that they had been assigned to one of three conditions: success, failure, or average performance. Debriefing was not successful in altering perception of performance. Subjects assigned to the success condition continued to rate their performance and abilities more favorably than did the other two groups. Subjects assigned to the failure condition continued to rate themselves as lacking in ability and as unsuccessful. The perseverance effects of initial impressions have been found with observers also.

Why are beliefs so persistent? One reason concerns information-processing factors—for example, biased search, recall, and integration of evidence. Although motivational and emotional factors may play a role, they do not seem to account for the research findings described previously. Confirmation biases, such as discounting contradictory information by offering alternative explanations, come into play. Offering explanations for beliefs makes these more enduring. "Thus the subject who suddenly finds herself confronted with evidence of her superior or inferior ability at discriminating suicide notes might search for some aspect of her background or personality that might account for such a talent or deficiency. The seemingly successful subject, for example, may credit her performance to her familiarity with the self-revealing poetry of an author who later committed suicide; the apparent failure may cite her own cheerful and optimistic disposition as an impediment to the empathetic set of task demands" (Einhorn, 1980, pp. 26–27). Beliefs are more likely to be altered if concrete information based on firsthand experience is provided that is compatible with current knowledge. Here, too, we see the importance of a true clinical apprenticeship that would offer such opportunities. Popular clinical beliefs receive consistent support from material in professional sources, especially those we selectively choose from the many available. Only by a deliberate search will we discover divergent views.

THE INFLUENCE OF PROFESSIONAL EDUCATION PROGRAMS

A number of changes could be made in clinical programs to upgrade the quality of decision making, as suggested earlier in the chapter in the discussion of PBL. (See also Hoge, Tomdora, & Stuart, 2003.) Richard McFall was so concerned about the quality of clinical psychology programs that he initiated a separate qualifying procedure (see Baker, McFall, & Shoman, 2008; Herbert, 2002; McFall, 1991, 2006; Ruark, 2008). There is a lack of attention in professional education to decision-making competencies, including kinds of errors and how to avoid them. Instructors may not be familiar with fallacies and biases that influence decisions; they may embrace an intuitive approach to practice and ignore analytic skills (e.g., Medawar, 1984, pp. 58–60). Economic, structural, and political factors that influence how problems are defined and handled may be ignored, including the influence of Big Pharma (see Chapter 2). Professionals as well as clients should learn how to spot and counter human service propaganda (see Chapter 4) and dysfunctional organizational stratagems. Some medical schools now offer related courses/websites (e.g., Wilkes & Hoffman, 2001). Valuable websites are available, such as www.PharmedOut.org. Political skills, such as how to form coalitions, will help you to pursue changes that benefit clients and create vibrant learning environments. A lack of such skills is one reason for the sense of helplessness and hopelessness among many clinicians in agency-based practice. Lipman (2003) highlights the importance of a community of inquiry. An educational environment in which controversial issues are routinely discussed and well-argued, conflicting points of view are welcomed fosters critical thinking and sound decisions. As Walton (2008a) suggests, questions are never out of place when the goal of a discussion is to arrive at the truth.

Clinical internships may not offer guided experience with high-quality corrective feedback. Supervisors may rely on indirect measures of trainees' skills in the form of process notes, brief written reports, or descriptions during supervisory meetings or case conferences, forgoing opportunities to listen to tape recordings of interviews with clients or to observe staff working with clients. Too rarely do students have multiple opportunities to observe trained staff working with clients. Mentors should share information about how they arrived at decisions as well as what the decisions are, so that novices have access to the reasoning process. Helpful questions should be modeled, both questions asked of clients and questions asked covertly. Research suggests the importance of active coaching, including offering guidance, requiring explanations, and evaluating progress. Few professional education programs require students to develop expertise in contingency analysis: skill in identifying and altering the relationships between environmental events and behaviors of interest, drawing on related empirical research in both applied and laboratory settings (e.g., Layng, 2009). Lack of such knowledge and skill may contribute to the dispositional bias—focusing on negative characteristics of clients and ignoring environmental variables (see Chapter 14). Programs vary in how they train students to evaluate their work with clients, ranging from reliance on vague, global methods to ongoing monitoring using specific, relevant progress indicators. Ongoing evaluation of such indicators enables timely decisions. Only via careful evaluation may harmful effects of intentions be detected.

SUMMARY

Domain-specific knowledge and skills may be vital in making well-reasoned decisions. If relevant information is available, possible discrepancies between what we know and what can be known may be large. If considerable information is available but little is used, clients may be harmed rather than helped. Practice- and policy-related research has increased, which makes choices as to whether to seek and use this knowledge more significant in relation to consequences for clients. With the invention of the systematic review and the process of evidence-based practice, clinicians now have more help in gaining rapid access to research findings. The accuracy of our self-assessment of our knowledge influences the decisions we make. Clinicians also differ in their goals in selecting material to read and workshops to attend. Some focus on entertainment value. Others focus on acquiring knowledge of value in helping clients. Decisions about what to read, see, or hear are influenced by ease of access of material and judged importance. Clinicians differ in the criteria used to assess the value of material. Some rely on scientific criteria—has a claim been critically tested, and if so, to what effect? Others rely on what's new or appeals to authority. Preferences influence what is learned and thus what is offered to clients.

Our skill in learning how to learn, as well as our attitudes about knowledge and learning, influences the gap between our current information and what is available that could contribute to well-reasoned decisions. Active learning skills such as comprehension monitoring enhance learning. Use of the principle of charity when reading or listening decreases the likelihood that valuable content will be prematurely discarded. The nature of professional education programs influences the quality of clinical decisions. Inclusion of a high-quality mentoring experience, as well as material concerning fallacies, contingency analysis, and the influence of the biomedical-industrial complex on professional practice, all discussed in an atmosphere that encourages critical appraisal of different positions, should enhance the quality of decisions and contribute to development of lifelong learning skills.

It should encourage asking questions about claims and a willingness to say, "I don't know," and to ask, "What's the evidence for your belief?" Professional education programs should provide students with effective learning-how-to-learn skills, including overcoming obstacles to making well-reasoned decisions, such as procrastination and lack of perseverance. Problem-based learning and evidence-based practice provide an educational format and a decision-making process designed to integrate evidentiary, ethical, and application issues in real time.

Taking Advantage of Research on Judgment, Problem Solving, and Decision Making

Clinical decision making requires choosing among different (often competing) goals and related courses of action. The lists of options (the "menus") related to a decision differ in number, variety, and whether they include feasible options that will help clients to attain outcomes they value. Lists differ in their noise level (number and vividness of irrelevant and misleading options). Misleading items may be in the list (those that direct you and your clients in unhelpful directions). Invalid assessment methods that do not measure what they presume to measure may be included. (See Lilienfeld, Lynn, & Lohr, 2003; Thyer & Pignotti, in press.) Variations in the rate of use of an intervention reflect the different decisions that may be made regarding a concern. For example, Gigerenzer (2002a) notes that in Maine, "the proportion of women who have had a hysterectomy by the age of 70 varies between communities from less than 20 percent to more than 70 percent" (p. 101). There are different kinds of problems, and different aspects of decision making differ in their importance in relation to the kind of problem. Decision making has been investigated in a variety of situations, including the laboratory (in which conditions can be controlled), as well as in interviews of experts and review of archival data. There is a rich literature on judgment, problem solving, and decision making in many different fields (e.g., see Baron, 2000; Gigerenzer, Hertwig, & Pachur, 2011; Gilovich, Griffin, & Kahneman, 2002; Koehler & Harvey, 2005; Salas & Klein, 2001). This indicates that:

- Expertise varies greatly.
- Domain-specific knowledge is important: both problem-related knowledge and self-knowledge influence success.

- Experts use different reasoning processes compared to novices (e.g., pattern recognition, mental simulations).
- Problem structuring is a critical phase: Some ways of structuring problems are better than others.
- Creative as well as critical thinking is required.
- Repeated practice providing corrective feedback is critical to developing informed intuition that allows us to respond effectively; skill in learning from experience is important, *not experience per se*, including learning from errors.
- Our goals influence our actions.
- We fall into a number of "intelligence traps"; we jump to conclusions (decide on one option too soon); errors of omission and commission occur.
- Experts, compared to novices, organize knowledge in a different way; they approach problems on a more abstract level and can more readily identify anomalies and additional information that would be helpful.
- Situation awareness (local rationality) is important (attending to the problem context).
- The strategies we use influence our success.
- Monitoring progress is important—for example, to catch false directions.
- Beliefs about what knowledge is and how to get it (our personal epistemology) influence success.
- How we decide to allocate our resources influences success (e.g., time spent in planning).
- We can learn to become better problem solvers.

Some people tend to think carefully, whereas others are more spontaneous. Some are avoidant; they try to avoid making decisions. Good problem solvers are more attentive to situational details and more tenacious compared to poor problem solvers, who are more likely to rely on unreasoned guessing and rationalizations and not to attend to detail. Ennis (1987) suggests that being sensitive to the feelings, level of knowledge, and degree of sophistication of others, as well as seriously considering other views, is important. Successful compared to unsuccessful problem solvers think more about their thinking. They critically review their assumptions and reasoning. They are their own best critics. They pay attention to data that contradict their assumptions. They ask questions about the accuracy of data, such as: What evidence supports this claim? What evidence contradicts it? Has it been critically tested? With what results? Are there well-argued alternative views? Research reveals two different kinds of intuition—informed intuition, based on extensive experience providing corrective feedback, and uninformed intuition, which is not accompanied by such experience. Characteristics of naturalistic decision-making settings include "time pressure, high stakes, experienced decision makers, inadequate information (information that is missing, ambiguous, or erroneous), ill-defined goals, poorly defined procedures, cue learning, context (e.g., higher-level goals, stress), dynamic conditions, and team coordination" (Klein, 1998, p. 4; Orasanu & Connolly, 1993).

There are different models of judgment and decision making:

> . . . normative models of thinking specify an ideal standard. The idea is to figure out what kind of thinking would bring us closest to achieving our personal goals, or the personal goals we would have "on reflection"—that is, after thinking about them carefully and well. Descriptive models specify what people in a particular culture actually do and how they deviate from the normative models. Prescriptive models are designs or inventions, whose purpose is to bring the results of actual thinking into closer conformity to the normative model. (Baron, 2000, p. 33)

One of the purposes of decision making is to reveal possibilities (Baron, 2000). As Jonathan Baron (1994) points out, the whole point of good thinking is to increase the probability of good outcomes. A good outcome is one that decision makers value; it results in valued goals (Baron, 2000). Consider the decisions in Exhibit 9.1. Klein (1998) suggests that effective decision makers do the best they can with what is knowable. Clearly this is not always done. Deficiencies identified in nursing students' decision-making skills included not making effective or efficient use of available information, errors in estimating risk and uncertainty, and difficulties selecting among alternative courses of action. Decisions differ in terms of how quickly they must be made, how experienced the person is making the decision, the kind of feedback offered, and time available to consider choices and outcomes (Connelly & Beach, 2000). We may have an incorrect model of how something, or some situation, functions. We may rely on misleading oversimplifications. Not only is it important to have relevant information, but it must also be organized so that we can take advantage of it when needed. It must allow us to adapt fluidly as needed, in real life, in real time. New goals may emerge during the course of decision making (Klein, 1998). Differences in how problems are framed (for example, to avoid negative events or to achieve positive benefits), how questions are posed, and how responses are gathered (by either closed or open questions) influence judgments. Outcome should be distinguished from the process used to achieve it; that is, a poor outcome may result from a good decision-making process.

Exhibit 9.1 Nurses, Information Use, and Clinical Decision Making—The Real World Potential for Evidence-Based Decisions in Nursing

Decision Type	Example of Clinical Questions/Choices
Intervention/effectiveness: Decisions that involve choosing among interventions.	Choosing a mattress for a frail elderly man who has been admitted with an acute bowel obstruction.
Targeting: A subcategory of intervention/effectiveness decisions outlined above, of the form "choosing which patient will benefit most from the intervention."	Deciding which patients should get antiembolic stockings.
Prevention: Deciding which intervention is most likely to prevent occurrence of a particular health state or outcome.	Choosing which management strategy is most likely to prevent recurrence of a healed leg ulcer.
Timing: Choosing the best time to deploy the intervention.	Choosing a time to begin asthma education for newly diagnosed patients with asthma.
Referral: Choosing to whom a patient's diagnosis or management should be referred.	Choosing that a patient's leg ulcer is arterial rather than venous and merits medical rather than nursing management in the community.
Communication: Choosing ways of delivering information to and receiving information from patients, families, or colleagues. Sometimes these decisions are specifically related to the communication of risks and benefits of different interventions or prognostic categories.	Choosing how to approach cardiac rehabilitation with an elderly patient who has had an acute myocardial infarction and lives alone, with her family nearby.
Service organization, delivery, and management: These types of decisions concern the configuration or processes of service delivery.	Choosing how to organize handover so that communication is most effective.
Assessment: Deciding that an assessment is required and/or what mode of assessment to use.	Deciding to use the Edinburgh Postnatal Depression screening tool.
Diagnosis: Classifying signs and symptoms as a basis for a management or treatment strategy.	Deciding whether thrush or another cause is the reason for a woman's sore and cracked nipples.
Information seeking: The choice to seek (or not to seek) further information before making a further clinical decision.	Deciding that a guideline for monitoring patients who have had their ACE inhibitor dosage adjusted may be of use, but choosing not to use it before asking a colleague.
Experimental, understanding, or hermeneutic: Relates to the interpretation of cues in the process of care.	Choosing how to reassure a patient who is worried about cardiac arrest after witnessing another patient arresting.

Source: From "Nurses, Information Use, and Clinical Decision Making: The real world potential for evidence-based decisions in nursing," by Thompson, C., Cullum, N., McCaughan, D., Sheldon, T., and Raynor, P., 2004, *Evidence Based Nursing, 7*, pp. 68–72.

PROBLEM SOLVING IS UNCERTAIN

Defining problems and making decisions in the helping professions is an uncertain activity. Uncertainty may concern: (1) the nature of the problem, (2) the outcomes desired, (3) what is needed to attain them, (4) the likelihood of attaining outcomes, and (5) the measures that will best reflect degree of success. Information about options may be missing, and accurate estimates of the probability that different alternatives will result in desired outcomes may be unknown. Preferences may change in the very process of being asked about them. Problems that confront clients (e.g., lack of housing or day care) are often difficult ones, which challenge the most skilled of helpers. They are often unstructured and untidy (Adams, 1974). Important information may be missing, and it is difficult to integrate different kinds of data. Knowledge may be available but not used. The true prevalence of a behavior or its natural history may not be known. Every source of information has a margin of error that may be small or large. We often do not know how great the range of error is or whether it is random or biased.

Even when a great deal is known, this knowledge is usually in the form of general principles that do not allow specific predictions about individuals (Dawes, 1994a). For example, although many convicted rapists rape again when released from prison, this does not allow you to accurately predict whether a particular person will rape again if released. Clinicians deal with samples of behavior. They often rely on small samples of self-report data gathered in an interview (a sample from one source). These samples may be biased and therefore misleading. Assessing the representativeness of samples to a population is a key helping skill. How likely is it that a sample (e.g., of behaviors, thoughts, feelings) accurately represents the population from which it is drawn? How likely is it that what you see during one hour in a residential center accurately reflects the usual pattern of interaction between staff and residents? Physicians usually work in a state of uncertainty about the true state of the patient. They can only estimate the probability that a client has a certain illness. Problems may have a variety of causes and potential solutions. Barriers that may be present are illustrated in Exhibit 9.2. Overlooking ignorance and uncertainty encourages attitudes (e.g., overconfidence) and problem-solving styles (e.g., jumping to conclusions) that may get in the way of helping clients or delude clients that help is at hand when it is not. This also will result in misinforming clients.

Situations Change

Situations evolve. They are not static. They may change from minute to minute, hour to hour, day to day, or week to week. Our initial hunch and the actions we take based on it influence later decisions. A second interview with a client may reveal an additional concern, such as substance abuse. Unless we recognize new information and rethink our initial hypotheses, we may make poor decisions. Debugging strategies may be needed to remind ourselves to attend to important changes in a situation that may call for new approaches to overcome an initial mind-set or framing of a situation. Woods and Cook (1999) suggest that assessing situations and formulating plans are interlinked; that is, as we change our views of a situation, we consider what plans may be of value. Failure to

Exhibit 9.2 Barriers to Problem Solving

1. Limited Knowledge	About the prevalence of a problem.
	About the causes of a problem.
	About what methods will be most effective in solving a problem.
2. Information Processing Barriers	We can consider only so many different kinds of data at one time.
	Inaccurate memory.
	We tend to process information sequentially rather than contextually.
	We may rely on misleading "rules."
	Reliance on questionable criteria to evaluate claims
3. Task Environment	Lack of resources.
	Overvalue of tradition (as preferable to change)
	Taboo topics (e.g., questioning claims).
	Distractions (constant interruptions).
	Time pressures.
	Reluctance to examine the results of policies, programs, and practices.
	Autocratic decision-making style.
4. Motivational Blocks	Value winning over learning.
	Vested interest in an outcome, conflicts of interest.
	Interest in predicting our environment.
	Cynicism.
	Lack of zeal.
5. Emotional Blocks	Fatigue.
	Anger.
	Anxiety.
	Low tolerance for ambiguity; inability to incubate.
	Appeal of vivid material.
6. Perceptual Blocks	Defining problem too narrowly.
	Overlooking alternative views.
	Stereotyping.
	Judging rather than generating ideas.
	We see what we expect to see.
7. Intellectual Blocks	Reliance on questionable criteria to evaluate claims.
	Failure to think critically about beliefs.
	Inflexible use of problem-solving strategies
	Lack of accurate information.
	Limited use of problem-solving languages (e.g., illustrations, models).
	Disdain for intellectual rigor.
	Valuing John Wayne thinking (strong pro/con positions with little reflection).
8. Cultural Blocks	Fear that the competition of ideas would harm the social bonding functions of false beliefs (see Chapter 4).
9. Expressive Blocks	Inadequate skill in writing and speaking clearly.
	Social anxiety.

Source: Adapted from *Conceptual Blockbusting: A Guide to Better Ideas* (3rd ed.), by J. L. Adams, 1986, Reading, MA: Addison-Wesley.

revise our views (becoming fixated on a certain hypothesis) is a key source of poor decisions. Elstein et al. (1978) found that the difference between expert diagnosticians and those who were not as accurate was that the experts held hypotheses tentatively, and were open to revising them as new information emerged.

STRUCTURING PROBLEMS IS A CRITICAL PHASE

Problem framing (clarifying and deciding how to structure a problem) is a critical step. Experts pay more attention to problem framing and structure problems at a deeper (more abstract) level compared to novices, who tend to accept problems as given (see Chapter 8). Different theories involve different problem framing. Consider homelessness. This could be viewed as: (1) the client's own fault (he or she is lazy); (2) a family problem (relatives are unwilling to help); (3) lack of low-cost housing; (4) a problem with service integration (services are not integrated); (5) due to a mental disorder; (6) a result of our basic economic structure (e.g., unskilled jobs have decreased); (7) discrimination based on racial prejudice; (8) a result of deregulation, which has led to an increase in poverty (as well as a vast increase in wealth for the very rich), millions losing their homes, and a decrease in services; and (9) some mix of these possibilities. Only by clarifying and redefining (restructuring) a problem may it be solved, or may you discover that there is no solution. Creative (bold guesses) and contextual thinking will often be needed to describe the problem space in a way that yields a solution. Only in this way may you discover interrelationships among different levels of influence (e.g., individual, family, community, agency, service system).

A problem well stated is a problem half solved.

—*Charles F. Kettering*

DOMAIN-SPECIFIC KNOWLEDGE AND SKILLS ARE IMPORTANT

Studies of decision making among physicians emphasize the importance of knowledge of content related to problems (see Chapter 5). The "possession of relevant bodies of information and a sufficiently broad experience with related problems to permit the determination of which information is pertinent, which clinical findings are significant, and how these findings are to be integrated into appropriate hypotheses and conclusions" were foundational components related to competence in clinical problem solving (Elstein et al., 1978, pp. x–xi). Let's say that you have been asked to help homeless people form self-help groups. What facts may be important to know? What theories and related concepts will be helpful? What skills do you need to use this knowledge effectively? (For example, you need critical appraisal skills to evaluate the soundness of related research; see Chapter 12.)

Knowledge that could be helpful may remain unused (inert). We may not remember what we know or transfer useful strategies from one area to another. Perhaps we never understood facts, concepts, or strategies in the first place. Content knowledge without performance skills to put this into use remains unused. This is known as the *parroting problem*; we can describe what should be done to solve a problem but cannot put this knowledge into effect. (See also discussion of experts compared to novices in Chapter 8.) Experts, compared to novices in an area, possess domain-specific knowledge and can move rapidly to identify what information is needed to solve a problem. They have valuable "scripts" that guide decision making (Hamm, 2003).

MANY INFLUENCES LIE OUTSIDE OUR AWARENESS

We are not necessarily aware of what influences the decisions we make, such as our goals or emotional reactions. The role of unconscious influences on our judgments, especially unrecognized environmental ones, is one of the better-supported findings within psychology. Two out of three sources of influence on our behavior (perception and associations) lie outside of our awareness. We may be unaware of contextual influences on the very goals we pursue in a situation (Gollwitzer, Bayer, & McCulloch, 2005). Emotions and perceptions may precede thoughts; associated cues are automatic in nature (they occur without our awareness) and influence behavior. Noticing an event does not mean that its influence is appreciated; appreciation requires awareness of a cause-effect relationship. Biasing influences may not be remembered. If we are not aware of our biases, we are less able to avoid them. We are typically unaware of the heuristics we use to respond rapidly to feedback in changing environments. The downside is that if our decisions are poor ones, then the automatic nature of the process makes it difficult to learn that we are wrong, and in what ways.

THE INFLUENCE OF GOALS AND CONFLICTS AMONG THEM

Our decisions are influenced by our goals of which we may or may not be aware; certain goals may be automatically triggered in situations in which they are often pursued. And goals may "become invulnerable to adverse situational influences" (Gollweitzer, Bayer, & McCulloch, 2005, p. 505). That is, we may pursue these even if we lose valuable opportunities in doing so. We overestimate the likelihood of preferred outcomes. Janis and Mann (1977) describe many disastrous results of the influence of motivational variables on decisions, such as the 1941 failure to take preventative action despite evidence that Pearl Harbor would be attacked. Tuchman (1984) discusses other historical examples such as the decision by the Trojans not to examine the wooden horse before allowing it into their city. Whether we make use of data affects what we perceive. For example, people are often incorrect in their answers about which way Lincoln's profile faces on a penny because they do not normally use this information. We may perceive without noticing; that is, just because something is perceived does not mean that it is noticed, and something can be noted without appreciating its significance in terms of how it affects behavior. Individual differences in valued goals (to help clients and avoid harm, to get through a busy day early) may influence what is noticed and what is not. So, too, may our emotional responses.

Meta-goals include maximizing accuracy, minimizing cognitive effort and negative emotions, and maximizing how easy it is to justify a decision (Payne & Bettman, 2005, p. 126). Competing goals in a clinical context include saving time and effort, helping clients, performing well, and avoiding errors. Goal conflict is a concern in many areas, including aviation, medical settings (such as anesthesiology), and child welfare practice. Competing goals in child welfare settings include providing services to parents and respecting their wishes, guarding the well-being of children who cannot protect themselves, and protecting oneself from lawsuits. Fears of malpractice may result in ordering unneeded tests. As one goal is pursued, another may be forgone. "Because local rationality revolves around how people pursue their goals, understanding performance at the sharp end depends on tracing interacting multiple goals and how they produce tradeoffs, dilemmas, and double binds" (Woods & Cook, 1999, p. 160). We know little about how trade-offs are usually represented or resolved in given situations. Consider a staff member in an agency who was required to make daily visits to the home of a father of a child who was physically abused. He arrives at the house and is told by the father that the child is sleeping and is fine. What are the trade-offs here? Trade-offs include dealing with an irate father whose statements are questioned by the request to see the child, time pressures to get on to other visits, and trying to protect the well-being of the child—is this child safe?

Vested interests in certain outcomes influence our decisions; we may assign exaggerated importance to some findings to protect a favored hypothesis. We are subject to wishful thinking (i.e., our preferences for an outcome increase our belief that it will occur) and to the illusion of control (simply making a prediction may increase our certainty that it will come true). Lack of interest in having a carefully thought out position or a wish to appear decisive (i.e., a John Wayne style) may compromise the quality of reasoning, as may a preference for mystery over mastery. An interest in understanding and predicting our environment encourages a readiness to overlook uncertainty and offer explanations for what are in fact chance occurrences. We may have unrealistic expectations and a desire for quick success.

INFLUENCE BY AFFECT

Our moods and affective reactions to different people or events influence our decisions (e.g., see Croskerry, Abbass, & Wu, 2008, 2010; Dunphy, Dunphy, Cantwell, Bourke, & Fleming, 2010). Our emotions offer rapid, often automatic information linked to fight-or-flight reactions. They influence how we respond to new material, or if we seek out certain material (Slovic, Finucane, Peters, & MacGregor, 2002). Slovic and his colleagues (2002) refer to reliance on feelings of goodness and badness in guiding judgments as the *affect heuristic*. Such feelings may influence our decisions outside of our awareness. Emotional reactions affect what we notice, what we recall, how we organize it, and what predictions we make. Even small changes in mood and arousal level may influence our judgments. For example, male subjects rated nudes as more attractive after a vigorous workout on an exercycle than they did before the workout (Cantor, Zillmann, & Bryant, 1975). Subjects who received a small gift rated TVs and cars more positively than those who received no gift (Isen, Shalker, Clark, & Karp, 1978). Descriptions of familiar people given while subjects were happy were charitable, loving, and generous, compared with the fault-finding descriptions given when subjects were angry (Bower & Cohen, 1982). Affect also influences memory; we recall events that match our current mood. We tend to think positive thoughts when we are in a good mood and negative thoughts when we are depressed. For example, we remember better those events that match our current mood and ask more questions about such events. Clinicians who are sad may attend more to risks and negative events than those who are happy, in which case risks and obstacles may be underemphasized. The clinician's mood is influenced by the client as well as by external factors, such as an argument with a significant other or an arduous commute. (For a review of the effects of mood on memory and decisions, see Schwartz, 2002.) Negative affect related to fear of failure or a seemingly insoluble problem may disrupt performance. Positive affect facilitates learning and problem solving; it seems to promote flexibility, which is an important aspect of creative thinking (see Labroo & Patrick, 2009; Nadler, Rabi, & Minda, 2010).

INFLUENCE BY TASK DEMANDS

The setting in which decisions are made influences our decisions. What are the problems to be solved or tasks to be completed? Task demands are emphasized in fast and frugal models of decision making. The concept of local rationality captures the idea that cognitive activity needs to be considered in view of the demands placed on practitioners by the problems that occur. "The expression of expertise and error, then, is governed by the interplay of particular problem demands inherent in the field of activity and the resources available to bring knowledge to bear in pursuit of the critical goals" (Woods & Cook, 1999, p. 161). The pressures created by managed care and related ethical dilemmas have received considerable attention. There are many opportunities to misrepresent a situation before making a decision that may only be obvious after we make it and compare our initial perspective with what resulted. In simulated aviation scenes, "less effective crews tended to simplify the situations they faced and were less sensitive to the constraints of the particular context they faced. Less effective crews were 'controlled by the task demands' and did not look ahead or prepare for what would come next. As a result, they were more likely to run out of time or encounter other cascading problems" (Woods & Cook, 1999, p. 155). Thus, how we direct our attention and what criteria we use to shift it is vital.

Different clinicians confront different problems. Some features of situations increase problem demands, such as time pressures, sources of irritability, conflicting goals, and unanticipated variations in pacing (Woods & Cook, 1999). Understanding demands "can reveal a great deal about the knowledge activation, attentional control or handling of multiple goals that is needed for successful performance" (p. 161). The notion of rationality favored by authors such as Gigerenzer, Klein, and Simon emphasizes the match between the problems we confront and the environment in which they occur (ecological rationality). This focus is also reflected in research that shows that the causes of errors are typically systemic (Reason, 1997, 2001); they are usually not caused by one person or one environmental characteristic. Rather, they are related to a number of such characteristics (see later discussion of errors). The emphasis on the contextual nature of decision making has implications for the extent to which a given decision-making procedure is generalizable with positive outcomes over a number of different situations; it depends on the similarity and the nature of the decisions and the contexts in which they are made.

CONFIRMATION BIASES ABOUND: PARTIALITY IN THE USE OF EVIDENCE

We tend to seek and overweigh evidence that supports our beliefs and ignore and underweigh contrary evidence (Nickerson, 1998). That is, we try to justify (confirm) our assumptions rather than to falsify them (seek counterexamples and test them as rigorously as possible). This is an example of partiality in the use of evidence, which can result in avoidable errors. Consider the study by Snyder and Swann (1978) in which students were asked to test the hypothesis that a person was either an extrovert or an introvert. Those who believed a person was an extrovert asked questions that prompted data in support of their view. Students who assumed that the person was an introvert selected questions that would prompt answers supporting this view. There was a self-fulfilling prophecy. This study was replicated with counselors with similar results (Dallas & Baron, 1985). That is, therapists selected questions that offered confirming evidence for their assumptions. Studies of medical reasoning show that overinterpretation is a common error. This refers to assigning new information to a favored hypothesis rather than exploring alternative accounts that more effectively explain data, or remembering this information separately (Elstein et al., 1978). Data that provide some support for and against opposing views increase confidence for holders of both views (Lord, Ross, & Lepper, 1979). As a result of considering only one hypothesis (e.g., that a child's behavior is a result of sexual abuse) and ignoring alternative hypotheses (e.g., that he or she has not been so abused and the behavior is related to other factors), false allegations of sexual abuse have occurred (Ceci & Bruck, 1995; DeYoung, 2004). Clinicians assign labels to clients based on the *Diagnostic and Statistical Manual of Mental Disorders IV-TR* (American Psychiatric Association, 2000). These labels may result in a selective search for data that confirm the label; contradictory data may be ignored. We use different standards to criticize opposing evidence than to evaluate supporting evidence. Confirmation biases may influence judgments in all phases of work with clients—defining problems, deciding on causes, and selecting plans. Such biases are less likely among experts (Klein, 1998).

SITUATION AWARENESS IS VITAL; ECOLOGICAL RATIONALITY

We make decisions about where to focus our attention (Durso & Gronlund, 1999). Situations change, often requiring adaptive actions (LaBerge, 1995). Situation awareness refers to the interlinking of pattern recognition and environmental factors. (See discussion of experts and novices in Chapter 8.) The intersection of the two points to a variety of ways in which our thinking may go astray. Knowledge may be available but unused. We may misread cues and take actions that worsen rather than improve the situations, as in the Chernobyl meltdown. Relevant knowledge may be available only if accurate pattern recognition occurs. If task demands are excessive, there may not be time to search our memories for patterns that facilitate successful task accomplishment. Woods and Cook (1999) use the term *mindset* to refer to loss of situational awareness, framing effects, and juggling multiple lines of thought and activity in time, including breakdowns in workload management and thematic vagabonding. The latter refers to a loss of coherence, in which multiple interacting themes are treated superficially and independently so we jump incoherently from one theme to the next. This may be because a mind-set is difficult to interrupt, our attention is influenced by irrelevant stimuli, or a breakdown occurs in setting priorities. For example, we may focus on irrelevant tasks. We may use standardized, routinized methods when these are not what is needed in a particular situation. We may not pay attention to the unique features of a situation, and so fail to realize that a change in approach is needed. One question here is: How much evidence should you require that a cue is wrong and should be overridden?

THERE ARE DIFFERENT DECISION-MAKING STYLES

It is generally argued that there are two basic kinds of decision-making styles: (1) a rapid intuitive style used with little effort and (2) a more deliberative analytic style (Kahneman, 2011). System 1 (intuition) is fast, parallel, automatic, effortless, associative, and slow-learning. System 2 (reasoning) is slow, serial, controlled, effortful, rule-governed, and flexible. Balla and his colleagues (2009) interviewed 35 general practitioners about 72 cases to explore the dual theory of cognition. Results supported use of both systems—instant problem framing consistent with intuitive thinking, focusing on risk and urgency of the case, followed by a second reflective phase in which initial judgments were reviewed. Salient features attended to included patient-relevant content (e.g., psychosocial background—terrible home life); patient label (patient believed it is an infection); red flags (she suddenly started weeping); recent intervention (e.g., recent surgery); and pattern (good pattern for flu). Reported use of different processes from system 1 included rapid judgments (79%), salient features recognized (90%), existing mental model (75%), use of rule of thumb (44%), framing efficient driver (100%), and exploring alternatives (93%). For system 2, subjects reported alternative options prioritizing (35%), new drivers (31%), and stopping rule (12%). Using system 2, problems were reframed and new decisions made in about a third of the cases. Drivers that influenced searching for more information included: (1) patient safety/risk reduction (e.g., outside usual pattern, young with risk factors for rare diseases, not to miss anything serious, cannot afford to be wrong on cancer, exclude red flags like glaucoma); (2) urgency of referral; (3) patient appearance/behavior; (4) perceived low-risk case; (5) label/diagnosis (e.g., aim for parsimony to provide unifying explanation); and (6) other (do no harm by putting elderly in hospital and just do what is safe).

WE USE SIMPLIFYING STRATEGIES (HEURISTICS)

The term *heuristic* refers to a rule of thumb (strategy). Our information is typically incomplete. We can consider only so much information at one time. The consequences of this may include: (1) selective perception (we do not necessarily see what is there); (2) sequential (rather than contextual) processing of information; (3) reliance on heuristics (rules of thumb) to reduce effort (e.g., frequently occurring cues, vivid case examples); and (4) faulty memory (our memories are inaccurate). In his discussion of bounded rationality over half a century ago, Simon (1955) suggested that we use heuristics (simplifying strategies) to solve decision problems. Research concerning naturalistic decision making shows that steps presumed to be of value in a rational model of problem solving and decision making, in which we identify alternatives, estimate the probability that each alternative will yield hoped-for outcomes, assign values to different options, and select the alternative with the greatest value, are often impossible to satisfy and are not needed to solve problems (Salas & Klein, 2001; Zsambok & Klein, 1997). We "satisfice" rather than optimize. Those with experience in an area that provided corrective feedback are able to quickly recognize important cues. (See also the later discussion of fast and frugal heuristics.)

APPROACHES FOCUSING ON BIAS

Nisbett and Ross (1980) and others, such as Tversky and Kahneman (1973), emphasized errors that result from use of simplifying heuristics. They suggested availability and representativeness (similarity) as reasons related to a variety of errors.

Availability

We often rely on what is available, such as a preferred theory or a vivid example. We seek information that is consistent with our preconceived notions; we tend to disregard conflicting evidence. Let us say that one of your clients has a substance abuse problem and that you recently went to workshop on self-esteem. This concept (self-esteem) is readily available in your thoughts. You may associate self-esteem with your client's problems and believe that low self-esteem is mainly responsible for this person's substance abuse. Availability influences judgments about causal relationships (Kahneman & Tversky, 1973). For example, observers tend to attribute the cause of other people's behavior to characteristics of the person rather than to situational factors (Batson, O'Quin, & Pych, 1982). The actor's behavior is more noticeable than more static situational events (see later discussion of observer-actor effects). We tend to exaggerate our own contributions to tasks; information about them is more available. We tend to overestimate the prevalence of illnesses that receive a great deal of media attention and underestimate the prevalence of illnesses that receive little media attention (Slovic, Fischhoff, & Lichtenstein, 1982a).

The Influence of Preconceptions and Preferred Theories

Preconceptions and theories influence how problems and possible resolutions are viewed. Often these are helpful. At other times they involve systematic errors (those in a biased direction, in contrast to random errors that may cancel each other out) and result in incorrect inferences "The impact of preconceptions is one of the better-demonstrated findings of twentieth-century psychology" (Nisbett & Ross, 1980, p. 67). Consider the classic study in which teachers are told that certain children in their classroom did very well on a nonverbal intelligence test that predicts intellectual blooming (Rosenthal & Jacobson, 1992). These children showed superior gains over the next 8 months. Actually, they were randomly selected. Many similar studies show that if teachers have low expectations about students the students will perform poorly, and if they have high expectations the students will perform well. Differences in expectations create different interactions. Teachers pay greater attention to students for whom they have high expectations (see R. Rosenthal, 1994). Our preconceptions and theories influence what events we notice or inquire about. The generation as well as the retrieval of data may be biased by preconceptions. Beliefs about the causes associated with a problem may result in selective inquiry during assessment.

Preconceptions can lead to incorrect inferences when (1) a theory is based on poor grounds (there is not adequate reason to believe that it is relevant), (2) a theory is used unconsciously, and (3) use of the theory "preempts examination of the data" (Nisbett & Ross, 1980, p. 71). All three biases are common in clinical practice. Practitioners often hold theories that have no empirical support as dearly as theories that do have support; they are often unaware of preconceptions that influence their decisions, and often do not check out their preconceptions by examining outcomes. Overconfidence in a theory increases the likelihood of biased preconceptions (Berner & Graber, 2008). The more ambiguous the data are, the more descriptions are influenced by preconceptions. We may be unaware of preconceptions that influence our decisions. Much of our understanding of the world is theory-based rather than data-based; our interpretations are inferences based on guesses about what may be true. Unwarranted confidence in a theory increases the chance of incorrect views. Only if we critically examine our assumptions may we identify flaws in our thinking and discover better options.

Stereotypes are a kind of preconception. They influence what we do and what we believe (e.g., Nelson, 2009). They save us time; we do not have to think about all the ways in which a client may not fit our conception. Stereotypes can be created remarkably quickly. For example, the fact that children were told that a visitor to their school was clumsy resulted in many of the children holding him responsible for knocking over a cake (when in fact he had not) (Leichtman & Ceci, 1995). We tend to overestimate the variability of in-groups (groups of which we are a member). Thus, we might assume too much knowledge from a sample of in-group members on some dimension about which we have little information. We tend to underestimate the degree of variability in out-groups (groups of which we are not a member). For example, people who are not gay or lesbian may underestimate the degree of variability among people who are gay or lesbian. On the other hand, gay men and lesbians may overestimate the degree of variability of gay or lesbian people.

Underestimating the variability of groups with which we are not familiar results in believing that we learn more (than we in fact do) from experience with one member of that group. If you have met one Native American, you may be inclined to make greater generalizations about what all Native Americans are like than if you have met many. If you have met many Native Americans from only one of the hundreds of different tribes, you may underestimate the degree of variability of behavior, values, and norms in other tribes. If we underestimate the degree of variability, we may lose a chance to identify clues about what a person is like or may do in certain situations. If we search only for evidence that supports a stereotype, we may miss more accurate alternative accounts. For example, Ceci and Bruck (1995) note, "Failure to test an alternative to a pet hunch can lead interviewers to ignore inconsistent evidence and to shape the contents of the interview to be consistent with their own beliefs" (p. 80). (See also discussion of stereotypes in Chapter 7.)

Achoring and Insufficient Adjustment

We tend to believe in initial judgments, even when we are aware that the knowledge we have access to has been arbitrarily selected—for example, by the spin of a roulette wheel. Adjustments from initial values are often inadequate. We often form impressions of clients quickly (Houts & Galante, 1985). For example, helpers make assumptions about clients' manageability and treatability that may influence questions asked and methods considered (Wills, 1978, 1982). Nisbett and Ross (1980) attribute primacy effects to our tendency to generate theories that bias the interpretation of data. These effects are encouraged by premature commitment to one assumption and insufficient revision of beliefs, as well as the tendency to believe (often falsely) in the consistency of behavior across different situations. One way to avoid anchoring effects is to consider an alternative estimate at another extreme. We are also influenced by recency—what we last see or hear. You may attend a workshop on child abuse and as a result suspect child abuse more readily in families. This, too, is a kind of influence based on availability.

Vividness

Nisbett and Ross (1980) emphasize the role of vividness of material in collecting, organizing, and interpreting data. Vivid information is more likely to be remembered than pallid information. The influence of vividness is illustrated by the finding that college students who spoke to four people were more swayed by the reports of these four individuals concerning the desirability of different psychology courses than were students who read a printout describing the course evaluations of 500 students (Borgida & Nisbett, 1977). Factors that contribute to vividness include emotional interest of material; the extent to which it provokes imagery and is concrete; and its sensory, temporal, or spatial proximity. Vivid case examples and testimonials are easy to recall and may crowd out data that, although less vivid, may be more informative, such as information on baseline rates of certain behaviors. Behaviors such as hitting and yelling are more vivid than are polite requests and following instructions. The client in the interview is more vivid than his or her home and neighborhood, which you may not see; this may contribute to our tendency to make the fundamental attribution error.

Practitioners often appeal to their experience: "I have seen this in my own practice." Clinicians may continue to use certain tests despite their questionable reliability and validity. In a survey of 500 clinical psychologists, they indicated that, in decisions about using a test, personal clinical experience with a test was more important than were data on reliability and validity (Wade & Baker, 1977). These clinicians emphasized the "subjective, insightful and experiential nature of the testing process" (p. 874). They gave more weight to their personal clinical experiences than to experimental evidence. (See also Lilienfeld, Lynn, & Lohr, 2003.) If a suspected murderer is called a "vicious killer," we may more readily believe that he was responsible for alleged crimes. Rook (1984) proposes that the heavy impact of negative exchanges in relationships that are basically positive may be due to the fact that positive exchanges become the expected background in such relationships; they are taken for granted and are less vivid. Events that do not take place are not as vivid. This type of information tends to be overlooked when it can be crucial. Sherlock Holmes solved a case based on the fact that a dog did not bark (Truzzi, 1976). Vivid information can be misleading, especially when duller but more informative material is not considered. Helpers often discount statistical information by citing a single case that supposedly contradicts this information. A vivid case example, unless it is known to be typical, ought to be given little weight in making decisions. A single example certainly should be given less weight than accurate relevant statistical information that contradicts the example.

Influence by Resemblance

We often make judgments based on the degree to which a characteristic seems to resemble or be similar to another characteristic or to a theory (Tversky & Kahneman, 1974). Relying on similarity is mainly an associative process in which we have associations with a certain characteristic. We have beliefs about what types of causes are associated with certain effects. For example, we may assume that causes resemble their effects, when this may not be so (Gilovitch & Savitsky, 2002). Overestimating the relationship between abuse as a child and abuse of one's own children reflects reliance on resemblance criteria. Other examples are:

- Foxes have remarkable lungs. Therefore, the lungs of a fox will remedy asthma.
- Turmeric (which is yellow) will cure jaundice.
- Unwillingness to discuss homosexual feelings reflects excessive interest in them. (Here and in the next example we see the assumption of opposites.)
- A generous action reflects underlying stinginess.

The problem is that similarity is not influenced by a number of factors we should consider: (1) whether a person/object belongs in a certain group, (2) the probability that an outcome was a result of a particular cause, and (3) the probability that a process will result in a certain outcome. Reliance on representative thinking may yield incorrect beliefs about the degree to which (1) outcomes reflect origins, (2) instances are representative of their categories, and (3) antecedents are representative of consequences. Reliance on similarity results in errors when we use clues that do not allow accurate predictions. For example, we may incorrectly assume that because a homeless child is similar to another client we just saw, similar causes are involved. We may search for consistent rather than informative data.

In representative thinking, some characteristic triggers an associated theory, belief, or schema. An example given by Howitt (1992) is assuming that a man abused his stepson because there is a correlation between being a stepfather and abuse of children. Consider also the example of a college admissions committee reviewing applicants given by Dawes (1988). One applicant was outstanding in all areas; however, she misspelled a word on her application. One committee member believed that this indicated that she was dyslexic, and her application was denied. Let's call misspelling a word c and the associated schema (dyslexia) the symbol S. We can then ask about conditional probabilities: What is the probability of c given S or S given c? The probability that members of S have characteristic c, given by $p(c \mid S)$, is likely. People with dyslexia often do misspell words. However, the probability that the characteristic c implies membership in S (dyslexia) is given by the conditional probability $p(S \mid c)$ (the probability that people with characteristic c are members of S), which is the inverse of $p(c \mid S)$. As Dawes points out, it is true that misspelling is a characteristic of dyslexia. However, probably many more students cannot spell certain words who are *not* dyslexic than who *are* dyslexic.

Thus, the basic problem with making probability judgments on the basis of representative characteristics is that "the schema accessed [dyslexia] may in fact be less probable, given the characteristic, than one not accessed when the schema not accessed has a much greater *extent* in the world than the accessed one" (Dawes, 1988, p. 70). The number of people who are *not* dyslexic is much larger than the number of people who *are* dyslexic. The problem is that when a schema (i.e., dyslexia) is accessed (considered), the actual extent of the class is usually not, resulting in faulty decisions. As Dawes points out, representative thinking does not distinguish between the probability of *c* given *S* and the probability of *S* given *c*. Most associations are *not* symmetrical. We can draw on rules of probability theory to avoid errors caused by representative thinking. Associative thinking may occur unnoticed (automatically, mindlessly) unless we question our assumptions, search for alternative possibilities, and review the evidentiary status of claims. Assessing the representativeness of samples to a population is a key helping skill. How likely is it that a sample (e.g., of behaviors, thoughts, feelings) accurately represents the population for which it is drawn? How likely is it that what you see during an hour in a residential center accurately reflects the usual pattern of interaction between staff and residents?

FAST AND FRUGAL HEURISTICS

There has been a shift to highlighting the adaptive nature of our decision making as it fits certain environments—a realization that hueristics often work well and save time and effort. Gigerenzer (2005) argues that many events that have been viewed as cognitive illusions are reasonable judgments given the environmental structure. Their use has been referred to as the "fast and frugal" approach to decision making (Gigerenzer, Hertwig, & Pachur, 2011). Such strategies often (but not always) suffice, and when ecologically relevant, may surpass more deliberative approaches. Advocates of the fast and frugal approach argue that rather than our limited information-processing capabilities being a handicap, they are an advantage, because they facilitate rapid decisions based on recognition of relevant environmental cues. They encourage attention to cues that are most relevant (situation awareness), so help to avoid errors introduced by too much information, including misleading and irrelevant data (see Exhibit 9.3). A key question is: "Are decisions most likely to help clients attain outcomes they value?"

Gigerenzer and his colleagues (2011) argue that availability and representativeness are labels for a wide variety of events, including ease of recall and number of instances. They argue that these are not theories but labels, surrogates for theories. He and his colleagues focus on the selection of heuristics in specific contexts—how do we select one in a given situation, and how effective is it? They argue that problems posed in laboratory experiments do not reflect real-life situations; for example, information search is ignored. They highlight the important distinction between cue validity (what is in the

Exhibit 9.3 Examples of Fast and Frugal Heuristics Useful in Solving Problems.

Heuristic	Definition	Surprising Finding
Recognition heuristic	If one of two alternatives is recognized, infer that it has the higher value on the criteria (if recognition validity > .5).	Systematic forgetting can be beneficial.
Fluency heuristic	If both alternatives are recognized but one is recognized faster, infer that it has the higher value on the criterion (if fluency validity > .5).	Less-is-more effect; systematic forgetting can be beneficial.
Take-the-best	Search through cues in order of validity, stop search as soon as a cue discriminates, and choose the alternative this cue favors.	Often predicts more accurately than multiple regression.
Tallying (unit-weight linear model)	To estimate a criterion simply count the number of positive cues.	Often predicts equally or more accurately than multiple regression.
Satisficing	Search through alternatives and choose the first one that exceeds your aspiration level.	Aspiration levels can lead to better choices than chance, even if they are arbitrary.
Equality heuristic	Allocate resources equally to each alternative (when there is high unpredictability).	Can outperform optimal asset allocation portfolios.
Default heuristic	If there is a default, do nothing (when defaults match those of the decision maker; when the consequences of a choice are hard to foresee).	Explains why mass mailing has little effect on organ donor registration; predicts behavior when trait and preference theories fail.

Note: For formal definitions, see references.

Source: Based on Gigerenzer and Brighton (2011), "Homo Heuristicus: Why Biased Minds Make Better Inferences," in G. Gigerenzer, R. Hertwig, and T. Pachur (Eds.), *Hueristics: The Foundations of Adoptive Behavior.* New York, NY: Oxford University Press.

mind) and ecological validity (what is in the environment). Consider the recognition heuristic: "If one of two objects is recognized and the other is not, then infer that the recognized object has the higher value with respect to the criterion." Such a strategy is fast because it can solve problems quickly and frugal because it requires little information and effort; but notice that it works when recognition validity is greater than .5.

Gigerenzer suggests that there are two kinds of search: an optimizing and a heuristic search. In the former there is a kind of sequential analysis. In the second, we do not try to optimize; we exploit characteristics of particular environments to make sound decisions. This view is a continuation of Simon's (1982) bounded rationality—that "satisficing" is sufficient in many situations—that the time and effort required to identify many alternatives and evaluate their soundness are not only unnecessary in many situations to arrive at a sound decision, but may actually result in more errors, cues that are most valuable are lost in a sea of data. Research regarding the development of expertise shows that primed decision making based on repeated past experiences providing corrective feedback enables speedy pattern recognition (Klein, 1998). Gigerenzer and his colleagues argue that the "heuristics and biases approach" (e.g., Nisbett & Ross, 1980) views rationality as logical instead of ecological. Typically, as they point out, optimization is not possible, let alone necessary; we rarely know all the factors influencing a behavior or event. Thus we have the "less is more" effect, in which accuracy "is always relative to the structure of the environment" (p. 9); error is confined to acceptable limits—for example, in making a prediction.

Gigerenzer (2005) suggests that a rule functions as a heuristic (rule of thumb) when it exploits our evolved capacities as well as structures of environments. All heuristics are domain specific to some degree, designed to solve certain kinds of problems. "Heuristics are not good or bad, rational or irrational, per se, but are only relative to an environment. In an environment, does a particular heuristic work well? The same holds true for optimization methods" (Gigerenzer et al., 2011, p. xix). Since these heuristics ignore information and enable fast decisions, they are called "fast and frugal." There is a trade-off between accuracy (good enough) and effort and time. A "take the best" approach is a form of one-reason decision making consisting of three building blocks: a search rule, a stopping rule, and a decision rule.

1. *Search by validity:* Search through cues in order of their validity, and look up the cue values of the cue with the highest validity first.
2. *One-reason stopping rule:* If one object has a positive cue value 1 and the other does not or is unknown, then stop the search and proceed to step 3. Otherwise include this cue and return to step 1. If no more cues are found, guess.
3. *One-reason decision making:* Predict that the object with the positive cue value 1 has a higher value on the criterion. (Gigerenzer & Goldstein, 1999, p. 74)

WE TEND TO MAKE CERTAIN KINDS OF ERRORS

What is an error? Consider this example from a study of error in ophthalmology:

A young boy with an enlarging right lower eyelid mass underwent three biopsies over an 8 month interval. The biopsies each showed chronic inflammation with eosinophils and necrosis. The anatomical diagnosis was descriptive and included the comment "consistent with eosinophilic granuloma." Treatment with external beam radiation on three separate occasions and several courses of a corticosteroid was unsuccessful. Usually eosinophilic granulomas are very sensitive to radiotherapy. When the pathology slides were reviewed elsewhere, the diagnosis of fungal cellulitis was made. The boy eventually lost his right eye, eyelids, facial skin and orbit. *Areas of concern:* A boy lost nearly a third of his face because three biopsies were misinterpreted as eosinophilic granuloma and cultures of the inflamed tissues were never taken. (Margo, 2005, p. 418)

Lipshitz (1997) defines decision errors as "deviations from some standard decision process that increase the likelihood of bad outcomes" (p. 152). (See Exhibit 9.4.) Woods and Cook (1999) suggest that "the label human error involves investigating how knowledge was, or could have been brought to bear in the evolving infinite" (p. 150). For example, we may use an oversimplification that is of value in some contexts in one in which it is not useful. They suggest that, by definition, experts do not make errors, because they are doing the best that could be done under the circumstances. Studies of decision making in professional contexts reveal a variety of errors, such as incorrect views of problems (e.g., missing physical causes). There are different systems for classifying errors in diagnosis. One highlights different dimensions of professional competence, such as faulty cognition and technical or integrative skills. Another emphasizes cognitive processes such as faulty hypotheses generation and information gathering

Exhibit 9.4 Problem-Solving Phases and Common Errors

Step	Common Errors
1. Clarify the problem.	• Jump to conclusions (overlook alternative views).
	• Seek to justify views rather than critically evaluate them.
	• Ignore environmental causes.
	• Gather irrelevant data.
	• Underestimate available problem-related research findings.
	• Overestimate personal problem-related knowledge.
	• Rely on invalid data (e.g., small biased samples).
	• Disregard conflicting evidence.
	• Stereotyping.
2. Search for solutions.	• Overlook options.
	• Look only for data that confirm assumptions.
	• Overlook constraints.
	• Overlook resources.
	• Do not revise views as needed based on new information.
	• See other items under Step 1.
3. Decide on a plan.	• Overlook promising options.
	• Overlook constraints.
	• Don't fully inform clients about options and their potential costs and benefits.
4. Implement plans.	• The "dilution" effect (i.e., offer ineffective version of plans).
	• Do not arrange for corrective feedback about outcome.

5. Evaluate results.	• Use vague outcome measures.
	• Use inaccurate measures.
	• Do not gather both subjective and objective measures.
	• Post hoc fallacy (assume that because there is a change, services were responsible).
	• Overlook harmful effects.
	• Do not revise plans as needed based on outcome data.
6. Try again?	• Give up too soon.
	• Fail to critically examine favored views.

Source: Adapted from *Social Work Practice: A Critical Thinker's Guide* (3rd ed.), by E. Gambrill, 2012, New York, NY: Oxford.

(Kassirer & Kopelman, 1989; see also Margo, 2005). Research regarding expert political judgment concerning real-world events within individuals' domains of expertise shows that they often fall prey to the following five errors or biases:

1. *Overconfidence.* There are large gaps between the subjective probabilities assigned to outcomes and the objective probabilities of those outcomes occurring (e.g., the illusion of knowledge).

2. *Cognitive conservatism.* Experts are too slow to update their beliefs.

3. *Certainty of hindsight.* Mistakes may be denied. "They tend to recall assigning higher subjective probabilities to those . . . outcomes that occur than they actually assigned before learning what occurred."

4. *Theory-driven standards of evidence and proof.* They "generally impose higher standards of evidence and proof on dissonant claims than they do on consonant ones." They use a double standard.

5. *Systematic evidence of incoherence in subjective probability judgments.* They "often judge the likelihood of the whole to be less, sometimes far less, than the sum of its parts." (Tetlock, 2003, pp. 233–234; see also Tetlock, 2005)

Reason (2001) distinguishes among mistakes, violations, lapses, and slips that may occur during planning, recalling intentions, carrying out a task, or monitoring. A violation entails knowingly omitting an important step. A lapse involves not recalling an intention to carry out an important task at the needed time. A slip entails unwittingly omitting an important task in a sequence and/or not detecting it. Common errors in different problem-solving phases can be seen in Exhibit 9.4. (See also Exhibit 8.1.) In a taxonomy of errors suggested by Zhang, Patel, Johnson, and Shortliffe (2004), a mistake occurs when behavior leads to a failure because of incorrect or incomplete knowledge; a slip occurs when the knowledge is correct but there is a failure. (See examples they give.) Attention has also been devoted to "patient error." Beutow and his colleagues

Exhibit 9.5 Examples of Patient Assertion Errors Identified in Nominal Group Interviews With Patients and Primary Health Care Professionals

2.1 Taciturnity	2.1.1 Nondisclosure of relevant information	Not updating contact information	"Not telling the doctor all your symptoms" (group 7)
	2.1.2 Nonquestioning	Not asking for clarification of confusing information	"Not questioning professionals if instructions are unclear or they do not understand" (group 10)
2.2 Verbosity	2.2.1 Excessive talk	Not giving the clinician sufficient time to meet concerns	"Telling doctor what I want but not giving much time for him to tell me what he would like" (group 3)
2.3 Extraneous talk	2.3.1 Irrelevant talk	Trying too hard to recall details	"No relationship with doctor, so just say 'yes' to everything" (group 1)
2.4 Erroneous talk	2.4.1 Inaccurate talk	Contradicting medical advice to family or friends	"Inaccurate/false responses" (group 2)
2.5 Inarticulateness	2.5.1 Inability to express thoughts clearly	Limited language skills; translation errors	"Inability to describe your sickness" (group 7)
2.6 Disrespect	2.6.1 Lack of caring	Lack of regard for interests of clinician	"Making one appointment for two to four people" (group 10)
	2.6.2 Discourtesy	Cell phone on during visits	"Not notifying if late or need to miss appointments" (group 10)
	2.6.3 Abusiveness	Violent patient	"Being drunk and abusive" (group 6)
2.7 Artfulness	2.7.1 Dishonesty	Distortion of information given	"Lying about symptoms to jump queue" (group 4)
	2.7.2 Pretense of sickness	Benefits of sick role	"Pretending to be ill to take the day from school" (group 7)
	2.7.3 Manipulation of system	False claims for compensation	"Seeks to manipulate the outflow of information from the medical record" (group 9)

Source: Beutow, S., Kiata, L., Liew, T., Kenealy, T., Dovey, S., and Elwyn, G. (2009). Patient error: A preliminary taxonomy. *Annals of Family Medicine,* 7, 223–231.

identified 70 types of patient errors using 11 nominal group interviews of patients and primary health care providers in New Zealand. Action errors (distinguished from mental errors) included attendance, assertiveness, and adherence. Exhibit 9.5 shows items included under "assertion errors."

Studies of decision making in child welfare show the effects of *ratcheting* (persisting with a point of view in spite of evidence that it is wrong) and *templating* (inappropriately applying correlational data to individual clients; Howitt, 1992; see also Munro, 1996). Errors may occur both in structuring problems and in drawing inferences. Medical students and even some practicing physicians hold various kinds of oversimplifications that create misconceptions (Feltovich, Spiro, & Coulson, 1989). Examples are:

- Seeing different entities as more similar than they actually are.
- Treating dynamic phenomena as static.
- Assuming that some general principle accounts for all of the phenomena.
- Treating multidimensional phenomena as unidimensional or according to a subset of dimensions.
- Treating continuous variables as discrete.
- Treating highly interconnected concepts as separable.
- Treating the whole as merely the sum of its parts. (Feltovich, Spiro, & Coulson, 1993, cited in Woods & Cook, 1999, p. 152)

Motivational and informational sources of error interact in various ways. We are most likely to miss biases in situations in which we are biased for (or against) a certain point of view and the informational source contains the same bias. Bias can intrude at any point in the judgmental process and may also occur because of interactions between different stages of data processing (Hogarth, 1980). "First, the acquisition of information from both the environment and memory can be biased. The crucial issue here is how certain information does or does not become salient. How we direct our attention influences what we see (and what we miss). Second, the manner in which we process information can be biased; for example, we may attempt to simplify a situation by using a misleading strategy. Third, the manner in which we are required to respond can introduce bias. Finally, the outcomes of our judgments can create bias in both: (1) interpretation of their significance (for example, is the outcome attributable to one's actions or simply a chance fluctuation?); and (2) learning relationships for predictive validity" (p. 158). There are individual differences in susceptibility to errors and biases: "Cognitive style—the strength of respondents' preferences for explanatory closure and parsimony—moderated the magnitude of several effects. Specifically, respondents who valued closure and parsimony highly were more prone to biases that were rooted in excessive faith in the predictive and explanatory power of their preconceptions—biases such as overconfidence, cognitive conservatism, certainty of hindsight and selective standards of evidence and proof . . . more 'open-minded,' lower-need-for-closure respondents . . . wound up being too imaginative and assigning too much subjective probability to too many scenarios (with the result that subjective probabilities summed to well above 1.0)" (Tetlock, 2003, p. 234).

Many errors occur because of confirmation biases (searching only for data in support of a preferred view) and reliance on questionable criteria such as popularity of a view for evaluating the accuracy of claims. Research on error shows that it is typically due to systemic factors, including poor training and poor interface between technology and human factors (e.g., Reason, 1997, 2001; see Exhibit 9.6). Often there is a cascade effect, in which one error, if not caught and countered, leads to another, in a chain that results in an unwanted consequence (Woolf, Kuzel, Dovey, & Phillips, 2004). This highlights the value of identifying the kinds of errors that occur in relation to a decision, so that early ones in a chain can be caught, thus cutting off the rest of the chain from occurring. "Because there are a set of contributors, multiple opportunities arise to redirect the trajectory away from disaster . . . an important part of safety is enhancing opportunities for people to recognize that a trajectory is heading closer to a poor outcome and to recover before negative consequences occur" (Woods & Cook, 1999, p. 144). This pattern suggests that "the label 'human error' should serve as the starting point for investigating how systems fail, not as a conclusion" (p. 144).

Exhibit 9.6 Examples of Contributing Factors to Errors

- Unfamiliarity with a potentially important situation that is novel or occurs infrequently
- Shortage of time for error detection and correction
- High level of noise (irrelevant cues)
- Mismatch between designer's and user's model of system
- No obvious means of reversing an unintended action
- A channel capacity overload, particularly one caused by the simultaneous presence of non-redundant information
- A need to unlearn a technique and apply one that requires the application of an opposing philosophy
- The need to transfer specific knowledge from one task to another without loss
- Ambiguity in required performance standards
- A mismatch between real and perceived risk
- Poor, ambiguous, or ill-timed feedback
- Operator inexperience—for example, a new employee
- Lack of needed information
- Little or no independent checking or testing of output
- A conflict between immediate and long-term objectives
- No diversity of information for accuracy checks
- An incentive to use other, less effective or more dangerous procedures
- Unreliable instrumentation that is not recognized as such
- Unclear allocation of responsibility
- No obvious way to track progress during a task
- Little or no intrinsic meaning in a task
- High-level emotional stress
- Ill health, especially fever
- Low workforce morale
- Inconsistency of meaning of displays and procedures
- Team members over those necessary to carry out tasks satisfactorily

Source: Adapted from *Managing the Risks of Organizational Accidents* (pp. 142–143), by J. Reason, 1997, Brookfield, VT: Ashgate. Reprinted with permission.

In errors of commission we *do* something that decreases the likelihood of discovering valuable options. We may:

- Look only for data that confirm our beliefs.
- Jump to conclusions.
- Stereotype people or theories.
- Misinterpret cues.
- Assume that correlation reflects causation.
- Prematurely discard a valuable opinion.

In errors of omission we *fail* to do something, which decreases the likelihood of discovering valuable options. We may:

- Not question initial assumptions.
- Fail to pose well-structured questions related to information needed to make decisions.
- Fail to seek out and critically appraise problem-related research findings.
- Ignore the role of environmental causes.
- Overlook cultural differences.
- Overlook client assets.

These two kinds of errors are interrelated. For example, jumping to conclusions (an error of commission) can occur only if you do not question initial assumptions (an error of omission). These errors may result in: (1) inaccurate descriptions, (2) incorrect estimates of covariations, (3) inaccurate descriptions of causal relationships, or (4) inaccurate predictions. Common defaults in thinking emphasized by David Perkins (1995) include:

- *Hasty thinking:* Impulsive and mindless; we don't reflect on what we think or do.
- *Narrow thinking:* Tendency to think in a narrow context; we overlook the big picture (e.g., my-side bias).
- *Fuzzy thinking:* Imprecise, unclear; we overlook key differences; we do not question vague terms (e.g., *support, ego strength*).
- *Sprawling thinking:* Wandering aimlessly in a disorganized manner without integrating data from diverse sources; we bounce from one view to another without ever deciding on an overview. (Perkins, 1995, p. 153)

They occur because of a lack of attention to planning, monitoring, and critical questioning. Consider the *Barnum effect*. This refers to accepting vague personality descriptions about ourselves that could be true of just about anybody. The very nature of clinical practice leaves room for many sources of avoidable error. Some errors result from a lack of information about how to help clients. Empirical knowledge related to clinical practice is fragmentary, and theory must be used to fill in the gaps. Decreasing gaps between available knowledge and its use is emphasized in evidence-based practice, including the design of innovative ways to decrease this gap (Greenhalgh, Robert, Macfarlane, Bate, & Kyriakidou, 2004).

MEMORY AS RECONSTRUCTIVE

We rely on our memory when processing and organizing data. Research shows that memory is a reconstructive process. "With the passage of time, with proper motivation, with the introduction of special kinds of interfering facts, the memory traces may change" (Loftus, 1980, p. 37; see also Ceci & Bruck, 1995; Loftus & Ketcham, 1994; Lynn et al., 2003). We tend to recall our successes and overlook our failures. This is one reason intuition may lead us astray. False memories can be created through biased interviewing methods (Ceci & Bruck, 1995; Ofshe & Watters, 1994). Simply being asked a question repeatedly can result in memories of events that did not happen (Ceci, Crotteau-Huffman, Smith, & Loftus, 1994; Ceci & Bruck, 1995). Our memories change in accord with our stereotypes. Consider a study in which subjects were read a description of some events in a woman's life (Gahagan, 1984, p. 93). Some subjects were told later that the woman had met a lesbian and started a homosexual relationship with her. Other subjects were told that she met a man and initiated a relationship with him. A third group received no information about sexual relationships. A week later, all participants were asked to recall details of the woman's earlier life. Subjects who were told that she had initiated a homosexual relationship showed strong distortion effects in their recall in accord with stereotypes about "typical characteristics of lesbians" (p. 93).

Memory may be imperfect because events were not accurately noted in the first place. Even if we accurately observed a sequence of events, our memory of these events may not remain accurate. Although some details may be accurately recalled, we may make up events to fill in gaps in our memory, to create what seem to be logical sequences of actions. We then imagine that we really saw these events. We thus may have false memories (e.g., Roediger & Bergman, 1998). The illusion of having a memory of an event can be created by including inaccurate descriptive data in a question. We may forget what happened in the past because of interfering events, which decrease attention to detail so that certain characteristics may not be noticed. Drugs and alcohol also affect memory. Another possibility is motivated forgetting, in which negative events are forgotten and positive ones remembered; happy times from a vacation tend to be recalled and sad times tend to be forgotten (Loftus, 1980, p. 711). Gamblers tend to remember instances when they have won and to forget about the times when they lost. Clinicians tend to recall their successes and to forget their failures. High anxiety interferes with remembering events; high arousal decreases attention to detail so that events may not be noticed. Considerable attention has been devoted to the study of memory, including discovery of strategies to jog memory. Methods include multiple probes, use of different question forms, hypnosis, and monetary incentives (Loftus & Ketcham, 1994; see also Baddeley, 1997; Halpern, 2003).

PERSPECTIVE MAKES A DIFFERENCE: SELF VERSUS OTHERS

We tend to make dispositional assumptions about others and infer environmental influences for our own behavior. This has a number of implications for empathy. Pronin and Ross (1999) explored the views of men and women after the end of a relationship. Participants perceived their own efforts in initiating a breakup as "significantly clearer, and less characterized by 'mixed signals' than the efforts of the person who initiated the breakup with them" (cited in Pronin, Puccio, & Ross, 2002, p. 646). This difference in perspective has been called "naive realism." It is an epistemological stance with the following characteristics (p. 647):

- I see stimuli, issues, and events as they are in objective reality and my social attitudes, beliefs, preferences, priorities, and the like follow from a relatively dispassionate . . . apprehension of the information or evidence at hand.
- Other rational social perceivers generally share my judgments and reactions— provided that they have had access to the same information that gave rise to my views, and provided that they too have processed that information in a reasonably thoughtful and open-minded fashion.
- The failure of a given individual or group to share my judgments and reactions arises from one of three possible sources: (1) the individual or group in question may have been exposed to a different sample of information . . . ; (2) the individual or group in question may be lazy, irrational, or otherwise unable or unwilling to proceed in a normative fashion from objective evidence to a reasonable conclusions; and (3) the individual or group in question may be biased (either in interpreting the evidence or in proceeding from evidence to conclusions) by ideology, self-interest, or some other distorting influence.

Implications of this kind of epistemology, suggested by Pronin et al. (2002), include overconfidence in our ability to persuade others and the *false polarization* effect (overestimating differences in views with adversaries; see also Ross & Ward, 1996). Observers tend to attribute the cause of other people's behavior to characteristics of the person rather than to situational factors (Batson, O'Quin, & Pych, 1982). The actor's behavior is more noticeable compared to more static situational events. We tend to exaggerate our own contributions to tasks. Consequences of insider-outsider differences and the naive realism perspective noted by these authors include the following: (1) we perceive our own self-knowledge and insight to be more accurate and complete than insights of others, (2) we perceive our knowledge of others to be more accurate and complete than other people's knowledge of ourselves, (3) we perceive the discrepancy between our self-knowledge and other people's knowledge of ourselves to be greater than the corresponding discrepancy between other people's self-knowledge and our knowledge of these other people, and (4) we perceive our group's knowledge of other groups to be more accurate and complete than other group's knowledge of our group (see also Dunning, Heath, & Suls, 2004).

THERE ARE CULTURAL DIFFERENCES

Some authors argue that "East Asians [Chinese, Japanese, and Koreans] have a more holistic, field-dependent attention mode and Westerners have a more focused analytic, field-independent attention mode" (Choi, Choi, & Norenzayan, 2005, p. 511). Comparisons of Westerners and East Asians, including Chinese, Japanese, and Koreans, on different kinds of cognitive tasks suggest a number of differences. Two modes of thinking were identified. In analytic thinking there is a "detachment of the object from its context, a preference to focus on attributes of the object and to assign the object to categories based on these attributes, and a tendency to use rules about the categories to predict and explain the object's behavior. Holistic thinking involves an orientation to the context as a whole, attention to relationship between the object and the context, and a preference for explaining the behavior of the object based on such relationships. Holistic thinking relies on experience rather than logic, and includes a dialectical orientation, meaning that there is an emphasis on change and a tolerance for contradiction" (p. 511).

Westerners possess a greater sense of control and "tend to explain behavior in terms of internal attributes, whereas East Asians explain behavior in terms of the interaction between internal attributes and situational factors. As a consequence, East Asians are less susceptible to the fundamental attribution error" (Choi et al., 2005, p. 511), the tendency to attribute behavior to dispositions of a person and to overlook situational factors (see also Chapter 14). These authors argue that East Asians have a more complex idea of causality. "Westerners are likely to confront conceptual conflicts or contradictions and 'polarize' their decision, that is, make a principled choice between opposing positions. In contrast, East Asians opt to avoid conflicts or contradictions and are quick to find a compromise solution between opposing positions" (p. 512). They suggest that cultural variations in analytic compared to holistic styles predict group differences in information search, including what information is relevant, where to locate it, and how to combine it (p. 512). See also *The Geography of Thought* (2003) by Richard Nisbett.

CREATIVITY AND INTUITION PLAY AN IMPORTANT ROLE

Successful problem solvers draw on their creative talents to discover options for solving problems. "The scientist and the artist, far from being engaged in opposed or incompatible activities, are both trying to extend our understanding of experience by the use of creative imagination subjected to critical control, and so both are using irrational as well as rational faculties. Both are exploring the unknown and trying to articulate the search and its findings. Both are seekers after truth who make indispensable use of intuition" (Magee, 1985, pp. 68–69; see also discussion of intuition in Chapter 4). Styles, attitudes, and strategies associated with creativity include:

- Readiness to explore and to change
- Attention to problem finding as well as problem solving
- Immersion in a task
- Restructuring of understanding
- A belief that knowing and understanding are products of one's intellectual efforts
- Withholding of judgment
- An emphasis on understanding
- Thinking in terms of opposites
- Valuing complexity, ambiguity, and uncertainty, combined with an interest in finding order
- Valuing feedback but not deferring to convention and social pressure
- Deferring closure in the early stages of creative tasks
- Commitment, as reflected in long hours devoted to work and total engagement
- Recognizing multiple perspectives on a topic (e.g., see Halpern, 2003)

FAILURES ARE INEVITABLE

Calls for ensuring certain outcomes are often made by politicians and administrators, such as "to ensure that no child be harmed in care." This is not possible. Even in the best of circumstances, given the uncertainty surrounding problems we confront and missing options for altering circumstances, failure to protect clients will occur. Some failures are avoidable, as suggested by the research by DePanfilis (2003) based on reviews of case records of children in care. (See also Bartholet, 2009.) Others are not. Calling for a perfection that is not possible can be demoralizing and can impede looking closely at outcomes (since we know we are unlikely to find such perfection). And bad outcomes do not necessarily reflect poor decisions. Illusions that we can always succeed are likely to result in feelings of regret that hinder rather than facilitate better decisions in the future (Kahneman, 1995). Reactions to commission (acting) are associated with greater regret than are reactions to omission (failing to act).

SOME BARRIERS ARE SELF-IMPOSED

Some barriers to problem solving are self-imposed, such as failures to revise our views when needed. The accuracy of our beliefs about the problems we confront affects our success in helping clients, as do our beliefs about ourselves (e.g., whether we think we can make a difference). Only if we are aware of our assumptions can we critically examine them; for example, pose related questions and seek and critically appraise relevant research. Motivational barriers include lack of interest in helping clients. You may believe that good intentions are enough to protect clients from harmful or ineffective services, although history shows they are not (see Chapter 1). Emotional barriers include fear of making mistakes and a low tolerance for uncertainty. Our moods influence how we process information (Bless, 2001; Finucane, Alhakami, Slovic, & Johnson, 2000). We may fear taking risks or feel helpless in the face of great need.

Intellectual barriers include inflexible use of problem-solving strategies that results in getting caught in "loops" (see Exhibit 9.2). Focusing on justifying our beliefs rather than on critiquing them is a major obstacle. This encourages confirmation biases, in which we seek only data that support our assumptions. A preoccupation with finding the cause of a problem can be a barrier, rather than asking how behaviors or events can be altered to attain desired outcomes (Feinstein, 1967). We may have ineffective interpersonal skills. Information that can contribute to sound decisions is unlikely to be shared with unempathic, judgmental helpers. Research concerning the causes of error in aviation as well as in medicine highlights the importance of effective communication skills and values that contribute to this. For example, arrogance on the part of the captain of an airplane may result in ignoring concerns raised by a copilot, which in turn results in a near miss or a crash. Decisions must often be made in high-stress situations involving many different people. Communication failure due to interpersonal conflicts and miscommunication are a key source of avoidable errors.

WE CAN LEARN TO BECOME BETTER DECISION MAKERS

We can draw on related research to learn how to make better and more timely decisions (e.g., Croskerry & Nimmo, 2011; Michiels, Thomas, Royen, & Coenen, 2011). Such research is of value in understanding how things go wrong (for example, by not attending to anomalies that may call a diagnosis into question). We can become familiar with barriers to problem solving and develop skills for avoiding them. We can acquire critical thinking values, knowledge, and skills that contribute to problem solving and decision making as well as skills involved in the process of evidence-based practice. (See Chapters 9 and 10.) We can acquire strategies for decreasing automatic stereotypes (Gollwitzer, Bayer, & McCulloch, 2005), become more aware of how we think, and make a rule to "consider the opposite" (Larrick, 2005). We can draw on both intuitive and analytic styles of reasoning.

We can pay more attention to our reasoning process (e.g., monitor our thinking by asking questions, such as, "How am I doing?" "Is this correct?" "How do I know this is true?" "What are my biases?" "Is there another way to approach this problem?" "Do I understand this point?"). These questions highlight the importance of self-correction in problem solving. Related behaviors can be thought of as self-governing processes (strategies we use to guide our thinking). They can help us to avoid common intelligence traps and to integrate both intuitive and analytic styles of thinking. Increasingly metacognitive levels of thought include:

1. *Tacit:* Thinking without thinking about it.
2. *Aware:* Thinking and being aware that you are thinking.
3. *Strategic:* Organizing your thinking by using strategies that enhance its efficacy.
4. *Reflective:* Reflecting on your thinking (pondering how to proceed and how to improve; Swartz & Perkins, 1990). Such reflection allows us to discover our "theories in action" (Schon, 1990).

Repeated practice opportunities involving real-life decisions in a context of corrective feedback contribute to developing rapid pattern recognition (see Chapter 8). We can, as Hogarth (2001) suggests, educate our intuition. We can take advantage of problem-based learning methods and become informed about how our work environments affect learning (e.g., see Richman-Hirsch, 2001).

LEARNING THROUGH MISTAKES

One of the greatest challenges in becoming a successful problem solver is reappraising the value of mistakes. We are often taught to hide rather than reveal them. Hiding them makes it less likely that we will avoid them in the future. Mistakes are inevitable and provide valuable learning opportunities if corrective feedback is provided (see discussion of acquiring expertise in Chapter 8). Failures and mistakes (less than hoped-for success) offer information that may yield better guesses next time around. They help us to learn about the nature of the problem (Popper, 1994).

> Only through our errors can we learn; and only he will learn who is ready to appreciate and even to cherish the errors of others as stepping stones towards truth, and who searches for his own errors: who tries to find them, since only when he has become aware of them can he free himself from them. (Popper, 1992, p. 149)

Popper (1998) suggests the following obligations:

1. To recognize that mistakes will be made; "it is impossible to avoid making mistakes."
2. To recognize that it is our duty to minimize avoidable mistakes.
3. To learn how to do better from recognizing our mistakes.
4. To be on the lookout for mistakes.
5. To embrace a self-critical attitude.
6. To welcome others pointing out our mistakes; we need others to discover and point out our mistakes; criticism by others is a necessity.
7. Objective criticism "must always be specific"; must give specific reasons why specific statements or specific hypotheses appear to be false, or specific arguments invalid. It must be guided by the idea of getting nearer to objective truth. In this sense it must be impersonal, but also sympathetic (pp. 64–65).

Unavoidable mistakes are those that could not have been anticipated. They occur despite taking advantage of available knowledge and critical thinking skills—in spite of making and acting on well-informed judgments. You may have worked with caregivers of an elderly relative to identify activities the relative enjoys but find that these activities do not function as reinforcers. Even though you and your clients do your best to identify reinforcers, you cannot know whether particular events will function as reinforcers until you try them out. Avoidable mistakes are mistakes that could have been avoided, for example, by being better informed regarding practice-related research findings, by thinking more critically about assumptions and their possible consequences, and by seeking help from someone more expert in an area. They may occur because of faulty decision-making styles, such as jumping to conclusions, and/or agency policies and procedures that interfere with sound decision making such as onerous and unhelpful documentation requirements. Communication failure is a key source of avoidable errors.

We may forget to include an important element in an intervention. (See discussion of common elements in Chorpita, Becker, & Daleiden, 2007.) We may not monitor progress so that we can detect need for change in a program.

Wu and his colleagues (Wu, Folkman, McPhee, & Lo, 2003) surveyed 254 internal medical house officers regarding their most significant mistake and their response to it. Kinds of mistakes included errors in diagnosis (33%), prescribing (29%), evaluation (21%), communication (5%), and procedural complications (11%). "Patients had serious adverse outcomes in 90% of the cases, including death in 31% of cases" (p. 221). "House officers who accepted responsibility for the mistake and discussed it were more likely to report constructive changes in practice. Residents were less likely to make constructive changes if they attributed the mistake to job overload. They were more likely to report defensive changes if they felt the institution was judgmental" (p. 221). Learning what caused a mistake can be difficult. For example, Margo (2005) found high interrater reliability in classifying diagnostic errors among three ophthalmologists, but marked disagreement about the root causes of the errors.

SUMMARY

Decision making is integral to helping clients. We make scores of decisions every day. Some are well reasoned. Others are not. We can take advantage of research concerning problem solving, decision making, and judgment to make better decisions—those that are likely to help clients attain outcomes they value. No matter what our intelligence, we are likely to fall into a variety of intelligence traps unless we develop values, knowledge, and skills that help us avoid them. Personal blocks to problem solving include emotional barriers, such as fear of taking risks, and motivational barriers, such as lack of interest in helping clients. Environmental obstacles include noisy offices, time pressures, and authoritarian administrative decision-making styles. Cultural blocks include a professional culture that punishes those who question bogus claims of effectiveness. We are subject to a variety of cognitive biases, such as looking only for data that support our beliefs (confirmation biases) and being influenced by misleading data. The good news is that we can become more effective problem solvers by taking advantage of debiasing strategies, including the process of evidence-based practice. We can learn how to avoid errors that get in the way of helping clients attain outcomes they value and avoiding harm—for example, by taking advantage of practice- and policy-related research findings.

10

Evidence-Based Practice: A Philosophy and Process for Making Informed Decisions

The goal of critical thinking is to arrive at well-reasoned decisions. Evidence-based practice (EBP) describes a process for facilitating this aim. It describes a philosophy and process designed to forward effective use of professional judgment in integrating information regarding each client's unique characteristics, circumstances, preferences, and actions, and external research findings. "It is a guide for thinking about how decisions should be made" (Haynes, Devereaux, & Guyatt, 2002, p. 1). Critical thinking and evidence-based practice require a willingness to say "I don't know"—to acknowledge that there may be a gap between your current knowledge and skills and what is needed to make sound decisions. It is a process for handling the uncertainty surrounding decisions that must be made in real life, in real time. Sources of uncertainty include limitations in current knowledge, lack of familiarity with what knowledge is available, and difficulties in distinguishing between personal ignorance and lack of competence and actual limitations of knowledge (Fox & Swazey, 1974). Uncertainties may be related to lack of information about problem-related causes, clients' ambivalence about pursuit of certain goals, and whether resources are available to help clients. A willingness to acknowledge that "I don't know," combined with taking steps to see if needed information is available, increases the likelihood that important uncertainties can be decreased or identified (Chalmers, 2004). This helps us to honor ethical obligations to involve clients as informed participants.

Although its philosophical roots are old, the blooming of EBP as a process attending to evidentiary, ethical, and application issues in all professional venues (education, practice/policy, and research) is fairly recent, facilitated by the Internet revolution. It is designed to break down the division between research, practice, and policy—highlighting the importance of attending to ethical issues. Evidence-based practice and health care arose because of troubling gaps between available knowledge and what is used by professionals. Gray (2001a) suggests that "at present, the process is marked by the following characteristics":

- Overenthusiastic adoption of interventions of unproven efficacy or even proven ineffectiveness.
- Failure to adopt interventions that do more good than harm, at a reasonable cost.
- Continuing to offer interventions demonstrated to be ineffective.
- Adoptions of interventions without adequate preparation such that the benefits demonstrated in a research setting cannot be reproduced in the ordinary service setting.
- Wide variation in the rates at which interventions are adopted or discarded (p. 366).

Critical thinking is integral to this process. In both critical thinking as well as EBP, attention is given to ethical issues. If we examine the values inherent in critical thinking suggested by Paul (1993; see Chapter 1), we see that they reflect those highlighted by the originators of EBP. Honesty and transparency (clear description of what is done to what effect) are emphasized in both. This applies to all venues of interest in the helping professions: professional education, practice and policy (what is done to what effect), and related research (its design, conduct, and reporting).

Descriptions of EBP differ in their breadth and attention to ethical issues, ranging from the broad, systemic philosophy and related evolving technology envisioned by its originators (e.g., Sackett, Richardson, Rosenberg, & Haynes, 1997) to narrow, fragmented views and total distortions (Gambrill, 2003, 2010). For example, views of evidence-based decision making are promoted that ignore hallmarks of this process, such as involving clients as informed participants. Given these many different views, it is important to review the vision of EBP and health care as described by its creators. Otherwise, potential benefits to clients and professionals may be lost. EBP involves the "conscientious, explicit and judicious use of current best evidence in making decisions about the care of individual [clients]" (Sackett, Rosenberg, Gray, Haynes, & Richardson, 1996). It involves "the integration of best research evidence with clinical expertise and [client] values" (Sackett, Straus, Richardson, Rosenberg, & Haynes, 2000). More attention has been given to client preferences and actions, because what clients do (e.g., carry out agreed-on tasks or fail to do so) often differs from their stated preferences, and our estimates of preferences are often wrong (Haynes, Devereaux, & Guyatt, 2002). (See Exhibit 10.1.)

EBP describes a process for and a professional educational format (problem-based learning) designed to help practitioners to link evidentiary, ethical, and application issues.

Exhibit 10.1 An Updated Model for Evidence-Based Clinical Decisions

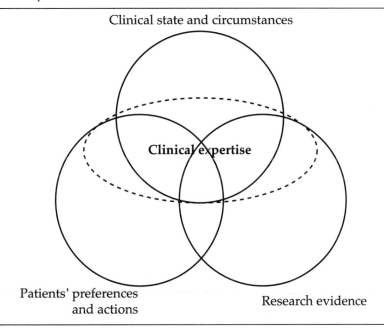

Clinical state and circumstances

Clinical expertise

Patients' preferences
and actions

Research evidence

Source: From "Clinical Expertise in the Era of Evidence-Based Medicine and Patient Choice [Editorial]," by R. B. Haynes, P. J. Devereaux, and G. H. Guyatt, 2002, *Evidence-Based Medicine, 7*, 36–38. Reprinted with permission.

(See description of problem-based learning in Chapter 8.) It is assumed that professionals often need information to make decisions—for example, concerning risk assessment or what services are most likely to help clients attain outcomes they value. Sackett et al. (1997) estimated that about two questions arise for every three patients physicians see, and that 30% of all questions remain unanswered (p. 8). We do not know how many questions arise in the course of work of other professionals or how many of these remain unanswered. Clinical expertise includes use of effective relationship skills and the experience of individual helpers to rapidly identify each client's unique circumstances, characteristics, and "their individual risks and benefits of potential interventions and their personal values and expectations" (Sackett et al., 2000, p. 1). Using clinical expertise, practitioners integrate information about a client's unique characteristics and circumstances, with external research findings, client expectations and values, and their preferences and actions (Haynes, Devereaux, & Guyatt, 2002; Sackett et al., 1997). Client values refer to "the unique preferences, concerns and expectations each [client] brings to an ... encounter and which must be integrated into clinical decisions if they are to serve the [client]" (Sackett et al., 2000, p. 1). Evidence-based health care refers to use of best current knowledge as evidence in decision making about groups and populations (see Gray, 2001a). Professional codes of ethics call for key characteristics of EBP, such as drawing on practice- and policy-related research and involving clients as informed participants.

AN ALTERNATIVE TO AUTHORITY-BASED PRACTICE

Evidence-based decision making arose as an alternative to authority-based decision making, in which consensus, anecdotal experience, or tradition are relied on to make decisions (see Exhibit 10.2). Given that EBP as described here is not the norm today, it is clear that alternative methods are popular and pose an obstacle to drawing on critical thinking skills to integrate evidentiary, ethical, and application concerns. Although misleading in the incorrect assumption that evidence-based practice means only that decisions made are based on evidence of their effectiveness, use of the term does call attention to the fact that available evidence may not be used or the current state of ignorance shared with clients. It is hoped that professionals who consider related research findings regarding decisions and inform clients about them will provide more effective and ethical care than those who rely on criteria such as anecdotal experience, available resources, or popularity. The following example illustrates reliance on authority-based criteria for selection of service methods:

Ms. Riverton has just been to a workshop on eye movement desensitization therapy. The workshop leader told the participants that this method "works and can be used for a broad range of problems." Ms. Riverton suggests to her supervisor at the mental health clinic where she works that agency staff should use this method. When asked why, she said because the workshop leader is a respected authority in the field. In this example, the authority of a workshop leader is appealed to. Evidence-based decision making involves use of quite different criteria; a key one is information about the accuracy of knowledge claims. Are they true?

Exhibit 10.2 Differences Between Authority-Based and Evidence-Based Practitioners

Authority-Based Practice	Evidence-Based Decision Making
• Clients are not informed or are misinformed.	• Clients are involved as informed participants.
• Ignores client preferences ("We know best").	• Seeks and considers client values and preferences.
• Does not pose specific questions about important decisions that must be made and does not search for and critically appraise what is found and share results with clients.	• Poses clear questions related to information needs, seeks related research findings, critically appraises them, and shares what is found with clients and others.
• Is motivated to appear well informed, to preserve status and reputation.	• Is motivated to help clients and to be an honest and competent broker of knowledge and ignorance.
• Ignores errors and mistakes.	• Seeks out errors and mistakes; values criticism as vital for learning.
• Accepts practice- and policy-related claims based on misleading criteria such as tradition or expert consensus.	• Relies on rigorous criteria to appraise practice claims and select practices and policies (e.g., those that control for biases).
• Relies on self-report of clients or anecdotal observations.	• Seeks out valid information concerning progress with a focus on outcomes of concern to clients.

THREE PHILOSOPHIES OF EVIDENCE-BASED PRACTICE

Evidence-based practice and social care involve a philosophy of ethics of professional practice and related enterprises, such as research and scholarly writing, a philosophy of science (epistemology—views about what knowledge is and how it can be gained), and a philosophy of technology. Ethics involves decisions regarding how and when to act; it involves standards of conduct. Epistemology involves views about knowledge and how to get it—or if we can. The philosophy of technology involves questions such as: Should we develop technology? What values should we draw on to make decisions? Should we examine the consequences of a given technology? Evidence-based practice encourages the integration of research and practice—for example, by highlighting the importance of clinicians critically appraising research reviews and developing a technology to help them to do so; "the leading figures in EBM [evidence-based medicine] . . . emphasized that clinicians had to use their scientific training and their judgment to interpret [guidelines], and individualize care accordingly" (Gray, 2001b, p. 26). EBP encourages clinicians to think for themselves—to develop critical appraisal skills. It offers practitioners and administrators a philosophy that is compatible with obligations described in professional codes of ethics, as well as an evolving technology for integrating evidentiary, ethical, and practical issues. EBP requires considering research findings related to important practice/policy decisions and sharing what is found (including nothing) with clients. Transparency and honesty regarding the evidentiary status of services is a hallmark of this philosophy. For example, the back cover of the seventh edition of *Clinical Evidence* (2002), the continually updated book distributed to physicians, states that "it provides a concise account of the current state of knowledge, ignorance, and uncertainty about the prevention and treatment of a wide range of clinical conditions." In what books describing practices in psychology, psychiatry, or social work do we find such a statement? To the contrary, we find books entitled *What Works in Child Welfare* (Kluger, Alexander, & Curtis, 2002) and *A Guide to Treatments That Work* (Nathan & Gorman, 2007).

STEPS IN EVIDENCE-BASED PRACTICE

Steps in evidence-based practice include the following:

1. Convert information needs related to practice decisions into answerable questions (see Chapter 11).
2. Track down, with maximum efficiency, the best evidence with which to answer them.

3.   Critically appraise that evidence for its validity, impact (size of effect), and applicability (usefulness in practice).

4.   Apply the results of this appraisal to practice/policy decisions. This involves deciding whether evidence found (if any) applies to the decision at hand (e.g., is a client similar to those studied? is there access to services described?) and considering client values and preferences in making decisions as well as other applicability issues.

5.   Evaluate our effectiveness and efficiency in carrying out steps 1 through 4 and seeking ways to improve them in the future. (Sackett et al., 2000, pp. 3–4)

Evidence-based practitioners take advantage of efficient technology for conducting electronic searches to locate the current best evidence regarding a specific question. There is an emphasis on information literacy and retrievability (Gray, 2001a).

Different Kinds of Questions

Different questions require different kinds of research methods to critically appraise proposed assumptions (e.g., Greenhalgh, 2010; Guyatt, Rennie, Meade, & Cook, 2008; Straus et al., 2005). These differences are reflected in the use of different "quality filters" to search for research findings, as described in Chapter 11. Kinds of questions include the following.

- *Effectiveness:* Do job training programs help clients get and maintain jobs? Are there harmful effects of such programs?
- *Prevention:* Do Head Start programs prevent school dropout?
- *Screening (risk/prognosis):* Does this measure accurately predict suicide attempts?
- *Description/assessment:* Do self-report data provide accurate descriptions of parenting practices?
- *Harm:* Does (or will) this intervention harm clients?
- *Cost:* How much does this program cost, compared to others?
- *Practice guidelines:* Are these practice guidelines valid, and are they applicable to my client/agency/community?
- *Self-development:* Am I keeping up-to-date? How can I keep up-to-date?

DIFFERENT STYLES OF EVIDENCE-BASED PRACTICE

Sackett and his colleagues (2000) distinguish between three different styles of EBP, all of which require integrating external research findings with the client's unique personal characteristics and environmental circumstances. All require Step 4 (see prior list of steps in EBP), but they vary in how other steps are carried out. They suggest that for problems encountered on an everyday basis, you should invest the time and energy necessary to carry out both searching and critical appraisal of reports found. For level 2 (problems encountered less often), they suggest that you seek out critical appraisals already prepared by others who describe and use explicit criteria for deciding what evidence they select and how they decide whether it is valid. Here, Step 3 can be omitted and Step 2 restricted to sources that have already undergone critical appraisal. A third style applies to problems encountered very infrequently, in which we "blindly seek, accept, and apply the recommendations we receive from authorities" (Sackett et al., 2000, p. 5). As they note, the trouble with this mode is that it is "blind" to whether the advice received from the experts "is authoritative (evidence-based, resulting from their operating in the appraising mode) or merely authoritarian (opinion-based, resulting from pride and prejudice)" (p. 5). One clue they suggest to distinguish which style is being used is a reluctance to describe related documentation. Lack of time may result in using style 2 with most problems.

EXAMPLES OF EVIDENCE-BASED DECISION MAKING

Claire provides counseling in a middle school in which many youth are referred for anger management problems. Her question is: In youth with anger management problems, is group anger management training compared to individual counseling more effective in helping youth to control their anger? This is an effectiveness question, so Claire was on the lookout for a systematic review of related randomized controlled trials. She searched in the Cochrane and Campbell databases; psycINFO; and ERIC, and found a meta-analysis of anger management programs for youth, which suggested that group counseling was effective in helping youth to decrease angry outbursts. She decided to suggest use of this approach to her clients. The youths said they preferred such a format.

Richard works in a child protection agency that uses a consensus-based risk assessment measure to estimate the likely recurrence of child abuse among parents alleged to have abused their children. This is based on the opinions of a group of experts on what they consider risk factors. His question was: Among parents alleged to have abused their children, are actuarial compared to consensus-based measures most accurate in predicting the likelihood of future abuse? Actuarial measures are based on empirical relationships between certain factors and the likelihood of an outcome, such as abuse. (See Chapter 15 for further discussion.) He looked in www.childwelfare.com as well as elsewhere on the Internet and discovered a report by Barber and his colleagues (2008) that concluded that an actuarial method was most accurate. An article he discovered by Johnson (2011) reported similar results.

Dr. Price works in a mental health crisis center. The administrator of this agency sent a memo to staff that he had heard that brief psychological debriefing was effective in decreasing post-traumatic stress disorder following a crisis, and suggested that his staff use this method. His question was: In clients experiencing a potentially traumatic event, is brief, one-hour psychological debriefing, compared to no service, more effective in preventing post-traumatic stress disorder? This also is an effectiveness question. He found a systematic review prepared by Rose, Bisson, Churchill, and Wessely (2002). To his surprise, this review concluded that not only was this method not effective, but there was some indication that it had harmful effects; one study reported that those receiving such counseling were more likely to experience stressful reactions a year later. Based on this review, he sent an e-mail to his colleagues questioning the use of this method for clients.

These examples illustrate distinctive features of evidence-based decision making. The clinicians posed well-structured questions related to information needs that guided an effective and efficient electronic search. Critical appraisal skills were used to review what was found. Many sources are available to guide this appraisal, including user-friendly checklists for different kinds of questions (e.g., Greenhalgh, 2010). A search for research findings may reveal that a practice method is harmful. Or you may discover that there is no research that critically appraises the effectiveness of an intervention or the accuracy of an assessment method, or that the research is too weak to draw an inference, and you and your clients must base decisions on other criteria, such as well-reasoned theory. All these are important findings related to decisions you and your clients make, and should be shared with clients.

ORIGINS OF EVIDENCE-BASED DECISION MAKING

Sackett and his colleagues (2000) suggest four realizations made possible by five recent developments for the rapid spread of evidence-based medicine. Realizations include (1) practitioner need for valid information about decisions they make; (2) the inadequacy of traditional sources for acquiring this information (e.g., because they are out-of-date, frequently wrong, overwhelming in their volume, variable in their validity); (3) the gap between assessment skills and clinical judgment "which increase with experience and our up-to-date knowledge and performance which decline" (p. 2); and (4) lack of time to locate, appraise, and integrate this evidence (p. 2). There were increasing gaps between information available on the Internet that could be of value to clients and clinicians and what was drawn on. Literature suggests that professionals do not draw on practice-related research findings to inform decisions (e.g., see Rosen, Proctor, Morrow-Howell, & Staudt, 1995). Not keeping up with new research findings related to important decisions renders knowledge increasingly out of date. As a result, decisions may be made that harm rather than help clients (e.g., Jacobson, Foxx, & Mulick, 2005). Five developments allowed improvement in this state of affairs:

1. The development of strategies for efficiently tracking down and appraising evidence (for its validity and relevance).
2. The creation of systematic reviews and concise summaries of the effects of health care (epitomized by the Cochrane Collaboration).
3. The creation of evidence-based journals of secondary publication.
4. The creation of information systems for bringing the foregoing to us in seconds.
5. The identification and application of effective strategies for lifelong learning and for improving our clinical performance. (Sackett et al., 2000, p. 3)

Variations in Services Offered

EBP and health care originated in medicine in part because of variations in services offered and their outcomes (Wennberg, 2002). Variations in services naturally raise questions such as "Are they of equal effectiveness?" and "Do some cause harm?"

Gaps Among Ethical, Evidentiary, and Application Concerns

Services found to be effective are often not used, and services of little value are often offered. Although interlinked in professional codes of ethics and accreditation standards, ethical and evidentiary issues are often worlds apart in practice. If professionals are not familiar with the evidentiary status of alternative practices and policies, they cannot pass this information on to their clients; they cannot honor informed consent obligations. If some alternatives are more effective than others in helping clients, and practice proceeds based on ignorance of this information, clients are deprived of opportunities to achieve hoped-for outcomes. Clients are typically not informed that recommended services have been found to be ineffective or harmful.

Increased Attention to Harming in the Name of Helping

The history of the helping professions shows that common practices thought to help people were found to harm them (e.g., see Sharpe & Faden, 1998; Valenstein, 1986). Such reports increased awareness that services designed to help clients, including assessment measures, may result in negative effects. For example, routine use of mammograms results in a high rate of false positives, with consequent unnecessary anxiety and invasive procedures such as biopsies (Gigerenzer, 2002a; Welch, Schwartz, & Woloshin, 2011). See also recent critiques of routine screenings for prostate cancer (Harris, 2011).

Limitations of Traditional Methods of Knowledge Dissemination

Gray (2001b) highlights the role of troubling gaps between obligations of researchers to report limitations of research, prepare systematic reviews, and accurately describe well-argued alternative views, and what we find in published literature. We find:

- Inflated claims: professional propaganda.
- Biased estimates of the prevalence of a concern: propagandistic advocacy in place of careful weighing of evidence.
- Hiding limitations of research.
- Preparing fragmented, incomplete literature reviews.
- Ignoring counterevidence to preferred views.
- Ignoring well-argued alternative perspectives and related evidence.
- Pseudoinquiry: little match between questions addressed and methods used to address them.
- Ad hominem rather than ad rem arguments.
- Ignoring unique knowledge of clients and service providers in making decisions about the appropriateness of practice guidelines.

Poor-quality research reviews continue to appear in professional journals as do continuing revelations of conflicts of interests between academic researchers and pharmaceutical companies resulting for example in inflated claims of positive results and censorship of negative findings (e.g., Bodenheimer, 2000; Brody, 2007).

In discussing the origins of EBP, Gray (2001b) emphasizes the increasing lack of confidence in data of potential use to clinicians: peer review, which he subtitles *feet of clay*, and flaws in books, editorials, and journal articles. Examples include submission bias, publication bias, methodological bias, abstract bias, and framing bias. In place of critical, systematic reviews of research we find incomplete, uncritical reviews (e.g., see Oxman & Guyatt, 1993). Most reviews do not tell us how they searched, where they searched, what criteria they used to review studies, and do not search for published as well as unpublished reports. Conclusions drawn based on unsystematic reviews are often quite misleading. As Rosenthal (1994) suggests in his description of *hyperclaiming* (telling others that proposed research is likely to achieve goals that it will not) and *causism* (implying a causal relationship when none has been established), "Bad science makes for bad ethics" (p. 128). Chalmers (1990) argues that failure to accurately describe research methods used is a form of scientific misconduct.

INVENTION OF THE SYSTEMATIC REVIEW

Recognition of limitations in narrative reviews of research related to practice questions encouraged invention of the systematic review for synthesizing research

Exhibit 10.3 Examples of Differences Between Inclusive, Rigorous (Systematic) Reviews and Haphazard Reviews

Haphazard Reviews	Systematic Reviews
1. The search process is not described.	1. The search process is clearly described.
2. The review omits many related studies.	2. All currently available research related to a practice question, both published and unpublished in all languages, is sought.
3. Criteria used to review research regarding different kinds of practice questions are not described.	3. Criteria used to appraise research related to different kinds of practice questions are clearly described.
4. Criteria used to appraise the quality of studies are not rigorous.	4. Criteria used to appraise research are rigorous (e.g., were evaluators of outcome blind to group assignment?).
5. Readers are not provided with sufficient information about each study to judge its quality for themselves.	5. Readers are provided with enough information about each study to judge its quality for themselves.
6. Claims of effectiveness and validity or inflated.	6. Claims are accompanied by descriptions of related evidence.

findings. Such reviews "state their objectives, ascertain as much of the available evidence as possible, use explicit quality criteria for inclusion or exclusion of studies found, use explicitly stated methods for combining data, produce reports which describe the processes of ascertainment, inclusion and exclusion, and combining data" (Gray, 2001b, p. 25). Differences between haphazard and systematic review can be seen in Exhibit 10.3.

The Internet Revolution

As Gray (2001b) notes, "The Internet stimulated the development of a number of software tools which allowed international organizations such as the Cochrane Collaboration to function effectively" (p. 25). The Cochrane Collaboration was created to prepare, maintain, and disseminate high-quality research reviews related to a specific practice/policy question. The Internet provides rapid access to research related to practice guidelines, including databases that facilitate speedy searches.

Other Factors

Gray (2001b) attributes part of the appeal of EBP to clinicians and to clients. "It is no longer feasible to feign knowledge: patients are just as likely to have searched for the evidence before they consult a clinician" (p. 27). Economic considerations were a factor. No matter what system of care exists, resources are limited with subsequent pressures to use them justly and wisely, including considering both individuals and populations (do all residents with a particular need have access to similar quality care?).

Other Views of Evidence-Based Practice

The most popular view is defining EBP as considering practice-related research in making decisions, including using practice guidelines (the EBPs approach). For example, Rosen and Proctor (2002) state that "we use evidence-based practice here primarily to denote that practitioners will select interventions on the basis of their empirically demonstrated links to the desired outcomes" (p. 743). Making decisions about individual clients is much more complex. There are many other considerations, such as the need to consider the unique circumstances and characteristics of each client, as suggested by the critiques of practice guidelines and manualized treatments (e.g., see Norcross, Beutler, & Levant, 2006). Practice guidelines are but one component of EBP, as can be seen by a review of topics in Sackett et al. (2000). The view that EBP consists of requiring practitioners to use empirically based treatments also omits attention to client values and their individual circumstances and resource constraints. The broad view of EBP involves searching for research related to important decisions and sharing what is found, including nothing, with clients. It involves a search not only for knowledge but also for ignorance. Such a search is required to involve clients as informed participants.

Many descriptions of EBP could be termed business as usual—for example, publication of unrigorous research reviews regarding practice claims, inflated claims of effectiveness, lack of attention to ethical concerns such as involving clients as informed participants, and neglect of application barriers. In addition to those who seek to forward EBP as envisioned by its originators in an atmosphere of open, rigorous critical inquiry (transparency and accountability), there will be those who adopt the external features of EBP (e.g., its language) and forgo the substance as the latest guise for authoritarian practice. Indications that EBP will be used as a new cloak for authority-based practice include material labeled as evidence-based that is not. The same product is offered in a different wrapper. A common reaction is simply relabeling the old as the new (as EBP), using the term *evidence-based* without the substance—for example, including uncritical reviews in sources labeled evidence-based. In many sources, we find no description of the unique process of EBP. Indeed, many (if not most) authors have used their discretion to misinform rather than inform readers about the origins and characteristics of EBP (Gambrill, 2011).

HALLMARKS AND IMPLICATIONS OF THE PHILOSOPHY OF EVIDENCE-BASED PRACTICE AND CARE

The philosophy and related technology of EBP have implications for all individuals and institutions involved with helping clients, including educators, researchers, practitioners/policymakers, and those who provide funding (see Gambrill, 2006). Research, practice, and educational issues are closely intertwined. For example, poor-quality reviews of research related to practice and policy questions may result in bogus practice guidelines that result in poor-quality services for clients. Clinicians may be misinformed about the evidentiary status of practice and policy claims, and so harm rather than help clients. Hallmarks and implications are interrelated. For example, promotion of transparency contributes to both knowledge flow and honoring ethical obligations.

Move Away From Authoritarian Practices and Policies

The key contribution of EBP is moving from authority-based professions to those in which ethical obligations to clients and students are honored and critical appraisal and honest brokering of knowledge and ignorance thrive. A preference for authority-based decision making is by no means limited to clinicians. It flourishes among researchers and academics as well. Examples include misrepresenting views, hiding limitations of research studies, ignoring counterevidence to preferred views, and not involving clients and clinicians as informed participants in decisions made (e.g., about whether to use a certain practice guideline) (Gambrill, 2012a). Indicators of the authority-based nature of practice include large gaps between what is said and what is done (e.g., professional codes of ethics and current practices and policies): for example, basing decisions on criteria such as consensus and tradition, lack of informed consent, and censorship of certain kinds of knowledge, such as variations in services and their outcomes.

Honor Ethical Obligations

Evidence-based practice has ethical implications for practitioners and policy makers as well as for researchers and educators (see Gambrill, 2006). Hallmarks include focusing on client concerns and hoped-for outcomes, attending to individual differences in client characteristics and circumstances, considering client values and expectations, and involving clients as informed participants in decision making (see prior list of steps). Ignoring research findings and forwarding bogus claims of effectiveness violate our obligation to provide informed consent, and may result in wasting money on ineffective services, harming clients in the name of helping them, and forgoing opportunities to attain hoped-for outcomes. A striking characteristic of EBP and related developments is the extent to which clients are involved in many different ways (e.g., Entwistle, Renfrew, Yearley, Forrester, & Lamont, 1998). One is reflected in the attention given to individual differences in client characteristics, circumstances, actions, values, and preferences in making decisions (see earlier description of EBP). A second is helping clients to develop critical appraisal skills. A third is encouraging client involvement in the design and critique of practice- and policy-related research (e.g., Hanley, Truesdale, King, Elbourne, & Chalmers, 2001). A fourth is attending to outcomes clients value, and a fifth is involving them as informed participants. A sixth is recognizing their unique knowledge in relation to application concerns.

The client-focused nature of evidence-based decision making requires helpers to attend to client interests—what are *their* desired outcomes; what information would *they* like; what are *their* preferences regarding practices and policies. Sharpe and Faden (1998) describe the struggle in medicine—a continuing one—to focus on client outcomes and highlight how recent this focus is and what a contentious issue it has been and continues to be. A concern for involving clients in making decisions that affect their lives emphasizes the importance of informed (in contrast to uninformed or misinformed) consent. EBP involves sharing responsibility for decision making in a context of recognized uncertainty. Decisions concerning the distribution of scarce resources require consideration of populations as well as individuals; decisions concerning populations may pose hardships for individual clients. EBP encourages programmatic research regarding error, both avoidable and unavoidable, its causes and consequences for clients and other involved parties, and exploration of methods designed to minimize avoidable errors, including agencywide risk management programs (e.g., Reason, 1997, 2001). A careful review of the circumstances related to mistakes allows us to plan how to minimize avoidable ones. Such attention helps us to minimize harming in the name of helping.

Making Practices, Policies, and Their Outcomes Transparent

Evidence-based practice encourages transparency of what is done to what effect in all venues of interest, including practice and policy, research, and professional education. EBP is a democratic endeavor, in which clients are appraised of the evidentiary status of services (e.g., the likelihood that they will do more good than harm). There is candidness and clarity in place of secrecy and obscurity. These characteristics are at odds with authority-based practice (e.g., see Chalmers, 1983; Gambrill, 1999). Involvement of clients as informed participants increases transparency. Transparency calls for blowing the whistle on pseudoscience, fraud, quackery, and professional propaganda (see Chapter 4). Increased transparency will highlight gaps between resources needed to attain hoped-for outcomes as suggested by related research and what is used, and thus may encourage advocacy on the part of clients and professionals for more effective services (e.g., see Domenighetti, Grilli, & Liberati, 1998). It will reveal services that are ineffective, allowing a more judicious distribution of scarce resources (see Eddy, 1994a, 1994b). It will reveal gaps between causes of client problems (e.g., poverty) and interventions used and promoted as of value. Identification of gaps will suggest ways to rearrange resources.

For example, why pay for ineffective training or services? Transparency will reveal the extent to which ethical obligations are met, such as involving clients as informed participants. Transparency encourages clear language, which should discourage propagandistic ploys that hide what is done to what effect. There is no longer a need to veil the lack of evidentiary status for practices and policies, the lack of focus on client outcomes, and failure to consider client preferences.

Increased transparency also has implications for the conduct, reporting, and dissemination of research findings. It requires accurate description of well-argued alternative views and related evidence and encourages rigorous testing of claims. Biases intrude, both on the part of researchers when conducting and reporting research and when preparing research reviews (e.g., Jadad & Enkin, 2007; MacCoun, 1998), as well as on the part of practitioners when making decisions. Reliance on conclusions of haphazard review will mislead both helpers and clients (e.g., see Littell, 2005). EBP calls for candid descriptions of limitations of research studies and use of methods that critically test questions addressed; it calls for systematic rather than haphazard reviews (see Cochrane and Campbell Collaboration's protocols). A key contribution of EBP is discouraging inflated claims of knowledge that mislead involved parties and hinder the development of knowledge. Consider terms such as *well-established* and *validated*, which convey a certainty that is not possible (see Chapter 4). Bogus claims of knowledge hinder exploration.

Encourage a Systemic Approach for Integrating Practical, Ethical, and Evidentiary Issues

Evidence-based practice involves a *systemic* approach to improving quality of services, including: (1) educating professionals who are lifelong learners, (2) involving clients as informed participants, (3) attending to management practices and policies that influence services including evidence-based purchase of services, (4) considering the implications of scarce resources, and (5) creating tools to address application challenges such as the development of strategies for efficiently tracking down and appraising evidence (for its validity and relevance) and the identification and application of effective strategies for lifelong learning and for improving clinical performance (Gray, 2001b). Quality of services is unlikely to improve in a fragmented approach—that is, without attending to *all* links in the system of service provision. Gray (2001a) suggests that performance (*P*) is directly related to an individual's motivation (M) and competence (C) and inversely related to the barriers (B) that individual has to overcome: $P = M \times C/B$. EBP encourages the creation of tools and training programs designed to develop and encourage use of critical appraisal skills. Related literature describes a wide variety of efforts to address application concerns.

Maximize Knowledge Flow

EBP and social care are designed to maximize knowledge flow. Exploring ways to diffuse and disseminate knowledge encourages knowledge flow, and related literature is rich in the variety of efforts described (e.g., Greenhalgh, Robert, Macfarlane, Bate, & Kyriakidou, 2004). In a culture in which knowledge flow is free, puffery (inflated claims of knowledge) is challenged and such challenges are welcomed. Gray (2001a) suggests that evidence-based organizations should include systems that are capable of providing evidence and promoting the use of evidence, including both explicit (created by researchers) and tacit (created by clinicians, clients, and managers). Clinicians and clients are involved as informed participants—there is no privileged knowledge in the sense of not sharing information about the evidentiary status of recommended practices and policies. Such sharing poses a threat to those who forward bogus claims and carry out pseudoinquiry, perhaps to gain funding and maintain status. Benefits of a free, efficient knowledge market include these seven:

1. Critical appraisal of claims of knowledge and ignorance.
2. Honoring informed consent obligations.
3. Increased staff morale, because decisions will be informed; staff are rewarded for sharing knowledge and are free to discuss problems, including errors, and to learn from colleagues and others throughout the world.
4. Increasing the ratio of informed to uninformed or misinformed decisions.
5. Recognizing uncertainty and ignorance. This is often swept under the rug, resulting in blaming staff for not acting on knowledge that does not (or did not) exist.
6. Decreasing bogus claims of knowledge that may result in harm to clients.
7. Lack of censorship of well-argued alternative views and counterevidence regarding popular views.

Identifying errors and mistakes and related factors, and using this information to minimize avoidable mistakes, contributes to knowledge flow. Thus, as Popper (1998) suggests, we have an obligation to recognize and learn from our mistakes. We learn from our mistakes, and we lose valuable learning opportunities by overlooking them. Research regarding errors shows that systemic causes (e.g., quality of staff training, agency policy) contribute heavily to mistakes and errors (e.g., Reason, 1997, 2001). Accountable complaint systems are another way to maximize knowledge flow. Evidence-based agencies encourage knowledge flow by using services found to maximize the likelihood of attaining outcomes that clients value and not using services of unknown effectiveness or those found to do more harm than good.

ALTERNATIVES TO EVIDENCE-BASED PRACTICE

There are many alternatives to evidence-based decision making. We could guess, use our intuition, toss a coin, ask our colleagues, or scan journals. Alternatives are suggested in Exhibit 10.4. Given that EBP as described in this chapter is not the norm today, it is clear that alternative methods are popular and pose an obstacle to drawing on critical thinking skills to integrate evidentiary, ethical, and application concerns.

OBJECTIONS TO EVIDENCE-BASED PRACTICE AND COUNTERARGUMENTS

There are many barriers to EBP, including the need to develop new skills, to candidly recognize ignorance as well as knowledge, and to create facilitative organization practices. Straus and McAlister (2000) suggest that some limitations of EBP are universal in helping efforts, such as lack of scientific evidence related to decisions and challenges in applying evidence to the care of individuals. Many objections result from misunderstandings and misrepresentations of EBP, including the following:

- Evidence-based practice denigrates clinical expertise.
- It ignores clients' values and preferences.
- It promotes a cookbook approach to medicine (e.g., ignores clients' unique circumstances and characteristics).
- It is simply a cost-cutting tool.
- It is an ivory-tower concept (it cannot be done).
- Only randomized controlled trials are considered.

Exhibit 10.4 Alternatives to Evidence-Based Practice

Basis for Clinical Decisions	Marker	Measuring Device	Units of Measurement
Eminence	Radiance of white hair	Luminometer	Optic density
Vehemence	Level of stridency	Audiometer	Decibels
Eloquence (or elegance)	Smoothness of tongue or nap of suit	Teflometer	Adhesion score
Nervousness	Litigation phobia level	Every conceivable test	Bank balance
Confidence	Bravado	Sweat test	No sweat

Source: Examples from "Seven Alternatives to Evidence Based Medicine," by D. Isaacs and D. Fitzgerald, 1999, *British Medical Journal, 319,* p. 1618. Reprinted with permission.

- It leads to therapeutic nihilism in the absence of evidence; theory won't be drawn on.
- We are already doing it; there is nothing new.

Reading original sources shows the incorrectness of these objections. (For detailed responses to 28 objections, see Gibbs and Gambrill, 2002.) Unique characteristics and circumstances of clients including cultural differences prohibit a cookbook approach. Review of research related to a question may show that effective programs will cost more, not less. Many (most?) practitioners do not search for external research findings related to important practice decisions. Many (most) do not inform clients about the criteria they use to select service methods or describe the risks and benefits of recommended services and alternatives. EBP calls on professionals to search for practice-related research findings and share what is found with clients. If no research findings are located, clients are so informed and well-argued practice theories are drawn on. The process of EBP and related tools, including checklists to guide critical appraisal of different kinds of research studies (e.g., CONSORT guidelines) and programs designed to help both professionals and clients critically review research, are new. Such tools have been applied to practice primarily during the past two decades. It is true that there is a preference for certain methodologies: methods that critically appraise claims so that we do not misinform ourselves and our clients. Randomized controlled trials are important in evaluating many kinds of questions such as those that concern effectiveness and prevention. Other research methods are required to investigate other kinds of questions, such as description questions.

Some claim that if you look diligently enough, you can always find a study that will support your conclusion and you can always find fault with a study that does not support favored views. Ethical reviewers seek all published and unpublished research that meets standards for inclusion in a review, regardless of whether that research supports or refutes their assumptions. Encouraging practitioners to integrate evidentiary, ethical, and application issues may clash with current practices in agencies; in authority-based agencies, staff may be punished for asking questions about the effectiveness of agency services. Resources required for EBP may be lacking. Professional codes of ethics require us to make informed decisions; thus, we are obligated to advocate for needed tools. Practitioners in all helping professions confront uncertainty; they all must struggle with deciding how (or if) research findings apply to a particular person.

CONTROVERSIES REGARDING EVIDENCE

Both the origins of EBP and objections to it reflect different views of evidence. Different opinions about how much we know reflect use of different criteria. When do we have enough to recommend a practice or policy? Do criteria for having enough differ in relation to different kinds of decisions? There are many kinds of evidence. (See Chapter 4 as well as Exhibit 10.5.) Concerns about inflated claims of effectiveness based on biased research studies were a key reason for the origin of EBP in health care. Inflated claims obscure uncertainties that, if shared, may influence decisions. Criteria suggested by the American Psychological Association (APA) Division 12, Clinical Psychology Taskforce for identifying a well-established intervention, consists of two well-designed randomized controlled trials (RCTs) showing positive outcomes. Within a fallibilistic approach to knowledge (see Chapter 4) we would say that a claim has been critically tested in two well-controlled randomized controlled trials and has passed both tests. This keeps uncertainty in view. Given the history of the helping professions (e.g., bogus claims of effectiveness and harming in the name of helping), isn't the most ethical road to make measured rather than inflated claims, so that professionals are not misled and in turn mislead clients?

A key way in which views of EBP differ is in the degree of rigor in evaluating knowledge claims. Consider the different conclusions concerning the effectiveness of Multisystemic Therapy (MST). This is widely claimed to be effective. Littell, Popa, and Forsythe (2005) conducted a systematic review of RCTs concerning MST and concluded that this program is no more effective than alternative interventions. Concerns identified in related studies included: (1) inconsistent reports on the number of cases randomly assigned, (2) unyoked designs, (3) unstandardized observation periods within studies, (4) unclear randomization procedures, (5) subjective definitions of treatment completion, and (6) no intention-to-treat analysis. This review, as well as many others, show that haphazard reviews come to different conclusions than do systematic reviews—typically, the former conclude that an intervention is effective (or more effective) than alternative interventions and systematic reviews concludes that there is no evidence for

Exhibit 10.5 Different Kinds of Evidence

- Legal regulations and related policies
- Ethical guidelines
- Folklore
- Common sense
- Practice wisdom (experiences, knowledge, and skills of professionals, including administrators)
- Cultural
- Superstition
- Medical
- Society's values
- A social care system, rules, resources, finances, organizational cultures
- Research findings, for example regarding prevalence and incidence of a problem
- Client's preferences, values, experiences, and circumstances
- Sources of problem framing (e.g., Big Pharma)

such claims. If there are no randomized controlled trials regarding an effectiveness question, we may have to rely on findings from a pre-post test. As this example illustrates, the term *best evidence* could refer to tests that differ greatly in the extent to which they critically appraise a claim.

Davies (2004) suggests that a broad view of evidence is needed to review policies, including (1) experience and expertise, (2) judgment, (3) resources, (4) values, (5) habits and traditions, (6) lobbyists and pressure groups, and (7) pragmatics and contingencies. He argues that we should consider all of these factors in making decisions about whether to implement a policy. Davies suggests six kinds of research related to evidence of policy impact: (1) implementation, (2) descriptive/analytical, (3) attitudinal, (4) statistical modeling, (5) economic/econometric, and (6) ethical.

SUMMARY

Current practices and policies in the helping professions reveal troubling gaps between obligations described in professional codes of ethics and what is done, and between responsibilities of researchers and scholars to be honest brokers of knowledge and ignorance and what we find—inflated claims, hiding limitations of research conducted. Clients are often harmed rather than helped because of neglect of research findings, and clients are typically not involved as informed participants. There are controversies about what evidence is and when there is enough to make a claim of effectiveness. Evidence-based decision making suggests a problem-solving process designed to decrease these gaps and to integrate ethical, evidentiary, and application concerns. It is assumed that we and our clients often need information to make important decisions. EBP describes a philosophy and process designed to help practitioners to gain needed information and to become lifelong learners. It is a process in which the uncertainty in making decisions is highlighted, efforts to decrease it are made, and clients are involved as informed participants. It is as much about the ethics of and pressures on academics and researchers as it is about the ethics and pressures on practitioners and agency administrators.

Evidence-based decision making calls for honest brokering of knowledge and ignorance—for example, clear descriptions of criteria used to make decisions. It encourages us to attend to ethical obligations (draw on practice- and policy-related literature, involve clients as informed participants, focus on outcomes clients value), and to be systemic (for example, address application obstacles such as agency cultures). Professional codes of ethics require drawing on practice- and policy-related research and involving clients as informed participants. The idea of integrating practice and research in professional contexts is not new, nor is attention to ethical issues as they relate to evidentiary ones. What is new about EBP is the description of an evolving philosophy and process designed to interlink evidentiary, ethical, and evidentiary concerns in all professional venues (practice/policy, research, and professional education).

There are many challenges and obstacles to EBP. In the everyday world, best practice may have to be based on shaky evidentiary grounds. Some objections to EBP arise because of lack of knowledge about the philosophy and process of EBP. It is important to distinguish between objections based on incorrect views of EBP and those based on an accurate understanding. Otherwise, we may prematurely discard promising approaches and lose opportunities to address real challenges.

Posing Questions and Searching for Answers

The first step in evidence-based practice (EBP) is a willingness to say, "I don't know"—to recognize the uncertainty in making decisions. As Chalmers (2004) suggests, evidence-based practice is a way of dealing honestly with the inherent uncertainty in helping clients. Not teaching physicians about clinical uncertainty has been referred to as "the greatest deficiency of medical education throughout the twentieth century" (quoted by Djulbegovic, 2004; Ludmerer, 1999). A second step is to acquire expertise in carrying out the steps in EBP. Skills are needed in evidence management, searching, appraisal, and storage (Gray, 2001a). A high level of EBP skills will allow you to use the original literature effectively. Challenges include gaining timely access to external research findings related to important practice and policy questions and critically appraising this knowledge (see also Thompson, Cullum, McCaughan, Sheldon, & Rayna, 2004). And competence does not guarantee good performance; the distinction between performance and competence is an old and continuing concern. Developing technology to address application problems has been a key contribution of evidence-based practice. This is an ongoing challenge. A review of 102 trials of interventions designed to help health professionals deliver services more effectively and efficiently shows that there are "no magic bullets" (Oxman, Thomson, Davis, & Haynes, 1995).

POSING WELL-STRUCTURED QUESTIONS RELATED TO INFORMATION NEEDS

A key step in evidence-based practice is translating information needs related to decisions into well-structured questions that facilitate the search for related research (e.g., Sackett et al., 2000). Reasons include the following (e.g., see Gibbs, 2003):

- Vague questions lead to vague answers; specific questions are needed to gain specific answers to guide decisions.
- If we do not pose clear questions about decisions, we may be less likely to seek and discover helpful research findings and change what we do; we may harm clients or offer clients ineffective methods.
- It is a countermeasure to arrogance, which interferes with learning and the integration of practice and research; if we seek answers we will discover how tentative answers are and how much we do not know.
- It can save time during an electronic search. The better formed the question, the more quickly may related literature or the lack of it be revealed.
- It is necessary for self-directed, lifelong learning.

Research in medicine suggests that physicians answer only a small percentage of questions that arise by consulting relevant research sources (e.g., Ely et al., 1999; Gorman & Helfand, 1995). There is a tendency to underestimate the difficulty in carrying out this step. The better formed the question, the greater the efficiency of searching should be, although, as search engines become more integrated, a search on Google with rough questions becomes more productive. The process of forming a question often begins with a vague general one and then proceeds to a well-built question. Sackett et al. (1997, 2000) suggest posing questions that describe the population of clients (P), the intervention you are interested in (I), what it may be compared to (including doing nothing) (C), and hoped-for outcomes (O) (PICO questions). Gibbs (2003) refers to these as COPES questions. First, they are Client Oriented. They are questions that affect clients' welfare. Second, they have Practical importance. They concern problems that arise in everyday practice. For example, child welfare staff assess risk. A question might be: "What types of clients present the greatest risk for child abuse?" Third, they guide an Electronic search for related research findings. (See Exhibit 11.1.) Fourth, hoped-for outcomes are identified. Synonyms may be used to facilitate a search. For example, other terms for abused children may be *maltreated children* or *mistreated children*. Sackett et al. (1997) suggest that a well-formed question should meet the following criteria:

- It concerns a problem of concern to clients.
- It affects a large number of clients.
- It is probably answerable by searching for related research findings.

Initial background reading may help you to focus your question. You may quickly locate relevant research by using Google.

Exhibit 11.1 Kinds of Questions and Corresponding Components of a Well-Structured Question

Question Type	Client Type and Problem	What You Might Do	Alternate Course of Action	Hoped-For Outcome	Quality Filter (Examples)
	Describe a group of similar clients. (Be specific.)	Use an intervention to prevent a problem; assess a problem; screen clients to assess risk.	Describe an alternative.	Valid measure? Accurate risk estimation? Accurate description of need?	Depends on kind of question (see Exhibit 11.2).
Effectiveness	In disoriented elderly persons who reside in a nursing home	Who receive reality orientation therapy	Compared to validation therapy	Which results in better orientation to time, place, and person?	Controlled trial; systematic review
Prevention	In sexually active high school students at high risk for pregnancy	Who are exposed to baby—think it over	Compared to didactic material on the use of birth control methods	Which group has fewer pregnancies during an academic year and more knowledge of birth control methods?	Controlled trial; systematic review
Assessment	In elderly nursing home residents who may be depressed or have Alzheimer's disease or dementia	Who complete a depression screening test	Compared to a short mental examination test	Which measure most efficiently and reliably discriminates between depression and dementia?	Validity interrater false positive
Description	In children	Raised with depressed mothers	Compared to mothers who are not depressed	Which group will have the greatest prevalence of developmental delays?	Survey Representative sample Qualitative analysis
Prediction	In preschool children	With antisocial behavior	Compared to children who do not display such behavior	What is the risk of antisocial behavior in adolescence?	Predictive validity
Risk	In mothers alleged to maltreat their children	Who complete an actuarial risk-assessment measure	Compared to a consensus-based measure	Which measure best predicts future abuse?	Risk assessment Sensitivity false positive
Harm	In adults	Who participate in a depression screening program	Compared with those who do not	Which results in the least harm?	Controlled trial systematic review
Cost-benefit	In offering parenting classes to mothers whose children have been removed from their care	Who will be purchasing services from another agency	Compared to offering such training in-house	Which is more cost-effective?	Cost-benefit ratio

Source: The first three questions are adapted from *Evidence-Based Practice for the Helping Professions* (p. 59), by L. E. Gibbs (2003), Pacific Grove, CA: Thomson/Brooks-Cole. The format of all questions is based on *Evidence-Based Medicine: How to Practice and Teach EBM* (p. 29), by D. L. Sackett, W. S. Richardson, W. Rosenberg, and R. B. Haynes (1997), New York: Churchill Livingstone.

Different Kinds of Questions

Different kinds of questions (about effectiveness, prevention, risk, assessment, or description) require different research methods to critically test them (see Chapter 12). A variety of questions may arise with one client or family. Let's say you work in a hospice and counsel grieving parents who have lost a child. Descriptive questions include: "What are the experiences of parents who lose a young child?" "How long do these last?" "Do they change over time, and if so, how?" Both survey data and qualitative research, such as focus groups, in-depth interviews, and participant observation, can be used to explore such questions. Research may be available that describes experiences of grieving parents based on a large, randomly drawn sample of such parents. A research report may describe the experiences of clients who seek bereavement counseling using in-depth interviews. Questions concerning risk may arise, such as, "In parents who have lost a young child, what is the risk of depression?" as well as questions about *effectiveness*: For parents who have lost a young child, is a support group more effective than no service in decreasing depression? *Prevention* questions may arise. For parents who have lost a young child, is brief counseling more effective than a support group in preventing depression from interfering with care of other children?

Effectiveness Questions

Many questions concern the effectiveness of service methods, such as given kinds of anger-management programs and the effectiveness of psychological debriefing in decreasing the likelihood of posttraumatic stress disorder. You may discover a systematic review or meta-analyses of randomized, controlled trials. You may locate the number needed to treat (NNT)—how many clients would have to receive an intervention for one to be helped. (See Bandolier's user-friendly guide describing how to calculate NNT; see also Furukawa, 1999.) (See also Chapter 10.)

Prevention Questions

Prevention questions direct attention to the future. These include questions about the effectiveness of early childhood visitation programs in preventing delinquency at later developmental stages. Examples are: "In young children, do early home visitation programs, compared with no service, influence the frequency of delinquency as adolescents?" "For parents who have lost a young child, is bereavement counseling or a support group more valuable in decreasing prolonged dysfunctional grieving?" Here too, well-designed randomized controlled trials control for more biases than do other kinds of studies (see discussion in Chapter 12).

Prediction (Risk/Prognosis) Questions

Professionals often attempt to estimate risk—for example, of future child maltreatment. A key question here is: What is the validity of the risk assessment measure? For example, what is the rate of false positives (clients incorrectly said to have some condition, such as to be suicidal), and false negatives (clients inaccurately said not to have this characteristic—to not be suicidal). A four-cell contingency table is of value in reviewing the accuracy of such measures (see Chapter 14). A well-built risk question is: In abused or neglected children placed in foster care, will an actuarial risk assessment measure provide a more accurate prediction than a consensus-based model regarding reabuse when children are returned to their biological parents?

Assessment Questions

Clinicians use a variety of assessment measures, such as the Beck Depression Inventory and the Conflict Tactics Scale (e.g., see Fischer & Corcoran, 2007). These measures differ in their reliability (for example, consistency of responses in absence of change) and validity (whether they measure what they purport to measure); see Chapter 13 for further discussion of reliability and validity. Inflated claims regarding the accuracy of assessment tools are common (see Lilienfeld, Lynn, & Lohr, 2003). The sample used to gather data and provide norms on a measure (scores of a certain group of individuals) may differ from clients with whom you work, and so these norms may not apply. A well-built assessment question is "In detecting frail elderly people who are depressed, is the Beck Depression Inventory or the Pleasant Events Schedule more accurate?"

Description Questions

Professionals also seek descriptive information, such as the experiences of caregivers of frail elderly relatives. A description question is "In those who care for dying relatives, what challenges arise and how are they handled?" Some description questions call for qualitative research, such as questions concerning experiences of people who have just lost an infant or who live in a nursing home. In-depth interviews, surveys, and focus groups may yield valuable information. Descriptive data involving large samples may provide information about the percentage of grieving parents who continue to grieve over the years. It may provide information about the percentage of divorces and other consequences and describe how parents cope with them. Here, too, we should consider the quality of related research.

Questions About Harm

Decisions may have to be made about how many people have to receive an assessment measure or service for one to be harmed. This is known as number needed to harm (NNH). Related questions are "How many people would we have to screen to identify one person who could benefit from help?" and "How many of these who are not at risk would be harmed by simply taking the test?" As Gray (2001a) suggests, any intervention, including assessment methods, may harm as well as help.

Questions About Costs and Benefits

Limited resources highlight the importance of cost-benefit analyses. What is the cost of offering one service compared to another, and how many people benefit from each service? Criteria for reviewing cost-benefit studies can be found in many sources (e.g., Guyatt, Meade, & Cook, 2008).

Questions About How to Encourage Lifelong Learning

Integrating practice and research requires lifelong learning. An example of a question here is: "In newly graduated professionals, will a journal club be more effective than a buddy system in maintaining evidence-based practice skills?"

Common Errors

Errors that may occur when posing questions include having more than one question in a question, trying to answer the question before stating it clearly, and posing vague questions. Students often confuse a practice/policy question (useful to guide a search) and a research question (specific to answering a question by collecting data) (Gibbs, 2003). Novices may pose different questions compared to experts in an area who are familiar with practice-related research. A lack of assessment knowledge and skills may contribute to overlooking important individual differences in a client's circumstances or characteristics. For example, posing an effectiveness question before discovering factors that contribute to depression (such as "In adults who are depressed, is cognitive-behavioral therapy more effective than medication in decreasing depression?") may overlook the fact that, for this client, recent losses in social support are uppermost, which suggests a different question (such as "In adults who are depressed because of a recent loss in social support, is a support group or individual counseling more effective in decreasing depression?").

Obstacles

Posing well-structured questions can be difficult. Thus, one obstacle is thinking it is easy and giving up when difficulty occurs. Ely and his coauthors (2002) conducted a qualitative study investigating obstacles to answering physicians' questions about patient care with evidence. Participants included nine academic/generalist doctors, 14 family doctors, and two medical librarians. They identified 59 obstacles. Those related to formulating questions included the following:

- Missing client data requiring an unnecessarily broad search. Ely and his coauthors note that questions that include demographic or clinical information and information about client preferences may help to focus the search; the kind of information that would be of value will vary depending on the question, and may not be clear until the search is underway.
- Inability to answer specific questions with general resources. A specific question is "What is this rash?" Vague cries for help, such as "I don't know what to do with this client," cannot be answered by a general resource.
- Uncertainty about the scope of the question and unidentified ancillary questions. For example, it may not be apparent that the original question should be expanded to include many related questions.
- Obstacles related to modifying the question:
  - Uncertainty about changing specific words in the question.
  - Unhelpful modifications resulting from flawed communication.
  - The need for modifications apparent only after the search has begun.
  - Difficulty modifying questions to fit a three- or four-part question format (client, intervention, comparison, and outcome).
  - Trying to solve too many questions at once or trying to answer the question while posing it.

Posing clear questions may be viewed as a threat. Questions are not benign, as illustrated by the fate of Socrates. Staff who pose questions in their agency may create discomfort among other staff, perhaps because they are doing something unfamiliar. Others may view the questioner as impertinent or disloyal to the agency or profession. Supervisors may not have experience in posing questions and may wonder why it is of value; learning to do so may not have been a part of their education. Other obstacles include lack of needed tools to search, a disinterest in considering criteria on which decisions are made, and fears that there are more questions than answers.

Options for addressing challenges include providing repeated guided experience in posing both clinical and research questions during professional education programs and providing continuing education opportunities that provide such skills. Learning by doing is emphasized in EBP. The more we use a skill, the more facility we gain with it, if we have access to corrective feedback. Unless we try to perform a certain skill we cannot determine our baseline competency level. Searching for related research findings may sound easy until we try to do it and run into obstacles. The need for change in a question is often revealed in the next step.

SEARCHING FOR RESEARCH FINDINGS RELATED TO INFORMATION NEEDS

A careful search requires seeking information that challenges (disconfirms) our assumptions as well as for information that supports them. Sackett et al. (2000) identiy different styles of evidence-based practice. They suggest that practice-related research should always be sought and critically appraised with questions that often arise (see Chapter 10). It is at this step that the most revolutionary changes have occurred to help searchers, including invention of the systematic review, creation of electronic databases of reviews such as the Cochrane and Campbell Collaboration libraries, and description of biases and their sources. (See Chapter 12.) Thousands of systematic reviews are included in each of these databases related to specific practice and/or policy questions. Here are some examples:

- Amphetamines for attention-deficit/hyperactivity disorder (ADHD) in adults.
- Day care centers for severe mental illness.
- Dietary advice for reducing cardiovascular risk.
- Discharge planning from hospital to home.
- Parent training support for intellectually disabled parents.
- Peer support telephone calls for improving health.

The Internet has revolutionized the search for information, making it speedier and more effective. Sources differ in the degree of quality control regarding accuracy of reporting of the evidentiary status of claims.

A search strategy consists of identifying relevant search terms including client type, proposed course of action, alternative action, and intended result. In addition, quality filters are included. Let's say you are working with a depressed elderly client. Search terms might include *depressed elderly*, *cognitive-behavioral methods* (compared to nothing), *decrease in depression*, and *systematic reviews*. Gibbs (2003) suggests using a thesaurus to identify related terms. Use of Boolean terms such as *and*, which retrieves only articles with both words (child abuse and single parents), and *or*, which locates all articles with either word (alcohol abuse or cocaine abuse), facilitates searches. Searches may be limited in a variety of ways— for example, by date. Parentheses can be used to group words, such as (*frail* and *elderly*). The term *NOT* excludes material containing certain words. Synonyms and key words can be combined by placing parentheses around OR statements, such as (parent training OR parent education). Truncating with asterisks (*) is used, as in (reduce*) for reduction.

Use of Quality Filters

Different kinds of questions require different kinds of research to critically appraise them, and related terms are of value in conducting a search. Such terms are referred to as *quality filters*. Examples are shown in Exhibit 11.2. Gibbs (2003) calls these

Exhibit 11.2 Examples of Quality Filters Regarding Different Kinds of Questions

Effectiveness and Preventiveness	Risk/Prognosis	Assessment	Description
Random	risk assessment	Interrater	Survey
OR	OR	OR	OR
Controlled	Predictive	Sensitivity	Representative
trial	validity	OR	sample
OR		Specificity	*Qualitative studies:*
Meta-analysis	OR	OR	Qualitative
OR	Receiver operat	False positive	analysis
Systematic	OR		OR
review	Sensitivity		Content analys
	OR		OR
	Specificity		In-depth interview
	OR		OR
	False positive		Focus group
	OR		
	Prognos		
	AND		
	Predict		

Source: See, for example, *Evidence-Based Practice for the Helping Professions* (p. 100), by L. E. Gibbs (2003), Pacific Grove, CA: Thomson/Brooks-Cole; and *PDQ Evidence-Based Principles and Practice*, by A. McKibbon, A. Eady, and S. Marks (1999), Hamilton, UK: B.C. Decker.

methodology-oriented locators for an evidence search (MOLES). If a question concerns effectiveness, quality filters include terms such as *random or controlled trials, meta-analysis,* or *systematic review.* Systematic reviews and meta-analyses include a search for and critical appraisal of related studies (see later discussion in this chapter). The better formed the question, the more likely it is that a search will be productive. Steps in searching include the following:

1. Form a well-structured question.
2. Select the appropriate quality filters related to question type.
3. Plan a search strategy (select the most appropriate bibliographic databases).
4. Conduct your search.
5. Evaluate the results and revise the strategy as needed.

If your search strategy results in too many hits, narrow the search by using more specific terms and more quality filters. If you get too little, widen the search by using more general terms. People differ in how they search. Some try a quick-and-dirty

Google search first. This is often productive. At other times, only a more systematic search may identify key studies related to a question. Ease of searching depends greatly on ready access to relevant databases. Information needs identified in working with clients can form the basis of critically appraised topics (CATs). A CAT is a brief (one-page) summary of the question raised, what was found, and the implications for clinical practice. Sackett and his colleagues (2000) recommend including the question that started the process and the search terms used to locate the paper. Next is a summary of the study methods and a table summarizing key results. Concerns important to bear in mind when using related information such as rare adverse effects, costs, or unusual elements of the critical appraisal are described also (Sackett et al., 2000, p. 88).

Relevant Sources

Searches will be more productive by focusing on sources that contain high-quality reviews. Different databases may have different rules about how search terms should be entered for maximum effect. Experience in using relevant databases is an important skill. An on-site informatist may be available to guide your search.

The Cochrane Library

The Cochrane Collaboration prepares, maintains, and disseminates high-quality reviews of research related to a particular practice question. It focuses on health concerns; however, many reviews are relevant to a wide variety of professionals. Examples are "Psychoeducation for Schizophrenia" (Pekkala & Merinder, 2004) and "Alarm Interventions for Nocturnal Enuresis in Children" (Glazener, Evans, and Petro, 2005). Cochrane and Campbell Collaboration reviews are based on a search for all high-quality research, published and unpublished, concerning a question, and critical appraisal of what is found. Journals are hand-searched. Abstracts of reviews are available without charge and can be searched. Reviews are prepared by people who are also responsible for identifying and incorporating new evidence as it becomes available. Entries include completed reviews, available in full-text, as well as protocols that are expressions of intent and include a brief outline of the topic and a submission deadline. Reviews are prepared and maintained based on standards in *The Cochrane Handbook* (Higgins & Green, 2009), which describes the process of creating systematic reviews. It is revised often to ensure that it remains up-to-date. The Cochrane Library also includes a Controlled Trials Register and the Cochrane Review Methodology Database, which is a bibliography of articles concerning research synthesis and practical aspects of preparing systematic reviews.

The Campbell Collaboration

The Campbell Collaboration is patterned after the Cochrane Collaboration; it prepares reviews related to education, social intervention, and criminal justice. Coordinating groups include communication and dissemination, crime and justice, education, social welfare, and a methods group. Like the Cochrane Collaboration, detailed instructions are followed for preparing high-quality reviews, and reviews are routinely updated. The Campbell Collaboration, like the Cochrane Collaboration, has an annual conference, and both are attended by methodologists as well as those interested in particular problem areas (www.campbellpenn.com).

The Internet

Google provides a key source for locating research findings. For example, a search on Google using the question "What is the prevalence of bedwetting among five-year-olds?" produced the answer of 16% in five seconds (www.emedicinehealth.com). Sources include websites concerned with a unique topic (e.g., ADHD); those concerned with fraud and quackery; those prepared by businesses (e.g., Zoloft); and websites concerned with harm (Americaniatrogenics.com). Material differs greatly in quality (accuracy of reports of research findings; e.g., Kunst, Groot, Latthe, Latthe, & Khan, 2002). Just because a source has a reputation for providing accurate appraisals does not guarantee that all material will be accurately presented. Thus, "buyer beware" applies. Criteria that can be used to appraise the likelihood that material is accurate include the source (does it have a reputation for critical appraisal and accurate presentation of well-argued alternative views?), clarity of writing, completeness of description of studies (e.g., sample size, measures used), and references that provide opportunities to follow up sources.

Examples of databases, together with their subject coverage and focus, are given in Exhibit 11.3. Some sites are available only by subscription. Databases relevant to the interpersonal helping professions include: PsychInfo, Social Science Citation Index, Social Work Abstracts, Sociological Abstracts, ERIC, Evidence-Based Mental Health, Medline, EMBASE, CINAHL (nursing and allied health professionals), Health Technology Assessment Program, Effective Health Care Bulletin, and Clinical Evidence. System for Information on Grey Literature in Europe (SIGLE) can be used to locate hard-to-find and nonconventional literature. Libraries are a key resource. Librarians should be skilled at informatics (searching for information related to a certain question in an efficient manner). Newspapers are another source. Governmental agencies provide free statistical information of potential value. (See examples of U.S. federal agencies and departments in Exhibit 11.4.)

Exhibit 11.3 Examples of Useful Websites

- *AMED* www.ovid.com/site/catalog/database. Alternative medicine, including complementary medicine, physiotherapy, occupational therapy, rehabilitation, podiatry, and palliative care (United Kingdom).

- *Bandolier.* www.medicine.ox.ac.uk/bandolier/ Bandolier contains bullet points (hence its title) of evidence-based medicine. Internet access is free.

- *Be-Evidence-Based.com.* www.be-evidence-based.com/ This is a database of research findings provided by the Center for Evidence-Based Social Services in the United Kingdom.

- *BestBETs.* http://www.bestbets.org/ Best Evidence Topics provide answers to clinical questions, using a systematic approach to reviewing the literature.

- *British Nursing Index.* www.proquest.com Nursing, midwifery, and health visiting (United Kingdom).

- *California Evidence-Based Clearinghouse for Child Welfare (CEBC).* www.cachildwelfareclearinghouse.org/

- *Center for Clinical Effectiveness.* www.mihsr.monash.org/cce/ This site offers evidence reports on a number of topics as well as links to similar websites, which are separated by category. You can submit clinical questions regarding patients and they will research this and respond to your question

- *Center for Evidence-Based Medicine.* www.cebm.net/ The website includes an EBM Toolbox for practicing and teaching EBM, the CATMaker (a software program allowing the user to create one-page summaries of evidence), a calendar of EBM events, and links to other EBM sites.

- *Center for Evidence-Based Mental Health.* www.cebmh.com/ This site provides materials to help develop skills in practicing EBMH. Also provided are links to other resources, including the full-text online journal *Evidence-Based Mental Health.*

- *Center for Evidence-Based Practice: Young Children With Challenging Behavior.* http://challengingbehavior. fmhi.usf.edu

- *Center for Health Evidence.* www.cche.net/ This website includes the User's Guides to the Medical Literature produced by JAMA.

- *Center for the Study and Prevention of Violence.* www.colorado.edu/cspv/blueprints

- *Child Trends.* www.childtrends.org

- *Child Welfare Information Gateway.* www.childwelfare.gov/

- *Childwelfare.com.* www.childwelfare.com/ This site was developed by Duncan Lindsey at UCLA and contains information related to child welfare.

- *Clinical Evidence.* clinicalevidence.bmj.com/ This site provides a concise account of the current state of knowledge, ignorance, and uncertainty about the prevention and treatment of a wide range of clinical conditions, based on careful searches of the literature.

- *Clinical Examination Research Interest Group.* www.sgim.org/index.cfm?pageId=588 This site describes the activities of the Clinical Examination Research Interest Group, which includes the Rational Clinical Examination Series published in JAMA.

- *Clinical Resources, Clinex Update Listserv, and Bibliography.* clinical.uthscsa.edu/clindx/ This lists evidenced-based articles on clinical diagnosis and the clinical examination.

- *ClinicalTrials.gov.* http://clinicaltrials.gov

- *Coalition for Evidence-Based Policy:* www.coalition4evidence.org

- *EBP Substance Abuse Database.* http://lib.adai.washington.edu/ebpsearch.htm

- *Effectiveness Matters.* This site is produced to complement *Effective Health Care* and provides updates on effectiveness. (See the electronic newsletter *Agency for Health Care Research on Quality* for material on purchasing.)

Exhibit 11.3 *(Continued)*

- *EQUATOR* www.equator-network.org. Network This is an international initiative designed to increase the value of medical research by promoting transparency and accurate reporting of studies.

- *ERIC* www.eric.ed.gov. This is a database of educational literature, sponsored by the U.S. Department of Education. It contains Resources in Education (RIE), Current Index to Journals in Education (CIJE) covering literature from over 775 journals (1966 onward), and ERIC Digest for overviews of educational topics.

- *Evidence-Based Behavioral Practice (EBBP)*. www.ebbp.org

- *Evidence-Based Group Work*. www.evidencebasedgroupwork.com/

- *Evidence-Based Healthcare*. www.evidencebasedhealthcare.org. Its purpose is to provide managers with the best evidence available about the financing, organization, and delivery of health care.

- *Evidence-Based Medicine*. http://ebm.bmj.com/ *Evidence-Based Medicine* is a journal released very other month that alerts clinicians to important advances in general and family practice, internal medicine, surgery, psychiatry, pediatrics, and obstetrics and gynecology.

- *Evidence-Based Mental Health*. http://ebmh.bmj.com/ *Evidence-Based Mental Health* is a journal that appears four times a year. It describes clinically relevant advances in treatment, diagnosis, etiology, prognosis/outcome research, quality improvement, continuing education, economic evaluation, and qualitative research.

- *Evidence-Based Nursing*. http://ebn.bmj.com/ *Evidence-Based Nursing* is a journal that appears four times a year. It describes clinically relevant advances in treatment, diagnosis, etiology, prognosis/outcome research, quality improvement, continuing education, economic evaluation, and qualitative research.

- *Evidence-Based Pediatrics*. www.med.umich.edu/pediatrics/ebm/ This site is a resource for evidence-based pediatrics provided through the University of Michigan. The site includes a list of CATs, a CAT template (step-by-step guide on how to create a CAT), guidelines for starting a journal club, and links to other websites.

- *Evidence-Based Practice Centers*. www.ahrq.gov/clinic/epc. The Agency for Health Care Policy and Research (AHCPR) has 12 centers in the United States for developing evidence reports and technology assessments of diagnostic and therapeutic interventions used in a variety of clinical conditions.

- *Matrix of Children's Evidence-Based Interventions*. www.nri-inc.org/reports_pubs/2006/EBPChildrensMatrix2006.pdf

- *MedlinePlus*. http://medlineplus.gov/

- *National Registry of Evidence-Based Programs and Practices (NREPP)*. www.nrepp.samhsa.gov/

- *Netting the Evidence*. www.shef.ac.uk/scharr/ir/netting/ This website provides a list of evidence-based practice resources available on the Internet.

- *NHS Centre for Reviews and Dissemination (CRD)*. www.york.ac.uk/inst/crd/ This is the sibling of the UK Cochrane Center. It produced reviews of the effectiveness and cost-effectiveness of health care interventions and provides access to several databases, including a database of structured abstracts of good-quality systematic reviews (DARE), which comment on the methodological features of published reviews and summarize the author's conclusions and any implications for health practice. It also provides the full-text *Effective Health Care Bulletin*, which is a bimonthly bulletin for decision makers that examines the effectiveness of a variety of health care interventions.

(Continued)

Exhibit 11.3 *(Continued)*

- *Ovid EBM.* www.ovid.com/ Ovid's goal is "to support and improve information access for researchers, clinicians, and students in scientific, medical, and academic communities worldwide by providing innovative and interlinked text retrieval software and database solutions."

- *PubMed.* www.ncbi.nlm.nih.gov/sites/entrez?db=pubmed PubMed is an Internet interface for Medline. Using the "Clinical Queries" feature in PubMed, you can restrict retrieval to articles most likely to answer your clinical question. This search is intended for clinicians and has built-in search filters based largely on Haynes et al's. four categories—therapy, diagnosis, etiology, prognosis.

- *PubMed: Medline.* www.nlm.nih.gov/pubs/factsheets/pubmed.html

- *Social Care Institute for Excellence (SCIE).* www.scie.org.uk Established in the United Kingdom in 2001 to provide reports regarding best practices in social care emphasizing value of services to consumers. SCIE produces "knowledge reviews" combining research knowledge with knowledge from practitioners and consumers.

- *Social Programs That Work.* www.evidencebasedprograms.org/

- *Suicide Prevention Research Center: Best Practice Registry.* www.sprc.org/featured_resources/bpr/index.asp

- *TRIP Database.* www.tripdatabase.com/ The TRIP Database searches over 75 sites of high-quality medical information. It provides direct, hyperlinked access to the largest collection of evidence-based material on the web as well as articles from journals such as the *BMJ, JAMA,* and *NEJM.*

Source: Adapted from Center for Evidence-Based Medicine, Toronto, Canada. http://ktclearinghouse.ca/cebm/resources/med

Examples of Centers and Organizations

The National Health Service (NHS) Research and Development Centre for Evidence-Based Medicine at the John Radcliffe Hospital in Oxford was the first of several similar centers in the United Kingdom. The aims are to promote an evidence-based approach and to provide support and resources to those who wish to make use of them (www.cebm.net). There are many other centers that can be located through the Internet.

Common Errors

Errors at this stage are related to the clarity and degree of precision of questions posed; they may be too narrow or too broad, resulting in too few or too many reports. Giving up too soon is a common error; it takes persistence to reframe search strategies more effectively. Lack of information about valuable websites may result in overlooking helpful resources.

Exhibit 11.4 Examples of U.S. Federal Agencies and Departments

Agency for Healthcare Research and Quality (AHRQ): www.ahrq.gov/

Best Practices Initiative, Department of Health and Human Services: www.osophs.dhhs .gov/ophs/Best/Practice/default.htm

Center for Information Technology: www.cit.nih.gov/home.asp

Center for Scientific Review (CSR): www.csr.hih.gov

Centers for Disease Control and Prevention (CDC): www.cdc.gov/

Centers for Medicare and Medicaid Services: http://cms.hhs.gov/default.asp

Educational Research and Improvement: www.ed.gov/offices/OERI/index.html

Faith-Based and Community Initiatives Office: http://whitehouse.gov/government/fbci

Food and Drug Administration (FDA): www.fda.gov/

General Accountability Office (GAO): www.gao.gov/

Health Resources and Services Administration: www.hrsa.gov/

Justice Programs Office: http://ojp.usdoj.gov/

National AIDS Policy Office: www.whitehosue.gov/onap/aids.html

National Center for Complementary and Alternative Medicine (NCCAM): http://nccam.nih.gov/

National Center for Research Resources (NCRR): www.ncrr.nih.gov/

National Center on Minority Health and Health Disparities (NCMHD): http://ncmhd/nih.gov/

National Clearing House on Child Abuse and Neglect Information: http://nccanch.act.hhs.gov

National Council on Disability: www.ncd.gov/

National Criminal Justice Reference Service (NCJRS): www.ncjrs.org

National Health Information Center: www.health.gov/NHIC/

National Institute of Child Health and Human Development (NICHD): www.nichd.nih.gov/

National Institute of Mental Health (NIMH): www.bnimh.nih.gov/

National Institute on Aging (NIA): www.ia.nih.gov/

National Institute on Alcohol Abuse and Alcoholism (NIAAA): www.niaaa.nih.gov/

National Institute on Deafness and Other Communication Disorders (NIDCD): www.nidcd.nih.gov/

National Institute on Drug Abuse (NIDA): www.nida.nih.gov/

National Institutes of Health (NIH): www.nih.gov/

National Library of Medicine (NLM): www.nlm.nih.gov/

Office of Justice Programs: www.ojp.usdoj.gov

Office of Scientific and Technical Information: www.osti.gov/ostipg.html

Office of the Surgeon General: www.osophs.dhhs.gov/ophs

Special Education and Rehabilitative Services: www.ed.gov/about/offices/list/osers/

Substance Abuse and Mental Health Services Administration: www.samhsa/gov/index/

Obstacles and Evolving Remedies

You may lack skills in avoiding inflated claims of what has been found, which are rampant. You may not be aware of important databases and may not have access to knowledgeable librarians. There may be no high-quality evidence related to a question. Gray (2001a) refers to this as the *relevance gap*. Another is failure to publish research results—the *publication gap*. A third is difficulty in finding published research—the *hunting gap*. Other gaps include the *quality gap* and the *good intention gap* (p. 101). Of the 59 obstacles to EBP identified by Ely and his colleagues (2002), the five they considered most important involved search problems:

1. Excessive time required to locate information.
2. Difficulty selecting an optimal search strategy.
3. Failure of a seemingly relevant resource to cover the topic.
4. Uncertainty about how to know when all relevant evidence has been found.
5. Inadequate synthesis of multiple sources of evidence into a conclusion that is clinically relevant.

The resources that enable an efficient search illustrate challenges that lie in the paths of those who would like to make evidence-informed decisions. For example, there may be no library in an agency (let alone a librarian) and no access to relevant databases. The importance of immediate access to needed databases is illustrated by the failure to use agency-based libraries even though they are conveniently located. There may be no access to a reference management system. Only via providing access to a "knowledge manager," as suggested by Gray (1998), may speedy access to relevant information be possible. This person's role would be to locate and critically appraise practice- and policy-related research findings in a timely manner. A central agency available to answer questions that arise should be created. Searching widely is one way to protect yourself from influence by bogus material from a single source. For example, compare material on the website of the American Psychiatric Association with material on the website of the International Society for Ethical Psychology and Psychiatry (http://psychintegrity.org).

CRITICALLY APPRAISING WHAT YOU FIND

Critically appraising the quality of different kinds of research is a key competency in EBP. As emphasized earlier, the kind of research that may provide evidence differs, depending on the question (e.g., see Guyatt, Oxman, Schunemann, Tugwell, & Knotterus, 2010). Some questions call for qualitative research methods, such as in-depth interviews. Questions pertaining to intervention, prevention, harm, or testing the accuracy of a diagnostic method may most carefully be explored using randomized controlled trials (Schulz, Altman, & Moher for the CONSORT Group, 2010). Often, a mix of qualitative and quantitative research may be best. Skill in critically appraising research related to different kinds of questions should be acquired during professional education programs. The EBM Toolkit is a Canadian-based collection of resources to support the practice of evidence-based medicine. It includes critical appraisal checklists, methodological filters, and other resources, and is located at www.med.ualberta.ca/ebm/ebm. htm. Workshops are available at a number of different sources. The Critical Appraisal Skills Program (CASP) in Oxford has been offering training programs for many years (www.phru.nhs.uk). The purpose of CASP is to help health service decision makers, and those who seek to influence decision makers, to develop evidence management skills—for example, to find, critically appraise, and change practice in line with research findings. CASP has also developed an interactive CD-ROM, which can be used in conjunction with workshops, in videoconferencing, as a stand-alone package, or to support learning, hopefully diffusing skills to a wider audience and providing opportunities for independent practice and learning.

There is no perfect study. All research has flaws that may compromise its value in exploring a question. Biases that may limit the value of findings are always of concern. Questions to ask of all research reports include the following:

- Is there a clear research question?
- Is the study design appropriate? Does it match the question?
- What is the sample size and source? Is the sample representative of the population?
- Are measures used valid and reliable?
- Are claims made accurate?
- Is the data analysis appropriate?
- Does the study offer information that can guide practice and policy decisions?

The research methods used may be appropriate for the question and be rigorous, but the findings may not apply to your clients or locale because of the sample or setting involved or the measures used.

Common Errors

Common errors include: (1) not critically appraising what you find, (2) becoming disheartened when you find little available or find conflicting evidence, and (3) misinterpreting a lack of evidence that a method is effective as evidence that it is not effective.

Obstacles and Evolving Remedies

You can save time by drawing on high-quality critical appraisals of evidence related to a question when these are available (e.g., the Cochrane and Campbell databases). Take advantage of user-friendly checklists to critically appraise different kinds of research (e.g., Greenhalgh, 2010). Statistical illiteracy is a key obstacle. Minimal statistical literacy suggested by Gigerenzer and his colleagues (Gigerenzer, Gaissmaier, Kurz-Milcke, Schwartz, & Woloshin, 2007) includes the following:

1. Understand that there is no certainty and no zero risk, but only risks that are more or less acceptable.
2. Understand what the risk is, the time frame and size of the risk, and whether it applies to the client.
3. Understand that screening tests may have benefits and harms.
4. Understand that screening tests can make two errors: false positives and false negatives.
5. Understand how to translate specificities, sensitivities, and other conditional probabilities into natural frequencies.
6. Understand that the goal of screening is not simply the early detection of disease; it is mortality reduction or improvement of quality of life.
7. Understand that interventions typically have benefits and harms.
8. Understand the size of those benefits and harms.
9. Be able to assess the quality of the evidence behind the numbers.
10. Recognize any conflicts of interest.

INTEGRATING RESEARCH FINDINGS WITH OTHER INFORMATION AND APPLYING THE FINDINGS

Do external research findings located apply to your client? What are the client's preferences? Do you have access to needed resources? This step requires integration of different kinds of information (evidence), drawing on clinical expertise. It requires integrating information concerning external research findings with characteristics of the client including their values and expectations, and his or her circumstances, and a consideration of application problems such as lack of resources, and deciding what to do together with the client. Evidence-based practice involves the "integration of best research evidence with clinical expertise and [client] values" (Sackett et al., 2000, p. 1).

> Increased expertise is reflected in many ways, but especially in more effective and efficient [assessment] and in the more thoughtful identification and

compassionate use of individual [clients'] predicaments, rights and preferences in making clinical decisions about their care. (Sackett et al., 1997)

Without clinical expertise, practice risks becoming tyrannized by external evidence, for even excellent external evidence may be inapplicable to or inappropriate for an individual patient. Without current best external evidence, practice risks becoming rapidly out of date, to the detriment of patients. (p. 2)

Research regarding a question may not clearly suggest a best practice. Client preferences and agency resources must be considered. Many application barriers may enter at this stage. Indeed, gathering information about their frequency and exact nature will be useful in planning how to decrease obstacles. Examples reported by my students include:

- Chaotic working space—shared phone, desk, and computer, and no private space for confidential conversations.
- Disparity between practice standards taught in school and (lower) agency expectations.
- The lack of planning of interventions on the part of administrators and program coordinators. This leads to counselors and support staff mainly working in crisis to deal with issues that arise. Also, without time for planning, support staff does not research promising practices that others may be using to address issues. Additionally, they do not look for any evidence as to the effectiveness of possible interventions before implementation.
- Providers feeling overwhelmed by the problems/issues that clients bring. This may be due to a large caseload, lack of resources to refer clients to, or the multitude of issues that clients are dealing with.
- Unsupportive administration (i.e., not attentive to line workers' needs, micromanagement).
- Unclear mission/goal of organization/agency (confusion regarding what staff is supposed to provide).
- Poor interagency communication and collaboration.

A review of research findings related to important questions may reveal that little or nothing is known. This will be true for many questions, including in medicine. Information may be available about certain kinds of clients but these clients may differ greatly from your client, and so findings may not apply. Resources available will limit options. Here, too, our obligations to inform clients and to consider their preferences provide a guide (e.g., helpers should clearly describe limitations in applying research findings in a particular situation). Questions include: Do research findings apply to my client? That is, is a client similar to clients included in related research findings? Can I use this practice method in my setting? (For example, are needed resources available?) If not, is there some other access to programs found to be most effective in seeking hoped-for outcomes? What alternatives are available? What does my client think about this method? Is it acceptable to clients? What if I don't find anything? (Glasziou, Del Mar, & Salisbury, 2003).

Many clinical decision aids are available via smart phone apps—for example, regarding prescribing (e.g., Wright, Sittig, Ash, Feblowitz, Meltzer, McMullen, et al., 2011). Some have automatic stop rules (e.g., if the user fails to ask a key question such as whether a drug being considered may interact adversely with another drug the patient is taking). Fast and frugal decision trees incorporate empirically derived rules (Gigerenzer, 2007).

Do Research Findings Apply to My Client?

A great deal of practice-related research consists of correlational research (e.g., describing the relationship between certain characteristics of parents and child abuse) and experimental research, describing differences among different groups (e.g., experimental and control). In neither case may the findings apply to a particular client. There is a continual strain between the scientific investigation of different events, such as child abuse, and dealing with the individual client. The focus of practice is on the individual client; science deals with generalities. Samples used in research studies may differ from a client. Norms on assessment measures may be available but not for people like your client. For example, your clients may be Latino and available norms may be for Caucasians. These norms may not represent responses of Latinos. Note, however, that norms should not necessarily be used as guidelines for selecting outcomes for individual clients; outcomes they seek may differ from normative criteria, and norms may not be optimal (e.g., low rates of positive feedback from teachers to students in classrooms). We must always consider the possible difference between those who participated in research related to a question of concern and our client. Will these differences influence the potential costs and benefits of an intervention? Certain differences may result in more harm than good if an intervention is used with a particular client.

The unique characteristics and circumstances of a client may suggest that a particular practice method should not be used because negative effects are likely or because such characteristics would render an intervention ineffective if it were applied at a certain time. For example, referring clients to parent-training programs who have a substance abuse problem may not be effective. Thus, there may be other problems (often referred to as comorbid) that influence the effectiveness of a method). Unique factors associated with a problem such as depression may influence the effectiveness of a given method (e.g., medication, increasing pleasant events, decreasing negative thoughts).

Knowledge of behavior and how it is influenced and what principles of behavior apply to all individuals will provide helpful guidelines (e.g., see Cooper, Heron, & Heward, 2008). If research findings apply to your client, are they important? Would they really make a difference in the decisions you and your clients make about how to attain hoped-for outcomes? Examples of questions suggested by Sheldon, Guyatt, and Haines (1998) about whether an intervention applies to a particular client include the following:

1. Is the relative risk reduction that is attributed to the intervention likely to be different in this case because of client characteristics?
2. What is the client's absolute risk of an adverse event without the intervention?
3. Is there some other problem or a contraindication that might reduce the benefit?
4. Are there social or cultural factors that might affect the suitability of a practice or policy or its acceptability?
5. What do the client and the client's family want?

How Definitive Are the Research Findings?

Reviews found may be high-quality systematic reviews or haphazard ones. (See Chapter 12.) In the former there may be strong evidence not to use a practice method or strong evidence to use one. More often there will be uncertainty about whether an intervention will do more good than harm. (See Exhibit 11.5.)

Will Benefits Outweigh Risks?

Every intervention, including assessment measures, has potential risks as well as benefits. Diagnostic tests may result in false positives or false negatives. Will the benefits of an intervention outweigh potential risks and costs? (See Exhibit 11.6.) What is the absolute risk reduction (ARR)? Let's say an oncologist is trying to convince a patient to take chemotherapy. She may say to her patient, "There is a 50% benefit of taking X; there are 50% fewer recurrences in 10 years." This is relative risk. Here is absolute risk: Out of 100 women who take X, three (instead of six who don't take X) will have a recurrence in 10 years. You can see why it is considered unethical to describe only relative risk reduction; it seems much more impressive. What is the number needed to treat (NNT)? (See Bandolier worksheet for calculating NNT.) How many clients have to receive a harm-reduction program to help one person? Interventions differ greatly in the NNT, ranging from 2 (fear of flying—standard exposure versus waiting list control) to hundreds (aspirin versus placebo for hip surgery = 232: www.cebm.utononto.ca/glossary/nntsPrint.htm, accessed March 10, 2004).

Exhibit 11.5 What to Believe? Perceptions of Disarray and Lack of Credibility Can Result From Conflicting Study Results in Medical Research

Source: F. M. Wolf (2000). "Summarizing Evidence for Clinical Use," by F. M. Wolf (2000), in J. P. Geyman, R. A. Deyo, & S. D. Ramsey (Eds.), *Evidence-Based Clinical Practice: Concepts and Approaches* (p. 136), edited by J. P. Geyman, R. A. Deyo, and S. D. Ramsey, Boston, MA: Butterworth-Heineman. Reprinted with permission from Copley News Service.

Is there any information about NNH (the number of individuals who would have to receive a service to harm one person)? A nomogram can be used to calculate the number needed to treat based on absolute risk in the absence of treatment (Guyatt & Rennie, 2002). "Using ARR and its reciprocal, the NNT, incorporates the influence of the changing baseline risk. If all we know is the ARR or the NNT, however, we remain ignorant of the size of the baseline risk. For example, an ARR of 5% (and a corresponding NNT of 20) may represent reduction of the risk of death from 10% to 5% (a RRR of 50%) or from 50% to 45% (a RRR of 10%)" (Guyatt & Rennie, 2002, p. 360). (See Exhibit 11.7.) The percentage of clients better in the control and better with treatment can be plotted on a L'Abbé plot of data for ready visual inspection.

Exhibit 11.6 Information Needed to Make a Decision Whether to Take a Drug: Benefits and Risks

In a study, 13,000 women age 35 and older who had never had breast cancer but were considered to be at high risk of getting it were given either Nolvadex or a placebo each day for 5 years. Women were considered to be at high risk if their chance of developing breast cancer over the next 5 years was estimated at 1.7% or higher (an estimate arrived at by using a risk calculator available at www.cancer.gov/bcrisktool). Here's what happened.

What Difference Did Nolvadex Make?	Starting Risk (Placebo Group)	Modified Risk (Nolvadex Group, 20 mg/day)
Did Nolvadex help?	3.3%	1.7%
Fewer Nolvadex users got invasive breast cancer (1.6% fewer due to drug)	33 in 1,000	17 in 1,000
No difference in death from breast cancer	About 0.09% in both groups	
Did Nolvadex have side effects?		
Life-threatening side effects	0.9 in 1,000	
Blood clots (in legs or lungs)	0.5%	1.0%
(additional 0.5% due to drug)	5 in 1,000	10 in 1,000
Invasive uterine cancer	0.5%	1.1%
(additional 0.6% due to drug)	5 in 1,000	11 in 1,000
Symptom side effects		
Hot flashes	69%	81%
(additional 12% due to drug)	690 in 1,000	810 in 1,000
Vaginal discharge	35%	55%
(additional 20% due to drug)	350 in 1,000	550 in 1,000
Cataracts that needed surgery	1.5%	`2.3%
(additional 0.8% due to drug)	15 in 1,000	23 in 1,000
Death from all causes combined	About 1.2% in both	
No difference between Nolvadex and placebo	groups	
	12 in 1,000	

Source: From *Know Your Chances: Understanding Health Statistics* (p. 78), by S. Woloshin, L. M. Schwartz, and G. Welch (2008), Berkeley, CA: University of California Press.

How Can I Help My Clients to Make Decisions?

Clients may not want to carry out a plan that seems to have the best chance of achieving hoped-for outcomes. Thus, the acceptability of plans must be considered. This will influence adherence to important procedural components associated with success. The lack of correlation between what someone says he or she wants (their preferences) and what he or she does (their actions), highlights the challenges of helping clients to discover their preferences. We often don't know what we want, and our preferences change in accord with a variety of factors, including the time at which we are asked about them in relation to a decision that has been made and the visibility of the consequences thereof. Although many people may say they wish to achieve a certain goal, when given instructions about how to plan their life to do so, their actions often do not reflect their stated preferences; that is, they don't do anything. Preferences are not necessarily logical (e.g., see Shaffer & Hulsey, 2009). In view of tendencies of some clients to match the goals and values of their therapists and other sources of behavioral confirmation in

Exhibit 11.7 Estimating the Size of the Treatment Effect

The 2 × 2 table

	Outcome		Risk of Outcome:
	+	−	
Treated (Y)	a	b	$Y = a/(a + b)$
Control (X)	c	d	$X = c/(c + d)$

Relative risk, or *Risk ratio* (RR), is the ratio of risk in the treated group (Y) to the risk in the control group (X): RR = Y/X

$$\frac{a/(a + b)}{c/(c + d)}$$

Relative risk reduction (RRR) is the percent reduction in risk in the treated group (Y) compared to the control group (X):

RRR = 1 − RR = 1 − Y/X × 100% or

RRR = [(X − Y)/X] × 100%

$$\frac{c/(c + d) - a/(a + b)}{c/c + d)}$$

Absolute risk reduction (ARR) is the difference in risk between the control group (X) and the treated group (Y):

$$\frac{c}{c + d} - \frac{a}{a + b}$$

Number needed to treat (NNT) is the inverse of the ARR:

NNT = 1/ARR = 1(X − Y)

Odds ratio (OR)

$$= \frac{a/b}{c/d} = \frac{ad}{cd}$$

Source: Adapted from G. Guyatt, D. Rennie, M. O. Meade, & D. J. Cook. (2008). *Users' guide to the medical literature: A manual for evidence-based clinical practice* (2nd Ed.). Chicago: American Medical Association.

the helping process, and in view of the influence of subtle influences such as question wording and order on the expression of preferences, a variety of methods of inquiry should be used to discover client preferences. Different surface wordings of identical problems influence judgments. Gains or losses that are certain are weighed more heavily than those that are uncertain. As discussed earlier, presentation of risks and benefits may be quite misleading (e.g., Gigerenzer & Gray, 2011). Only relative risk may be given to encourage a client to take a medication. How decisions are framed (in terms of gains or losses) influences decisions (e.g., Edwards, Elwyn, Covey, Matthews, & Pill, 2001).

Helping clients discover their preferences may require involving them in a decision analysis. Shared decision making between clients and professionals is increasingly emphasized. Many decisions aids are available that inform clients about risks and benefits of different options (including doing nothing) (e.g., O'Connor et al., 2007; O'Connor et al., 2009). (See also tools such as drug fact sheet in Exhibit 11.6.) Formats include interactive videos, personal computers, audiotapes, audio-guided workbooks, and pamphlets. (See, for example, *Ottawa Personal Family Decision Guide*, decisionaid .ohri.ca/decguide.html). Such aids can personalize information by allowing clients to ask questions *important to them*. Clients differ in how risk-averse they are and in the importance given to particular outcomes. Many decisions involve unique individual trade-offs between risks and benefits, both short and long term. Client decision aids can help an individual weigh factors according to his or her unique values while being accurately informed about possible consequences of different options, including the uncertainty associated with each option. Woltman and her colleagues (2011) developed an electronic decision support system to enhance shared decision making between community mental health clients and their case managers.

Reviews of the literature suggest that such aids increase clients' involvement and are more likely to lead to informed, value-based decisions (O'Connor et al., 2009). They prevent overuse of options that informed patients do not value (O'Connor et al., 2007). Use of discretionary surgery decreased. Use of decision aids improves accuracy of risk perception but does not necessarily improve general or specific health outcomes. See Shaffer and Hulsey (2009) for a discussion of why this may be so. Decision aids can highlight important data often overlooked, such as absolute risk. Eddy (1990) suggests use of a cost-utility matrix to help clients arrive at individual decisions. Occasions when discovering client preferences is especially important include those in which:

- Options have major differences in outcomes or complications.
- Decisions require making trade-offs between short-term and long-term outcomes.
- One choice can result in a small chance of a grave outcome.
- There are marginal differences in outcomes between options.

Benefits of decision aids noted by O'Connor (2001) include the following:

- Reducing the proportion of clients who are uncertain about what to choose.
- Increasing clients' knowledge of the problem, options, and outcomes.
- Creating realistic expectations (perceived probabilities) of outcomes.
- Improving the agreement between choices and a client's values.
- Reducing some elements of decisional conflict (feeling uncertain, uninformed, unclear about values, and unsupported in decision making).
- Increasing participation in decision making without adversely affecting anxiety (O'Connor, 2001; see also O'Connor et al., 2009).

We should involve clients as informed participants (see Exhibit 11.8). Scales have been developed to measure client involvement (Elwyn et al., 2003).

Exhibit 11.8 Evidence-Informed Client Choice

Agency: _____

Client: _____

Date: _____

Referral agency: _____

Program within agency: _____

Staff member within agency who will offer program: _____

A. *Related External Research*

___ 1. Research shows that this program will help people like me to attain hoped-for outcomes.

___ 2. This program has never been rigorously tested in relation to hoped-for outcomes.

___ 3. Research shows that other programs that help people like me have been critically tested and found to attain hoped-for outcomes.

___ 4. Research shows that this program is likely to have harmful effects (e.g., decrease hoped-for outcomes).

B. *Agency's Background Regarding Use of This Method*

___ 1. The agency to which I have been referred has a track record of success in using this program with people like me.

___ 2. The staff member who will work with me has a track record of success in using this method with people like me.

Adapted from "Evidence-Informed Patient Choice," by V. A. Entwistle, T. A. Sheldon, A. J. Sowden, & I. A. Watt, 1998, *International Journal of Technology Assessment in Health Care, 14*, pp. 212–215.

Can I Use This Method in My Agency?

Can a plan be carried out in a way that maximizes success? Are needed resources available? Do providers have the skills required to carry out plans? Can needed resources be created? Are those responsible for offering services competent to do so? How do you know? Competence in applying a method does not necessarily reflect competence to teach others, such as parents (McGimsey, Greene, & Lutzker, 1995). Consultation skills are required to teach others successfully, such as providing a rationale for methods used, demonstrating steps while describing them, arranging role-plays for each step, and providing corrective feedback. There may be vital differences in provider adherence to practice guidelines that decrease the safety and effectiveness of an intervention. Current service patterns may limit options. Questions Sackett et al. (1997) suggest for deciding whether to implement a guideline include the following:

- What barriers exist to its implementation? Can they be overcome?
- Can you enlist the collaboration of key colleagues?
- Can you meet the educational, administrative, and economic conditions that are likely to determine the success or failure of implementing the strategy?

- Is there a high-quality systematic review of related evidence?
- Are there influential local exemplars already implementing the strategy?
- Is there consistent information from all relevant sources?
- Are there opportunities for discussions about the intervention with an expert?
- Are guidelines in a user-friendly format? Can I use it without extensive outside collaboration?
- Is there freedom from conflict with economic and administrative incentives and patient and community expectations? (p. 182)

Problems may have to be redefined from helping clients attain needed resources to helping them to bear up under the strain of not having them, or involving clients with similar concerns in advocacy efforts to acquire better services.

Are Alternative Options Available?

Are other options available—perhaps another agency to which a client could be referred? Perhaps self-help programs are available. Here, too, familiarity with practice-related research can facilitate decisions.

What If the Experts Disagree?

We rely on the assertions of experts, those with presumed special knowledge, on an everyday basis. Given this dependence, how can we make wise decisions regarding the accuracy and candidness with which an expert describes controversies and uncertainties? In some situations we could seek and review the quality of evidence for ourselves. In some cases checking the evidentiary status of claims by experts is fairly easy. Suppose a lecturer claims that psychiatric classifications are valid categories and provide intervention guidelines. You could check this by reading critiques of this classification system (e.g., Angell, 2011; Houts, 2002; Kutchins & Kirk, 1997) and by reading the introduction to the *DSM*, in which its purpose is described. At other times, checking accuracy will require greater effort, such as critically reviewing the quality of a review concerning a method. At other times it may not be possible, due to time constraints. How dependent are you on the advice of experts in your work? How can you check the expertise (knowledge) and ethics (honesty regarding controversies and uncertainties) of an expert? How do recommendations of clinical experts compare to what is suggested, based on results of carefully controlled research (Antman, Lau, Kuplenick, Mosteller, & Chalmers, 1992)? Indicators of honesty include: (1) accurate description of controversies in an area, including methodological and conceptual problems; (2) accurate description of well-argued disliked views; (3) critical appraisal of both preferred and alternative views; and (4) inclusion of references to sources cited, so readers can look these up.

What If Clients Prefer an Untested Method?

What if your client prefers a method that has not been tested or that has been tested and has been found to be ineffective or harmful? Most interventions used in the helping professions have not been tested; we don't know if they are effective, not effective, or harmful. Certainly you should not use a method shown to be harmful. What about untested methods? If there is an effective method, you could describe the costs and benefits of using this compared to an ineffective method. Untested methods are routinely offered in both health and social care. Whether you should offer them depends on many factors, including acceptability to clients and scarcity of resources in your agency.

What If I Do Not Find Any Related Research?

What if there is no research that can guide decisions? What do you do if you have searched for information related to an important question and find nothing? Let us assume that your search has been a high-quality one and that no one else could find anything, either. You should share what you find (including nothing) with your clients and draw on empirically grounded practice theory to guide your work. Providing effective, empathic responses is called for here. Evidence-based practice involves sharing ignorance and uncertainty as well as knowledge in a context of ongoing support, and drawing on practice theory to guide decisions in the context of shared uncertainties.

What If Related Research Is of Poor Quality?

This will be a common finding. Consider, for example, the review of research regarding family preservation programs by Lindsey, Martin, and Doh (2002). This shows that such programs, promoted as effective by "advocacy research," are not effective. Many other areas could be cited concerning lack of effectiveness of programs assumed to help clients, including intensive case management services for the elderly found to do more harm than good—mortality increased (Blenkner, Bloom, & Nielson, 1971). Other examples of harm in the name of helping include Scared Straight programs (Petrosino et al., 2003). Your search will often reveal that there is uncertainty regarding the effectiveness of a method. For example, if there are no randomized controlled trials regarding an effectiveness question, then we may move down the list. This is what we must do in the everyday world, since most interventions used in fields such as psychology and social work have not been critically tested. Thus, instead of well-designed randomized controlled trials regarding an intervention, we may have to rely on findings from a pre-post test that is subject to many rival explanations regarding the cause of change (see Chapter 12). The term *best evidence* could refer to a variety of different kinds of tests that differ greatly in their ability to critically test claims. Whatever you find you should share with your clients, and you will have to draw on practice theory as needed.

What If Research Is Available but It Has Not Been Critically Appraised?

One course of action is to critically appraise the literature for yourself. In the everyday world, you may not have time to do this. Perhaps you can contact someone who works in the field. If this concerns a problem that occurs often, involve interested others in critically appraising it. In the United Kingdom, physicians can contact a source that will carry out a search for research findings related to a question. Questions asked are tracked and those that are raised often can guide selection of topics for systematic reviews (Glasziou, 2005; personal communication).

Balancing Individual and Population Perspectives

One of the most challenging aspects of practice is considering both individuals and populations. Ethical issues regarding the distribution of scarce resources are often over-looked. However, there is only so much money and time. Decisions made about populations often limit options of individuals.

Common Errors

Common errors in integrating information from diverse sources are related to common cognitive biases discussed throughout this book, such as overconfidence, influence by redundant information, and confirmation biases. Eagerness to help clients may encourage unfounded confidence in methods suggested. Lack of reliability and validity of information is often overlooked, resulting in faulty inferences. Jumping to conclusions may result in oversimplification of the causes of a client's concerns. Or the opposite may occur, as in posing a variety of different causes, none of which provide intervention implications. Lack of evidence may be shared with the client in an unempathic manner. Many components of EBP are designed to minimize biases such as jumping to conclusions—for example, by using quality filters when reviewing external research findings related to a question.

Obstacles and Evolving Remedies

Helping professionals to learn from their experience in ways that improve the accuracy of future decisions is a key priority. Hogarth (1987) proposes four sources of mistakes in decision making: (1) selective perception, (2) imperfect information processing, (3) inaccurate calculations due to cognitive limitations, and (4) incorrect reconstructions of events because of biases and faulty memory or both. (See also Chapter 9.) EBP highlights the play of bias and uncertainty involved in helping clients and attempts to give helpers and clients the knowledge and skills to handle them honestly and constructively. Consider the attention given to helping both clients and helpers to enhance their critical appraisal skills and to use quality filters in reviewing research findings related to practice questions (see Exhibit 11.2). Biases intrude both on the part of researchers when preparing research reviews and at the practitioner level when making decisions (e.g., see Chapter 12). Consider assessment. Clinicians have to decide what characteristics of clients and their contexts to attend to and how to weigh them. They have to decide what information to gather and how they will do this (see Chapter 13). Preferred practice theories may influence sound integration of individual expertise, external evidence, and client values and expectations. The time and effort devoted to making a decision should depend on the potential consequences in relation to making a faulty or good decision and what is needed, based on prior experience. There are many sources of innumeracy, as described in Chapters 14 and 15.

We can draw on literature investigating expertise to encourage valuable strategies including "educating our intuition" and discouraging premature closure (see Chapter 4). Experts in an area rely on primed decision making as a result of extensive experience offering corrective feedback (see Chapter 8). Use of clinical pathways and smart phones with built-in decision aids, such as flowcharts, can be helpful, and many are in use. Such aids can be used to prompt valuable behaviors, to critique a decision (for example, purchasing services from an agency that does not use evidence-informed practices), to make a differential diagnosis, to match a client's unique circumstances and characteristics with a certain service program, to suggest unconsidered options, and to interpret different assessment pictures (Guyatt & Rennie, 2002). And just as the narratives of clients may help us to understand how we can improve services, so the narratives of practitioners may help us to identify challenges and opportunities to providing quality services to clients (Greenhalgh & Hurwitz, 1998).

EVALUATING AND LEARNING FROM WHAT HAPPENS

Evaluating the effects of services has many advantages: (1) both you and your clients receive ongoing feedback about degree of success; (2) plans can be changed in a timely manner, depending on outcomes; (3) positive feedback increases clients' motivation; and (4) the relationship between services and outcomes can be explored (e.g., see Lambert & Shimokawa, 2011; Miller et al., 2006). Evaluation helps you and your clients to avoid faulty decisions based on incorrect estimates of progress and related factors. Timely corrective feedback is essential to catching and correcting harmful unintended effects at an early point. For example, one of my students had her field placement in a hospital. She discovered that a young girl with beta thalassemia (an inherited chronic illness) was not doing well, even though she was following her prescribed treatment regimen. The student discovered this because she monitored both the girl's compliance and the results of her lab tests. The lack of expected match between compliance and the lab results led to the discovery that a treatment change recommended a year before had never been implemented, a discovery that may have saved this girl's life. Clients have a right to know whether they benefit from or are harmed by services. Involving clients as informed participants and preventing avoidable harm are ethical obligations of professionals. Fulfilling these obligations requires tracking outcomes of importance on an ongoing basis, using valid measures rather than relying on misleading surrogates, such as process measures (number of sessions attended). Reliance on surrogate end points may be misleading (Gotzsche, Liberati, Torri, & Rossetti, 1996).

Different choices have different opportunity costs, such as not discovering early on that services have harmful effects. "All genuine evaluations produce findings that are better than speculation" (Berk & Rossi, 1990, p. 34; see also Rossi, Lipsey, & Freeman, 2003). Some evaluation methods are more likely than others to avoid biases that get in the way of accurately estimating progress and what was responsible for it. Ways to fool yourself and your clients about degree of progress include selecting measures because they are easy to use even though they are not related to client concerns and are not sensitive to change. Concerns about cost, acceptability to clients, and feasibility will limit options. You will often have a choice between feedback that can improve the soundness of future decisions and feedback that prevents debugging (identifying and remedying errors; Bransford & Stein, 1984). Measures used should be relevant (meaningful to clients and significant others), specific (clearly described), sensitive (reflect changes that occur), feasible (possible to obtain), unintrusive (not interfere with service provision), valid (measure what they are supposed to measure), and reliable (show consistency over different measurements in the absence of change). There is a rich literature suggesting valid, feasible ways to evaluate different kinds of outcomes, including complex ones, such as quality of life. This includes different kinds of single-case designs to answer questions such as: "Is there change? Is one intervention better than another (e.g., relaxation training compared to decreasing negative thoughts)? Is there change within a session (for example, in anxiety)?" Such designs differ from case studies and anecdotal reports in carefully tracking clearly described outcomes of interest over time (see Bloom, Fischer, & Orme, 2009).

Advantages of single-case designs include flexibility and detailed information concerning a single individual. Requirements include clear description of hoped-for outcomes and their repeated measurement in different phases, such as baseline and intervention. Inclusion of a baseline allows you and your clients to compare results with preintervention levels of a concern. Experimental N of 1 trials are ideal in discovering what method works best for a given client when the external research is murky or does not apply well to a client. Here, you and your clients agree to test a practice method regarding its effectiveness in attaining outcomes clients value. Following a baseline, alternative services are offered, or a service and a placebo. However, N of 1 trials may be done in a haphazard way. If so, as Sackett and his colleagues (2000) note, conclusions about effects may be quite misleading for a variety of reasons:

1. Many concerns are self-limited and improve on their own.
2. Extreme levels of a measure or symptom, if untreated and remeasured later, often return to or toward the normal range.
3. The placebo effect can lead to substantial relief of symptoms.
4. Our own and our clients' expectations can bias our conclusions about whether a treatment worked.
5. Clients may exaggerate the benefits of treatment. (Sackett et al., 2000, pp. 150–151)

In all of these instances, any interventions that take place in the interim, even if quite useless, will appear effective (Sackett et al., 2000, p. 151).

Objections to obtaining corrective feedback often are related to misconceptions about careful evaluation, such as the view that this requires selection of trivial outcomes or measures—the belief that rigor requires rigor mortis. Related literature demonstrates that this is not so. Clients like the feedback they receive from careful evaluation (Campbell, 1988). In a quality assurance review program that graphed the progress toward each goal for more than 2,000 psychiatric patients, clients reported that they appreciated the careful evaluation of progress (Bullmore, Joyce, Marks, & Connolly, 1992). The alternative to careful evaluation is basing decisions on guesstimates (uninformed guesses) that may mislead both you and your clients.

Sources of Error in Estimating Progress and Making Judgments About Related Causes

Biases that may lead us astray in estimating progress and what was responsible for it include the following:

- Being swayed by hindsight bias (see Chapter 15).
- Being overconfident.

- Engaging in wishful thinking.
- Having an illusion of control.
- Overlooking the role of chance (coincidences).
- Overlooking confounding causes, such as regression effects (see Chapter 15).
- Attributing success to our own efforts and failure to other factors.
- Seeking only data that support preferred views (confirmation bias).
- Relying on observed rather than relative frequency (see Chapter 15).
- Overlooking the interaction between predictions and their consequences (see Chapter 15).
- Mistaking correlation for causation (see Chapter 14).
- Relying on misleading criteria such as testimonials (see Chapter 4).

What you think is a result of intervention may be the result of a confounding factor such as maturation or history (see Chapter 12). Positive outcomes may be due to the act of treatment rather than the treatment itself (i.e., a placebo effect). Negative as well as positive placebo effects may occur. The former have a negative impact on outcome and/or result in negative side effects. These may be related to subtle signs of inattention. One or more of the following reactive effects may contribute to the placebo effect:

- *Hello–good-bye effect:* Clients present themselves as worse than they really are when they seek help and as better than they really are when the service has ended. This leads to overestimating progress (Hathaway, 1948).
- *Hawthorne effect:* Improvements may result from being the focus of attention—for example, going to a well-known clinic or being seen by a famous therapist.
- *Rosenthal effect:* We tend to give observers what we think they want—to please people we like or respect.
- *Observer bias:* The observer's expectations may result in biased data.
- *Social desirability effect:* We tend to offer accounts viewed as appropriate. For example, clients may underreport drinking.

Extreme values tend to become less extreme on repeated assessment. If you do unusually well on a test, you are likely to do less well the next time around. Conversely, if you do very poorly, you are likely to do better the next time. These are called *regression effects*. There is a regression (a return) toward the mean (your average performance level). Overlooking these effects can lead to faulty judgments. We tend to attribute success to our skills and failure to chance. Use of vague or irrelevant feedback obscures the true relationship (or lack thereof) between our judgments and outcomes. We tend to focus on our hits and overlook our misses. To accurately estimate your track record (or anyone else's), you must examine both hits and misses, as well as what would have happened without intervention (see Chapter 17). We tend to forget that actions taken as a result of predictions influence the outcomes.

Familiarity with common biases may help you avoid them and their negative effects, such as continuing harmful or ineffective programs. Many of these biases also influence decisions in other helping phases (e.g., assessment). Ongoing tracking of progress provides feedback that can correct inaccurate views due to one or more biases. The vaguer the outcome measures, the more likely that bias will creep in, because there is less chance for corrective feedback.

Obstacles and Evolving Remedies

Lack of time and training in selecting relevant, feasible progress indicators interferes with evaluation that can guide decision making. Fears about revealing lack of progress or harmful effects may discourage careful evaluation. Evaluation is a highly political process; it is not for the timid (Baer, 2003). Some of my master's students tell me that they are not allowed to evaluate services in their agency. As Oxman et al. (1995) suggest, there are no magic bullets. Calls for accountability and the transparency of results that this requires, as well as selection of user-friendly, valid tools for assessing progress, will facilitate evaluation. Client involvement may be critical to making services and outcomes more visible to all interested parties. (See Domenighetti, Grilli, & Liberati, 1998.) The philosophy of evidence-based practice encourages the participation of clients as informed participants. Keeping track of the questions you ask, the critical appraisal of related research, and client progress over time will be of value in learning how to improve future decisions. (See discussion of CATs.)

EVALUATING YOUR SKILLS IN EVIDENCE-BASED PRACTICE

Questions that encourage self-development of evidence-based practice knowledge and skills are illustrated in Exhibit 11.9. Gray (2001a) suggests use of the following prompts when reviewing your scanning strategy:

- How many hours each week do I want to spend scanning for new knowledge?
- What sources of knowledge do I want to scan regularly?
- What sources of information will I exclude?
- How can I ensure that I do not miss important new knowledge using this strategy?
- What checklists can I use to ensure that I stick to my scanning objectives? (A weekly checklist is useful.)

Exhibit 11.9 Self-Evaluation Questions

A. Asking Answerable Questions

1. Am I asking any practice questions at all?
2. Am I asking well-formed (four-part) questions?
3. Am I using a "map" to locate my knowledge gaps and articulate questions?
4. Can I get myself unstuck when asking questions?
5. Do I have a working method to save my questions for later answering?
6. Is my success rate of asking answerable questions rising?
7. Am I modeling the asking of answerable questions for others?

B. Finding the Best External Evidence

1. Am I searching at all?
2. Do I know the best sources of current evidence for decisions I make?
3. Do I have immediate access to searching hardware, software, and the best evidence for questions that arise?
4. Am I finding useful external evidence from a widening array of sources?
5. Am I becoming more efficient in my searching?
6. How do my searches compare with those of research librarians or colleagues who have a passion for providing best current care?

C. Critically Appraising Evidence for Its Validity and Usefulness

1. Am I critically appraising external evidence at all?
2. Are the critical appraisal guides becoming easier for me to apply?
3. Am I becoming more accurate and efficient in applying critical appraisal measures such as pretest probabilities and NNTs?

D. Integrating Critical Appraisal With Clinical Expertise and Applying the Results

1. Am I integrating my critical appraisals in my practice at all?
2. Am I becoming more accurate and efficient in adjusting some of the critical appraisal measures to fit my clients?
3. Can I explain (and resolve) disagreements about management decisions in terms of this integration?
4. Have I conducted any clinical decision analyses?
5. Have I carried out any audits of my diagnostic, therapeutic, or other EBP performance?

E. Relationship Skills

1. Am I seeking feedback after each meeting from clients regarding their perceptions of my empathy and the helpfulness of sessions? (See feedback scale developed by David Burns.)
2. Are my empathy ratings from clients improving?

F. Self-Evaluation and Helping Others Learn Evidence-Based Practice

1. Am I helping others learn how to ask well-structured questions?
2, Am I raising more questions regarding claims made that affect services clients receive and receiving more positive responses?
3. Am I teaching and modeling searching skills?
4. Am I teaching and modeling critical appraisal skills?
5. Am I teaching and modeling the integration of best evidence with my clinical expertise and my clients' preferences?
6. Am I helping others enhance their skills in offering empathic and disarming responses?
7. Am I using fewer unjustifiable excuses? (See McDowell, 2000; Pope & Vasquez, 2007.)
8. Do I admit more often that "I was wrong"?

Source: Parts A, B, C, D, and F adapted from *Evidence-Based Medicine: How to Practice and Teach EBM* (pp. 220–228), by D. L. Sackett, S. E. Straus, W. S. Richardson, W. Rosenberg, and R. B. Haynes, 2000, New York, NY: Churchill Livingstone. Reprinted with permission.

- Is there anyone else who could develop, or has developed already, a scanning strategy with whom I could share the load?
- How can I review the benefits and weaknesses of this strategy at the end of the year? (Gray, 2001a, p. 111)

Try out your skills by identifying an important decision you must make. What kind of question is it? What is your best answer before searching for related research? What did you discover? Gray (2001a) emphasizes the importance of information storage and retrieval skills; if you can't find information when you need it, it is not of value to clients. Possibilities include a user-friendly computer reference system.

THE QUESTION OF MOTIVATION

Some helpers seem to be motivated already. But, if we are not, how do we get motivated? Does being aware of harming in the name of helping help us to get motivated? Many professionals seem to be quite aware of harm in the name of helping but do not seem to think this applies to their practices and policies. Our motivation is related to our values and our skills in getting motivated. We must believe that it is important to prevent harming in the name of helping and to provide services most likely to benefit clients (given that they are acceptable to clients), to be motivated, and related environmental contingencies must support this commitment. We must be willing to recognize gaps in our background knowledge and what may be available—to recognize our ignorance. We must be willing to acknowledge uncertainty—to say, "I don't know." We also must have the "courage to fail" (Fox & Swazey, 1974), the courage to recognize that we will make mistakes, and a commitment to learn from them.

If we work in environments in which supervisors and administrators have little interest in determining whether clients are helped or harmed (indeed, they may block such efforts), it may be difficult to maintain values and behaviors related to evidence-based practice. We may get worn down as our efforts are not reinforced, or are punished, for example, by supervisors. We may even forget valuable ways of acting, such as asking hard questions—we may come to think of such questions as irrelevant or out of place. Questions that can help us to remain faithful to our ethical principles include:

- Will it help clients if I promote assessment measures of dubious or untested validity?
- Will it help clients if I hide the evidentiary status of service programs?
- Will it help clients if I use outcome measures that are not valid?

- Will it help clients if I attribute troubled or troubling behavior to alleged pathological characteristics of clients ("mental disorders") and ignore environmental factors empirically shown to influence related behaviors?

SUMMARY

Key steps in EBP include posing well-formed questions regarding information needed to make important decisions; seeking efficiently and effectively electronically for related research; critically appraising what is found (or drawing on high-quality critical reviews prepared by others); using practice expertise to integrate diverse sources of information, including knowledge about the clients' values, expectations, preferences, and available resources; and making a decision together with clients about what to do, trying it out, evaluating what happens, and learning from this experience how to do better the next time. These steps increase the likelihood that you and your clients will be well informed about the kinds and levels of uncertainties associated with decisions. Although the steps involved in evidence-based practice may sound simple and straightforward, they are often difficult and sometimes impossible to carry out successfully in the real world. There are many challenges, including learning new skills and acquiring access to needed resources, such as databases, and arranging for ongoing feedback to keep skills well honed. Access to efficient search engines is vital. Perhaps the greatest challenge is a willingness to recognize gaps in your current knowledge regarding decisions that must be made and what may be out there—a willingness to say, "I don't know," and a commitment to your clients to see what is out there.

12

Critical Appraisal of Practice- and Policy-Related Research: The Need for Skepticism

Simply because something appears in print does not mean that it is accurate. Indeed, flaws in published research were key to the development of evidence-based practice (EBP) and policy, as described in Chapter 10. Thornley and Adams (1998) reviewed data in 2,000 trials on the Cochrane Schizophrenia Group's register and found consistently poor quality of reporting, which they suggest "is likely to have resulted in an overly optimistic estimation of the effects of treatment" (p. 1181). Less rigorous studies report more positive findings compared to research that controls for biases. Consider the history of facilitated communication. This intervention method is designed to increase verbal communication among people with disabilities. Initial anecdotal and pre-post reports suggested that this was effective. Later, more rigorous studies found no effect (Jacobson, Mulick, & Schwartz, 1995). As Rosenbaum (2002) suggests, we should also be skeptical of the skeptics. Just because someone says a study is flawed does not mean that it is. Learning to critically appraise different kinds of research studies for yourself frees you from misleading influences by others, including researchers, academics, and journalists, allowing you to accurately inform your clients about the potential of given options for attaining outcomes they value. Encouraging clinicians to do this is a key aim of evidence-based practice.

Being informed about different kinds of research and their advantages and disadvantages, including biases that result in misleading results, will help you to draw on practice- and policy-related research in an informed manner. This kind of research savvy is closely related to honoring ethical obligations to clients. Without this you may recommend ineffective or harmful methods and overlook effective programs. And you will be a pushover for those who use social-psychological persuasion strategies and informal fallacies to influence what you do (see Chapters 5 and 6). For example, phrases such

Exhibit 12.1 The Major Types of Studies Found in the Medical Literature

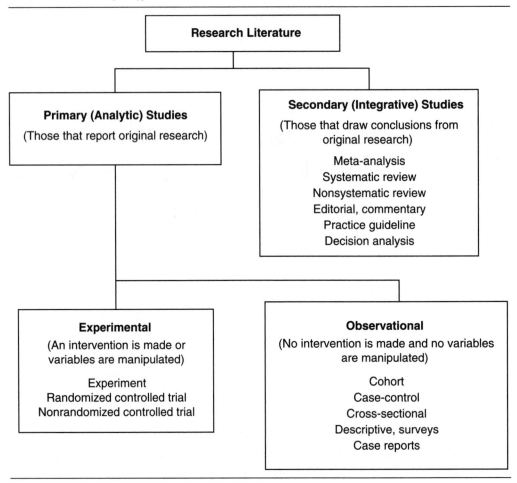

Source: From "Critical Appraisal of the Literature," by W. F. Miser, 1999, *Journal of the American Board of Family Practice, 12*, pp. 315–333. Reprinted with permission of the American Board of Family Medicine.

as "has not been established" may really mean that a medication has been tested with equivocal results (Meier, 2004).

There are many kinds of research reports (see Exhibit 12.1). They differ in their purpose (the questions raised) and the likelihood that the method used can provide accurate information about the question (see Exhibit 12.2). Examples include:

Analytic: Designed to make causal inferences about relationships—for example, between certain risk factors, such as poverty, and an outcome such as child abuse. Two or more groups are compared.

Descriptive: Designed to provide information about the prevalence or incidence of a problem or about the distribution of certain characteristics in a group.

Prospective: Subjects are selected and followed up.

Retrospective: Events of interest have already occurred (children have been abused) and data are collected from case records or recall, as in case-control studies.

Contemporary comparison: Groups that experience a risk factor at the same time are compared.

Different kinds of research design control for different kinds of biases, which may result in misleading conclusions (see Exhibit 12.2). Sackett (1979) identified 35 different kinds of biases in case-control studies. Many sources provide more detail, including the user-friendly book *How to Read a Paper* (Greenhalgh, 2010) and sources that provide more detail, such as Guyatt, Mead, Cook, and Rennie (2008).

Exhibit 12.2 Types of Studies

The types of studies that give the best evidence are different for different types of questions. In every case, however, the best evidence comes from studies in which the methods used maximize the chance of eliminating bias. The study designs that best suit different question types are as follows:

Question	Best Study Designs	Description
Intervention	Randomized controlled trial (RCT)	Subjects are randomly allocated to treatment or control groups and outcomes assessed.
Etiology and risk factors	Randomized controlled trial	As etiololgy questions are similar to intervention questions, the ideal study type is an RCT. However, it is usually not ethical or practical to conduct such a trial to assess harmful outcomes.
	Cohort study	Outcomes are compared for matched groups with and without exposure to risk factor (prospective study).
	Case-control study	Subjects with and without outcome of interest are compared for previous exposure or risk factor (retrospective study).
Frequency and rate	Cohort study	As above.
	Cross-sectional study	Measurement of condition in a representative (preferably random) sample of people.
Diagnosis	Cross-sectional study with random or consecutive sample	Preferably an independent, blind, comparison with gold standard test.
Prognosis and prediction	Cohort/survival study	Long-term follow-up of a representative cohort.
Phenomena	Qualitative	Narrative analysis or focus group; designed to assess the range of issues (rather than their quantification).

Source: From *Evidence-Based Medicine Workbook* (p. 41), by P. Glasziou, C. Del Mar, and J. Salisbury, 2003, London: BMJ. Reprinted with permission.

COMMON MYTHS THAT HINDER CRITICAL APPRAISAL

A variety of myths may hinder critical appraisal of the quality of research on which practice recommendations are made.

It Is Too Difficult for Me to Learn

The ease of identifying some key characteristics of rigorous studies regarding certain kinds of practice questions is suggested by the fact that social workers wanted their physicians to rely on the results of randomized controlled trials (RCTs) when making recommendations about treatment methods (Gambrill & Gibbs, 2002). However, individuals relied on weak criteria, such as intuition, when making decisions about their clients. Checklists and scales have been developed to enhance reporting of different kinds of research such as CONSORT (Schulz, Altman, & Moher for the CONSORT Group, 2010) and PRISMA (Liberati et al., 2009) as well as to appraise different kinds of research. Failure to satisfy a critical feature (such as blind assessment of outcome) suggests that overall scores should not be used, since one critical flaw may be canceled out by many less important characteristics.

All Research Is Equally Sound

All research is not equally informative. Research designs differ in the questions that can be carefully explored; they differ in the extent to which biases are controlled for, that may contribute to incorrect conclusions. A variety of errors can be and are made in designing and interpreting research. Because of this, you may conclude that a method was effective when it was not; it may even be harmful. You may conclude that a method was not effective when it is effective. A research design may be used that cannot critically test the question raised. Chalmers (2003) defines reliable studies as "those in which the effects of policies and practices are unlikely to be confused with the effects of biases or chance" (p. 28). Less rigorous studies report more positive results than do more rigorous studies (e.g., see Lindsey, Martin, & Doh, 2002; Schulz, Chalmers, Hayes, & Altman, 1995).

I Should Trust the Experts

You will often have to depend on the experts. Depending on experts is risky because experts may all be biased in a certain direction. That is, they may share a bias toward a commonly favored view of a certain problem and how to minimize it. In fact, experts in an area prepare more biased reviews than do individuals who are well trained in methodological issues but who do not work in that area (Oxman & Guyatt, 1993). But you can learn about criteria of value in discovering whether people are honest experts. Do they, for example, use clear language that you can understand? Do they describe well-argued alternatives and describe contradictory evidence to preferred views?

Intuition Is a Better Guide

First, we must distinguish between informed and uninformed intuition. (See Chapter 4.) Informed intuition based on repeated experiences providing corrective feedback is quite different from merely guessing. We also must distinguish the kind of task involved. Does it require identifying the most effective method? Does it involve diagnosing a client? Myths that hinder critical appraisal include the belief that intuition provides a sound guide to what is effective. Chalmers (2003) points out that "as Donald Campbell (1969) noted many years ago, selectively designating some interventions as 'experiments'—a term loaded with negative associations—ignores the reality that policy makers and practitioners are experimenting on other people most of the time. The problem is that their experiments are usually poorly controlled. Dr. Spock's ill-founded advice [to let babies sleep on their stomachs] would probably not be conceptualized by many people as a poorly controlled experiment, yet that is just what is was" (p. 30). Later research showed that stomach-sleeping was one of the causes of sudden infant death syndrome (SIDS).

Only Certain Kinds of Research Must Be Rigorous

Another myth is that only certain kinds of research must be rigorous to avoid biased results. A concern to avoid biases that may result in misleading conclusions is relevant to all research, including qualitative research. For example, a number of authors describe errors resulting from not checking assumptions when using various kinds of qualitative research (see later discussion of qualitative research).

One or Two Studies Can Yield Conclusive Findings

Yet another myth is that one or two well-controlled studies yield the truth. Such an assumption reflects a justification approach to knowledge, in which we assume that certainty is possible (see Chapter 4).

A Study Must Be Perfect to Be Useful

Yet another myth is that a study must be perfect to yield valuable findings. All studies are flawed. The question is, are the flaws so great that they preclude any sound conclusions?

Quantitative Research Is Best/Qualitative Research Is Best

Another myth is that quantitative research is better than qualitative research, or vice versa. It depends on the question. And pursuit of many questions is informed by both kinds of research. Consider, for example, *Labeling the Mentally Retarded* (1973) by Jane Mercer, in which community surveys, official records, and unstructured interviews were all used. Multimethod studies are often used.

THE QUESTION OF BIAS

The notion of bias is central to critically appraising the quality of practice- and policy-related research. Bias is a systematic leaning to one side that distorts the accuracy of results. Bias can be of two types: (1) systematic, in which errors are made in a certain direction, or (2) random fluctuations. It has long been of interest. Consider Francis Bacon's (1620/1985) four idols of the mind:

> The Idols of the Tribe have their foundation in human nature itself, and in the tribe or race of men. For it is a false assertion that the sense of man is the measure of things . . . and the human understanding is like a false mirror, which receiving rays irregularly, distorts and discolors the nature of things by mingling its own nature with it.
>
> The Idols of the Cave are the idols of the individual man. For everyone (besides the errors common to human nature in general) has a cave or den of his own, which refracts and discolors the light of nature; owing either to his own proper and peculiar nature; or to its education and conversation with others; or to the reading of books, and the authority of those whom he esteems and admires; or to the differences of impressions, accordingly as they take place in a mind preoccupied and predisposed or in a mind indifferent and settled.
>
> There are also Idols formed by the intercourse and association of men with each other, which I call Idols of the Market-place, on account of the commerce and consort of men there. And therefore the ill and unfit choice of words wonderfully obstructs the understanding. . . . But words plainly force and overrule the understanding . . . and throw all into confusion, and lead men away into numberless empty controversies and idle fancies.
>
> Lastly, there are Idols, which have immigrated into men's minds from the various dogmas of philosophies and also from wrong laws of demonstration. These I call Idols of the Theater, because in my judgment all the received

systems are but so many stage-plays, representing worlds of their own creation after an unreal and scenic fashion.

Biases occur in the design of research (for example, what question is asked); in how it is conducted (rigorously or sloppily) and interpreted (accurately or not); in how it is reported (e.g., clearly or not); and in how it is used. (See Jadad & Enkin, 2007.) There are publication biases. For example, studies reporting negative results are less likely to be published than studies reporting positive results: "Studies that show a statistically significant effect of treatment are more likely to be published, more likely to be published in English, more likely to be cited by other authors, and more likely to produce multiple publications than other studies" (Sterne, Egger, & Smith, 2001, p. 198). Examples of biases in published research include: "*submission* bias (research workers are more strongly motivated to complete, and submit for publication, positive results), *publication bias* (editors are more likely to publish positive studies), *methodological bias* (methodological errors such as flawed randomization produce positive biases), *abstracting bias* (abstracts emphasize positive results), and *framing bias* (relative risk data produce a positive bias)" (Gray, 2001b, p. 24). Jadad and Enkin (2007) provide the most exhaustive and entertaining description of bias in all stages. Other biases include *outcome choice bias* (selection of outcomes that are easy to measure rather than those that are most relevant). Biases in the uptake phase include those introduced by personal preferences (e.g., does it challenge a favored theory?) and *geographic bias* (judged by country or origin of the author). Jadad and Enkin (2007) include *belligerence bias*, which results from being difficult just for the sake of being difficult. *Empiricism bias* refers to over- or underestimating the value of a report because it contradicts clinical experience. *Careless reader bias* is another one (readers do not read important sections of an article). The steps involved in evidence-based practice are designed to decrease confirmation biases, such as looking only for data that support a preferred theory.

Bias and Validity

Biases may influence both internal and external validity. Internal validity refers to the extent to which a design allows you to critically test and come up with an accurate answer concerning the causal relationships between some intervention and an outcome. Threats to internal validity have been masterfully described by Campbell and Stanley (1963; see Exhibit 12.3). (See also Shadish, Cook, & Campbell, 2002.) These threats are rival hypotheses to the assumption that a method was effective, for example. Biases include *selection bias* (e.g., biased allocation to experimental and control groups),

Exhibit 12.3 Possible Confounding Causes (Rival Explanations) for Change

---

1. *History.* Events that occur between the first and second measurement, in addition to the experimental variables, may account for changes (e.g., clients may get help elsewhere).

2. *Maturation.* Simply growing older or living longer may be responsible, especially when long periods of time are involved.

3. *Instrumentation.* The way that something is measured changes (e.g., observers may change how they record).

4. *Testing effects.* Assessment may result in change.

5. *Mortality.* There may be a differential loss of people from different groups.

6. *Regression.* Extreme scores tend to return to the mean.

7. *Self-selection bias.* Clients are often self-selected rather than randomly selected. They may differ in critical ways from the population they are assumed to represent and differ from clients in a comparison group.

8. *Helper selection bias.* Social workers may select certain kinds of clients to receive certain methods.

9. *Interaction effects.* Only certain clients may benefit from certain services, and others may even be harmed.

Source: Based on *Experimental and Quasi-Experimental Designs for Research,* by D. T. Campbell and J. C. Stanley, 1963, Chicago, IL: Rand McNally.

performance bias (unequal provision of care apart from the methods under evaluation), *detection bias* (biased assessment of outcome), and *attrition bias* (biased occurrence and handling of deviations from a protocol and loss to follow-up). *Confounders* may occur— variables that are related to a causal factor of interest and some outcome(s) that are not represented equally in two different groups. *Zero time bias* may occur, in which people in a prospective study are enrolled in a way that results in systematic differences between groups (as in prospective cohort studies). Well-designed randomized controlled trials contain more control for different kinds of biases compared to weaker studies, such as quasi-experimental studies. Unless a study is replicated, we are not sure whether there were problems (flaws) that resulted in misleading findings. History illustrates that many results based on a single study could not be replicated and were found to be false.

External validity refers to the extent to which you can generalize the findings in a study to other circumstances. These other circumstances may include other kinds of clients (e.g., age, risk factors, severity of problem); settings; services offered (e.g., timing, number of sessions or dosage, other concurrent services); kinds of outcomes reviewed; or length of follow-up (Juni, Altman, & Egger, 2001, p. 42). To what extent can you generalize the causal relationship found in a study to different times, places, and people, and different operational definitions of interventions and outcomes? Farrington (2003) uses the term *descriptive validity* to refer to "the adequacy of the presentation of key features of an evaluation in a research report." Unblinded rating of outcome can result in misleading conclusions of effectiveness. The literature on experimenter and subject biases highlights the importance of research that controls for these (e.g., Rosenthal, 1994). For example, we tend to give socially desirable responses, to present ourselves in a good light. Knowing a hypothesis creates a tendency to encourage the very responses that we are investigating. Experimenter effects are not necessarily intentional; even when we do not intend to skew results in a certain way, this may occur. Experimenter biases influence results in a number of ways. If the experimenters know the group a subject is in, they may change their behavior—for example, subtly lead the person in a certain direction. This is why it is vital in randomized controlled trials for raters of outcome to be blind—unaware of the group to which a person is assigned.

QUESTIONS TO ASK ABOUT ALL RESEARCH

Certain questions are important to raise across all research because of the potential for flaws that may result in misleading conclusions. These include concerns about the size and source of samples used, whether there is a comparison group, the accuracy and validity of measures used, and the appropriateness of data analysis. Answers to these characteristics will shed light on both the internal and external validity of a study. Methodological quality criteria suggested by Cook and Campbell (1979) as well as Shadish, Cook, and Campbell (2002) include four criteria: statistical conclusion validity, internal validity, construct validity, and external validity. The term *validity* refers to the accuracy of assumptions in relation to causes and effects. Classic criteria for assuming a causal relationship include: (1) the cause precedes the effect, (2) the cause is related to the effect, and (3) other plausible alternatives of the effect can be excluded (John Stuart Mill, 1911). As Farrington (2003) notes, "If threats to valid causal inference cannot be ruled out in the design, they should at least be measured and their importance estimated" (pp. 51–52). Too often the limitations of studies are not mentioned, are glossed over, or are minimized. Flaws in traditional methods of dissemination, including peer-reviewed journals, were one of the reasons for the origins of evidence-based practice (Altman, 2002). Poor reporting of a randomized controlled trial does not necessarily mean that a trial was poorly constructed; it may be only poorly reported (e.g., Soares et al., 2004).

Is the Research Question Clear?

Do the authors clearly describe their research question, or is this vague or confusing? Examples of clear research questions are: "What factors contribute to the reabuse of children returned to their biological parents?" or "Do substance abuse programs to which parents are referred help them to decrease alcohol consumption compared to no intervention?" Unclear questions do not allow for clear tests at the point of data analysis, set in advance.

What Kind of Question Is It?

Does the article address the effectiveness of a practice method? Is it an assessment question? Does it describe a new risk assessment measure for depression in the elderly? What kind of question does it concern? (See Exhibit 11.1 in Chapter 11.)

Is It Relevant to My Clients? Is It Important?

Does the information apply to your clients? If you knew the answer, could you and your clients make more informed decisions? Does it concern outcomes of interest to your clients? Have key ones been omitted? Is the setting similar to your practice setting? Are the clients similar?

Who Sponsored the Study?

Sponsorship of a study may suggest possible biases (see also discussion of propaganda in Chapter 4). Sponsorship of research or a continuing education program by a company with a vested interest in a product, such as a pharmaceutical company, encourages presentation of biased material (e.g., see Brody, 2007).

Does the Research Method Used Match the Question Raised?

Can the research method used address the question? Different questions require different research methods (see Exhibit 12.2). That is why discussing whether qualitative or quantitative research is best is unproductive—it depends on the question. Oxman and Guyatt (1993) suggest a scale ranging from 1 (not at all) to 6 (ideal) in relation to the potential that a research method can critically test a question.

Is There a Comparison Group?

Critically testing certain kinds of questions requires a comparison. A hallmark of randomized controlled trials is distributing clients to two or more different conditions. An intervention group (cognitive-behavioral therapy for depression) may be compared to a no-treatment group or to a comparison group (interpersonal therapy). Only if we have a comparison can we identify which might be better than the other. If all we have is a pre-post test describing how depressed people are before and after some intervention, there is no comparison with a group receiving no service or a different service. Thus, there could be a variety of other reasons for any changes seen (see Exhibit 12.3).

Is the Study Design Rigorous?

The general research method may be appropriate but be carried out in a sloppy, unrigorous manner that allows the play of many biases. Farrington (2003) suggests five methodological criteria: (1) *internal validity*—demonstrating that the intervention caused an effect on the outcome: (2) *descriptive validity*—without information about key features of research it is hard to include the results in a systematic review; (3) *statistical conclusion validity*; (4) *construct validity*; and (5) *external validity*. He suggests that these occur in order of importance, at least concerning systematic reviews of impact evaluations. He views information about the external validity of a single research project as "the least important to a systematic reviewer since the main aims of a systematic review and meta-analyses include establishing the external validity or generalizability of results over different conditions and investigating factors that explain heterogeneity in effect size among different evaluation studies" (p. 61).

What Is the Sample Size and Source?

Most research involves a sample that is assumed to be characteristic of the population from which it is drawn. Selection biases are one kind of bias related to how subjects were selected. Does the sample on which a study was based offer a sound opportunity to answer questions raised? (Some research deals with an entire population, such as all graduates of the University of California at Berkeley's social work master's degree program in the year 2004.) A key question is: "Can we accurately generalize from a sample to the population from which it is drawn, or from one population to another (other year)?" Does the sample represent the population to which generalizations will be made? Questions that arise include the following:

- Is the sample selection process clearly described?
- How was the sample selected?
- From what population was it selected?
- Is it representative of the population?
- Were subjects lost for follow-up?

The answers to these questions provide clues about biases that may limit the value of a study to answer questions. For example, small samples drawn by convenience, rather than by random selection, in which each individual has an equal chance of selection, may not provide information that reflects characteristics of the population of interest. Often researchers do not clearly describe the source of their sample. A number of filtering decisions may be made to obtain a final sample. CONSORT guidelines for reporting randomized controlled trials include a flowchart for describing samples used. We can see how many people were excluded at different points and for what reasons. Readers can review for themselves possible sources of bias in the final sample, on which conclusions are based.

Sample size and the critical testing of hypotheses are closely related. That is, some studies do not find effects—not because there are no effects to be found, but because the sample size does not have the power to test whether there is an association. As Farrington (2003) notes, "a statistically significant result could indicate a large effect in a small sample or a small effect in a large sample" (p. 52). Researchers should base selection of their sample size on the power needed to obtain a significant result. On the other hand, use of a large sample may yield many significant differences, which may not be illuminating. Clear description of the source of samples used is important in qualitative as well as quantitative research.

Are Measures Used Reliable and Valid?

Measures of concepts, such as self-esteem and substance abuse, are used in research. Do they measure what they purport to measure? Are they relevant to your clients? The validity of measures is a key concern in all research. Reliability refers to the consistency of ratings—for example, between different administrations of an assessment measure for an individual at different times (stability), or between two observers of an interaction at the same time (interrater reliability). Validity refers to the extent to which a measure reflects what it is designed to measure. There are many different kinds, as discussed in Chapter 13. Reliability places an upward boundary on validity. That is, a measure cannot be valid if it is not reliable (cannot be consistently assessed). And a measure may be reliable but invalid, perhaps because of shared biases among raters. Research using one kind of data (self-report) may present an inaccurate picture. For example, observation of children's behavior on the playground to identify instances of bullying may not match a student's self-report.

Did Authors Report Attrition (Dropout Rates)?

In many studies, some subjects drop out over the course of the study. This number should be reported, and is reflected in "intention-to-treat" analysis. This is "an analysis of a study where participants are analyzed according to the group to which they were initially allocated. This is regardless of whether or not they dropped out, fully complied with the treatment, or crossed over and received the other treatment. It protects against attrition bias" (Center for Reviews and Dissemination, University of York, UK, April 4, 2004).

Was There Any Follow-Up—If So, How Long?

An intervention may be effective in the short term but not in the long term. How long were subjects followed up? The effects of many programs are short-term.

Are Procedures Clearly Described?

Are practice methods used clearly described? If not, it will not be possible to replicate them. For example, in effectiveness studies, only if methods are clearly described can readers determine exactly what was done and whether methods were offered in an optimal manner.

Are the Data Analyses Sound?

Statistics are tools used to explore whether there is a relationship between two or more variables. We ask what is the probability of finding an association by chance in samples of different sizes (e.g., see Hoyle, Harris, & Judd, 2002). We do this by estimating the probability of getting a result in a sample of a certain size. We could make two kinds of errors. We may assume that there is a relationship when there is not (Type I error) or assume there is no relationship when there is (Type II error). The term *statistical significance* refers to whether a test falls below a certain probability (e.g., .01 or .05). You should have some rudimentary knowledge of statistics so you can ask cogent questions in terms of the adequacy of statistical analyses. Examples of ways to cheat on statistical tests when preparing reports suggested by Greenhalgh (2010) include:

- Go fishing—do lots of correlations and report only those that are significant.
- Do not adjust for baseline difference.
- Ignore withdrawals and nonresponders.
- Ignore outliers (see also *Harlot Pie* by Sackett and Oxman, 2003).

Researchers as well as practitioners make mistakes in how they word findings. For example, rather than stating that there was "no statistically significant difference," they may say that there was "no difference/change" (Weisburd, Lum, & Yang, 2003). Statistical testing is not without controversy. Complex statistical methods will not correct major flaws in the design or conduct of a study (Penston, 2010). This is why care in planning studies is so important. In addition to insufficient sample size to critically test the relationship between two or more variables, another problem is the use of inappropriate methods of statistical analysis, which may result in bogus claims. Different statistical tests make different assumptions about variables in relation to their underlying distribution.

A statistical method may be used that requires interval data (reflecting continuous data in which points are separated by equal intervals) for ordinal data, in which you can rank order differences but, in fact, don't have any idea about how much difference there is between points. It's like using a rubber ruler. Many constructs are continuous. Consider drinking—one could have no drinks, one drink, or many drinks per day. However, often this is treated as a binary variable (categorically defined); either one is or is not an alcoholic; a continuous variable is transformed into a binary one. Data is lost in changing a continuous variable to a dichotomous one—individual variations are omitted. Research texts describe a number of problems in relation to inappropriate use of statistical tests, such as fishing (running many tests to see if any would be significant). For example, you may read an article that uses many variables with a large sample and claims that it found 15 significant differences. The question is: How many correlations were run? A certain percentage would be significant by chance.

Are Claims Made Accurate?

Problems in any of the characteristics previously described, such as samples and measures used, may not allow clear conclusions. Inflated claims are common. That is why is it important to learn how to critically appraise research findings for yourself. Do claims made match the kind of design used? For example, pre-post tests cannot tell us whether the intervention was responsible for the results, because there is no comparison group. Yet the author may say, "Our results show that X was effective."

Are Findings Clinically Important?

Will research findings be of value in helping clients? People differ in their views about when there is enough evidence to recommend use of service or to recommend that a program not be used because it is harmful. For example, even a modest reduction in future delinquency may be important (e.g., Weisburd, Lum, & Yang, 2003). Many kinds of evidence come into play in making decisions (see Chapter 10). What may be true of a group may not be true of an individual. Thus, aggregate studies must be interpreted with caution in relation to generalizing to an individual. Otherwise you may make the *ecological fallacy*—assume that what is true of a group is true of an individual.

Did the Authors Describe Any Special Interests and Their Biases?

We should be informed about any special interests of authors that may bias conclusions, including the development of practice guidelines and diagnostic classification systems such as the *DSM*. For example, all *DSM-IV-TR* task force members of sections on mood disorders and schizophrenia had financial ties to drug companies. Did a drug company fund the study? Midanik (2006) describes the influence of the biomedical view of alcohol abuse on funding patterns.

WHAT ABOUT HIERARCHIES OF EVIDENCE?

Many different hierarchies of evidence have been proposed. A common hierarchy for levels of evidence for effectiveness studies lists systematic reviews first, followed by well-designed randomized controlled trials, quasi-experiments, controlled observational studies, and expert opinion. Making informed policy and practice decisions requires many other kinds of evidence, including economic, ethical, implementation, descriptive, analytical, attitudinal, and impact evidence. (See Davies, 2004.) Policy making is influenced by many kinds of evidence, including related values and resources. Hierarchies should not be rigidly used. Glasziou, Vandenbroucke, and Chalmers (2004) note that "criteria designed to guide inferences about the main effects of treatment have been uncritically applied to questions about etiology, diagnosis, prognosis, or adverse effects" (p. 39). A key point they make is that whatever the kind of report, including case studies, it is important to do a systematic review. Balanced assessments should draw on a variety of types of research, and different questions require different types of evidence (see also GRADE guidelines; Guyatt, Oxman, Schunemann, Tugwell, & Knottnerus, 2011).

QUESTIONS ABOUT EFFECTIVENESS AND PREVENTION

How can you discover if a practice or policy does more good than harm? You could ask your colleagues what they think. But on what do they base their views? Examples of effectiveness questions are:

- In youth with antisocial behavior, is group cognitive-behavioral training or individual counseling more effective in decreasing such behaviors and increasing positive behaviors?
- In young adults diagnosed with AIDS, are education and group support more effective than individual counseling in increasing safe-sex behaviors?

A key concern with testing effectiveness questions is: Is there a comparison group that allows us to determine whether different results would be attained with different groups? Various sources of bias in different stages regarding an RCT are illustrated in Exhibit 12.4. Is a new drug compared with a diluted dosage of a rival medication? Is sample size sufficient? Has a test been ended early? What does *effective* mean? For example, is the claim based on a 3-point difference on a 60-point scale? (Woloshin & Schwartz, 2011). Just as we can ask about number needed to treat (NNT), we can ask about number needed to harm (NNH). That is, how many people would have to receive a service for one to be harmed?

Exhibit 12.4 Examples of Potential Bias in Randomized Controlled Trials

During Planning

Choice of question bias
Regulator bias (e.g., institutional review board requirements)
Selection bias

During Conduct

Ascertainment bias (not blinded)
Population choice bias (may be overly narrow)
Intervention choice bias
Comparison (or control) group choice bias
Outcome choice bias (relevant and/or just easy to measure)

During Reporting

Dropouts not reported
Protocol violations not reported
Selective reporting of results
Data dredging bias

During Dissemination

Publication bias
Language bias
Time lag bias

During Uptake

Careless reader bias (do not read key sections of a report)
Rivalry bias (do not like author so ignore article)
Personal habit bias (over- or underrate study because disagrees with personal beliefs)
Clinical practice bias (disregard because disagrees with clinical experience)
Prominent author bias (overrate value of studies by well-known authors)
Printed word bias (overrate just because it is printed)
Flashy title bias
Geographic bias (judgment based on location)
Favored design bias (I do not like your design)
Small trial bias (underestimate value of small trial)
Vested interest bias (e.g., uptake will decrease my profits)
Belligerence bias (underrate value for sake of being difficult)
Empiricism bias (underrate because it challenges readers clinical experience)
Institution bias (we don't do things that way)

Source: Based on Randomized Controlled Trials: Questions, Answers and Musings (2nd ed.), by A. R. Jadad and M. W. Enkin, 2007, Malden, MA: Blackwell.

Randomized Controlled Trials

In experimental designs such as randomized controlled clinical trials there is a comparison between different groups, which may include an experimental group that receives a special treatment (the independent variable) and a control group, in which there is no special treatment. Or a comparison group receiving a different service may be used; two different methods may be compared. Factorial experimental designs explore the effects of more than one independent variable. Interaction effects are often of great interest here—for example, among personality, peer rejection of youth, and school environment. Random distribution of subjects to different groups using an effective randomization procedure is a key feature of rigorous experimental designs. Random distribution of subjects to groups is designed to minimize selection bias—differences in outcomes due to differences in subjects in different groups. (See CONSORT guidelines, www.consortstatement.com.) You should always review *how* subjects were randomly distributed to groups, because some methods of random distribution do not guard against selection biases that may skew results.

> Randomisation in clinical trials is the use of a chance procedure, such as coin tossing or computer-generated random numbers, to generate an allocation sequence. It ensures that participants have a prespecified (very often an equal) chance of being assigned to the experimental or control group. This means that the groups are likely to be balanced for known as well as unknown and unmeasured confounding variables. To protect against selection bias, concealment of the randomly-generated allocation sequence is essential. This is because foreknowledge of group assignments leaves the allocation sequence subject to possible manipulation by researchers and participants. Randomisation without allocation concealment does not guarantee protection against selection bias. (Center for Reviews and Dissemination, University of York, April 4, 2004)

Without a comparison group (for example, a group that did not receive a service), we do not know what would have happened in the absence of a service. (See Exhibit 12.5.) A briefer scale, the Jadad Scale, takes 5 minutes to complete. (See Jadad & Enkin, 2007.) Failure to question the effectiveness of an intervention has been responsible for much harm in the past, including the blinding of 10,000 babies by giving them oxygen at birth (Silverman, 1980). Joan McCord investigated the effectiveness of special services to youth designed to prevent delinquency, and found that such services resulted in more harm than good (see McCord, 2003). "Had there been no control group, evaluators might have concluded that the program was beneficial because so many of the treatment boys were better adjusted than anticipated. Or because two-thirds reported beneficial effects for themselves, evaluators might have judged that the program was effective. But these judgments would have been contrary to objective evidence that the program resulted in adverse outcomes for many of the participants" (McCord, 2003, p. 22). Blinding is a key method designed to decrease ascertainment bias.

> Blinding is used to keep the participants, investigators and outcome assessors ignorant about which interventions participants are receiving during a study.

Exhibit 12.5 Validity Screen for an Article About Therapy

1. Is the study a randomized controlled trial?	Yes (go on)	No (stop)
How were patients selected for the trial?		
Were they properly randomized into groups using concealed assignment?		
2. Are the subjects in the study similar to mine?	Yes (go on)	No (stop)
3. Are the participants who entered the trial properly accounted for at its conclusion?	Yes (go on)	No (stop)
Was follow-up complete and were few lost to follow-up compared with the number of bad outcomes?		
Were patients analyzed in the groups to which they were initially randomized (intention-to-treat analysis)?		
4. Was everyone involved in the study (subjects and investigators) blind to treatment?	Yes	No
5. Were the intervention and control groups similar at the start of the trial?	Yes	No
6. Were the groups treated equally (aside from the experimental intervention)?	Yes	No
7. Are the results clinically as well as statistically significant?	Yes	No
Were the outcomes measured clinically important?		
8. If a negative trial, was a power analysis done?	Yes	No
9. Were other factors present that might have affected the outcome?	Yes	No
10. Are the treatment benefits worth the potential harms and costs?	Yes	No

Note: A "stop" answer to any of the questions should prompt you to seriously question whether the results of the study are valid and whether you should use this intervention.

Source: From "Critical Appraisal of the Literature," by W. F. Miser, 1999, *Journal of the American Board of Family Practice, 12*, pp. 315–333. Reprinted with permission of the American Board of Family Medicine.

In single blind studies only the participants are blind to their group allocations, while in double-blind studies both the participants and investigators are blind. Blinding of outcome assessment can often be done even when blinding of participants and caregivers cannot. Blinding is used to protect against performance and detection bias. It may also contribute to adequate allocation concealment. However, the success of blinding procedures is infrequently checked and it may be overestimated. (Center for Reviews and Dissemination, University of York, UK, 2004)

Farrington (2003) suggests that the SMS developed by Sherman, Farrington, Welsh, and MacKenzie (2002) is the most influential methodological quality scale in criminology. This scale was used to rate prevention programs using 10 criteria on a scale from

0 to 5: (1) adequacy of sampling, (2) adequacy of sample size, (3) pretreatment measures of outcome, (4) adequacy of comparison groups, (5) controls for prior group differences, (6) adequacy of measurement of variables, (7) attrition, (8) postintervention measurement, (9) adequacy of statistical analyses, and (10) testing of alternative explanations. Brounstein and his colleagues (Brounstein, Emshoff, Hill, & Stoil, 1997) used this scale to review 440 evaluations. Only 30% received a score of 3 to 5, on a scale ranging from 0 (no confidence in results), to 5 (high confidence in results; Farrington, 2003, p. 57). It is difficult to carry out experiments in applied settings. However, we should not overlook the fact that hundreds of investigators do manage to carry out controlled studies that provide rigorous tests of claims in real-life settings. See, for example, Cochrane and Campbell databases.

Effect size is one statistic used to describe the effects of an intervention in an experimental study. This indicates the strength of a relationship between, or among, two or more variables. Effect sizes range from 0 to 1. Larger effect sizes suggest stronger relationships. Cohen (1977) suggests that small effect sizes are about .2, medium ones about .5, and large effect sizes about .8 or greater. Effect sizes should be reported. These can be calculated in different ways, all of which are designed to describe the relationship between the effect found in the intervention group and the effect found in a comparison group. One is to divide the mean difference between the experimental and control group in a study by the standard deviation of the control or alternative treatment group. The narrower the confidence interval, the stronger the effect size (see later discussion; the odds ratio refers to the odds of an event happening in one group, expressed as a proportion of the odds of that event happening in another [e.g., control] group). An odds ratio of 1.0 indicates that there is no relationship. (See also discussion of relative and absolute risk reduction and number needed to treat in Chapter 11.)

N of 1 randomized controlled trials involve the detailed description of an individual over a period of time and provide useful information about effectiveness (see Chapter 11). Questions Guyatt and Rennie (2002) suggest for deciding on the feasibility of such a study include: "(1) Is the client eager to collaborate? (2) Does the program have a rapid onset and offset? (3) Is an optimal duration of service feasible? (4) What important targets of service should be measured? and (5) What dictates the end?" (p. 278). Single-case studies provide vital feedback. In quasi-experimental studies allocation of participants to different groups is arranged by the researcher, but there is no genuine randomization and allocation concealment; thus, selection biases are of concern as well as a number of other biases, depending on the design (see Exhibit 12.3). Pre-post studies are one variety; they do not include a comparison group, so we cannot determine causation. Time-series designs are another kind of quasi-experimental study (see Campbell & Stanley, 1963).

Observational Studies

In observational studies, unlike RCTs, assignment of subjects to different groups is not under the control of the investigator. Different groups are self-selected or are "natural experiments." Subjects are not randomly assigned to different services or exposed to different kinds of risks. Such exposure or service occurs by choice or circumstance. Examples include exposure to lead in houses and to family violence. Those who are exposed and those who are not exposed may differ in important ways, thus introducing selection biases.

> An observational study concerns treatments, interventions, or policies and the effects they cause and in this respect it resembles an experiment. A study without a treatment is neither an experiment nor an observational study. Most public opinion polls, most forecasting efforts, most studies of fairness and discrimination, and many other important empirical studies are neither experiments nor observational studies. (Rosenbaum, 2002, pp. 1–2)

Experimental studies may be impossible to conduct because of ethical or logistic reasons. They may not be necessary. They may be inappropriate or inadequate. Important roles for observational methods suggested by Gray (2001a), based on Black (1994), include the following reasons:

1. Some interventions have an impact so large that observational data are sufficient to show it.
2. Infrequent, adverse outcomes would be detected only by RCTs so large that they are rarely conducted. Observational methods such as postmarketing surveillance of medicines are the only alternative.
3. Observational data provide a realistic means of assessing the long-term outcome of interventions beyond the time scale of many trials. An example is long-term effects of neuroleptic medication.
4. Clinicians often will be opposed to an RCT; observational approaches can be used to show clinical uncertainty and pave the way for a trial.
5. Some important aspects of care cannot be subjected to a randomized trial for practical and ethical reasons. (Adapted from Black, 1994)

Observational studies include (1) cohort studies, (2) case-control studies, (3) pre-post studies, and (4) case series. This order reflects the level of evidence provided regarding effectiveness questions, although there are exceptions (see discussion, for example, of case-control studies). Observational studies may be descriptive or analytical. Analytical studies include cohort and case-control studies. Observational studies differ in their *ecological validity*; that is, the extent to which the study is carried out in contexts that are similar or identical to the everyday life experiences of those involved. A variety of strategies are used to detect hidden biases in observational studies, such as inclusion of a number of control groups to try to identify hidden covariates (characteristics that influence the results other than the one focused on). And as Rosenbaum (2002) suggests, "even when it is not possible to remove bias through adjustment or detect bias through careful design, it is nonetheless possible to give quantitative expression to the magnitude of uncertainties about bias, a technique called *sensitivity analysis*" (p. 11).

Cohort Studies

In cohort studies, a group of individuals who have experienced a certain situation (for example, witnessed domestic violence) is compared with a group of people who have not been so exposed. Both groups are followed up to determine the association between exposure and an outcome (such as subsequent abuse of one's own children). Cohort studies are prospective and analytical. Because of lack of random assignment they are prone to a number of biases, such as lack of control over risk assignment and uneven loss to follow-up. Cohort studies are often used to describe different kinds of risk. Questions to ask include the following (Gray, 2001a; Center for Reviews and Dissemination, University of York, UK, 2004).

- Is there sufficient description of the groups (how they were recruited) and the distribution of prognostic factors?
- Are the groups assembled at a similar point in relation to (for example) their disorder progression? (Were decisions made that could have included or excluded more severe cases?)
- Is the intervention/treatment reliably ascertained?
- Were the groups comparable on all important confounding factors?
- Was there adequate adjustment for the effects of these confounding variables?
- Were measures used valid?
- Was a dose-response relationship between intervention and outcome demonstrated?
- Was outcome assessment blind to exposure status?
- Was the presence of co-occurring disorders considered?
- Was follow-up long enough for the outcomes to occur?
- What proportion of the cohort was followed up?
- Were dropout rates and reasons for dropout similar across intervention and unexposed groups?

Gray (2001a) notes that "the main abuse of a cohort study is to assess the effectiveness of a particular intervention when a more appropriate method would be an RCT" (p. 150).

Case-Control (Case-Referent) Studies

In a retrospective case-control study we start with people who have a particular characteristic (a certain illness) and look back in time in relation to certain outcomes. Samples may be small in such studies yet suggest strong relationships. Consider the case-referent study reporting a relationship between the drug diethylstilbestrol (DES) given to pregnant women and vaginal cancer. Herbst, Ulfelder, and Poskanzer (1971) included eight women who had vaginal cancer and 32 who did not in relation to use of DES during pregnancies. Seven had taken DES in the group with vaginal cancer and none had taken it in the referent group. This study illustrates the value of case-referent studies regarding rare conditions or for risk factors that have long development phases. Suggested criteria for reviewing case-control studies are:

- Is the case definition explicit?
- Has the illness state of clients been reliably assessed and validated?
- Were the controls randomly selected from the population of the cases?
- How comparable are the cases and controls with respect to potential confounding factors?
- Were interventions and other exposures assessed in the same way for cases and controls?
- How was the response rate defined?
- Were the nonresponse rates and reasons for nonresponse the same in both groups?
- Is it possible that overmatching has occurred, in that cases and controls were matched on factors related to exposure?
- Was an appropriate statistical analysis used (matched or unmatched)?" (Center for Reviews and Dissemination, University of York, 2004, Phase 5, p. 11)

Cross-Sectional Studies

In a cross-sectional study, a snapshot is taken of people at a particular time. Such studies may be used to describe the frequency or rate of a behavior or to try to identify the relationship between one or more factors and a problem, such as child abuse. Unfortunately, such research does not show which came first.

Pre-Post Studies (Before and After)

In pre-post studies, responses are compared before and after some intervention. Such designs do not provide information about the causal relationship between an intervention and an outcome unless, perhaps, the change is very large and is replicated.

Case-Series Studies

Another kind of clinical study consists of describing characteristics of a series of case examples. Because of the lack of comparison, we cannot make assumptions about causes. Questions for reviewing case-series studies include the following:

- Is the study based on a representative sample selected from a relevant population?
- Are the criteria for inclusion explicit?
- Did all individuals enter the study at a similar point in their disorder progression?
- Was follow-up long enough for important events to occur?
- Were outcomes assessed using objective criteria or was blinding used?
- If comparisons of subseries are being made, was there sufficient description of the series and the distribution of prognostic factors? (Center for Reviews and Dissemination, University of York, 2004, Phase 5, p. 11)

A case report is essentially an anecdotal report—a description of a single case. Such reports differ greatly in their rigor.

Questions About Harm

Just as we can ask about number needed to treat (NNT), we can ask about number needed to harm (NNH). That is, how many people would have to receive a service for one to be harmed? Many studies do not offer any information about possible harms of interventions, including assessment and diagnostic measures. Petrosino, Turpin-Petrosino, and Finckenauer (2000) presented a meta-analysis of seven randomized experiments regarding recidivism data concerning Scared Straight programs. All seven indicated that these programs were harmful; that is, the experimental group had higher recidivism rates. More recent reviews, including more studies, have arrived at the same conclusion (see Petrosino et al., 2003).

SYSTEMATIC REVIEWS AND META-ANALYSES

There are vast differences between haphazard reviews (incomplete and uncritical—garbage in, garbage out) and rigorous, exhaustive reviews (Littell, Corcoran, & Pillai, 2008; Littell, 2008). In systematic reviews, there is a search for all evidence related to questions and a critical assessment of what is found. For example, Cochrane review groups search for research reports, published and unpublished, related to a specific question. The search process is carefully described, so that readers are apprised of how this was conducted. (See also Campbell Collaboration reviews.) Authors describe how they searched, where they searched, and what criteria they used to appraise the quality of studies. Systematic reviews involve the following basic components: (1) state the objectives of the research, (2) define eligibility criteria for studies to be included, (3) identify all potentially eligible studies, (4) apply eligibility criteria, (5) assemble the most complete data set feasible, (6) analyze this data set using statistical synthesis and sensitivity analysis if appropriate and possible, and (7) prepare a structured report of the research (Chalmers, 2003, p. 25). Rigorous reviews "are designed to minimize the likelihood that the effects of interventions will be confused with the effects of biases and chance" (Chalmers, 2003, p. 22).

Systematic reviews are of value in relation to all questions. A meta-analysis is a systematic review that includes quantification of effect sizes in the summarization of results from many studies. Meta-analyses differ greatly in their quality. Components of quality ones are shown in Exhibit 12.6. Differences in the transparency and rigor of research reviews are illustrated by reviews of multisystemic therapy (MST). Most sources, describe this as an effective treatment. Based on a systematic review, Littell, Popa, and Forsythe (2005) argue that this program is no more effective than other programs. Critical appraisal of a study takes a great deal of time. That is probably why it is often not done. The abstract and discussion sections of reports become the least important, and the method and results sections become of key concern (Rosenthal, 2001).

The logo of the Cochrane Collaboration illustrates a program that is effective (see Cochrane website). This visual description allows you to quickly see how many studies fall to the left or to the right of the midline. It is called a "forest plot." The odds ratios and 95% confidence intervals for effects of home visiting on child injury (Roberts, Kramer, & Suissa, 1996) are illustrated in Exhibit 12.7. The solid line running down the center indicates the point where there is no difference between treatment and control groups (an odds ratio of 1). The odds ratio refers to the odds of an event in an exposed group compared to the odds of the same event in a group not exposed. Odds refers to the ratio of probability of occurrence to nonoccurrence of the event. Each horizontal line represents one trial, and the length of each line represents

Exhibit 12.6 Steps in Determining the Validity of a Meta-Analysis

1. Was the literature search done well?		
a. Was it comprehensive?	Yes	No
b. Were the search methods systematic and clearly described?	Yes	No
c. Were the key words used in the search described?	Yes	No
d. Was the issue of publication bias addressed?	Yes	No
2. Was the method for selecting articles clear, systematic, and appropriate?	Yes	No
a. Were there clear, preestablished inclusion and exclusion criteria for evaluation?	Yes	No
b. Was selection systematic?	Yes	No
i. Was the population defined?	Yes	No
ii. Was the exposure/intervention clearly described?	Yes	No
iii. Were all outcomes described and were they compatible?	Yes	No
c. Was selection done blindly and in random order?	Yes	No
d. Was the selection process reliable?	Yes	No
i. Were at least two independent selectors used?	Yes	No
ii. Was the extent of selection disagreement evaluated?	Yes	No
3. Was the quality of primary studies evaluated?	Yes	No
a. Did all studies, published or not, have the same standard applied?	Yes	No
b. Were at least two independent evaluators used and was the interrater agreement assessed and adequate?	Yes	No
c. Were the evaluators blinded to authors, institutions, and results of the primary studies?	Yes	No
4. Were results from the studies combined appropriately?	Yes	No
a. Were the studies similar enough to combine results?	Yes	No
i. Were the study designs, populations, exposures, outcomes, and direction of effect similar in the combined studies?	Yes	No
b. Was a test for heterogeneity done and was its p value nonsignificant?	Yes	No
5. Was a statistical combination (meta-analysis) done properly?	Yes	No
a. Were the methods of the studies similar?	Yes	No
b. Was the possibility of chance differences statistically addressed?	Yes	No
i. Was a test for homogeneity done?	Yes	No
c. Were appropriate statistical analyses performed?	Yes	No
d. Were sensitivity analyses used?	Yes	No
6. Are the results important?	Yes	No
a. Was the effect strong?	Yes	No
i. Was the odds ratio large?	Yes	No
ii. Were the results reported in a clinically meaningful manner, such as the absolute difference or the number needed to treat?	Yes	No
b. Are the results likely to be reproducible and generalizable?	Yes	No
c. Were all clinically important consequences considered?	Yes	No
d. Are the benefits worth the harm and costs?	Yes	No

Source: From "Applying a Meta-Analysis to Daily Clinical Practice," by W. F. Miser, 2000, in *Evidence-Based Clinical Practice: Concepts and Approaches* (p. 60), edited by J. P. Geyman, R. A. Deyo, and S. D. Ramsey, Boston: Butterworth-Heinemann. Reprinted with permission.

the confidence interval (CI). This shows the precision of the estimate. The shorter this is, the less the variability of results in a study. The longer it is, the greater the variability. If a confidence interval crosses the vertical line, then the range of estimated effects of the treatment include the possibility both of getting better and of getting worse. Generally, if the whole CI is on the left of the line, the treatment improves the situation. The confidence interval "quantifies the uncertainty in measurement. It is usually reported as a 95% CI, which is the range of values within which we can be 95% sure that the true value for the whole population lies" (Sackett et al., 2000, p. 245). The pooled estimate shown at the bottom is 0.74. Criticisms of meta-analysis suggested by Rosenthal (2001) include the following points:

Exhibit 12.7 Odds Ratios and 95% Confidence Intervals for Effects of Home Visiting on Child Injury

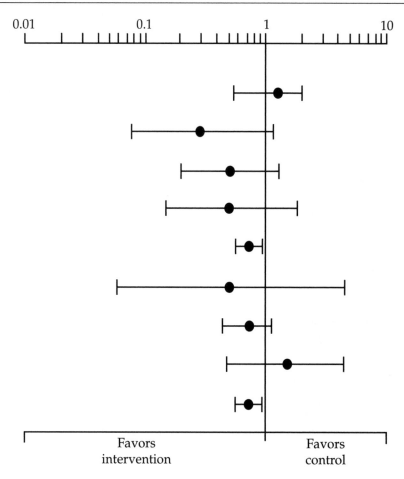

Source: From "Does More Visiting Prevent Child Head Injury? A Systematic Review of Randomized Controlled Trials," by I. Roberts, M. S. Kramer, and S. Suissa, 1966, *British Medical Journal, 312,* pp. 29–33.

1. Retrievability bias.
2. Overemphasis on a single value rather than a description of central tendency and variability in findings.
3. Glossing over important details.
4. Overlooking heterogeneity of studies.
5. Overlooking heterogeneity of outcomes and the potential contributions of moderating variables (such as psychotherapy).
6. Inclusion of poorly designed studies that contain many sources of bias.
7. Inclusion of multiple dependent variables (outcomes) with different effect sizes, perhaps due to variables such as different laboratories. (Workshop on meta-analysis, March 2000, University of California–Berkeley; see also Lipsey, 2003; Littell, Corcoran, & Pillai, 2008)

QUESTIONS ABOUT PREVALENCE AND INCIDENCE (FREQUENCY AND RATE)

Making informed decisions may require accurate information regarding the incidence and prevalence of a concern. *Prevalence* refers to the number of people in a population who currently have a condition or attribute. *Incidence* refers to the number of people in a population who develop an attribute within a year. Prevalence and incidence are of interest in trying to understand the frequency of a certain condition. Epidemiology is the "study of the distribution and determinants of health-related states or events in specified populations, and the application of this study to control of health problems" (Last, 1988, p. 42). Descriptive epidemiology is the study of the occurrence of illness or other health-related characteristic (e.g., person, place, or time). Analytic studies examine associations—for example, between certain risks and outcomes. Descriptive studies do not test hypotheses. Analytic studies do test hypotheses.

Let us say that a parent seeks help because she is worried about her child being abducted by a stranger. She has read a report in the newspaper saying that stranger abduction is common and parents should be careful. Because of this she rarely allows her children to go out unaccompanied. She and her husband disagree about this—he believes that his wife is overly concerned and because of this is depriving their child of freedom and opportunities to learn and grow. As with other decisions, we can translate information needs into well-formed questions that allow us to search electronically, efficiently, and effectively for related literature. The following questions may guide a search:

- In suburban neighborhoods, what is the incidence and prevalence of stranger abduction of young children?
- Do the media exaggerate the prevalence of stranger abduction?

Other kinds of questions that are relevant here include: "For young children, are there effective, preventative steps that can be taken to decrease stranger abduction?" and "Under what circumstances does stranger abduction occur?" Ecological studies are descriptive in nature and use data collected for a variety of purposes, including administrative needs. An example is comparison of the different rates of child abuse in different communities that have different levels of social support. Both cohort studies and cross-sectional studies may be used to gather information about frequency or rate.

QUESTIONS ABOUT CAUSES

A well-formed question might be: "In elementary school children who are a classroom management problem, what are common causes?" We could use a variety of methods to try to identify related factors. We could create a survey and ask teachers what they think. We could hold focus groups. We could compare this with results of a descriptive and functional analysis of classroom contingencies (e.g., Alberto & Troutman, 2013; Watson & Steege, 2003). The latter form of investigation suggests that being under- or overchallenged may contribute to disruptive behavior in a classroom (problems in curriculum design), and/or classroom contingencies may maintain such behavior (being reinforced for inappropriate behavior and ignoring desired behaviors). Would a survey or use of focus groups reveal the same data? (See Exhibit 12.8 for questions to raise concerning articles about causation.)

Surveys

Surveys are used for many purposes, including describing the prevalence of certain conditions, such as depression, to gather people's views about quality of care and services, and to try to identify causes using complex statistical tools, such as regression analysis. The purpose of correlational research is to investigate the relationship between two or more variables using statistical analysis. Pearson product-moment correlation coefficients are typically used as the statistic to represent the degree of association. This ranges from -1 to $+1$, both indicating a perfect correlation. For example, we may ask: "What is the relationship between college grade-point average (GPA), scores on the Graduate Record Examination (GRE), and performance in graduate school?" Do

Exhibit 12.8 Validity Screen for an Article About Causation

1.	Was a clearly defined comparison group or those at risk for the outcome of interest included?	Yes (go on)	No (stop)
2.	Were the outcomes and exposures measured in the same way in the groups compared?	Yes (go on)	No (stop)
3.	Were the observers blinded to the exposure of outcome and to the outcome?	Yes (go on)	No (stop)
4.	Was follow-up sufficiently long and complete?	Yes (go on)	No (stop)
5.	Is the temporal relationship correct? (Does the exposure to the agent precede the outcome?)	Yes (go on)	No (stop)
6.	Is there a dose-response gradient? (As the quantity or the duration of exposure increases, does the risk of outcome increase?)	Yes (go on)	No (stop)
7.	How strong is the association between exposure and outcome? (Is the relative risk or odds ratio large?)	Yes (go on)	No (stop)

Note: A "stop" answer to any of the questions should prompt you to question whether the results of the study are valid and whether the item in question is really a causative factor.

Source: From "Critical Appraisal of the Literature," by W. F. Miser, 1999, *Journal of the American Board of Family Practice, 12,* pp. 315–333. Reprinted with permission of the American Board of Family Medicine.

GPA and GRE scores predict performance in graduate school? Correlational designs differ in their ecological validity (the extent to which findings can be generalized to other groups). We cannot draw causal assumptions based on correlational data; associations do not necessarily reflect causal relationships (see Chapter 14). There may be some other variable that is responsible for the association. It could even be that there is reverse association. Gray (2001a) suggests the following questions in critically appraising survey data:

- How was the population to be surveyed chosen? Was it the whole population or a sample?
- If a sample, how was the sample chosen? Was it a random sample or was it stratified, to ensure that all sectors of the population were represented?
- Was a validated questionnaire used? Did the authors of the survey mention the possibility of different results being obtained by different interviewers, if interviewers were used?
- What procedures were used to verify the data?
- Were the conclusions drawn from the survey all based on the data, or did those carrying out the survey infer conclusions? Inference is acceptable, but it must be clearly distinguished from results derived solely from the data. (Gray, 2001a, p. 153)

QUESTIONS REGARDING EXPERIENCES

Examples of questions that arise here include:

- For social workers in child welfare agencies, what are current sources of strain and perceived causes?
- In elderly clients entering a nursing home, what are their feelings and thoughts?

Different Kinds of Qualitative Research

Qualitative research may be of many different kinds, including case studies, narrative analyses, focus groups and participant observation. There is a concern to describe people's experiences as they see them. Examples of different kinds of qualitative research include participant observation, unstructured interviews, and hermeneutic reading of texts. For example, Bourgois and his fellow investigators (Bourgois, Lettiere, & Quesada, 2003) spent time with homeless people in San Francisco over a period of years. Case studies consist of detailed descriptions of individuals, groups, organizations, or neighborhoods. As Becker (1996) suggests, "we always describe how they [other people] interpret the events they participate in, so the only question is not whether we should, but how accurately we do it." He suggests that "it is inevitably epistemologically dangerous to guess at what could be observed directly. The danger is that we will guess wrong, that what looks reasonable to us will not be what looked reasonable to them" (p. 58). As Becker notes, "The variety of things called ethnographic aren't all alike, and in fact may be at odds with each other over epistemological details" (p. 57).

Data gathered via participant-observation may be more valid than information collected on self-report surveys that people are paid to complete. Consider the question "What kinds of risks (if any) do street addicts take?" In their article describing HIV risk among homeless heroin addicts in San Francisco, Bourgois, Lettiere, and Quesada (2003) found that "Virtually all our network members have told us that they distort their risky behavior on questionnaires" (p. 270). Campbell (1996) agrees with Becker about overstretching quantitative research: "Quantitative data often represents low-cost, mass-produced research and is often wrong. The others' meanings as inferred from questionnaire averages are overly determined by the ethnocentric subjectivity of the researcher" (p. 161). As Campbell (1996) notes, "questionnaires, fixed interviews, and experimental designs limit the dimensions of inquiry in advance. Often this precludes learning information that would have discredited the validity of the quantitative results and the hypotheses that guided the research" (p. 162). Campbell considers the "most ubiquitous source of error in efforts to know the other" to be "to interpret as a cultural difference what is in reality a failure of communication. . . . I personally am convinced that many of the cultural differences reported by psychologists and others using questionnaires or tests come from failures of communication misreported as differences" (p. 165). A checklist for critically appraising a qualitative research report follows (see other sources for additional descriptions of qualitative research methods):

1. Did the paper describe an important clinical problem addressed via a clearly formulated question?
2. Was a qualitative approach appropriate?
3. How were (a) the setting and (b) the subjects selected?
4. What was the researcher's perspective, and has this been taken into account?
5. What methods did the researcher use for collecting data and are these described in enough detail?
6. What methods did the researcher use to analyze the data and what quality-control measures were implemented?
7. Are the results credible and, if so, are they clinically important?
8. What conclusions were drawn, and are they justified by the results?
9. Are the findings of the study transferable to other clinical settings? (Greenhalgh, 2010, pp. 168–173)

QUESTIONS ABOUT DIAGNOSIS AND SCREENING

The professional literature describes scores of tests. The key question here is "Can a test accurately detect a certain condition or characteristics, such as depression in an elderly client, and at what cost?" Tests may provide helpful guidelines or be misleading—appear to inform but do the opposite, perhaps harm rather than help clients. Consider the example of the reflex dilation test. In Britain, it was suggested that a simple medical test could be used to demonstrate that buggery or other forms of anal penetration had occurred. Here is the description:

> Reflex dilation well described in forensic texts . . . usually occurs within about 30 seconds of separating the buttocks. Recent controversy has helped our understanding of what is now seen as an important sign of traumatic penetration of the anus as occurs in abuse, but also following medical and surgical manipulation. . . . The diameter of the symmetrical relaxation of the anal sphincter is variable and should be estimated. This is a dramatic sign which once seen is easily recognized. . . . The sign is not always easily reproducible on second and third examinations and there appear to be factors, at present, which may modify the eliciting of this physical sign. The sign in most cases gradually disappears when abuse stops. (Hanks, Hobbs, & Wynne, 1988, p. 153)

News of this test spread quickly, and because of this test, many children were removed from their homes on the grounds that they were being sexually abused—when this was not true. (Questions that should have been asked are described in the next section.) "Diagnostic tests are done when patients are symptomatic, whereas screening tests are done on nonsymptomatic clients" (Elmore & Boyko, 2000, p. 83). (See also Knottnerus, 2002.) Tests may be used to predict future behavior. They should be used to revise subjective estimates concerning a client—that is, to change a decision about how a client should be treated. Clinicians tend to overestimate the predictive accuracy of test results. One cause of this error is ignoring base-rate data (see Chapter 15). The predictive accuracy of a test depends on the initial risk of a condition in the person receiving the test. The probability that a client with a positive (or negative) test result for dementia actually has dementia depends on the prevalence of dementia in the population from which the client was selected—that is, on the pretest probability that a client has dementia. Because there is little appreciation of this point, predictive accuracy often is overestimated.

Critically Appraising Reports of Diagnostic Accuracy

Here too, a variety of biases as well as incomplete reporting of how a test was developed and tested can lead to problems in interpreting accuracy. Classification is involved in testing—placing people into categories. Surprisingly few reference standards are clear for making unequivocal classifications. Claims of accuracy are often inflated. The best type of evidence in relation to how test results relate to benefits of treatment is a randomized controlled trial. If these are not available, cohort studies may provide information. Bossuyt and his colleagues (2003) describe standards for reporting diagnostic accuracy. Both a checklist and flowchart are included to help readers to evaluate the potential for bias in a study and to judge the applicability of findings. Questions suggested by Greenhalgh (2010) for critically appraising related articles include the following:

1. Is this test potentially relevant to my practice?
2. Has the test been compared with a true gold standard?
3. Did this validation study include an appropriate spectrum of clients?
4. Has workup bias been avoided?
5. Has expectation bias been avoided?
6. Was the test shown to be reproducible both within and between observers?
7. What are the features of the test as derived from this validation study?
8. Were confidence intervals given for sensitivity, specificity, and other features of the test?

9. Has a sensible "normal range" been derived from those results?
10. Has this test been placed in the context of other potential tests in the diagnostic sequence for the condition (pp. 104–108)?

These questions were not raised in reviewing the accuracy of the reflex dilation test. As a result, many people were harmed. The false positive rate was not reported (the percentage of persons inaccurately identified as having a characteristic). Nor was the false negative rate reported (the percentage of persons inaccurately identified as not having a characteristic; see Exhibit 12.9).

Key concepts in reviewing tests include the following. (See also discussion of absolute and relative risk reduction and number needed to treat in Chapter 11.)

- *Sensitivity:* Among those known to have a problem, the proportion whom a test or measure said had the problem.
- *Specificity:* Among those known not to have a problem, the proportion whom the test or measure has said did not have the problem.
- *Pretest probability (prevalence):* The probability that an individual has the disorder before the test is carried out.
- *Post-test probability:* The probability that an individual with a specific test result has the target conditions (posttest odds/[1 + post-test odds]).
- *Pretest odds:* The odds that an individual has the disorder before the test is carried out (pretest probability/[1 – pretest probability])
- *Post-test odds:* The odds that a patient has the disorder after being tested (pretest odds × LR [likelihood ratio]).
- *Positive predictive value (PPV):* The proportion of individuals with positive test results who have the target condition. This equals the posttest probability, given a positive test result.
- *Negative predictive value (NPV):* The proportion of individuals with negative test results who do not have the target condition. This equals 1 minus the posttest probability, given a negative test result.
- *Likelihood ratio:* Measure of a test result's ability to modify pretest probabilities. Likelihood ratios indicate how many times more likely a test result is in a client with a disorder compared with a person free of the disorder. A likelihood ratio of 1 indicates that a test is totally uninformative. "A likelihood ratio of greater than 1 indicates that the test is associated with the presence of the disease whereas a likelihood ratio less than 1 indicates that the test result is associated with the absence of disease. The further likelihood ratios are from 1 the stronger the evidence for the presence or absence of disease. Likelihood ratios above 10 and below 0.1 are considered to provide strong evidence to

Exhibit 12.9 Definitions and Calculations for a Perfect (Gold Standard) Diagnostic Test: Definitions of Sensitivity, Specificity, Predictive Values, and Posttest Disorder

Test	Disorder Present	Disorder Absent	Total
Test Positive	A	B	A + B
Test Negative	C	D	C + D
Total	A + C	B + D	N = (A + B + C + D)

Definitions

Sensitivity: A/(A + C)

Specificity: D/(D + B)

False negative rate: C/(C + A)

False positive rate: B/(B + D)

Positive predictive value: A/(A + B)

Negative predictive value: D/(C + D)

Pretest disease probability: (A + C)/(A + B + C + D)

Posttest disease probability, positive results: A/(A + C)

Posttest disease probability, negative result: C/(C + D)

	Disorder Present	Disorder Absent	Total
Test Positive	100	0	100
Test Negative	0	100	100
Total	100	100	200

Calculations:
Sensitivity: 100/(100 + 0) = 100%
Specificity: 100/(100 + 0) = 100%
Positive predictive value: 100%
Posttest disease probability, negative test: 0%

Source: From "Assessing Accuracy of Diagnostic and Screening Tests," by J. G. Elmore and E. J. Boyko, 2000, in *Evidence-Based Clinical Practice: Concepts and Approaches* (p. 85), edited by J. P. Geyman, R. A. Deyo, and S. D. Ramsey, Boston, MA: Butterworth-Heinemann. Reprinted with permission.

rule in or rule out diagnosis respectively in most circumstances" (Deeks & Altman, 2004, p. 168).

- *Likelihood ratio of a positive test result (LR+):* The ratio of the true positive rate to the false positive rate: sensitivity/(1 − specificity).
- *Likelihood of a negative test result (LR−):* The ratio of the false negative rate to the true negative rate: (1 − sensitivity)/specificity. (adapted from Pewsner et al., 2004)

These concepts can be illustrated by a four-cell contingency table (see Exhibit 12.9). "In clinical practice it is essential to know how a particular test result predicts the risk of abnormality. Sensitivities and specificities do not do this: they describe how abnormality (or normality) predicts particular test results. Predictive values do give probabilities of abnormality for particular test results, but depend on the prevalence of abnormality in the study sample. . . ." (Deeks & Altman, 2004, p. 169). Only if a test increases accuracy of understanding should it be used. Will test results change what would be done? Often in social work, psychology, and psychiatry, there is no gold standard against which to compare a test. An example of a gold standard is reviewing an X-ray to detect pneumonia when someone has a cough. We should consider pretest estimates. (See Chapter 15.)

Screening

Screening is a key public health strategy that has been broadened to concerns such as depression and anxiety. The President's New Freedom Commission on Mental Health (2005) recommends universal screening (see Lenzer, 2004). Requirements for an ideal screening program include the following:

- The benefit of testing outweighs the harm.
- The [disorder] is serious, with a high burden of suffering.
- The natural history of the [disorder] is understood.
- The [disorder] occurs frequently.
- Effective treatment exists, and early treatment is more effective than late treatment.
- The test is easy to administer.
- The test is inexpensive.
- The test is safe.
- The test is acceptable to participants.
- The sensitivity, specificity, and other operating characteristics of the test are acceptable. (Elmore & Boyko, 2000, p. 89; based on Jekel, Elmore, & Katz 1996; see also Gray, 2001a)

QUESTIONS ABOUT PROGNOSIS, RISK, AND PROTECTIVE FACTORS (PREDICTION)

Both prognosis and risk project into the future; related tests attempt to predict events in the future. For example, depending on a diagnosis of depression, one has a certain prognosis, which in turn is related to certain protective and risk factors. Risk assessment is of interest in a number of areas, including suicide and violent acts such as domestic and child abuse. Thousands of children are on "at risk" registers on the assumption that they are at a continuing risk of abuse. Thus, both prognosis and prediction have a forward orientation—they look into the future, and as with all such looks, there will be errors. We can and do make errors in identifying risks and protective factors in diagnosis and in prognosis. (See Chapter 15.) Errors in earlier stages (e.g., assessment) may result in errors at later stages (selection of service plans). Examples of questions here are:

- In elderly, frail clients living alone, what is the risk of hip fracture?
- In young children abused by their parents, what is the risk of future abuse?
- In young children rejected by their peers, what is the risk of developing problems in adolescence?
- In young adults who have unprotected sexual intercourse with multiple partners, what is the risk of developing AIDS?

Prognostic studies include clinical studies of variables that predict future events, as well as epidemiological studies of risk factors. In ecological (aggregate) studies, secondary data is often used to identify associations in a population group between risk factors and outcomes of interest, such as depression. Generalization from aggregate data to individuals is problematic because of the likelihood of the ecological fallacy (assuming what is true for a group is true for an individual). Actuarial methods (using the results of empirical investigations of the relationships between certain characteristics and an outcome) are superior to intuitive methods for making accurate predictions in a number of areas (e.g., see Chapter 15). Both cohort and case control studies have been used to try to identify and quantify risk and protective factors. Problems include naturally occurring fluctuations. Accurately communicating risks to clients is a challenge (e.g., Paling, 2006).

Critically Appraising Related Research

Guyatt and Rennie (2002) suggest the following questions concerning articles on prognosis:
    Are the results valid?
- Was the sample of clients representative?
- Were the [clients] sufficiently homogeneous with respect to prognostic risk?
- Was follow-up sufficiently complete?
- Were objective and unbiased outcome criteria used?

    What are the results?
- How likely are the outcomes over time?
- How precise are the estimates of likelihood?

How can I apply the results to [client] care?

- Were the study [clients] and their management similar to those in my practice?
- Was the follow-up sufficiently long?
- Can I use the results [in my setting]? (p. 144)

Both absolute and relative risk should be given. The latter often sounds impressive in relation to risk reduction compared to absolute risk reduction (see Chapter 15).

QUESTIONS ABOUT PRACTICE GUIDELINES

Many sources purport to describe practice guidelines. Indeed, this term has become a buzzword, together with terms such as *best practice, empirically validated methods,* and *evidence-based practice.* There is a spirited controversy regarding the usefulness of practice guidelines—for example, do they allow for variations in client characteristics? (See Chapter 2.) Clients often have multiple concerns, rendering use of guidelines more complex. The quality of the relationship yields different outcomes even when using the same guidelines. Inflated claims are common regarding the effectiveness of guidelines (Grilli, Magrini, Penna, Mura, & Liberati, 2000). Thus, it is important to learn how to evaluate their quality. Bogus claims may occur because those who make them (1) are uninformed about the limitations of the research design in critically testing a question, (2) are aware of this, but do not care, (3) care but need a publication, and/or (4) are on the payroll of a corporation with a profit motive. Conflicts of interest between creators of guidelines and Big Pharma are rife (e.g., Cosgrove et al., 2009). Questions concerning the development of a guideline include the following:

- Were all important decisions, options, and outcomes clearly described? For example, has a well-tested alternative, such as the use of contingency management for altering behavior of children labeled ADHD, been ignored?
- Is there a rigorous effort to identify and locate all related research? Were studies located carefully appraised using rigorous criteria?
- Are the benefits and risks clearly described, as well as costs for each outcome of interest, including the views of different stakeholders (e.g., see Lawrie, McIntosh, & Rao, 2000)?
- Does the guideline apply to your clients?

Greenhalgh (2010) recommends inquiring whether the preparation and publication of the guidelines involve a significant conflict of interest.

The American Psychological Association Task Force (1995) on psychological intervention recommended that if two randomized controlled trials show the effectiveness of an intervention, then this method has been "established" as valid. Notice the justificationary nature of such a claim (certainty is suggested by the term *established*). Objections to task force recommendations were raised by both practitioners and researchers. Critics suggested that "transportability" issues were downplayed (problems of using guidelines tested in controlled settings in the "real world"). A program may not achieve the same results when used in real-life settings. Lawrie, McIntosh, and Rao (2000) suggest the following questions in reviewing the potential usefulness of a clinical guideline. (1) Is the guideline valid? (2) Is it important? (e.g., is there currently a large variation in practice? Does the guideline contain new evidence or old research findings that are not acted on? Would use of a guideline have major effects on outcomes?) and (3) Can I use it in caring for my clients? As Gray (2001a) emphasizes, staff and clients are the experts regarding application barriers. They are in a position to identify, and indeed to reflect in their behaviors, application barriers, such as beliefs about what methods are effective. (See discussion of the common elements approach in psychotherapy as an alternative to use of practice guidelines; Chorpita et al., 2007.)

CONTROVERSIAL ISSUES

There are differences of opinion, even within a particular research tradition, regarding questions about evidence, best methods, and how to interpret results (e.g., see Becker, 1996). The research design used to explore a question reflects the researchers' views about knowledge and how it can be gained, and their views concerning honest brokering of knowledge and ignorance. Inflated claims are common. Keep in mind that just because a program has been found to be effective or ineffective in critical tests does not warrant claims of certainty. Also, dimensions other than evidentiary status, such as importance of outcomes to clients and acceptability of methods, should be considered.

OBSTACLES

Obstacles to acquiring skills in critically appraising research and using these to enhance the quality of services include both personal and environmental ones. Research courses are given separately from practice courses in most professional education programs. This discourages integration of practice and research. This is not the case with problem-based learning, now used in many professional schools (see Chapter 8). Agencies may discourage evidence-informed practice and not provide necessary training and tools, including access to needed databases. Exploration of how to address application problems is an active area of research with many exciting developments, such as involving clients as informed participants in making decisions (see Coulter, 2002; Coulter, Parsons, & Askham, 2008; Edwards & Elwyn, 2001; Gravel, Légaré, & Graham, 2006).

SUMMARY

Different questions require different kinds of research methods to critically test assumptions. Some questions are exploratory and descriptive. Their intent is to describe the relationships among different variables. A question may be: "What is the relationship between certain characteristics of a helper (e.g., warmth) and service outcome?" Another question may be: "What are characteristics of single parents on welfare who succeed in getting a job and getting off welfare, compared to people who do not?" Some kinds of research (experimental studies) involve testing a hypothesis. Their aim is to identify causal relationships among variables in a rigorous manner.

Research methods differ in the degree to which sources of bias are present. A key concern is the match between a question and the likelihood that the method used to test it can do so. Currently, literature in the helping professions abounds with poor matches. Evidence-informed practice encourages attention to the limitations of research designs. One of the key reasons for the origin of EBP was a concern about flaws in published research, such as inflated claims of knowledge (see Chapter 10). Bogus claims are problematic; they may result in selection of ineffective or harmful methods and neglect of effective methods. A variety of tools and entire enterprises, such as the Cochrane and Campbell collaborations, have been developed to help practitioners draw on research related to life-affecting decisions. These include user-friendly checklists for critically appraising the quality of different kinds of research.

PART IV

Applying Critical Thinking Skills to Clinical Decisions

13

Making Decisions About Data Collection

The purpose of assessment is to make sound decisions—for example, whether to use a certain remedy. Interrelated goals include: (1) clarifying concerns; (2) detecting characteristics that influence problems; and (3) selecting outcomes that, if achieved, would minimize concerns (Nay, 1979) (see also Hunsley & Nash, 2008). Decisions are made about what data to collect, how to gather it, when to stop, and how to combine data. These decisions influence the accuracy of accounts offered and thus options for achieving outcomes clients value. Thus, accuracy of measures is vital. This chapter offers an overview of sources of bias in collecting data. No matter how good our reasoning skills are, if we base our decisions on inaccurate data we will be less likely to help clients. Common errors are shown in Exhibit 13.1. Preferred-practice theories guide what we look for and what we notice as well as how we process and organize data. Theories differ along a number of dimensions, including the attention devoted to the past and present; the unit of concern (individual, family, or community); the attention devoted to environmental and personal characteristics; and the degree of optimism concerning how much change is possible. Consider depression. Major grand narratives include biomedical views, social interactional perspectives, and psychological views. A practice theory emphasizing dispositional characteristics encourages collection of data about psychological factors, such as repressed anger based on past experiences of loss. A theory that emphasizes external causes encourages collection of data about environmental influences, such as a decrease in pleasant events and an increase in negative ones. Theories differ in their evidentiary status—the extent to which they have been critically tested regarding their value in helping.

Decisions are often made on the basis of quite limited data. Karen Budd and her colleagues (Budd, Poindexter, Feliz, & Naik-Polan, 2001) critically reviewed the content and legal relevance of clinical evaluations of parents conducted in child abuse and neglect ($n = 190$) mental health evaluation reports.

Exhibit 13.1 Common Errors in Gathering Assessment Data: Being Forewarned Is Being Prepared

- Gathering irrelevant data (e.g., redundant data).
- Gathering only data that support preconceived views (confirmation biases).
- Overlooking the role of environmental factors.
- Overlooking cultural differences that influence the validity of data.
- Forgoing opportunities to observe behavior in real life or role-plays when needed to clarify clients' concerns and circumstances.
- Not involving significant others in collecting data.
- Vagueness (data do not clarify concerns and circumstances).
- Not describing setting events, antecedents, and consequences related to behaviors of interest, including alternative positive behaviors.
- Relying on unsupported opinions of other professionals.
- Relying on unsupported data in case records.
- Relying on biased, unrepresentative samples (sampling too narrowly, for example, observing behavior on only one occasion that does not provide information about what usually occurs).
- Using invalid measures (they do not measure what they are supposed to measure).

Evaluations of parents typically were completed in a single session, rarely included a home visit, used few if any sources of information other than the parent, often cited no previous written reports, rarely used behavioral methods, stated purposes in general rather than specific terms, emphasized weaknesses over strengths in reporting results, and often neglected to describe the parent's caregiving qualities or the child's relationship with the parent. (Budd et al., 2001, p. 93)

Clinicians differ in how much information they seek before they stop searching. Many clinicians gather more data than needed; as the amount increases, so may confidence in its usefulness, even though accuracy is not increased. The collection of data appears to have a self-reinforcing function, since it is often unclear how additional data will be useful in making more accurate decisions. Our subjective uncertainty may be decreased—even though objective uncertainty is not—by collecting additional data. Irrelevant as well as relevant data may be influential. Each source of information is subject to error. This may be random (unsystematic, varying) or systematic (biased in one direction). Sources of random error include measurement changes (observers may fluctuate in their ratings) and changes in client characteristics (for example, in mood). Sources of systematic error include *demand characteristics* (characteristics of a situation that encourage responses in one direction). For example, we tend to present ourselves in a good light; this is known as the *social desirability effect*. Both random and systematic error may interfere with discovering a client's true score on a measure. Many errors involve or result in inappropriate speculation (assuming that what is can be discovered simply by thinking about it). Data collection is influenced by clinicians' knowledge and related beliefs, their goals, the resources available, and their relationship skills. Selection of assessment methods may be based on sound reasons such as empirical research concerning the accuracy of a source. On the other hand, selection may be based on questionable grounds, such as personal preferences contradicted by empirical data about the accuracy of a given source. Measures used reflect an underlining theory regarding causes. There are many competing grand narratives regarding alleged causes of behaviors, feelings, and environmental circumstances. The view favored influences the creation and use of diagnostic and assessment measures. Thus, key questions are: What is the theory related to a recommended measure? Has it been tested? If so, with what results?

Some methods such as phrenology were enormously popular for years and many famous people, including Walt Whitman, sought the services of a phrenologist (see Exhibit 1.1). Although claimed to be accurate and relevant, tests may be neither. (See Exhibit 13.2.) For example, you may not be informed that colonoscopies miss many cancers (Kolata, 2008). Evidence that propaganda regarding assessment measures thrives is illustrated by the hundreds of methods promoted as accurate that have not been tested to determine if they do more harm than good, and the many that have been tested and found to be inaccurate or to do more harm than good that are still used. The points raised here apply not only to claims that appear in the media, but also to material in professional newsletters, in books, and in peer-reviewed journals. Here again, we see bold assertions (exaggerated claims of knowledge) and suppression of counterevidence and well-argued alternatives. Here, too, propaganda may stem from others (the media and professional publications), from ourselves (inflated assessment of our own knowledge), and from interactions between these sources.

Mistaken beliefs about a source of data may limit selections. You may believe that observation of interaction in structured or natural contexts is useless, since this drastically alters usual interaction patterns. This is not necessarily true (see later discussion of use of observation). Some data may be collected from existing sources, such as case records; other material is gathered during interviews. Skill in posing well-formed questions regarding assessment needs that allow you to search effectively and efficiently for related research is valuable (see Chapters 10 and 11).

DECISIONS AND OPTIONS

Assessment is used to understand (describe) clients and their circumstances, and to make predictions about them. Involved decisions include the following:

- What data will be most helpful in making sound decisions—for example, about factors related to hoped-for outcomes and whether they can be attained?

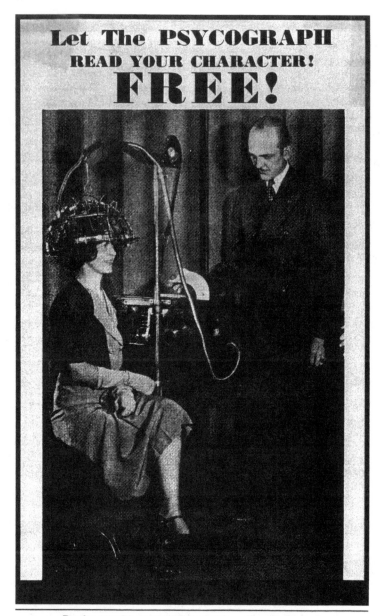

Brochure used to promote Psycograph readings in theaters.

Exhibit 13.2 Examples of a Dubious Assessment Method: The First Psycograph

Source: From *Quack: Tales of Medical Fraud from the Museum of Questionable Medical Devices* (p. 145), by B. McCoy, 2000, Santa Monica, CA: Santa Monica Press.

- How can I obtain such data?
- What criteria will I use to decide I have enough information?
- What should I do if I obtain contradictory data?
- What criteria should I use to check the accuracy of data?
- How can I avoid inaccurate and incomplete accounts?

Assessment methods can be harmful as well as helpful. For example, they may provide misleading estimates of problem severity and misleading directions for accurate understanding of a client and their concerns. Quick tests for the flu are often inaccurate (Pollack, 2009). Severe depression among the elderly is often missed (Brown, McAvay, Rane, Moses, & Bruce, 2003; Goleman, 1995). Falls among the elderly may be due to incorrect vision corrections (e.g., see Campbell, Sanderson, & Robertson, 2010; Voermans, Snijders, Schoon, & Bloem, 2007). Less intrusive but equally accurate methods may not be mentioned or accurately described because a doctor is not trained to carry them out effectively or because insurance companies do not pay for such methods. Here, as well as in other helping phases, specialized knowledge may be required and critical thinking skills needed to weigh the accuracy of claims and soundness of different views and to integrate different kinds of information, such as findings from external research and the unique circumstances and characteristics of a client. Informed selection of assessment methods maximizes opportunities to discover alternative behaviors that will successfully compete with disliked behaviors.

Knowledge about different assessment frameworks and measures will help you to select referral sources that use evidence-informed methods and to evaluate data gathered by others. Informed consent obligations require sharing uncertainties regarding possible harms and benefits associated with use of a method such as a screening test for depression or mammogram for breast cancer (e.g., Welch, Schwartz, & Woloshin, 2011). Not sharing uncertainties may hide the fact that decisions involve a value judgment about how to balance risks and harms.

- Does a risk assessment measure accurately predict further likelihood of child abuse?
- Does an anxiety measure accurately identify clients who have a level of anxiety that warrants referral to counseling?
- Does a measure designed to assess the effects of traumatic life experiences accurately identify those who could benefit from counseling?

Judging whether a particular measure provides reliable and valid data requires skills in locating related research as well as knowledge and skill in critically appraising what you find. Such skills will help you to decide whether a measure provides accurate data.

Decisions will also be influenced by client preferences and feasibility (whether it is possible to use a method). Clients may not be willing to use certain methods. You may not have skills in administering and interpreting a measure. Some sources, such as self-report, are easy to use and are flexible in the range of content provided; however, accuracy varies considerably. In addition to deciding on sources of data (e.g., self-report, observation), you and your clients will decide on a type of measure (e.g., frequency, duration, latency).

SOURCES OF INFLUENCE ON WHAT CLINICIANS SEE AND REPORT

Our judgments and decisions are influenced by many variables as discussed in Chapter 9. Perception is selective. As a consequence, we may not see all there is to see and may see what is not present. Consider the experiment by Chabris and Simons (2009) in which observers failed to see a gorilla crossing the stage. Our temporary moods, either positive or negative, affect our decisions, as illustrated in Chapter 9. Different decisions may be made about a client who is seen at the end of a hectic day than may be made if the same client had been interviewed at the beginning of that day. As discussed in Chapter 8, experts see more compared to novices in an area. Professionals are influenced by what they read and see both in the media and in professional sources, including direct-to-consumer advertising of pharmaceutical products.

Preferred Theories, Vividness, and Chance

We seek information that is consistent with our preferred theories and preconceptions and tend to disregard contradictory information, as suggested in earlier chapters (although this does not apply to experts in an area). People who are informed that an instructor is warm perceive him differently than people who are told that the same instructor is cold (Kelley, 1950). The more ambiguous a situation, the more preconceptions and biases affect what is seen. Abercrombie (1960) describes a radiologist who examined an X-ray of a child with a persistent cough. The radiologist discounted a button observed on the X-ray, assuming that the button was on the boy's vest—in fact, the button was inside of the boy and was causing his cough.

We are influenced by the vividness of material. It is easy to recall bizarre behavior and pay attention to this while ignoring less vivid appropriate behavior. We overestimate risks that get attention in the media and underestimate risks that do not receive attention. Some scholars suggest that we live in a culture of fear in which we are daily warned about the latest risks and dangers (e.g., Furedi, 2006). Frequency may or may not be a sound guide to decisions. (See discussion of fast and frugal heuristics in Chapter 10.)

Chance availability may affect our decisions—that is, certain events may just happen to be present when thinking about a problem, and these influence what we attend to (Hogarth, 1987). Clinicians in certain settings are exposed to particular kinds of clients, which may predispose them to make certain assumptions. For example, a nurse may see many depressed patients and so be primed to attend to signs of depression. Base-rate data that is abstract tend to be ignored (see Chapter 15).

Sample Bias

The samples to which we have access are usually biased. Few samples are random, in which each element of the population has an equal chance of being selected. Only a small percentage of people who experience distress or who engage in deviant behavior may seek help from a clinician. Those with such problems who do seek help or are referred to clinicians thus represent a biased sample of the total population of individuals who evidence certain behaviors. If a sample is randomly selected, there is less likelihood that it will be biased. The general failure to understand this is illustrated by the cabinet officer who did not accept the results of a poll that he did not like because people were chosen at random (Tversky & Kahneman, 1971).

Clinicians must often make generalizations from single instances to larger populations. For example, a psychologist may make generalizations about a person on the basis of one meeting. Generalizations about a mother's parenting skills may be made on the basis of her self-report during one interview. A lack of appreciation for sample size and sample bias can lead to incorrect judgments. The larger the sample, the more likely it is to reflect the characteristics of the population from which it is drawn. People have little appreciation of the importance of the law of large numbers. We are willing to make strong inferences based on few data. This tendency offers one explanation for disagreements about how to describe certain events—each person may be using a different sample to generalize from, and each sample may be small (as well as biased). Some clinicians use verbal report in the interviews as their only data source, neglecting other sources such as role-play and observation in real-life settings. They have but a tiny sample of behavior and a tiny sample in just one situation—the interview—which is not a real-life setting. Yet they may remain confident in their ability to make accurate generalizations about clients on the basis of small, biased samples. The empirical literature does not support this belief (see later discussion of method variance). The size of the sample on which decisions are based can often be substantially increased by drawing on samples collected by others that are described in professional journals and books. For example, consider a clinician who is working with a client who is having trouble finding a job, but the clinician has worked with only a handful of such clients previously. Becoming familiar with related research may reveal promising programs.

Agency Policy/Social Pressures/Resources

Agency administrators have beliefs and preferred policies that influence the kind of staff they hire and, consequently, the kind of data gathered. These preferences are revealed in steps that are taken to facilitate (or hamper) collection of certain kinds of data. For example, agencies may discourage home visits and observation of family members at home because of related costs. Peers and supervisors may exert pressures to gather certain kinds of data and to ignore other sources. Staff may not have access to relevant databases allowing speedy searches for research findings regarding the most valid assessment methods for a client with a given concern. Let's say that Mrs. Compana is worried that because her mother has Alzheimer's disease, she herself will be so diagnosed. A question is: In people with a parent who has Alzheimer's disease, what is their risk of developing this?

The Quality of Feedback

The timing and relevance of feedback obtained about the accuracy of observations influence descriptions. Helpful feedback provides opportunities to correct initial assumptions. Corrective feedback is vital to development of expertise—to the development of informed intuition (see Chapter 8).

Inattention to Nonoccurrences

Events that do not occur tend to be ignored, even though these events may be highly relevant. We may fail to note that a certain bizarre behavior does not occur in 95% of contexts, attending instead to the small percentage of situations in which it does occur. Overlooking situations in which it does not occur deprives clinicians of valuable information about environmental influences on behavior.

Not Distinguishing Between Description and Inference

A basic distinction in collecting data is between inference and description. A descriptive statement can be confirmed by reference to the real world. For example, if a counselor states, "The teenager sat between his parents," she could point to evidence for this. An inference involves extrapolation; it cannot be confirmed or rejected without other information that is not present via observation. If this counselor said, "The youth purposely sat between his parents in order to separate them as a team" or "because of his unresolved Oedipal complex," she would be making inferences. Although distinguishing between descriptions and inferences sounds easy, in fact some clinicians may lack this skill; that is, they cannot distinguish between descriptions and inferences. This may cloud their thinking in a number of ways, including confusion between what actually happened in a situation and interpretations of what happened. For example, a clinician might say that a husband is hostile toward his wife. When asked to give examples, he may say, "He does not like her." A further question may yield "He is aggressive and punishing toward his wife." Note that we still do not have any clear example of the referents for the term *hostile*.

The difficulty of distinguishing between descriptions and inferences is shown by Abercrombie's (1960) efforts to enhance the critical thinking skills of medical students. (Her description of the diplomatic skills required to succeed in this task is fascinating.) She showed the students X-rays of two hands and asked them to list the differences between them. The students typically reported that one X-ray showed an older hand than did the other. This inference was made swiftly on the basis of certain preconceptions related to the fact that one X-ray was smaller than the other. "During the discussion it became clear that the apparently 'factual' statement that 'B is an older hand than A' is an inference which had been arrived at as a result of picking up a number of clues, calling on past experience and information which was more or less relevant, ignoring the limitations of their knowledge, and inadequately testing hypotheses to estimate the probability of their being correct. The inferences the students had made were not arrived at as a result of a series of logical steps, but swiftly and almost unconsciously. The validity of the inferences was usually not inquired into, indeed the process was usually accompanied by a feeling of certainty of being right, and consequently the discussion of incompatible views sometimes became very heated" (Abercrombie, 1960, p. 105).

Communication Skills

The quality of a clinician's relationship skills influence what clients share (see Chapter 2). The better such skills, the more likely clients will be to share relevant material. Thus, skill in forming positive alliances with clients influences quality of information gathered.

DIFFERENT KINDS OF EVIDENCE

Clinicians draw on various kinds of evidence in making decisions. Each type of evidence has strengths and weaknesses in relation to accuracy.

Real Evidence

Actual objects may be "offered to prove their own existence or to allow an inference to be drawn from their existence" (Smith & Hunsaker, 1972, p. 112), as in circumstantial evidence. Staff may show an attending psychiatrist broken objects in a patient's room to support their statement that "the patient is out of control."

Hearsay Evidence

This refers to reports that are based on what someone heard someone else say; the presenter of the information did not see the event himself, he is merely reporting what someone else told him. There are elaborate rules concerning acceptance of hearsay evidence in courts of law. Hearsay evidence is relied on extensively in clinical practice. Sources of inaccuracy include limitations in the perception of the original witness and bias on the part of the "reporter." A major problem with hearsay evidence is that the original witnesses cannot be interviewed to probe the credibility of their perceptions. Clinicians often discount sources of error in accepting hearsay evidence.

Expert Witnesses

Expert witnesses are assumed to have special knowledge concerning a particular matter, which allows them to offer well-founded, authoritative opinions (conclusions based on facts). Clinicians are often called on to testify as experts in hearings concerning child custody and allegations of sexual abuse. Weighty consequences rest on the accuracy of such testimony. Experts testify regarding psychological characteristics of a person, for example: Did they have road rage? Do they have a personality disorder? How expert such individuals really are has been the subject of many spirited discussions. Do "experts" have knowledge that allow them to make accurate assertions? The topic of expert testimony has received considerable critical attention over the past years (e.g., see Ceci & Hembrooke, 1998; Dawes, 1994a; Faust & Ziskin, 2012; Gigerenzer, 2002a; McCann, Shindler, & Hammond, 2003). Consider the overturning of murder convictions because of flawed expert testimony ("Sally Clark Freed," 2003). We can protect ourselves from being misled by alleged expert testimony by being informed about factors that influence the accuracy of such reports (e.g., Lindsey, 2004). This also applies to eyewitness accounts. Being informed about related research should increase skepticism among all involved parties about the accuracy of such reports.

The *Daubert v. Merrell Dow Pharmaceuticals, Inc.* (1993) ruling describes requirements for expert testimony (see also *Frye v. United States*, 1923). The American Psychological Association provides ethical guidelines for clinicians who serve as expert witnesses (2002). The rules of hearsay evidence are less stringent in expert testimony, in which a clinician may rely on data gathered from significant others as well as archival records. Lawyers and judges may raise questions about the reliability and validity of such evidence. Whether these questions will be profitable depends partly on whether an expert has insider knowledge that cannot be checked. For example, only a psychiatrist may have access to a patient's behavior in the hospital, or other witnesses may be present who also have insider knowledge and who may confirm or contradict the psychiatrist's testimony.

Circumstantial Evidence

Here, the existence of an object or a certain circumstance is used to infer that certain facts are true. Only one person may have had an opportunity to start a fire on a certain occasion. Thus, although no one witnessed a youth starting a fire, opportunity may be used as circumstantial evidence that he is guilty.

Reluctant Evidence

Information may be provided under duress; that is, respondents may be reluctant participants in offering information. Intentional misrepresentation or denials may be offered. As always, the demand characteristics of the setting in which data are collected should be considered.

Factual Evidence

This refers to potentially verifiable statements that describe people or objects. Factual evidence is descriptive rather than evaluative or explanatory. Statistics may be used to support a claim, or observational data describing interaction may be offered.

Firsthand Reports/Eyewitness Accounts

Clinicians have to evaluate the accuracy of reports by eyewitnesses. Such reports include descriptions of facts directly witnessed by an individual. The possibility of inaccurate accounts is of major concern in courts of law, in which special procedures such as cross-examination and use of multiple witnesses are designed to reveal inaccurate accounts (e.g., see Cutler, 2009; Walton, 2008b; Weiser, 2011). Consider the following example concerning a young freelance photographer:

> Dillen's initial arrest was little more than a misunderstanding. What is significant is the fact that the arrest resulted in a mug-shot photograph of Robert Dillen in the files of the Dormont police. By chance, one investigating

officer thought he noticed an uncanny resemblance between Dillen and a composite sketch made by holdup victim, Diane Jones. Several weeks after the holdup, Diane Jones was asked to look at a set of ten mug-shot photographs, one of which was Dillen's. It was Dillen's that she identified.

Copies of Dillen's photographs were then sent to other police departments, where they were identified by the witnesses and victims of 13 different crimes, leading subsequently to the identification of Dillen in a live lineup by several witnesses and finally to an identification in court by a 16-year-old victim of rape and abduction. Dillen was eventually proved innocent. (Hall, Loftus, & Tousignant, 1984, pp. 124–125)

Errors in observation can be revealed by staging an interaction and asking witnesses to describe what they saw. This kind of demonstration is often used in law schools to illustrate the limitations of eyewitness testimony—a kind of testimony that is considered superior to other kinds of evidence. Many studies demonstrate that false memories can be created (Loftus, 2004). The accuracy of witness reports may differ because of characteristics of the event itself (such as exposure), characteristics of the witness (such as amount of stress or fear), and instructions. As Loftus (1980) points out, someone who is thinking, "How can I get myself out of this situation?" (p. 32) will be less attentive to characteristics of faces than will someone who observes people carefully. Prior knowledge and the expectations of the witness influence what is perceived. Testimony may be discounted on faulty grounds. For example, if a person cannot recall peripheral details of an incident, his testimony regarding identification of a suspect in a lineup may be discredited, even though memory for such details is not correlated with accurate identification (Wells & Lindsay, 1983). The confidence with which memories are reported is a predictor of whether the report will be believed (but not of how accurate the report is). This confidence in turn is influenced by response biases when reporting memories.

Some people have a conservative bias; they are reluctant to identify someone unless they are very sure of the identification. Other people have the opposite tendency— they act more certain than they actually are. Greater credibility is accorded to an account if a person has previously freely admitted a memory failure on another item. Verbal qualifiers (such as "I think" or "I guess") increase skepticism on the part of listeners concerning accuracy of reports. These qualifiers are cues that a "reporter is in a state of reconstructive memory" (p. 32). There is an extensive literature on using cues to decide whether a person's confession is false (Kassin & Gudjonsson, 2004) or he or she is lying (Vrij, Granhag, & Porter, 2010). The research on eyewitness testimony is relevant to the concerns of clinicians in evaluating the accuracy of reports. As we have seen, there are many paradoxes in this area—all is not what it seems. Confidence does not necessarily reflect accuracy, and hesitancy does not necessarily reflect a lack of accuracy. Memory changes, false memories may be created, and the very review of its contents may create changes in our memories (see later discussion of self-report data) (see also Cutler, 2009).

NOT FOR RESEARCHERS ALONE: CONCERNS ABOUT RELIABILITY AND VALIDITY

Concerns about validity and factors that influence this (e.g., reliability) are not confined to researchers. They are also relevant to clinical practice. If you rely on irrelevant or inaccurate measures, you may select ineffective or harmful plans because of faulty assumptions. If you rely on an inaccurate measure of social skill, you may assume incorrectly that a client has the skills required to succeed in certain situations when he does not, resulting in punishing consequences such as rejection. Dishion, Burraston, and Li (2003) found that method variance (use of different methods to assess a given factor) accounted for 50% of observed variation in descriptions of parenting behavior. Method variance can occur because of different views and reporting styles of different respondents using different methods to gather data (e.g., self-report, self-monitoring, observation). Dishion and Granic (2004) emphasize the value of naturalistic observation (observation in real-life contexts such as the playground) in decreasing misleading effects of relying on one method (e.g., self-report): "When only one method is used, one introduces a mono method bias" (p. 146; see also Cook & Campbell, 1979).

Validity concerns the question: Does the measure reflect the characteristic it is supposed to measure? For example, does behavior in a role-play correspond to what a client does in similar real-life situations? A measure is valid to the extent to which it reflects the concept or object it is supposed to measure. Consider, for example, the Beck Depression Inventory. To what extent does a client's score reflect his or her depression? What is the likelihood that a client who scores high on a suicide potential scale will attempt suicide in the next 6 weeks? (See discussion of the predictive value of tests in Chapter 15.) There are many different kinds of validity, and it is helpful to be familiar with these (Campbell & Stanley, 1963). Direct (e.g., observing teacher-student interaction) in contrast to indirect measures (e.g., asking a student to complete a questionnaire assumed to offer information about classroom behavior) are typically more valid. Confusion sometimes arises about issues of validity and the extent to which measures from different sources offer similar accounts. Different responses (overt behavior, feelings, thoughts) may or may not be related to certain events. Clients may report being anxious but show no physiological signs of anxiety. This does not mean that their reports are inaccurate.

For these individuals, the experience of anxiety may be cognitive rather than physical. Types of validity and reliability include the following:

- *Predictive validity:* This refers to the extent to which a measure accurately predicts behavior at a later time. For example, how accurately does a measure of suicidal potential predict suicide attempts?
- *Concurrent validity:* This refers to the extent to which a measure correlates with a valid measure gathered at the same time; for example, do responses on a questionnaire concerning social behavior correlate with behavior in real-life contexts? Concurrent and predictive validity are sometimes referred to as criterion validity. In both, scores on a measure are compared to a criterion that is assumed to be accurate. For example, scores on a self-report measure of social skill could be compared with behavior in a role-play simulation.
- *Content validity:* This reflects the degree to which a measure adequately samples the domain being assessed. For example, does an inventory used to assess parenting skills include an adequate sample of such skills?
- *Construct validity:* This term refers to the degree to which a measure successfully measures a theoretical construct—the degree to which results of a measure correspond with assumptions about the measure. The finding that depressed people report more negative thoughts on a questionnaire compared to nondepressed people adds an increment of construct validity to a measure. Evidence should be available showing that different methods of assessing a construct (e.g., direct observation and self-report) yield similar results (convergent validity) and that similar methods of measuring different constructs (e.g., aggression and altruism) yield different results (discriminant validity). That is, evidence should be available that a construct can be distinguished from other *different* constructs.
- *Face validity:* This term refers to the extent to which items included on a measure make sense "on the face of it." Can you accurately guess the meaning (purpose) of an item?
- *Convergent validity:* This refers to the extent to which different measures of the same construct correlate with each other. Measures of the same construct should correlate with each other.
- *Discriminant validity:* Measures of divergent constructs should not be highly correlated. For example, if a measure of depression correlates highly and positively with a measure of happiness, something is wrong.
- *Reliability:* This term refers to the consistency of results (in the absence of real change) provided by the same person at different times (time-based reliability, stability), by two different raters of the same events (individual-based reliability,

as in interrater reliability), or by parallel forms or split halves of a measure (item-bound reliability). For example, the reliability of a questionnaire could be evaluated by asking people to complete it at two different times. As noted in the discussion of eyewitness testimony, interrater reliability may be low. Sources of error include changes in ratings due to fatigue, lack of sufficient training, and different preconceptions. Homogeneity is a kind of item-bound reliability assessing the degree to which all the items on a test measure the same characteristics. Many concepts such as loneliness are multifactorial (more than one factor is involved).

Reliability places an upward boundary on validity. For example, if responses on a questionnaire vary from time to time (in the absence of real change), it will not be possible to use results of a measure to predict what a person will do in the future. Reliability can be assessed in a number of ways, all of which yield some measure of consistency. In test-retest reliability, the scores of the same individuals at different times are correlated with each other. Correlations may range from –1 to +1. The size of the correlation coefficient indicates the degree of association. A zero correlation indicates a complete absence of consistency. A correlation of +1 indicates a perfect positive correlation. The stability (reliability of a measure at different times) of some measures is high. That is, you can ask a client to complete a questionnaire this week and 5 weeks from now and obtain similar results (in the absence of real change). Other measures have low stability. Coefficients of reliability are usually sufficient if they are .80 or better. However, the higher the better.

The degree to which different sources provide similar or identical reports is typically used as a sign that a description is accurate. Both a husband and a wife may offer identical reports concerning the husband's drinking pattern. Both staff members in a retirement home, as well as other residents, may offer similar reports about a resident's behavior. Inconsistent reports call for further investigation; they may indicate that one or more of the sources is inaccurate. Agreement between two or more witnesses of an event is often considered indicative of accuracy; however, all these witnesses may have been influenced by a similar biasing effect that distorted the accuracy of all descriptions. For example, the appearance of a suspect in a particular lineup may influence all observers' reactions similarly (Wells, Lindsay, & Ferguson, 1979). Talking together about an event may increase agreement but not accuracy. Consistency of data may result in overestimation of the informativeness of material. Reliability of measures used and of psychiatric diagnosis is often low (Kutchins & Kirk, 1997; Kirk, 2010). Agreement between different clinicians and agreement between different ratings of the same person at different times may be modest in other fields, such as medicine.

Other important characteristics include sensitivity, utility, and feasibility. The *sensitivity* of measures is important to consider; that is, will a measure reflect changes that occur? Insensitive measures will not offer information about progress or factors related to client concerns and circumstances. The *utility* of a measure is determined by its cost (time, effort, expense) balanced against information provided. *Feasibility* is related to utility. Some measures will not be feasible to gather. For example, clients who cannot read will not be able to complete written questionnaires. Utility may be compromised by the absence of empirically derived norms for a measure. *Norms* offer information about the typical (or average) performance of a group of individuals. You can compare your clients' results with those of similar clients. Cut points may be used to decide whether a client is in the typical range on a given characteristic or to make predictions about future behavior. Their placement will affect the rate of false positives and false negatives. Placing people into categories based on cut-points may encourage errors, such as pathologizing clients because what is in reality a continuous dimension (e.g., number of tantrums per week) is shifted to a categorical description as in the *Diagnostic and Statistical Manual of Mental Disorders* (American Psychiatric Association, 2000).

Be sure to consider the representativeness of norms in relation to your client. How similar is the client to the people whose norms were obtained? Are there cultural differences? The more representative the sample is to your client, the greater the utility of the measures in relation to a client. Thus, nomothetic approaches to assessment (standardized across clients) may not offer the most accurate, relevant information for individuals. Norms may reflect low levels of hoped-for behavior (e.g., a low rate of positive feedback). They may not offer the detail needed to understand a client; what is "anger" for a particular client? And they may not take account of cultural differences. Idiographic measures (those specific to an individual) may offer more accurate information.

QUESTIONABLE ASSESSMENT METHODS

Many tests used by professionals are pseudoscientific; that is, there is no evidence that they are accurate and do more good than harm; there is no evidence that they contribute to accurate assessment (Lilienfeld, Lynn, & Lohr, 2003; Thyer & Pignotti, 2010). Are claims of value accurate? (See Exhibit 13.3.) If we read a claim that a measure is reliable and valid, is this true? What kind of reliability and validity were assessed? Are claims made about its usefulness sound? As readers, we should be skeptical, because limitations are often not candidly acknowledged. Criteria to consider include: (1) reliability, (2) validity, (3) sensitivity, (4) utility, (5) feasibility, and (6)

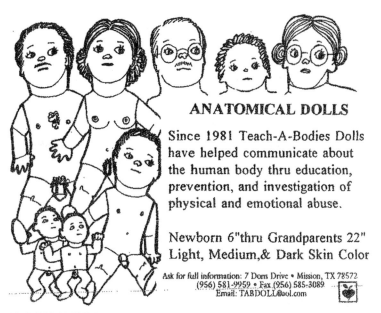

Exhibit 13.3 Examples of Advertisement for Anatomical Dolls

Source: NASW News, 44(8), September 1999, p. 24.

relevance. A fluid understanding of reliability and validity concerns as they apply to practice methods will help you to critically appraise measures. For example, standardization in how a measure is administered and interpreted is important, not just for scientific purposes, but also to increase the accuracy with which a test is used. (See, for example, guidelines of the American Psychological Association regarding use of tests.) Rarely will you find a statement such as the following: "We examined only inter-item reliability (correlation among items). We do not know if the measure is stable. That is, we do not know whether a person who takes the inventory today will get a different score four weeks from now in the absence of intervention."

Unstable measures cannot accurately reflect change that may result from provision of services. It may be assumed that positive changes have occurred when there has been no change. Has the validity and reliability of a test been independently investigated? Have only the creators of a test investigated its reliability and validity? Does a measure provide accurate information about clients in real-life situations? Responsibility for gathering such evidence falls, not to those who raise questions regarding the accuracy and reliability of a measure, but to those who forward claims about it. Hunsley, Lee, and Wood (2003) describe a number of assessment techniques that they regard as questionable based on a review of related empirical literature. These tests include the Rorschach inkblot test, the Thematic Apperception Test, projective drawings, anatomically detailed dolls, and the Myers-Briggs type indicator.

SOURCES OF DATA

No matter what our preferred practice framework, we have a limited number of sources of information: (1) various forms of self-report (e.g., what clients or others say, written measures); (2) self-monitoring (clients or significant others keep track of some behaviors, thoughts, feelings, or events in real life); (3) observation in role-plays or real life; and (4) physiological measures. Case records contain information based on one or more of these sources. Each method has advantages and disadvantages and certain requisites. Some clinicians depend on self-report as their main source of information. Observation, when feasible, may be needed to supplement self-report. Inaccurate assumptions about helpful methods may discourage their use. For example, some clinicians may not use client self-monitoring (see later discussion) on the grounds that clients will not do it. True, some will not, but others will. Another source of data that is often neglected is observation of interaction between a client and his or her significant others (student and teacher, peers on a playground).

Self-Reports

Self-report gathered during interviews is the most widely used assessment method. People have unique knowledge about themselves—what they have done in the past, and their future hopes and fears. The narrative tradition is perhaps the oldest in our history. We hear stories from the time of our childhood and we read them in books and newspapers. We learn of life's challenges as well as of possibilities for dealing with them in the stories we hear and tell. We each have our stories, which may change over time. Clients have their stories. The stories of different family members about events may be quite different. A professional enters the stage at a particular point in the story flow of a client, family, neighborhood, community, or organization and becomes part of the story—how large remains to be seen, depending in part on the professional's skill in establishing trust, offering hope, and understanding the points of view of the participants. What seems simple can be complex. Different players may have different agendas and understandings of events, which if not recognized will impede an outcome that is valued by all players.

Self-reports may not be accurate (e.g., Schnelle, 1974). Familiarity with sources of bias and error will be helpful in reducing distortion in self-reports of events that may be obtainable no other way (Stone et al., 1999). Disadvantages of self-report include the possibility that clients cannot provide the requested information, are not willing to provide it, or present inaccurate views. Information may not be accessible to clients. Perhaps they forgot some sequence of events or never noted a sequence of events accurately. Clients may not understand a question and so report incorrect information. Inaccurate accounts may be offered because of embarrassment over a lack of information or fear about the consequences of providing accurate accounts. Reports are influenced by clients' perceptions of how they are expected to behave.

Thinking Critically About Self-Report Data

When assessing the accuracy of self-reports consider the following questions:

- Does the situation encourage an honest answer?
- Does the client have access to the information?
- Can the client comprehend the question?
- Does the client have the verbal skills required to answer questions?
- Is the interviewer familiar with and skilled in avoiding interviewer biases?

Often, people do not accurately observe the relationship between behavior and environmental events and instead offer reports based on biased assumptions. Self-reports may tell us more about what people think they have perceived rather than about what actually happened. In a classic study, Weiss and Brown (1977) investigated the accuracy with which women identified factors that influenced their mood. For a 2-month period, subjects recorded their mood twice a day and also kept track of several factors that might affect mood (for example, amount of sleep, the weather, health, sexual activity, and day of the week). The subjects reported their views about the relative influence of these factors on their mood at the end of the 2-month period. Multiple regression analyses were performed on the mood score of each subject to derive objective weights for each factor. Analysis of the results indicated that there were large discrepancies between these objective weights and the average subjective weights. In fact, the overall correlation between objective and subjective weights was slightly negative. Weiss and Brown (1977) also examined data for individual subjects. This analysis revealed a similar pattern; subjects were not accurate in assessing the relative effects of certain factors on their mood; they mistook strong influences for weak ones, and weak influences for strong ones. In some cases, they failed to distinguish between positive and negative influences. This study was followed by another one in which undergraduate students were asked to estimate the impact of the same factors on a person's mood. The relative weights obtained were identical to those reported by the women in the original study. Participants' daily experience of emotional ups and downs and their concomitants, even the daily recording of these events, gave them no advantage in estimating the correlates of their moods.

A great deal of information is available on some subjects, such as parents' reports about the behavior of their children. For example, social desirability influences parental reports in terms of placing the information in a positive light—for example, in line with socially accepted child-rearing practices. Parents' perceptions shift over time in line with cultural stereotypes and popular books. Parents cited problems with "sibling rivalry" more often after Dr. Spock's (1945) book appeared (Robbins, 1963). Clients may have difficulty giving specific examples of behaviors of concern. Research on memory offers some intriguing explanations of why clients often find it difficult to offer specific examples. One way large amounts of information can be handled is to summarize inconsistencies in experiences. A wife who has had difficulty with her husband for months or years may focus on certain regularities in her experience and relate them to a theme that represents these ("He is bad tempered"). (See other sources for more details, e.g., Baddeley, 2005; Woll, 2002.)

Repeated suggestions that a certain event occurred (when it did not) may result in inaccurate reports. For example, 58% of preschool children produced false stories to at least one fictitious event after 10 weeks of thinking about both real and fictitious events (Ceci, Crotteau-Huffman, Smith, & Loftus, 1994). Consider the false report from Bill, a 4-year-old.

> My brother Colin was trying to get Blowtorch [an action figurine] from me, and I wouldn't let him take it from me, so he pushed me into the wood pile where the mousetrap was. And then my finger got caught in it. And then we went to the hospital. And my mommy, daddy, and Colin drove me there, to the hospital in our van, because it was far away. And the doctor put a bandage on this finger (indicating). (Ceci & Bruck, 1995, p. 219)

As this example suggests, the very process of thinking about a question may alter our memories (see also Loftus & Ketcham, 1994; Lynn, Lock, Loftus, Krakow, & Lilienfeld, 2003). Consider critiques of recovered memory therapy. Memories may be false, creating havoc in people's lives as well as in the lives of those they accuse (see Ofshe & Watters, 1994). This is not to say that all memories of past abuse are false. It is to say that some are, especially those that violate what we know about how memory works. Also, we must examine all four possible relationships between whether someone who reports being abused as a child remembers abuse, and whether it really occurred (Dawes, 1994b). This is usually not done, resulting in false estimates. Client characteristics that influence self-reports include:

- Desire to give socially desirable answers.
- Lack of understanding of the questions.
- Faulty memory.
- Anxiety.
- No true opinions or preferences.
- Distracted because of poor timing of the interview.
- Misunderstandings about the purpose of the interview.

The Importance of the Questions Asked

Questions are used to clarify client statements and to refine and check clinical assumptions. The accuracy of self-reports is influenced by questions asked and characteristics of the interviewer. The more specific the question, the more likely the answer is to be correct if the responder has no reason to hide the truth. Preferred theories influence choice of questions. Which questions are asked, how they are asked, and when they are asked all have an effect on the response received. Sources of interviewer bias include:

- Questions or terms may be vague or ambiguous.
- A particular sequence of questions may suggest certain answers.
- Too many questions may be asked (the inquisitor).
- Unwarranted assumptions may be implicit in questions asked, as in leading questions.
- More than one question may be embedded in a single question.
- Interviewer preferences, emotional reactions, and biases may influence what is noted.
- Answers may be misunderstood.
- Recording errors may be made.

The questions you ask reflect your beliefs about what is and is not important. We tend to ask questions that confirm our beliefs. This confirmatory bias may result in overlooking contradictory data and alternative (more accurate) views. The response format used influences what is reported. Clients may give different reports if you ask closed-end questions calling for a "yes/no" answer than if you ask open-ended questions. Some people have an acquiescent response set (a tendency to say "yes"). Use of inexact adverbs such as *often* or *seldom* can give an illusion of precision and agreement that does not exist. We differ in our interpretation of vague terms such as *frequent* or *seldom* (Pepper, 1981; Teigen & Brun, 2003a, 2003b). Questions asked reflect preconceptions about clients. How they are asked (for example, wording, order, concreteness) influences both the expression and the formation of values by affecting how we frame problems and how confident we are in our judgments (Fischhoff, Slovic, & Lichtenstein, 1980; see Exhibit 13.4).

Identification of values and goals is a key concern in counseling. Given the influence of subtle social psychological processes in therapy, it could be argued that non-directive methods are the most manipulative of all methods because preconceptions of the inquirer are not shared with clients. The purpose of motivational interviewing and the various methods it incorporates from diverse sources is to engage clients in a change process (see Norcross, Krebs, & Prochaska, 2011). One way to overcome subtle priming effects on clients is to ask about values and goals in a variety of ways, to coax

Exhibit 13.4 Ways an Elicitor May Affect a Respondent's Judgments of Value

---

Framing the issue:

Is there a problem?

What options and consequences are relevant?

How should options and consequences be viewed?

How should values be measured?

Influencing the respondent's views:

Altering the salience of perspectives

Altering the importance of perspectives

Changing confidence in expressed values:

Misattributing the source

Changing the apparent degree of coherence

Changing the respondent:

Altering perspectives

Creating perspectives

Source: Adapted from "Knowing What You Want: Measuring Labile Values," by B. Fischhoff, P. Slovic, and S. Lichtenstein, 1980, in *Cognitive Processes in Choice and Decision Behavior* (p. 123), edited by T. S. Wallsten, Hillsdale, NJ: Erlbaum. Copyright 1980 by Lawrence Erlbaum Associates. Reprinted with permission.

out inconsistencies that can then be clarified. We often do not know what we want, as suggested by the saying, "Be careful what you wish for, because you might get it," and by research showing a marked discrepancy between what we say we want (our preferences) and the actions we take (or do not) to attain related goals. For example, thousands of people pay for advice they do not follow.

Inconsistent reports on the part of clients may be due to differences among interviewers. "When two different examiners get variations in a history from the same patient, they often assume that the patient is unreliable or perverse. In many instances, however, the fault lies with the examiners, not with the client. Differences in reports regarding history may arise from many aspects of the examining procedure. Among the major sources of variability is the specificity with which details of symptoms are noted" (Feinstein, 1967, p. 318). Research concerning witness testimony indicates that allowing people to offer an open narrative account results in greater accuracy than does asking many questions. The demand characteristics of the situation (what clients think others want to hear) influence reports.

Memories may be modified during the process of an interview. Question comprehension and information retrieval through memory search are related. An example of the influence of questions on memory changes is provided by a study of Loftus and Palmer (1974). Subjects watched a film of a traffic accident at an intersection; they were later asked, "How fast was [the car] going when it ran the stop sign?" For some subjects, no stop sign appeared in the film. However, many of these subjects reported that they had seen a stop sign in the pictures viewed. This misleading question introduced information that was not initially available into reconstructed memory. More recent research supports the creation of false memories (e.g., Loftus, 2004). Memories are not permanent—they are altered as new information is introduced and motivations change. Each time a memory is retrieved, the potential is there for substitution or alteration; "the contents of the interview may not reflect a person's earlier experience and attitudes so much as their current picture of the past" (Loftus, 1980, p. 50); "misinformation can alter memory by creating new visual memories for details that were presented only verbally" (Belli & Loftus, 1996, p. 165).

Checklists and Personality Inventories

Checklists and personality inventories are forms of self-report and are susceptible to sources of error and bias similar to those described in the discussion of verbal reports (e.g., see Fischer & Corcoran, 2007; Segal & Hersen, 2010). The use of self-report inventories typically involves the assumption that the client's report provides accurate accounts of feelings, attitudes, behaviors, and related events. In fact, they may not reflect experiences either in the past or present. Scales allowing only yes or no answers may yield different answers than those that allow a range of answers. Concerns about personality tests are similar to those used in educational settings. That is, tests may be used for both predictive as well as prescriptive purposes; however, they may not offer correct predictions concerning future behavior, nor may they offer guidelines about how to achieve desired outcomes. For example, test results may offer no information about the reasons for a given score, whether correct or incorrect, healthy or not. Normative data allowing comparison of a client with others may not be available. Checklists tend to emphasize problems rather than resources (e.g., see Eyberg & Ross, 1978). Overall scores are often used to describe a client, encouraging trait conceptions that obscure the situational variability of behavior. Personality tests, as well as intelligence tests, may be used in a static manner to describe a client at a given time, rather than in a process manner to reflect where the client can go. Tests are subject to faking of responses. Problems of reliability and validity are often overlooked.

Self-Monitoring

Self-monitoring, in which clients keep track of behaviors, thoughts, feelings, and the circumstances related to them in real-life settings, offers another potential source of information (e.g., see Bloom, Fischer, & Orme, 2009; Watson & Tharp, 2007). Depressed clients may keep track of negative thoughts as well as the situations in which they occur; clients who complain about anxiety may note the circumstances related to changes in anxiety level and rate their subjective anxiety level. Benjamin Franklin used self-monitoring to keep track of various virtues such as temperance ("Eat not to dullness") and tranquility ("Be not disturbed by trifles"; Silverman, 1986). Smartphones facilitate self-monitoring. Such data can be plotted for review. Advantages of self-monitoring include lack of expense, lack of intrusion by outside observers, and helping clients to explore the relationship of behaviors, thoughts, and feelings to environmental events such as the reactions of other people. Whether clients will gather information and how representative this information will be depends partly on whether a feasible data-gathering method is designed that matches client skills and opportunities and whether the client understands the procedures involved in and the purpose of monitoring.

Variables that influence the reactivity of self-recording (that is, the degree to which recording a behavior alters how often it occurs) include the motivation the client has to change a behavior and the nature of the behavior monitored. The timing of self-recording (whether it occurs before or after a behavior of concern, such as smoking) and the kind of recording device used also influence reactivity. Setting performance goals and offering reinforcement for attaining these increase the reactive effects of self-monitoring. Many steps can be taken to increase the accuracy of self-monitoring, such as clearly defining what is to be recorded. Self-anchored scales can be used to assess events (such as urges and negative thoughts). These are individually tailored for each client. A client may choose to monitor her depression on a scale ranging from 1 (slightly down) to 5 (very depressed). Advantages include flexibility in designing a scale that matches the unique circumstances of each client. Because these are individually constructed, no norms are available allowing comparison of the client's responses with those of others. In addition, no information may be available about reliability and validity.

Monitoring the Behavior of Significant Others

Clients may gather useful information regarding significant others. Factors that affect accuracy of self-monitoring also affect the accuracy of information noted about the behavior of others. If people know their behavior is being observed, there may be reactive effects, as there are in self-monitoring. The observer's behavior may change as a result of observing someone else.

The Use of Structured Analogues

Analogues (role-plays) include those in which clients interact together but do so in an artificial setting (such as the office), as well as contexts in which clients participate in role-playing with someone other than a real-life participant (such as with a psychologist rather than a parent; Heyman & Slep, 2004; Kerig & Lindahl, 2004). They are used to access relevant interactions. Dismissal of such data because of concerns about faking of behavior has been found to be unbased. Dishion and Granic (2004) observe: "In fact, it appears that a hallmark of a disturbed relationship is the inability to fake good under the watchful eye of outside observers" (p. 145). Advantages of the use of analogues include convenience and efficiency. Information can be gathered without going into the natural environment. The more similar the role-play is to real-life conditions, the more likely behavior seen will be representative of that in real life. Role-plays are used both in assessment of social interactions and in developing effective social skills.

Observation in the Natural Environment

Advantages of observation in real-life settings include the opportunity to view clients in their natural environments. Disadvantages include cost and inconvenience, restriction of observed data to overt behavior, intrusiveness, and reactive effects of observation (that is, being observed may alter interactions). For example, when parents were aware they were being observed, they played more, were more positive in their verbal behaviors, and structured their children's activities more than when they were unaware of being observed (Zegiob, Arnold, & Forehand, 1975). Such effects are usually temporary, and many steps can be taken to increase the likelihood of gaining representative data (Hartman, Barrios, & Wood, 2004). Detailed observation of family interaction is a key data collection method used by researchers at the Oregon Research Institute in their exploration concerning antisocial behavior of children and adolescents (Reid, Patterson, & Snyder, 2002). The Living in Familiar Environments (LIFE) Coding System is used to describe both depressive and aggressive behaviors (Hops, Davis, & Longoria, 1995). The latter include behaviors indicating anger or irritability, such as yelling and verbal criticism and threats. The former include crying, looking down, and self-derogatory and complaining behaviors. Davis, Sheeber, and Hops (2002) view these two classes of behavior as distinct forms of conflict behavior (p. 176). Observation of parent-child behavior is a key part of assessment in many behavioral parent training programs. A variety of coding systems have been developed for observing students in classroom settings (Volpe, DiPerna, Hintze, & Shapiro, 2005). (See also www.incredibleyears.com.)

Many clinicians are not trained how to carefully observe interaction—to identify specific behaviors, as well as related cues and consequences. Lack of training increases the likelihood of biased observation (Hartman, Barrios, & Wood, 2004). The same objective situation may create different emotional reactions; because of different past experiences, two people may see an event quite differently. Use of handheld computers allows data collection and analysis of interaction patterns in a time-efficient manner (Richard & Lauterbach, 2004). Decisions must be made about what, when, where, how long, and whom to observe, as well as how to remain unobtrusive. The more vague the categories used to describe behaviors, the lower the reliability in coding behaviors; vague terms make it difficult or impossible for observers to agree on referents. Overlooking the value of observation contributes to the fundamental attribution error, in which problems are incorrectly attributed to clients' personal characteristics and related environmental circumstances are overlooked. (For further information, see Reid, Patterson, & Snyder, 2002; Rosenbaum, 2002.) Criteria for observing and judging observational reports suggested by Ennis (1987) include:

- Minimal inferences required.
- Short time interval between observation and report.
- Report by observer, rather than someone else (that is, not hearsay).
- If a report is based on a record, it is generally best that:
    - The record was close in time to the observation.
    - The record was made by the observer.
    - The record was made by the reporter.
    - The statement was believed by the reporter, either because of a prior belief in its correctness or because of a belief that the observer was habitually correct.
- Corroboration.
- Possibility of corroboration.
- Conditions of good access.
- Competent use of technology, if technology is useful.
- Satisfaction by observer (and reporter, if a different person) of credibility criteria. (Ennis, 1987, p. 13)

Case Records

Case records are often consulted to gather information. Records take time to write and to read and have important purposes such as facilitating clinical decision makng. Deficiencies of case records include missing or vague information, a focus on pathology, and neglect of client assets. Written reports are based on one or more sources of information already discussed and so may reflect errors associated with them. Often, the source of information is not noted. If a case record states that "Mrs. M. is an alcoholic," does it give the source of this information? Did the author of this report directly witness related behavior? If so, where? How often did he or she witness it? What does *alcoholic* mean? Clinicians are often willing to accept vague statements in case records without asking such questions. Tallent (1988) has written an engaging and valuable book on psychological report writing in which pitfalls in recording are described. As he notes, these are remarkably persistent over time (see Tallent, 4th edition, 1993). His research was based on a survey of psychologists, psychiatrists, and social workers concerning problems with psychological reports. He divided pitfalls in recording into five categories:

1. *Problems of content* included omission of essential information, inclusion of irrelevant data, and unnecessary duplication.

2. *Problems of interpretation* referred to overspeculation, unlabeled speculation, and inadequate differentiation. Examples of unlabeled speculation were drawing conclusions from insufficient data, expressing theory as fact, and not relating inferences to the tests they presumably are derived from. Overspeculation is a kind of irresponsible interpretation, and seems to irritate readers. "Facts, inferences, speculations are often mixed and not labeled" (Tallent, 1988, p. 31). "The distinctions between reasonable deduction from the data, speculative extrapolations from the data, and the psychologist's clinical impression are not clear" (p. 31). Inadequate differentiation refers to reports that deal in generalities: "They tend to present generalizations that might apply to anyone rather than to the particular individual" (p. 32).

3. *Problems of attitude and orientation* included complaints about lack of practical use, exhibitionism, excessive authoritativeness, test oriented rather than client oriented, and overly theoretical. Concerns included the following: "A lack of humility. I never cease to be amazed by the confidence some psychologists have in their tests and in their own abilities to interpret them. To accept such reports the psychiatrist would have to lose what little intelligence he or she is supposed to have" (1988, pp. 33–34). "They often are too theoretical or academic in language to be comprehensible or meaningful in terms of future treatment goals for the client. They occasionally give us the feeling that no client was present at the time" (p. 34).

4. *Problems of communication* included vagueness, unnecessary length (wordiness), excessive technicality and complexity, style problems, poor organization, and hedging. Complaints included the following: "Often padded with meaningless multi-syllable words to lengthen report" (1988, p. 36). "They are too often written in a horrible psychologese—so that clients 'manifest overt aggressive hostility in an impulsive manner'—when, in fact, they punch you on the nose" (p. 36). "They suffer mainly from vagueness, double-talk and universality without enough of an attempt being made to specify more precisely what sets this person off from other people (and what does not)" (p. 37). "Too often

they are so poorly organized that the reader has a difficult time to get a clear psychological picture of the client" (p. 39). "When several tests have been administered, many psychologists cannot integrate the findings without giving separate results for each test" (p. 39). "They too often are riddled with qualification—'it appears that,' 'it may well be,' 'the test reports indicate.' This is fine when speculation is being introduced, but many reports merely convey the inadequacy and timidity of the writer" (p. 39).

5. *Problems of science and profession* referred to criticism based on characteristics of research and professions rather than of individuals. Examples included lack of agreement as to how reports should be written, inadequate theories of behavior, and unreliability of diagnostic categories. Problems of role conduct were also mentioned: "They frequently do not mind their own business and go beyond their ken—invading territory properly allocated to the MD" (1988, p. 41). Many social workers reported that psychologists invade the realm of the psychiatrist.

These various pitfalls become downfalls, as Tallent (1988, p. 233) suggested, in the courtroom, when lawyers critique a clinician's credibility and conclusions. Problems with validity and reliability that are overlooked by clinicians are often the focus in court. Errors that are especially common include overinterpretation, omission of needed information, and hedging.

Physiological and Biological Markers (DNA) Measures

Physiological measures are often used for assessment and evaluation of progress, especially in behavioral medicine. Measures include pulse rate, blood pressure, muscle tension, respiration rates, Palmer sweat index, and urine analysis. Here, too, questions of reliability and validity are important. For example, accuracy of urine analysis in relation to drug use varies widely over different laboratories. Reports may be deliberately falsified. Tests of genes are widely promoted. Do these offer valuable information?

Other Sources

Police reports, school records, and other sources of archival data may be used. Sources of error here include missing information and changes in procedures that may result in spurious increases or decreases in reported frequency. Clients may be referred to other professionals, for example, to evaluate special skills or abilities. How valid are assessment methods used? Are inferences well reasoned? Are claims made on questionable grounds (e.g., what is usual practice)? Don't be intimidated by credentials and degrees. If you are working with people who are indeed professionals, they will welcome questions about their assumptions and will take the initiative in telling you about any limitations of tests used and assumptions made.

WEIGHING THE VALUE OF DATA

Variables that influence judgments about the accuracy of data include recency (how recent an observation was), the source, and the capability of the source to offer the data presented. Other criteria include:

- Expertise
- Lack of conflict of interest
- Agreement among sources
- Reputation (e.g., for careful habits)
- Use of established procedures
- Known risk to reputation
- Ability to give reasons

Reliability

As discussed earlier in this chapter, a measure cannot be valid if responses vary in consistency. Claims of reliability should be accompanied by facts and figures: What kind of reliability was measured? Was this appropriate? Were other kinds assessed? Were reliability ratings .80 or above?

Validity

What evidence is there that a measure accurately assesses what it is purported to measure? Here too, we should be given information regarding the kind of validity assessed (see prior discussion), as well as facts and figures, such as the correlation between a gold standard and a measure that should be .80 or higher (for example, between role-played exchanges and a self-report instrument). As with reliability, published reports often make claims about validity but provide no related facts and figures.

Relevance

"So what?" Are data collected relevant? Do they help to clarify hoped-for outcomes and related factors? Clinical decisions are influenced by irrelevant as well as by relevant data.

Collection of additional material is not necessarily helpful and may decrease accuracy as well as take time to gather and record it.

What's Missing?

Another helpful rule is to ask, "What is missing?" For example, data for some of the four cells in a contingency table are often missing (see Chapter 14). We tend to collect data that support our preconceptions and favored theories unless we make it a habit to explore alternative well-argued views. You may be tempted to rely on measures that are available and easy to use but are irrelevant or misleading. Compromises will often be necessary between feasibility and accuracy. You will often have to settle for measures that, although imprecise, provide helpful guidelines. Accuracy can be improved by using multiple methods, relying especially on those most likely to offer accurate, relevant data. Decisions about trade-offs between harms and benefits of particular methods usually involve subjective judgments that cannot be answered solely on evidentiary grounds. (Challenges in integrating data are discussed in Chapter 11.)

RECORDING AND STORING INFORMATION

Clinicians are required to keep records, and, depending on where they work, may spend considerable time recording. Munro (2011) estimates that social workers in child welfare in the United Kingdom spend 60% of their time on documentation requirements, allowing all too little time for face-to-face contact with families and children. Computerized recording is becoming common. Guidelines for recording are offered in Exhibit 13.5. Lapses in memory highlight the value of records. The importance of case records is affirmed by court rulings that inadequate records hinder the development of treatment plans (e.g., see *Whitree v. New York State*, 1968). Records are helpful to the extent to which they fulfill the purposes of recording: These include administrative, case planning, and supervisory functions. Information should be easy to locate. Information retrieval skills are vital to evidence-based practice to gain swift access to information needed in case records (for example, about progress), as well as access to research findings related to important decisions. Well-designed forms permit ready location of material as well as reminders to include helpful data.

Exhibit 13.5 Quality Check of Psychological Reports

	Yes	No
1. The report meets ethical and legal responsibilities to the client and community, and (as applicable) to other professionals and agencies.	☐	☐
2. Material is up-to-date.	☐	☐
3. Presenting concerns are clearly described as well as how the client arrived at your office (for example, who referred the client).	☐	☐
4. Clear examples of client concerns and related circumstances are given.	☐	☐
5. Sources of assessment data relied on are clearly described.	☐	☐
6. The evidentiary status of assessment and intervention methods used are clearly described.	☐	☐
7. Hoped-for outcomes are clearly described.	☐	☐
8. Conclusions are supported by data.	☐	☐
9. Speculation is within reason and is labeled as such.	☐	☐
10. There is an absence of jargon, stereotypes, and overly technical or complex language.	☐	☐
11. Language used is clear and unambiguous.	☐	☐
12. The record includes a clear description of degree of progress.	☐	☐
13. Outcome(s) focused on is/are directly related to presenting concerns.	☐	☐
14. Measures used to describe progress are clear and relevant.	☐	☐
15. The report is concise and well organized.	☐	☐
16. Uninformative labels are avoided.	☐	☐
17. All important information is given, including demographic data, relevant historical information, and current life circumstances.	☐	☐
18. Self-report is complemented by observation when relevant and feasible.	☐	☐
19. Client assets and social supports are noted.	☐	☐
20. Intervention methods are clearly described.	☐	☐

Source: Items 1 through 11 are from *Psychological Report Writing* (3rd ed., p. 244), by N. Tallent, 1988, Englewood Cliffs, NJ: Prentice Hall. Copyright 1988 by Prentice Hall.

SUMMARY

Gathering data is a key step in clinical decision making. Decisions are made about what data to collect, how to gather data, and when to stop. Sources of information include self-report; self-monitoring; observation (in interviews, in analogue situations, or in real life); personality inventories; physiological measures; and case records. Each source has advantages and disadvantages. Familiarity with the strengths and weaknesses of each will be helpful in selecting those that offer accurate data. Some clinicians confine their attention to self-report, forgoing other valuable sources such as self-monitoring and observation in real-life settings that may correct biases in self-report data. Practice theories guide how clients and their circumstances are viewed, which in turn affects what data are gathered. We are influenced by our preconceptions. We often pay undue attention to data that are vivid (high-intensity temper tantrums) and ignore data that do not have this quality yet nevertheless may be helpful (e.g., failure of parents to reinforce positive behaviors). Broad generalizations may be based on small samples, reflecting an insensitivity to the size of the samples on which inferences are based.

Many studies highlight the difficulty of distinguishing between inferences and descriptions; when descriptions are asked for, inferences may be offered. Clinicians often gather too much data, and they tend to be overly confident of the accuracy of data gathered and assumptions made. Combining data from different sources is a challenge. Taking advantage of related research findings regarding the accuracy of different sources, including errors associated with various kinds of data, will help you to avoid errors. The value of data is related to its reliability, validity, and completeness. As in other problem-solving situations, what is missing may not be obvious—but may be critical in understanding clients and their potential for change.

14

Discovering Causes of Clients' Problems: Common Biases

Clinical practice requires making judgments about the causes of clients' concerns. The history of public health, medicine, psychiatry, and psychology is strewn with fascinating examples of skilled (and not so skilled) detective work in the identification of causes. The time lag between identification of a causative factor and acceptance of this information is often discouragingly long. Consider the lag in implementing knowledge that scurvy could be prevented by eating citrus fruit (Carpenter, 1986) or that fatal infections could be avoided by having physicians wash their hands after examining each patient (Sinclair, 1909). Consider also the belief that tuberculosis was inherited.

Assessment is integrally related to intervention; that is, how concerns are structured and what causal factors are assumed to be important influence selection of intervention methods. Indeed, if plans are not successful, assessment errors could be a reason. Beliefs about how events are related stem from many sources. Some originate from summaries of empirical data; some rest on informed expert opinion or systematic observation; others are based on myths, fables, metaphors, and maxims that may or may not reflect reality (Nisbett & Ross, 1980, p. 117). Focusing on incorrect causes of a problem may worsen a situation. Consider the client who complained about abdominal pains at bedtime (Valins & Nisbett, 1972). The therapist interpreted these as pains related to sexual anxiety. As a result, the client became concerned about her emotional stability. Her anxiety and her negative image of herself increased. Later, a relative suggested that her pain might be caused by an allergic reaction to tomatoes; the client stopped eating tomatoes, and the pains disappeared.

Cues that may be used to infer causality include temporal order, contiguity in time and space, similarity of cause and effect, covariation, and availability of alternative possibilities (Einhorn & Hogarth, 1986). The presumed cause must occur before the presumed effect; the correlation must be consistent; and it must be shown that a third variable is not responsible for the relationship between the two variables. Attention to only one of these conditions can result in post hoc reasoning—the assumption that because one event follows another, it is caused by it (the post hoc ergo propter hoc fallacy—or the fallacy of the consequent). Haynes (1992) argues that constant conjunction (two events always occur together) is not applicable to the social sciences because of the complexity of causes related to behavior; past events may influence current behaviors (Haynes & O'Brien, 2000). Variables related to client concerns may be *necessary* (a condition that must be present if the effect occurs), *sufficient* (a condition that by itself will bring about change), or *necessary and sufficient* (a condition that must be present for an effect to occur and one that by itself will bring about an effect). Many different kinds of causes are possible:

- *Sufficient cause:* Y occurs whenever X occurs: therefore, X is sufficient to cause Y; X must precede Y if X is a cause of Y.
- *Insufficient cause:* That cause that, *by itself*, is insufficient to produce the effect, but can function as a causal variable in combination with other variables.
- *Necessary cause:* Y never occurs without X.
- *Necessary and sufficient cause:* Y occurs whenever X occurs, and Y never occurs without X.
- *First cause:* That cause upon which all others depend—the earliest event in a causal chain.
- *Principal cause:* That cause upon which the effect *primarily* depends.
- *Immediate cause:* That cause that produces the effect without any intervening events.
- *Mediate cause:* A cause that produces its effect only through another cause (Haynes, 1992, p. 26).

Assessment is an ongoing feature of clinical practice; additional information concerning causal factors usually is gained as work proceeds. These data may or may not require changes in decisions. Elstein and his colleagues (1978) reported that physicians generated hypotheses early in the process of thinking about a problem, and that only a few were considered. Kuipers and Kassirer (1984) found that expert physicians used only factors considered particularly relevant about a case; they restricted their attention to a relatively small model. Research describing how decisions are made in the natural environment (e.g., Zsambok & Klein, 1997) shows that experts in an area do not review a variety of alternatives before reaching a decision; they quickly arrive at an option based on situation awareness (on the recognition of patterns) as discussed in Chapter 9. Findings regarding use of fast and frugal heuristics support this finding (Gigerenzer, Hertwig, & Pachur, 2011). Such research raises questions about programs that recommend a long search. This should be reassuring to clinicians who must make decisions in a timely manner. However, in novel situations in which an option is not readily obvious, a more analytic style of thinking may be required.

CHALLENGES

Causal factors differ in how long it takes for a cause to affect behavior (latency) and the time required to stabilize an effect (equilibrium). Causal effects may depend on critical periods such as developmental stage. Identifying the causes of behavior is difficult because (1) they may be unknown; (2) they occur at different levels (e.g., physiological, psychological, sociological); (3) they interact in complex or simple ways; (4) they change over time; and (5) they are influenced by chance occurrences (Haynes, 1992). Assessment requires the integration of diverse sources of data, which is difficult. Different aspects of a concern (onset, duration, intensity) may be influenced by different causes. A variety of fallacies occur as shown in Exhibit 14.1.

Clients often have multiple problems that are interrelated in a variety of ways. These may include relationship problems, addiction problems, as well as problems with anxiety and anger. Identical forms of behavior may have different functions (be maintained by different contingencies). A given problem may develop via different

Exhibit 14.1 Fallacies Related to Causal Reasoning

- Inferring cause from correlation
- Post hoc ergo propter hoc (or after this, therefore because of this)
- Confounding necessary and sufficient cause
- Argumentum ad ignorantiam (or arguing from ignorance)
- Fallacy of division (community/individual fallacy, Rose's fallacy)
- Fallacy of accident
- Fallacy of composition
- Confusion of cause and effect
- Domino or slippery slope fallacy
- Perfectionist fallacy
- Irrelevant conclusion (irrelevant thesis, fallacy of diversion, red herring)
- False dilemma
- Ad populum (or appealing to the people)
- Objectionable vagueness
- Equivocation

Source: Based on *Evidence-Based Practice: Logic and Critical Thinking in Medicine* (p. 54), by M. Janicek and D. L. Hitchcock, 2005, Chicago, IL: American Medical Association.

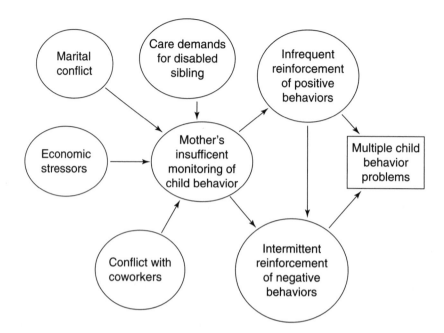

Exhibit 14.2 A Model Illustrating Extended Systems Variables Affecting a Child's Behavior Problems

Source: From *Principles and Practice of Behavioral Assessment* (p. 188), by S. N. Haynes and W. H. O'Brien, 2000, New York: Kluwer Academic/Plenum Publishers. Reprinted with permission.

pathways and manifest itself in a variety of ways (see Exhibit 14.2). (For a detailed discussion of the complexity of causal relationships, see Haynes, 1992, and Haynes & O'Brien, 2000.)

A given cause may affect behavior differently at different times and places. Rarely can we point to necessary and sufficient conditions related to problems. Contributory causes often come into play that create the total set of conditions necessary and sufficient for an effect. The strength of causal variables differs among individuals with the same concerns. People differ on:

- The number of variables that influence a behavior.
- Variables that influence the onset, magnitude, and duration of behavior.
- The relative strength of individual causal variables.
- The role of mediating variables.
- Predispositions and vulnerability to particular events.
- The setting generality of causal relationships.
- The paths through which causal effects occur. (Haynes, 1992, p. 108)

Beliefs about causes differ in the extent to which they are compatible with empirical findings about behavior; for instance, claims of levitation (the ability to float in the air) are not compatible with the laws of gravity. Ideally, intervention should focus on key causal variables. This requires estimating the weights of different factors. Identification of causes is not necessarily explanatory; that is, the cause of an illness (such as cancer) may be known, and the symptoms and associated pathology may be identifiable, but the etiology may not be understood. Thus, causes differ in the level of explanatory completeness they offer. People use different criteria to decide when an explanation is at hand (e.g., it allows accurate prediction—it makes sense). Causes may be difficult to identify because of a lag in effect, as between smoking and the development of lung cancer.

Kuhn (1993) examined the kind of evidence used to support theories about alleged causes of a problem. She divided this into three kinds. One was *genuine evidence*. Criteria here were: (a) it is distinguishable from description of the causal inference itself, and (b) it bears on its correctness. Kinds of covariation evidence included: (1) correspondence (evidence that does no more than note a co-occurrence of antecedent and outcome), (2) covariation (there is a comparison or quantification), and (3) correlated change (does b change after a?). In appealing to evidence external to the causal sequence, we go beyond the antecedent and outcome themselves to invoke some additional, external factor such as appealing to external evidence (counterfactual arguments). Kinds of indirect evidence coded included: (1) analogy (particular to particular), (2) assumption (general to particular), (3) discounting (elimination of alternatives), and (4) partial discounting. Another major category included *pseudoevidence*. Kuhn describes pseudoevidence as taking the form of scenario or general script depicting how the phenomena might occur. They are usually expressed in general terms. Defining characteristics that distinguish pseudoevidence from genuine evidence is that, in contrast to the latter, pseudoevidence cannot be sharply distinguished from description of the causal sequence itself. There are generalized scripts and scripts as unfalsifiable illustrations. Here subjects equate evidence with examples. An example is viewed as sufficient to account for the phenomenon and counterexamples are dismissed as exceptions. It is assumed that because the examples are proved, the theory is proved. Last, Kuhn used a category of *no evidence* (either genuine or pseudo) offered in relation to the theory proposed. Included here are: (a) implications that evidence is unnecessary or irrelevant, (b) assertions not connected to a causal theory, or (c) citing the phenomenon itself as evidence regarding its cause.

DIFFERENT THEORIES EMPHASIZE DIFFERENT CAUSES

Assumptions about causes are influenced by practice theories; these theories guide selection and organization of material. Premature acceptance of one kind of explanation may interfere with discovering alternative views that yield intervention knowledge. Explanations differ in the system level(s) to which they appeal (e.g., biological,

Exhibit 14.3 Ways in Which Theories of Behavior Differ

Degree to which behavior is viewed as knowable.

Goals pursued (e.g., explanation and interpretation alone, understanding based on prediction and influence).

Criteria used to evaluate claims (e.g., tradition, consensus, scientific).

Range of problems addressed with success.

Causal importance attributed to psychological factors (e.g., feelings/thoughts).

Causal importance attributed to biomedical factors (e.g., genetic and/or brain differences).

Attention devoted to evolutionary influences.

Importance attributed to developmental stages.

Range of environmental factors considered (e.g., family, community, society).

Importance attributed to past experiences.

Degree of optimism about how much change is possible.

Degree to which related assumptions can be critically tested.

Degree of empirical support (evidence for and against a theory).

Note: The terms explanation and theory are used interchangeably.

psychological, sociological) and how integrative they are (the extent to which relationships among different factors are recognized) (see Exhibit 14.3). Contextual theories encourage a broad search for causes, including attention to the role of significant others (individuals who influence clients), community characteristics, and even global influences such as the biomedical-industrial complex (Petryna, Lakoff, & Kleinman, 2006). Consider the classic study by Wahler (1980) in which he found that the nature of a mother's social contacts outside the home influenced the quality of her interaction with her children at home. Reid, Patterson, and Snyder (2002) describe the effect of environmental factors such as poverty on family interaction patterns and resulting behaviors, such as antisocial behavior of children and adolescents. Galea et al. (2011) links the role of poverty to mortality. A contextual (ecological) view of excessive alcohol use would entail far more than a description of individual characteristics that may encourage related behaviors including attention to neighborhood characteristics and promotion of alcohol in the media. A given theory may be applied to an increasing range of concerns, even though it may not be the most appropriate one in these many instances. Seeking feedback regarding the effects of intervention will decrease this tendency.

Different views of behavior have different consequences in relation to how people are treated. Controversies include the relative importance attributed to biological, psychological, and environmental factors, and how the environment is defined. Consider different views concerning the cause of attention-deficit/hyperactivity disorder (ADHD). Some investigators assume that related behaviors are caused by a brain disease (Barkley et al., 2002). Others argue that our capitalistic consumer-oriented society, which encourages competition, a focus on the self, and use of medications, encourages promoting (mis)behaviors on the part of children as psychiatric problems, overlooking changes in work and family life, such as less time spent by parents with their children and dulling school environments (Timimi & Taylor, 2004; Timini, 2008). These views have different intervention implications (e.g., medication compared to altering environmental circumstances). Some systems and beliefs are institutionalized in a society and have been referred to as "grand narratives"—for example, the great religions of the world, major political ideologies such as capitalism, and biomedicine (Davey & Seale, 2002). There is general agreement that behavior varies; that it is influenced by a variety of variables; that it can be analyzed at different levels (e.g., physiological, psychological, sociological); and that there is a great deal of individual variation in response to different environmental risks, resulting in different degrees of vulnerability and resilience (e.g., Jensen & Fraser, 2011; Worthman, Plotsky, Schlecter, & Cummings, 2010). Examples of variables that may come into play include temperamental and other genetic influences, past experiences, risk experiences and how we view them, protective features that counteract risks, and later circumstances. Views that emphasize the interactions among genes, organisms, and their environments differ in how reciprocal these relationships are assumed to be and in the range of environmental events considered.

A biomedical grand narrative dominates practice in many areas. The client is viewed as having an illness (mental) in need of a diagnosis and treatment (Conrad, 2007; Conrad & Potter, 2000). Hallmarks of a disease include a known etiology (cause), a predictable course, and a progression in severity if left untreated. Factors focused on may include biochemical changes, brain damage, and genetic differences. Beliefs that "something in the blood" or "something in the food" is related to mental illness have a long history and are reflected in current treatments, some of which are of dubious value (Skrabanek, 1990). The finding of biochemical abnormalities related to certain behavior patterns only establishes that abnormalities in biochemistry are present, not that they cause the behavior. (See critiques of neuroimaging methods, Leo & Cohen, 2003; Vul et al., 2009.) And the finding that medication decreases anxiety or depression does not show that biomedical factors are responsible for anxiety and depression. Mirowsky and Ross (2003) argue that biochemical changes may result from stress caused by limited opportunities due to discrimination. Adverse life events affect the length of telomeres (Drury et al., 2011; Tyrka, Price, Kao, Porton, & Marsella, 2010). (For a critique of biomedical approaches to deviant behavior, see Boyle, 2002; Gorenstein, 1992; Moncrieff, 2008.) In 1999 the U.S. surgeon general concluded that there was no anatomical, biochemical, or functional sign that reliably distinguishes between the brains of mental patients and those of others. Still, at that time, hundreds of problems in living were claimed to be mental illnesses. This remains true today. There are indications that the brain is altered, perhaps forever, by taking neuroleptic medication (e.g., see Whittaker, 2010).

Physical abnormalities in the brain may be assumed to be responsible for certain kinds of troubled or troubling behavior. Even when brain damage can be detected, it does not necessarily indicate that it causes any particular behavioral pattern. Problems with these kinds of explanations include limited intervention knowledge and predictive validity. Alberto and Troutman (1990) argue that biophysical explanations give teachers excuses not to teach. Such explanations are incomplete. For instance, environmental factors may also be important.

> To say that Rachel can't walk, talk, or feed herself because she is retarded tells us nothing about the conditions under which Rachel might learn to perform these behaviors. . . . Even apparently constitutional differences in temperament are so vulnerable to environmental influences as to provide only limited information about how a child is apt to behave under given conditions. (Alberto & Troutman, 1990, p. 9)

Human experience is complex, affected not only by inheritance, but by unique environmental circumstances as shown even in infant and twin studies (Plomin, 2011). Kleinman and Fitz-Henry (2007) argue that biological reductionism fails "to account for the enormous complexity of human social experience—war, genocide, structural violence, poverty and displacement—and the highly nuanced subjective states that those experiences engender . . . or even the more 'routine' violence of social neglect and institutionalized racism" (p. 53). Anthropologists highlight the interplay of individuals and their unique circumstances. Experience "has as much to do with collective reality [e.g., dependence on medication] as it does with individual translations and transformations of those realities. It is simultaneously social and subjective, collective and individual" (Kleinman & Fitz-Henry, 2007, p. 53).

Currently there is great interest in searching for genetic markers for physical and psychological signs and symptoms. Some argue that genotype (genetic makeup) can never be separated from phenotype (visible characteristics that result from the interaction between the genotype and the environment), because both the environment and random developmental factors affect how genotype is expressed (Lewontin, 1991, 1995, 2009; Strohman, 2003). People with a common genetic history often share a similar environmental history. Even when a genetic influence is found, it may account for only a small portion of the variance in understanding a problem or behavior. Although many people accept the findings of twin studies purporting to show a strong hereditary component to developing schizophrenia, others do not, pointing out methodological flaws (e.g., see Boyle, 2002). An epigenetic approach is now widely accepted.

> Certainly genes are essential for defining any phenotype but by themselves they remain just inert materials. In order for genetic information to be

replicated or "decoded" and used to assemble phenotypes, the DNA must first be manipulated by systems of enzymes and small molecules that constitute the efficient cause for constructing phenotypes. Nearly all biologists now acknowledge that reality—an epigenetic system, so named because of its ability to activate and silence elements of DNA and thereby to produce specific patterns of gene expression and proteins in a context-dependent (time and place) manner. (Strohman, 2003, p. 190)

In developmental explanations there is an "unfolding" metaphor, in which the role of internal characteristics is emphasized (e.g., see Sameroff, Lewis, & Miller, 2000). The term *development* refers to "the process of continual change during the lifetime of an organism" (Lewontin, 1995, p. 121). There has been great interest in developmental psychopathology. Some argue that what are viewed as developmental changes in fact reflect changing environments. Variables such as age and social class are "marker variables" that correlate with many problems but do not explain them or provide intervention guidelines (Baer, 1984, 1987). The similarities of circumstances for many people at a given age in a society may lead one to assume (incorrectly) that biological development is responsible, overlooking the role of similar contingencies. Acceptance of a stage theory of development may get in the way of identifying environmental factors that can be rearranged. That is, it may be incorrectly assumed that a person is stuck in a given stage and there is nothing to do but wait for time to pass. Some scholars suggest that acceptance of Piagetian stages resulted in withholding valuable learning experiences from children, on the grounds that they were not ready.

Psychoanalytic views emphasize the role of early childhood experiences and related unconscious influences on behavior, thoughts, and feelings. In cognitive explanations, a causal role is attributed to thoughts. There is an interest in identifying and altering mental events such as expectations, schemas (views of the self and world), and attributions. In behavioral views, theory, actions, thoughts, and feelings are considered to be largely a function of our learning history. Varied social histories result in a wide range of behavior. Thus, in this approach behavior always "makes sense" (Layng, 2009). Behavior that may seem quite bizarre typically serves adaptive functions, but only when contingencies of reinforcement (relationships between behaviors and their consequences) are clarified may they become apparent. Biochemical and genetic influences are assumed to play a role; however, their interaction with learning variables is emphasized. Variations in behavioral views reflect different assumptions about the causes of behavior and what intervention should focus on (e.g., thoughts and/or environmental factors), and also different preferred methodologies (the intensive study of individuals or the study of group differences). In social learning theory, it is assumed that our expectations, goals, and standards are important influences on behavior (Bandura, 1986). Thoughts are considered to play an important role in the complex processes that affect attention and in the degree to which different kinds of interventions are effective. In a radical behavioral view, rather than appealing to feelings and thoughts as explanations for behavior, they are viewed as requiring explanation themselves (e.g., Skinner, 1974).

Lewontin (1994) emphasizes the importance of examining the metaphors we use to think about behavior, such as potential, fitness, development, and adaptation. He contends that common metaphors such as potential and innate capacity are wrong. "There are differences among genotypes, with different consequences in different environments, but there is no way in general, over environments, to rate these innate or intrinsic properties from 'bad' to 'good,' 'high' to 'low,' 'small' to 'big.' There is complete environmental contingency" (1994, p. 19). Furthermore, we play a great role in creating our environments. Lewontin notes that the metaphor of adaptation implies that there is an autonomously determined world to which we change in order to fit. He suggests that based on what little we know about genes, organisms, and environment, a more accurate metaphor is that of construction. "If we want to understand evolution, we must understand it as construction because the actual situation is that organisms make their own environments. They define them. They create them. They change them. They interpret them" (1994, p. 36).

ASSESSING COVARIATIONS

Clinical assessment involves the description of covariations among behaviors, environmental events, and/or personality traits—depending on your preferred practice model. You may note that only when a client fails to state her preferences in a number of social exchanges do angry outbursts occur. We have beliefs (which may or may not be correct) about what kind of traits go together. A clinician may believe that dependent people have a high need for social approval. Beliefs about covariations (what events tend to go together) influence selection of presumed causes, and beliefs about causes influence our judgment of covariations. Assumptions about the strength of association between variables are influenced by their correlation as well as by the implied causal clues in how variables are labeled (Einhorn & Hogarth, 1985). For example, when people were asked to assess the relationship between two variables on a scatterplot, the correlation had to be high to enable a relationship to be perceived (Jennings, Amabile, & Ross, 1982). However, when variables were given labels, the degree of correlation required to see a relationship was much lower.

Confusions between covariation and causation are often easy to spot. That both swimming and ice cream consumption increase in the summer does not mean that one leads to the other. Mistaken assumptions of covariations may not be so easy to spot if they complement beliefs about what events go together, as in the assumption that parental substance abuse will result in similar behavior on the part of their children. The history of science is a fascinating compendium of faulty assumptions of causal effects based on correlations. Even the great British statistician Pearson assumed that a correlation of .50 between a parent's tendency to develop tuberculosis and his or her children's tendency to contract tuberculosis reflected evidence for a hereditary cause of this disease (Blum, 1978). Another example of confusion between covariations and causation can be seen in superstitious behavior. A client may be convinced, for example, that because she had a dream that her mother would die, she is in some way responsible for the death of her mother, which happened shortly after the dream. Thus, mistaken assumptions about covariations may result in incorrect causal assumptions, as reflected in superstitious beliefs, including those related to the effectiveness of the services we offer. Terms that describe personality traits, such as dependent and aggressive, supposedly convey information about the consistency of behavior. Behavior is considered to be a function of both personality characteristics and situational circumstances. Roberts and DelVecchio (2000) reported that personality consistency peaks in one's fifties (about .75). The "big five" factors (e.g., openness, conscientiousness, extraversion, agreeableness, and neuroticism) have been found to predict behaviors in different cultures (e.g., see Church, Katigbak, Reyes, Salanga, Miramontes, & Adams, 2008). (See also Mischel, 2004; Mischel, Shoda, & Mendoza-Denton, 2002.)

The Influence of Preconceptions/Practice Theories

Assumed covariations are influenced by preconceptions about the origins of given behaviors that may have no relation to the true level of covariation of two events. Practice theories are one important source of preconceptions (see prior discussion). We attend to factors that are compatible with our favored practice theory. A clinician favoring cognitive accounts who interviews a depressed woman will attend to her thoughts—what she says to herself. A clinician who emphasizes the role of environmental contingencies will gather information about what the client does, what events she enjoys, what recent changes have occurred in the frequency of these events, and recent factors in her life that may relate to a change in pleasant events. A psychiatrist who favors medical explanations may emphasize a client's medication regime—what medication she is taking (if any) and what changes should be made. A psychoanalytic clinician might concentrate on exploring her past, searching for material that may relate to current complaints. Knowledge about research findings pertinent to client complaints will influence questions asked and what is noticed and therefore what data are at hand when assessing covariations and making causal analyses. Lack of knowledge about the relationship between certain signs and symptoms and underlying causes may result in incorrect decisions.

Illusory Correlations

The influence of preconceptions is highlighted by research on illusory correlations. Clinicians tend to overestimate the degree of covariation between variables, resulting in illusions of validity and reliability. Classic studies by Chapman and Chapman (1967, 1969) illustrate that expectations based on theories and semantic associations overwhelm the influence of data that do not match these expectations or even refute them. They started with the question of how clinicians can persist in reporting associations between certain responses on projective tests and specific clinical symptoms, when research has shown that there is little or no association between these signs and symptoms. In one study, the reports of 32 practicing clinicians who analyzed the Rorschach protocols of homosexual men were reviewed (1969). These clinicians listed signs that had face validity but were empirically invalid as responses characteristic of homosexual men. That is, they selected signs based on "what seemed to go together"—on what ought to exist—rather than on empirically determined associations between signs and the criteria. Clinicians were more likely to report illusory correlations than were lay observers. Illusory correlations are influenced by assumptions about what goes together. We tend to overestimate the size of correlations between factors we believe go together and to underestimate the degree of covariation when we do not have any preconceptions about the relationship between two or more factors (Jennings, Amabile, & Ross, 1982). This tendency is increased by the confirmation bias (not attending to data that do not support a position—ignoring negative instances) and not reviewing all four cells of a contingency table (see later discussion).

Clinicians who believe that behavior is determined mostly by personal characteristics will be less likely to notice correlations between environmental factors and behavior. Shweder (1977) suggests that we tend to blur the distinction between likeness and co-occurrence. Expectations of consistency encourage illusory correlations. That is, we tend to assume that people behave in trait-consistent ways. One reason for this is that "we tend to see most people in a limited number of roles and situations and thus are exposed to a more consistent sample of behavior than we would obtain from a true random sample of a person's behavioral repertoire" (Nisbett & Ross, 1980, p. 107; see also discussion of actor-observer differences in Chapter 9). Apparent discrepancies are readily explained away. Subjective feelings of control are enhanced by the belief that other people are consistent in their traits and thus are predictable.

The ability to detect covariations in specific domains may be greater because we have many opportunities to observe such covariation. Take, for example, the relation between making certain changes in steering when driving a car. In this situation, we benefit from immediate feedback about the effects of our actions.

Experience involving corrective feedback offers an opportunity to observe covariations and helps to correct the influence of inaccurate preconceptions regarding what ought to go together. This highlights the importance of arranging feedback about our assumptions. If preconceptions are rigid and feedback is vague or irrelevant, experience may do little to change incorrect notions, especially in areas such as clinical practice, in which indicators of progress are often vague and outcome often is not systematically monitored. Research regarding fast and frugal heuristics shows that we often do make rapid and accurate decisions, for example, based on the *recognition heuristic*. "If one of two alternatives is recognized, infer that it has the higher value on the criterion" (if recognition validity is greater than .5) (Gigerenzer & Brighton, 2011).

Misunderstanding Probabilities

We tend to focus on hits when estimating covariation; negative instances tend to be disregarded. Consider the belief that there is a relationship between worry about an event and the event occurring. Parents may worry about whether their teenage children will arrive home safely, without getting into a car accident. So, if a mother worries and then her daughter is involved in an accident, the mother (as well as the press) may attribute this coincidence to clairvoyance or some other mystical power. Headlines may read: "Mother Worries—Daughter Injured." As Jensen (1989) notes, only the hits (worry followed by accident) receive attention; false alarms, misses, and correct rejections are ignored. In fact, no judgment of association can legitimately be made without considering all four of the possibilities illustrated in Exhibit 14.4. The risk of an accident if the mother worried would have to be compared to the risk in the absence of worry. In assessing covariations, pointing only to particular cases is misleading. The tendency to discount negative instances is responsible for beliefs in suspect causes such as prayer

Exhibit 14.4 Contingency Table

		Worry	
		Yes	No
		Hit	Miss
	Yes	(Correct positive)	(Incorrect negative)
		(a)	(b)
Accident			
		False alarm	Correct rejection
	No	(Incorrect positive)	(Correct negative)
		(c)	(d)

Source: Based on "Pathologies of Science, Precognition and Modern Psychophysics" (p. 158), by D. D. Jensen, 1989, *The Skeptical Inquirer, 13,* pp.147–160. Reprinted with permission.

and worry. People who say that their prayers are answered may not pay attention to times when their prayers were not answered. That is, they may not keep track of all the times they prayed, noting the outcome of each. "Answered prayers" are more vivid— they may say, "What a coincidence." The confirmation bias (the tendency to selectively search only for evidence that supports preconceptions) encourages a focus on hits. (See Roberts, Ahmed, & Hall, 2004.)

Covariations (and thus causal relationships) often are assumed between certain personal and environmental characteristics (for example, personality traits or recent life changes and problems), and between certain symptoms (e.g., fevers) and diagnostic categories. Decisions about the association between variables often are made without considering the necessary probabilities, for example, symptoms are far more common than diseases. The result is overestimation of pathology. The use of the terms *symptom* and *disease* in this section does not imply acceptance of a biomedical model of problems. These terms are used here because many clinicians use this grand narrative to understand psychological problems. The *DSM-IV-TR* (*Diagnostic and Statistical Manual of Mental Disorders*, American Psychiatric Association, 2000) is based on the assumption that the hundreds of behaviors, thoughts, and feelings described in this source reflect a "mental disorder." Data concerning the diagnostic accuracy of medical tests are often overlooked, resulting in incorrect decisions. Consider overestimates of the accuracy of screening tests such as mammograms (Welch, Schwartz, & Woloshin, 2011). Smedslund (1963) found that nurses tended to focus on joint occurrences of symptom and disease when they were asked to determine whether there was a relationship between symptoms and the disease. Each nurse received a pack of 100 cards, which supposedly depicted excerpts from the files of 100 patients. The presence or absence of the symptom and the presence or absence of the disease were noted on each card in the ratios shown in Exhibit 14.5. About 85% of the nurses said that there was a relationship between the symptoms and the disease, and most justified their claims by noting the number of cards in which both the symptom and the disease were present

Exhibit 14.5 Correlation-Relevant Frequency Information on the Relationship Between a Hypothetical Symptom and Disease in 100 Hypothetical Patients

| | | Disease | | |
		Present	Absent	Total
Symptoms	Present	37	33	70
	Absent	17	13	30
	Total	54	46	

Source: Based on "The Concept of Correlation in Adults," by J. Smedslund, 1963, *Scandinavian Journal of Psychology, 4,* pp. 165–173.

(37); that is, they tended to focus on joint occurrences of symptom and disease and to ignore other combinations.

The probability of A given B is usually not equal to the probability of B given A. For example, the probability of being a male if a person is a head of state is quite different than the probability of being a head of state if a person is a male (Bar-Hillel, 1983). Dawes (1982) reported that the probability of being a chronic smoker if a person develops lung cancer is about .99; the probability of developing lung cancer if a person is a chronic smoker is .10 (people probably die of something else first) (p. 42). Not distinguishing between two such probabilities is known as "the confusion of the inverse." Another source of incorrect estimates is not distinguishing between compound probabilities (the probability of this and that) and conditional probabilities (the probability of this given that). A second principle is as follows: $P(A|B) = P(A,B)/P(B)$. "Simple, and hence conditional, probabilities can be inferred from compound probabilities, but not vice versa. But compound probabilities can be inferred via principle 2 only when both conditional and simple probabilities are known. If just simple or just conditional probabilities are known, however, no other type of probability can be inferred" (Dawes, 1982, pp. 43–44). Consider the probability of being addicted to heroin (A) if a person smokes marijuana (B). This equals the probability of both being addicted to heroin and smoking marijuana (A,B) divided by the probability of smoking marijuana (B). "It is decidedly not equal to $P(A,B)/P(A)$—the probability of both smoking pot and being addicted to heroin divided by the probability of being addicted to heroin; hence the fact that most heroin addicts (A) also smoke pot (A,B) is an irrational justification for draconian marijuana laws" (Dawes, 1982, p. 43).

A third principle is that "the probability of a symptom is equal to the compound probability of the symptom and the disease plus the compound probability of the symptom without the disease: $P(S) = P(S,D) + P(S, \overline{D})$." Dawes uses the example that "the probability of seeing dragonflies on the Rorschach (S) is equal to the probability of seeing dragonflies and being schizophrenic (S,D) plus the probability of seeing dragonflies and not being schizophrenic $(S,\overline{D}$; p. 43). If the probability of the sign without the problem—$P(S,\overline{D})$—is quite high, the probability of the problem given the sign—$P(D|S)$—may be very low, even though $P(S|D)$ is high. This can be presented in a contingency table (see Exhibit 14.4). Determining the probability of a sign given the problem and the probability of the sign without the problem involves comparisons between the columns, whereas the probability of the problem given the sign and probability of the problem without the sign involve row comparisons." Thus, as Dawes notes, if it were known that all schizophrenic patients in a clinic saw dragonflies on the Rorschach and only 10% of nonschizophrenic clients did, but the proportion of clients who were schizophrenics were *not* known, then there would be no way to assess the likelihood that someone who saw dragonflies was schizophrenic.

The probability of a sign or symptom is greater than the probability of a disease or problem because signs are common to many problems; that is, $P(S \mid D) > P(D \mid S)$. Dawes (1982) points out that it is only because so many women have neither cancer nor a positive reading that there is such high agreement between mammogram results and the occurrence of breast cancer. People may believe that the probability of cancer given a positive mammogram is equal to the probability of a positive reading given cancer (Dawes, 1982). Diagnosis is confused with prognosis (Einhorn, 1988). So a positive mammogram is less diagnostic than is presented by many professionals. This results in the performance of too many biopsies (Thornton, Edwards, & Baum, 2003; Welch et al., 2011; see also discussion of using frequencies to correctly interpret test results in Chapter 15). The research that clinicians draw on may overestimate the correlation between variables (spurious correlations) or underestimate this.

Consider also reports of being abused as a child and whether an individual was in fact abused. We must examine all four cells (Dawes, 1994b). We must consider who have and have not reported abuse, and who have actually been abused and those who have not been abused. In everyday practice, only one row of a four-cell contingency table is available to counselors. We do not know who would be represented in the other row (not caught). As Dawes points out, we do not think in comparative terms. "We match (often from memory) rather than compare" (p. 4). Statements that sound convincing may in fact be quite inaccurate. The only way to avoid these errors, as Dawes notes, is to make it a habit to elaborate joint probabilities (to use the information in all four cells of a 2 × 2 contingency table); see also Hastie and Dawes (2001) and the discussion of sensitivity and specificity in Chapter 12.

CAUSAL ANALYSIS

Different cues draw "attention to different aspects of causal strength" (Einhorn & Hogarth, 1985, p. 323). Constant conjunction is represented by cells a and d in Exhibit 14.4; cells b and c represent instances that disconfirm constant conjunction or support alternative accounts. Temporal order is reflected in which variable is selected as causative. Inaccurate assumptions may occur because of a failure to consider alternative explanations or because of false assumptions based on contiguity in time and space. The fallacy of false cause is committed when an event is inaccurately assumed to be the cause of some other event. Consider the case of Clever Hans, the wonder horse (reported by Stanovich, 1998). Clever Hans supposedly could solve mathematical problems. When presented with a problem by his trainer, he would tap out the answers with his hoof. Many testimonials were offered in support of his amazing ability. A psychologist, Oskar Pfungst, decided to study the horse's ability. He systematically altered conditions to search for alternative explanations. This exploration revealed that Clever Hans was an astute observer of human behavior. He watched the head of his trainer as he tapped out his answer. His trainer would tilt his head slightly as Hans approached the correct answer, and Clever Hans would then stop. What are in fact the results of self-selection are often mistakenly attributed to other factors, as in the assumption that since student achievement is superior in private school, private schools are better than public schools.

Conflicts between degree of statistical correlation and cues to causality (such as similarity between two variables) may result in either spurious correlation or an incorrect assumption that variables are not related, based on low or no correlation. Agreement is often confused with accuracy. Although much attention is often devoted during graduate training to sources of and warnings about spurious correlations, little attention may be given to the opposite concern. Quite different causes may be identified by changing which "causal field" is emphasized (Mackie, 1974). For example, clinicians who emphasize dispositional causes focus on a different causal field than do systems-oriented clinicians, who attend to environmental as well as personal causes. Beliefs about which events are causally related to each other influence data selection, as well as data processing and organization. If you believe that childhood experiences account for a client's feelings of loneliness, insight therapy may be selected to increase awareness of how past experiences relate to this concern. Based on this causal analysis, recent environmental changes (such as loss of friends) may be overlooked. A focus on one cause alone may result in inaccurate judgments. This is one reason for holding interdisciplinary case conferences, in which the biases of one kind of professional may be neutralized by the biases of other kinds of professionals. For example, many factors are related to relapse in depression. A focus on only one may result in incorrect assumptions.

Clinicians, like other people, are adept at creating explanations. Once an account is offered, it may bias subsequent search for data. When asked to explain which factors affect their behavior in a situation, people often overlook correct sources of influence and identify irrelevant ones. The particular causes identified depend partly on how advanced knowledge is in an area. For example, causes proposed for explaining variations in behavior change over time; few, if any, clinicians now rely on examination of bumps on the head (see discussion of phrenology in Gamwell & Tomes, 1995). Widespread belief in the occult (Schultz, 1989) and the popularity of a variety of other beliefs illustrate the readiness with which suspect causes are accepted (e.g., see Shermer, 1997). Rules of thumb (heuristics) may increase or decrease the likelihood of identifying accurate causal assumptions.

There is nothing odd or negative about weighing data in relation to causal theories. The problem arises when we invent ad hoc theories and overlook factors that would allow us to make accurate predictions. This tendency may be heightened in an eclectic approach to practice, which increases the likelihood of holding many ad hoc theories or notions. The more tenuous a theory is, the less it should be relied on when assessing data and the more attention should be focused on data. Just as a causal model may not be used in situations in which it is appropriate, it may be applied in situations in which it is inappropriate (Nisbett & Ross, 1980, p. 135).

SOURCES OF ERROR

Influence by initial impressions as well as overlooking the unreliability of data may result in errors. A deterministic causal relationship may be assumed in situations in which the relations are probabilistic, as in the gambler's fallacy (see Chapter 15). Lack of knowledge about empirical data describing interactions between behavior and environmental variables may compromise the quality of judgments. For example, a clinician may be unaware of the ways in which schedules of reinforcement influence behavior and may misattribute the cause of a child's misbehavior in the classroom to personal characteristics—overlooking the role of scheduling effects in the environment (e.g., different patterns of reinforcement for behaviors offered by different teachers; see Alberto & Troutman, 2013). Lack of knowledge about the effects of prescribed drugs may result in missing the true cause of an elderly client's confusion. Sources of errors that may result in inaccurate or incomplete problem structuring are illustrated in Exhibit 14.6.

Misleading Reliance on Similarity

We have beliefs about what types of causal factors are associated with certain effects. One source of error in inferring causal relationships is the assumption that factors related to an event resemble that event. (See also Chapter 10.) In reality, "causes and effects may bear little or no resemblance to one another" (Nisbett & Ross, 1980, p. 117). Everyday explanations of deviant behaviors often rely on causal assumptions based on resemblance, as in bad seed arguments. Nisbett and Ross (1980) note that many causal assumptions within psychoanalytic theory rely on the assumption that symptoms may have identical or opposite characteristics to their psychic causes. Timidity may be presumed to reflect underlying aggressive or hostile tendencies. The form of a behavior may not reveal its function (cause).

Exhibit 14.6 Sources of Error That May Result in Inaccurate or Incomplete Problem Structuring

Source	Description
1. Partiality in the use of evidence	Overlooking, distorting, or discounting contradictory evidence. Giving favored treatment to favored beliefs (see, for example, items 2 to 7).
2. Rationalizing rather than reasoning justifying rather than critiquing	Focusing on building a case for a position rather than gathering information impartially. This is an example of item 1.
3. Focusing on irrelevant or incorrect evidence	Selecting irrelevant or marginally relevant reasons to support beliefs or actions. The conclusion may have nothing to do with the reasons provided.
4. Jumping to conclusions	Failing to treat a belief or conclusion as a hypothesis requiring scrutiny.
5. Unwarranted persistence	Not changing your mind even when there is compelling evidence to do so.
6. Categorical rather than probabilistic reasoning	Reducing options to two possibilities (either_____ or _____).
7. Confusing naming with explaining (e.g., diagnosing rather than contextually assessing)	Assuming that giving something a name (e.g., bipolar personality disorder) explains it and offers intervention leverage.
8. Confusing correlation with causation	Assuming that an association between two or more events indicates causation.
9. Confusing shared with distinguishing characteristics	Focusing on characteristics that may not distinguish among different groups or causes.
10 Faulty generalization	Relying on small or biased samples; assuming that what is true of the whole is true of the parts, or vice versa.
11. Stereotyping	Incorrectly estimating the degree of variability in a group.
12. Influence by consistent data	Being influenced by data that do not offer any new information but are merely consistent with data already available.
13. Lack of domain-specific knowledge	Not having information needed to clarify and understand problems (e.g., facts, concepts, theories). This source of error is related to many others in this list.
14. Confusing form and function	Mistakenly assuming that similar forms of behavior have similar functions and that different forms of behavior reflect different functions.
15. Simplistic accounts	Relying on accounts that ignore important causes and/or overlook uncertainties.
16. Vagueness	Vaguely describing problems, causes, and hope for outcomes.
17. Uncritical acceptance of explanations	Accepting explanations without evaluating them and comparing them with well-argued alternative accounts; not checking whether a belief is consistent with known facts; selecting untestable beliefs.

(continued)

Exhibit 14.6 (*continued*)

Source	Description
18. Assuming that a weak argument is not true	Assuming that because you cannot offer a convincing argument, a claim is false.
19. Reliance on ad hoc explanations	Making up explanations as you go along, even though they may contradict one another or be circular (explain nothing).
20. Incorrect weighing of different contributors	Not weighing contributing factors in relation to their importance.
21. Misuse of speculation	Believing that you can find out what is going on just by thinking about it.
22. Overcomplex accounts	Relying on needlessly complicated accounts that obscure causes.
23. Ecological fallacy	Assuming that an association between two variables on a group level is also true on an individual level.
24. Confusing correlations and base rates	Incorrectly assuming that a correlation reflects the base rate.
25. Relying on questionable criteria for evaluating the accuracy of claims	Examples include consensus, anecdotal experience, and tradition.
26. Using a general rule that is not applicable to a particular situation	Assuming that because agency administrators are usually fair that a particular administrator was fair on a certain occasion.

Note: The sources of error described may be (and usually are) not related to intentions; caring about people is not enough to avoid them.

Favored Theories

Our theories influence selection of causes. Many clinicians believe in the disease model of substance abuse as well as in the addictive personality. A counselor who accepts this model will focus on dispositional causes (see later discussion of dispositional bias). Other perspectives focus on identifying environmental as well as personal factors that may be related to substance abuse, and do not view it as a disease (e.g., Heyman, 2009; Peele, 1999). Consider the client described by Layng (2009) who, when she was about to be discharged from a psychiatric unit, started to accuse people of being the devil. Most staff believed that this was further evidence of her "mental illness." One staff person sat down with her and started to talk to her, offering statements such as, "The devil does do bad things to people." In the course of this conversation, it became obvious that "the devil" referred to her husband to whom she would return when discharged and whom she feared. This example illustrates that behavior makes sense but that we must care enough to take the time to understand the sense it makes in terms of environmental circumstances. Behavior that results in psychiatric diagnoses, including hallucinations and delusions, may make perfect sense when their function (meaning) is understood. Such understanding, as Layng (2009) points out, is complicated by our metaphorical use of language. Understanding the functions of odd behavior usually takes time both in discussions with clients and significant others as well as in careful observation in related environments. Does managed care provide the time for such assessment? Do clinicians learn how to carry out a constructional assessment (Goldiamond, 1974)?

Theories that are appropriate in some situations may be inappropriately applied in other contexts. Theories that are familiar are more available and are therefore more likely to be influential than are unfamiliar theories. The tendency to be more confident than there is good reason to be about theories compounds their distorting effects. The following quote from Popper (1959) is apt:

> I found that those of my friends who were admirers of Marx, Freud, and Adler, were impressed by a number of points common to these theories, and especially by their apparent explanatory power. These theories appeared to be able to explain practically everything that happened within the fields to which they referred. The study of any of them seemed to have the effect of an intellectual conversion or revelation, opening your eyes to a new truth hidden from those not yet initiated. Once your eyes were thus opened, you saw confirming instances everywhere: the world was full of verifications of the theory. A Marxist could not open a newspaper without finding on every page confirming evidence for his interpretation of history; not only in the news, but also in its presentation—which revealed the class bias of the paper—and especially of course in what the paper did not say. The Freudian analysts emphasized that their theories were constantly verified by their "clinical observations."

Theories influence what we recall as well as what data we note and how we organize data. The influence of preferred theories is illustrated by a study (Plous & Zimbardo, 1986) in which clinicians were asked to list the most likely explanations for three different problems—a sleep disturbance involving nightmares, severe headaches, and depression—variously portrayed by actors in vignettes. Some referred to the therapist, some to the client, and some to the therapist's closest friend of the same sex. Psychoanalysts made more dispositional attributions and fewer situational or mixed attributions than did behavioral therapists. Nontherapists (college students) made the highest number of both dispositional and situational or mixed attributions. Psychoanalysts made significantly more dispositional attributions in relation to their friends and clients than they did for their own behavior. Medical training was associated with the attributional bias of psychoanalysts; those with medical training gave more dispositional attributions than did clinicians without such training.

Metaphors We Use

Metaphors and similes influence how we view our experiences (Lakoff & Dean, 2004; Lakoff & Johnson, 1980). If we think of arguments as war, we may respond to arguments by trying to win and view others as opponents. Advertisers take advantage of metaphors and myths (e.g., Scott, Stanford, & Thompson, 2004). Szasz (1987) argues that the very concept of "mental illness" is a metaphorical device used to (falsely) equate physical with mental illness. The sickness metaphor is prevalent in clinical practice, in such statements as "They have a sick relationship" and "She is an alcoholic." Metaphors may be helpful in revealing factors related to clients' concerns and how best to attain related outcomes. On the other hand, they may result in negative outcomes such as medicalizing moral dilemmas, imposing unwanted services on people, and overlooking environmental causes of stress and depression (e.g., Cohen & Timimi, 2008; MacCoun & Reuter, 2001; Szasz, 1994). For example, because of the use of the illness metaphor, dispositional attributions may be made ("alcoholism as disease" metaphor) or people who have committed violent crimes may be excused on the grounds that they are mentally ill and thus not responsible for their behavior.

Partiality in the Use of Evidence—The Confirmation Bias

Attending to only some important data and overlooking other data is perhaps the most common source of error in clinical decision making (see Exhibit 14.6). Physicians who make incorrect decisions discount evidence that contradicts a favored hypothesis (Elstein et al., 1978). New information is assigned to a favored hypothesis rather than offering a new causal account that could more effectively account for this data. Terms referring to this tendency include conservation, overinterpretation, and assimilation. Well-argued alternatives may be ignored. Diagnoses based on the DSM-IV-TR (Diagnostic and Statistical Manual of Mental Disorders, American Psychiatric Association, 2000) are usually made as a result of attending to a few prototypic characteristics. Vested interest in a view compromises the ability to weigh evidence and sample data objectively. For example, research that offers mixed evidence in relation to a favored hypothesis increases belief in initial views (Lord, Ross, & Lepper, 1979). Decisions made by journal reviewers of manuscripts are in the direction of preferred-practice theories (e.g., Mahoney, 1977). Nor are researchers immune to the influence of their assumptions—elaborate precautions are taken to avoid this influence. (See Chapter 12.) The study of experimenter effects has yielded a great deal of information about such influences.

Oversimplifications

All descriptions of behavior are, to a greater or lesser extent, simplifications regarding causes and perhaps of related complaints and behaviors. And a complete description, even if possible, may not be needed to attain hoped-for outcomes. What is needed is an account that allows us to discover if there is a problem of concern and, if so, to identify its nature and whether it can be addressed while doing more good than harm. The belief that there is only one cause of behavior when there are many may result in faulty causal assumptions. Ignoring important causes decreases the likelihood of choosing effective intervention. (See also discussion of predigested thinking in Chapter 5.)

Avoidable oversimplifications prevent discovery of needed information. Examples are: (1) "It's in the genes," (2) "It's in the brain," (3) "It's due to low self-esteem," (4) "She had a past trauma," and (5) "She is bipolar." The assertion that depression is a brain disease is an oversimplification on both conceptual and empirical grounds. Related research shows that environmental factors play a key role and that there are many kinds of depression and sadness (Luyten et al., 2006). A school social worker may attribute poor academic performance to low self-esteem because a student often "puts herself down" (has a high frequency of negative self-statements). This assessment is incomplete (Foxx & Roland, 2005). No mention is given to possible environmental influences such as a punitive teacher.

Mistaking Correlation and Causation

The fallacy of false cause may occur because correlations are mistaken for causes (e.g., see Shanks, 2005). We may assume that because two variables (brain and foot size) covary, one causes the other. Although we may scoff at the idea that brain size causes foot size, other mistaken assumptions based on confusions between correlations and causation may not be so obvious. The history of the professions provides many illustrations of the confusion between correlation and causation. For example, people used to think that tuberculosis was inherited because people who lived together often got it. Consider also the common assumption that low self-esteem causes problems such as depression. In fact, both low self-esteem and depression may be related to other variables such as a high frequency of punishing experiences and a low frequency of positive feedback in the past and the present. Some argue that because depression improves after taking medication, this shows that it is a brain disease. This confuses correlation with causation. Our tendency to overestimate correlations heightens our susceptibility to this error.

Confusing Causes and Their Effects

Is depression a cause of marital conflict, or is marital conflict a cause of depression? Is cognitive disorientation a result of being homeless, or does being homeless contribute to cognitive disorientation? Tavris (1992) argues that the depression that many women complain of is often a result of gender role expectations (e.g., that women be the major caretaker of children) that limit women's opportunities for well-paid work. The fundamental attribution error may result in mistaking effects for causes. Consider Jimmy, a 12-year-old African American student referred because of apathy, indifference, and inattentiveness to classroom activities (Sue & Sue, 1990, p. 44). The counselor believed that Jimmy harbored repressed rage that needed to be ventilated and dealt with. He believed that Jimmy's inability to express his anger led him to adopt a passive-aggressive means of expressing hostility (i.e., inattentiveness, daydreaming, falling asleep) and recommended that Jimmy be seen for intensive counseling to discover the basis of his anger. After 6 months of counseling, the counselor realized that Jimmy's fatigue, passivity, and fatalism were a result of poverty. He came from a home of extreme poverty, where hunger, lack of sleep, and overcrowding sapped his energy and motivation.

The Fundamental Attribution Error

The fundamental attribution error (the tendency to attribute behavior to qualities of people rather than to situational events) results in overlooking related environmental events. "Every day, people make harmful and damaging judgments about themselves, or harmful judgments about their spouses even to the point of severing marriages, because they wrongly attribute a current crisis to stable personal dispositions instead of transient pressures" (Nisbett & Ross, 1980, p. 252). An example of the willingness to ascribe behavior to stable dispositions is offered by a study conducted by Jones and Harris (1967). People who read an essay advocating or opposing Castro's leadership of Cuba inferred that the author of the essay believed in the view described even when they were told that the theme of the essay was dictated by someone else. In another study that highlights our tendency to ignore or underestimate situational influences, subjects were recruited for a game involving tests of general knowledge (Ross, Amabile, & Steinmetz, 1977). They took part either as participants or as observers and were randomly assigned to these roles. Subjects were aware of this random distribution. Questioners could ask any questions as long as they knew the answer themselves. After completing the game, the observers, contestants, and questioners were all asked to rate contestants and questioners on their general knowledge and other competence-related items. The contestants received lower ratings by all parties despite the fact that they had little opportunity to display their knowledge because of the situational factor of random distribution.

One effect of preconceptions is the tendency to perceive greater consistency in behavior than exists. The influence of the context in which exchanges take place is often overlooked by clinicians. (See also discussion of biases in self-report data in Chapter 13.) Clinicians typically observe clients in interviews. Client behavior is more available than their environments when clinicians think about causes. The situation is the reverse from the actor's point of view; that is, to the actor, it is the situation that is more vivid. This probably explains why actors attribute a greater role to environmental variables when offering reasons for their own behavior than do people who observe the actors.

Underestimating the Role of Chance: Readiness to Explain Coincidences

Many events simply happen by chance; chance and randomness are much more likely to occur than we think (Falk, 1981). Most people, however, do not appreciate the prevalence of randomness, and readily offer explanations for events that are actually a result of chance. We underestimate the ease with which outcomes can adequately be explained (Paulos, 1988). Our need for control encourages a search for explanations for events that offer an illusion of control (Langer, 1975). One of the problems with offering explanations is that they influence what we see and assume on subsequent occasions, even when they are incorrect. Outcomes that are really the result of chance tend to be attributed to personal characteristics, such as skill or its lack.

Vividness

People who are unusually prominent in some way are more likely to be considered to have a causal role. Someone who is visually prominent in a discussion is viewed as having an influential role in the outcome of the discussion (Taylor & Fiske, 1975). The proximity of one event to another may lead us to believe that a causal relationship exists. The effects of repeated affirmation of a point and the use of emotional terms on judgments offer additional examples of the role of vividness. Clinicians tend to select their most vivid case examples when discussing causal attribution. Such biased selection (attempted proof by selected instances) may result in incorrect inferences. Events that have a small probability (they occur rarely) tend to be overestimated (Tversky & Kahneman, 1981). If a rare event is associated with a particularly negative outcome, it may receive undue attention. Attention may be focused on situations in which excessive drinking occurs; situations in which it does not occur may be ignored. This biased focus encourages an overemphasis on problems and limits understanding of situations in which drinking does not occur.

Ignoring Base-Rate Information

Information about how many people act a certain way in a situation is often disregarded when trying to determine why a particular person acts in a certain manner. For example, in Milgram's study of obedience (1963), data on the percentage of subjects who delivered high shocks to people had little impact on judgments made by individual subjects; even though they knew that delivering high shocks was the modal response, they still made strong negative judgments about those who delivered high shocks (Miller, Gillen, Schenker, & Redlove, 1973). Information about normative behavior may be dismissed even though such information would be helpful. Consensus information is underutilized in self-perception. Subjects who were informed that feelings of depression such as the Sunday blues were the rule, not the exception, were no less inclined to inaccurately attribute their mood to personal inadequacy and weakness (Nisbett, Borgida, Crandall, & Reed, 1976). Nisbett and Ross (1980) suggest that consensus information is ignored because it is less vivid than information about events or people. In the false consensus effect, we make the assumption that the percentage of people who would act and believe as we would is higher than it actually is. The more other people's behavior differs from our own, the more likely we are to regard their behavior as unusual and as revealing of personal dispositions (Ross, Greene, & House, 1977). The tendency to associate with people who are similar and the greater ease of recalling our own beliefs and actions encourage this false consensus. Since the practice of many clinicians involves clients who are quite different from themselves, such effects are likely to encourage incorrect inferences of pathology.

The Self-Fulfilling Prophecy

There is a self-fulfilling prophecy—our expectations influence what befalls us. Clinicians often have advance descriptions of a client, perhaps from a referral source or case record. These descriptions may create expectations about a client, which then influence the exchange that occurs. Consider the study by Snyder, Tanke, and Berscheid (1977), in which men were asked to speak to an unknown woman over the phone. Men in one group were told that the woman was very attractive; the men in the other group were told that she was unattractive. After speaking to the woman, they rated the woman on a number of traits. The conversations were recorded, and the interactions were rated by observers who could hear only the man or only the woman and knew nothing about the attractiveness manipulation. The observers rated the "attractive woman" as being more confident and more animated, enjoying the conversation and liking the partner. The "unattractive woman" was rated as more sensitive, trusting, kind, genuine, and modest. Men who were told they were speaking to an attractive woman were rated as more sociable, sexually warm, interesting, independent, permissive, bold, outgoing, humorous, socially adept, and pleased with the conversation. These results indicated that the men behaved differently in the two different conditions. Snyder and Thomsen (1988) suggest that self-fulfilling prophecies are especially likely to occur in situations of unequal power, such as therapist-client relationships. Many clients can readily be persuaded that the therapist's impressions are accurate.

Overconfidence

Overconfidence concerning the accuracy of our causal assumptions discourages a search for disconfirming data (e.g., Arkes, 2001; Berner & Graber, 2008). Depending on the quality of corrective feedback, experience may or may not be an accurate guide (see Chapter 9). Personnel managers, for example, do not see how applicants they reject would have performed. Customs inspectors do not know about false negatives—travelers who had illegal or declarable goods and who passed through customs unnoticed—and are thus overconfident of their skills in spotting contraband. Clinicians usually do not find out how effective other methods would have been with a client. (See also Klayman, Soll, Gonzales-Vallejo, & Barlas, 1999.) Predicting the future is quite different from understanding the past; ignoring this difference is responsible in part for the overconfidence clinicians have in their intuitive abilities. There is an "overestimation of contingency" (the assumption of particular causal relationships) and an illusion of certainty. "There is an essential difference between the consequent-antecedent process of looking backward versus the antecedent-consequence process of looking forward" (Dawes, 1993). Retrospective memory is biased—"we interpret past events in a manner consistent with our present beliefs concerning stability and change in the human life course. The result is gross overestimation of the strength and consistency of the 'patterns' we observe retrospectively—hence, overconfidence in what we 'know.'" Thus, prediction is not equivalent to understanding and explanation. In retrospective review (looking back from a consequent—a client has been labeled a schizophrenic), we are free to search for enumerable antecedent causes resulting in post hoc reasoning. (See Dawes, 1993, for more detail.) Dawes uses the example of examining the black box after an airplane crash to discover causes. As he suggests, we do not know how many planes arrived safely in which similar factors occurred, and there is no way to find out. Our theory of what happened or what caused an outcome (such as being depressed) encourages an organization of memories that fits this theory. (See research regarding retrospective memory, Loftus, 2004.)

Confusing Naming and Explaining

Naming (offering a diagnosis for an observed pattern of behavior) may be confused with explaining. That is, it is assumed that because something has been named, it has also been explained (see discussion of empathic explanations in Chapter 3). This is rarely the case in the field of psychology, although it may be so in the field of medicine (such as when a physician determines that a patient has tuberculosis). Pseudoexplanations involve a confusion of naming and explaining and can result in frustration, because although helpful information now seems to be on hand, in fact none has been added.

Confusing Content and Structure (Form and Function)

Errors may occur because of confusion between content and structure. Content may differ while structure remains the same; this is difficult to appreciate (Einhorn, 1980b). The distinction between form (the typology of a behavior) and function (what maintains the behavior, why it occurs) is a basic one in applied behavior analysis (Fisher, Piazza, & Roane, 2011). Focusing on the form of behavior (hitting) and overlooking its function (removing demands) may result in incomplete accounts. (See earlier discussion of the client who accused people of being the devil.) This error is less likely in theories that emphasize the distinction between form (the typology of behavior) and function (what maintains the behavior—why it occurs). Simply describing behavior does not provide information about its function (why it occurs). The context in which behavior occurs must also be explored. If you know the circumstances in which a client is likely to engage in certain behaviors, you have information about how the environment might be altered to influence these behaviors. Ignoring context encourages excessive focus on personal causes. For example, individual counseling may be recommended for an adolescent having problems at school that are related to the reactions of her peers and teachers as well as to the economic stress experienced by her single parent. A problem-oriented curricular design (e.g., aging, health, anxiety, depression, family violence) may discourage recognition of similar contingencies of reinforcement that apply to different concerns. There are no courses in the physics department on the physics of refrigerators, the physics of air conditioners, and so forth, because there is agreement on a certain core of structural relationships (Blalock, 1984). Many graduate programs do not require students to take a course in basic behavioral principles that cuts across all problem areas in terms of potential application. This is not to say that specialized content, for example, about developmental tasks or changes at different ages is unimportant.

Dead-End and Incomplete Accounts

Dead-end accounts are those that do not provide guidelines for achieving valued outcomes. They get in the way of discovering promising options. An example is attributing a client's troubling behavior to angry feelings without discovering environmental factors related to these feelings. After-the-fact accounts describing what people did (and why) may sound profound, but do not provide before-the-fact information that helps you and your clients to select effective plans. Dead-end accounts may be incomplete (omit crucial causes). Incomplete accounts include only some pieces of a puzzle. They may focus on thoughts without relating them to what people do in specific situations. Another kind of incomplete account is assuming that behavior causes another behavior, without asking about the causes of both. Self-esteem is often accepted as a cause of behavior. But where does self-esteem come from? You may assume that your success in a job interview is due to high self-efficacy (an expectation that you will succeed). A more complete account would include information about your history in related situations such as past successful experiences (Baumeister, Campbell, Krueger, & Vohs, 2003). We feel confident in situations in which we do well.

Problems With Memory

Events may not be accurately noted in the first place. And just because a sequence of events is accurately observed does not mean that the memory of these events will remain accurate. Distortions may and do creep in over time. Errors of construction occur (see Chapter 9).

Other Sources of Error

An event is more likely to be selected as a cause if it is presented as the subject of a sentence than as the object (Pryor & Kriss, 1977). "Thus, Sue is more likely to be identified as the causal agent in her preference for a restaurant if subjects are told that she likes the restaurant than if they are told that the restaurant is liked by Sue" (Nisbett & Ross, 1980, p. 127). The influence of surface wordings on clinical judgments needs further investigation. There is every reason to suppose that such influences occur in clinical practice as they do in other settings.

Inconsistent use of rules may result in errors. A rule may be used appropriately in some instances but be overlooked in other situations in which it would be helpful. This tendency toward inconsistency offers an advantage to actuarial methods of prediction (see Chapter 15). Errors may occur because uncertainties are overlooked or ignored. Sources of uncertainty in clinical practice include potential effectiveness of intervention methods, validity of measures, and longevity of gains. Uncertainties are viewed as so important to consider that a website has been created, the United Kingdom Database of Uncertainties About the Effects of Treatments (DUETs). Causal inferences may be incorrect because premises are untrue or because the form of the argument is incorrect. The factual soundness of an argument (its plausibility) as well as its logical soundness should be considered as discussed in Chapter 3. Just as an explanation may be oversimplified, it may be overly complex, obscuring key variables.

A DISPOSITIONAL BIAS

Clinicians make decisions about problem framing—what kind of problem, where it lies, and what causes it. Dispositional bias refers to the tendency to attribute the cause and locus of problems to the client rather than to environmental events or to the interaction of personal and environmental factors (see earlier discussion of the fundamental attribution error). The dispositional bias of clinicians has received a great deal of attention. The following discussion of factors related to this source of error is based on Batson, O'Quin, and Pych (1982). More recent research supports this earlier discussion. Four factors involve characteristics of the observer (the clinician) and three result from being in a helper role.

1. *In their role as an observer, clinicians tend to focus on the client.* It is the client who is interviewed; the client is salient in the interview context, and such focus encourages dispositional attributions. For example, Storms (1973) found that when observers of an interaction were shown a replay of the situation from a participant's point of view, they made more situational attributions. In another study, undergraduates listened to an audiotape of a peer-counseling session (Snyder, Shenkel, & Schmidt, 1976). The client depicted on the tape presented her problem as being related to her situation. Her problem was viewed as more situational by observers asked to take the client's role and was viewed in more dispositional terms by subjects instructed to take the role of a peer counselor. "These results are quite consistent with the suggestion that people who identify with the helper role are prone to adopt an observer set and, as a result, to make more dispositional attributions" (Batson, O'Quin, & Pych, 1982, p. 65). Such findings are compatible with self-other differences described in Chapter 9.

2. *Information gathered is selective, or the "office-bound helper."* Many counselors see their clients only in the office, which may result in incorrect assumptions about the consistency of behavior. They do not see clients in other situations, in which behavior may differ considerably from that seen in the interview. Behavior that is the direct result of the unusual situation of being in a client role may be inaccurately assumed to reflect behavior in other situations. Agency policy may prohibit home visits. Even when home visits do occur, the sample of behavior gathered may be small, and little care may be exercised to ensure that a representative sample is gathered. This is not to say that real-life observation is always relevant or ethical. It is to say that, even though it might be both relevant and ethical, it is often not used as a source of assessment information (e.g., see Budd et al., 2001). In some agencies, one clinician may see a child

and another clinician may see the child's parents. This practice discounts the mutual influence processes between children and their parents.

3. *Practice theories influence attributions.* The preferred practice theories of many clinicians encourage dispositional attributions. Many clinicians favor a sign approach to assessment, in which behaviors are viewed as signs of hypothetical internal dispositions. This contrasts with a sample approach to assessment, in which behaviors are viewed as important in their own right as a sample of a broader class of actions. Compared to behaviorally oriented clinicians, psychodynamically oriented clinicians viewed a person as significantly more maladjusted and viewed his problems in more dispositional terms when the person was labeled a patient than when he was referred to as a job applicant (Langer & Abelson, 1974). The label "patient" created a dispositional bias on the part of psychodynamically oriented counselors.

4. *Situational information provided by the client is discounted.* Information that clients provide about situations related to their concerns may be discounted. Batson and his colleagues (1982) suggest that counselors are especially likely to discount information that indicates the problem is situational. They identify three factors that contribute to this tendency. First, clinicians are aware of people's tendency to make situational attributions for their behaviors, and there may be an attempt to correct for this bias by emphasizing dispositional causes. Second, labels and diagnoses applied to clients encourage dispositional attributions by compromising the client's credibility as a provider of accurate information. A clinician may have read in a case record that a client has a history of being hospitalized for schizophrenia, and subsequently emphasize personal limitations as causal factors. Many studies illustrate the influence of third-party information on clinical decisions. In a study by Batson (1975), counselors who received information that a client had low scores on self-awareness and high scores on manipulation made fewer situational attributions, even though this client presented evidence that the problem was situational. Third, offering a situational attribution for a problem is usually less damaging to one's self-esteem. Thus, a client who blames a problem on the situation may be assumed to be acting in his own best interest and, for this reason, his statements may be discounted.

5. *Professional training encourages dispositional attributions.* Trained helpers are more likely to make dispositional attributions concerning clients' problems than are untrained helpers. Batson and his colleagues (1982) found this true of different types of helpers; for example, clinical psychologists as well as social workers. They conclude that there is "a pervasive tendency for trained helpers, however trained, to perceive clients' problems as more dispositional than do people

without training" (p. 69). As the authors note, such differences in attribution may be due to selection effects (people who are prone to make such attributions choose helper roles) rather than to socialization effects of training. Most clinicians are trained in how to use the classifications of "mental disorders" in the *DSM*. Such training increases use of these categories (Pottick, Wakefield, Kirk, & Tian, 2003); such labels are required for third-party payment. They focus on alleged characteristics of the individual.

6. *Calling a healthy person sick is less serious than calling a sick person healthy.* Clinicians are supposed to protect society from people who may be dangerous. Physicians are trained to be conservative; they are trained that it is better to call a healthy person sick than to call a sick person healthy. If a social worker attributes child abuse to dispositional characteristics of a mother and removes a child, at least the child will not be harmed by the parent (although harm may result from the foster parents and/or from the trauma of separation; e.g., see DePanfilis, 2003). On the other hand, if a situational cause is assumed (such as stress, which could be relieved) and the child is left in the home and abused, there may be an uproar in the press. In this kind of situation, possible problems with other living contexts, such as the foster home, are much less vivid at the point of making a decision about whether to remove a child, since the foster home is often unknown. On the other hand, the injuries to the child, the child's reactions to these injuries, and a parent who may be uncooperative and angry are all very vivid.

7. *Resources available relate mostly to changing the client.* Batson and his colleagues (1982) argue that helpers want to succeed but are aware that success is more likely if they change the client's situation. However, they realize that often this will not be possible. This is especially true in social work, in which many problems are related to environmental problems over which social workers have little control, such as poor housing, poor education, lack of day care, and unemployment. So helpers concentrate instead on dispositional accounts—accounts that may enable them to help. Batson, O'Quin, and Pych (1982) base their views on the assumption that clinicians believe that they are better able to help with dispositional than with situational problems. They cite three reasons for their beliefs. One is that helpers have more immediate access to clients than to their clients' environments. A second reason is that changing the environment is more difficult: "to change a sick situation may involve legal or political action affecting many people and costing much money and time" (p. 71). The third reason is that resources available are geared toward personal characteristics rather than situational causes. "The majority of our societal resources are directed toward helping individuals adapt

to their social environments; far fewer are directed toward changing the social environments that breed poverty, crime, depression, and despair" (p. 71). Currently we are infatuated with taking pills to solve problems; the focus is on presumed biochemical imbalances of individuals, overlooking environmental circumstances (e.g., Herzberg, 2009).

Availability of resources influences attributions for client's problems. For example, in a study by Batson, Jones, and Cochran (1979), some of the subjects received a list of referral sources that emphasized the dispositional nature of problems, such as a mental hospital, a residential treatment center, a mental health clinic, group therapy, and a family counseling service. Other subjects received a list of resources emphasizing environmental contributors, such as a career information center, an ombudsman, and a community coalition. Subjects who received the former list were more likely to view the client's problems in dispositional terms. Again, vividness is an influential factor: the client's presence compared with an unseen environment. This tendency is compounded by the fact that many clinicians do not know how to carry out contingency analyses in order to identify environmental factors that contribute to problems (Cooper, Heron, & Heward, 2008). Not having such skills, the influence of environmental contingencies may be overlooked. The long-term effects of decisions made, based on resources available, produces a vicious cycle; the more problems are viewed in dispositional terms, the more services compatible with this view will be requested.

USE AND MISUSE OF INTUITION

The view of intuition as a "responsiveness to information that is not consciously represented, but which nevertheless guides inquiry toward productive and often profound insights" (Bowers, 1987, p. 73) is compatible with the differences found between experts and novices. (See Chapters 4 and 8.) Experts use mental simulations and patterns based on experience providing corrective feedback that they may no longer be able to easily describe. The tacit nature of such knowledge encourages attributions for productive solutions to intuition. Basing decisions on what feels right in the absence of tacit knowledge plus relevant research findings may result in decisions that do not help clients. "Real clinical expertise based on sound, concrete, situational understanding must be distinguished from arbitrary subjectivity, guessing, mystical intuition, instinct, routine, or habit" (Gordon, 1988, p. 278).

All serious thinking calls on both searchlike processes and the sudden recognition of familiar patterns. Without recognition based on previous experience, search through complex spaces would proceed in snaillike fashion. Informed intuition exploits the knowledge we have gained through our past searches. Hence we would expect what in fact occurs, that the expert will often be able to proceed intuitively in attacking a problem that requires painful search for the novice. And we would expect also that in most problem situations combining aspects of novelty with familiar components, intuition and search will be cooperative in reaching solutions (Simon, 1990, p. 203).

IMPROVING THE ACCURACY OF CAUSAL ASSUMPTIONS

Tools and rules of thumb that can be used to improve the accuracy of causal assumptions share a focus on increasing awareness of our reasoning process—making implicit processes explicit, so that we can examine our assumptions. Examples include asking questions, such as, "What's missing?" or "Do I need more information?" Guidelines include attending to context (getting the total picture), questioning initial assumptions, paying attention to anomalies, and changing representations (restructuring situations). This will require making use of both systems of reasoning: intuitive and analytic (see Chapter 9).

Take Advantage of Helpful Tools

Cognitive maps, flowcharts, contingency tables, and tree structures can be used to describe the relationships among variables. Drawing a graph of the presumed relationship between two characteristics (daily mood and daily number of pleasant events) or making a contingency table may help to identify assumptions and alternative possibilities (see Exhibit 14.4). Flowcharts can be used to illustrate the steps involved in making a decision and to highlight data needed and common errors at each point (e.g., Rzepnicki & Johnson, 2005). Venn diagrams provide an aid for analysis of arguments.

Make Assumptions Explicit

If we do not make our assumptions explicit, we cannot examine their accuracy. Drawing cognitive maps of possible interrelationships among concepts may be helpful in clarifying implicit assumptions that influence decisions.

Clearly Describe Relevant Events

Clinical decisions often involve estimating probabilities—for example, the likelihood that a client's depression is related to recent environmental changes. Probabilities may be easier to estimate if relevant events are clearly described—for example, the exact nature of recent environmental changes. Clear description of concerns and related factors are vital to clarifying vague terms such as depression, anxiety, and poor communication. Vague descriptions of concerns may make it impossible to discover related factors. Keep in mind that behavior usually makes sense but only when we understand the functions of behavior and other contextual variables. Another way to get bogged down is to focus on problems rather than related factors—for example, focusing on elder abuse per se, rather than identifying and addressing related factors.

Watch Out for the Fundamental Attribution Error

We tend to focus on attributes of the person and to overlook environmental variables (i.e., fall into the fundamental attribution error). This, combined with the greater vividness of negative behaviors, often results in pathologizing clients. To avoid doing this, consider the context in which behaviors of concern occur (or their lack).

Be Data Focused

Speculative thinking may be relied on "to solve problems which can only be solved by the observation and interpretation of facts. . . . The belief that one can find out something about real things by speculation alone is one of the most long-lived delusions in human thought" (Thouless, 1974, p. 78). We often are guilty of the contrary-to-fact hypothesis, in which we state "with an unreasonable degree of certainty the results of events that might have occurred that did not" (Seech, 1993, p. 131). An example is: "She felt sad because of her neighbor's family problems. If only she hadn't gotten married at such an early age, she would be a happier woman today" (p. 131). Speculation is valuable in discovering new possibilities but it does not offer information about whether these insights are correct. What is cannot be deduced from what ought to be. Speculation is not without its effects, since our beliefs influence what we look for. Expectations based on theories and semantic associations may overwhelm the influence of data that do not match these expectations or that even refute them. This tendency is encouraged by confirmation biases (seeking data that confirm our beliefs and overlooking data that do not). For example, we often attend to only the positive-positive cell of a four-cell contingency table (see earlier discussion in this chapter).

There is nothing odd or negative about weighing data in relation to available theories. The problem arises when we invent ad hoc accounts for the purpose at hand and overlook points of view (causes) that would have predicted other events or relationships, and never reconsider them when our initial beliefs are shown to be incorrect (Einhorn, 1980b). This tendency may be heightened in eclectic practice, in which we use ad hoc theories or notions that may contradict each other.

Being data focused rather than theory focused will help you to avoid premature and excessive reliance on dubious accounts (Einhorn, 1980b). The more tenuous a theory is, the less you should rely on it when reviewing data, and the more attention you should pay to the data. What exactly is the problem? Exactly how is it manifested? What factors have been found to be associated with it in related high-quality research reports?

Focus on Informative Data

The data you gather could be (1) relevant (help you and your clients select effective service plans), (2) irrelevant, or (3) misleading. Focus on relevant data. Irrelevant data may lead you astray. A few worthless items can dilute the effect of one helpful item. In thinking about what a particular person might do in a situation, we tend to disregard data that describe how people usually act, even though this may help us to predict what an individual would do. Ask: "Is this data relevant here?" How so? We tend to focus on vivid events and to overlook those that are important but not vivid.

Assess Rather Than Diagnose; Explain Rather Than Name

Problem solving can be likened to walking along an unknown path with many dead ends. One kind of dead end is simply naming (e.g., labeling) something (a problem or behavior of interest). Suppose that you see a homeless person on the street gesturing oddly and talking to himself. You may think, "He is mentally ill." Is this label helpful? Does it decrease uncertainty about how you might be able to be of help?

> Intervention programs cannot be based solely on a diagnostic or classification category such as "depression" or "attention-deficit disorder" because such topographically based [description of form] diagnoses do not identify which of many possible determinants are operational for a particular client. Diagnoses typically provide only an array of possible causal factors. The generalizability of the suggested variables and weights to a particular client cannot be presumed.
>
> Diagnosis can facilitate the design of intervention programs only if any of three conditions are met: (1) specific causal paths are invariably associated with specific diagnostic categories, (2) a hierarchy of the most probable paths or their weights is associated with specific diagnostic categories, and/ or (3) effective interventions are available for specific diagnostic categories regardless of within-category variance in causality. These conditions are seldom met. (Haynes, 1992, p. 109)

Assessing rather than diagnosing will help you avoid explanatory fictions (terms that seem to offer information but do not). Pseudoexplanations (circular accounts) are prime examples. In a circular account, we use a behavior to infer an explanation and appeal to the same behavior to support our explanation (no additional information is provided). For example, a teacher may explain a student's hitting other children by stating that he is aggressive and, when asked how she knows, may say, "Because he hits other children." A lack of situation awareness—failing to elaborate the "problem space" (to pursue a contextual analysis) is a principal cause of ineffective problem solving (Nickerson, Perkins, & Smith, 1985; Salas & Klein, 2001; Zsambok & Klein, 1997).

Avoid the Single-Cause Fallacy: Ask, "What's Missing?"

Just as an explanation may be overly complex and obscure options, it may be incomplete (overlook causes) and obscure options. We may assume (incorrectly) that different problems have one cause. Rarely is behavior related to one cause. For example, investigations of relapse in depression suggest many related factors. Simplistic accounts in which complex problems such as family violence are attributed to one factor (e.g., past history of violence) can be misleading. Thinking in either/or terms and ignoring or discounting important uncertainties encourage selection of simplistic accounts. Ask yourself: Does my account consider major influences? Have I left out important influences?

Avoid Unnecessarily Complex Accounts

Just as an account may be overly simple (overlook causes related to a problem), it may be overly complex (unnecessary concepts may be used that get in the way of discovering causes). This is why parsimony is emphasized in science, as described in Chapter 4. Although general "sensitizing concepts" can be helpful in the exploratory stage of problem solving, they must be clarified to understand a client's concerns and options for resolving them, including a client's unique subjectivity (meanings of the client's experiences). (See, for example, Biehl, Good, & Kleinman, 2007.) We tend to believe that vague, jargon-filled accounts are more profound than clearly stated ones (Armstrong, 1980). McCabe and Castel (2008) found that subjects who read a manuscript with a picture of a brain were more impressed with the evidentiary status of the claims made in the article than were subjects who read the same manuscript without the picture.

Watch Out for Illusory Correlations

Mistaken assumptions about causes may be due to incorrect estimates of the degree to which two or more events covary. (See prior discussion of assessing covariations.)

Covariations (and thus causal relationships) are often assumed between certain characteristics (e.g., personality traits or recent life changes) and problems or between certain symptoms and diagnostic categories (e.g., vigilance for danger and generalized anxiety disorder). Corrective feedback offers an opportunity to change misleading beliefs about what "ought" to go together.

Pay Attention to Base Rates

Base rates indicate the prevalence of a behavior or event in a population. Only about half of parents who were abused as children abuse their own children (estimates range from 40% to 60%). We tend to rely on data about a particular case and to ignore base-rate probabilities. Imagine that you have just left a staff position in a shelter for battered women where 90% of clients seeking services had been abused. You are now working in a community mental health center in which the base rate of battered women is much lower, say 10%. Ignoring differences in base rates may result in incorrect assumptions—that clients have been battered when they have not been. Base-rate data are not as vivid as characteristics of the client whom you see during interviews. It thus is easy to overlook this information, even though it is important to consider when making decisions. If we rely on resemblance criteria (similarity) to evaluate probability, we may overlook prior probability (base-rate data; Tversky & Kahneman, 1974; see also Chapter 15).

Watch Out for Sample Bias

Decisions are made on the basis of samples of behavior or conditions. We may often make generalizations about what clients do in real-life contexts based on how they act during interviews. Inaccurate assumptions may result from overgeneralizations based on small, biased samples.

Search for Alternative Accounts

We tend to be influenced by what we first think. Keep in mind that you could be wrong. Make it a habit to question initial assumptions. We tend to seek data that confirm our views and not to look for evidence against them. This is known as the confirmatory bias or self-fulfilling prophecy. This style of search often results in faulty judgments (Nickerson, 1998). Studies of medical decisions show that overinterpretation is a key source of error (contradictory evidence is ignored or is incorrectly assumed to support preferred views; Elstein et al., 1978). We use different standards to criticize evidence against our views than we use to evaluate evidence that supports them. Evidence that is mixed (it provides some support for and some against favored views) increases the confidence of believers of both views (Lord, Ross, & Lepper, 1979). We readily think up causes. We have an investment in understanding and predicting what happens around us. A premature focus on one possibility will get in the way of considering alternative views. Unless your assumptions about causes provide guidelines for removing complaints, or unless you must act quickly (shoot from the hip), consider alternative possibilities.

Enhance Your Understanding of Probabilities

Misunderstanding about probabilities may result in faulty problem structuring. Different kinds of probabilities include: (1) compound (probability of X and Y), (2) conditional (probability of X given Y), and (3) simple (X). In the conjunction fallacy, we overlook the fact that the probabilities of A and B both occurring must be less than the simple probability of A or the simple probability of B. (For a critique of this as a fallacy, see Gigerenzer, 2007.) We may ignore base-rate data. Dawes (1988) gives the example of assuming that low self-esteem (c) results in problems (P) and related symptoms (S) because people who consult counselors regarding problems have low self-esteem. This confuses $P(c \mid S)$—the probability of low self-esteem, given problems—and $P(S \mid c)$ the probability of problems given low self-esteem. As Dawes points out, we do not know $P(S \mid c)$ is high "because clients come to [counselors] because they have problems" (p. 76). The counselors' experience is conditional on S. Also, as Dawes points out, people's self-esteem may be poor because they have problems. Readers of books on sexual abuse are often asked to review a long list of symptoms to check for indicators of sexual abuse. One problem here is assuming that the probability of a symptom (e.g., suicidal thoughts) is the same as the probability of an underlying problem or experience (e.g., sexual abuse as a child; Ofshe & Watters, 1994). Symptoms such as depression are much more common than any one underlying cause. When we do not consider this, we are subject to illusory correlations (e.g., between symptoms and presumed causes). Another problem is that certain symptoms may not be independent but are assumed to be so when making an overall estimate. (See also prior discussion of probabilities in this chapter.)

Watch Your Language

The role of language is discussed at many points in this book. Language influences how successful we are in communicating with ourselves as well as with clients and colleagues. Some uses of language have an almost magical quality, as when we label a behavior and think that we have explained it when we have not (see the earlier discussion of naming compared to explaining). It is easy to slip from describing someone ("She complains about being lonely") to a causal inference ("She has a dependent personality") that provides little or no intervention leverage. We tend to convert trait names (e.g., aggressive) into presumed causes (e.g., aggressive personality) that get in the way of understanding clients and their concerns and circumstances. Psychobabble (vague jargon) obscures rather than clarifies.

Acquire Domain-Specific Knowledge and Skills

Specialized content knowledge and skills may be necessary to accurately assess concerns and related circumstances and options in order to help a client achieve hoped-for outcomes. You may have to search for and critically appraise related research findings to discover promising options. If you are unaware of the influence of schedules of reinforcement on behavior, you may mistakenly attribute the cause of problems to personal characteristics (low self-esteem), overlooking the role of scheduling effects. Lack of knowledge about the psychological effects of certain physical illnesses or drugs may result in incorrect assumptions about the cause of an elderly client's depression.

Be Aware of What You Don't Know (Ignorance as a Kind of Knowledge)

Be honest about gaps in your knowledge related to decisions you and your clients make. Available knowledge about how to help clients attain certain outcomes is usually incomplete. Sources of uncertainty include potential effectiveness of different methods, the accuracy of assessment and evaluation measures, and the future course of certain behavior patterns. Recognizing our ignorance and the uncertainties involved in making decisions can help us to avoid misleading influences of overconfidence. Witte, Witte, and Kerwin (1994) offered a course on medical ignorance at the University of Arizona School of Medicine to highlight the importance of knowing what is not known as well as what is. Carroll (2001) has his students ask "ignorance" questions based on their reading of texts. These highlight what they do not know or what the text may not include. Proctor and Schriebinger (2008) suggest that the study of ignorance is just as important as the study of knowledge.

Watch Out for Redundant Data

Our tendency to collect redundant information encourages a false sense of overconfidence. You may, for example, ask a client who complains of depression about her past history of depression. In selectively scanning for depression, you may overlook periods of happiness and related factors (see Exhibit 14.6).

Be Flexible

One definition of rationality is changing your mind when data indicate that you should. Our tendency to be overconfident of our judgments and to look for data that confirm our views (confirmatory biases) contributes to unwarranted persistence. Change your mind when you have good reason to do so.

Avoid False Dilemmas

We often think in either/or terms when searching for causes and selecting plans. We may think it must be either x or y when in fact we should consider a number of possibilities. Thinking in either/or terms may result in overlooking promising options.

Restructure the Problem

Restructuring problems may be useful with ill-defined goals. Let us say that you accept a client's goal of being happier but feel stymied as to how to pursue this goal. Recognizing that this goal is the outcome of a number of different behaviors and situations encourages a focus on pursuit of these changes as a route to being happier. The questions "What would that look like?" and "How would you know that the goal is met?" can help you to be specific. Different kinds of metaphors and analogies can be used to simplify problems and to avoid a fixation on one problem structure or view that hinders solution of a problem.

Decrease Compartmentalization

Repeated practice in clinical decision making with corrective feedback —focusing on the process as well as the product—will encourage generalization of helpful skills. (See discussion of problem-based learning in Chapter 10.) Questions that encourage generalization of content and procedural knowledge from one domain to another include "How could I apply that to this?" and "Could I use that to understand this problem?"

Use Effective Troubleshooting Skills

Skill in troubleshooting is one of the competency clusters that distinguishes effective from ineffective decision makers. Setbacks and mistakes are responded to as opportunities to use helpful strategies, such as asking questions that allow us to get unstuck (for example, "Why did I make this mistake?" "How could I avoid it in the future?" "How can I break this down into smaller steps?" "What do I need to know here?" "How can I rearrange information here?").

Cultivate Positive Moods

Research suggests that the mood of the therapist influences decisions made (Salovey & Turk, 1988). Negative moods increase a focus on negative events and may thus encourage clinicians to pathologize clients. Biasing effects of positive moods include underplaying the severity of concerns and encouraging clients to take risks they are not ready for. Given research that suggests that many clinicians err in seeing too much pathology and overlook client assets, and that support and belief in client's potential for change facilitates progress, if we have to err, a positive bias is likely to result in the least damaging errors. Turk and Salovey (1986) suggest the use of a bias inoculation procedure in which clinicians receive experience in how their moods influence their memories. You could briefly reflect on your mood before each interview as a check on possible bias and as a cue to alter your mood or at least be aware of it.

Use Helpful Rules of Thumb

Useful rules of thumb to minimize errors in causal assumptions include the following:

1. *Search for alternative explanations.* Causal assumptions may be retained even though they do not fit the data, as illustrated in the failure of debriefing described in Chapter 9 (see also the classic study by Ross and Lepper, 1980). Use the rule to "never rely on one way of asking" (Edwards & von Winterfeldt, 1986, p. 657) to counteract this tendency. Incomplete or inaccurate assumptions may be discovered by searching for alternative explanations; this will counteract tendencies to focus on vivid but misleading cues and to look only for evidence that confirms favored assumptions. Bromley (1977) recommends inclusion of a heading of "Alternative Accounts" in case records.

2. *Pay attention to sources of uncertainty.* Clinical decisions are made in a context of uncertainty. Overlooking uncertainty does not make it go away. Decisions are more likely to be accurate if it is recognized. The process of evidence-based practice is designed to reveal and if possible decrease uncertainty, such as attending to the false positive rate of an assessment measure.

3. *Seek disconfirming information.* Our tendency to discount contradictory information highlights the value of seeking disconfirming information. Let's say that a psychologist believes that problems with children are always related to marital difficulties and is confronted with a family in which no evidence of marital difficulties can be found. Reasons to discount this lack of evidence may be readily created. He may say, "They seem happy, but there are problems—I just haven't found them," rather than using disconfirming data to question

his assumptions. A belief that a certain effect always occurs is usually an oversimplification. Although marital problems may accompany child problems in many cases, in other instances they may not.

4. *Pay attention to context (environmental causes).* Be sure to explore the possible role of environmental variables related to client concerns. Axis IV of the *DSM* focuses on psychosocial and environmental problems such as housing problems, poverty, inadequate access to health resources, and unemployment. Considering relevant events from the client's point of view may help you to discover important environmental factors. When relevant and feasible, observe clients in real-life settings or in role-play. Relying on self-report alone encourages a dispositional bias.

5. *Examine all four cells of contingency tables.* Incorrect assumptions about causes often occur because attention is focused on one cell (usually the positive-positive cell) of a four-cell contingency table.

6. *Ask "what if."* Asking "what if" questions should help you to avoid errors due to premature closure about causes. These include questions such as "What if X caused Y, rather than Y caused X?" or "What if X had never happened—would Y still have occurred?" If well-argued alternative explanations can readily be offered, the original account is questionable.

SUMMARY

A key aspect of clinical practice is identifying the cause of client concerns. Effective searches may require critical thinking skills and creativity as well as specialized knowledge based on experience that provides corrective feedback. Practice theories guide both the collection and the processing of data. Causal analysis requires the integration of different kinds of data, a task that is subject to a variety of errors. Research on clinical decision making indicates that hypotheses about client concerns are arrived at quite early and that, although a great deal of data is collected, decisions are based on a modest amount of data; we do not use all the data gathered. Decisions are influenced by irrelevant as well as by relevant data. Assumptions about covariations—what events go together and how strongly they are associated—influence our assumptions. Common errors in assessing how closely two or more events are related include ignoring nonoccurrences, preconceptions about which events are related, and attempted proof by selected instances. The fundamental attribution error in which causes are mistakenly attributed to the client rather than to situational variables is common. It is easier to label a client with borderline personality than to find out data about her life and environment. We often assume that behavior is more consistent than it actually is; we overlook the variability of behavior in different situations.

In exploring the relationship between personal characteristics and environmental variables and client concerns, we tend to give undue attention to the present-present cell of contingency tables, the cell that represents having both a presumed characteristic and the problem; this results in overestimates of pathology. Our interest in having control over our environment encourages a readiness to offer explanations for chance occurrences. We are influenced by vivid events that may lead us astray, and we tend to be overconfident in our assumptions. Or we may underestimate our knowledge and attribute sound decisions to our (un)informed intuition. An important distinction here is between informed intuition and the kind that relies on "inspiration without perspiration"—uninformed hunches. Research concerning sources of error in assessing covariations and making causal assumptions can be used to suggest guidelines for improving accuracy. These include making assumptions explicit, searching for alternative explanations, and taking advantage of tools such as clinical decision aids.

CHAPTER

15

⮕◦⬤◦⬅

Making Predictions:
Improving the Odds

Making choices and predictions is a routine part of clinical practice. Choices are made between different views of client concerns, different interventions, and different outcomes to pursue. These choices involve implicit or explicit predictions as to which alternatives are best. Some predictions concern what clients will do in the future, such as: Will this man rape again if released from jail? Will a client kill herself over the weekend? Will this father participate in treatment plans? Other predictions concern the potential effectiveness of intervention methods: Will cognitive-behavioral therapy help this depressed client? How long will positive gains be maintained? Decisions about which intervention to use should be based on predictions about a client's likely future in response to different procedures or without any intervention, and an evaluation of the acceptability of each alternative to the client. Different effects that are important to consider include both short-term and long-term consequences for clients as well as for their significant others (those who interact with and influence clients). Often, there is no access to such information. Interventions focused on the individual usually do little or nothing to alter social, political, and economic factors that contribute to clients' concerns, as many critics of psychotherapy have emphasized (see Chapter 2). For clinicians who work in agencies, vague policies allow wide discretion in making choices in accord with each clinician's unique beliefs about what criteria should be relied on (e.g., popularity, evidentiary status, personal preferences). Consider this reply of a field instructor to one of my students, who had asked her, "Is play therapy effective?" (This was the method offered to all clients at this agency.) "I don't care about research," she said. "I am here doing this because it is what I like to do."

Predictions are closely related to causal assumptions, and typically concern the prediction of some clinical variable of interest, such as prognosis or recidivism based on characteristics such as history, age, and quality of social support available. "Other things being equal, the greater the predictive validity of some variable, the greater its causal relevance" (Einhorn & Hogarth, 1985, p. 320). Correlation coefficients often are used as measures of predictive accuracy. (Possible misinterpretations of correlations are discussed in Chapter 14.) Predictions differ in complexity and the nature of feedback required and available to check their accuracy. The more complex, the more aids such as actuarial models are valuable (see later discussion). The more vague and delayed the feedback about the consequences of predictions and choices, the less help is offered for improving future predictions. Clinicians often disagree about the criteria that should be used to assess outcome.

Measures used to make predictions include self-reports, test scores, ratings based on observation, and impressions gathered in interviews. Prediction rules may be more effective in ruling out a problem (e.g., influenza) than in ruling it in (Michaels, Thomas, Royen, & Coenen, 2011). Problems of reliability may be overlooked when evaluating the usefulness of data. For instance, you might assume that a small difference in scores reflects a true difference, when the difference is a result of an unreliable measure. This might result in inaccurate classification of clients (such as assuming that clients are clinically depressed when they are not) or faulty selection of an intervention (deciding to intervene because it is assumed that a measure indicates pathology when no such condition exists). The predictive accuracy of a measure, such as a suicide potential scale, may be unknown. Judgments are made under considerable uncertainty in attempts to maximize some values while minimizing associated costs. How much we value an outcome is often confused with the probability that it will occur (Elstein, 1988). It is not surprising, given the high degree of uncertainty in making predictions and choices, that clinicians may protest that they do not make predictions or avoid making them through delay, inattention, or refusal (Corbin, 1980). The tendency to put off difficult decisions was one of the major reasons for the development of permanency planning procedures in child welfare—procedures designed to encourage social workers to arrive at a case plan for children in a timely manner (Stein & Gambrill, 1977).

We weigh information in terms of whether we think it is causally related to a criterion; we ask "Is it meaningful to us?" rather than "Does it help us to predict which clients will benefit most from a service?" Clinicians choose practice methods on the basis of what they believe will work. But what does that mean? Does it mean that it is helpful to the people who believe in it? If this criterion is used, then we would have to say that appeal to many beliefs, including astrology, is valuable. The popularity of astrology would leave no doubt that it does work: "to most people astrological ideas have undeniable beauty and appeal, the birth chart is nonjudgmental, the interpretation is unfalsifiable, and astrologers tend to be nice people." The distinction between utility and validity explains the conflict between astrologers and critics of astrology. "Critics see a lack of factual evidence and conclude it doesn't work, whereas astrologers see that it helps people and conclude that it does work" (Dean, 1987, p. 178). Both are right and both are guilty of not wanting to know what the other is talking about. Explanations do not necessarily yield predictions, and predictions may not yield accurate explanations, even when the predictions are accurate. Some interventions in medicine are effective, but the process through which success is achieved is unknown. Accurately predicting an individual's future may not be possible, even though considerable information is available about his developmental history. Consider the following case report (based on Morgan, 1982; Pilpel, 1976).

CASE WORKER'S REPORT

Subject: The "C" Family

1. R.C., male, age 43. Unstable personality. Irregular employment during past 8 years; frequently makes unreasonable demands of employer and threatens to resign. Very bitter toward former coworkers. Easily irritated. Has minimal contact with his children, but evinces marked hostility toward elder son. Appears to be in poor health. (confidential: Medical records reveal condition of advanced tertiary syphilis, date of infection unknown.)
2. J.C., female, age 38. Unemployed. Known to have had many extramarital affairs. Estranged from R.C. for a number of years. (CONFIDENTIAL: Medical records reveal no sign of venereal infection.) Shows only an erratic interest in her children. Has difficulty handling money matters.
3. W.C., male, age 18. Weak constitution; bouts of respiratory illness. Disciplinary problems in school. Poor student. Frequently fails examinations despite special tutoring. Evinces self-destructive tendencies.
4. J.S.C., male, age 12. May be son of J.C. and one of her lovers. Submissive and indecisive. Appears intimidated by rest of family. Does well in school, however. Appears to hero-worship his brother.

Analysis

1. The Cs present clear symptoms of family disintegration. R.C. and J.C. married despite initial strong opposition from the former's parents, who did not attend the wedding; latter's parents seem to have been unenthusiastic about the union even though they acquiesced to it. The birth of W.C. 7½ months after the

marriage ceremony did nothing to ameliorate the situation, and his "premature" arrival may be partly responsible, along with Oedipal factors, for R.C.'s obvious hostility to him.

2. Both J.C. and R.C. move in a subculture of sexual promiscuity not at all conducive to family stability. Extramarital adventures appear probable for the period between births of W.C. and J.S.C. and certain for the years following. Cohabitation within the marriage seems to have ceased at least 9 or 10 years ago.

3. Parental neglect of the children in terms of psychological and emotional nurture has been fairly chronic throughout. It has been aggravated by blatant favoritism toward the younger child on the part of both J.C. and R.C. W.C. shows clear signs of maladjustment. His misbehavior at his first school is said to have become "legendary." In his secondary school he was usually at the bottom of his class. He appears to have repressed his anger (understandable) toward his parents and turned it against himself. Seems prone to depression. Recently he jumped off a 30-foot-high bridge while playing with his brother and a cousin, on the theory, as he explained it, that he would grab onto the top of a nearby fir tree and thereby break his fall. Instead, he fell 30 feet to the bottom of the ravine, rupturing a kidney, which caused him to be laid up for 6 weeks.

4. J.S.C. suffers from a marked lack of self-direction. He tries very hard to please and be agreeable, sensing himself inadequate to deal with the three high-powered personalities around him. His autonomy seems seriously impaired.

Prognoses

Poor. R.C.'s health will continue to deteriorate. J.C.'s indiscreet sexual dalliance seems likely to continue also. In any case, the neglect of the children will not abate. J.C. and R.C. essentially lead separate lives now, observing only the formalities of a marriage relationship. Neither has a compelling interest in their sons, and neither seems competent to handle family finances. W.C. seems certain to have further severe problems of adjustment ahead of him, and he is ill-equipped to cope with them. J.S.C. seems to have a chance for healthy development, but he must overcome his timidity and avoid mimicking his brother's dubious exploits.

Summary

For all practical purposes this family has ceased to exist as a viable social unit.
—26 September 1893

Updates

> R.C. died in 1895.
> J.C. died in 1921.
> J.S.C. became a stockbroker in 1900.
> W.C. became Prime Minister of Great Britain in 1940.

Review of hundreds of predictions over years show that we are not very successful in making accurate predictions (Tetlock, 2005). Several methods have been used to explore how clinicians combine data and which data they use. One method is to ask them to describe what they do and why they do it as they make decisions. Another approach is to ask clinicians to review a set of profiles that include a set number of variables and to predict the criterion status (for example, psychotic) of people who produced these profiles. Some studies have found that models based on randomly determined regression weights and unit weighting (using coefficients with equal weights) outperform clinical predictions and models based on these (Dawes & Corrigan, 1974; Wainer, 1976). Research in this area suggests that clinicians' reasoning has the same shortcomings as that of others, including stockbrokers, physicians, intelligence analysts, and electrical engineers.

ACTUARIAL COMPARED TO CLINICAL JUDGMENT

Diagnosis, assessment, and prediction are interrelated. That is, predictions about a client (such as degree of dangerousness, likelihood of relapse, likelihood that a given intervention will be successful) are related to how problems are framed and related assumptions about causal factors. Different sources of data are considered in making predictions (implicit or explicit) about a clients' future behavior. Both assessment and prediction require the integration of diverse sources of data and the selection of relevant rather than irrelevant variables. Here is where many sources of inaccuracy creep in. Prediction involves forward inference (reasoning from present causes to future outcomes), whereas assessment (or diagnostic inference) often involves backward inference (reasoning from symptoms and signs to prior causes). Assessment and prediction are closely related in that "success in predicting the future depends to a considerable degree on making sense of the past" (Einhorn & Hogarth, 1985, p. 313). Errors in assessment may result in incorrect predictions as a result of a confusion between "diagnostic and prognostic probabilities." (See later section on use of test results.) One of the oldest controversies in the field of psychology concerns clinical versus statistical judgment. Clinical judgment draws on a variety of data sources, including impressions gained during interviews. Judgments are intuitively arrived at on the basis of assumptions that often (if not typically) remain implicit rather than explicit. Meehl (1954) made a persuasive case for the superiority of actuarial methods over intuition, and an even more persuasive case can be made today in relation to many kinds of judgments. That is, we can improve the accuracy of judgments in relation to some decisions by taking advantage of known empirical relationships in combining diverse sources of data. Statistical or actuarial judgment involves the systematic combination of data from a variety of sources. Sources may include life history data, test scores, ratings of behavior, and subjective judgments based on information gained during interviews. Judgments are based on empirically determined relationships between sources of data and an outcome, such as job success.

The topic of actuarial versus clinical judgment is a hot one, and those who advocate use of actuarial methods when they are superior in accuracy to clinical inference often are attacked as advocating complete reliance on such methods. This is not what is being advocated (Dawes, Faust, & Meehl, 1989). In the actuarial approach, error is accepted, which decreases the likelihood that it will be ignored. Acceptance of error decreases possibilities of lost opportunities to predict an outcome and the illusion of control—assuming that accurate predictions can be made when they cannot. Quinsey, Harris, Rice, and Cormier (2006) describe 15 arguments against actuarial risk appraisal and responses to these. There are over 136 studies demonstrating the superior predictive accuracy of actuarial methods in a variety of areas, including diagnosis of medical versus psychiatric disorders; description of personality; and prediction of treatment outcome, violent behavior, length of hospitalization, and future child maltreatment (e.g., Grove & Meehl, 1996; Grove, Zald, Lebow, Snitz, & Nelson, 2000; Johnson, 2011; Barber, Shlonsky, Black, Goodman, & Trocmé, 2008). Actuarial judgments have been found to be superior to clinical judgments in many areas, even though they rely on linear models for what may be nonlinear relationships among variables. Clinicians are better at selecting and coding information than they are at integrating it, and this may be one of the reasons decisions made by actuarial methods are often more accurate than those based on clinical inference. It is difficult to combine different sources of information, as must be done in clinical contexts in which environmental, psychological, developmental, and biological factors all may be considered.

PREDICTION, CHOICE, AND PROBABILITY

Making predictions and choices requires the assessment of probabilities. Probability can be viewed as a quantified opinion. The probability assigned to an event represents a subjective degree of belief that it will occur, and can be expressed on a continuous scale ranging from 0 to 1. Only the endpoints of the scale are certain; degrees of uncertainty are represented by the points in between. A psychiatrist may predict that there is a 70% probability that a patient admitted to a psychiatric emergency service is a danger to others if released. Information may be available about the informativeness of certain indicators that can be used to make estimates as in use of actuarial methods and fast and frugal decision trees (Gigerenzer, 2007). In many cases probabilities based on reliable data are not available and clinicians have to rely on their subjective probabilities, estimates of the likelihood of given outcomes such as whether a depressed client will make another suicide attempt in the near future. Typically, they can only guess at the relative importance of different predictors. Even in areas in which extensive research has been carried out to identify criteria of value in making prediction, for example, about future child abuse, results may be disappointing. Current actuarial systems, although superior to consensus-based systems for predicting risk of future harm to children, increase accuracy by classifying children into categories of potential harm such as: high, moderate, and low (Johnson, 2011; Barber et al., 2008). And this occurs with only a certain degree of accuracy. Next, a careful assessment is needed. In *Against Prediction*, Harcourt (2007) critiques use of actuarial methods in the criminal justice system.

Clinicians differ in the kinds of data used and in the weighting of these data. One clinician may base predictions on perusal of genograms, whereas another may base them on a contingency analysis of family interactions. A variety of models have been developed for making choices. In the *compensatory model*, weights are assigned to each variable and the weighted values are summed. Another model is the *conjunctive model*, in which cut-points are set in relation to each dimension, and any alternative that falls below these points is dropped. The placement of the cut-point influences the relative number of successes and failures; the higher the cut-point, the greater the proportion of successes to failures. The lower the criteria of success, the more successes will be observed, regardless of predictive ability and the location of the cut-point. In the *disjunctive model,* a high score on one or several dimensions compensates for a low score on a variable. Past decisions can be used to create a model for current decisions. Clinical rather than actuarial judgments are typically used in combining test results with other sources of data to arrive at judgments.

Clinicians and clients must also assign value or worth (subjective utilities) to outcomes; these represent the relative desirability of different outcomes. How much weight should be given to protecting potential rape victims, and how much to maximizing freedom of those who have a history of rape? How much weight will a client give to the probability of a false positive on a diagnostic test such as a mammogram? How will a client balance benefits and risks of a proposed intervention? Clinicians often help clients to clarify their values. (See discussion of decision aids in Chapter 11.) Descriptions of personal values are influenced by many variables, including the questions asked, their sequence, and how responses are obtained (Soman, 2005). We often do not know what we want. Indeed, the gap between clients' statements of their preferences and related actions is so great that it is considered a major concern in evidence-based practice (see Chapter 10). Conflict often occurs between minimizing costs and maximizing gains. A cost-benefit analysis by a client may reveal that the costs of stopping drinking outweigh the potential benefits. Ideally, gains would be maximized and costs minimized as well as efficiency maintained in terms of time, money, and effort devoted to making a decision. The assessment of probabilities and subjective utilities are interdependent. Certain outcomes are assessed as more valuable than uncertain outcomes. We believe that we are more likely than other people to have good things befall us and less likely to experience maladies. Potential losses are more influential than are potential gains; that is, we are risk-averse.

CHALLENGES IN ASSESSING RISK

Prediction of risk is of concern in many areas, ranging from flying in airplanes and building nuclear plants to deciding whether to leave a child in a home in which he has been neglected and deciding whether to get a mammogram. Risks differ in the degree of certainty that they will occur, knowledge about how to reduce them, and their severity, timing, and type (e.g., see Martinic & Leigh, 2004). Individual risk may differ from population-derived risks. We fall into the ecological fallacy when we assume that what is a risk factor to most people is a risk factor for an individual. Gigerenzer (2002a) highlights four sources of uncertainty: (1) the illusion of certainty, (2) ignorance of risk, (3) miscommunication of risk, and (4) clouded thinking. The first point is addressed in Chapter 4—that is, a justification approach to knowledge in which it is assumed that we can arrive at certain truth, for example, by piling up examples. Ignorance of risk refers to being uninformed about the risks associated with different decisions, such as having a mammogram or attending an anxiety screening day. The third point, miscommunication of risk, refers to not knowing how to communicate risk in an understandable way. For example, a physician may know the risks associated with a certain test but not be able to clearly communicate this knowledge to a patient so that the patient can make an informed decision (Paling, 2006). The fourth kind of innumeracy, clouded thinking, refers to knowing the risks but not knowing how to draw correct inferences from them. "For instance, physicians often know the error rates of a clinical test and the base rate of a disease, but not how to infer from this information the chances that a patient with a positive test actually has the disease" (p. 25). Such problems are easily solved by using natural frequencies, as discussed later in this chapter. Statistical innumeracy is very high among professionals as well as clients. That is, given relevant figures, answers are strikingly incorrect, usually by overestimating pathology (Gigerenzer, 2002a). Let's take an example:

> At the beginning of one continuing education session, 160 gynecologists were provided with the relevant health statistics needed to derive the answer

to this question in the form of conditional probabilities, which is the form in which medical studies usually report test statistics (Gigerenzer et al., 2007):

Assume that you conduct breast cancer screening using mammography in a certain region. You know the following information about the women in this region:

> The probability that a woman has breast cancer is 1% (prevalence).
> If a woman has breast cancer, the probability that she tests positive is 90% (sensitivity).
> If a woman does not have breast cancer, the probability that she nevertheless tested positive is 9% (false positive rate).

A woman tests positive. She wants to know from you whether this means that she has breast cancer for sure, or what the chances are. What is the best answer?

> (A) The probability that she has breast cancer is about 81%.
> (B) Out of 10 women with a positive mammogram, about 9 have breast cancer.
> (C) Out of 10 women with a positive mammogram, about 1 has breast cancer.
> (D) The probability that she has breast cancer is about 1%.

The best answer is (C); that is, only about 1 out of every 10 women who tests positive in screening actually has breast cancer. The other 9 are falsely alarmed; that is, they receive a positive test result although they do not have breast cancer. Only 21% of the gynecologists found the best answer; the majority (60%) disconcertingly chose "9 out of 10" or "81%," thus grossly overestimating the probability of cancer. Another troubling result was the high variability in physicians' estimates, which ranged between a 1% and 90% chance of cancer. (Wegwarth & Gigerenzer, 2011)

People differ in how they evaluate different kinds of risks. We are risk-averse; we worry more about what we will lose than what we will gain. An illustration of this tendency can be seen in a study by McNeil, Pauker, Sox, and Tversky (1982) concerning preference for surgery or radiation therapy for lung cancer. One group of subjects received statistics that showed the percentage of patients that survived for different lengths of time after treatment. The other group received mortality statistics (percentage of patients who died). When the choice was posed in terms of mortality, 42% selected radiation therapy over surgery; only 25% of patients who received survival statistics selected radiation therapy over surgery. The advantages of surgery relative to radiation therapy loomed larger in the minds of respondents when framed in terms of the probability of survival than they did when stated in terms of the probability of death. The observed effect occurred with physicians as well as patients.

At the other end of the pole are those who seek risks—they engage in risky behavior. Examples include skydivers, mountain climbers, and high-stakes gamblers. Research regarding risks shows that:

1.   Voluntary risks are viewed as less risky than those that are not voluntary.
2.   Natural risks are assumed to be less hazardous than artificial risks.
3.   We tend to overestimate the risks of events that kill or injure a great number of people and underestimate the risks associated with less vivid conditions or events that in fact affect many more people, such as asthma.
4.   We tend to consider risks to be less if we think that we have control over them.
5.   We tend to think that things that we cannot see and that are associated with dreaded outcomes, such as radioactive waste and AIDS, are riskier than events that involve known risks or less dreaded outcomes such as auto accidents (Halpern, 2003, p. 299).

Thus, as Halpern (2003) notes, "personal risk perceptions are not the same as scientific risk estimates" (p. 299).

Selection of interventions is influenced by the perceived risk associated with different options. Over the past few decades, there has been enormous interest in identifying risk factors for certain diseases, including alleged mental illnesses. Some argue that we live in a risk society (Beck, 1992). Advertisers take full advantage of our fears and hopes (e.g., see Exhibit 15.1). A public health perspective seeks to identify risks for certain future conditions—for example, through screening programs—and promotes behaviors to decrease them. The importance of some screening programs is suggested by the fact that you could have an illness without feeling ill or you may feel ill without having an illness (Gray, 2001a). But do screening programs do more good than harm? Will screening all residents of the United States for mental illness do more good than harm? (Lenzer, 2004; President's New Freedom Commission on Mental Health, retrieved September 9, 2005). See also controversies related to screening nonsymptomatic individuals for prostate, breast, and cervical cancer (Welch, Schwartz, & Woloshin, 2011).

Statistical illiteracy hinders conversion of information regarding risk into language that helps clients understand "Is this likely to happen to me?" Advertisers inflate benefits

Exhibit 15.1 Comic-strip formats (like radio commercials) afforded ads a time dimension. Even a staid baking company might lure newspaper readers into the "almost hypnotic" sequence of squares that told of a marriage imperiled by "bargain bread."

Source: Marchand, R. (1985, p. 113). *Advertising the American Dream: Making Way for Modernity, 1920–1940.* Berkeley, CA: University of California Press.

of remedies promoted and hide adverse effects to entice the unwary to use their products (Gambrill, 2012a). Different ways to present benefits/risks include the following:

- *Absolute risk reduction:* The absolute risk reduction is the proportion of patients who die without treatment minus those who die with treatment. Let's say that drug X reduces the number of people who die from 41 to 32 in 1,000. The absolute risk reduction is 9 in 1,000, which is 0.9%.
- *Relative risk reduction:* The relative risk reduction is the absolute risk reduction divided by the proportion of patients who die without treatment. For the preceding data, the relative risk reduction is 9 divided by 41, which is 22%. Drug X reduces the risk of dying by 22%.
- *Number needed to treat:* The number of people who must participate in a treatment to save one life is the number needed to treat (NNT). This number can be derived from the absolute risk reduction. The number of people who needed to be treated to save one life is 111, because 9 in 1,000 deaths (which is about 1 in 111) are prevented by the drug.

Relative risk reduction looks more impressive than absolute risk reduction. Relative risks are larger numbers than absolute risks and suggest higher benefits than really exist. Presenting only relative risks is viewed as unethical in the medical literature. Gigerenzer (2002a) views use of absolute risks as a mind tool that makes the actual benefits more understandable.

USING TEST RESULTS

It is estimated that in general practice medically unexplained, physical symptoms comprise up to half of all new referrals. Clinicians use tests to decrease uncertainty. Tests may be used to assess risk or to predict future behavior. You may estimate the likelihood that a client has a problem, such as depression or tuberculosis. This is known as the initial base rate probability. You then may consider whether asking a client to take a test will be of value. "To what extent will test results decrease uncertainty about an assessment or diagnosis? Tests should be used to revise subjective estimates—that is, to change a decision about how a client should be treated. Let's say, based on an interview, you suspect that an elderly client has Alzheimer's disease and you obtain psychological test results. The results should be used to choose among different intervention options in light of the new estimate based on the test results. That is, estimates of the probability that the client has Alzheimer's disease will be revised. Clinicians may either fail to revise or incorrectly revise their probability estimates when thinking about additional data.

These kinds of problems are harder than we realize. They are also typical of the problems clinicians confront, although in fields such as psychiatry, social work, and psychology, less information is available about base rates and test accuracy. Two kinds of odds should be considered (Arkes, 1981). One kind consists of prior odds—odds before additional information about a client is available. Obtaining more information (data that are useful in decreasing uncertainty) should change these prior odds.

It serves little purpose to ask a client to take a test that will not change what would be done, depending on what the test reveals, perhaps because there is no effective intervention. Thus, taking a test is useful only if it moves a client across an "action threshold"— the point at which a different action will be taken, depending on what is revealed. In making this decision it is important to consider whether a test has been normed and in what way. Has it been tested for validity on clients with a known condition? Has a test of depression been normed using a sample of people known to be depressed by criterion indicators? The predictive accuracy of a test depends on the initial risk of a condition in the person receiving the test. The probability that a client with a positive (or negative) test result for dementia actually has dementia depends on the prevalence of dementia in the population from which the patient was selected—that is, on the pretest probability that a client has dementia. Because there is little appreciation of this point, predictive accuracy is often overestimated. What percentage of applicants would succeed on the job anyway without any testing procedure? If 90% would, then testing does not add much information.

A test will have different accuracy readings in a population in which there is a much smaller percentage of individuals with known depression. If used in such a population, there will be a high false positive rate. That is, there will be a high rate of individuals labeled with the condition (depression) who do not have it. Let's say a social worker works in an agency where staff see a high frequency of children who have been sexually abused. If such a test is used in an agency that sees a wide variety of children with a much lower base rate of sexual abuse, there will be a high rate of false positives. Thus, you should ask: "How will this test perform with my clients? Does the pretest probability for my clients differ from the pretest probability of clients who were subjects in the study for which the test was developed?" We can estimate a test's performance in distinguishing between clients with and without a certain condition by using likelihood ratios. A likelihood ratio of 1 indicates that a test is totally uninformative. The consequence of a positive or negative test will be different depending on the pretest probability of a condition. Cut-points are used to try to balance the kinds of errors that occur. A receiver operating characteristic (ROC) analysis can be used.

Professionals tend to make certain kinds of misinterpretations of test results. Incorrect information given to clients regarding test results for HIV is illustrated in the following example:

Session 1: The Counselor Was a Female Social Worker

Sensitivity?

- False negatives really never occur. Although, if I think about the literature, there were reports of such cases.
- I don't know exactly how many.
- It happened only once or twice.

False positives?

- No, because the test is repeated; it is absolutely certain.
- If there are antibodies, the test identifies them unambiguously and with absolute certainty.
- No, it is absolutely impossible that there are false positives; because it is repeated, the test is absolutely certain.

Prevalence?

- I can't tell you this exactly.
- Between about 1 in 500 and 1 in 1,000.

Positive predictive value?

- As I have now told you repeatedly, the test is absolutely certain.

The counselor was aware that HIV tests can lead to a few false negatives, but incorrectly informed Ebert that there are not false positives. Ebert asked for clarification twice, in order to make sure that he correctly understood that a false positive is impossible. The counselor asserted that a positive test result means, with absolute certainty, that the client has the virus. (Gigerenzer, 2002a, pp. 129–130)

Test sensitivity (the test's accuracy in correctly identifying people who have a disorder) may be confused with *test specificity* (accuracy of a test in correctly identifying people who do not have a disorder), resulting in incorrect predictions. Test sensitivity is often incorrectly equated with the predictive value of a positive test result, and test specificity is incorrectly equated with the predictive value of a negative test result (Beck, Byyny, & Adams, 1981; Elstein, 1988; see Chapter 12). Steurer and his colleagues (Steurer, Fischer, Bachmann Koller, & ter Riet, 2002) found that Swiss general practitioners "were unable to interpret correctly numerical information on the diagnostic accuracy of the screening test." Only 22% of these doctors selected the correct answer for the posttest probability of a positive screening test. They grossly overestimated the value of a positive result alone. They tended to overestimate information derived from tests and to underestimate information from a client's clinical history. Physicians vastly overestimate the predictive accuracy of screening tests such as mammograms (Gigerenzer, 2002a; Welch, Schwartz, & Woloshin, 2011).

Errors concerning the predictive accuracy of tests are also a result of confusion between two different conditional probabilities. We tend to confuse *retrospective accuracy*, the probability of a positive test given that the person has a condition, and *predictive accuracy*, the probability of a condition given a positive test result. Retrospective accuracy is determined by reviewing test results after the true condition is known. Predictive accuracy refers to the probability of having a condition given a positive test result and the probability of not having a condition given a negative test. It is predictive accuracy that is important when confronted with a test result on an individual (see Chapter 14 for further discussion). Another source of error in making predictions is the assumption that the accuracy of a test can be represented by one number. In fact, test accuracy will vary greatly, depending on whether a test is used as a screening device in which there are large numbers of people who do not have some condition of interest or whether it is used for clients with known signs or symptoms. In the latter case, the true positive and true negative rates are much higher than in the broad screening situation, so there will be fewer false positives and false negatives. Overlooking this difference results in overestimations of test accuracy in screening situations, resulting in a high percentage of false positives. An example of a "drug facts box" that includes information allowing an informed decision about the benefits and risks associated with taking a drug can be seen in Chapter 11, Exhibit 11.6.

SOURCES OF ERROR

There are many sources of error in trying to make accurate predictions, including overlooking the effects of confounding causes, such as the play of chance and misleading effects of small biased samples. Many of the same factors that result in misleading beliefs about causes are also at play when making predictions.

Preconceptions

Predictions are made based on concepts and data that are available; here again we are influenced by practice theories and preconceptions. Hearing a persuasive causal explanation of an event increases a belief that an outcome associated with that event will occur (Tversky & Kahneman, 1983). The causal coherence of a scenario is used to assess the likelihood of its occurrence; that is, causal persuasiveness is confused with outcome (Hogarth, 1987, p. 49). Behaviors that have occurred with a high frequency in a certain situation in the past are likely to do so again, other factors being equal. It is when available cues do not reflect the true frequency of an event or result in ignoring the importance of other events (such as nonoccurrences) that these result in errors. Anchoring effects are influential in all stages of decision making, including making predictions. Since initial judgments are often wrong, actions taken based on these may be incorrect. Initial judgments can be remarkably resistant to change. For example, even though subjects were told that initial estimates they received were based on random information such as the throw of dice, they did not alter their estimates (Tversky & Kahneman, 1974). Adjustments in predictions are often made on the basis of information that is initially available, thus compounding possible biasing effects of initial judgments (Hogarth, 1980, p. 47).

Framing Effects

Posing a decision in a certain way influences our decisions (e.g., Soman, 2005). Emphasizing potential benefits of a choice increases the likelihood that the decision maker will say yes. Conversely, we are more likely to say no when possible negatives are emphasized (Dawes, 1988). Framing effects are more powerful where important decisions are being made, such as whether to undergo a surgical procedure. Consider the following example:

> *Counselor:* Perhaps I can help you with your decision. We know that two thirds of those who get treatment at Anderson Hospital for the Chemically Dependent remain chemical-free for two years. We also know that one third of those treated at Luther Hospital's Chemical Dependency Unit return to chemicals within two years.
>
> *Client:* I think I'll choose Anderson because, from what you have said, my chances seem better there.

How We Represent Problems

Gigerenzer (2002a) emphasizes the importance of how we represent problems in relation to the likelihood of understanding them. (See later discussion of using natural frequencies rather than probabilities.)

Overlooking the Importance of Base-Rate Data

The earlier discussion highlighted the importance of considering base-rate data (the general prevalence of a behavior or event in the population) in making predictions.

Normative data tends to be ignored in making predictions, not only in relation to other people but in relation to self-perception as well. If we are informed that most other individuals act in a certain way in a situation and are then asked what a particular person will do in that context, we tend to ignore normative data in arriving at a judgment. A helpful rule of thumb is to find out what is known about the most frequent outcome in a situation and to attend to these data when making predictions. Because of preconceptions about what things go together, clinicians often overlook base-rate data, assuming that they have nothing to do with case data. Often, clinicians do not have access to base-rate information; such data may be difficult or impossible to acquire. Ignoring base-rate data when they are available can result in overestimating clinical success; the question of how many cases would be successful anyhow is overlooked (see later section on feedback).

The attention topics receive in the media influence estimates of the prevalence of events. For example, the relative frequencies of cancer and homicides are overestimated, whereas the relative frequencies of asthma and diabetes, which receive less media attention, are underestimated (Lichtenstein, Slovic, Fischhoff, Layman, & Coombs, 1978). If the media and the professional literature devote a great deal of attention to children of alcoholics, this may lead clinicians to overestimate their prevalence. Consider also the attention given to stranger abduction of children. A review article in *Public Interest* indicated that the prevalence of abductions by strangers has been grossly overestimated by special-interest groups and that once correct figures become available, later correction of inflated figures may do little or nothing to correct initial, inaccurate estimates (Best, 1988). Overestimating the prevalence of a problem is not without effects. The result may be redistribution of clinical and other resources away from areas where need is greater. We tend to worry about what has recently happened and to let events slip from our minds as the events recede into the past. Clinicians may worry more about whether they should report a threat by a client against a significant other immediately after a lurid description of a crime committed by another client when the clinician did not warn the involved party. The purchase of earthquake insurance increases right after an earthquake (Slovic, Kunreuther, & White, 1974).

Overlooking Regression Effects

Overlooking regression effects can result in errors. Extreme effects will usually not be so extreme when they are reassessed. If a client does unusually well on a test, she is likely to do less well the next time around; or conversely, if she does very poorly, she is likely to do better the next time around. "The implication of the regression phenomenon is that when prediction is based on sources with imperfect predictive ability, predictions should be less extreme than the information generated by the sources. The term 'regression phenomenon' simply means that in the presence of imperfect predictive sources, predictions should be regressed toward the mean" (Hogarth, 1980, p. 35). Both reliability and validity problems add to the regression effect. For example, lack of reliability may lead to predictions that are too extreme. This is a special problem in clinical contexts in which clinicians are heavily influenced by cues that have an extreme value; extremes stand out—they are vivid. Essentially, "a failure to understand chance fluctuations leads to judgmental errors" (Hogarth, 1980, p. 35).

Expecting extreme values to be less marked on repeated assessment helps avoid this source of error. Superstitious beliefs may result from overlooking regression effects. Superstitions are beliefs about the causal relationship between two or more events (for example, carrying a rabbit's foot and avoiding bad luck) that are not true. An example described by Kahneman and Tversky (1973) concerns Israeli flight instructors who were encouraged to use positive reinforcement and to avoid punishment to help pilots learn to fly. After doing so, they argued that these methods were not effective since it was their experience that praise of superior performance resulted in less effective outcomes on the next efforts, while criticism of poor performance produced improved performance on subsequent attempts. They concluded that punishment was more effective than positive reinforcement in increasing desired behaviors. Some argue that unwarranted belief in the effectiveness of most practices is superstitious in nature, given that there is no evidence that most practices do more good than harm.

Errors in Estimating Joint Probabilities

Clinical practice often requires the assessment of joint probabilities. Let's say that a psychologist in a student counseling center wants to determine the probability that a student (a) will select journalism as a college major, (b) become unhappy with his choice, and (c) change to engineering. This involves estimating the probability of conjunctive events. Such events are usually overestimated. For example, when different groups of subjects were asked to estimate the probabilities of (a), both (a) and (b), and all three, they gave the following average estimates: .21 for (a); .39 for (a) and (b); and .42 for all three—(a), (b), and (c) (Slovic, Fischhoff, & Lichtenstein, 1976). However, the joint probability of two events cannot be greater than the smaller of the probabilities that are associated with the events (see section on overlooking important probabilities in Chapter 14).

Relying on Irrelevant Data

Irrelevant data increase the probability of incorrect predictions; a few worthless items can dilute the effect of one helpful item. The influence of irrelevant data is illustrated in a study in which social work graduate students were asked to estimate the likelihood that some people were child abusers. Inclusion of information that the person "fixes up cars in his spare time" and "once ran away from home as a boy" decreased the effects of data that he has "sadomasochistic sexual fantasies" (see Nisbett & Ross, 1980, p. 155). Irrelevant material about this person tended to make him less similar to someone who might abuse his child. A rule of thumb here is to ask whether data have any real predictive value.

Influence by Redundant Data

Sources of assessment data are not necessarily independent. Take, for example, the prediction of intelligence. Data concerning grade point average, intelligence test scores, recommendations, and past employment are not independent sources of information; they are related, which decreases the amount of information each source offers. Clinicians often overlook the redundancy of data in making predictions; that is, the more data sources they have available, even though these are not independent, the more confident they feel in their predictions. Consider the study of Oskamp (1965), in which the judgments of clinical psychologists were studied as a function of the amount of data they received. These clinicians were asked to make a prediction based on a case study and to indicate their degree of confidence in these judgments under different conditions in relation to the amount of data they received. As the data they received increased, so did their confidence in their judgments. There was, however, no increase in predictive accuracy. Kahneman and Tversky (1973) refer to the influence by the consistency of redundant data and the influences of extreme values of predictive cues as the *illusion of validity*—both increase confidence in judgments even though both are inversely related to the predictive accuracy of data sources. Our tendency to overestimate the degree of covariation between variables adds to the illusion of validity.

Underestimating the Play of Chance

Errors in prediction often occur because of misperception of chance fluctuations. Clinicians tend to overestimate their ability to make accurate predictions. For example, they often fail to appreciate the random variability in behavior that may be beyond any current models of explanation. We may believe that the immediate future will compensate for unusual outcomes by reversing these patterns and base predictions on such beliefs (Nisbett & Ross, 1980). This source of error is known as the gambler's fallacy, because gamblers often make this error. The *gambler's fallacy* refers to the belief that the next event in a sequence that is probabilistic in nature, such as flipping a coin, will redress prior imbalances. It is assumed, for example, that the outcome of tossing a coin on one occasion influences the outcome on the next occasions; that if three heads in a row appear, the next flip will yield tails. This belief is exploited by gambling casinos, as well as by those who claim to have paranormal power. Clinicians are also subject to this source of error. Making predictions can lead to an illusion of control—a feeling that there is control over a future that is indeed uncertain (see later discussion of feedback).

Hindsight Bias

We have a tendency to say that "we knew it all along" when a certain outcome occurs, especially when it is consistent with our preconceptions. In fact, we often cannot recall what we predicted before an outcome is known, or misrecall in a biased direction. This encourages overestimates of predictability (e.g., overestimating the relationship between returning a child to the home of his biological parents and subsequent child abuse). Knowledge of an outcome encourages the view that it was inevitable—that we should have known what the outcome would be, even though there was no way we could have known the outcome beforehand. We tend to assume that outcomes are consistent with our preconceptions—"I knew it all along." Another characteristic of hindsight bias is a tendency to assume a direct relationship between an outcome and certain causes when, in fact, no evidence is offered for or against such an assumption (Fischhoff, 1975). Since explanations are readily created, possible accounts are usually always at hand. Hindsight bias often results in blaming people for what appear to be errors that could have been avoided; looking back, knowing the outcome that occurred, it is assumed that "he should have known." It also results in praising people for what were just lucky guesses (Hastie & Dawes, 2001; Hogarth, 1980). There are benefits from hindsight bias; it helps us to remember associations that work as well as ones that do not work.

Outcome Bias

We tend to judge the quality of a process by its outcome. Use of vague or irrelevant feedback obscures the true relationship (or lack thereof) between predictions and outcomes. Those who have been told there is a poor outcome evaluate the decision or action more negatively. This is referred to as outcome bias. For example, Caplan, Posner, and Cheney (1991) found an inverse relationship between the severity of outcome and the judgments on the part of anesthesiologists concerning the appropriateness of care. Cases in which there were bad outcomes were rated as substandard while the very same behaviors, if they resulted in neutral outcomes, were rated as being up to standard. Information about outcome biased the evaluation of the process followed (Woods & Cook, 1999, p. 146). People view an outcome as more probable when they are given knowledge of an outcome. Research concerning physicians' decisions about whether to recommend estrogen replacement therapy for menopausal women suggests that physicians feel more responsible for negative outcomes that are a result of their direct actions (for example, cancers that result from the treatment) than they do for negative outcomes that just happen (for example, bone fractures due to osteoporosis; see Elstein, 1988). Preferences for methods that have the smallest maximum loss may decrease attention to methods that would result in maximum gains.

These kinds of biases, including hindsight bias referred to earlier, show that we tend to confuse and overlook differences between information available about outcome at one time and information available at another time. Thus, "experiments on hindsight bias have shown that: (1) people overestimate what they would have known in foresight, (2) they also overestimate what others knew in foresight, and (3) they actually misremember what they themselves knew in foresight" (Woods & Cook, 1999, p. 146). As these authors note, all three have implications for error analysis in terms of incorrect memories and estimates of what information was available when the decision was made and what information is available after we know that an error occurred. Hindsight bias results in misperceptions and incorrect analysis of the reasons the mistake was made in the first place. "In general, we react after the fact as if the knowledge we now possess was available to the operators then. This oversimplifies or trivializes the situation confronting the practitioners, and masks the processes affecting practitioner behavior before the fact. As a result, hindsight and outcome bias block our ability to see the deeper story of systematic factors that predictably shape human performance" (p. 147).

Overlooking the Interaction Between Predictions and Related Actions

The interactive nature between the actions we take as a result of the predictions we make may obscure the true relationship between the effects of our actions and outcomes (Einhorn, 1988). We tend to forget that actions taken as a result of predictions influence the outcomes. Consider the prediction that the banks will fail, followed by a run on the banks and their subsequent failure. If you believe you can help a group, you may extend greater effort, which may increase the probability of a positive outcome. If an applicant is accepted for a job, opportunities on the job may ensure future success. Those who are rejected do not have these opportunities.

Other Factors

Clinical predictions are also influenced by preferences for certain outcomes; the probability of desired outcomes is judged to be higher than is justified by information available. This has been called wishful thinking (Hogarth, 1980). Predictions and causal analyses differ depending on question format. Thus, the response mode influences judgments (Slovic, Fischhoff, & Lichtenstein, 1982b). Data presented in the form of "no" (negative terms) is more difficult to comprehend than data presented in positive terms. Faulty memory influenced by preconceptions may result in errors in recall about factors related to an outcome. These errors will obscure the relationship between predictor variables and outcomes. Trying to recall events is an active process in which accounts are often reconstructed. Feedback may be ignored, especially if this contradicts predictions and favored value systems on which these predictions are based. The tendency to be overconfident about the accuracy of our predictions is as common among experts as it is among other people (Tetlock, 2005). Overconfidence resulting from flawed self-assessments influences decisions in many areas, including our health and how much we think we know (Dunning, Heath, & Suls, 2004; Kruger & Dunning, 1999). Physicians are very confident of grossly inaccurate estimates of the accuracy of tests (see Wegwarth & Gigerenzer, 2011). Success tends to be attributed to personal skill, and failure tends to be attributed to chance. The confusion between a conditional probability and its inverse (confusion of the inverse) is likely to result in inaccurate predictions of pathology. The probability of a sign given a disorder is not necessarily equal to the probability of the disorder given the sign; the probability of the sign is usually higher than the probability of the disorder. If $P(S \mid D)$ and $P(D \mid S)$ are confused, many more clients will be falsely diagnosed as having a disorder that they do not have (Eddy, 1982).

Errors may occur because of vague and shifting criteria for judging alternatives. Being overloaded with information reduces the consistency of judgments; one form of presentation (such as charts) is usually selected, and others (such as the text) are ignored. This lack of consistency is one of the reasons that actuarial judgments are often superior to clinical judgments. We are influenced by the degree of similarity between the characteristics of an event, object, person, and the class to which it belongs. Resemblance is a valid indicator only to the extent that data sources are not redundant or that it does not result in ignoring other information (Hogarth, 1980, p. 31). Information that is inconsistent with our stereotypes of what characteristics are predictive of a given event is often ignored.

INCREASING THE ACCURACY OF PREDICTIONS

One step you can take to enhance the accuracy of predictions is to clearly describe possible risks and gains of alternatives and to make explicit predictions. Few clinicians offer specific probabilities in making predictions, even though predictions become more accurate if this is done (Einhorn & Hogarth, 1978). Rather than offering vague predictions (such as "I think insight therapy will be effective"), you could predict that there is an 80% chance that a certain intervention will be successful in increasing positive exchanges in a family. Comparison of outcomes with specific predictions offers more fine-grained feedback about accuracy than do vague predictions, such as "There will be improvement." Considering maximum possible gains from a method may help counteract undue attention to minimizing risks associated with different options.

Visual representations can be helpful. Fast and frugal decision trees enhance accurate predictions (Gigerenzer, 2007). Attending to reliability and validity of measures will enhance accuracy, as will taking advantage of statistical tools. Use of actuarial methods will increase the consistency with which known relationships between predictors and an outcome, such as the risk of future abuse, are considered. Although some clinicians believe that relying on a predictive equation dehumanizes clients, this view ignores the human costs of error that result from not using these tools (Dawes, Faust, & Meehl, 1989). The tendency to focus on the conjunction of two events (such as certain kinds of dreams and negative events) may be checked by paying attention to disconfirming combinations in a four-cell contingency table (see Chapter 14). Asking about all four cells can help you to avoid focusing only on hits. Keeping in mind the possible harm avoided by asking questions about tests and interventions encourages raising such questions. Consider the harm to children and their families by removing children from their homes based on an invalid test (Hobbs & Wynne, 1989).

Decreasing reliance on memory will increase the accuracy of predictions. Because of confirmation biases, we tend to remember data that support our assumptions and may even recall data that were not present that support assumptions, and we may forget data that were present that do not support our views. Keeping good records will decrease errors due to memory lapses. Collecting data about degree of progress will improve the quality of feedback. Treatment manuals increase the fidelity with which interventions are implemented, which should enhance the accuracy of predicted outcome if this is related to fidelity.

Use Natural Frequencies

Thinking in terms of natural frequencies rather than probabilities can help us to overcome innumeracy, as illustrated by Gigerenzer (2002a). Let's say that the following information is available about asymptomatic women aged 40 to 50 in a given region who participate in mammography screening:

The probability that one of these women has breast cancer is 0.8 percent. If a woman has breast cancer, the probability is 90 percent that she will have a positive mammogram. If a woman does not have breast cancer, the probability is 7 percent that she will still have a positive mammogram. Imagine a woman who has a positive mammogram. What is the probability that she actually has breast cancer?

Here is the problem in natural frequencies:

> Eight out of every 1,000 women have breast cancer. Of these 8 women with breast cancer, 7 will have a positive mammogram. Of the remaining 992 women who don't have breast cancer, some 70 will still have a positive mammogram. Imagine a sample of women who have positive mammograms in screening. How many of these women actually have breast cancer? (Gigerenzer, 2002a, p. 42)

Here is the depiction of both natural frequencies and probabilities (p. 45):

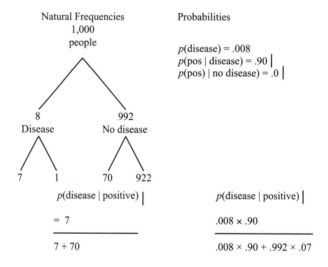

Let's take another example:

> To diagnose colorectal cancer, the hemoccult test—among others—is conducted to detect occult blood in the stool. This test is used from a particular age on, but also in routine screening for early detection of colorectal cancer. Imagine you conduct a screening using the hemoccult test in a certain region. For symptom-free people over 50 years old who participate in screening using the hemoccult test, the following information is available for this region:
>
> Conditional Probabilities Format—First 24 Participants
>
> The probability that one of these people has colorectal cancer is 0.3 percent. If a person has colorectal cancer, the probability is 50 percent that he will

have a positive hemoccult test. If a person does not have colorectal cancer, the probability is 3 percent that he will still have a positive hemoccult test. Imagine a person (over age 50, no symptoms) who has a positive hemoccult test in your screening. What is the probability that this person actually has colorectal cancer? _____ percent. (Gigerenzer, 2002a, p. 104)

Natural Frequencies Format—Remaining 24 Participants

Thirty out of every 10,000 people have colorectal cancer. Of these 30 people with colorectal cancer, 15 will have a positive hemoccult test. Of the remaining 9,970 people without colorectal cancer, 300 will still have a positive hemoccult test. Imagine a sample of people (over age 50, no symptoms) who have positive hemoccult tests in your screening. How many of these people actually have colorectal cancer? ___ out of ___. (Gigerenzer, 2002a, pp. 104–105)

Here we have the natural frequency depicted (p. 107).

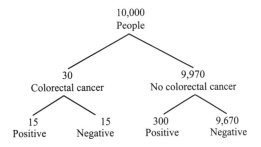

Seek Feedback

One of the many choices you make is how (or if) to explore the accuracy of your decisions, including predictions. Clinical judgments typically involve continuous rather than discrete evaluation, and thus many opportunities for gaining corrective feedback are available. The more rapid and continuous the feedback, the more sensitive and valid the measures of progress; the more closely outcomes are related to decisions made, the more opportunities we have to learn how to make better decisions in the future. Feedback from clients regarding each session enhances outcome (Lambert & Shimokawa, 2011). Feedback may be irrelevant to learning; outcomes observed may offer inaccurate or incomplete data about predictions, which may result in overconfidence in judgments. (See discussion of wicked environments in Chapter 8.) Clearly describing objectives and keeping track of progress on an ongoing basis will be helpful in assessing the accuracy of judgments. If feedback is delayed—for example, whether a rapist will rape again when released from prison—a precursor of later behavior, such as urges, could be monitored. What and how to measure outcome is a hotly debated issue. Choices are influenced by practice perspectives. Measures used include therapist opinions, self-report of clients, self-monitoring, role-playing, observation of behavior in real-life settings, and archival records, such as hospital admissions (see Chapter 13). Feedback that is vague, irrelevant, or delayed hinders discovery of relationships between predictions and outcomes. Selection of sensitive, relevant outcome indicators often requires creativity, as well as a knowledge of practice-related literature about options. (See Chapter 11 for further detail.)

Use Absolute Risk

Always ask for the absolute risk. Absolute risk is always in relation to a number (e.g., 1 out of 10, 1 out of 1,000, etc.). Relative risk is highly misleading. Gigerenzer (2002a) views absolute risk as an important tool in our adaptive tool box.

THE FALLACY THAT PREVENTION IS ALWAYS BETTER THAN CURE

This fallacy is highlighted by Skrabanek and McCormick in *Follies and Fallacies in Medicine* (1998). They point out that prevention has a price and that this price may be more costly than any subsequent problems (p. 87). In his article "The Arrogance of Preventive Medicine," Sackett (2002) emphasizes (1) aggressive assertiveness (e.g., pursuing healthy asymptomatic individuals for intervention); (2) presumption (confidence that the preventive interventions will, on average, do more good than harm); and (3) attacking those who question the value of prevention. Many kinds of preventive advice encourage us to avoid certain behaviors, such as smoking and eating fats. Prevention efforts in public health make heavy use of screening measures. "This activity, usually regarded as prevention, is nothing of the sort: it is the early diagnosis of disease" (Skrabanek & McCormick, 1998, p. 88). These authors highlight the original requirements by Wilson and Jungner (1968), which include that the disease should be both common and serious and that an effective treatment is available. They also note, "If a disease is uncommon in the population being screened even good tests will throw up a large number of false positives; each of these has to be further investigated and carries a direct cost" of overdiagnosis and overtreatment and related burdens of unnecessary anxiety (p. 88). "It has become usual to describe diseases for which there is no known necessary or sufficient cause as multi-factorial in origin" (p. 91). Each measure carries with it possibilities for error. This applies to medical as well as to psychological tests. For example, Skrabanek and McCormick (1998) note that an incorrect sample may be included on a smear, which misses cancer cells. This could result in false negatives. Abnormalities are much more common than we would think and much more common than the disease (e.g., Welch, 2004).

SUMMARY

Predictions are one of the products of clinical judgments. Predictions made are related to causal assumptions and typically involve the prediction of a criterion variable, such as likelihood of relapse, based on a number of factors. For example, a psychiatrist may predict whether a homeless, mentally ill person will make another suicide attempt in the near future. Clinical prediction involves the integration of different kinds of data—a task that is difficult. Predictions must be made under considerable uncertainty in terms of the relationship between predictor variables and a criterion such as the likelihood that an intervention will be effective. There is controversy over what criteria to use to evaluate outcome—for example, client self-report, opinion of the clinician, and/or changes in real-life behavior. Comparison of statistical versus clinical prediction shows that actuarial methods are often more accurate than clinical inference. Competing values must be considered—for example, to protect potential victims from assault and to maximize freedom of the potentially assaultive individual. Given the importance of and uncertainties surrounding the predictions that clinicians make, it is not surprising that they delay or avoid making them.

Making predictions and choices requires the assessment of probabilities. We are prone to making certain kinds of errors, such as the confusion of the inverse (assuming that the probability of a sign given a disorder is the same as the probability of the disorder given the sign). Other sources of error include overlooking the unreliability of data, being influenced by the consistency of redundant data, and using vague and shifting criteria for evaluating options. Ignoring consensus information and base-rate data is a common source of error. Relevant data are often ignored because of our limitations in considering many different sources. We are prone to hindsight bias; knowledge of an outcome encourages a view that it was inevitable. We tend to focus on our hits and ignore our misses. Errors may arise from irrelevant, delayed, or vague feedback concerning the accuracy of decisions. Here, too, being forewarned is being prepared; that is, if we are aware of common sources of error, we can take steps to minimize them. We can use natural frequencies to estimate risk. Visual representations can help us to attend to sources of uncertainty. We can make precise estimates of probable success and monitor progress in an ongoing fashion.

CHAPTER

16

◆━◆◆◆━◆

Enhancing the Quality of Case Conferences, Team Meetings, and Organizational Culture

Making decisions often involves discussions with other professionals, as well as with clients and their significant others. Sources of error discussed in previous chapters may occur during these conversations. Many problems are complex, requiring input for different kinds of professionals, including a physician, a pharmacist, a nurse, a social worker, a financial counselor, and a dietician. In addition, values and preferences of clients and their significant others must be considered. A physician, a social worker, a physical therapist, an occupational therapist, and a nurse may all work together to help frail elderly clients. Social workers and nurses work closely together in hospice work. Increasing attention has been given to enhancing the quality of decisions made in multidisciplinary teams (e.g., Willens, Cripps, Wilson, Wolff, & Rothman, 2011). Creation of a multidisciplinary team increases the likelihood of considering the pros and cons of different approaches and thus of informed consent on the part of clients and their significant others (Head, Bogers, Serruys, Takkenberg, & Kappetein, 2011). Interdisciplinary teams differ in their autonomy, level of confidence in their effectiveness, impact of their work, and perceived value of their work (Levi, 2007). Professional practice is increasingly being organized by teams, highlighting the importance of clear communication between team members, who often work in high-stress environments such as emergency room departments. As noted in earlier chapters, communication problems are common and are a key source of avoidable errors that often have harmful consequences (e.g., McKnight, Stetson, Bakken, Curran, & Cimino, 2002). Staff may have different views regarding what is needed to create a safety culture, for example (see Manojlovich et al., 2011).

The involvement of different professionals with different helping approaches and perhaps varying interests, highlights the potential for misunderstandings and conflict.

Examples of decisions made in a team include the following (Jaarsma, 2005): appropriate diagnosis; optimal medical management, including discharge planning and length of follow-up; how to address barriers to participation; and how to track change in signs and symptoms (for example, daily weighing, telemonitoring). Discussions in team meetings may not result in sound decisions. The classic article by Paul Meehl, "Why I Do Not Attend Case Conferences" (1973), offers reasons why. He suggests that "many intelligent, educated, sane, rational persons seem to undergo a kind of intellectual deterioration when they gather around a table in one room" (p. 227). His impressions described in 1973 are supported by in-depth studies of dialogue in case conferences. For example, a study of decisions made in case conferences concerning child abuse found that, rather than a balanced search for the truth, these involved premature closure in assignment of responsibility for the abuse (Dingwall, Eekelaar, & Murray, 1983).

Case conferences represent a complex social situation in which participants have different goals, skills, values, styles of interaction, practice theories, prejudices, and biases. The setting in which they take place influences what occurs, as do the tasks addressed; the physical environment (for example, comfortable or uncomfortable, noisy or quiet); and the particular pressures (for example, to contain costs). The overall agency climate and culture influences the nature of team meetings and case conferences—for example, do administrators model critical appraisal of practices and policies (Gray, 2001a)? Team meetings and case conferences are an ideal setting for the use of persuasion strategies that are not likely to further the quality of discussion. Opinions may be changed and actions taken on the basis of appeals to emotion rather than in response to sound arguments. Meehl (1973) notes that clinicians take on questions to which they would never consider offering blithe answers in other contexts (for example, suggesting complex psychodiagnostic accounts even though they have had only a brief exposure to a client and little evidence has been offered to support their accounts).

CHARACTERISTICS THAT DECREASE THE QUALITY OF DECISIONS IN GROUP MEETINGS

Some concerns such as the sick-sick fallacy and use of pseudoauthority are discussed in Chapter 7. Sharing the values and skills of evidence-based practice, including transparency and critical appraisal, should facilitate decision making in interdisciplinary teams. This will contribute to a culture of thoughtfulness in which differences of opinion are viewed as learning opportunities, critical appraisal is valued, and there is a sincere interest in understanding other points of view.

Attributing Value to All Contributions

There may be a reluctance to criticize anyone's views, even though these may be uninformative or inaccurate. Practice-related research may be ignored or disregarded: "The prestigious thing to do is to contribute ideas to the conference . . . whether or not the quality of evidence available is adequate to support the view offered" (Meehl, 1973, p. 235). The tendency to be impressed by plausible-sounding but uninformative explanations is encouraged by not asking questions such as: "What evidence is there for this view?" or "How does this help us understand and know what to do about this problem?" "In order to maintain the fiction that everybody's ideas are worthwhile, it is necessary to lower the standards for what is evidential. As a result, a causal anecdote about one senile uncle remembered from childhood is given the same group interest and intellectual respect that is accorded to the citation of a high quality experimental or field actuarial study" (p. 228).

Statements that are uninformative because they are true of all people may be made (Kadushin, 1963), such as: "She has intrapsychic conflicts." (This is called the Barnum Effect.) Along the same lines, the vagueness of astrological descriptions allows readers to see themselves in such accounts and so consider them accurate and meaningful. Such statements, even though flawed, may succeed in persuading others to accept a dubious account. Fallacies may be recognized but not pointed out because they bolster a favored position. Questions may facilitate or hinder decision making. They can be divided into three categories in terms of forwarding critical appraisal: (1) irrelevant, (2) possibly relevant, and (3) very relevant. So, we should ask, "Will the answer make any difference in helping clients attain outcomes they value?" Questions sometimes are posed not to contribute to making an informed decision based on sound arguments and evidence, but to do the opposite—to sidetrack a discussion by encouraging distracting emotional reactions. Such questions have a point, but it is not to arrive at sound decisions.

Confusing the Consistency of and Differential Weight of a Sign

Someone may point out that a certain diagnosis is consistent with a characteristic when it is also consistent with other possibilities that the group is trying to distinguish among. Let's say you and your colleagues are trying to decide which of two parents abused a child and each of the parents has a history of abuse as a child. Pointing out that the mother has a past history of abuse is not informative, since the father also has such a history. Meehl (1973) suggests that this error "illustrates one of the generic features of case conferences in psychiatry, namely, the tendency to mention things that don't make any difference one way or the other" (Meehl, 1973, p. 231). (See also Chapter 7 for discussion of other classification concerns.)

Ignoring Uncertainty and Innumeracy

Unreliability of measures may be neglected when interpreting score changes or difference scores. Relatively small differences (for example, in before-and-after measures) may reflect unreliable measures rather than a true difference. Whether the measures are valid is another question. If the reliability of a measure is questionable, then small differences should be interpreted with caution or ignored. Ignoring the size and representatives of samples used to infer traits or tendencies is another common error. Inferences are often based on small, unrepresentative samples of behavior. For example, a judgment about a resident of a nursing home may be based on a 15-minute observation in an interview (see the discussion of the law of large numbers in Chapter 13). There are many ways in which samples may be unrepresentative. Behavior may have been sampled in a context that differs from the one in which problems occur. Aggressiveness of a child at home may be the problem, but perhaps the only data available may have been gathered at school. Behavior in this situation may not reflect behavior at home. Furthermore, since no information is offered about the antecedents and consequences of behavior labeled aggressive, little is known about the circumstances in which such behavior takes place. (For descriptions of conducting a functional analysis of behavior, see, for example, Cooper, Heron, & Heward, 2007.)

Errors may occur because of lack of understanding about how probability applies to individual cases. Estimates of prior probability (for example, the base rate for a diagnosis of schizophrenia in a particular population) and the degree of leverage added by a given characteristic (such as history of hospitalization) often are neglected. Decisions may be based on intuition even though actuarial methods are more accurate (see Chapter 15). Let's say a decision must be made about whether to accept an applicant for clinical training who has a low college grade point average. Someone may say, "Let's interview him," assuming an interview would yield better predictions, when actuarial data shows that it will not. This is called the "interview error" (Dawes, 1994a). Clearly, there are instances in which other factors should be considered. However, overriding empirical data results in more misclassifications than correct ones.

Inappropriate Minimizing of Signs or Symptoms

This fallacy occurs when a behavior is excused on the grounds that anyone would do it. The question is—would anyone do it? Thinking about doing something and doing it are two different things. We are influenced by our personal biases when selecting characteristics viewed as normal as well as when deciding what is pathological. This fallacy is the opposite of the sick-sick fallacy, and is illustrated by the nurse who attempted to belittle the importance of a patient's hallucinations by telling the group that she herself had had an imaginary companion as a child (Meehl, 1973). Both tendencies may be encouraged by lack of knowledge about norms and a reluctance to seek such data. (See also discussion of the rule of optimism in Chapter 7.)

Cheap Shots

Some tactics can be called cheap shots because of their failure to advance informed decision making. Like other kinds of strategies, they may be subtle or obvious (Edwards, 1938). Cheap shots often are used by people in power. Negative labels (such as "nitpicker") may be used to refer to someone in order to discredit a position. This ploy is made more effective by including actions that attempt to convince listeners that the person using the negative label does so only because he or she has been forced to by the supposed facts. A sad expression of inevitability may be assumed or a joking manner used so that the negative label will leave its mark but the name-caller can deny that he or she meant it that way. A possible remedy here is to ignore the cheap shot and reintroduce the question at hand. This remedy is suitable unless the name-calling has a negative effect on the decision-making process. There are two situations in which it may have such an effect. One is when the recipient of the name is a client or significant other who may be stigmatized in terms of decisions made about her or him. Another is when the negative name is attached to one of the decision makers, whose views are then ignored as a result, even though they are sound.

Ridicule may be communicated in how something is said as well as by what is said. A roll of the eyes may change the impact of a statement. A look of shared commiseration and strained long-suffering directed toward other participants (raised eyebrows and a sigh) may accompany a statement. Remedies here include restating a position clearly, noting why it should be taken seriously (for example, regarding possible consequences for clients). If the ridicule is offered by a person in authority, others in the group could ask for more appropriate criticism of the position. The success of these remedies depends on several factors, such as the cogency of a point, the views of others, and the status of the ridiculer. Those who use ridicule may attempt to make the target appear pedantic for continuing to uphold an "ill-advised" position. A more subtle but no more admirable tactic is to make negative innuendoes about a position without offering any evidence for them—to imply, for example, that a certain action will have bad effects. Emotional appeals and innuendoes may be used to encourage others to discount disliked cogent points. Force or intimidation is sometimes used to gain compliance in place of offering sound reasons to create conviction. Threats of removal of resources or punishing consequences, such as loss of a job, may be made. Whistle-blower protection laws are designed to help those who expose practices and policies that harm clients and are deceptive.

Equating the Softheaded with the Softhearted

An interest in critically appraising claims that affect clients' lives may be viewed as cold and unfeeling, whereas a regard for vagueness, non sequiturs, and tolerance of fallacies may be considered a mark of caring and compassion. Actuarial methods for making decisions may be abandoned because of a concern that a client will not receive optimal treatment, even though, over all clients, more accurate decisions result from actuarial decision methods than from relying on consensus (e.g., Grove & Meehl, 1996). Such a departure from what research shows is best not only increases the chances of making a mistake for an individual client, but may increase inaccurate predictions for other clients as well (Meehl, 1973). Unless there is a sound method that allows you to discriminate between cases in which intuition or consensus would be the optimal method for making a decision and cases in which it would be more accurate to rely on actuarial methods, neglect of actuarial methods that have a better success rate will decrease the accuracy of decisions. Sympathy is not a sound reason to abandon well-tested actuarial methods for making predictions.

Other Concerns

Different standards of evidence are often used to support a favored position than are used to critique opposing views; that is, more rigorous evidence is requested when considering perspectives other than our own. For example, inferences based on projective tests may be offered with no corroborative evidence to support a diagnosis. In contrast, data based on observation of behavior in real-life settings may be requested in support of alternative views of a client's problem. It may be assumed that only a certain kind of professional is qualified to offer certain information. Psychiatrists may assume that the role of psychologists is mainly to offer assessment data based on psychological tests, and that they have little else to contribute. The degree that a professional has does not necessarily indicate areas of competence.

The "spun glass theory of the mind" refers to the belief that people are very fragile and should be treated as such; that relatively minor deprivations, rejections, or failure experiences play a causative role in major traumas (Meehl, 1973, p. 253). Meehl (1973) suggests that such a belief may have countertherapeutic effects in protecting clients from engaging with reality or not offering them effective intervention methods. For example, one clinician objected to interviewing a client in a new setting who was about to be discharged, on the grounds that this unusual situation might undo the successful effects of therapy.

The fallacy of uncertain consequences involves the argument that because the consequences related to an option (such as selection of a given intervention) are uncertain, it should not be used—it would be too risky. Uncertainty is our constant companion. The fallacy of uncertain consequences occurs when no data are offered showing a high likelihood of anticipated risks (Michalos, 1971, p. 100). The crummy criterion fallacy occurs when the criteria used to assess the soundness of an argument are weak or inappropriate. Meehl (1973) offers the example of dismissing psychological test results on the basis that these do not agree with the assessment of a psychiatrist who held a 10-minute interview with a client.

WHY IS THE QUALITY OF DISCUSSION IN CASE CONFERENCES OFTEN POOR?

Reasons for the poor quality of many case conferences are related to the factors discussed at the beginning of this chapter; case conferences are complex social contexts in which people have different goals, values, styles, and skills, and in which they are influenced by the particular setting and the pressures within it. Reluctance to hurt or embarrass people encourages some of the problems described in the previous sections. Meehl calls this the "buddy-buddy syndrome." It results from the false belief that high-quality discussions cannot occur unless harsh or discourteous methods are used. This is not so.

> If it is argued that you can't prevent people who have nothing significant to contribute from talking without being cruel or discourteous, I submit that this is empirically false. I point to case conferences in other specialties like neurology and internal medicine, where, so far as I have observed, there is no social discourtesy or cruelty manifested by those in charge; but the general atmosphere is nevertheless one which says, in effect, "Unless you know what you are talking about and have reason to think that you are saying something really educational for the rest of us or beneficial to the patient, you would be well advised to remain silent. Mere yakking for yakking's sake is not valued in this club." I have rarely had to listen to trivia, confused mentation, plain ignorance, or irrelevancies when I have attended case conferences in internal medicine or neurology or the clinicopathological conference on the medical service. If an atmosphere of decent intellectual scholarly standards can be created and maintained on those services, I cannot think it is impossible to approximate the same thing in clinical psychology and psychiatry. (Meehl, 1973, p. 284)

Participants have different goals. These may be explicit or implicit and may be shared or competitive (if some goals are achieved, others may not be). The explicit goal of case conferences is to make decisions, such as what intervention should be recommended or whether to transfer a client to another facility. The manifest purpose of the group may not be the real one. Take "rubber-stamp groups." The ostensible purpose is to arrive at a decision. In reality, the decision has already been made; the purpose of the meeting is to simply go through the motions of having a discussion about a matter that has already been decided. Strains and differences among goals account for some of the odd happenings at group meetings. Personal goals that often do not contribute to sound decisions include the following: show how bright you are, avoid anyone knowing you don't know what you are doing, impress your superiors, be as invisible as possible, skewer your boss or most disliked colleague, and win your point. Goals in most groups include maintaining positive relations, regulating intimacy and accessibility, appearing normal, maintaining claims to roles, and controlling information presented.

Misunderstandings may occur because participants have different values. For example, a psychologist may focus on harm done to a victim of rape whereas a lawyer may focus on protecting the rights of the accused. Fallacies that occur may not be recognized. Case material may be presented in a disorganized fashion, which makes sound decision making difficult or impossible. An agreed-on format for case presentations can encourage descriptions that make it easier to catch errors. This should include a description of how the client came to the attention of an agency or clinician. Although this may be obvious in some contexts, in other settings, such as schools, child protection, and community mental health centers, it is not obvious. For example, significant others (those who interact with and influence a client) may have encouraged a client to seek help against the client's wishes. Such information is important in recognizing coercive elements in initial contacts. Topics in need of discussion can be noted on the form.

Disagreements and differences of opinion are inevitable; however, many clinicians do not learn to discuss differences in a helpful fashion. For those who lack skills and positive experiences with discussions of differences, disagreements may create feelings of anxiety or anger. For example, master's degree students in the School of Social Welfare at the University of California at Berkeley had been interested for years in forming a panel of clinicians with different perspectives and having these individuals discuss a case or some common questions. Some instructors who were approached turned them down on the grounds that a discussion of differences would be divisive. The terms *discussion* and *debate* seemed to be associated with *oppositional*, *destructive*, and *confrontational*, rather than with inquiring and stimulating.

The term *argument* as used in lay language typically refers to a disagreement between two people—emotions are high, and language may be abusive. There is disregard for the feelings of others. Winning is the object, rather than finding the truth, and there is a resistance to new ideas. Discussions, dialogues, and debates are centered on issues rather than on people. (See discussion of arguments in Chapter 3.) The purpose of a case conference is not to protect the self-esteem of the head of the psychology department—it is to determine if Mr. Richards is ready to be discharged from the hospital or whether Mrs. Sansom, who is dying, requires a more protective setting. The focus should be on finding the best route to achieving outcomes valued by clients. There is an openness to new ideas rather than a resistance to these, no matter what their source—whether offered by a low-status person, perhaps a social worker in a medical conference, or by a high-power person, perhaps the head physician on a service unit. Emotion is at a functional level.

Participants may not realize that their biases encourage them to ignore contradictory information. Consider the prevalence of groupthink (overlooking deficits in a preferred view because of lack of consideration of disadvantages and well-argued alternatives). Indicators suggested by Janis and Mann (1977) include the following:

- *Illusion of invulnerability:* Members ignore obvious danger, take extreme risk, and are overly optimistic.
- *Collective rationalization:* Members discredit and explain away warnings contrary to group thinking.
- *Illusion of morality:* Members believe their decisions are morally correct, ignoring the ethical consequences.
- *Excessive stereotyping:* The group constructs negative stereotypes of rivals outside the group.
- *Pressure for conformity:* Members pressure any in the group who express arguments against the group's stereotypes, illusions, or commitments, viewing such opposition as disloyalty.
- *Self-censorship:* Members withhold their dissenting views and counterarguments.
- *Illusion of unanimity:* Members perceive falsely that everyone agrees with the group's decision; silence is seen as consent.
- *Mind guards:* Some members appoint themselves to the role of protecting the group from adverse information that might threaten group complacency.

Group characteristics that contribute to groupthink include high cohesiveness, an insulation from outside influence, authoritarian leadership styles, and high stress. Pressure for conformity has long been studied with sobering findings (e.g., Asch, 1956; Zimbardo, 2007). Recognizing the value of minority views in discovering solutions should lessen tendencies to squelch them (e.g., Nemeth & Goncalo, 2005).

Pfohl (1978) found that diagnostic team members usually passed over contradictory information and, when directly confronted with contradictory evidence, would ask the group "to look beyond this irrelevant 'fact,' to grasp the whole picture of a patient's problem" (p. 175). Contradictory evidence to a position may be transformed into additional evidence for a preferred diagnosis; for example, by interpreting a client's statements as denials that yield further evidence for a diagnosis. Errors are particularly likely when a practice theory is used that can account for anything—even contradictory claims. The high status of some participants in case conferences increases the probability that errors they make will be accepted. Decker (1987) suggests that even if defense lawyers are present at commitment hearings, reliance on knowledge about the patient's behavior in the hospital (to which lawyers do not have access unless they locate and use another insider) gives the upper hand to psychiatrists. False biographical material may be used to bolster a position, and this may remain standing unless challenged.

Fallacies may be recognized but not commented on because of past failures to improve the quality of discussions. The power structure in a group may be such that no matter how cogent a point, it will not be persuasive because of the apathy and fear of most participants. Or diplomatic skills that are useful in countering or neutralizing fallacies may be lacking. A history of harsh criticism for speaking up in case conferences or fear of negative evaluation discourages participation. Silence, when confronted with faulty assumptions that may harm clients, no matter what the cause—including a past history of being harshly criticized in a group—calls for thinking about the implications for clients. (See discussion of the ethics of excuses in Chapter 17.) Feeling helpless and saying nothing in a group setting, even though understandable in terms of an unpleasant past history, is an ethical concern if this results in decisions that harm clients. Participants may lack skills in focusing on shared goals (see Fisher & Ury, 1991). Ideological biases may interfere with balanced consideration of different perspectives. If there are no incentives to alter such biases, the level of discourse may remain at a low level. Some discussions are not so much arguments but an exchange of opinions. That is, there may be so little clarification of claims and grounds for these, that no one knows what is being discussed. Topics discussed may be of little or no interest to participants. There may be little shared sense of working together toward helping clients receive high-quality services.

The fact that people sit around a table does not necessarily mean that they will be listened to if they speak. Whether others listen and whether an opportunity to speak is even given depend on factors such as status in a group. Studies of decision making in predicting the dangerousness of psychiatric patients suggest that effective neutralizing of information contradictory to a preferred diagnosis is based largely on the authority and control of the psychiatrist over other team members (Pfohl, 1978) (see also Dingwall, Eekelaar, & Murray, 1983). Psychiatrists use a variety of tactics to control interaction, including interruption of team members in the process of interviewing a patient and disrupting the timing of the presentation of information. Participants often have different frames of reference and knowledge bases for viewing a concern. A psychiatrist may focus on biomedical causes; a social worker may emphasize environmental causes. An administrator may be concerned about the precedent a decision may set. Use of different frames of reference may result in misunderstandings.

DENUNCIATIONS AND PITCHES

Some investigators who examined case conferences conclude that these can most accurately be described as contexts in which someone is prematurely assumed to be responsible for an act, such as child maltreatment, and then a denunciation effort is made to bolster this account. "A successful denunciation establishes the act as one typically committed by persons of a 'bad' character and constructs a biography of the actor that indicates such a character. A successful pitch normalizes the act and the biography" (Emerson, 1969, p. 156). Participants who disagree with a position may be ignored and emotional language used to encourage acceptance of a preferred position. The wrong person may be accused of perpetrating the abuse or neglect, resulting in further abuse.

An Example of a Case Conference[1]

The participants in this conference included a social worker (SW), her senior (SSW), a health visitor (HV), her nursing officer (NO), a medical social worker (MSW), two policemen (PC1 and PC2), two physicians (CONS1 and CONS2), a registrar (REG), a medical student, and a secretary. The family involved included the mother, Mrs. Hancock; her live-in boyfriend, Mr. Finnegan; Mary Walsh, who lived with the family and helped out with the children following the mother's recent accident; Lindy Oates, the eight-month-old baby brought to the hospital; and three other children (Dingwall et al., 1983, pp. 152–153; all names used throughout this case are fictitious).

> The child came to casualty at 5 p.m. . . . The boyfriend had come home and said that he had held the child up because it was crying and had discovered a lot of bruises. He didn't know how they had got there and he called the GP [general practitioner]. The GP had said that he had been called only because of a cough and a runny nose. The only prior admitted incident was that the child fell off the sofa and had a bruised cheek. The mother was living with a twenty-six-year-old boyfriend called Finnegan but the child was a child of her former boyfriend. The mother had had her hand in plaster because she had broken her wrist after falling on ice. They were living with three other children in the house. There was somebody else living in the house as a kind of help for them who was known to the social services. On examination the baby was crying. She had a torn upper frenulum . . . and was covered in bruises. . . . These were on the mouth, the chest and the upper abdomen and they were usually circular. Some of them

[1]*Source*: From *The Protection of Children: State Intervention and Family Life* (pp. 152–65), by R. Dingwall, J. Eekelaar, and T. Murray, 1983, Oxford, England: Basil Blackwell. Copyright 1983 by Basil Blackwell, R. Dingwall, J. Eekelaar, and T. Murray.

were recent, only a few hours old but others had been there a few days. No other abnormality had been found and there was no bone injury. The child had been admitted for observation. . . . Everybody commented how wary the child was when anyone approached the cot. . . . She looked suspicious and afraid . . . and sometimes she cried if anybody tried to touch her. (pp. 153–154)

There was agreement based on the clinical evidence as well as on the social context (that is, irregular cohabitation, previous contact with social services) that the injuries resulted from maltreatment. The discussion then focused on identifying the person guilty of this abuse.

MSW: This is complicated by the fact that there are three adults in the house. No one knows very much about Finnegan. She (Mrs. Hancock) claims that she wants to marry him and that he is wonderful with children. Mary Walsh is a vulnerable person who has been known to the social services and she has been the main caretaker of the child. It's a complicated situation.

The senior social worker runs over Mrs. Hancock's record. She is known to the department but not as a persistent or highly dependent client. Mary Walsh is linked to a known child abuser, her sister-in-law, Bridget; she is tied into a group for whom child mistreatment is a natural way of life. The social worker points to Mary Walsh's record of satisfactory child caretaking and to their ignorance of Martin Finnegan's past, but none of these challenges is pursued. The authors believe that the identification of Mary Walsh as the person responsible for the abuse was the expected outcome of the reasoning process that characterizes the system in which these kinds of cases are reviewed. "Once Lindy Oates had been adequately characterized as a victim, Mary seemed to be the person least responsible for her own actions and therefore most likely to have perpetrated the injuries. Moreover, her prosecution left Mrs. Hancock's household/family intact and the children out of state care. The decision gives effect to the liberal principles on which child protection operates" (p. 165; see Chapter 7 for a discussion of the rule of optimism). When a "total denunciation is initiated, those who hold other views must be brought into line or discredited" (Emerson, 1969, pp. 140–141).

And what was the outcome? Mary Walsh was arrested and was prosecuted on a charge of bodily harm. The case was dismissed. "About two weeks after this hearing, Lindy Oates was admitted to hospital with two skull fractures, a broken arm, and three broken ribs. Her brother had bruising in 19 separate places. It emerged that Martin Finnegan had, five years previously, been convicted of causing grievous bodily harm to his own daughter. He pleaded guilty to the assaults on Lindy and her brother and was jailed for four years" (p. 165).

ENHANCING THE QUALITY OF CASE CONFERENCES AND TEAM MEETINGS

A number of steps can be taken to enhance the quality of team meetings and case conferences.

Use Effective Communication Skills

Effective use of critical thinking skills requires complementary social skills. Presenting ideas in a positive manner involves avoiding unnecessary negative comments about other views, recognizing common interests, and praising other people's good ideas. Avoid temptations to make hostile or sarcastic comments. Points can be persuasively made without resorting to put-downs, which, although they may temporarily impress people by their wit, may not win friends or influence people. Colleagues may not appreciate others who ferret out vagueness and identify fallacies in reasoning, even though this is helpful in avoiding clinical errors that may harm clients. For example, one of my graduate students said that the chief psychiatrist at a case conference became quite irritated when she questioned the clarity of a term he used. Rather than clarify the term, he asked the student, "Don't they teach you that at Berkeley?" He attempted to use his prestige and authority in an ad hominem attack on the student and the school. Be prepared that you may be liked less if you question dubious statements even when you are diplomatic. Cultural differences should be considered. Gaining the attention of the group will require skill in identifying appropriate opportunities to enter a discussion. Holding the floor against interruption attempts is an important skill (see Gambrill, 2006). Humor can be used for many different purposes, including encouraging others to relax, defusing aggressive reactions, relieving embarrassment, reminding people of social rules, introducing risky topics, and unmasking pretensions. A sense of humor helps to keep things in perspective. And empathy and warmth are vital with colleagues as they are with clients. Familiarity with common fallacies and social persuasion strategies will be valuable in identifying and countering methods others may use to discourage critical appraisal of claims (see Chapter 6).

Present Ideas Clearly and Persuasively

How ideas are presented as well as what is said influences the persuasiveness of a message. Rather than using brief words and phrases, you may increase your effectiveness by using elaborated opinion statements; these start with a pronoun and contain a compound sentence, such as: "Well, I think _____ because of _____." Use persuasive examples and describe reasons for your position. Practice helps in presenting views clearly and persuasively. Smiling or giggling when discussing a serious topic will dilute the impact of what is said. Seating position may influence persuasiveness. Past research found that even avowed feminists did not perceive women who sat at the head of a table as leaders (Porter & Geis, 1981). Eye contact with others will enhance the credibility of statements (unless this is culturally inappropriate). Preparation of critically appraised topics (CATs) will facilitate sharing of important information (see Chapter 11). The "humble inquirer and doubter" approach that Benjamin Franklin found so useful in having others consider his views may be effective in some groups. Franklin "resolved never to advance any view as certainly correct, but rather to express himself in terms of 'modest diffidence'" (Silverman, 1986, p. xix). In other groups, phrases that minimize the importance of what is said (such as, "I don't know if this is important, but" or "this may not be significant, but") may encourage others to tune out rather than tune in.

Do Not Take Things Personally

Assuming the best rather than the worst about other people's intentions can help us to identify and move beyond fallacies and stratagems without becoming overly emotional. Stressful work environments may encourage harsh, inappropriate reactions. Certainly there are times when a direct request for a behavior change is called for; one of the reasons unconstructive behaviors persist, such as belittling and ad hominem comments, is because no one does anything to discourage them.

Prepare for Meetings

You can prepare for meetings by posing well-formed questions regarding decisions that must be made at case conferences, and searching for and critically appraising related research. Posing questions and seeking related research allows you to share what you find at the meeting. Distribute a critically appraised topic (CAT; see Chapter 11) beforehand so participants can read it before they arrive. This kind of preparation will be helpful in weighing the evidentiary status of different views during meetings.

The likelihood of offering sound arguments can be increased by practicing how to present views, by anticipating counterarguments, and by being prepared with responses. A search for accurate explanations requires an open exploration and critique of well-argued alternatives. Those with privileged access to relevant data will have an advantage, since their statements cannot be checked. Case records should be reviewed before case conferences to check statements based on these records for accuracy. People who use an authoritarian decision-making style and who make use of propaganda methods will try to discourage putting things in writing, usually by claiming that it is unnecessary, foolish, a waste of time, or dangerous. This is not to say that noting things in writing is always a good idea. Clearly it is not, for example, if a policy is to be flexibly implemented.

Clarify Vague Terms

Vague terms are often used in case conferences. Unless these are clarified, their relevance cannot be judged—although we should never be more precise that we have to be, as Popper (1994) suggests. Metaphors should be clarified in terms of how they apply to a discussion. The same is true for fables and descriptions of personal experiences. Such descriptions may be psychologically moving but may not contribute to making sound decisions. Vague statements such as "she's mentally ill," and vague labels such as "borderline personality" or "depressive syndrome" should be clarified. Abstractions sometimes hide a lack of related evidence.

Distinguish Between Strong Opinions and Bias

Strong opinions may be mistaken for bias (Scriven, 1976). People can accurately be called biased only if their reasons for holding a position are matters of prejudice and they cannot be convinced to alter their position when presented with more accurate premises or inferences. The style of presentation may be misleading in distinguishing between someone who is biased and someone who has strong opinions. Strong bias may pass unchallenged because of the style of presentation. For example, someone who is biased may disguise this by acting as if he has been forced into accepting a position against his will; that it is the last thing he would do if his hands were free (which they are). Conversely, someone who is open to a discussion of different perspectives may appear biased because of strong assertion of a point of view. People with a point of view who are interested in discovering what is true will be interested in hearing criticism and diverging views. "Someone can be said to represent a point of view rather than a bias if s/he strives to (a) identify his/her interests; (b) open them to examination; (c) encourage discussion; and (d) take into serious consideration dissenting points of view" (MacLean, 1981, p. 148).

Focus on Common Goals

Fisher and Ury (1991) stress the importance of focusing on common goals, especially in contentious atmospheres. They suggest that this is helpful in encouraging understanding of other views and in keeping emotion in reasonable bounds, even in response to people who are masters of giving others "aggro" (aggravation). Rather than dwelling on a negative reaction, such as name-calling, focus on the common goal (to arrive at well-reasoned decisions).

Increase Knowledge of Group Process

Many behaviors that occur in groups are the result of particular kinds of group process and structure. For example, groups have different leadership patterns and different norms. Being familiar with group process and structure should increase your effectiveness in groups (e.g., see Levi, 2007). This should decrease tendencies to take things personally or blame others (reactions that get in the way of cooperative problem solving). Some of the concerns already mentioned can be avoided by establishing norms for discussion, such as taking responsibility for providing reasons for assertions, welcoming criticism, thanking others for pointing out mistakes in one's thinking, and not hogging the floor. Different people can take the role of facilitator, orchestrating effective discussion, including encouraging critical appraisal of views. Strategies suggested by Janis and Mann (1977) to avoid groupthink include the following guidelines:

1. The group should be aware of the causes and consequences of groupthink.
2. The leader should be neutral when assigning a decision-making task to a group, initially withholding preferences and expectations. This practice will be especially effective if the leader consistently encourages an atmosphere of open inquiry.
3. The leader should give high priority to airing objections and doubts, and be accepting of criticism.
4. Groups should always consider well-argued unpopular alternatives, assigning the role of devil's advocate to several strong members of the group.
5. Sometimes it is useful to divide the group into two separate deliberative bodies as options are evaluated.
6. Spend a sizable amount of time surveying all warning signals from rival groups and organizations.
7. After reaching a preliminary consensus on a decision, all residual doubts should be expressed and the matter reconsidered.
8. Outside experts should be included in vital decision making.
9. Tentative decisions should be discussed with trusted colleagues not in the decision-making group.
10. The organization should routinely follow the administrative practice of establishing several independent decision-making groups to work on the same critical issue or policy.

Agreeing on an agenda at the beginning of a meeting is useful in clarifying goals and increasing the probability that they are met. Such agreement offers an opportunity to reaffirm the focus of a discussion if people get off the track. Agreeing on norms that facilitate well-reasoned ethical decisions is another valuable practice. Examples include the following: (1) no one should interrupt another speaker, (2) no one person should hog the floor, (3) speakers are responsible for describing how points raised relate to the topic being discussed, and (4) empirical claims should be accompanied by a description of their related evidence. Agreement on a well-designed case presentation format should save time by clearly presenting relevant data, decreasing discussion of extraneous data, and helping to ensure inclusion of data that contribute to well-reasoned decisions, such as information about environmental factors related to hoped-for outcomes. Another helpful norm is to take a vote on controversial issues; otherwise, a consensus in favor of a position may be assumed when there is none, or there may be a consensus, but in favor of a competing position. One group member can be selected to introduce alternative perspectives in groups in which there tends to be premature closure, and to remind the group that they should not attack (or ignore) people who introduce different views but respond to points raised in a constructively critical manner (Janis, 1982). This role can be assumed by a different person each week.

Know Who You Are Dealing With: Be Politically Savvy

It helps to be familiar with preferred decision making and interactional styles of group participants (e.g., French & Raven, 1959; Jehn, 2004). The manifest purpose of group meetings may be to discuss a change in procedure or policy; decisions may really be made outside the group. For example, a small cohort may run things in a hospital by laying the groundwork for support of preferred positions prior to meetings. This may be done by meeting together and agreeing on a position and by seeking the support of others who are sympathetic to a position prior to the group meeting. Seeking solutions to difficult clinical questions may be hampered by naysayers who may comment, "It won't work," "We've tried that in the past and it failed," "There's no time," "We don't have the resources," "You don't understand our system," or "That's the way we've been doing it for years." Typically, no evidence—or only weak support—is provided for such statements. Such statements may be made not because a solution is not desired, but because no possible solution can be envisioned.

It may not be possible to change a disliked or dysfunctional style; however, critical thinking skills and related interpersonal competencies can be used to mute the effects of styles that compromise the quality of decision making. Group members can model effective decision making such as asking about the evidentiary status of recommended methods. Some people possess critical thinking skills as well as helpful interpersonal competencies, but use these only when they must, in order to reach their goals. I have been quite amazed to see that someone who is usually attacking and demeaning in a discussion, and who makes use of dishonest strategies (such as misrepresenting positions), can act quite differently (courteous, attentive, even ingratiating) in settings in which such offensive strategies would be quickly identified and countered. Rather than assuming a pained, patronizing expression when colleagues speak, there is attentive interest with an expression that wise words are being spoken.

The preferred style of some individuals is to make unsupported pronouncements and to act as if support is offered when it is not (begging the question). This method is used mostly by those who occupy a power position in the group—taking advantage of participants' reluctance to question a person in such a role. Pronouncers may assume a patronizing or offended stance if asked to support their views. Some people try to encourage others to go along with a position by forecasting vague negative outcomes if disliked options are selected. If others are not swayed by one negative forecast, additional scare tactics may be invoked to create fear and worry. Intimidators may first try to neutralize disliked positions (for example, by ignoring them or by using patronizing responses) and, if this fails, then try to intimidate participants. A colleague may say that if cognitive-behavioral methods are used to treat depression, rather than medication, the client may make another suicide attempt. The question is: Is there evidence that such an attempt would be more likely if those methods were used? Is there counterevidence?

Enhance Critical Thinking Skills

Being familiar with formal and informal fallacies increases the likelihood that you can identify them and move the discussion to sounder points. Having names or numbers for the fallacies helps in recognizing them, and may even be of value in discouraging a fallacy with humor. When I pointed out to one of my colleagues who had the habit of distorting positions and then attacking the distorted version that he had just committed number 19 of Thouless's (1974) list of 38 dishonest tricks of debate, everyone laughed, and he dropped his straw man argument. Case conferences provide one of many opportunities to hone critical thinking skills and related interpersonal competencies. Fallacies are bound to occur. A "fallacy or stratagem of the week" can be selected for special focus.

Be Sure You Understand Other Points of View

Only if you understand another point of view can you accurately identify flaws and strengths in that position. If this guideline had been used by participants in the case conference described earlier in this chapter, the true culprit might have been identified as being responsible for the abuse of Lindy, and subsequent abuse might have been avoided. We can offer cogent counterarguments only if we understand other views. A focus on common goals (helping clients) encourages attention to other perspectives. We are less likely to blame others for actions, statements, and styles that we do not like if we try to see things from their points of view. Empathic reactions increase recognition of environmental factors that influence others (Regan & Totten, 1975), and reduce prejudice toward others (Batson et al., 1997).

THE INFLUENCE OF ORGANIZATION CULTURE AND CLIMATE

Organizations develop cultures and climates. Certain values are preferred, and certain norms and rules are followed. Components of culture include history, contingencies in effect, patterns of communication, decision-making styles, philosophy, myths, and stories. Organizations are influenced by their external environments, including funding sources and legal regulations (see Exhibit 16.1). Staff are influenced by accepted policies and preferred management practices—for example, a top-down or

Exhibit 16.1 Factors That Influence Clinical Practice

Source	Influencing Contributory Factors
Agency context	Funding sources Legal and administrative regulations Economic and regulatory context
Organizational policies and management practices	Financial resources and constraints Organizational structure Policy standards and goals Safety culture and priorities
Work environment	Staffing levels and skills mix Workload and shift patterns Design, availability, and maintenance of equipment Administrative and managerial support
Team characteristics	Verbal communication Written communication Supervision and seeking help Team structure (congruence, consistency, leadership, etc.)
Individual (staff) factors	Competence (knowledge and skills) Physical and mental health
Task requirements	Task design and clarity of structure Availability and use of protocols Availability and accuracy of test results
Client characteristics	Complexity and seriousness of concerns Language and communication Personality and environmental circumstances

Source: Adapted from "The Investigation and Analysis of Clinical Incidents," by C. Vincent and S. Taylor-Adams, 2001, in *Clinical Risk Management: Enhancing Patient Safety* (2nd ed., p. 442), edited by C. Vincent, London, UK: BMJ. Reprinted with permission.

a participatory decision-making style. Policies influence staffing levels, adequacy of training, and overall workload, which in turn affect staff stress levels. Organizations differ in the quality of services offered and in the quality of training opportunities and supervision provided to staff (see Exhibit 16.2). A description of services in Wales and England reported that half of the patients in intensive care receive suboptimal care (Kmietowicz, 2005). Agencies differ in their policies about introducing innovative technologies and in how well they match the competence of staff to the tasks they confront. All these factors influence the overall task environment, which in turn influences decisions made. Although status (ranking) is important in all organizations, the criteria on which it is based differ in different organizations—for example, longevity of service, charisma, expertise, or coercive power. Contingencies may not support behaviors that forward evidence-informed decisions and related critical thinking skills. Organizations have different ways of handling conflict, uncertainty, and less than hoped-for success. They differ in the extent to which they seek clear, accurate information about service outcomes and use this information to improve services, and in the extent to which they encourage a culture of thoughtfulness in which critical discussion is valued (see Reason, 1997).

If we can have worker incompetence, is there such a thing as organizational incompetence? Examples include: (1) lack of any means of checking whether key tasks are carried out; (2) not checking the quality of communication with clients; (3) lack of feedback on important decisions, so staff cannot learn how to improve future performance; (4) not using interventions that have been shown to be effective; (5) continuing to use services that have been shown to be ineffective; and (6) using interventions that have been found to harm clients. What is considered incompetence will depend on goals pursued. For example, a chief administrator who values only his salary and doesn't care

Exhibit 16.2   Strategies to Increase the Good-to-Harm Ratio Regarding Intervention

Type of Intervention	Strategy
Does more good than harm.	• Promote use if it is affordable. • Take steps to increase good and decrease harm to make ratio more favorable.
Does more harm than good.	• Stop them starting. • Slow them starting. • Start to stop them if it is not possible to increase good and decrease harm sufficiently to convert them into interventions that do more good than harm.
Of unknown effect.	• Stop them starting. • Promote the conduct of RCTs both for new interventions and for interventions already in practice.

Source: From *Evidence-Based Healthcare* (2nd ed., p. 48), by J. A. M. Gray, 2001a, New York, NY: Churchill Livingstone. Reprinted with permission.

about clients may not consider harming clients a sign of organizational incompetence (unless such harm is readily discoverable). To what extent are errors tolerated, or glossed over because of callousness? Singer (1978) suggests that incompetence, callousness, and planned error explain error related behaviors in organizations. He suggests that "In cases where there is an unwillingness to take action, the second category occurs, errors of callousness" (p. 31). "When key people within organizations or institutions are made aware of a problem, persistent or exceptional, and do not take steps to correct it or to rectify injustices, we have errors of callousness" (p. 31). We frequently rationalize our behavior, that is, give a reason as to why it occurred. When are such rationalizations unethical? We should ask these questions regarding bureaucrats—those who are in high-level administrative places, as well as line staff.

Creating a Learning Organization

Knowledge can grow only in an open environment, in which clients and staff are free to raise questions (express criticism) about practices and policies and their outcomes. Criticism provides information that may help to minimize avoidable mistakes. Learning organizations are characterized by ongoing improvement in the quality of decisions as well as the development of new knowledge, including new ways of using and managing knowledge developed by others. Gray (2001a) suggests that knowledge in an organization can be increased by transforming tacit into explicit knowledge (see discussion of intuition in Chapter 4). The notion of a learning organization suggests an active pursuit of the flow of knowledge and developing more knowledge, rather than a passive stance that characterizes many organizations. An evidence-informed organization is one in which staff at all levels "are able to find—appraise, and use knowledge from research evidence" (p. 249). Gray (2001a) characterizes the evidence-based organization as having "an obsession with finding, appraising, and using research-based knowledge as evidence in decision making" (p. 250).

In an evidence-informed organization, the evidentiary status of practices is considered in addition to client characteristics and circumstances, including their values and preferences. There is a concern to allocate resources equitably, and in ways in which they can do the most good for the least cost (Øvretveit, 1995, p. 121). Evidentiary status alone does not imply that a practice or policy should be adopted; there are many other considerations, such as client preferences, needs of different populations, and resources available which affect the cost-benefit balance, as described in Chapter 11. Administrators have a responsibility to create a work environment in which behaviors that contribute to positive outcomes for clients are maximized and behaviors that diminish such outcomes are minimized.

Learning from Errors

Settings differ in how easy it is to make, recognize, cover up, and remedy mistakes. In discussing errors we should consider the extent to which employees control their own work lives. Some agencies take advantage of opportunities to learn how to improve services from a review of factors related to adverse events. Others ignore such opportunities. Research regarding error highlights its inevitability and its many related causes:

- Human fallibility can be moderated up to a point, but it can never be eliminated entirely. It is a fixed part of the human condition, partly because errors, in many contexts, serve a useful function (for example, trial-and-error learning in knowledge-based situations).
- Different error types have different psychological causes, occur in different parts of the organization, and require different methods of management.
- Safety-critical errors happen at all levels of the system, not just at the sharp end.
- Measures that involve sanctions, threats, fear, appeals, and the like have only a very limited effectiveness. And, in some cases, they can do more harm—to morale, self-respect, and a sense of justice—than good.
- Errors are a product of a chain of causes in which the precipitating psychological factors—momentary inattention, misjudgement, forgetfulness, preoccupation— are often the last and least manageable links in the chain.
- The evidence from a large number of accident inquiries indicates that bad events are more often the result of error-prone situations and error-prone activities than they are of error-prone people. Such people do, of course, exist, but they seldom remain at the hazardous sharp end for very long. Quite often, they get promoted to management. (Reason, 1997, p. 129)

Staff willingness to identify mistakes is influenced by agency culture. Ineffective error management strategies include:

- They "firefight" the last error rather than anticipating and preventing the next one.
- They focus on active failures rather than latent conditions.
- They focus on the personal, rather than the situational contributions to error.
- They rely heavily on exhortations and disciplinary sanctions.
- They employ blame-laden and essentially meaningless terms such as *carelessness*, *bad attitude*, and *irresponsibility*.
- They do not distinguish adequately between random and systematic error-causing factors.

- They are generally not informed by current human factors, knowledge regarding error, and accident causation. (Reason, 1997, p. 126)

Reason (1997) identifies a variety of factors that influence how safety is handled. These include *safety-specific factors*, such as policy concerning incident and accident reporting and emergency resources. *Management factors* include how change is handled, quality of leadership, and communication. Other factors are policies regarding hiring and placement, purchasing, and degree of control over purchasing. *Technical factors* also influence how safety is handled, such as compatibility of human and system interfaces. *Procedural factors* include standards, rules, and operating procedures. *Training characteristics* influence safety. For example, is there a close match between training offered and competencies required? If reporting mistakes is punished, few will do it. However, if agency policy recognizes that mistakes will be made and that they are vital for learning how to do better in the future, and staff are encouraged to discuss them with their supervisors at an early point, they are less likely to result in further negative effects, and they provide an opportunity to learn how to decrease avoidable mistakes. (See the classic study by Bosk, 1979.)

Strategies suggested to make incident reporting work are illustrated in Exhibit 16.3. A key reason errors and mistakes continue to occur is that no one takes steps to identify

Exhibit 16.3 Making Adverse Incident Reporting Work

1. Training for all staff on risk management and incident reporting.
2. Continuing education on the aims and importance of risk management and incident reporting.
3. A clear statement that all staff are responsible for reporting.
4. A clear description of reportable incidents and indicators, drawn up in consultation with staff.
5. User-friendly incident reporting forms.
6. Clear description of reporting procedures.
7. Encouragement of staff to report an incident even if they are not sure whether it is necessary to do so.
8. A designated person on shift who is responsible for making sure that any incident that occurs during that time is reported.
9. A policy of no blame and no disciplinary action except in cases of gross misconduct, repeated errors despite retraining, or criminal negligence.
10. Regular feedback to staff describing the action taken as a result of their reports.
11. Design of corrective strategies to reduce undesirable incidents in the future.
12. Inclusion in clinical practice of specific corrective strategies by general consensus.
13. Evaluation of the efficacy of corrective strategies.

Source: Adapted from "Clinical Incident Reporting," by J. Secker-Walker and S. Taylor-Adams, 2001, in *Clinical Risk Management: Enhancing Patient Safety* (2nd ed., p. 434), edited by C. Vincent, London, UK: BMJ. Reprinted with permission.

them, bring them to people's attention, discover their causes, and involve others in trying to minimize avoidable ones. Organizations have a great deal to gain in the short term by encouraging the view that errors are caused by a particular individual, but much to lose in the long run in terms of discovering and altering systemic causes. Consider, for example, the many instances in which the death of a child in state care is attributed to a single staff person. This hinders exploration of agency culture and climate to identify related factors. The causes of errors are typically systemic. We cannot understand them, in most cases, by looking solely at one individual.

Encourage Accountability

The prevalence and variety of avoidable errors are related to agency policies regarding transparency and accountability. To what extent are known errors tolerated? To what extent do staff fail to acknowledge and rectify known errors? Related forms of denial Singer (1978) proposes include blaming the victim, trivializing error, no response, out-right cover-ups, reinterpreting errors as correct, and bureaucratic diffusion of responsibility. Staff may claim that certain errors are unavoidable when they are avoidable, or protest that errors have only minor consequences when they have major ones, including killing people. Singer (1978) suggests, "Hidden by bureaucratic complexity, decision-makers increasingly take overt chances with the lives of individuals, groups, or whole populations, themselves shielded from the consequences of their actions by various forms of organizational assumed liability" (Singer, 1978, p. 31). Most corporations have legal departments to protect the corporation and those in it from adverse events, such as lawsuits. What is the responsibility of those in leadership positions to honestly represent the quality of services provided? To what extent are they complicit in cover-ups that prevent improvement in services? Singer (1978) suggests that "probabilism"—the view that most bad things won't happen—has replaced the view that we have a choice. He argues that this is used as a substitute for thinking and to obscure moral responsibility. Consider continuing to offer services that have been found to harm clients. Is this an example of "planned tolerable error"—the view that not that many people will be hurt?

SUMMARY

Clinical decisions are made or rubber-stamped in case conferences. The case conference has been the subject of lively critiques, such as the classic chapter by Meehl, in which he identified characteristics that dilute the quality of decisions made, including rewarding gold and garbage alike. Rather than being a setting in which there is a reasoned discussion of well-argued alternatives, case conferences and team meetings may reflect emotional pitches for or against particular views. Factors that encourage the use of low-level appeals and irrelevant statements include the buddy-buddy syndrome (people are reluctant to hurt or embarrass others), a feeling of powerlessness, social anxiety, lack of effective social skills, vested interests, and failure to recognize fallacies. Effective communication skills are important complements to critical thinking skills. An emphasis on shared values (helping clients) will encourage consideration of different perspectives, as will staying focused on the task at hand—making decisions that benefit clients. Other steps that can be taken to increase the quality of case conferences include learning to identify and counter fallacies (such as polarized thinking, straw person arguments, and appeals based on emotion rather than reason) and encouraging helpful group practices, such as setting agendas. Sharing the values, knowledge, and skills as well as the products (e.g., CATs) of evidence-informed practice will facilitate effective team decision making.

The Future

CHAPTER
17

≍⬧≍

Overcoming Personal Obstacles to Critical Thinking

A variety of personal obstacles may interfere with making sound decisions. Avoidable errors may occur because you do not keep up-to-date with new developments or you overlook important client characteristics or circumstances. Errors in communication may result in inaccurate accounts of client concerns. Blau (1988) suggests that errors may occur because of clinicians' character flaws or neurotic conflicts, such as inappropriate intimacy with clients, breaches of confidentiality, lying to clients, and not seeking consultation when needed. You may become cynically resigned to poor practice standards. Dysfunctional work environments and/or lifestyles (e.g., not getting enough sleep) contribute to such reactions. Lack of interest in having a carefully thought-out position or a wish to appear decisive may compromise the quality of decisions. Brookfield (1987) suggests that adult learners may view learning to think critically as a journey into ambiguity and uncertainty.

Other obstacles include a low tolerance for uncertainty, a tendency to make premature judgments, unrealistic expectations, and a desire for quick success (Adams, 1974). Barriers to the development of intelligence suggested by Sternberg (1987) include the following (pp. 212–221):

- Lack of motivation or impulse control
- Inability to translate thought into action
- Lack of perseverance and follow-through
- Procrastination
- Distractibility and lack of concentration
- Spreading yourself too thick or too thin
- Lack of goal orientation
- Fear of failure
- Excessive self-pity; wallowing in personal difficulties

- Excessive dependency
- Inability to see the forest for the trees
- Lack of balance between critical, analytic thinking and creative, intuitive thinking
- Flawed self-assessments (e.g., overestimates of what you know)

Attitudes many authors view as vital for critical thinking include curiosity, skepticism, open-mindedness, and a disposition to be both systematic and flexible. (See also Chapter 1.) Good problem solvers are more attentive to situational details and are more tenacious.

ENCOURAGE VALUES COMPATIBLE WITH ETHICAL OBLIGATIONS TO CLIENTS

Thinking critically about decisions may require changing how you weigh certain outcomes. You may value entertainment more than gaining knowledge of use to your clients; you may be more concerned with appearing expert than learning from colleagues. Values that encourage well-reasoned decisions include an interest in helping clients and avoiding harming them, and in honoring professional codes of ethics. Valuing discovery of accurate accounts and tolerance for differences increase the likelihood of creative solutions (Perkins, 1988).

CHANGE A PREFERENCE FOR MYSTERY TO ONE FOR BEING WELL INFORMED

One indicator of a preference for mystery is a disinterest in practice-related research findings that, if drawn on, would improve the quality of services. A disinterest in clear description of the evidentiary status of claims that affects clients' lives is partly the result of professional education programs that promote obscurity over clarity. Some clinicians receive more of an indoctrination than an education in which critical appraisal of claims is encouraged, including seeking disconfirming evidence regarding preferred views (Gambrill, 1997). A disinterest in available knowledge that can decrease uncertainty may be related to a search for final answers, or the false belief that drawing on practice-related research allows no room for creativity and judgment. On the contrary, drawing on clinical expertise is needed to fill in gaps in knowledge and, together with your clients, to determine whether research findings apply. A preference for obscurity may be related to the imposter syndrome, a belief on the part of therapists that they are not who they pretend to be. Gibbs and DeVries found that about a fifth of a sample of 62 clinicians frequently feel like fakes (reported in DeAngelis, 1987, p. 14). If clinicians do not seek and use empirically based content and procedural knowledge to help clients attain outcomes their clients value, they do misrepresent themselves to clients.

OFFER CLIENTS THE SAME QUALITY OF SERVICES YOU WOULD LIKE

Compartmentalization of standards is one of the striking characteristics about human beings. Clinicians who rely on intuition want their physician to rely on results of randomized controlled trials when making treatment recommendations (see Chapter 1 for results of the "Is what's good for the goose good for the gander?" test). Does this apply to you? (See later discussion of excuses.)

REVIEW COMPROMISES AND RECOGNIZE SIGNS OF DEPLETION

The realities of day-to-day practice may result in changes in what you hope to accomplish. A mismatch between our skills and the tasks we confront may result in a mentality of powerlessness or an unrealistic sense of omnipotence. Personal control tends to be abandoned when performance demands and associated risks are excessive (Bandura, 1986). It is important to review compromises and recognize signs of depletion including nattering (complaining without trying to improve things). Signs of omnipotence include making no attempt to draw on practice-related research and a view of therapy as totally an art. Those who follow the latter path ignore the distinction between collective and individual ignorance. Clinical students usually start graduate education with ideals and enthusiasm. After encountering limited progress, they may revise their expectations downward—especially in relation to social reform goals. Original standards may become dimmer, harder to recall, or even forgotten, as new, less hopeful ones replace them. Related factors include lack of high-quality supervision, dysfunctional managed care requirements, lack of resources (including time), heavy caseloads, and onerous documentation requirements. Clinicians may decide that clients are really worse off than they thought—sicker and harder to change. This view is encouraged by the promotion of more and more behaviors and feelings as mental illnesses requiring medication (Angell, 2011). Graduate training may encourage this view via emphasizing diagnosis of mental illness (see Chapter 7). Blaming the client or the agency for limited success removes responsibility from clinicians' shoulders. Previous interests in increasing equity in the world by helping those who struggle with poverty, poor housing, high-crime neighborhoods, domestic violence, lack of health care, and poor education may be abandoned as it becomes obvious that individually focused counseling results in little or no headway in decreasing these problems (Cohen & Timimi, 2008). Ashton and Webb (1986) studied teachers' sense of efficacy and its relation to student achievement, and found marked changes over a few years, even in idealistic students.

Efforts to improve competencies may be abandoned because of a lack of effective learning skills, including identification of clear goals, intermediate steps, and progress indicators. The work environment may offer few, if any, opportunities for continued learning. Education programs differ in opportunities offered to evaluate whether skills have been acquired. It is difficult for busy practitioners to keep up with research findings related to life-affecting questions that arise daily. Indeed, this was a key reason for the invention of the systematic review (e.g., Cochrane and Campbell databases). Another way to give up is not to evaluate client progress in a systematic way—to accept a feeling of what works rather than gathering data to explore degree of progress. You may believe that careful evaluation of progress will be too time-consuming or cannot offer helpful information. Neither of these beliefs is true (e.g., Bloom, Fischer, & Orme, 2009).

Are You Burned Out?

Symptoms of burnout include cynicism, depression, a loss of motivation and energy, and a numbing of feeling (Maslach et al., 2001). Indicators include emotional exhaustion, depersonalization, and reduced personal accomplishment. There may be a cynical resignation to poor practices and policies. Burnout may result from an imbalance between client needs and available resources for meeting them. Indicators include sleepiness during sessions; drifting attention; being late for meetings; annoyance with clients; feelings of relief when a client cancels; sardonic or humorous references to clients; increased irritability with staff, family, and clients; and disillusionment with work (p. 284). We may even become numb to the misery of others. Use these indicators as cues that something must be changed in your personal or work life. Perhaps you do not carefully evaluate progress with your clients and become discouraged because your effectiveness is unknown. Burnout is associated with a higher frequency of mistakes (Campbell & Cornett, 2002).

RECOGNIZE UNCERTAINTY AND AMBIGUITY

Uncertainty is an inherent part of clinical practice—indeed, of life itself (Marris, 1996). Consider the questions: How accurate is this client's self-report? Will this client carry out agreed-on tasks? Will this intervention be more (or less) effective than another for this client? How long should follow-up services be provided in order to maintain gains? How uncertainty is handled influences the quality of decisions. In opting for all, some clinicians opt for ignoring what information is available. Acknowledging uncertainty does not mean that decisions are not made: It means that steps are taken to decrease it. Ignoring uncertainty may result in overlooking valuable options. Hallmarks of evidence-informed practice include recognizing the uncertainty involved in making decisions and taking steps to reduce it, such as drawing on practice- and policy-related research. It is a way to handle the inevitable uncertainty in the helping process in an ethical, informed participatory manner. Even when well equipped with knowledge and tools, lack of time to locate needed information may contribute to avoidable uncertainty. Uncertainty may breed a temptation to deny it, perhaps fearing that its recognition would stifle needed action. We may deny uncertainty by ignoring individual differences or framing a problem in a way that hides uncertainty. Cassell (1991) suggests that "to disengage from the patient [for example, by ignoring knowledge about their unique circumstances and characteristics] is to lose the ultimate source of knowledge in medicine" (p. 232). We do not see what is there to be seen. Inflated estimates of judgmental accuracy may in part be an adaptive reaction to uncertainty; overconfidence encourages needed action, despite doubts about outcomes (Fischhoff, 1975).

ACQUIRE HELPFUL VIEWS ABOUT KNOWLEDGE AND HOW TO GET IT

Our beliefs about how we can learn and how much control we have over what we learn are integrally related to our potential to learn (Hofer, 2001). Both a belief that we have little control over what we learn and a lack of knowledge about how to do so will hinder learning. We may believe that acquiring new knowledge requires little effort or that others (rather than we ourselves) are responsible for what we learn. Intuitive beliefs are often difficult to modify. Properties of beliefs that influence how difficult it may be to alter them include their strength (confidence in a belief—willingness to act on a belief), longevity (how long it has been held), and value (how important it is to us). Once a belief is formed, we are likely to fall prey to confirmation bias—a selective search for confirming data.

View Learning as an Active Process

In problem-based learning, the focus is on the *process* of decision making. (See critique of the bucket theory of learning and discussion of problem-based learning in Chapter 8.)

Learning is an active process in which we question views and compare perspectives. Lifelong learning requires arranging opportunities to critically assess our knowledge and skills and using corrective feedback to enhance future success. Seek colleagues who are skilled in offering constructive feedback, for example, who offer clear instructions concerning helpful changes. Active learning requires seeking feedback about your competencies and the outcomes clients attain.

Value Errors and Lack of Success as Learning Opportunities

Assumptions may not be questioned because of fear of discovering errors. Errors and lack of success are inevitable. The constructive way to view mistakes is as an opportunity to learn. We learn by risking and then responding to feedback on our performance. This feedback helps us to discover what we understand and what we do not, what we can do and what we cannot. Changing one's view of errors as rare and as occasions for blame to one of recognizing and using them as learning opportunities is vital. Skill in troubleshooting is one of the cluster of skills that distinguish novices from experts; responding to setbacks as opportunities to learn focuses attention on problem solving. Our reactions to feedback, including errors, are influenced by how secure we feel.

Recognizing Your Knowledge Gaps

We are unlikely to be interested in acquiring new knowledge if we are satisfied with our current knowledge. Dissatisfaction with current views is a valuable source of motivation for looking further—for example, for alternative, more effective methods. I often have been told "I already do that" when I am discussing the topic of identifying clear objectives. Further inquiry often reveals that the speaker does not have the related skills. A false belief that a skill is already present will get in the way of acquiring new competencies. Perkinson (1993), as well as others, stresses that "students must become critical of their own performances and their own understandings—while remaining confident in their ability to do better if they are to continue growing" (pp. 40–41). The importance of thinking about why theories do not work has been emphasized by many writers (e.g., Schon, 1990). "Developing theories in use is one of the most important ways critical thinking can be practiced at the workplace. It requires practitioners to reflect on the reasons why espoused theories are not working and to seek alternative forms of practice" (Brookfield, 1987, p. 154). It requires us to distinguish between which theories we think we rely on and which ones we actually use—which may be a surprising revelation.

Cultivate an Open Mind

Many writers stress the relationship between effective reasoning and an attitude toward the truth. Effective reasoning "presupposes a questioning attitude, an openness to both arguments and facts, and a willingness to modify one's beliefs in the light of evidence that they should be modified. In other words, it presupposes a commitment to the truth insofar as the truth can be ascertained" (Nickerson, 1986b, p. 12). Integral to this commitment is the understanding that beliefs should be reexamined from time to time, and that there will be no clear answers for many questions or no way to find out what the answers are. "That is not to say that reasoning serves no purpose in such cases, but simply to suggest that some issues must be decided on the basis of preferences, tastes, or weakly held opinions regarding what the truth might be. The reasonable person will surely reason about such issues, but having reasoned, will recognize the tenuous nature of the basis of any conclusions drawn or decisions reached" (pp. 12–13). Practice-related beliefs are often difficult to alter because they are linked to a worldview; a preferred approach to understanding reality. Conceptions of behavior and how it can be changed form a basic part of our beliefs about the nature of human beings, and thus have emotional connotations. If a view is proposed that differs from an accepted view in significant ways, the new perspective may be rejected out of hand. The more clearly an issue or situation is described, the easier it is to identify related beliefs. Often it is only when specific situations are considered that differences emerge. For example, we may agree on the value of client self-determination, but disagree as to how this should be implemented in specific cases.

Identifying knowledge gaps requires an openness to reviewing background knowledge and skills and candidly comparing these with what the literature suggests is needed to help clients.

> Intellectually, critical thinking is challenging because we must prepare the way for new ideas by rooting out old ones, by breaking down remnants from popular, if incoherent, illogical and insupportable ideologies and prejudices of the day. Until we have thought deeply and critically we are apt to be persuaded by deeply flawed ideas. . . .
>
> We must learn in other words, something quite new to us: to identify not with the content of our beliefs but with the integrity of the process by which we arrived at them. We must come to define ourselves, and actually respond in everyday contexts, as people who reason their way into, and can be reasoned out of, beliefs. Only then will we feel unthreatened when others question our beliefs, only then will we welcome their questions as a reminder

of the need to be ready to test and retest our beliefs daily at the bar of reason, only then will we learn to think within multiple points of view, with a sense of global perspective. (Paul, 1993, p. xii)

Basic to this process is a willingness to challenge ideas and conceptions, to adopt a view of knowledge as tentative, and to view theories as tools rather than dogma to be guarded. People differ in how open they are to examining their beliefs. Those with closed minds are limited to alternatives 1 and 4 in the following list (Hayakawa, 1978, p. 232): "1. he may accept the speaker and accept his statement; 2. he may accept the speaker but reject his statement; 3. he may reject the speaker but accept his statement; 4. he may reject the speaker and reject his statement."

Beliefs differ in their evidentiary status as well as in how clearly they are formulated and how accessible they are in our consciousness. Data tend to be interpreted in ways that make it consistent with current views. Whether a belief is true or false may have great or little impact on the tenability of other beliefs. If knowledge of a subject is quite limited, inconsistencies in beliefs may not be recognized. One way to avoid inconsistencies is not to recognize them—to simply add new beliefs without altering old ones. This has been called the *add-on* principle (Harmon, 1986). The principle of *negative undermining* states that we should stop believing something whenever we do not have adequate reasons to believe it (p. 39). The principle of *positive undermining* states that "you should stop believing something whenever you believe that your reasons for believing it are not good" (p. 39). Harmon suggests that we are also influenced by the principle of *clutter avoidance*—the mind should not be cluttered with trivialities (p. 55).

A willingness to question beliefs requires curiosity and an interest in discovering what is true. A disinterest in examining practice beliefs may be related to a reluctance to accept responsibility for decisions. It is not unusual to hear clinicians say, "I don't make decisions. Clients make their own decisions." This stance overlooks the social-influence process inherent in clinical practice. (See Chapter 2.) A belief on the part of clinicians that they do not make decisions is a key indicator of a sense of powerlessness (or failure to take responsibility) that develops when we lack decision-making skills.

Seek Help When You Need It

The very process of evidence-based practice confronts us repeatedly with our ignorance. That is, we translate our information needs related to important decisions we must make into clear, well-structured questions that allow us to see whether there are any research findings that shed light on these questions. A reluctance to recognize that we need help will be a major obstacle, as illustrated by how difficult it is for students to say, "I don't know" (Damer, 1995).

IMPROVE SELF-MANAGEMENT SKILLS

The first 10 obstacles to the full development of intelligence, described at the beginning of this chapter, are related to a lack of self-management skills. Self-management involves rearranging the environment and behavior in order to attain valued goals (Watson & Tharp, 2007). Steps include identifying specific goals, planning how to achieve these, acting on plans, and monitoring progress. The Premack Principle can be used to increase desired behaviors; high-probability behaviors can be used to reinforce low-probability behaviors (Premack, 1965). Rather than having a cup of coffee before starting a disliked task (such as recording), complete a modest amount of recording (close to baseline) before having your coffee. Precommitment strategies can be used to avoid future temptations such as momentary moods and distractions. For example, you could make a commitment to spend 1 hour each week seeking practice-related research, and this time could be protected from interruptions by planning ahead. Skills such as self-monitoring are a valuable component of effective problem solving. Self-change methods have been used to help clients attain a wide range of hoped-for outcomes; clinicians can also take advantage of these methods.

Increase Time-Management Skills

People who are productive engage in metaplanning. A review of your schedule often reveals room for improvement (Maher & Cook, 1985; Watson & Tharp, 2007). Here are six helpful guidelines:

1. Distinguish between tasks that must be done and discretionary tasks that do not have to be completed on a given day.
2. Delegate responsibilities to others.
3. Select a pleasing variety of tasks each day—some that can be easily accomplished and some that will be more challenging.
4. Arrange some distraction-free time each day.
5. Make realistic daily plans.
6. If possible, allow time for necessary documentation between interviews.

You may assume that your workdays must have a crisis mentality; this attitude will interfere with systematic attention to clients. A closer examination may reveal opportunities for some distraction-free time. Feeling disorganized may be a result of not planning the day in terms of priorities—what must be done versus what could be done (discretionary activities)—being careful not to overload the must-do category. If procrastination is a problem, develop self-management skills to overcome it. If delegating responsibility is difficult, explore the reasons for this. Use the most efficient means of communication to ease work tasks.

Enhance Stress-Management Skills

Stress may result from too much work, personal problems, a job that is boring or too demanding in terms of the match between required and available skills, or an over-sensitivity to negative evaluations (see Exhibit 17.1). Excessive workloads contribute to errors. For example, "A consultant pediatrician facing allegations of misconduct in overstating and exaggerating reports of child abuse was running a unit that was grossly understaffed at the time, the General Medical Council heard last week" (Dyer, 2005, p. 1105; see also Barling, Kelloway, & Frone, 2004). Different stressors may influence our problem-solving capability in different ways (e.g., Hammond, 2000; Matthews, 2001). Too little or too much interest, anxiety, or anger can get in the way of making informed decisions. Use feelings as clues to contingencies (Skinner, 1974); what is happening (or has happened) related to feeling angry or anxious, for example? Perhaps someone ignored your comment in a meeting. Excessive interest in an outcome may interfere with the careful weighing of evidence and make it difficult to manage impatience, anxiety, or anger. Both behavioral and cognitive coping skills can be of value in avoiding and regulating arousal (see Exhibit 17.2). Stressors differ in how easily they can be controlled and in their frequency, timing, intensity, and duration.

Situations initially appraised as threatening can be reframed as unimportant by asking questions such as "Does this really matter?" and "Will it make any difference

Exhibit 17.1 Sources of Stress and Remedies

Source	Remedy
• Negative thoughts	Replace with positive task-oriented thoughts.
• Ineffective social skills	Acquire effective social skills.
• Overwork	Plan more manageable work load (for instance, delegate responsibility).
• Fatigue	Check balance between work and recreation.
• Lack of positive feedback from colleagues	Arrange support group.
• Lack of self-reinforcement for accomplishments	Increase self-reinforcement.
• Muscle tension	Use relaxation skills.
• Lack of knowledge	Acquire needed information.
• Lack of clinical skills	Acquire helpful skills.
• Lack of positive feedback from clients	Enhance evaluation skills.
• Lack of needed resources	Problem-solve to determine if added resources can be acquired.
• Unrealistic expectations	Encourage realistic expectations.
• Lack of resources	Advocate for additional resources.

Exhibit 17.2 Coping Skills Used by Hospice Nurses

Rational Action
> Identified a couple of different solutions.
> Accepted my limitations.
> Did what I knew had to be done.
> Tried to learn from the situation.
> Discussed the situation with peer or team member.
> Drew on past experience of similar situation.
> Tried not to act too hastily.
> Told myself I had done well.
> Told myself that I was not responsible.

Fantasized Action
> Wished that I could change the way I felt.
> Wished that I could change what happened.
> Imagined a better time or place than the one I was in.
> Wished that the situation would go away or be over.
> Wished I were a stronger person.

Emotional Avoidance
> Kept my feelings to myself.
> Tried to forget the whole thing.

Professionalism
> Assured myself that the dying are needy.
> Told myself that dying is a natural process.
> Chose my words carefully with the patient.

Emotional Response
> Took deep breaths and/or meditated.
> Waited to see what would happen.

Anticipated Coping
> Anticipated difficulty and prepared myself emotionally.
> Talked to someone to find out more about the situation.
> Made up a plan of action and followed it.
> Tried to appreciate some humorous aspect of the situation.
> Asked someone I respected for advice and followed it.
> Examined my goals regarding the patient.
> Just took one step at a time.

Conflicted Behavior
> Avoided being with people for a while.
> Slept more than usual.
> Felt better by eating, drinking, or smoking.
> Turned to some other activity to take my mind off things.
> Sought emotional support from family and friends.

Meditation
> Prayed.
> Hoped a miracle would happen.
> Looked for the silver lining.
> Rediscovered what is important in life.
> Examined my goals regarding the patient.
> Focused on what I might learn about life from the patient.

Concerned Behavior
> Went over the problem trying to understand it.
> Talked to someone who could do something.

Source: Adapted from "Stress and Coping Among Hospice Nurses: Test of an Analytic Model," by D. A. Chiriboga, G. Jenkins, and J. Bailey, 1983, *Nursing Research, 32*, pp. 294–299. Reprinted with permission.

10 years from now?" Ignoring minor irritations and acquiring skills in requesting behavior changes and responding to criticism will decrease reactions of anger that interfere with making well-reasoned decisions. Emotional reactions can be regulated by keeping things in perspective. "Whenever you are in doubt or when the self becomes too much with you, try the following experiment: Recall the face of the poorest and most helpless man you have ever seen and ask yourself if the step you contemplate is going to be of any use to him. Then you will find your doubts and your self melting away" (Gandhi in Burgess, 1984, p. 38). Anxiety in social situations may be related to a lack of social skills. If this is the case, the most effective way to alter such reactions is to acquire and use helpful skills. Take advantage of your clinical assessment skills to help yourself to achieve desired goals.

INCREASE COMMUNICATION SKILLS

Clinical practice involves exchanges with clients, their significant others, fellow workers, administrative staff, and various other professionals who may become involved in a case. The importance of communication skills has been emphasized throughout this book. The quality of your skills for handling challenges that arise in social situations will influence the quality of your decisions. Failures of communication are a key cause of avoidable errors. Thus developing effective skills in this area is vital to making sound decisions (Elliott et al., 2011; Katz, 2002). A variety of assertive skills are needed, such as making and refusing requests, posing questions, and accepting and giving corrective feedback. Avoidable errors may occur because of vague instructions, a failure to raise questions, and defensive reactions to corrective feedback. A focus on helping clients will encourage attention to corrective feedback. Effective relationship skills will add to your confidence and comfort in exchanges, even difficult ones. Knowledge about cultural differences in interactional styles may be needed (Smith, Rodrigues, & Bernal, 2011).

Examples of relevant social skills include praising others and offering encouragement, offering criticism in a constructive manner, disagreeing with others in a nonabrasive manner, supporting positive alternatives to negative behaviors, requesting changes in annoying behavior without becoming unpleasant, and responding effectively to criticism (see Gambrill, 2012b). Making evidence-informed decisions requires questioning claims your colleagues make. Use of diplomatic methods may avoid bad feelings. Let's say a colleague makes a sweeping generalization such as "Cognitive methods help everyone." Rather than saying, "That's clearly not true" (not that you would), you could say, "Do you think they work better for some clients than others?" That is, you could introduce the idea of comparison. You could use a Columbo style: "Could it be . . . ?"

Communication skills are of value with clients as well as colleagues. In both situations poor communication skills may create avoidable conflicts, resulting in failure to gain (or transmit) important information. Consider examples described by Kottler and Blau (1989, pp. 80–81):

- Distracting mannerisms or facial expressions.
- Poor attending skills and eye contact.
- Difficulty following and focusing the direction of statements.
- The use of closed-ended questions and an interrogative style that create defensive reactions.
- Frequent interruptions.
- Noting surface messages of what is said rather than deeper-level messages.
- Relying exclusively on the content of communications rather than on affect or process.
- Using excessive self-disclosure and inappropriately putting the focus on oneself.
- Exaggerated passivity in style.
- Difficulty tolerating silence.
- Appearing unduly cold, aloof, and wooden in appearance.
- Appearing too friendly, seductive, and informal.
- Being aggressive or punitive in confrontations.

Empathy and warmth are important with colleagues as well as with clients. They create the context in which other important elements of effective services are offered, such as clarifying goals and planning services. Lapses in empathy include (1) telling people what they should feel (e.g., "That's not the way to feel when you see her"); (2) an interrogative interview style; (3) overinterpretation; (4) self-disclosure that distracts attention from pursuit of goals; (5) encouragement of dependence by offering excessive help; and (6) negativity (criticizing clients). Examples of physicians' poor attempts at empathy when they must deliver bad news to patients are as follows:

One 72-year-old woman with breast cancer confided to her consultant surgeon that she did not want to lose her breast, only to be told, "At your age, what do you need a breast for?"

A woman of 40 with the same disease asked a different hospital consultant if there was any way she could avoid a mastectomy. He said, "There is not much there worth keeping, is there?"

An elderly man with terminal lung cancer was asked by a junior hospital doctor why he was crying, and explained that he did not want to die.

The house officer's unsympathetic response was: "Well, we all have to die sometime." (Collins, 1988, p. A7)

Effective social skills can be used to avoid conflicts during team meetings as well as to resolve conflicts in a constructive manner. Clear description of the exact nature of a conflict (for example, what each party wants, what indicators will be used to determine whether goals are met) is helpful (Fisher & Ury, 1991). Ennis (1987) suggests that being sensitive to the feelings, levels of knowledge, and degrees of sophistication of others, as well as seriously considering other views, is important (see also Colón-Emeric, Ammarell, Bailey, Corazzini, & Utley-Smith, 2006; McKnight, Stetson, Bakken, Curran, & Cimino, 2002). A troubleshooting checklist for reviewing situations is offered in Exhibit 17.3. Some clinicians overreact when they are criticized; they become anxious or angry, and are less able and willing to consider alternative views. Confrontational rather than cooperative methods may be used to persuade colleagues to accept favored positions. Questions raised by clients or colleagues about the effectiveness of proposed methods or degree of progress may be met with defensive responses rather than informed answers. Oversensitivity to negative feedback decreases the likelihood that divergent views will be shared or defended in the face of criticism, and increases the likelihood of overreactions to criticism. Excessive reactions to negative evaluation or to being ignored may be related to unrealistic expectations such as expecting to please everyone. One reason people do not speak up in case conferences is because of a concern about what others will think of their ideas, of their style of presentation, or of the way they look. Focus on the benefits to clients of taking an active role in discovering and critiquing assumptions in order to arrive at well-reasoned decisions.

Increase Awareness of Transference and Countertransference Effects

Awareness of how you tend to respond to certain kinds of people may help you to avoid dysfunctional reactions (Hayes, Gelso, & Hummel, 2011). One of the goals of clinical training programs is to help clinicians become aware of transference effects (how clients respond to clinicians, based on their past experiences) as well as countertransference

Exhibit 17.3 Troubleshooting Checklist

1. Were my goals achievable? Did I focus on common goals?
2. Did I plan how to achieve my goals?
3. What thoughts and behaviors did I attend to? Were they relevant or irrelevant? Distracting or helpful?
4. What should I have done more of?
5. What should I have done less of?
6. Did I consider other perspectives?
7. Were special skills required that I don't have?

effects (how clinicians tend to relate to different clients). Not recognizing such effects may result in errors such as misattributing a lack of progress to environmental obsta-cles and overlooking relationship factors. Kottler and Blau (1989) discuss a number of errors that may result from lack of awareness of countertransference effects, including premature termination of treatment due to an unrecognized dislike for clients. Thus, either underinvestment or overinvestment in clients may result in poor decisions. Errors described by Herbert Strean in one of his cases that he attributed to his negative attitude toward a client (cited in Kottler & Blau, 1989, p. 132) include:

- He lost his objectivity and let himself be pulled into the client's manipulative ploys.
- Because of feelings of threat, jealousy, and competition, he perpetuated a continual power struggle.
- He often made the correct interpretation or said the right words, but in a tone of voice that was more hostile than empathic.
- He spent much of the time trying to prove to the client (flashbacks to his father) that he knew what he was doing.
- Although he was aware that his countertransference feelings were getting in the way, he could not monitor or confront them sufficiently, nor did he seek supervision or therapy to resolve them.
- He retreated behind the mask of cold, objective analyst in order to be punitive, rather than adopting a posture of empathy and support.

Such errors may also occur with colleagues.

ENCOURAGE REALISTIC EXPECTATIONS

Clinicians are not immune to unrealistic expectations. These may concern colleagues ("I have to please everyone"), as well as clients ("I have to help everyone"). Albert Ellis offered a variant on his classic list of irrational assumptions that applies to practitioners:

- I have to be successful with all of my clients practically all of the time.
- I must be an outstanding therapist, clearly better than other therapists I know or hear about.
- I have to be greatly respected and loved by all my clients.
- Since I am doing my best and working so hard as a therapist, my clients should be equally hardworking and responsible, should listen to me carefully, and should always push themselves to change.

- Because I am a person in my own right, I must be able to enjoy myself during therapy sessions and to use these sessions to solve my personal problems as much as to help clients with their problems. (Cordes, 1983, p. 22)

A belief that "I have to be successful with all of my clients" may contribute to burnout. Unrealistic beliefs may be due to expectations for success that cannot be realized, because individual counseling cannot alter many problems (such as homelessness), as suggested in Chapter 2. They may be due to intemperate expectations on the part of government officials, such as "Ensure that no child be harmed in care." Waiting for an ideal alternative may result in unnecessary delays in choosing among available options. Critical thinking values and skills will enhance recognition of the limits and potentials of clinical practice—of the inevitable uncertainty associated with decisions. The expectation to succeed all the time can be satisfied only by ignoring lack of success. Problems differ in their potential for resolution, even by expert clinicians. It is unrealistic to expect clinicians to resolve problems such as poverty, lack of access to medical care, and lack of job opportunities. An understanding of social, political, and economic factors related to social and personal problems protects you from assuming potentials for change via individually based services such as counseling and therapy that do not exist and that may result in the demoralization associated with burnout.

DEVELOP POSITIVE ALTERNATIVES TO CHALLENGING SITUATIONS

One of your greatest sources of discouragement may be the discrepancy between services needed and services available. For example, money may not be provided for in-home services, requiring clients to enter residential care. Neither money nor services may be available to help an abusive parent lessen external stresses related to her abusive behavior. Money may not be available to gather information needed to decrease avoidable errors and alter onerous conditions such as long waiting times for clients. Indeed, funding for services has decreased. What can be done in such situations? As with any problem, it can be handled in either a constructive or a dysfunctional manner. One dysfunctional response assumes that what is must always be; there is a *fatalism* that nothing can be done to alter conditions. I have been struck by the prevalence of reactions, such as, "There is nothing we can do," "We have too many cases," "We have no power," and "We have to make decisions quickly." There is a feeling of hopelessness and helplessness, even among graduate students. Or there is a utopianism—only if all is changed is the effort worthwhile. *Goal displacement* is another kind of dysfunctional reaction. This involves focusing on concerns that are not of key importance to clients. For example, you may recommend that a client participate in counseling, even though this will do nothing to address environmental circumstances related to problems. If you do this often enough, you may convince yourself that this is appropriate. Constructive ways of handling discrepancies between services needed and those available include: (1) offering what help you can related to the problems of greatest concern to clients; (2) taking what steps you can to decrease discrepancies (e.g., bringing them to the attention of administrators and legislators and forming a group of other interested colleagues to pursue a specific change); and (3) joining advocacy groups to pursue needed changes (e.g., Cohen & Timimi, 2008).

Focusing on helping clients, including what to do when resources are not available, will help us to choose the best course of action in difficult circumstances. As Archie Cochrane (1992) noted, outcome "is certainly not the whole story" (p. 95). The manner in which services are provided, including kindliness and the ability to communicate, matter also. He suggests, "We all recognize quality when we see it and particularly when we receive it" (p. 95). Consider the example he gives in *Effectiveness and Efficiency* (1999). As a prisoner of war during World War II, he took care of other prisoners of war. He was with a dying soldier who was in great pain. Neither spoke a word of the other's language. There was no pain medication. He took the man in his arms and held him until he died. "In despair, and purely instinctively, I sat on his bed and took him in my arms. The effect was almost magical; he quieted at once and died peacefully a few hours later. I was still with him, half asleep and very stiff. I believe that by personal intervention I improved the quality of care dramatically in this case, and I know it was based on instinct and not on reason" (pp. 94–95).

WHAT ABOUT SELF-EFFICACY AND SELF-ESTEEM?

Considerable attention has been devoted to examining the influence of judgments of efficacy on performance (Bandura, 1986, 1997).

> A lack of confidence in our ability to solve problems can manifest itself in a variety of ways; for example it may be reflected by a lack of interest, fear of exploring new domains, and fear of criticism. These feelings can interfere with solving a problem and can prevent us from engaging in activities that might improve our problem-solving skills. . . . The tendency to avoid new areas becomes especially strong when others are performing well while we experience considerable difficulty. A common way to define such difficulties is simply to assume we are inept or slow and others are talented. An alternative perspective is that everyone experiences difficulty when first learning about a new area. (Bransford & Stein, 1984, p. 123)

Performance efficacy refers to the belief that a certain behavior can be performed. *Outcome efficacy* is a judgment of the likely effect of a behavior. Judgments of efficacy influence how long we persist at a task and how much effort we make. Success in real-life situations is the most influential source of accurate efficacy expectations (Baumeister et al., 2003). Perceptions of self-efficacy influence our thoughts and emotions as well as the goals we pursue. Some people have a "let me out of here" approach when confronting difficult problems. "Over time, the let me out of here approach can result in self-fulfilling prophecies. For example, people who initially have difficulty solving math problems may come to believe that they have no math ability; they may therefore avoid situations in which they must deal with math problems. Since such individuals receive little practice with math because they avoid it, their initial hypothesis about not being able to solve math problems is likely to come true. In general, it seems clear that people who avoid dealing with problems place limitations on themselves that are not necessarily there to begin with" (Bransford & Stein, 1984, p. 4). Fear of failure interferes with focused attention on problems.

Self-efficacy and self-esteem are not necessarily correlated with actual skill levels. (See research on flawed self-assessment in Dunning, Heath, and Suls, 2004.) Simply raising self-esteem is unlikely to improve skilled performance, as suggested in the title of Baumeister et al.'s review (2003): "Does self-esteem cause better performance, interpersonal success, happiness, or healthier lifestyles? Answer: No, no, probably, sporadically." (See also Foxx & Roland, 2005.) Self-assessment on the part of physicians is not highly correlated with actual performance (Tousignant & DesMarchais, 2002). Facilitators tend to overestimate the skills of their students (Whitfield & Xie, 2002). Thus, as Baumeister and his colleagues (2003) conclude, raising self-esteem should not be an end in itself. Self-efficacy can be enhanced by acquiring additional skills.

Low levels of outcome efficacy pose an obstacle to decision making in several ways. Helpful views may not be presented in a case conference, or may be presented in an ineffective manner. Just as the boldness with which comments are made does not necessarily reflect their soundness, so, too, the diffidence with which comments are made does not necessarily reflect a lack of cogency. Low self-efficacy is associated with negative affect, which reduces the quality of problem solving. Positive emotions encourage flexibility and creativity and enhance helpfulness and generosity, which should add to effectiveness in both interviews and case conferences. Low self-efficacy increases vulnerability to fears of negative evaluation. Both extremes of self-esteem, excessive and limited, may interfere with making well-informed decisions, by encouraging a reluctance to examine beliefs. Evaluations of personal efficacy and self-esteem are not necessarily related (Bandura, 1986). If clinicians are effective in certain situations but do not value their related skills, they may still have low self-esteem.

EXAMINE RATIONALIZATIONS/EXCUSES

When our skills and resources do not match the challenges we confront, we seek reasons. Difficult situations may breed excuses that preserve self-esteem and help us live with our limitations (McDowell, 2000; Snyder, Higgins, & Stucky, 1983). We may create self-imposed obstacles to high-quality performance (consistently get insufficient sleep) to avoid failure. Such strategies help us to preserve self-esteem and personal control. They help us "to negotiate reality" (Higgins, Snyder, & Berglas, 1990). Alternatives to self-handicapping reactions are suggested in Exhibit 17.4. Excuses can be defined as "explanations or actions that lessen the negative implications of an actor's performance, thereby maintaining a positive image for oneself and others" (p. 45). There are many ways to deny responsibility. Offering rationalizations and excuses is an everyday part of life. Related literature overlaps with literature on self-protection, self-deception, and the deception of others. This literature suggests challenges to critical thinking and fulfilling ethical components of EBP as well as possible remedies. There are many ways in which we create a disconnect between our actions and the harm we create or contribute to (Bandura, 1999; Fetherstonhaugh et al., 1997). Popular excuses for avoiding responsibility for harming others are: (1) I didn't know, (2) I was just following orders (from my supervisor or from an evil administrator), and (3) I was just doing what others do, using the same standards of care (even though abysmal). We could deny there is a problem. We can offer an excuse and provide what we know to be merely Band-Aid help. Excuses given by social workers for less-than-optimal service include lack of resources and high

Exhibit 17.4 Self-Handicapping Strategies and Constructive Alternatives

Self-Handicapping Strategies	Constructive Alternatives
• Become fatalistic; focus on problems. Natter (complain without taking action to correct disliked situations).	• Seek positive alternatives. Identify the specific changes you would like, as well as how these could be attained, and take steps in that direction.
• Blame others/blame yourself.	• Same as above.
• Decide there is little help that can be offered and do your job in a "routinized," uncaring manner.	• Offer whatever help you can to clients and meet with others to explore what changes could be made to improve services.
• Assume a self-congratulatory position (congratulate yourself on services offered even though none have been provided).	• Carefully evaluate progress and be honest about results.
• Claim you do not make decisions.	• Recognize the decisions you make, identify factors that limit your options, and meet with others to see how obstacles could be decreased.
• Struggle on by yourself.	• Involve others in seeking positive changes; form coalitions. A group has more power than an individual.

caseloads. These may reflect reality. Caseloads may be high. Many objectives are difficult to attain. Resources are often lacking. We may reframe negative outcomes as deserved because of moral lapses on the part of the harmed ("They deserve it"). We may use cleansing language that obscures suffering and coercion (e.g., use of the term *relocated* to refer to forced evictions).

We may resort to pseudoscientific practices, such as assigning uninformative diagnostic labels to clients in order to relieve our discomfort when confronted with unsolvable problems (Houts, 2002). If an incorrect decision is made, one or more of the following accounts could be offered:

- It was not possible to get all the information.
- This was a difficult case; anyone would have had trouble.
- I was pressed for time.
- I didn't have the authority to make a decision.
- I was tired.
- My graduate education didn't prepare me for this kind of client.
- Other people make the same mistakes.

Excuses that astrologers offered when they made a wrong statement about a client include these four examples (Dean, 1986–1987, p. 173):

1. Client does not know himself. (This shifts the blame from astrology to the participants.)
2. Astrologer is not infallible.
3. Another factor is responsible. (This puts the blame on the ambiguity of the birth chart.)
4. Manifestation is not typical.

We tend to attribute our successes to our own efforts and abilities and our failures to external influences, such as luck or test difficulty. Excuses are especially likely to occur when we hold ourselves responsible for a negative outcome but still want to believe that we are good people. Excuses serve many functions, including preserving self-esteem, smoothing social exchanges, and helping people to live with their limitations; they function as self-handicapping strategies if they reduce options for achieving valued clinical goals. To the extent that excuses relieve us from assuming undue responsibility for clients and encourage reasonable risk taking, they are helpful. To the extent that they prevent us from recognizing limitations that could be altered—for example, by keeping up with practice-related research—they are not helpful. Reframing strategies may be used to mute the negative consequences of an action; harm may be underestimated ("He wasn't really harmed"), victims may be derogated ("He's not worth helping"), or the source of the negative feedback may be attacked ("My supervisor doesn't have experience with such clients") (Bandura, 1999). Such strategies are encouraged by our tendency to question the accuracy of negative feedback. Acts of omission may be excused by denying there was any need for action, as in the famous Kitty Genovese case, in which witnesses to the slaying of a young woman did not become involved; they said they thought it was a lovers' quarrel or that it was not their responsibility (Rosenthal, 1964). "Transformed responsibility excuses" decrease responsibility for actions. For example, consensus-raising tactics may be used; a clinician can protest that others would have acted in the same way. He can say that he was coerced, or shortcomings can be attributed to others to avoid threats to himself; that is, projection can be used (Snyder, Higgins, & Stucky, 1983, p. 97). Use of projection is illustrated by research that shows that when people receive negative feedback, they describe others as having the negative characteristics (Holmes, 1978).

A temporary inconsistency in performance may be appealed to in order to decrease responsibility. Variations include the intentionality plea ("I didn't mean to do it") and effort-lowering statements ("I didn't try") (Semin & Manstead, 1983). Self-handicapping strategies, such as expecting to fail, may be used to remove responsibility for possible low performance (Arkin & Oleson, 1998). Excuses may save time in the short term, but cost time in the long run. For example, not evaluating practice and not keeping up with practice-related research saves time in the short run but may cost time in the long run, both for clients and clinicians, because ineffective methods are used. Excuses are self-handicapping if they pose an obstacle to detecting and acting on options for achieving goals clients value (if they get in the way of recognizing limitations that could be altered). So, when you offer an excuse, ask, "Does this work for me (and my clients) or against me (and my clients)?" and "Does this increase or decrease the likelihood of providing needed services and liking my work?" Professional codes of ethics provide a guide here.

When confronted with demonstrably poor services, we can refer to our ethical obligations to discover our professional responsibility. For example, codes of ethics obligate us to perform competently. If our agency culture prevents such practice (it is incompetent), aren't we obligated to do something about it? When are rationalizations unethical? Is it okay just to throw up our hands and say we cannot do anything? Failure to perform competently as a professional means two different things. First, there is failure to apply correctly the body of theoretical knowledge on which professional action rests. Failures of this sort are errors in techniques. For surgeons, we have identified two varieties of this type of error—technical and judgmental. Second, there is failure to follow the code of conduct on which professional action rests. Failures of this sort are moral in nature (Bosk, 1979, p. 168).

Excuses and Self-Deception

Richard Paul (1993) suggests that we consistently deceive ourselves about the state, degree, and nature of our knowledge, our freedom, and our character (Paul, 1993, p. xiii). Some authors argue that we have multiple selves developed in relation to multiple contexts (e.g., work, home, and recreational life) that we routinely inhabit, and that these multiple selves may not communicate with each other. For example, we may not compare the professional self and the moral self to determine if we act consistently (honor certain obligations in different contexts). Kurzban (2010) argues that we are all hypocrites. If the essence of self-deception is not knowing when we are deceiving ourselves, as Baron (2000) suggests, what is possible? For example, when confronted with the fact that they use different standards of evidence when making decisions about their own health than they do with clients, some professionals dismiss this discrepancy by saying that "medicine is different" from psychology or social work (Gambrill & Gibbs, 2002). Is it different? Is it so different that we do not have to concern ourselves with informed consent obligations—sharing with a client the risks and benefits of recommended methods as well as the risks and benefits of well-argued alternatives. The self-deceived can be classified into two categories: (1) those whose values match their self-deception and (2) those whose values do not reflect a match. The latter, unlike the former, can be enlightened (enlightened according to their own values), whereas the former, because there is a match between their self-deception and their values, cannot be changed by appealing to (revealing) the lack of correspondence between their beliefs and their actions.

There are those who want to help clients but do not know how. And there are those who really do not care about clients. Other methods will be required, such as evidence-informed organizational cultures, to alter the behavior of those who do not care. I suggest that self-deception in the two different instances just described serves different functions, is created by different histories, and requires different remedies. Self-deception can be viewed as a form of self-propaganda. (See discussion of propaganda in Chapter 4.) Possible remedies when our values do not match our actions include both those designed to decrease our vulnerability to sociological propaganda (including material from professional organizations) and those that allow us to break out of self-propaganda—self-deceptions that do not match our values (see Chapter 18). We can increase empathy for clients by attending to data illustrating harming in the name of helping.

SUMMARY

A variety of personal obstacles may hinder sound decision making. Making well-reasoned decisions may be hampered by a lack of self-knowledge. This includes knowledge of personal strengths and limitations. We overestimate our competence. Motivational and attitudinal obstacles may compromise the quality of reasoning. These include careless-ness, lack of interest in having a well-reasoned position, a wish to appear decisive, and a vested interest in a certain outcome. You may have dysfunctional reactions to mis-takes and lack of success and a low tolerance for uncertainty. Ideals about what can be accomplished may be replaced by a pessimistic view. Once-valued goals, such as taking small steps to rectify inequities in service delivery, may be abandoned. Some obstacles to critical thinking, such as procrastination and distractibility, are related to a lack of self-management skills. Effective stress-management and time-management skills are important in facilitating sound decisions. Effective communication skills are vital in exchanges involved in making decisions. Perhaps the most important obstacle is a reluc-tance to examine competencies and the accuracy of beliefs. Lack of awareness of the relationship between favored views and related political, economic, and social influ-ences is an obstacle to critically examining beliefs—we assume we have created them and we overlook external influences. The excuses we use for lack of success may be barriers to offering clients high-quality services. Guidelines describing how to alter the personal obstacles discussed in this chapter are available; indeed, many clinicians often use these with their clients.

CHAPTER

18

Maintaining Critical Thinking Skills

Both personal and environmental obstacles may chip away at critical thinking values and skills that contribute to evidence-based practice (EBP). These include characteristics of the practice environment, such as funding patterns and, limited resources. There may be conflicts between professional values and agency practices. (See Exhibit 18.1.) Agency administrators may pressure staff to continue use of ineffective or harmful methods rather than practices and policies that have been critically tested and found to help clients. We are bombarded with inflated claims from professional newsletters, colleagues, and the media. Prevailing opinion is another obstacle—influence by standards of practice, opinion leaders, professional education, and advocacy (for example, by pharmaceutical companies). Other barriers include feelings of incompetency regarding new practices, the need to act, and information overload. Suggestions for maintaining helpful values and skills that contribute to lifelong learning are offered in this chapter.

GENERALIZING AND MAINTAINING CRITICAL THINKING SKILLS

Having critical thinking knowledge and skills does not mean that they will be used. Cultivating related values and arranging for the generalization and maintenance of such knowledge and skills is also needed. Without transfer training and arrangement of supportive tools and contingencies, the use of new knowledge and skills may be confined to the situations in which training was offered. Including a variety of situations in training and acquiring useful self-questioning skills such as asking, "Could I be wrong?" or "How am I doing?" encourages transfer (Halpern, 2003; Haskell, 2001).

Exhibit 18.1 Barriers to More Client-Centered Care

Overarching barriers:
- Evidence about risks, benefits, and outcomes lacking for many complex conditions or where people have multiple problems.
- Diseases associated with aging in industrialized societies may require lifestyle interventions rather than medical care.
- Concern of policy makers that client-centered care will increase health care demands and costs.

Client-level barriers:
- Lack of confidence in ability to make judgments about information concerning potential benefits and risks.
- Emotions about illness lead to preference for external decision maker.
- Lack of understanding of options and potential impact on health and well-being.
- Health status precludes active role.
- Multiple decisions may be required.
- May be seeking complementary or alternative care and not want to share details with health professional.

Health professional–level barriers:
- Lack of time to explore client preferences.
- Lack of skills to explore client preferences.
- Unconvinced that client-centered care or shared decision making is appropriate or provides the best outcomes.
- Preference for role of benevolent patriarch/matriarch rather than client-centered facilitator.
- Unaware that client values can differ from those of the health professional.
- Lack of knowledge, skills, or capacity to provide social support and care rather than health care.

Organizational/system-level barriers:
- Lack of awareness that behaviors of multiple providers interact and may adversely affect clients.
- Lack of a single designated coordinator of care.
- System designed for acute care rather than ongoing management of chronic problems.
- Care required may be social support rather than health care, and health system is not well constructed to provide this care.
- Reimbursement systems may not be well aligned with the type of care required or chosen.

Interactional barriers:
- Relationship between client and health professional not well established.
- Poor communication between client and health professional.
- Client may be receiving care from multiple providers who are unaware of or do not communicate with each other.

Source: Adapted from "How Will Health Care Professionals and Patients Work Together in 2020?" by R. Hertwig, H. Buchan, D. A. Davis, W. Gaissmaier, M. Harter, K. Kolpatzik, F. Legare, N. Schmacke, and H. Wormer, 2011, in *Better Doctors, Better Patients, Better Decisions: Envisioning Health Care 2020* (p. 320), edited by G. Gigerenzer and J. A. M. Gray, Cambridge, MA: MIT Press.

Remember the Benefits of Critical Thinking

The quality of decisions is an ethical as well as a practical enterprise. Clinical decisions have life-affecting consequences; they offer or limit opportunities for clients and significant others to enhance the quality of their lives. The history of the helping professions clearly indicates the need for boundaries on the individual discretion of clinicians in the selection of objectives (making sure clients value them) and procedures (choosing those that, while least intrusive, are most effective and efficient and acceptable to clients), and in being accountable to clients by monitoring progress, so that timely, sound decisions can be made about what to do next. As we have more information about what practices and policies are effective and which ones are ineffective or harmful, lack of knowledge about this research becomes ever more problematic. Remembering the benefits of critical thinking—arriving at well-reasoned decisions that contribute to helping clients and avoiding harm—should encourage you to take advantage of critical thinking skills. Involving clients as informed participants is a key benefit. Large variations in helping efforts and harming in the name of helping contributed to the development of evidence-based practice. Use of critical thinking knowledge and skills will help you to avoid variations that are ineffective or harmful. Awareness of informal fallacies and persuasion strategies that advertisers, politicians, and professional organizations use to promote dubious claims can help you to avoid their influence.

Clients will benefit by receiving effective assessment and intervention methods. Clinicians will benefit by increased success in helping clients attain outcomes they value. Whether colleagues will be thankful will depend on your skills in diplomacy; their values (e.g., avoiding harm to clients) and beliefs about knowledge (how or if it can be gained); and on other personal and environmental factors discussed in previous chapters. They are more likely to value and support critical appraisal that contributes to high-quality services if goals are shared (e.g., to involve clients in decision making as informed participants). Use of sound decision-making methods can move clinical practice further along the continuum of effectiveness, from deterioration effects to neither harming nor helping to offering the best help possible.

Encourage Related Goals and Beliefs

For some people, it is more important to avoid doubt and to appear consistent than it is to discover the best answer to a question. Some people do not believe in the value of thinking. "If people do not believe that thinking is useful, they will not think. This is perhaps the major argument we hear against thinking about things like nuclear war, religion, and morals: 'These matters are beyond me. They are best left to experts who are capable of thinking about them—if anyone'" (Baron, 1985a, p. 259). Beliefs that discourage critical thinking include the following: that changing one's mind is a sign of weakness, considering alternatives leads to confusion and despair, quick decision making is a sign of strength or wisdom, truth is determined by authority, and we cannot influence what happens to us by trying to understand events. A quote from Nickerson (1987) is apt here. "I believe that often, when people in positions of authority (parents, teachers, managers, military leaders) say that they wish that the people over whom they have authority (children, students, employees, subordinates) could think, they mean that they wish their charges or subordinates were more skilled at accomplishing goals set, or at least endorsed, by their superiors. Seldom do they have in mind a concept of thinking that is sufficiently broad to include the questioning of the goals themselves and the authorities that have set them" (p. 34).

Only when we clarify our beliefs can we critically examine them. Research on human judgment shows that we are often unaware of how we are influenced. Propagandists take full advantage of this fact—even creating beliefs that we have arrived at a certain view ourselves, when indeed our views are created by others (Ellul, 1965). We may change our opinions without knowing we have done so. For example, listeners' opinions on busing of school children could be altered from pro to con or from con to pro by an eloquent speaker, without listeners realizing that their opinions had shifted (Goethals & Reckman, 1973). Clearly describing the reasoning process involved in making a decision increases the likelihood of avoiding errors and identifying values that influence decisions.

Arrange a Supportive Environment

Even the strongest repertoire can be eroded in an unsupportive environment. Unless there are prompts and incentives to use critical thinking skills, they erode. Gray (2001a) has written an excellent guide for arranging supportive practice environments. He describes what is required at the administrative and management levels to create an evidence-based agency. Not all will warm to his recommendations. For example, he suggests that such an agency must "have an obsession for evaluation." Such an "obsession" is viewed as essential to integrate practice and research. Arranging and maintaining a supportive environment will be easier with expertise in contingency analysis— knowledge and skill in rearranging the relationships between behaviors of interest and environmental events (e.g., Cooper et al., 2008). Helpful questions include: What consequences support desired behaviors? What events punish these? How can I increase reinforcement of critical thinking skills? What prompts could I arrange? Are necessary tools available? Are undesired behaviors reinforced? Arrange prompts and incentives for use of knowledge and skills that encourage sound decisions, such as posing well-formed questions related to information needs.

Woo kindred spirits to work together to create conditions that foster critical thinking. Evaluate your progress in drawing on clinically relevant research by reviewing the list of items in Exhibit 11.9. Are personal obstacles getting in the way (see Chapter 17)? If so, what kind, and how can you minimize them? Monthly meetings can be held to review decisions with others who model critical appraisal of claims and assumptions. You could start a journal club in which members take turns searching for research findings related to life-affecting questions and sharing what they find (for example, by preparing CATs—

see Chapter 11). You can keep critical appraisal skills well honed by referring to user-friendly checklists to review the quality of different kinds of research (see Chapter 12).

Be Politically and Organizationally Savvy

Some clinicians forgo having a voice in what happens in an organization or in their community because they believe that politics is beneath (or above) them. This decision will be a welcome one to those who wield power. Skill in recognizing various kinds of political tactics is useful in anticipating and exerting countercontrol. Politics—the effort to gain or maintain power—is an integral part of everyday life; political action is often necessary to achieve desired goals. Political skills are important, especially those in working with others toward mutually valued aims, such as enhancing the quality of services. We have a choice about how to react in settings in which low-level appeals are tolerated or even encouraged—appeals that diminish opportunities to help others. Conditions that compromise the quality of decisions may be ignored; disliked situations may be tolerated with little or no effort made to improve matters. Or we can work together with others to create an environment that facilitates sound decisions. True, such action requires time and effort in the short run; however, in the long run, it should save time and enhance quality of service. And such a road is more satisfying than just complaining. Let's say there is a policy against observing clients and significant others in real-life settings, such as classrooms and playgrounds, but research suggests that such naturalistic observation provides valuable guidelines for selecting plans (e.g., Reid, Patterson, & Snyder, 2002). Not gathering such data when possible and needed may increase the likelihood of the fundamental attribution error (attributing behaviors to personality dispositions of clients and overlooking environmental causes). You and your colleagues could lobby to change the policy based on evidentiary grounds. You can give copies to your colleagues of the results of studies showing that observation of interaction between clients and significant others can provide important data (see Chapter 13).

A request for change is more likely to receive a favorable reaction if it involves a small change and is compatible with current beliefs and goals; you will be more successful if you focus on shared interests such as helping clients (Fisher & Ury, 1991). Anticipate objections, prepare counterarguments, and seek the support of colleagues. If many people work together to achieve a change, it is more likely to occur than if one person pursues it alone. The Internet provides a way to link people in pursuit of change. Understanding organizations—how they work, how they change, and why change is often difficult—will suggest both opportunities and obstacles to introducing innovations. Examine both the formal system (e.g., written agency policies) and the informal system (e.g., preferred communication styles) to explore options for change. The informal system includes practices that are not codified in writing, such as, "Keep records general to protect confidentiality." The implementation of a formal rule may not reflect its intention. For example, written service agreements may be prepared but may not contain ingredients that facilitate case planning and clarification of expectations, such as clear descriptions of hoped-for outcomes.

You also have a choice about how involved to be in professional organizations—for example, to work together with others to increase statistical literacy among both clients and professionals so clients can be involved as informed (rather than uninformed or mis-informed) participants (Smith, 2011) and to clarify ethical codes. Professionals are man-dated to honor codes of ethics. Typically these codes are vague, requiring (and allowing) varied and discretionary interpretations. Consider this statement in the NASW Code of Ethics (National Association of Social Workers, 2008): "The social worker should accept responsibility or employment only on the basis of existing competence or the intention to acquire the necessary competence." What criteria are to be used to evaluate competence? Does "competence" imply being up-to-date with practice-related empirical literature and sharing this information with clients? Or does it mean using services con-sistent with standards in a community (which may be poor)? You could join an organiza-tion that encourages integration of research and practice.

Pay Attention to Process as Well as to Outcome

Instructional methods that require review and revision of plans are more effective than are others in encouraging generalization. In this kind of learning the emphasis is on the process rather than on the product of problem solving. The format for problem-based learning described in Chapter 8 emphasizes process. Research concerning personal con-trol suggests the advantages of focusing on process (How can I do it?) rather than out-come (Can I do it?) (Langer, 1983, 2009). Focusing solely on outcome may increase anxiety and divert attention from exploring how problems can be solved. And, if skills required to enhance the quality of decisions are absent, increased calls for accountability will not improve practice and, indeed, may have a negative effect (Lerner & Tetlock, 1999). A process orientation encourages active involvement in grappling with the chal-lenges of practice; it highlights the relationship between process and outcome, and in so doing, should be more fruitful in generating valuable ideas. A sole focus on outcome may encourage a sense of incompetence—a belief that there is no relationship between what we can do (our behavior) and what may be achieved (hoped-for outcomes); it may encourage a mindless approach to problems that results in lost opportunities to help clients. "Since the attention of outcome-oriented individuals is directed toward the goal of the task and their own ability to accomplish it, they may be relatively 'mindless' concerning actual methods of performing the task, at least in comparison to process-oriented individuals" (Langer, 1983, p. 131).

Create a Plan of Action for Continued Learning

Continued learning over your career is one of the joys of being a professional. You can design personal experiments to enhance decision-making skills (Neuringer, 1981). These are more likely to succeed if you take advantage of self-management skills such as identifying clear goals and progress indicators and planning a step-by-step agenda. (See Watson & Tharp, 2007.) You can consult sources that publish evidence-informed articles in your area and review material on relevant blogs. Many excellent blogs are available regarding medications, such as http://carlatpsychiatry.blogspot.com, http://brodyhooked.blogspot, www.pharmedout.org, and www.criticalthink.org. Valuable websites for keeping up with evidentiary concerns include DUETs and the EQUATOR Network. (See also Chapters 11 and 12.)

Increase Opportunities for Corrective Feedback

Most clinical exchanges take place in private. Disadvantages that result from this privacy range from lost opportunities to gain corrective feedback from colleagues to the practice of outright quackery and sexual abuse of clients. Monitoring progress with each client will improve the quality of decisions; next steps can be based on detailed data about degree of progress. (See discussion of N of 1 studies in Chapter 12.) Only via careful description of degree of change may harmful effects of interventions be discovered (e.g., Vyse, 2005). Methods that can be used to keep track of progress are described in a number of sources (e.g., Bloom et al., 2009). Colleagues who are skilled in use of a particular method can help others to improve their skills based on observation of interviews or review of audiotaped or videotaped exchanges with clients.

Take Advantage of Helpful Tools and Select Effective Training Programs

Attention to application obstacles is a hallmark of evidence-informed practice. This includes the creation of tools to facilitate the integration of practice and research, such as electronic databases, and use of apps on smart phones to gather and share information and to make decisions. Flowcharts can be used to review the source of samples in research reports (e.g., CONSORT guidelines) and to make fast and frugal decisions (Gigerenzer, 2007). Brief checklists have been used to decrease errors and enhance quality of care (Ely, Graber, & Croskerry, 2011; Gawande, 2010). Seek continuing education programs that use formats that enhance learning and generalization of skills. Traditional methods of dissemination, such as continuing education programs, do little to change professional behavior (Forsetlund et al., 2009). Problem-based learning is designed to help practitioners to integrate diverse sources of information

(Straus, Richardson, Glasziou, & Haynes, 2005). (For critiques of traditional continuing education programs, see Wright, 2005.)

Perkins (1987) suggests putting up a poster (now an app on a smartphone) that lists important components of a *thinking frame* (a guide to organizing and supporting thinking). Effective *metacognitive skills* (deciding which strategies to use in making decisions and how much time to devote to a decision) will save time and effort. Aids such as actuarial methods can be used to increase well-informed decisions. Take advantage of computer testing and graphing of data concerning progress when appropriate (see Richard & Lauterbach, 2004). Even brief programs may be helpful in counteracting error-producing strategies (Gigerenzer, 2002a; Larrick, 2005). Fong, Kravitz, and Nisbett (1986) found that brief instruction concerning the law of large numbers helped subjects to improve their statistical reasoning. (See also Agrawal, Saluja, & Kaczorowski, 2004.)

Practice Critical Thinking Skills

Both personal and work environments offer opportunities to practice critical thinking skills, including propaganda spotting: reading the newspaper and professional journals, using the Internet, watching TV, attending case conferences (e.g., Frankfurt, 2005). Watch how others handle situations in which fallacies occur to discover options. Having names for the different fallacies will make it easier to identify them. Practice will make the use of critical thinking skills more fluid.

Enhance Your Skills in Propaganda Spotting (Self and Other)

We are surrounded by propaganda—material that encourages belief and action with the least thought possible (Ellul, 1965). It is impossible to avoid, but we do have a choice whether to try to minimize its effects or just "go with the flow" (e.g., see Angell, 2009; Gøtzsche, & Jørgensen, 2011). We can enhance our skills in avoiding influence by dubious claims and emotional appeals, motivated by a desire to offer clients the best services possible rather than being a patsy for bogus claims promoted by self-interested sources such as the biomedical-industrial complex. Also, propaganda spotting can be fun. We may not be aware of influences on our beliefs and actions. Many writers, both past and present, such as Foucault (1981), emphasize the extent to which influence is not necessarily consciously used and we are not necessarily aware of influence attempts. Interrelated kinds of propaganda include deep propaganda that obscures political, economic, and social contingencies that influence troubled and troubling behaviors, and the questionable accuracy of common assumptions—for example, that hundreds of behaviors are biologically based mental illnesses requiring the help of experts (see Chapters 1 and 2). Related literature highlights the prevalence of propaganda and our vulnerability to it (Angell, 2011; Gambrill, 2012a; Pratkanis, 2007; Pratkanis & Aronson, 2001), as well as the need to enhance transparency and accuracy of reporting (e.g., Wormer, 2011). Structural factors related to personal and social problems often are not mentioned in newspaper reports or professional sources (see Chapter 2). Ownership of the major media by a few companies is not encouraging in terms of describing alternative well-argued views that conflict with vested interests (Bagdikian, 2004).

We can keep a copy of Carl Sagan's Baloney Detection Kit (see Sagan, 1995) on our desk or a cue card listing Hugh Rank's (1984) common propaganda cues: "Hi," "Trust me," "You need," "Hurry," "Buy" (see also Rank, 1982). We can become familiar with informal fallacies, such as glittering generalizations, name-calling, plain-folks appeal, and card stacking, and their use to encourage beliefs and actions with the least thought possible (Gambrill & Gibbs, 2009); we can read Thouless's *Straight and Crooked Thinking: Thirty-Eight Dishonest Tricks of Debate* (1974). We can choose a "fallacy of the week" from Fallacy Files (www.fallacyfiles.org) to practice detecting and avoiding its influence. We can join others who share our interest to spot bogus claims—for example, the most outrageous pitch of the month. All professional schools should offer courses on human services propaganda to help professionals avoid unwanted influence (Wilkes & Hoffman, 2001). The study of ploys and pitches used in pharmaceutical ads and by pharmaceutical reps in their interaction with professionals is receiving greater attention. PharmedOut (www.pharmedout.org) contains user-friendly educational material to help us avoid such pitches. Pitches include appeal to experts (e.g., "Dr. X at Best Evidence Medical Center has been using our new drug for four months") and giving gifts. Drug reps are carefully trained in relationship building. Professional education programs should offer courses on the history of harming in the name of helping in the professions and help professionals handle uncertainty and highlight the value of attending to ignorance as well as knowledge. Witte, Witte, and Kerwin (1994) describe a course offered entitled Medical Ignorance. (See discussion of knowledge as ignorance in Chapter 4.)

We can decrease self-propaganda by making the effects of our decisions and criteria on which we base them more visible. We can:

- Thank others for pointing out mistakes in our thinking.
- Become informed about common informal fallacies and cognitive biases, such as wishful thinking and hindsight bias, and learn how to avoid them.
- Examine the correspondence between our values and our actions by taking the "Is what's good for the goose good for the gander?" test (see Chapter 1).
- Take time for empathic reflection (what if I were in her shoes?) and correct empathic dysfunctions (under- or overinvolvement) that contribute to a detachment that harms clients (Halpern, 2001).

- Read client narratives and view photographs of harmful consequences that result from poor decisions.
- Explore personal excuses that result in and hide harms to others. (See Chapter 17.)

A MENU FOR CONTINUED LEARNING

Many tips have been described in previous chapters. Fourteen key examples are high-lighted here:

1. *Place clients' interests front and center.* A focus on helping clients and avoiding harm should serve as a key centering point that will help you to avoid directions that do not match related values.

2. *Look for disconfirming evidence.* Make it a habit to search for disconfirming evidence, such as counterexamples and counterarguments (Mussweiler, Strack, & Pfeiffer, 2000). Bromley (1977) recommends inclusion of an "Alternative Hypotheses" heading in clinical records. This may help to counter the influence of initial assumptions, which may be incorrect. Take advantage of sources devoted to exposure of bogus claims that may harm clients, such as the Alliance for Human Research Protection, International Society for Ethical Psychology and Psychiatry, Healthy Skepticism (see Mansfield, 2003), and AdWatch (www.consumerreports.org).

3. *Increase intellectual and emotional empathy.* Understanding other views has several advantages. One is identifying flaws in your thinking. Misunderstandings are less likely and cogent counterarguments are more likely when we understand other perspectives. A focus on common goals (for example, to help clients) will encourage attention to other positions. Empathy for others decreases the likelihood of "sins of service" such as apathy, brush-off, coldness, condescension, robotism, rule book, and runaround (Gorman, 1999). Here, too, take advantage of websites that highlight costs of bogus claims and corruption (such as Transparency International at www.transparency.org).

4. *Enhance your communication skills.* The harmful effects of miscommunication have been highlighted throughout this book. Developing effective communication skills will enhance the likelihood of making sound, participatory decisions. Such skills include giving feedback in a positive manner (e.g., Cantillon & Sargeant, 2008).

5. *Pay attention to context.* The tendency to attribute client concerns to dispositional causes has been often noted in this book. This tendency deflects attention from environmental factors related to social and personal problems.

One way to combat this bias is to enhance empathic reactions—to put yourself in other people's shoes. Another is to become informed about environmental causes of personal and social problems, including poor nutrition and health care (e.g., see Gentry, Poirier, Wilkinson, Nhean, Nyborn, & Siegel, 2011; Zarocostas, 2007) and obstacles to shared decision making (Gravel, Légaré, & Graham, 2006).

6. *Pay attention to words.* Different meanings for words and failure to clarify these or to recognize their emotional influences can result in errors and muddled discussions. Nickerson (1986b) argues, "It is never inappropriate to ask what someone means by a specified word in a particular context" (p. 130). On the other hand, Popper warns us about being more precise than we need to be and about trying to arrive at "the truth" by arguing about the definition of words. Research on the helping process reveals how clinicians use words to influence patients' decisions:

> Doctors realized that the words they chose to present the evidence could have a strong influence on the patient's decision. They effectively limited the options while seeming to invite the patient to make the decision. The contributors framed these themes with phrases such as "It's how you put it over," and "It depends on how you feed information to people." The semantics then affect the way in which evidence is implemented by swaying the patient in a particular direction. (Freeman & Sweeney, 2001)

7. *Watch out for vivid data.* We tend to overlook the importance of nonoccurrences. It is easy to ignore good behavior and focus on more vivid disliked behaviors. Make it a habit to ask about events that do not occur.

8. *Beware of personally relevant data.* One of the themes throughout this book is the influence of emotions and self-interest on judgments. "Perhaps there are no greater impediments to effective reasoning than those that derive from a confusion between reasoning and rationalizing, or, to make the same distinction in other terms, between weighing evidence on the one hand and defending a position or making a case on the other. This is the problem of our frequent failure, perhaps our inability, to assess evidence objectively and without bias when we have a vested interest in the outcome of a debate" (Nickerson, 1986a, p. 362). Use emotional and personally relevant material as a reminder to be especially vigilant. Being informed about research findings regarding the influence of mood and emotion on judgments may increase the likelihood that this source of error will be minimized.

9. *Complement critical thinking skills with knowledge.* Familiarity with relevant knowledge in a domain is often vital in making accurate decisions. "The first rule of effective reasoning is to get your facts straight" (Nickerson, 1986b, p. 132). Critical thinking skills, as well as good intentions and supportive skills, may be enough when little is known about how to help a client (that is, when either nothing is known or research indicates that it does not matter what is done as long as you develop a supportive alliance). Offering support is not enough when more can be done. For example, I recently saw a client who had been seeing a therapist for depression for over a year. She reported that her therapist was using supportive counseling. There was no focus on acquiring skills that could be used in daily life to decrease depression. A careful assessment revealed many specific changes that could be made to decrease her depression; far more help than supportive counseling was needed and was available. Effective learning skills and the process of evidence-informed practice make it possible to gain maximum payoff for time spent locating and appraising relevant research findings (see Chapters 9 and 10).

10. *Overcome statistical innumeracy.* Examples of statistical innumeracy that harms clients have been given throughout this book. Valuable tools such as using natural frequencies are available to overcome this avoidable source of error. What is the false positive rate of a test? What is the false negative rate? What are the overall costs and benefits of taking a test?

11. *Ask questions with a high payoff value.* Questions differ in the likelihood that helpful information will be revealed by the answers. Asking questions that have maximum utility will save time. One helpful question is: "What's missing?" What is not discussed may be most important in making decisions (e.g., "What is the absolute risk?") (see Paling, 2006).

12. *Move beyond the illusion of understanding.* Some assumptions contribute real understanding; others provide merely a feeling of understanding and are not helpful when applied to real-life problems. The need to act may encourage excessive belief in the appropriateness of actions taken. Accepting beliefs based on a feeling of understanding is encouraged by the expectation that we should have explanations for almost anything, without significant effort to arrive at these accounts. Pressures on clinicians, often self-imposed, to appear more expert than is warranted encourage this tendency. Accepting views only because they make sense may result in a fragmented, eclectic approach to practice—an unintegrated, unevidence-informed mix of assumptions that is used to make decisions rather than a cohesive, empirically informed practice theory.

13. *Be your own best critic.* We learn how to do better only by being willing to candidly examine our limitations as well as our strengths. Only in this way can we correct flaws in our self-assessment that may get in the way of offering high-quality services to clients and use mistakes as learning opportunities (Flannelly & Flannelly, 2000).

14. *Catch and counter reemerging falsehoods that diminish the quality of services.* One of the most common and hardy is the belief that reason and caring are incompatible. The rational individual is painted as cold, unfeeling, and missing the boat in relation to understanding the qualitative, subjective, rich-textured side of life. It is argued that one cannot be a critical thinker and a caring person at the same time. Reason and passion are pitted against one another as if they were adversaries. Caring without careful reasoning is not caring at all, especially in the helping professions, as illustrated by the history of harming in the name of helping in these professions. "A passionate drive for clarity, accuracy, and fair-mindedness, a fervor for getting to the bottom of things, to the deepest root issues, for listening sympathetically to opposition points of view, a compelling drive to seek out evidence, an intense aversion to contradiction, sloppy thinking, inconsistent application of standards, a devotion to truth as against self-interest—these are essential commitments of the rational person" (Paul, 1993, p. 348).

Another hardy falsehood is that because our interpretations of the meanings of events intrude between what is in the world and what we see, science (testing as well as guessing) is no better than, and not as valuable as, use of uninformed intuition. Critical tests are painted as sterile, narrow, and unfaithful to reality, and subjective methods are presented as rich, meaningful, and representative of reality. In fact, the elaborate methodologies used in scientific investigation are because of concern with the very issue subjectivists claim is ignored in scientific inquiry—a concern to tease out misleading, biasing effects that may result in faulty conclusions (see Chapter 4). Methods of inquiry (quantitative and or qualitative) differ in the kinds of questions that can be answered and in the kinds of answers offered (see Chapter 12). Science deals with questions that are possible to critically test. This is not to say that other kinds of questions and related methods do not have value or that intuition is not vital for coming up with ideas and how to test them. (See also discussion of informed intuition in Chapter 9.)

Another falsehood is the belief that you have to be an expert in an area to critically evaluate related claims. On the contrary, critical thinking values, knowledge, and skills can be applied to any area if authors and speakers clearly describe claims and related assumptions and data. Some clinicians believe that the therapeutic process is essentially unknowable, implying that it is useless to try to identify specific elements that contribute to success. Literature related to the therapeutic process belies this assumption (Norcross, 2011). In moments of discouragement, it may be tempting to slip into this belief and to abandon efforts to discover what is knowable in this complex area. A belief that there are no answers discourages a search for answers; "any advance, personal or scientific, depends on the assumption that what is not yet known is knowable" (Langer, 1983, p. 119). Yet another belief is that if errors are inevitable there is no use trying to avoid them. Errors are part and parcel of learning how to refine our skills and are more likely to be avoided if we accept their inevitability. Many *are* avoidable.

REVIEW PREFERRED PRACTICE THEORIES

Some clinicians do not distinguish between theories of different empirical status—embracing those with none as readily as those with considerable evidentiary status (Meehl, 1973). A helpful theory consists of a set of concepts and proposed interrelationships that are of value in understanding a broad array of phenomena.

TAKE TIME-OUTS TO REFLECT ON YOUR WORK

In this day and age of excessive workloads, it is ever more important to take occasional time-outs to think about your work in relation to the big picture. This picture will often reveal troubling gaps between what clients need and what they get and the manner in which they receive it. Many clinicians work in agencies in which problems clients confront, such as lack of stable housing, health care, and employment opportunities, are related to social, political, and economic factors. However, services offered may focus on individuals, ignoring environmental causes of concerns. These helpers may believe, with good reason, that they provide only a Band-Aid in terms of what is needed. Candid recognition of gaps is vital so you do not become (or remain) a fellow traveler in the Band-Aid mode without taking steps, together with others, to try to decrease gaps in needed services. Indeed, in describing the philosophy of evidence-based practice, Guyatt and Rennie (2002) suggest that when physicians observe that their patients' well-being is influenced by the quality of their environment, they have an obligation to advocate for positive changes.

Occasional time-outs for reflection on your work will allow you to think about the excuses you adopt for inadequate services. Do excuses result in lost opportunities for constructive change that can be made within the constraints of a given setting, including working together with colleagues and clients to create needed changes in your work setting, as well as steps that can be taken outside work, such as forming coalitions and lobbying legislators?

DEVELOP COURAGE

As emphasized throughout this book, when the resources we have do not match what is needed to help clients, there are three options: (1) ignore the gap, (2) just complain, or (3) take active steps to close the gap. Caring as well as courage are required to take the high road. These are a powerful duo. Caring about clients yields courage to act on their behalf.

SUMMARY

Maintaining critical thinking values, knowledge, and skills that contribute to evidence-informed practice should not be left to chance. Transfer of new skills to other areas can be facilitated by developing useful self-management skills, by focusing on the process rather than on the product of thinking (using the steps in evidence-based practice), and by practicing skills in different situations. Reviewing the benefits of critical thinking and awareness of the prevalence of propaganda in the helping professions, such as bogus claims of benefit and hiding of adverse side effects both in the media and in professional sources, should be a reminder of the importance of using critical thinking skills in day-to-day practice. Increasing the quality of feedback about the degree of progress offers fine-grained data on results of clinical decisions. Arranging a supportive environment and cultivating realistic expectations will be helpful in maintaining skills. Increasing your statistical literacy will decrease the likelihood that you will be taken in (and in turn take in your clients) by bogus claims of effectiveness. Focusing on helping clients and avoiding harm will provide a deep well of courage to ask hard questions.

References

Abbott, A. (1988). *The system of professions: An essay on the division of expert labor.* Chicago, IL: University of Chicago Press.

Abel, G., & Glinert, L. H. (2008). Chemotherapy as language: Sound symbolism in cancer medication names. *Social Science and Medicine, 66*(8), 1863–1969.

Abercrombie, M. L. J. (1960). *The anatomy of judgement.* New York, NY: Basic Books.

Abramowitz, S. I., & Murray, J. (1983). Race effects in psychotherapy. In J. Murray & P. R. Abramson (Eds.), *Bias in psychotherapy.* New York, NY: Praeger.

Adams, J. L. (1974). *Conceptual blockbusting: A guide to better ideas.* New York, NY: W.H. Freeman.

Adams, J. L. (1986). *Conceptual blockbusting: A guide to better ideas* (3rd ed.). Reading, MA: Addison-Wesley.

Addis, M. E., & Krasnow, A. D. (2000). A national survey of practicing psychologists' attitudes towards psychotherapy treatment manuals. *Journal of Consulting and Clinical Psychology, 68,* 331–339.

Agrawal, S., Saluja, I., & Kaczorowski, J. (2004). A prospective before-and-after trial of an educational intervention about pharmaceutical marketing. *Academic Medicine, 79,* 1046–1050.

Alberto, P. A., & Troutman, A. C. (1990). *Applied behavior analysis for teachers* (5th ed.). Columbus, OH: Merrill.

Alberto, P. A., & Troutman, A. C. (2013). *Applied behavior analysis for teachers* (9th ed.). Upper Saddle River, NJ: Merrill/Pearson.

Altman, D. G. (2002). Poor-quality medical research: What can journals do? *Journal of the American Medical Association, 287,* 2765–2767.

Altman, D. G., Machin, D., Bryant, T. N., & Gardner, M. J. (Eds.). (2000). *Statistics with confidence: Confidence intervals and statistical guidelines.* London, UK: BMJ Books.

American Psychiatric Association. (2000). *Diagnostic and statistical manual of mental disorders* (4th ed., text rev.). Washington, DC: Author.

American Psychological Association Task Force. (1995). Training in and dissemination of empirically validated psychological treatment: Report and recommendations of the task force on Promotion and Dissemination of Psychological Procedures of Division 12 (Clinical Psychology). *Clinical Psychologist, 48,* 3–23.

Anastasi, A., & Urbina, S. (1996). *Psychological testing* (7th ed.). Upper Saddle River, NJ: Prentice Hall.

Angell, M. (2004). *The truth about drug companies: How they deceived us and what to do about it.* New York, NY: Random House.

Angell, M. (2009, August 10). Drug companies & doctors: A story of corruption. *New York Review of Books,* 1/15.

Angell, M. (2011). The illusions of psychiatry. *New York Review of Books,* 7/14.

Antman, E. M., Lau, J., Kupelnick, B., Mosteller, F., & Chalmers, T. C. (1992). A comparison of results of meta-analyses of randomized controlled trials and recommendations of clinical experts: Treatments for myocardial infarction. *Journal of the American Medical Association, 268,* 240–248.

Antonuccio, D. O., Burns, D. D., & Danton, W. G. (2002). Antidepressants: A triumph of marketing over science. *Prevention & Treatment, 5,* 1–17.

Applbaum, K. (2009a). Getting to yes: Corporate power and the creation of psychopharmaceutical blockbuster. *Culture and Medical Psychiatry, 33,* 185–215.

Applbaum, K. (2009b). "Consumers as patients!" Shared decision-making and treatment non-compliance as business opportunity. *Transcultural Psychiatry, 48,* 107–130.

Argyris, C., & Schon, D. A. (1974). *Theory in practice: Increasing professional effectiveness.* San Francisco, CA: Jossey-Bass.

Arkes, H. (1981). Impediments to accurate clinical judgment and possible ways to minimize their impact. *Journal of Consulting and Clinical Psychology, 49,* 323–330.

Arkes, H. R. (2001). Overconfidence in judgmental forecasting. In J. S. Armstrong (Ed.), *Principles of forecasting handbook* (pp. 495–515). Boston, MA: Kluwer.

Arkin, R. M., & Oleson, K. C. (1998). Self-handicapping. In J. M. Darley & J. Cooper (Eds.), *Attribution and social interaction: The legacy of Edward E. Jones* (pp. 313–347). Washington, DC: American Psychological Association.

Armstrong, J. C. (1980). Unintelligible management research and academic prestige. *Interfaces, 10,* 80–86.

Aronson, J. K. (2003). Anecdotes as evidence: We need guidelines for reporting anecdotes of suspected adverse drug reactions. *BMJ, 326,* 1346.

Asch, S. E. (1956). Studies of independence and conformity: Minority of one against a unanimous majority. *Psychological Monographs, 70*(9, Whole No. 416).

Ashton, P. T., & Webb, R. B. (1986). *Making a difference: Teachers' sense of efficacy and student achievement.* New York, NY: Longman.

Asimov, I. (1989). The relativity of wrong. *The Skeptical Inquirer, 14,* 35–44.

Averill, J. (1982). *Anger and aggression: Implications for theories of emotion.* New York, NY: Springer-Verlag.

Bacon, F. (1620/1985). Appendix 4: Idols of the mind. In J. Pitcher (Ed.), *Francis Bacon: The essays*. New York, NY: Penguin Books.

Baddeley, A. D. (2001). Is working memory still working? *American Psychologist, 56*, 851–864.

Baddeley, A. D. (2005). *Human memory: Theory and practice* (Rev. ed.). Hove, UK: Psychology Press.

Baddeley, A. D., Conway, M.A., & Aggleton, J. P. (2002). *Episodic memory: New directions in research*. New York, NY: Oxford University Press.

Badinter, E. (1980). *Mother love, myth and reality*. New York, NY: Macmillan.

Baer, D. M. (1984). Future directions: Or, is it useful to ask, "Where did we go wrong?" before we go? In R. F. Dangel & R. A. Polster (Eds.), *Parent training: Foundations of research and practice* (pp. 547–557). New York, NY: Guilford.

Baer, D. M. (1987). Weak contingencies, strong contingencies, and many behaviors to change. *Journal of Applied Behavior Analysis, 20*, 335–337.

Baer, D. M. (2003). Program evaluation: Arduous, impossible, or political? In H. E. Briggs & T. L. Rzepnicki (Eds.), *Using evidence in social work practice: Behavioral perspectives* (pp. 310–322). Chicago, IL: Lyceum.

Bagdikian, B. H. (2004). *The new media*. Boston, MA: Beacon Press.

Baker, T. B., McFall, R. M., & Shoham, V. (2008). Current status and future prospects of clinical psychology: Toward a scientifically principled approach to mental and behavioral health care. *Psychological Science in the Public Interest, 9*, 67–103.

Balko, R. (2006). *Overkill: The rise of paramilitary police raids in America*. Washington, DC: The Cato Institute.

Balla, J. I., Heneghan, C., Glasziou, P., Thompson, M., & Balla, M. E. (2009). A model for reflection for good clinical practice. *Journal of Evaluation in Clinical Practice, 15*, 964–969.

Bandolier. (2003, January). Magnetic insoles for foot pain: Randomized trial results. Comment on M. H. Winemiller et al. (2003). Effect of magnetic vs. sham-magnetic insoles on plantar heel pain: A randomized controlled trial. *Journal of the American Medical Association, 290*, 1474–1478.

Bandura, A. (1978). On paradigms and recycled ideologies. *Cognitive Therapy and Research, 2*, 79–103.

Bandura, A. (1986). *Social foundations of thought and action*. Englewood Cliffs, NJ: Prentice Hall.

Bandura, A. (1997). *Self-efficacy: The exercise of control*. New York, NY: W.H. Freeman.

Bandura, A. (1999). Moral disengagement in the perpetration of inhumanities. *Personality and Social Psychology Review, 3*, 193–209.

Barber, J., Shlonsky, A., Black, T., Goodman, D., & Trocmé, N. (2008). Reliability and predictive validity of a risk assessment tool. *Journal of Public Child Welfare2, 173–195*.

Barbour, V., Clark, J., Jones, S., Norton, M., Simpson, P., E Veitch, E. (2011). Why drug safety should not take a back seat to efficacy. *PLoS Medicine, 8,* e1001097.

Bar-Hillel, M. (1983). The base-rate fallacy controversy. In R. W. Scholz (Ed.), *Decision making under uncertainty* (pp. 39–62). New York, NY: Elsevier.

Barkley, R. A., Cook, E. H., Diamond, A., Zametkin, A., Thapar, A., Teeter, A., et al. (2002). International Consensus Statement on ADHD. *Clinical Child and Family Psychology Review, 5,* 89–111.

Barling, J., Kelloway, E. K., & Frone, M. R. (2004). *Handbook of work stress.* Thousand Oaks, CA: Sage.

Barnes, J. (1984). *The complete works of Aristotle: The revised Oxford translation.* Princeton, NJ: Princeton University Press.

Barnett, R., & Rivers, C. (2004). *Same differences: How gender myths are hurting our relationships, our children, and our jobs.* New York, NY: Basic Books.

Baron, J. (1981). Reflective thinking as a goal of education. *Intelligence, 5,* 291–309.

Baron, J. (1985a). *Rationality and intelligence.* Cambridge, UK: Cambridge University Press.

Baron, J. (1985b). What kind of intelligence components are fundamental? In S. F. Chipman, J. W. Segal, & R. Glaser (Eds.), *Thinking and learning skills: Vol. 2. Research and open questions.* Hillsdale, NJ: Erlbaum.

Baron, J. (1994). *Thinking and deciding.* New York, NY: Cambridge University Press.

Baron, J. (2000). *Thinking and deciding* (3rd ed.). New York, NY: Cambridge University Press.

Baron, J. (2005). Normative models of judgment and decision making. In D. J. Koehler & N. Harvey (Eds.), *Blackwell handbook of judgment and decision making* (pp. 19–36). Malden, MA: Blackwell.

Barrett, S., Jarvis, W. T., Kroger, M., & London, W. H. (2002). *Consumer health: A guide to intelligent decisions* (7th ed.). New York, NY: McGraw-Hill.

Barrows, H. S. (1994). *Practice-based learning: Problem-based learning applied to medical education.* Springfield, IL: Southern Illinois University School of Medicine.

Bartholet, E. (2009). The racial disproportionality movement in child welfare: False facts and dangerous directions. *Arizona Law Review, 51,* 871–932.

Basaglia, Franco. (1987). *Psychiatry inside out: Selected writings of Franco Basaglia.* N. Scheper-Hughes & A. M. Lovell (Eds.). New York, NY: Columbia University Press.

Batson, C. D. (1975). Attribution as a mediator of bias in helping. *Journal of Personality and Social Psychology, 72,* 455–466.

Batson, C. D., Jones, C. H., & Cochran, P. J. (1979). Attributional bias in counselors' diagnosis: The effects of resources on perception of need. *Journal of Applied Social Psychology, 9,* 377–393.

Batson, C. D., O'Quin, K., & Pych, V. (1982). An attribution theory analysis of trained helpers' inferences about clients' needs. In T. A. Wills (Ed.), *Basic processes in helping relationships* (pp. 59–80). New York, NY: Academic Press.

Batson, C. D., Polycarpoum, P., Harmon-Jones, E., Imhoff, H. J., Mitchener, E. C., Bednar, L. L., et al. (1997). Empathy and attitudes: Can feeling for a member of a stigmatized group improve feelings toward the group? *Journal of Personality and Social Psychology, 72*, 105–118.

Bauer, H. H. (2004). Science in the 21st century: Knowledge monopolies and research cartels. *Journal of Scientific Exploration, 18*, 643–660.

Baumeister, R. F., Campbell, J. D., Krueger, J. I., & Vohs, K. D. (2003). Does high self-esteem cause better performance, interpersonal success, happiness, or healthier life-styles? *Psychological Science in the Public Interest, 4*, 1–44.

Bayer, R. (1987). Politics, science and problems of psychiatric nomenclature: A case study of the American Psychiatric Association referendum on homosexuality. In H. T. Englehart & A. L. Caplan (Eds.), *Case studies in the resolution and closure of disputes in science and technology* (pp. 381–400). New York, NY: Cambridge University Press.

Beck, A. T. (1976). *Cognitive therapy and the emotional disorders*. New York, NY: International Universities Press.

Beck, U. (1992). *Risk society: Towards a new modernity*. Newbury Park, CA: Sage Publications.

Beck, P., Byyny, R. L., & Adams, K. S. (1981). *Case exercises in clinical reasoning*. Chicago, IL: Yearbook Medical.

Becker, H. S. (1996). The epistemology of qualitative research. In R. Jessor, A. Colby, & R. A. Shweder (Eds.), *Ethnography and human development: Context and meaning in social inquiry* (pp. 53–71). Chicago, IL: University of Chicago Press.

Beit-Hallahmi, B. (1987). The psychotherapy subculture: Practice and ideology. *Social Science Information, 26*, 475–492.

Bekelman, J. E., Li, Y., & Gross, C. P. (2003). Scope and impact of financial conflicts of interest in biomedical research: A systematic review. *Journal of the American Medical Association, 289*, 454–465.

Bell, T., & Linn, M. C. (2002). Beliefs about science: How does science instruction contribute? In B. K. Hofer & P. R. Pintrich (Eds.), *Personal epistemology: The psychology of beliefs about knowledge and learning* (pp. 321–346). Mahwah, NJ: Erlbaum.

Belli, R. F., & Loftus, E. F. (1996). The pliability of autobiographical memory: Misinformation and the false memory problem. In D. C. Rubin (Ed.), *Remembering our past: Studies in autobiographical memory* (pp. 157–179). New York, NY: Cambridge University Press.

Benedetti, F. (2009). *Placebo effects: Understanding the mechanisms in health and disease*. New York, NY: Oxford University Press.

Bereiter, C., & Scardamalia, M. (1985). Cognitive coping strategies and the problems of "inert" knowledge. In S. F. Chipman, J. W. Segal, & R. Glaser (Eds.),

Thinking and learning skills: Vol. 2. Research and open questions. San Francisco, CA: Jossey-Bass.

Berger, P. L., & Luckman, T. (1966). *The social construction of reality.* New York, NY: Doubleday.

Berk, R. A., & Rossi, P. H. (1990). *Thinking about program evaluation.* Newbury Park, CA: Sage.

Berner, E. S., & Graber, M. L. (2008). Overconfidence as a cause of diagnostic error in medicine. *American Journal of Medicine, 121,* s2–23.

Bérubé, A. (1992). *Coming out under fire: The history of gay men and women in World War II.* New York, NY: Free Press.

Best, J. (1988). Missing children, misleading statistics. *Public Interest, 92,* 84–92.

Best, J. (2004). *More damned lies and statistics: How numbers confuse public issues.* Berkeley, CA: University of California Press.

Best, J. (2008). *Stat-spotting: A field guide to identifying dubious data.* Berkeley, CA: University of California Press.

Beutler, L. E. (2000). Davie and Goliath: When empirical and clinical standards of practice meet. *American Psychologist, 55,* 997–1007.

Beutow, S., Kiata, L., Liew, T., Kenealy, T., Dovey, S., & Elwyn, G. (2009). Patient error: A preliminary taxonomy. *Annals of Family Medicine, 7,* 223–231.

Beyerstein, B. L. (1990). Brainscams: Neuromythologies of the new age. *International Journal of Mental Health, 19,* 27–36.

Bhandari, M., Busse, J. W., Jackowski, D., Montori, V. M., Schünemann, H., et al. (2004). Association between industry funding and statistically significant pro-industry findings in medical and surgical randomized trials. *Canadian Medical Association Journal, 170,* 477–480.

Biehl, J., Good, B., & Kleinman, A. (Eds.). (2007). *Subjectivity: Ethnographic investigations.* Berkeley, CA: University of California Press.

Black, N. (1994). Experimental and observational methods of evaluation. *BMJ, 309,* 540.

Blackmore, S. (1987). The elusive open mind: Ten years of negative research in parapsychology. *The Skeptical Inquirer, 11,* 244–255.

Blackmore, S. (1991). Keynote, annual meeting of CSICOP (Committee for the Scientific Investigation of Claims of the Paranormal).

Blalock, H. M, Jr. (1984). *Basic dilemmas in the social sciences.* Beverly Hills, CA: Sage.

Blau, P. M. (1960). Orientation toward clients in a public welfare agency. *Administrative Science Quarterly, 5,* 341–361.

Blau, T. H. (1988). *Psychology tradeoff: The technique and style of doing therapy.* New York, NY: Brunner/Mazel.

Blenkner, M., Bloom, M., & Nielson, M. (1971). A research and demonstration project of protective services. *Social Casework, 52,* 483–499.

Bless, H. (2001). The consequences of mood on the processing of social information. In A. Tesser & N. Schwarz (Eds.), *Blackwell handbook of social psychology: Intraindividual processes* (pp. 391–421). Oxford, UK: Blackwell.

Bloom, M., Fischer, J., & Orme, J. G. (2009). *Evaluating practice: Guidelines for the accountable professional* (6th ed.). Upper Sadde River, NJ: Pearson.

Blum, J. (1978). *Pseudoscience and mental ability*. New York, NY: Monthly Review Press.

Bodenheimer, T. (2000). Disease management in the American market. *BMJ, 320,* 563–566.

Bogner, M. S. (Ed.). (1994). *Human error in medicine*. Hillsdale, NJ: Erlbaum.

Boren, J. H. (1972). *When in doubt, mumble: A bureaucrat's handbook*. New York, NY: Van Nostrand Reinhold.

Borgida, E., & Nisbett, R. E. (1977). The differential impact of abstract vs. concrete information on decisions. *Journal of Applied Social Psychology, 7,* 258–271.

Bosk, C. L. (1979). *Forgive and remember: Managing medical failure*. Chicago, IL: University of Chicago Press.

Bossuyt, P. M., Reitsma, J. B., Bruns, D. E., Gatsonis, C. A., Glasziou, P. P., Irwig, L. M., et al. (2003). Towards complete and accurate reporting of studies of diagnostic accuracy: The STARD initiative. *BMJ, 326,* 41–44.

Bourgois, P., Lettiere, M., & Quesada, J. (2003). Social misery and the sanctions of substance abuse: Confronting HIV risk among homeless heroin addicts in San Francisco. In J. D. Orcutt & D. R. Rudy (Eds.), *Drugs, alcohol, and social problems* (pp. 257–278). New York, NY: Oxford University Press.

Bower, G. H., & Cohen, P. R. (1982). Emotional influences in memory and thinking: Data and theory. In M. S. Clark & S. T. Fiske (Eds.), *Affect and cognition* (pp. 291–332). Hillsdale, NJ: Erlbaum.

Bowers, K. S. (1987). Intuition and discovery. In P. Stern (Ed.), *Theories of the unconscious and theories of the self* (pp. 71–90). Hillsdale, NJ: Analytic Press.

Boyle, M. (2002). *Schizophrenia: A scientific delusion?* (2nd ed.). London, UK: Routledge.

Braddock, C. H., Edwards, K. A., Hasenberg, N. M., Laidley, T. L., & Levinson, W. (1999). Informed decision making in outpatient practice: Time to get back to basics. *Journal of the American Medical Association, 282,* 2313–2320.

Bransford, J. D., & Stein, B. S. (1984). *The IDEAL problem solver: A guide for improving thinking, learning, and creativity*. New York, NY: W.H. Freeman.

Broad, W., & Wade, N. (1982). *Betrayers of the truth*. New York, NY: Simon & Schuster.

Brock, T. C., & Green, M. C. (Eds.). (2005). *Persuasion: Psychological insights and perspectives* (2nd ed.). Thousand Oaks, CA: Sage.

Brody, H. (2007). *Hooked: Ethics, the medical profession and the pharmaceutical industry*. New York, NY: Rowman & Littlefield.

Bromley, D. B. (1977). *Personality description and ordinary language*. New York, NY: John Wiley & Sons.

Bromley, D. B. (1986). *The case-study method in psychology and related disciplines.* New York, NY: John Wiley & Sons.

Brookfield, S. (1995). *Becoming a critically reflective teacher.* San Francisco, CA: Jossey-Bass.

Brookfield, S. D. (1987). *Developing critical thinkers: Challenging adults to explore alternative ways of thinking and acting.* San Francisco, CA: Jossey-Bass.

Brounstein, P. J., Emshoff, J. G., Hill, G. A., & Stoil, M. J. (1997). Assessment of methodological practices in the evaluation of alcohol and other drug (AOD) abuse prevention. *Journal of Health and Social Policy, 9,* 1–19.

Brown, E. L., McAvay, G., Raue, P. J., Moses, S., & Bruce, M. L. (2003). Recognition of depression among elderly patients of home care services. *Psychiatric Services, 54,* 208–213.

Bryant, G. D., & Norman, G. R. (1980). Expressions of probability: Words and numbers. *New England Journal of Medicine, 302,* 411.

Budd, K. S., Poindexter, L. M., Feliz, E. D., & Naik-Polan, A. T. (2001). Clinical assessment of parents in child protection cases: An empirical analysis. *Law and Human Behavior, 25,* 93–108.

Buetow, S., Kiata, L., Leiw, T, Kenealy, T., Dovey, S., & Elwyn, G. (2009). Patient error: A preliminary taxonomy. *Annals of Family Medicine, 7,* 223–231.

Buie, J. (1987). Newspaper's tone, errors irk sources. *APA Monitor, 18,* 23.

Buie, J. (1989). Psychologists defend reimbursement rights. *APA Monitor, 20,* 25.

Bullmore, E., Joyce, H., Marks, I. M., & Connolly, J. (1992). A computerized quality assurance system (QAS) on a general psychiatric ward: Towards efficient clinical audit. *Journal of Mental Health, 1,* 257–263.

Bunge, M. (1984). What is pseudoscience? *The Skeptical Inquirer, 9,* 36–47.

Bunge, M. (2003). The pseudoscience concept, dispensable in professional practice, is required to evaluate research projects: A reply to Richard J. MacNally. *The Scientific Review of Mental Health Practice, 2,* 111–114.

Burgess, P. H. (1984). *The sayings of Mahatma Gandhi.* Singapore: Graham Brash.

Burnham, J. C. (1987). *How superstition won and science lost. Popularizing science and health in the United States.* New Brunswick, NJ: Rutgers University Press.

Burns, D. D. (1999). *Feeling good: The new mood therapy* (2nd ed.). New York, NY: Avon.

Busfield, J. (Ed.). (2001). *Rethinking the sociology of mental health.* Malden, MA: Blackwell.

Campbell, A. J., Sanderson, G., & Robertson, M C. (2010). Poor vision and falls. Correcting vision can help, but do so with care. Editorial. *BMJ, 340:*c2456.

Campbell, D. A., & Cornett, P. L. (2002). How stress and burnout produce medical mistakes. In M. M. Rosenthal & K. M. Sutcliffe (Eds.), *Medical error: What do we know? What do we do?* (pp. 37–57). San Francisco, CA: Jossey-Bass.

Campbell, D. T. (1969). Reforms as experiments. *American Psychologist, 24*, 409–429.

Campbell, D. T. (1996). Can we overcome worldview incommensurability/relativity in trying to understand the other? In R. Jessor, A. Colby, & R. A. Shweder (Eds.), *Ethnography and human development: Context and meaning in social inquiry* (pp. 153–172). Chicago, IL: University of Chicago Press.

Campbell, D. T., & Stanley, J. C. (1963). *Experimental and quasi-experimental design for research.* Chicago, IL: Rand McNally.

Campbell, J. A. (1988). Client acceptance of single-system evaluation procedures. *Social Work Research and Abstracts, 24*, 21–22.

Campione, J. C. (1989). Assisted assessment: A taxonomy of approaches and an outline of strengths and weaknesses. *Journal of Learning Disabilities, 22*, 151–165.

Cantillon, P., & Sargeant, J. (2008). Giving feedback in clinical settings. *BMJ, 337*:a1961.

Cantor, J. R., Zillmann, D., & Bryant, J. (1975). Enhancement of experienced sexual arousal in response to erotic stimuli through misattribution of unrelated residual excitation. *Journal of Personality and Social Psychology, 32*, 69–75.

Cantor, N. (1982). "Everyday" versus normative models of clinical and social judgment. In G. Weary & H. L. Mirels (Eds.), *Integrations of clinical and social psychology* (pp. 27–47). New York, NY: Oxford University Press.

Caplin, R. A., Posner, K., & Cheney, F. W. (1991). Effect of outcome on physician judgments of appropriateness of care. *Journal of the American Medical Association, 265*, 1957–1960.

Carlat, D. J. (2010). *Unhinged: The trouble with psychiatry—a doctor's revelations about a profession in crisis.* New York, NY: Free Press.

Carpenter, K. J. (1986). *The history of scurvy & vitamin C.* New York, NY: Cambridge University Press.

Carroll, D. W. (2001). Using ignorance questions to promote thinking skills. *Teaching of Psychology, 28*, 98–100.

Carroll, L. (1946). *Alice in wonderland* and *Through the looking glass.* Kingston, TN: Kingsport Press.

Cassell, E. J. (1991). *The nature of suffering and the goals of medicine.* New York, NY: Oxford University Press.

Ceci, S. J., & Bruck, M. (1995). *Jeopardy in the courtroom: A scientific analysis of children's testimony.* Washington, DC: American Psychological Association.

Ceci, S. J., Crotteau-Huffman, M., Smith, E., & Loftus, E. W. (1994). Repeatedly thinking about non-events. *Consciousness and Cognition, 3*, 388–407.

Ceci, S., & Hembrooke, H. (Eds.). (1998). *Expert witnesses in child abuse cases.* Washington, DC: American Psychological Association.

Center for Reviews and Dissemination (CRD), University of York, UK (2004, April 4).

Chabris, C., & Simons, D. (2009). *The invisible gorilla: How our intuitions deceive us*. New York, NY: Broadway Paperbacks.

Chalmers, I. (1983). Scientific inquiry and authoritarianism in perinatal care and education. *Birth, 10*, 151–166.

Chalmers, I. (1990). Underreporting research limitations is scientific misconduct. *Journal of the American Medical Association, 263*, 1405–1408.

Chalmers, I. (2003). Trying to do more good than harm in policy and practice: The role of rigorous, transparent, up-to-date evaluations. *The ANNALS of the American Academy of Political and Social Science, 589*, 22–40.

Chalmers, I. (2004). Well informed uncertainties about the effects of treatment. *BMJ, 328*, 475–476.

Chapman, L. J. (1967). Illusory correlation in observational report. *Journal of Verbal Learning and Verbal Behavior, 6*, 151–155.

Chapman, L. J., & Chapman, J. P. (1967). Genesis of popular but erroneous diagnostic observations. *Journal of Abnormal Psychology, 72*, 193–204.

Chapman, L. J., & Chapman, J. P. (1969). Illusory correlation as an obstacle to the use of valid psychodiagnostic signs. *Journal of Abnormal Psychology, 74*, 271–280.

Charatan, F. (2011). US senate criticizes home health companies for "gaming" Medicare. *BMJ, 343*:d6454.

Charlton, B. G. (2010), The cancer of bureaucracy. *Medical Hypotheses, 74*, 961–965.

Chase, W. G., & Simon, H. A. (1973). Perception in chess. *Cognitive Psychology, 1*, 55–81.

Chauncey, G. (1995). *Gay New York: Gender, urban culture, and the making of the gay male world, 1890–1940*. New York, NY: Basic Books.

Chelton, L. G., & Bonney, W. C. (1987). Addiction, affects, and selfobject theory. *Psychotherapy: Theory, Research and Practice, 24*, 40–46.

Chi, M. T. H., Feltovich, P. J., & Glaser, R. (1980). Categorization and representation of physics problems by experts and novices. *Cognitive Science, 5*, 121–152.

Chiriboga, D. A., Jenkins, G., & Bailey, J. (1983). Stress and coping among hospice nurses: Test of an analytic model. *Nursing Research, 32*, 294–299.

Choi, I., Choi, J. A., & Norenzayan, A. (2005). Culture and decisions. In D. J. Koehler & N. Harvey (Eds.), *Blackwell handbook of judgment & decision making* (pp. 504–524). Malden, MA: Blackwell.

Chorpita, B. F., Becker, K. D., & Daleiden, E. L. (2007). Understanding the common elements of evidence-based practice: Misconceptions and clinical examples. *Journal of the American Academy of Child and Adolescent Psychiatry, 46*, 647–652.

Christensen, A., & Jacobson, N. S. (1994). Who (or what) can do psychotherapy: The status of and challenge of nonprofessional therapies. *Psychological Science, 5*, 8–14.

Church, A. T., Katigbak, M. S., Reyes, J. A., Salanga, M. G., Miramontes, L. A., & Adams, M. B. (2008). Prediction and cross-situational consistency of daily behavior across cultures: Testing trade and cultural psychology perspectives. *Journal of Research and Personality, 42*, 1199–1215.

Cialdini, R. B. (1984). *Influence: The new psychology of modern persuasion*. New York, NY: Quill.

Cialdini, R. B. (2001). *Influence: Science and practice* (4th ed.). New York, NY: Harper.

Cialdini, R. B. (2008). *Influence: Science and practice* (5th ed.). Boston, MA: Pearson.

Cialdini, R. B., & Sagarin, B. J. (2005). Principles of interpersonal influence. In T. C. Brock & M. C. Green (Eds.), *Persuasion: Psychological insights and perspectives* (2nd ed., pp. 143–170). Thousand Oaks, CA: Sage.

Cirino, R. (1971). *Don't blame the people*. New York, NY: Random House.

Clarke, A. E., Mamo, L., Fosket, J. R., Fishman, J. R., & Shim, J. K. (Eds.). (2010). *Biomedicalization: Technoscience, health, and illness in the U.S.* Durham, NC: Duke University Press.

Clarkin, J. F., & Levy, K. N. (2004). The influence of client variables on psychotherapy. In M. J. Lambert (Ed.), *Bergin and Garfield's handbook of psychotherapy and behavior change* (5th ed., pp. 194–226). Hoboken, NJ: John Wiley & Sons.

Clinical evidence: The international source of the best available evidence for effective health care. (2002, 7th ed.). London, UK: BMJ Publishing Group.

Cochrane, A. L. (1972/1999). *Effectiveness and efficiency: Random reflections on health services*. Cambridge, UK: Royal Society of Medicine Press and Nuffield Trust, Cambridge University Press.

Cohen, C. I., & Timimi, S. (Eds.). (2008). *Liberatory psychiatry: philosophy, politics, and mental health*. New York, NY: Cambridge University Press.

Cohen, D., & Jacobs, D. (1998). A model consent form for psychiatric drug treatment. *International Journal of Risk & Safety in Medicine, 11*, 161–164.

Cohen, J. (1977). *Statistical power analysis for the behavioral sciences*. New York, NY: Academic Press.

Cohen, L., Sargent, M., & Sechrest, L. (1986). Use of psychotherapy research by professional psychologists. *American Psychologist, 41*, 198–206.

Collins, R. (1988, August 7). Lessons in compassion for student doctors. *The Sunday New York Times*, A7.

Colliver, J. A. (2000). Effectiveness of problem-based learning curricula: Research and theory. *Academic Medicine, 75*, 259–266.

Colman, A. M. (1987). *Facts, fallacies, and fraud in psychology*. London, UK: Hutchinson.

Colón-Emeric, C. S., Ammarell, N., Bailey, D., Corazzini, K., & Utley-Smith, Q. (2006). Patterns of medical and nursing staff communication in nursing homes:

Implications and insights from complexity science. *Quality Health Research*, *16*, 173–188.

Combs, J. E., & Nimmo, D. D. (1993). *The new propaganda: The dictatorship of palaver in contemporary politics*. New York, NY: Longman.

Connelly, T., & Beach, L. R. (2000). The theory of image theory: An examination of the central conceptual structure. In T. Connolley, H. R. Arkes, & K. R. Hammond (Eds.), *Judgment and decision making: An interdisciplinary reader* (2nd ed., pp. 755–766). New York, NY: Cambridge University Press.

Conrad, P. (2001). Genetic optimism: Framing genes and mental illness in the news. *Culture, Medicine and Psychiatry*, *25*, 225–247.

Conrad, P. (2007). *The medicalization of society: On the transformation of human conditions into treatable disorders*. Baltimore, MD: Johns Hopkins University Press.

Conrad, P., & Potter, D. (2000). From hyperactive children to ADHD adults: Observations on the expansion of medical categories. *Social Problems*, *47*, 559–582.

Conrad, P., & Schneider, J. W. (1992). *Deviance and medicalization: From badness to sickness*. Philadelphia, PA: Temple University Press.

Cook, T. D., & Campbell, D. T. (1979). *Quasi-experimentation: Design analysis issues for field settings*. Boston, MA: Houghton Mifflin.

Cooper, J. O., Heron, T. E., & Heward, W. L. (2008). *Applied behavior analysis* (2nd ed.). Upper Saddle River, NJ: Pearson/Merrill-Prentice Hall.

Corbin, R. M. (1980). Decisions that might not get made. In T. S. Wallsten (Ed.), *Cognitive processes in choice and decision behavior* (pp. 47–67). Hillsdale, NJ: Erlbaum.

Cordes, C. (1983). Don't be your most difficult client. *APA Monitor*, *14*(11), 22.

Cosgrove, L., Bursztajn, H. J., Krimsky, S., Anaya, M., & Walker, J. (2009). Conflicts of interest and disclosure in the American Psychiatric Association's clinical practice guidelines. *Psychotherapy and Psychosomatics*, *78*, 228–232.

Cottle, M. (1999). Selling shyness. *New Republic* (Aug. 2).

Coulter, A. (2002). *The autonomous patient: Ending paternalism in medical care*. London, UK: Nuffield Trust.

Coulter, A., Parsons, S., & Askham, J. (2008). *Where are the patients in decision-making about their own care?* World Health Organization. Copenhagen, Denmark: WHO Regional Office for Europe.

Cowan, N. (2005). *Working memory capacity*. New York Psychology Press.

Creadick, A. G. (2010). *Perfectly average: The pursuit of normality in postwar America*. Amherst, MA: University of Massachusetts Press.

Croskerry, P. (2009). Clinical cognition and diagnostic error: Applications of a dual process model of reasoning. *Advances in Health Science Education*, *14*, 27–35.

Croskerry, P., & Nimmo, G. R. (2011). Better clinical decision making and reducing diagnostic error. *Journal of the Royal College Physicians of Edinburgh*, *41*, 155–162.

Croskerry, P., Abbass, A., & Wu, A. W. (2008). How doctors feel: Affective issues in patient safety. *Lancet, 372*, 1205–1206.

Croskerry, P., Abbass, A., & Wu, A. W. (2010). Emotional influences in patient safety. *Journal of Patient Safety, 6*, 1–7.

Cutler, B. L. (Ed.) (2009). *Expert testimony on the psychology of eyewitness identification.* New York, NY: Oxford University Press.

Dallas, M. E., & Baron, R. S. (1985). Do psychotherapists use a confirmatory strategy during interviewing? *Journal of Social and Clinical Psychology, 3*, 106–122.

Damer, T. E. (1995). *Attacking faulty reasoning: A practical guide to fallacy free argument* (3rd ed.). Belmont, CA: Wadsworth.

Darley, J. M., & Cooper, J. (Eds.). (1998). *Attribution processes, person perception, and social interaction: The legacy of Edward E. Jones.* Washington, DC: American Psychological Association.

Darley, J. M., & Gross, P. H. (1983). A hypothesis-confirming bias in labeling effects. *Journal of Personality and Social Psychology, 44*, 20–37.

Daubert v. Merrell Dow Pharmaceuticals (1993). 509 U.S. 579.

Davey, B., & Seale, C. (Eds.). (2002). *Experiencing and explaining disease* (3rd ed.). Bristol, PA: Open University Press.

Davies, P. (2004, February 19). Is evidence-based government possible? Jerry Lee lecture, 4th Annual Campbell Collaboration Colloquium, Washington, DC.

Davis, B., Sheeber, L., & Hops, H. (2002). Coercive family processes and adolescent depression. In J. B. Reid, G.R. Patterson, & J. Snyder (Eds.), *Antisocial behavior in children and adolescents: A developmental analysis and model for intervention* (pp. 173–192). Washington, DC: American Psychological Association.

Dawes, R. M. (1982). The value of being explicit when making clinical decisions. In T. A. Wills (Ed.), *Basic processes in helping relationships* (pp. 37–58). Orlando, FL: Academic Press.

Dawes, R. M. (1988). *Rational choice in an uncertain world.* Orlando, FL: Harcourt Brace Jovanovich.

Dawes, R. M. (1993). Prediction of the future versus an understanding of the past: A basic asymmetry. *American Journal of Psychology, 106*, 1–24.

Dawes, R. M. (1994a). *House of cards: Psychology and psychotherapy built on myth.* New York, NY: Free Press.

Dawes, R. M. (1994b). On the necessity of examining all four cells in a 2 3 2 table. In *Making better decisions* (Vol. 1, pp. 2–4). Pacific Grove, CA: Brooks/Cole.

Dawes, R. M. (2001). *Everyday irrationality: How pseudo-scientists, lunatics and the rest of us systematically fail to think rationally.* Boulder, CO: Westview Press.

Dawes, R. M., & Corrigan, B. (1974). Linear models in decision making. *Psychological Bulletin, 81*, 95–106.

Dawes, R. M., Faust, D., & Meehl, P. E. (1989). Clinical versus actuarial judgment. *Science*, *243*, 1668–1674.

Dawes, R. M., Faust, D., & Meehl, P. E. (2002). Clinical versus actuarial judgment. In T. Gilovich & D. Griffin (Eds.), *Heuristics and biases: The psychology of intuitive judgment* (pp. 716–729). New York, NY: Cambridge University Press.

Dean, G. (1986–1987). Does astrology need to be true? Part 1: A look at the real thing. *The Skeptical Inquirer*, *11*, 166–185.

Dean, G. (1987). Does astrology need to be true? Part 2: The answer is no. *The Skeptical Inquirer*, *12*, 257–273.

DeAngelis, T. (1987). Therapists who feel as if they're not therapists: The imposter syndrome. *APA Monitor*, *18*, 14.

Decker, F. H. (1987). Psychiatric management of legal defense in periodic commitment hearings. *Social Problems*, *34*, 156–171.

Deeks, J. J., & Altman, D. G. (2004). Diagnostic tests 4: Likelihood ratios. *BMJ*, *329*, 168–169.

Delamothe, T. (2011). Editor's choice: We need to talk about nursing. *BMJ*, *342*:d3416.

DeMott, B. (1990). *The imperial middle: Why Americans can't think straight about class.* New York, NY: William Morrow.

DePanfilis, D. (2003). Review of IAIU investigations of suspected child abuse and neglect. In *DYFS out-of-home care settings in New Jersey: Final report.* Baltimore, MD: School of Social Work. College Park, MD: University of Maryland.

Dewey, J. (1933). *How we think: A restatement of the relation of reflective thinking to the education process.* Boston, MA: Heath.

Deyo, R. A. (2002). Cascade effects of medical technology. *Annual Review of Public Health*, *23*, 23–44.

Deyo, R. A., Simon, G., & Omenn, G. S. (1997). The messenger under attack—intimidation of researchers by special interest groups. *New England Journal of Medicine*, *336*, 1176–1180.

DeYoung, M. (2004). *The day care ritual abuse moral panic.* Jefferson, NC: McFarland.

Diaz, F. J., & de Leon, J. (2002). Excessive anti-psychotic dosing in two US state hospitals. *Journal of Clinical Psychiatry*, *63*, 998–1003.

Didi-Huberman, G. (1982/2003). *Invention of hysteria: Charcot and the photographic iconography of the Salpetriere.* Cambridge, MA: MIT Press.

Dillard, J. P., & Pfau, M. (Eds.). (2002). *The persuasion handbook: Developments in theory and practice.* Thousand Oaks, CA: Sage.

Dingwall, R., Eekelaar, J., & Murray, T. (1983). *The protection of children: State intervention and family life.* Oxford, UK: Basil Blackwell.

Dishion, T. J., Burraston, B., & Li, F. (2003). A multimethod and multitrait analysis of family management practices: Convergent and predictive validity. In Z. Sloboda, &

W. J. Bukoski (Eds.), *Handbook of drug abuse prevention: Theory, science and practice* (pp. 587–608). New York, NY: Kluwer Academic/Plenum Press.

Dishion, T., & Granic, I. (2004). Naturalistic observation of relationship processes. In S. N. Haynes & E. M. Heiby (Eds.), *Comprehensive handbook of psychological assessment* (Ed. M. Hersen). *Vol. 3: Behavioral Assessment* (pp. 143–161). Hoboken, NJ: John Wiley & Sons.

Ditto, P. H., & Lopez, D. F. (1992). Motivated skepticism: Use of differential decision criteria for preferred and nonpreferred conclusions. *Journal of Personality and Social Psychology, 62,* 568–584.

Djulbegovic, B. (2004). Lifting the fog of uncertainty from the practice of medicine. *BMJ, 329,* 1419–1420.

Domenighetti, G., Grilli, R., & Liberati, A. (1998). Promoting consumers' demand for evidence based medicine. *International Journal of Technology Assessment in Health Care, 14*(11), 97–105.

Donovan, P. (2004). *No way of knowing: Crime, urban legends, and the Internet.* New York, NY: Routledge.

Doust, J., & Del Mar, C. (2004). Why do doctors use treatments that do not work? For many reasons—including their inability to stand idle and do nothing. *BMJ, 328,* 474–475.

Dovey, S. M., Meyers, D. S., Phillips, R. L., Green, L. A., Fryer, G. E., Galliher, J. M., et al. (2002). A preliminary taxonomy of medical errors in family practice. *Quality and Safety in Health Care, 11,* 233–238.

Druckman, D., & Bjork, R. A. (Eds.). (1991). *In the mind's eye: Enhancing human performance.* Washington, DC: National Academy Press.

Drury, S. S., Theall, K., Gleason, M. M., Smyke, A. T., Vivo, D., Wong, J. Y. Y., et al. (2011). Telomere length and early severe social deprivation: Linking early adversity and cellular aging. *Molecular Psychiatry,* 1–9 (http://dx.doi.org/10.1038/mp)

Duesberg, P., Mandrioli, D., McCormack, A., & Nicholson, J. M. (2011). Is carcinogenesis a form of speciation? *Cell Cycle, 10,* 2100–2114.

Duncan, B. (1976). Differential social perception and attribution of intergroup violence: Testing the lower limits of stereotyping blacks. *Journal of Personality and Social Psychology, 34,* 590–598.

Duncan, B. L., Miller, S. D., Wampold, B. E., & Hubble, M. A. (Eds.). (2010). *The heart & soul of change: What works in therapy* (2nd ed.). Washington, DC: American Psychological Association.

Dunning, D., Heath, C., & Suls, J. M. (2004). Flawed self-assessment: Implications for health, education, and the work place. *Psychological Science in the Public Interest, 5,* 69–106.

Dunphy, B., Dunphy, S., Cantwell, R., Bourke, S., & Fleming, M. (2010). Evidence based-practice and affect: The impact of physician attitudes on outcomes associated

with clinical reasoning and decision-making. *Australian Journal of Educational &
Developmental Psychology, 10*, 56–64.

Dunphy, B. C., Cantwell, R., Bourke, S., Fleming, M., Smith, B., Joseph, K. S., &
Dunphy, S. (2009). Cognitive elements in clinical decision-making toward a cogni-
tive model for medical education and understanding clinical reasoning. *Advances in
Health Sciences Education*, DOI 10.1007/s10459-009-9194-y

Durso, F. T., & Gronlund, S. D. (1999). Situation awareness. In F. T. Durso, R. S.
Nickerson, R. W. Schvaneveldt, S. T. Dumais, D. S. Lindsay, & M. T. H. Chi
(Eds.), *Handbook of applied cognition* (pp. 283–314). New York, NY: John Wiley
& Sons.

Dyer, C. (2005). News roundup: Doctor was "near to breaking point" when she exaggerated abuse. *BMJ, 330*, 1105.

Eagle, G. (2002). The political conundrums of post-traumatic stress disorder. In D. Hook
& G. Eagle (Eds.), *Psychopathology and social prejudice* (pp. 75–91). Cape Town,
South Africa: University of Cape Town Press.

Eddy, D. M. (1982). Probabilistic reasoning in clinical medicine: Problems and opportunities. In D. Kahneman, P. Slovic, & A. Tversky (Eds.), *Judgment under uncertainty:
Heuristics and biases*. New York, NY: Cambridge University Press.

Eddy, D. M. (1990). Comparing benefits and harms: The balance sheet. *Journal of the
American Medical Association, 263*, 2493, 2498, 2501.

Eddy, D. M. (1993). Three battles to watching the 1990s. *Journal of the American Medical
Association, 270*, 520–526.

Eddy, D. M. (1994a). Principles for making difficult decisions in difficult times. *Journal
of the American Medical Association, 271*, 1792–1798.

Eddy, D. M. (1994b). Rationing resources while improving quality. *Journal of the American Medical Association, 272*, 817–824.

Edgley, C., & Brissett, D. (1999). *A nation of meddlers*. Boulder, CO: Westview Press.

Edmondson, R. (1984). *Rhetoric in sociology*. New York, NY: Macmillan.

Edwards, A., & Elwyn, G. (2001). *Evidence-informed patient choice: Inevitable or impossible?* New York, NY: Oxford University Press.

Edwards, A., Elwyn, G., & Mulley, A. (2002). Explaining risks: Turning numerical data
into meaningful pictures. *BMJ, 324*, 827–830.

Edwards, A. G., Elwyn, G., Covey, J., Matthews, E., & Pill, R. (2001). Presenting risk
information—A review of the effects of "framing" and other manipulations on
patient outcomes. *Journal of Health Communication, 6*, 61–82.

Edwards, V. (1938). *Group leader's guide to propaganda analysis*. New York, NY: Institute
for Propaganda Analysis.

Edwards, W., & von Winterfeldt, D. (1986). On cognitive illusions and their implications. In H. R. Arkes & R. R. Hammond (Eds.), *Judgment and decision making: An
interdisciplinary reader* (pp. 642–679). Cambridge, UK: Cambridge University Press.

Ehrenreich, B., & Ehrenreich, J. (1977). The professional managerial class. *Radical America, 11*, 7–31.

Einhorn, H. J. (1980a). Learning from experience and suboptimal rules in decision making. In T. S. Wallsten (Ed.), *Cognitive processes in choice and decision behavior.* Hillsdale, NJ: Erlbaum.

Einhorn, H. J. (1980b). Overconfidence in judgment. In R. A. Shweder (Ed.), *New directions for methodology in social and behavioral science, No. 4. Fallible judgment in behavioral research* (pp. 1–16). San Francisco, CA: Jossey-Bass.

Einhorn, H. J. (1988). Diagnosis and causality in clinical and statistical prediction. In D. C. Turk & P. Salovey (Eds.), *Reasoning, inference and judgment in clinical psychology* (pp. 51–72). New York, NY: Free Press.

Einhorn, H. J., & Hogarth, R. M. (1978). Confidence in judgment: Persistence of the illusion of validity. *Psychological Review, 85*, 395–416.

Einhorn, H. J., & Hogarth, R. M. (1985). Prediction, diagnosis, causal thinking in forecasting. In G. Wright (Ed.), *Behavioral decision making* (pp. 311–328). New York, NY: Plenum.

Einhorn, H. J., & Hogarth, R. M. (1986). Judging probable cause. *Psychological Bulletin, 99*, 3–19.

Electronic Handbook of Legal Medicine. www.medlit.net/textbook

Elliott, R., Bohart, A. C., Greenberg, L. S., Watson, J. C., & Greenberg, L. S. (2011). Empathy. In J. C. Norcross (Ed.), *Psychotherapy relationships that work: Evidence-based responsiveness* (2nd ed., pp. 132–152). New York, NY: Oxford University Press.

Ellis, A., & Grieger, R. (1977). *Handbook of rational-emotive therapy.* New York, NY: Springer.

Ellul, J. (1965). *Propaganda: The formation of men's attitudes.* New York, NY: Vintage.

Elmore, J. G., & Boyko, E. J. (2000). Assessing accuracy of diagnostic and screening tests. In J. P. Geyman, R. A. Deyo, & S. D. Ramsey (Eds.), *Evidence-based clinical practice: Concepts and approaches* (pp. 83–93). Boston, MA: Butterworth-Heinemann.

Elstein, A. S. (1988). Cognitive processes in clinical inference and decision making. In D. C. Turk & P. Salovey (Eds.), *Reasoning, inference, and judgment in clinical psychology* (pp. 17–50). New York, NY: Free Press.

Elstein, A. S., Shulman, L. S., Sprafka, S. A., Allal, L., Gordon, M., Jason, H., et al. (1978). *Medical problem solving: An analysis of clinical reasoning.* Cambridge, MA: Harvard University Press.

Elwyn, G., Edwards, A., Wensing, M., Hood, K., Atwell, C., & Grol, R. (2003). Shared decision making: Developing the OPTION scale for measuring patient involvement. *Quality and Safety of Health Care, 12*, 93–99.

Ely, J. W., Graber, M. L., & Croskerry, P. (2011). Checklists for reducing diagnostic errors. *Academic Medicine, 86*, 307–313.

Ely, J. W., Osheroff, J. A., Ebell, M. H., Bergus, G. R., Levy, B. T., Chambliss, M. L., & Evans, E. R. (1999). Analysis of questions asked by family doctors regarding patient care. *BMJ, 319*, 358–361.

Ely, J. W., Osheroff, J. A., Ebell, M. H., Chambliss, M. L., Vinson, D. C., Stevermer, J. J., & Pifer, E. A. (2002). Obstacles to answering doctors' questions about patient care with evidence: Qualitative study. *BMJ, 324,* 710–718.

Emerson, R. M. (1969). *Judging delinquents: Context and process in juvenile court.* New York, NY: Aldine.

Engel, S. M. (1994). *With good reason: An introduction to informal fallacies* (5th ed.). New York, NY: St. Martin's Press.

Ennis, R. H. (1987). A taxonomy of critical thinking dispositions and abilities. In J. B. Baron & R. J. Sternberg (Eds.), *Teaching thinking skills, theory, and practice* (pp. 9–26). New York, NY: W.H. Freeman.

Entwistle, N. (1987). A model of the teaching-learning process. In J. T. Richardson, M. W. Eysenck, & D. W. Piper (Eds.), *Student learning: Research in education and cognitive psychology* (pp. 13–28). Milton Keynes, UK: Society for Research into Higher Education and Open University Press.

Entwistle, V. A., Renfrew, M. J., Yearley, S., Forrester, J., & Lamont, T. (1998). Lay perspectives: Advantages for health research. *BMJ, 316,* 463–466.

Entwistle, V. A., Sheldon, T. A., Sowden, A. J., & Watt, I. A. (1998). Evidence-informed patient choice. *International Journal of Technology Assessment in Health Care, 14,* 212–215.

Erault, M. (1994). *Developing professional knowledge and confidence.* London, UK: Falmer.

Expert Group on Learning from Adverse Events in the NHS. (2000). *An organization with a memory.* London, UK: Stationery Office.

Ewen, S. (1976). *Captains of consciousness: Advertising and the social roots of the consumer culture.* New York, NY: McGraw Hill.

Eyberg, S. M., & Ross, A. W. (1978). Assessment of child behavior problems: The validation of a new inventory. *Journal of Clinical Psychology, 16,* 113–116.

Fabrigar, L. R., Smith, S. M., & Brannon, L. A. (1999). Applications of social cognition: Attitudes as cognitive structures. In F. T. Durso (Ed.), *Handbook of applied cognition* (pp. 173–206). New York, NY: John Wiley & Sons.

Falk, R. (1981). On coincidences. *The Skeptical Inquirer, 6,* 18–31.

Farrington, D. P. (2003). Methodological quality standards for evaluation research. *The ANNALS of the American Academy of Political and Social Science, 587,* 49–68.

Faust, D., & Ziskin, J. (2012). *Ziskin's coping with psychiatric and psychological testimony.* New York, NY: Oxford University Press.

Fearnside, W. W., & Holther, W. G. (1959). *Fallacy: The counterfeit of argument.* Englewood Cliffs, NJ: Prentice Hall.

Feinstein, A. R. (1967). *Judgment.* Baltimore, MD: Williams & Wilkins.

Feltovich, P. J., Johnson, P. E., Moller, J. H., & Swanson, D. B. (1984). The role and development of medical knowledge in diagnostic expertise. In W. J. Clancey

& E. H. Shortliffe (Eds.), *Readings in medical artificial intelligence: The first decade* (pp. 275–319). Reading, MA: Addison-Wesley.

Feltovich, P. J., Spiro, R. J., & Coulson, R. (1989). The nature of conceptual understanding in biomedicine: The keep structure of complex ideas and the development of misconceptions. In D. A. Evans & V. L. Patel (Eds.), *Cognitive science in medicine: Biomedical modeling* (pp. 113–172). Cambridge, MA: MIT Press.

Feltovich, P. J., Spiro, R. J., & Coulson, R. L. (1993). Learning, teaching, and testing for complex conceptual understanding. In N. Frederickson, R. Mislevy, & I. Bejar (Eds.), *Test theory for a new generation of tests* (pp. 181–218). Hillsdale, NJ: Lawrence Erlbaum.

Fenton, M., Brice, A., & Chalmers, I. (2009). Harvesting and publishing patients' unanswered questions about the effects of treatments. In P. Littlejohns & M. Rawlins (Eds.), *Patients, the public and priorities in healthcare* (pp. 165–180). Abingdon, Oxon, UK: Radcliffe.

Fetherstonhaugh, D., Slovic, P., Johnson, S. M., & Friedrich, J. (1997). Insensitivity to the value of human life: A study of psychophysical numbing. *Journal of Risk and Uncertainty, 14*(3), 282–300.

Fiks, A. G., Hughes, C. C., Gafen, A., Guevara, J. P., & Barg, F. K. (2011). Contrasting parents' and pediatricians' perspectives on shared decision-making in ADHD. *Pediatrics, 127*, e188–e196.

Fingarette, H. (1988). *Heavy drinking: The myth of alcoholism as a disease*. Berkeley, CA: University of California Press.

Finucane, M. L., Alhakami, A., Slovic, P., & Johnson, S. M. (2000). The affect heuristic in judgments of risk and benefits. *Journal of Behavioral Decision Making, 13*, 1–17.

Firestone, R. W., & Seiden, R. H. (1987). Microsuicide and suicidal threats of everyday life. *Psychotherapy, 24*, 31–39.

Fischhoff, B. (1975). Hindsight foresight: The effect of outcome knowledge on judgment under uncertainty. *Journal of Experimental Psychology: Human Perception and Performance, 1*, 288–299.

Fischhoff, B., Slovic, P., & Lichtenstein, S. (1980). Knowing what you want: Measuring labile values. In T. S. Wallsten (Ed.), *Cognitive processes in choice and decision behavior* (pp. 117–141). Hillsdale, NJ: Erlbaum.

Fisher, J. & Corcoran, K. (2007). *Measures for clinical practice and research: A sourcebook*. New York, NY: Oxford University Press.

Fisher, R., & Ury, W. (1991). *Getting to yes: Negotiating agreement without giving in* (2nd ed.). New York, NY: Penguin.

Fisher, W. W., Piazza, C. C., & Roane, H. S. (2011). *Handbook of applied behavior analysis*. New York, NY: Guilford.

Flannelly, L. T., & Flannelly, K. J. (2000). Reducing people's judgment bias about their level of knowledge. *Psychological Record, 50,* 587–600.

Flew, A. (1985). *Thinking about social thinking.* Oxford, UK: Blackwell.

Fong, G. T., Kravitz, D. H., & Nisbett, R. E. (1986). The effects of statistical training on thinking about everyday problems. *Cognitive Psychology, 18,* 253–292.

Forsetlung, L., Bjømdal, A., Rashidian, A., Jamtvedt, G., O'Brien, M. A., Wolf, F., Davis, D., Odgaard-Jensen, J., & Oxman, A. D. (2009). Continuing education meetings and workshops: Effects on professional practice and health care outcomes. *Cochrane Library Issue 2.*

Foucault, M. (1981). *Power-knowledge: Selected interviews and other writings, 1972–1977.* New York, NY: Pantheon.

Foucault, M. (1973). *The birth of the clinic: An archeology of medical perception.* New York, NY: Pantheon.

Fox, R. C., & Swazey, J. P. (1974). *The courage to fail: A social view of organ transplants and dialysis.* Chicago, IL: University of Chicago Press.

Foxx, R. M., & Roland, C. E. (2005). The self-esteem fallacy. In J. W. Jacobson, R. M. Foxx, & J. A. Mulick (Eds.), *Controversial therapies for developmental disabilities: Fad, fashion, and science in professional practice* (pp. 101–112). Mahwah, NJ: Erlbaum.

Francis, A. (2010a, April 21). DSM5 temper dysregulation—Good intentions, bad solution. *Psychiatric Times.*

Francis, A. (2010b). The first draft of DSM-V: If accepted, will fan the flames of false positive diagnoses. *BMJ, 340:*c1168.

Francis, A. (2010c, July 23). New guidelines for diagnosing Alzheimer's wishful thinking with dangerous consequences. *Psychiatric Times.*

Francis, A. (2010d, July 6). Normality is an endangered species: Psychiatric fads and overdiagnosis. *Psychiatric Times.*

Frank, J. D., & Frank, J. B. (1991). *Persuasion and healing: A comparative study of psychotherapy* (3rd ed.). Baltimore, MD: John Hopkins Press.

Frankfurt, H. G. (2005). *On bullshit.* Princeton, NJ: Princeton University Press.

Frazer, J. G. (1925). *The golden bough: A study in magic and religion.* London, UK: Macmillan.

Freeman, A. C., & Sweeney, K. (2001). Why general practitioners do not implement evidence: qualitative study. *BMJ, 323,* 1100–1102.

French, J. R. P., Jr., & Raven, B. (1959). The bases of social power. In D. Cartwright (Ed.), *Studies in social power* (pp. 150–167). Ann Arbor, MI: University of Michigan, Institute for Social Research.

Friedson, E. (Ed.). (1973). *Professions and their prospects.* Beverly Hills, CA: Sage.

Friedson, E. (1994). *Professionalism reborn? Theory, prophecy, and policy.* Chicago, IL: University of Chicago Press.

From the president. (1986, November). *NASW News, 31*, 2.

From the president. (1987, April). *NASW News, 32*, 2.

Fromm, E. (1963). *Escape from freedom*. New York, NY: Holt, Rinehart & Winston.

Frye v. United States, 293 F 1013 (DC Cir. 1923).

Fugh-Berman, A., & Ahari, S. (2007, April). Following the script: How drug reps make friends and influence doctors. *PloS Medicine, 4*(4), e150.

Furedi, F. (2006). *Culture of fear revisited: Risk taking and the morality of low expectation*. New York, NY: Continuum.

Furnham, A. F. (1988). Lay theories: Everyday understanding of problems in the social sciences. New York, NY: Pergamon.

Furukawa, T. A. (1999). From effect size into number needed to treat. *The Lancet, 353*, 1680.

Gahagan, J. (1984). *Social interaction and its management*. London, UK: Methuen.

Gaissmaier, W. & Gigerenzer, G. (2011). When misinformed patients try to make informed health decisions. In G. Gigerenzer, & J. A. M. Gray (Eds.), *Better doctors, better patients, better decisions* (pp. 29-43). Cambridge, MA: MIT Press.

Galea, S., Tracy, M., Hoggatt, K. J., DiMaggio, C., & Karpati, A. (2011). Estimated deaths attributable to social factors in the United States. *American Journal of Public Health, 10*, online ahead of print, June 16.

Gallup Organization. (2001). The Americans' belief in psychic and paranormal phenomena is up over the last decade. Retrieved July 3, 2001.

Gambrill, E. (1999). Evidence based practice: an alternative to authority-based practice. *Families in society, 80*, 341–350.

Gambrill, E. (2002). Educational policy and accreditation standards: Do they work for clients? *Journal of Social Work Education*, 226–239.

Gambrill, E. (2003). Evidence based practice: Implications for knowledge development and use in social work. In A. Rosen & E. K. Proctor (Eds.), *Developing practice guidelines for social work interventions: Issues, methods and research agenda* (pp. 37–58). New York, NY: Columbia University Press.

Gambrill, E. (2006). Evidence based practice: Choices ahead. *Research on Social Work Practice, 16*, 338–357.

Gambrill, E. (2010). Evidence-informed practice: antidote to propaganda in the helping professions? *Research on Social Work Practice, 20*, 302–320.

Gambrill, E. (2011). Evidence-based practice and the ethics of discretion. *Journal of Social Work, 11*, 26–48.

Gambrill, E. (2012a). *Propaganda in the helping profession*. New York, NY: Oxford University Press.

Gambrill, E. (2012b). *Social work practice: A critical thinker's guide* (3rd ed.). New York, NY: Oxford University Press.

Gambrill, E. D. (1997). Social work education: Possible futures. In M. Reisch & E. Gambrill (Eds.), *Social work in the 21st century* (pp. 317–327). Thousand Oaks, CA: Pine Forge Press.

Gambrill, E. D., & Gibbs, L. (2002). Making practice decisions: Is what's good for the goose good for the gander? *Ethical Human Sciences & Services, 4,* 31–46.

Gambrill, E., & Gibbs, L. (2009). *Critical thinking for helping professionals: A skills based workbook* (3rd ed.). New York, NY: Oxford University Press.

Gambrill, E., & Reiman, A. (2011, May 25). A propaganda index for reviewing manuscripts: An exploratory study. *PloS ONE.*

Gambrill, E., & Shlonsky, A. (2001). The need for comprehensive risk management systems in child welfare. *Children and Youth Services Review, 23,* 79–107.

Gamwell, L., & Tomes, N. (1995). *Madness in America: Cultural and medical perceptions of mental illness before 1914.* Ithaca, NY: Cornell University Press.

Gandhi, A. G., Murphy-Graham, E., Petrosino, A., Chrismer, S. S., & Weiss, C. H. (2007). The devil is in the details. *Evaluation Review, 31,* 43–74.

Ganzach, Y. (2000). The weighing of pathological and non-pathological information in clinical judgment. *Acta Psychologica, 104,* 87–101.

Garb, H. N. (1998). *Studying the clinician: Judgment, research and psychological assessment.* Washington, DC: American Psychological Association.

Gardner, M. (1957). *Fads and fallacies in the name of science.* New York, NY: Dover.

Gawande, A. (2010). *The checklist manifesto: How to get things right.* New York, NY: Metropolitan Books.

Gelles, R. J. (1982). Applying research on family violence to clinical practice. *Journal of Marriage and the Family, 44*(1), 9–20.

Gellner, E. (1992). *Postmodernism, reason, and religion.* New York, NY: Routledge.

Gentry, E., Poirier, K., Wilkinson, T., Nhean, S., Nyborn, J., & Siegel, M. (2011). Alcohol advertising at Boston subway stations: An assessment of exposure by race and socioeconomic status. *American Journal of Public Health, 101:*1936–1941.

Gergen, K. J. (1987). Introduction: Toward a metapsychology. In H. J. Stam, T. B. Rogers, & K. J. Gergen (Eds.), *The analysis of psychological theory: Metapsychological perspectives* (pp. 115–130). Cambridge, MA: Hemisphere.

Gibbs, L. (1991). *Scientific reasoning for social workers.* New York, NY: McGraw-Hill.

Gibbs, L. (2003). *Evidence-based practice for the helping professions.* Pacific Grove, CA: Brooks/Cole.

Gibbs, L., & Gambrill, E. (2002). Evidence-based practice: Counterarguments to objections. *Research on Social Work Practice, 14,* 452–476.

Gigerenzer, G. (2002a). *Calculated risks: How to know when numbers deceive you.* New York, NY: Simon & Schuster.

Gigerenzer, G. (2002b). *Reckoning with risk: Learning to live with uncertainty*. New York, NY: Penguin.

Gigerenzer, G. (2005). Fast and frugal heuristics: The tools of bounded rationality. In D. J. Koehler & N. Harvey (Eds.), *The Blackwell handbook of judgment and decision-making* (pp. 62–88). Malden, MA: Blackwell.

Gigerenzer, G. (2007). *Gut feelings: The intelligence of the unconscious*. New York, NY: Viking.

Gigerenzer, G., & Brighton, H. (2011). Homo heuristicus: Why biased minds make better inferences. In G. Gigerenzer, R. Hertwig, & T. Pachur (Eds.), *Heuristics: The foundations of adaptive behavior* (pp. 2–27). New York, NY: Oxford University Press.

Gigerenzer, G., Gaissmaier, W., Kurz-Milcke, E., Schwartz, L. M., & Woloshin, S. (2007). Helping doctors and patients make sense of health statistics. *Psychological Science in the Public Interest, 8*, 53–96.

Gigerenzer, G., & Goldstein, D. G. (1999). Betting on one good reason: The take the best heuristic. In G. Gigerenzer, P. M. Todd, & ABC Research Group (Eds.), *Simple heuristics that make us smart* (pp. 75–95). New York, NY: Oxford University Press.

Gigerenzer, G., & Gray, J. A. M. (Eds.). (2011). *Better doctors, better patients, better decisions: Envisioning health care 2020*. Cambridge, MA: MIT Press.

Gigerenzer, G., Hertwig, R., & Pachur, T. (Eds.). (2011). *Heuristics: The foundations of adaptive behavior*. New York, NY: Oxford University Press.

Gilbert, P. (1994). Male violence: Toward an integration. In J. Archer (Ed.), *Male violence* (pp. 352–389). London, UK: Routledge.

Gilovich, T. (1991). *How we know what isn't so: The fallibility of human reason in everyday life*. New York, NY: Macmillan.

Gilovich, T., & Griffin, D. (2002). Introduction—Heuristics and biases: Then and now. In T. Gilovich, D. Griffin, & D. Kahneman (Eds.), *Heuristics and biases: The psychology of intuitive judgement* (pp. 1–18). New York, NY: Cambridge.

Gilovich, T., Griffin, D., & Kahneman, D. (Eds.). (2002). *Heuristics and biases: The psychology of intuitive judgement*. New York, NY: Cambridge University Press.

Gilovich, T., & Savitsky, K. (2002). Like goes with like: The role of representativeness in erroneous and pseudo-scientific beliefs. In T. Gilovich, D. Griffin, & D. Kahneman (Eds.), *Heuristics and biases: The psychology of intuitive judgement* (pp. 616–624). New York, NY: Cambridge.

Glasziou, P., Del Mar, C., & Salisbury, J. (2003). *Evidence-based medicine workbook*. London, UK: BMJ.

Glasziou, P., Vandenbroucke, E. J., & Chalmers, I. (2004). Assessing the quality of research. *BMJ, 328*, 39–41.

Glazener, C. M. A., Evans, J. H., & Petro, R. E. (2005). Alarm interventions for nocturnal enuresis in children. *Cochrane Library*, Issue 2. Chichester, UK: John Wiley & Sons.

Goethals, G. R., & Reckman, R. F. (1973). The perception of consistency in attitudes. *Journal of Experimental Social Psychology*, 9, 491–501.

Goldberg, L. R. (1959). The effectiveness of clinicians' judgements: The diagnosis of organic brain damage from the Bender-Gestalt test. *Journal of Consulting Psychology*, 23, 25–33.

Goldberg, R. L. (1970). Man vs. model of man: A rationale, plus some evidence, for a method of improving on clinical inference. *Psychological Bulletin*, 73, 422–432.

Goldfried, M. R. (2011). Generating research questions from clinical experience: Therapists' experiences in using CBT for panic disorder. *Behavior Therapist*, 34, 57–62.

Goldiamond, I. (1974). Toward a constructional approach to social problems: Ethical and constitutional issues raised by applied behavior analysis. *Behaviorism*, 2, 1–84.

Goldiamond, I. (1984). Training parent trainers and ethicists in nonlinear analysis of behavior. In R. F. Dangel & R. A. Polster (Eds.), *Parent training: Foundations of research and practice* (pp. 504–546). New York, NY: Guilford.

Goldstein, A. P. (1980). Relationship enhancement methods. In F. H. Kanfer & A. P. Goldstein (Eds.), *Helping people change: A textbook of methods* (pp. 18–57). Elmsford, NY: Pergamon.

Goldstein, D. G., & Gigerenzer, G. (1999). The recognition heuristic: How ignorance makes us smart. In G. Gigerenzer, P. M. Todd, & ABC Research group. *Simple heuristics that make us smart* (pp. 37–58). New York, NY: Oxford University Press.

Goleman, D. (1995). Depression in the old can be deadly, but the symptoms are often missed. *New York Times*, September 6.

Gollwitzer, P. M. (1999). Implementation intentions: Strong effects of simple plans. *American Psychologist*, 54, 493–503.

Gollwitzer, P. M., Bayer, U. C., & McCulloch, K. C. (2005). The control of the unwanted. In R. R. Hassin, J. S. Uleman, & J. A. Bargh (Eds.), *The new unconscious* (pp. 485–515). New York, NY: Oxford University Press.

Gondolf, E. W., & Fisher, E. R. (1988). *Battered women as survivors: An alternative to treating learned helplessness*. Lexington, MA: Lexington Books.

Goodman, D., Brownlee, S., Chang, C. H., & Fisher, E. (2010). Regional and racial variation in primary care and the quality of care among Medicare beneficiaries. http://www.rwjf.org/pr/product. Downloaded 10/23/11.

Gordon, D. R. (1988). Clinical science and clinical expertise: Changing boundaries between art and science in medicine. In M. Lock & D. R. Gordon (Eds.), *Biomedicine examined (culture, illness, and healing)* (pp. 257–295). New York, NY: Springer.

Gorenstein, E. E. (1992). *The science of mental illness*. New York, NY: Academic Press.

Gorman, D. M. (1998). The irrelevance of evidence in the development of school-based drug prevention policy, 1986–1996. *Evaluation Review, 22*(1), 118–146.

Gorman, D. M., & Huber, J. C. (2009). The social construction of "evidence-based" drug prevention programs: A reanalysis of data from the Drug Abuse Resistance Education (DARE) Program. *Evaluation Review, 33,* 396–414.

Gorman, D. M., Conde, E., & Huber, J. C., Jr. (2007). The creation of evidence in "evidence-based" drug prevention: A Critique of the Strengthening Families Program Plus Life Skills Training Evaluation. *Drug and Alcohol Review, 26,* 585–593.

Gorman, M. (1999). Avoiding the seven deadly sins, or technology and the future of library service in academic libraries. In D. S. Montanelli, & P. F. Stenstrom (Eds.), *People come first: User-centered academic library service, 6–7.* Chicago, IL: Association of College and Research Libraries.

Gorman, P. N., & Helfand, M. (1995). Information seeking in primary care: How physicians choose which clinical questions to pursue and which to leave unanswered. *Medical Decision Making, 15,* 113–119.

Gottlieb, S. (2003). One in three doctors don't tell patients about services they can't have. *BMJ, 327,* 123.

Gøtzsche, P. C., & Jørgensen, K. J. (2011). The breast screening program and misinforming the public. *J R Socialized Medicine, 104,* 361–369.

Gøtzsche, P. C., Liberati, A., Torri, V., & Rossetti, L. (1996). Beware of surrogate endpoints. *International Journal of Technology Assessment in Health Care, 12,* 238–246.

Goulding, R. (2004). One in twelve older people are prescribed the wrong drug. *Archives of Internal Medicine, 164,* 305–312.

GRADE Working Group. (2004). Grading quality of evidence and strength of recommendations. *BMJ, 328,* 1490.

Gravel, K., Légaré, F., & Graham, I. D. (2006). Barriers and facilitators to implementing shared decision-making in clinical practice: A systematic review of health professionals' perceptions. *Implementation Science, 1,* 2006:16 doi:10.1186. Downloaded 10/23/11.

Gray, J. A. M. (1998). Where is the chief knowledge officer? *BMJ, 317,* 832.

Gray, J. A. M. (2001a). *Evidence-based healthcare: How to make health policy and management decisions* (2nd ed.). New York, NY: Churchill Livingstone.

Gray, J. A. M. (2001b). Evidence-based medicine for professionals. In A. Edwards & G. Elwyn (Eds.), *Evidence-based patient choice: Inevitable or impossible?* (pp. 19–33). New York, NY: Oxford University Press.

Gray, W. D. (1991). *Thinking critically about new age ideas.* Belmont, CA: Wadsworth.

Gray-Little, B., & Kaplan, D. (2000). Race and ethnicity in psychotherapy research. In C. R. Snyder & R. E. Ingram (Eds.), *Handbook of psychological change* (pp. 591–613). New York, NY: John Wiley & Sons.

Greenberg, S. A. (2009). How citation distortions create unfounded authority: Analysis of a citation network. *BMJ, 339*:b2680.

Greenhalgh, T. (2010). *How to read a paper: The basis of evidence-based medicine* (3rd ed.). London: BMJ Press.

Greenhalgh, T., & Hurwitz, B. (1998). *Narrative based medicine: Dialogue and discourse in clinical practice*. London, UK: BMJ Press.

Greenhalgh, T., Robert, G., Macfarlane, F., Bate, P., & Kyriakidou, O. (2004). Diffusion of innovations in service organizations: systematic review and recommendations. *The Milbank Quarterly, 82*, 581–629.

Greenwald, G. (2009). *Drug decriminalization in Portugal: Lessons for creating fair and successful drug policies*. Retrieved Jan. 28, 2011 from the Cato Institute website www.cato.org/pub.

Gresham, F., & MacMillan, D. (1997). Denial and defensiveness in the place of fact and reason: Rejoinder to Smith and Lovaas. *Behavioral Disorders, 22*(4), 219–230.

Grice, H. P. (1975). Logic and conversation. In P. Cole & J. Morgan (Eds.), *Syntax and semantics* (Vol. 2, pp. 41–58). New York, NY: Academic Press.

Grilli, R., Magrini, N., Penna, A., Mura, G., & Liberati, A. (2000). Practice guidelines developed by specialty societies: The need for a critical appraisal. *The Lancet, 355*, 103–106.

Gross, P. R., & Levitt, N. (1994). *Higher superstition: The academic left and its quarrels with science*. Baltimore, MD: Johns Hopkins University Press.

Grove, W. M., & Meehl, P. E. (1996). Comparative efficiency of informal (subjective, impressionistic) and formal (mechanical, algorithmic) prediction procedures: The clinical-statistical controversy. *Psychology, Public Policy & Law, 2*, 293–323.

Grove, W. M., Zald, D. H., Lebow, B. S., Snitz, B. E., & Nelson, C. (2000). Clinical vs. mechanical prediction: A meta-analysis. *Psychological Assessment, 12*, 19–30.

Gusfield, J. R. (2003). Constructing the ownership of social problems: Fun and profit in the welfare state. In J. D. Orcutt & D. R. Ruby (Eds.), *Drugs, alcohol, and social problems* (pp. 7–18). New York, NY: Rowman & Littlefield.

Guyatt, G. H., Meade, M. O., Jaeschke, R. Z., Cook, D. J., & Haynes, R. B. (2000). Practitioners of evidence-based care: Not all clinicians need to appraise evidence from scratch but need some skills. *BMJ, 320*, 954–955.

Guyatt, G. H., Oxman, A. D., Schunemann, H. J., Tugwell, P., & Knotterus, A. (Eds.) (2011). GRADE guidelines: A new series of articles in the *Journal of Clinical Epidemiology. Journal of Clinical Epidemiology, 64*, 380–382.

Guyatt, G. H., Oxman, A. D., Vist, G. E., Kunz, R., Falck-Ytter, Y., Alonso-Coello, P., & Schünemann, H. (2008. GADE: An emerging consensus on rating quality of evidence and strength of recommendations. *BMJ, 336*, 924–926.

Guyatt, G., & Rennie, D. (2002). *User's guide to the medical literature: A manual for evidence-based clinical practice*. The Evidence-Based Medicine Working Group JAMA & Archives. Chicago, IL: American Medical Association.

Guyatt, G., Rennie, D., Meade, M., & Cook, D. J. (2008). *Users' guides to the medical literature: A manual for evidence-based clinical practice* (2nd ed.). The Evidence-Based Medicine Working Group JAMA & Archives. Chicago, IL: American Medical Association.

Hagert, G., & Waern, Y. (1986). On implicit assumptions in reasoning. In T. Myers, K. Brown, & B. McGonigle (Eds.), *Reasoning and discourse* (pp. 95–115). Orlando, FL: Academic Press.

Hakim, D. (2011). A disabled boy's death and a system in disarray. *New York Times*, June 5.

Hall, D. F., Loftus, E. F., & Tousignant, J. P. (1984). Post-event information and changes in recollection for a national event. In G. L. Wells & E. F. Loftus (Eds.), *Eyewitness testimony: Psychological perspectives* (pp. 124–141). Cambridge, UK: Cambridge University Press.

Halpern, D. F. (1998). Teaching critical thinking for transfer across domains: Dispositions, skills, structure, training, and meta-cognitive monitoring. *American Psychologist, 53,* 449–455.

Halpern, D. F. (2003). *Thought & knowledge: An introduction to critical thinking* (4th ed.). Mahwah, NJ: Erlbaum.

Halpern, J. (2001). *From detached concern to empathy: Humanizing medical practice*. New York, NY: Oxford University Press.

Hamblin, C. L. (1970). *Fallacies*. London, UK: Methuen.

Hamm, R. M. (2003). Medical decisions scripts: Combining cognitive scripts and judgment strategies to account fully for medical decision making. In D. Hardman & L. Macchi (Eds.), *Thinking: Psychological perspectives on reasoning, judgment and decision making* (pp. 315–345). New York, NY: John Wiley & Sons.

Hammond, K. R. (1996). *Human judgment and social policy: Irreducible uncertainty, inevitable error, and unavoidable injustice*. New York, NY: Oxford University Press.

Hammond, K. R. (2000). *Judgments under stress*. New York, NY: Oxford University Press.

Hanks, H., Hobbs, C. J., & Wynne, J. M. (1988). Early signs and recognition of sexual abuse in the pre-school child. In K. Browne, C. Davies, & P. Stratton (Eds.), *Early prediction and prevention of child abuse* (pp. 139–160). Chichester, UK: John Wiley & Sons.

Hanley, B., Truesdale, A., King, A., Elbourne, D., & Chalmers, I. (2001). Involving consumers in designing, conducting, and interpreting randomised controlled trials: Questionnaire survey. *BMJ, 322,* 519–523.

Hansen, H. V., & Pinto, R. C. (Eds.). (1995). *Fallacies: Classical and contemporary readings*. University Park, PA: Pennsylvania State University Press.

Harcourt, B. E. (2007). *Against prediction: Punishing and policing in an actuarial age.* Chicago, IL: University of Chicago Press.

Harmon, G. (1986). *Change in view: Principles of Reasoning.* Cambridge, MA: MIT Press.

Harris, G. (2004, May 14). Pfizer to pay $430 million over promoting drug to doctors. *New York Times,* p. 1.

Harris, G. (2011, July 10). New for aspiring doctors, the people skills test. *New York Times,* p. 260.

Harris, G. (2011, Oct. 7). U.S. panel says no to prostate test for healthy men: Sharp dissent is seen. *New York Times,* pp. 1, 3.

Hartman, D. P., Barrios, B. A., & Wood, D. D. (2004). Principles of behavioral observation. In S. N. Haynes & E. M. Heiby (Eds.), *Comprehensive handbook of psychological assessment: Vol. 3. Behavioral assessment.* Hoboken, NJ: John Wiley & Sons.

Haskell, R. E. (2001). *Transfer of learning: Cognition, instruction, & reasoning.* San Diego, CA: Academic Press.

Hastie, R., & Dawes, R. (2001). *Rational choice in an uncertain world: The psychology of judgment and decision making.* Thousand Oaks, CA: Sage.

Hathaway, S. R. (1948). Some considerations relative to nondirective counseling. *Journal of Clinical Psychology, 4,* 226–231.

Hayakawa, S. I. (1978). *Language in thought and action* (4th ed.). New York, NY: Harcourt Brace Jovanovich.

Hayek, F. A. (1967). *Studies in philosophy, politics and economics.* London: Routledge & Kegan Paul.

Hayek, F. A. (1976). *Law, legislation and liberty: Vol. 2. The mirage of social justice.* Chicago, IL: University of Chicago Press.

Hayes, J. A., Gelso, C. J., & Hummel, A. M. (2011). Managing countertransference. *Psychotherapy, 48,* 88–97.

Hayes-Roth, F., Klahr, P., & Mostow, D. J. (1981). Advice taking and knowledge refinement: An iterative view of skill acquisition. In J. R. Anderson (Ed.), *Cognitive skills and their acquisition* (pp. 231–253). Hillsdale, NJ: Erlbaum.

Haynes, R. B., Devereaux, P. J., & Guyatt, G. H. (2002). Editorial: Clinical expertise in the era of evidence-based medicine and patient choice. *Evidence-Based Medicine, 7,* 36–38.

Haynes, S. N. (1992). *Models of causality and psychopathology: Toward dynamic, synthetic and nonlinear models of behavior disorders.* New York, NY: Macmillan.

Haynes, S. N., & O'Brien, W. H. (2000). *Principles and practice of behavioral assessment.* New York, NY: Kluwer Academic/Plenum.

Head, S. J., Bogers, A. J. J. C., Serruys, P. W., Takkenberg, J. J. M., & Kappetein, A. P. (2011). A crucial factor in shared decision making: The team approach. *The Lancet, 377,* 1836.

Healy, D. (2003). Lines of evidence on the risk of suicide with selected serotonin reuptake inhibitors. *Psychotherapy and Psychosomatics, 72*, 71–79.

Hellman, L. D., Morrison, T. L., & Abramowitz, S. I. (1987). Therapist flexibility/rigidity and work stress. *Professional Psychology, 18*, 21–27.

Herbert, R. (2002). We'd like to thank the academy. *Observer, 15*, 1/23–28. Washington, DC: American Psychological Association.

Herbst, A. L., Ulfelder, H., & Poskanzer, D. C. (1971). Adenocarcinoma of the vagina: Association of maternal stilbestrol therapy with tumor appearances in young women. *New England Journal of Medicine, 284*, 878–881.

Heritage, J., & Clayman, S. (2010). *Talk in action: Interactions, identities, and institutions.* Malden, MA: Blackwell.

Herron, W. G., & Rouslin, S. (1984). *Issues in psychotherapy.* Washington, DC: Oryn Publications.

Hertwig, R., Buchan, H., Davis, D. A., Gaissmaier, W., Harter, M., Kolpatzik, K., . . . Wormer, H. (2011). How will health care professionals and patients work together in 2020? A manifesto for change. In G. Gigerenzer & J. A. M. Gray (Eds.), *Better doctors, better patients, better decisions: Envisioning health care 2020* (pp. 317–338). Cambridge, MA: MIT Press.

Herzberg, D. (2009). *Happy pills in America: From Miltown to Prozac.* Baltimore, MD: Johns Hopkins University Press.

Heyman, G. M. (2009). *Addiction: A disorder of choice.* Cambridge, MA: Harvard University Press.

Heyman, R. E., & Slep, A. M. S. (2004). Analogue behavioral observation. In S. N. Haynes & E. M. Heiby (Eds.); M. Hersen (Editor in chief), *Comprehensive handbook of psychological assessment: Vol. 3. Behavioral assessment* (pp. 162–180). Hoboken, NJ: John Wiley & Sons.

Higgins, J. P. T., & Green, S. (Eds.). (2009). Cochrane handbook for systematic reviews of interventions. www.cochrane.org/resources/handbook (version 5.1.0, March, 2011)

Higgins, R. L., Snyder, C. R., & Berglas, S. (1990). *Self-handicapping: The paradox that isn't.* New York, NY: Plenum Press.

Hillebrandt, D., & Imray, C. (2004). Minerva. *BMJ, 328*, 1210.

Hinds, P. J. (1999). The curse of expertise: The effects of expertise and debiasing methods on prediction of novice performance. *Journal of Experimental Psychology: Applied, 5*, 205–221.

Hobbs, C. J., & Wynne, J. M. (1989). Sexual abuse of English boys and girls: The importance of anal examination. *Child Abuse and Neglect, 13*, 195–210.

Hobbs, N. (1975). *The futures of children: Recommendations of the Project on Classification of Exceptional Children.* San Francisco, CA: Jossey-Bass.

Hodgkinson, G. P., & Sparrow, P. R. (2002). *The competent organization: A psychological analysis of the strategic management process*. Buckingham, UK: Open University Press.

Hofer, B. K. (2001). Personal epistemology research: Implications for learning and teaching. *Journal of Educational Psychology Review, 13*, 353–383.

Hofer, B. K., & Pintrich, P. R. (Eds.). (2002). *Personal epistemology: The psychology of beliefs about knowledge and knowing*. Mahwah, NJ: Erlbaum.

Hogarth, R. M. (1980). *Judgment and choice: The psychology of decisions*. New York, NY: John Wiley & Sons.

Hogarth, R. M. (1987). *Judgement and choice: The psychology of decision* (2nd ed.). New York, NY: John Wiley & Sons.

Hogarth, R. M. (2001). *Educating intuition*. Chicago, IL: University of Chicago Press.

Hoge, M. A., Tomdora, J., & Stuart, G. W. (2003). Training in evidence-based practice. *Psychiatric Clinics of North America, 26*, 851–865.

Holland, J. H., Holyoak, K. J., Nisbett, R. E., & Thagard, P. R. (1986). *Induction: Processes of inference, learning, and discovery*. Cambridge, MA: MIT Press.

Holmes, D. S. (1978). Projection as a defense mechanism. *Psychological Bulletin, 85*, 677–688.

Holmes, T. H. (2004). Ten categories of statistical errors: A guide for research in endocrinology and metabolism. *American Journal of Endrocrinological Metabolism 286*, e495–e501.

Hook, D., & Eagle, G. (Eds.). (2002). *Psychopathology and social prejudice*. Lansdowne, South Africa: University of Cape Town Press.

Hops, H., Davis, B., & Longoria, N. (1995). Methodological issues in direct observation: Illustrations with the Living in Familiar Environments (LIFE) coding system. *Journal of Clinical Child Psychology, 24*, 193–203.

Houts, A. C. (1984). Effects of clinical, theoretical orientation and patient explanatory bias on initial clinical judgments. *Professional Psychology: Research and Practice, 15*, 284–293.

Houts, A. C. (2002). Discovery, invention, and the expansion of the modern diagnostic and statistical manuals of mental disorders. In L. E. Beutler & M. L. Malik (Eds.), *Rethinking the DSM: A psychological perspective* (pp. 17–65). Washington, DC: American Psychological Association.

Houts, A. C., & Galante, M. (1985). The impact of evaluative disposition and subsequent information on clinical impressions. *Journal of Social and Clinical Psychology, 3*, 201–212.

Howitt, D. (1992). *Child abuse errors: When good intentions go wrong*. New York, NY: Harvester Wheatsheaf.

Hoyle, R. H., Harris, M. J., & Judd, C. M. (2002). *Research methods in social relations*. Pacific Grove, CA: Wadsworth.

Huber, R. B. (1963). *Influencing through argument*. New York, NY: David McKay.

Huck, S. W., & Sandler, H. M. (1979). *Rival hypotheses: Alternative interpretations of data based conclusions.* New York, NY: Harper & Row.

Huff, D. (1954). *How to lie with statistics.* New York, NY: Norton.

Hughes, C. E., & Stevens, A. (2010). What can we learn from the Portuguese decriminalization of illicit drugs? *British Journal of Criminology, 50,* 999–1022.

Hunsley, J., Lee, C. M., & Wood, J. M. (2003). Controversial and questionable assessment techniques. In S. O. Lilienfeld, S. J. Lynn, & J. M. Lohr (Eds.), *Science and pseudoscience in clinical psychology* (pp. 39–76). New York, NY: Guilford.

Hunsley, J., & Mash, E. J. (Eds.). (2008). *The science and art of clinical assessment.* New York, NY: Oxford University Press.

Hyman, R. (1961). On prior information and creativity. *Psychological Reports, 9,* 151–161.

Illich, I. (1976). *Limits to medicine: Medical nemesis, the expropriation of health.* London, UK: Boyars.

Illich, I., Zola, I. K., McNight, J., Caplan, J. A., & Shaiken, H. (1977). *Disabling professions.* Salem, NH: Marion Boyers.

Illouz, E. (2008). *Saving the modern soul: Therapy, emotions, and the culture of self-help.* Berkeley, CA: University of California Press.

Imel, Z. E., Wampold, B. E., Miller, S. D., & Fleming, R. R. (2008). Distinctions without a difference: Direct comparisons of psychotherapies for alcohol use disorders. *Psychology of Addictive Behaviors, 22,* 533–543.

Ioannidis, J. P. A. (2005). Why most published research findings are false. *PloS Medicine, 2*(8), e124.

Ioannidis, J. P. A. (2008). Why most discovered true associations are inflated. *Epidemiology, 19,* 640-648.

Isaacs, D., & Fitzgerald, D. (1999). Seven alternatives to evidence based medicine. *BMJ, 319,* 1618.

Isen, A. M., Shalker, T. E., Clark, M., & Karp, L. (1978). Affect, accessibility of material in memory, and behavior: A cognitive loop? *Journal of Personality and Social Psychology, 36,* 1–12.

Jaarsma, T. (2005). Inter-professional team approach to patients with heart failure. *Heart, 91,* 832–838.

Jacobs, J. (1985). "In the best interests of the child": Official court reports as an artifact of negotiated reality in children's assessment centers. *Clinical Sociology Review, 3,* 88–108.

Jacobson, J. W., Foxx, R. M., & Mulick, J. A. (Eds.). (2005). *Controversial therapies for developmental disabilities: Fad, fashion, and science in professional practice.* Mahwah, NJ: Erlbaum.

Jacobson, J. W., Mulick, J. A., & Schwartz, A. A. (1995). A history of facilitated communication: Science, pseudoscience, and antiscience working group on facilitated communication. *American Psychologist, 50,* 750–765.

Jadad, A. R., & Enkin, M. W. (2007). *Randomized controlled trials: Questions, answers and musings* (2nd ed.). Malden, MA: Blackwell.

James, W. (1975). *Pragmatism*. Cambridge, MA: Harvard University Press.

Janicek, M., & Hitchcock, D. L. (2005). *Evidence-based practice: Logic and critical thinking in medicine*. Chicago, IL: American Medical Association.

Janis, I. L. (1982). *Groupthink: Psychological studies of policy decisions and fiascos* (2nd ed.). Boston, MA: Houghton Mifflin.

Janis, I. L., & Mann, L. (1977). *Decision making: A psychological analysis of conflict, choice and commitment*. New York, NY: Free Press.

Janofsky, M. (2001, June 19). Therapists are sentenced in girl's "rebirthing" death. *The New York Times*, A12.

Janson, D. (1988, April 22). End to suit denied in shooting death. *The New York Times*, AI13/2.

Jarvis, W. T. (1990). *Dubious dentistry: A dental continuing education course*. Loma Linda University School of Dentistry, Loma Linda, CA: Loma Linda University School of Dentistry.

Jehn, K. A. (2004). A qualitative analysis of conflict types and dimensions in organizational groups. *Administrative Science Quarterly, 42*(3), 530–557.

Jekel, J., Elmore, J. G., & Katz, D. (1996). *Epidemiology, biostatistics, and preventive medicine*. Philadelphia, PA: Saunders.

Jennings, D. L., Amabile, T. M., & Ross, L. (1982). Informal covariation assessment: Data-based versus theory-based judgments. In D. Kahneman, P. Slovic, & A. Tversky (Eds.), *Judgment under uncertainty: Heuristics and biases* (pp. 211–230). New York, NY: Cambridge University Press.

Jensen, D. D. (1989). Pathologies of science, precognition and modern psychophysics. *The Skeptical Inquirer, 13*, 147–160.

Jensen, J. M., & Fraser, M. W. (2011). *Social policy for children and families: A risk and resilience perspective* (2nd ed.). Thousand Oaks, CA: Sage.

Johnson, A. (2009, June 30). Cost effectiveness of cancer drugs is questioned. *Wall Street Journal*.

Johnson, D. M. (1972). *A systematic introduction to the psychology of thinking*. New York, NY: Harper & Row.

Johnson, E. J. (1988). Expertise and decision under uncertainty: Performance and process. In M. T. H. Chi, R. Glaser, & M. J. Farr (Eds.), *The nature of expertise* (pp. 209–228). Hillsdale, NJ: Erlbaum.

Johnson, E. J., et al. (2005). Making better decisions: From measuring to constructing preferences. *Health Psychology, 24*, s17–s22.

AU: List a
authors?

Johnson, W. L. (2011). The validity and reliability of the California Family Risk Assessment under practice conditions in the field: A prospective study. *Child Abuse & Neglect, 35*, 18–28.

Johnson-Laird, P. N. (1983). *Mental models: Towards a cognitive science of language, inference, and consciousness.* Cambridge, MA: Harvard University Press.

Johnson-Laird, P. N. (1985). Logical thinking: Does it occur in daily life? Can it be taught? In S. F. Chipman, J. W. Segal, & R. Glaser (Eds.), *Thinking and learning skills: Vol. 2. Research and open questions* (pp. 293–318). Hillsdale, NJ: Erlbaum.

Jones, E. E., & Harris, V. A. (1967). The attribution of attitudes. *Journal of Experimental Social Psychology, 3*, 1–24.

Jordan, C., & Franklin, C. (2003). *Clinical assessment for social workers: Quantitative and qualitative methods* (2nd ed.). Chicago, IL: Lyceum.

Jordan, J. S., Harvey, J. H., & Weary, G. (1988). Attributional biases in clinical decision making. In D. C. Turk & P. Salovey (Eds.), *Reasoning, inference, and judgement in clinical psychology* (pp. 93–106). New York, NY: Free Press.

Jørgensen, K. J., & Gøtzsche, P. C. (2004). Presentation on websites of possible benefits and harms from screening for breast cancer: Cross sectional study. *BMJ, 328*, 148–155.

Judson, H. F. (2004). *The great betrayal: Fraud in science.* New York, NY: Harcourt.

Juni, P., Altman, D. G., & Egger, M. (2001). Assessing the quality of controlled clinical trials. *BMJ, 323*, 42–46.

Kadushin, A. (1963). Diagnosis and evaluation for (almost) all occasions. *Social Work, 8*, 12–19.

Kahane, H. (1971). *Logic and contemporary rhetoric: The use of reason in everyday life.* Belmont, CA: Wadsworth.

Kahane, H. (1995). *Logic and contemporary rhetoric: The use of reason in everyday life* (7th ed.). Belmont, CA: Wadsworth.

Kahane, H., & Cavender, N. (1998). *Logic and contemporary rhetoric: The use of reason in everyday life* (8th ed.). New York, NY: Wadsworth.

Kahneman, D. (1995). Varieties of counterfactual thinking. In N. J. Roese & J. M. Olsen (Eds.), *What might have been: Social psychology of counterfactual thinking* (pp. 375–396). Mahwah, NJ: Erlbaum.

Kahneman, D. (2011). *Thinking fast and slow.* New York, NY: Farrar, Straus & Giroux.

Kahneman, D., & Klein, G. (2009). Conditions for intuitive expertise: A failure to disagree. *American Psychologist, 64*, 515–526.

Kahneman, D., & Tversky, A. (1973). On the psychology of prediction. *Psychological Review, 80*, 237–251.

Kananen, L., Surakka, A., Pirkola, S., Survisaari, J., Lonnqvist, J., & Peltonen, L., et al. (2010). Childhood adversities are associated with shorter telomere length at adult age both in individuals with an anxiety disorder and controls, *PloS ONE, 5*: e10826.

Karger, H. J. (1983). Science, research and social work: Who controls the profession? *Social Work, 28*, 200–205.

Karsh, B-T., Weinger, M. B., Abbott, P. A., & Wears, R. I. (2010). Health information technology: Fallacies and sober realities. *Journal of the American Medical Association, 17*, 617–623.

Kassin, S. M., & Gudjonsson, G. H. (2004). The psychology of confessions. A review of the literature & issues. *Psychological Science in the Public Interest, 5*, 33–67.

Kassirer, J. P. (2005). *On the take: How medicine's complicity with big business can endanger your health.* New York, NY: Oxford University Press.

Kassirer, J. P., & Kopelman, K. I. (1989). Cognitive errors in diagnosis, instantiation, classification, and consequences. *American Journal of Medicine, 86*, 433–441.

Katz, J. (2002). *The silent world of doctor and patient.* Baltimore, MD: John Hopkins University Press.

Kaufman, M. (2006, July 21). Medication errors harming millions, report says. Extensive national study finds widespread, costly mistakes in giving and taking medicine. *The Washington Post.*

Keefe, R. (2000). *Theories of vagueness.* New York, NY: Cambridge University Press.

Kelley, G. A. (1955). *The psychology of personal constructs.* New York, NY: Norton.

Kelley, H. H. (1950). The warm-cold variable of first impressions of persons. *Journal of Personality, 18*, 431–439.

Kelly, I. W., Culver, R., & Loptson, P. J. (1989). Astrology and science: An examination of the evidence. In S. K. Biswas, D. C. V. Malik, & C. V. Vishveshwara (Eds.), *Cosmic perspectives.* New York, NY: Cambridge University Press.

Kenrick, D. T., & Gutierres, S. E. (1980). Contrast effects in judgments of attractiveness: When beauty becomes a social problem. *Journal of Personality and Social Psychology, 38*, 131–140.

Kerig, P. K., & Lindahl, K. M. (Eds.). (2004). *Family observational coding systems: Resources for systemic research.* Mahwah, NJ: Erlbaum.

Kerwin, A., & Witte, M. (1983). Map of ignorance (Q-Cubed Programs): What is ignorance? Retrieved from www.ignorance.medicine.arizona.edu/ignorance.html

Kessler, R. C., and the WHO World Mental Health Survey Consortium. (2004). Prevalence, severity, and unmet need for treatment of mental disorders in the World Health Organization world mental health surveys. *Journal of the American Medical Association, 291*, 2581–2590.

Kiesler, D. J. (1966). Some myths of psychotherapy research and the search for a paradigm. *Psychological Bulletin, 65*, 110–136.

King, L. S. (1981). *Medical thinking: A historical preface*. Princeton, NJ: Princeton University Press.

King, P. M., & Kitchener, K. S. (2002). The reflective judgment model: Twenty years of research on epistemic cognition. In B. K. Hofer & P. R. Pintrich (Eds.), *Personal epistemology: The psychology of beliefs about knowledge and knowing* (pp. 37–61). Mahwah, NJ: Erlbaum.

Kirk, S. (2010). Science and politics in the evolution of the DSM. Seabury Lecture. University of California, Berkeley, April.

Kirk, S. A., & Kutchins, H. (1992a). Five arguments for using DSM-III-R and why they are wrong. In E. Gambrill & R. Pruger (Eds.), *Controversial issues in social work* (pp. 146–154). Boston, MA: Allyn & Bacon.

Kirk, S. A., & Kutchins, H. (1992b). *The selling of DSM: The rhetoric of science in psychiatry*. New York, NY: Aldine de Gruyter.

Kirsch, I. (2010). *The emperor's new drugs: Exploding the antidepressant myth*. New York, NY: Basic Books.

Kirsch, I., & Sapirstein, G. (1999). Listening to Prozac but hearing placebo: A meta-analysis of antidepressant medications. In I. Kirsch (Ed.), *How expectancies shape experience* (pp. 303–320). Washington, DC: American Psychological Association.

Klayman, J. (1995). Varieties of confirmation bias. *Psychology of Learning and Motivation, 32*, 385–418.

Klayman, J., Soll, J. B., Gonzales-Vallejo, C., & Barlas, S. (1999). Overconfidence: It depends on how, what, and whom you ask. *Organizational Behavior and Human Decision Processes, 79*, 216–247.

Klein, G. (1998). *Sources of power: How people make decisions*. Cambridge, MA: MIT Press.

Kleinman, A., & Fitz-Henry, E. (2007). The experiential basis of subjectivity. In J. Biehl, B. Good, & A.. Kleinman (Eds.), *Subjectivity: Ethnographic investigation* (pp. 52–65). Berkeley, CA: University of California Press.

Klemp, G. O., & McClelland, D. C. (1986). What characterizes intelligent functioning among senior managers. In R. G. Sternberg & R. K. Wagner (Eds.), *Practical intelligence: Nature and origins of competence in the everyday world* (pp. 31–50). Cambridge, UK: Cambridge University Press.

Kline, N. (1962). Factifuging. *The Lancet*, 1396–1399.

Kluger, M. P., Alexander, G., & Curtis, P. A. (2002). *What works in child welfare*. Washington, D.C.: CWLA Press.

Kmietowicz, Z. (2005). Half of patients in intensive care receive suboptimal care. *BMJ, 330*, 1101.

Knishinsky, A. (1982). *The effects of scarcity of material and exclusivity of information on industrial buyer perceived risk in provoking a purchase decision* (Unpublished doctoral dissertation). Arizona State University, Tempe.

Knottnerus, J. A. (Ed.). (2002). *The evidence base of clinical diagnosis*. London, UK: BMJ.

Koberg, D., & Bagnall, J. (1976). *The universal traveler: A soft system guide to creativity, problem-solving and the process of reaching goals*. Los Altos, CA: Kaufman.

Koehler, D. J., & Harvey, N. (Eds.). (2005). *The Blackwell handbook of judgment and decision making*. Oxford, UK: Blackwell.

Koh, G. C-H, Khoo, H. E., Wong, M. L., & Koh, D. (2008). The effects of problem-based learning during medical school on physician competency: A systematic review. *CMAJ, 178,* 34–41.

Kohn, A. (1988). *False prophets: Fraud and error in science and medicine*. New York, NY: Basil Blackwell.

Kolata, G. (2008). Colonoscopies miss many cancers study finds. *New York Times,* Dec. 15.

Kolata, G. (2011, July 8). How bright promise in cancer testing fell apart. *The New York Times,* A1/A14.

Kondro, W., & Sibbald, B. (2004). Drug company experts advised staff to withhold data about SSRI use in children. *Canadian Medical Association, 170*(5), 783.

Kopta, S. M., Newman, F. L., McGovern, M. P., & Sandrock, D. (1986). Psychological orientations: A comparison of conceptualizations, interventions, and treatment plan costs. *Journal of Consulting and Clinical Psychology, 54,* 369–374.

Korotitsch, W. J., & Nelson-Gray, R. O. (1999). An overview of self-monitoring research in assessment and treatment. *Psychological Assessment, 11,* 415–425.

Korzybski, A. (1980). *Science and sanity: An introduction to nonaristotelian systems and general semantics* (4th ed.). Lakeville, CT: Institute of General Semantics.

Kottler, J. A., & Blau, D. S. (1989). *The imperfect therapist: Learning from failure in therapeutic practice*. San Francisco, CA: Jossey-Bass.

Kruger, J., & Dunning, D. (1999). Unskilled and unaware of it: How difficulties in recognizing one's own incompetence lead to inflated self-assessments. *Journal of Personality and Social Psychology, 77,* 1121–1134.

Kruskal, W., & Mosteller, F. (1981). Ideas of representative sampling. In D. Fiske (Ed.), *New directions for methodology of social and behavioral science: No. 9. Problems with language imprecision* (pp. 3–24). San Francisco, CA: Jossey-Bass.

Kuhn, D. (1991). *The skills of argument*. New York, NY: Cambridge University Press.

Kuhn, D. (1993). Connecting scientific and informal reasoning. *Merrill-Palmer Quarterly, 39,* 74–103.

Kuhn, D. (1993). Science as argument: Implications for thinking and learning scientific thinking. *Science Education, 77,* 319–337.

Kuhn, T. S. (1962/1970). *The structure of scientific revolutions* (2nd ed.). Chicago, IL: University of Chicago Press.

Kuhn, T. S. (1996). Logic of discovery or psychology of research? In I. Lakatos & A. Musgrave (Eds.), *Criticism and the growth of knowledge* (pp. 1–23). Cambridge, MA: Cambridge University Press.

Kuipers, B., & Kassirer, J. P. (1984). Causal reasoning in medicine: Analysis of a protocol. *Cognitive Science, 8,* 363–385.

Kuno, E., & Rothbard, A. B. (2002). Racial disparities in anti-psychotic prescription patterns for patients with schizophrenia. *American Journal of Psychiatry, 159,* 567–572.

Kunst, H., Groot, D., Latthe, P. M., Latthe, M., & Khan, K. S. (2002). Accuracy of information on apparently credible websites: Survey of five common health topics. *BMJ, 324,* 581–582.

Kurzban, R. (2010). *Why everyone (else) is a hypocrite: Evolution and the modular mind.* Princeton, NJ: Princeton University Press.

Kutchins, H., & Kirk, S. A. (1997). *Making us crazy: DSM: The psychiatric bible and the creation of mental disorders.* New York, NY: Free Press.

LaBerge, D. (1995). *Attentional processing: The brain's art of mindfulness.* Cambridge, MA: Harvard University Press.

Labroo, A., & Patrick, V. M. (2009). Psychological distancing: Why happiness helps you see the big picture. *Journal of Consumer Research, 35,* 800–809.

Lacasse, J. R., & Gomory, T. (2003). Is graduate social work education promoting a critical approach to mental health practice? *Journal of Social Work Education, 39,* 383–408.

Lacasse, J. R., & Leo, J. (2005). Serotonin and depression: A disconnect between the advertisements and the scientific literature. *PloS Medicine, 2,* e392.

Lakoff, G., & Dean, H. (2004). *Don't think of an elephant! Know your values and frame the debate: The essential guide for progressives.* White River Junction, VT: Chelsea Green.

Lakoff, G., & Johnson, M. (1980). *Metaphors we live by.* Chicago, IL: University of Chicago Press.

Lakoff, R. T. (2001). *The language war.* Berkeley, CA: University of California Press.

Lambert, M. J., & Barley, D. E. (2002). Research summary on the therapeutic relationship and psychotherapy outcome. In J. C. Norcross (Ed.), *Psychotherapy relationships that work: Therapists' contributions and responsiveness to patients* (pp. 17–32). New York, NY: Oxford University Press.

Lambert, M. J., & Ogles, B. M. (2004). The efficacy and effectiveness of psychotherapy. In M. J. Lambert (Ed.), *Bergin and Garfield's handbook of psychotherapy and behavior change* (5th ed., pp. 139–293). Hoboken, NJ: John Wiley & Sons.

Lambert, M. J., & Shimokawa, K. (2011). Collecting client feedback. In J. C. Norcross (Ed.), *Psychotherapy relationships that work: Evidence-based responsiveness* (2nd ed., pp. 203–223). New York, NY: Oxford University Press.

Landers, S. (1987). LD definition disputed. *APA Monitor, 18*(12), 35.

Lang, S. (1998). *Challenges.* New York, NY: Springer.

Langer, E. (2009). *Counterclockwise: mindful health and the power of possibility.* New York: Ballantine Books.

Langer, E. J. (1975). The illusion of control. *Journal of Personality and Social Psychology, 32*, 311–328.

Langer, E. J. (1983). *The psychology of control.* Newbury Park, CA: Sage.

Langer, E. J., & Abelson, R. P. (1974). A patient by any other name: Clinician group difference in labeling bias. *Journal of Consulting and Clinical Psychology, 42*, 4–9.

Larrick, R. P. (2005). Debiasing. In D. J. Koehler & N. Harvey (Eds.), *Blackwell handbook of judgement and decision making* (pp. 316–337). Malden, MA: Blackwell.

Larson, M. S. (1977). *The rise of professionalism: A sociological analysis.* Berkeley, CA: University of California Press.

Last, J. M. (1988). *A dictionary of epidemiology* (2nd ed.). New York, NY: Oxford University Press.

Lawrie, S. M., McIntosh, A. M., & Rao, S. (2000). *Critical appraisal for psychiatry.* New York, NY: Churchill Livingstone.

Layng, J. (2009). In search for an effective clinical behavior analysis. The nonlinear thinking of Israel Goldiamond. *Behavior Analysis, 32*, 163–184.

Leape, L., Lawthers, A. G., Brennan, T. A., et al. (1993). Preventing medical injury. *Qualitative Review Bulletin, 19*, 144–149.

Leiby, J. (1978). *A history of social welfare and social work in the United States.* New York, NY: Columbia University Press.

Leichtman, M. D., & Ceci, S. J. (1995). The effects of stereotypes and suggestions on preschoolers' reports. *Developmental Psychology, 31*, 568–578.

Lemert, E. M. (1951). *Social pathology.* New York, NY: McGraw-Hill.

Lenrow, P. (1978). Dilemmas of professional helping: Continuities and discontinuities with folk helping roles. In L. Wipse (Ed.), *Altruism, sympathy and helping: psychological and sociological principles* (pp. 263–290). Orlando, FL: Academic Press.

Lenzer, J. (2004). Bush launches controversial mental health plan. *BMJ, 329*, 367.

Leo, J., & Cohen, D. (2003). Broken brains or flawed studies? A critical review of ADHD neuroimaging research. *Journal of Mind and Behavior, 24*, 29–56.

Lerner, J. S., & Tetlock, P. E. (1999). Accounting for the effects of accountability. *Psychological Bulletin, 125*, 255–75.

Lesgold, A., Rubinson, H., Feltovich, P., Glaser, R., Klopfer, D., & Wang, Y. (1988). Expertise in a complex skill: Diagnosing x-ray pictures. In M. T. H. Chi, R. Glaser, & M. Farr (Eds.), *The nature of expertise* (pp. 311–342). Hillsdale, NJ: Erlbaum.

Letter to the editor. (1986). *NASW News, 31*, 15.

Levi, D. J. (2007). *Group dynamics for teams* (2nd ed.). Thousand Oaks, CA: Sage.

Levy, C. J. (2002, December 13). State to survey mentally ill in residences. *The New York Times*, 1.

Levy, C. J. (2003, May 20). Doctor admits he did needless surgery on the mentally ill. *The New York Times*.

Lewis, C. (1987). The humanitarian theory of punishment: Issues in religion and psychotherapy, (13)1. Retrieved February 9, 2012, from https://ojs.lib.byu.edu/spc/index.php/IssueSINReligionAndPsychotherapy/article/view/273/272.

Lewontin, R. C. (1991). *Biology as ideology: The doctrine of DNA*. New York, NY: HarperCollins.

Lewontin, R. C. (1994). *Inside and outside: Gene, environment, and organism*. Worcester, MA: Clark University Press.

Lewontin, R. C. (1995). Genes, environment and organisms. In R. B. Silvers (Ed.), *Hidden histories of science* (pp. 115–139). New York, NY: New York Review of Books.

Lewontin, R. C. (2009). Where are the genes? www.councilforresponsiblegenetics.org Downloaded 10/1/2011.

Liberati, A., Altman, D. G., Tetzlaff, J., Mulrow, C., Gotzsche, P. C., & Ioannides, J. P. A., et al. (2009). The PRISMA statement for reporting systematic reviews and meta-analyses of studies that evaluate health care interventions: Explanation and elaboration. *PloS Medicine, 6*, e1000100.

Lichtenstein, S., & Slovic, P. (2006). *The construction of preference*. Cambridge, UK: Cambridge University Press.

Lichtenstein, S., Slovic, P., Fischhoff, B., Layman, M., & Coombs, C. (1978). Judged frequency of lethal events. *Journal of Experimental Psychology: Human Learning and Memory, 4*, 551–578.

Lilienfeld, S. O. (2002). When worlds collide: Social science, politics, and the Rind et al. (1998) child sexual abuse meta-analysis. *American Psychologist, 57*, 176–188.

Lilienfeld, S. O., Lynn, S. J., & Lohr, J. M. (2003). *Science and pseudoscience in clinical psychology*. New York, NY: Guilford.

Limb, M. (2011). *Science* asks researchers to withdraw paper on chronic fatigue syndrome and retrovirus. *BMJ, 342*:d3505.

Lindsey, D., Martin, S., & Doh, J. (2002). The failure of intensive casework services to reduce foster care placements: An examination of family preservation studies. *Children and Youth Services Review, 24*, 743–775.

Lindsey, S. (2004). Statistical scientific evidence and expertise in the courtroom. In E. Kurz-Milcke & G. Gigerenzer (Eds.), *Experts in science and society* (pp. 269–279). New York, NY: Kluwer Academic/Plenum.

Lipman, M. (2003). *Thinking in education* (2nd ed.). Cambridge, UK: Cambridge University Press.

Lipsey, M. W. (2003). Those confounded moderators in meta-analysis: Good, bad and ugly. *The ANNALS of the American Academy of Political and Social Science, 587,* 69–81.

Lipshitz, R. (1997). Naturalistic decision making perspectives on decision making. In C. Zsambok & G. Klein (Eds.), *Naturalistic decision making* (pp. 151–162). Mahwah, NJ: Erlbaum.

Lipton, J. P., & Hershaft, A. M. (1985). On the widespread acceptance of dubious medical findings. *Journal of Health and Social Behavior, 26,* 336–351.

Littell, J. (2008). Evidence-based or biased? The quality of published reviews of evidence-based practice. *Children and Youth Services Review, 30,* 1299–1317.

Littell, J. (2005). Lessons from a systematic review of effects of multisystemic therapy. *Children and Youth Services Review, 27,* 429.

Littell, J. H., Corcoran, J., & Pillai, V. (2008). *Systematic reviews and meta-analysis.* New York, NY: Oxford University Press.

Littell, J. H., Popa, M., & Forsythe, B. (2005). Multisystemic therapy for social, emotional, and behavioral problems in youth age 10–17. *Cochrane Database of Systematic Reviews, 4.* Chichester, UK: John Wiley & Sons.

Ljung, B-M., Chew, K., Deng, G., Matsumura, K., Waldman, F., & Smith, H. (2006). Fine needle aspiration techniques for the characterization of breast cancers. *Cancer, 74,* 1000–1005.

Lo, B., & Field, M. J. (Eds.). (2009). *Conflict of interest in medical research, education and practice.* Institute of Medicine. Washington, DC: National Academy Press.

Lock, M. (1982). Popular conceptions of mental health in Japan. In A. J. Marsella & G. M. White (Eds.), *Cultural conceptions of mental health and therapy* (pp. 215–234). Norwell, MA: D. Reidel.

Lock, M. (1993). *Encounters with aging: Mythologies of menopause in Japan and North America.* Berkeley, CA: University of California Press.

Loeske, D. R. (1999). *Thinking about social problems: An introduction to constructionist perspectives.* New York, NY: Aldine de Gruyter.

Loftus, E. F. (1980). *Memory: Surprising new insights into how we remember and why we forget.* Reading, MA: Addison-Wesley.

Loftus, E. F. (1996). *Eyewitness testimony* (5th printing). Cambridge, MA: Harvard University Press.

Loftus, E. F. (1997). Creating false memories. *Scientific American, 277,* 70–75.

Loftus, E. F. (2004). Memories of things unseen. *Current Directions in Psychological Science, 17,* 145–147.

Loftus, E. F., & Doyle, J. M. (1997). *Eyewitness testimony: Civil and criminal.* Charlottesville, VA: Lexis Law Pub.

Loftus, E. F., & Guyer, M. J. (2002). Who abused Jane Doe? The hazards of the single case history, Part 1. *The Skeptical Inquirer, 26,* 22–32.

Loftus, E. F., & Ketcham, K. E. (1983). The malleability of eyewitness accounts. In S. M. A. Lloyd-Bostock & B. R. Clifford (Eds.), *Evaluating witness evidence: Recent psychological research and new perspectives* (pp. 159–172). New York: Wiley.

Loftus, E., & Ketcham, K. (1994). *The myth of repressed memory: False memories and allegations of abuse.* New York, NY: St. Martin's Press.

Loftus, E., & Palmer, J. (1974). Reconstruction of automobile destruction: An example of the interaction between language and memory. *Journal of Verbal Learning and Verbal Behavior, 13,* 585–589.

Lord, C., Ross, L., & Lepper, M. R. (1979). Biased assimilation and attitude polarization: The effects of prior theories on subsequently considered evidence. *Journal of Personality and Social Psychology, 37,* 2098–2109.

Luborsky, L., Diguer, L., Seligman, D. A., Rosenthal, R., Krause, E. D., Johnson, S., Schweizer, E. (1999). The researchers' own therapy allegiances: A "wildcard" in comparisons of treatment efficacy. *Clinical Psychology: Science and Practice, 6,* 95–106.

Luck, J., & Peabody, J. W. (2002). Using standardized patients to measure physicians' practice: Validation study using audio recordings. *BMJ, 325,* 67–92.

Ludmerer, K. M. (1999). *Time to heal.* New York, NY: Oxford University Press.

Luyten, S. J., Blatt, B., Van HoudenHove, B., & Corvelyn, J. (2006). Depression, research and treatment: Are we skating to where the puck is going? *Clinical Psychology Review, 26,* 985–999.

Lynn, S. J., Lock, T., Loftus, E. E., Krackow, E., & Lilienfeld, S. O. (2003). The remembrance of things past: Problematic memory recovery techniques in psychotherapy. In S. O. Lilienfled, S. J. Lynn, & J. M. Lohr (Eds.), *Science and pseudoscience in clinical psychology* (pp. 250–239). New York, NY: Guilford.

MacCoun, R. J. (1998). Biases in the interpretation and use of research results. *Annual Review of Psychology, 49,* 259–287.

MacCoun, R. J. (2001). American distortion of Dutch drug statistics. *Society, 38,* 23–26.

MacCoun, R. J., & Reuter, P. (2001). *Drug war heresies: Learning from other vices, times, & places.* New York, NY: Cambridge University Press.

Mackie, J. L. (1974). *The cement of the universe: A study of causation.* Oxford, UK: Clarendon Press.

MacLean, E. (1981). *Between the lines: How to detect bias and propaganda in the news and everyday life.* Montreal, Canada: Black Rose Books.

MacLehose, R. R., Reeves, B. C, Harvey, I. M., Sheldon, T. A., Russell, I. T., & Black, A. M. (2000). A systematic review of comparisons of effect sizes derived from randomized and non-randomized studies. *Health Technology Assessment, 4*(34), 1–154.

Maclure, M. (1985). Popperian refutation in epidemiology. *American Journal of Epidemiology, 121,* 343–350.

Magee, J. (1985). *Philosophy in the real world.* LaSalle, IL: Open Court.

Maguire, G. P., & Rutter, D. R. (1976). History-taking for medical students. I. Deficiencies in performance. *The Lancet, 11*, Sept., 556–560.

Maher, C. A., & Cook, S. A. (1985). Time management. In C. A. Maher (Ed.), *Professional self-management: Techniques for special service providers* (pp. 23–43). Baltimore, MD: Brooks.

Mahoney, M. J. (1997). Publication prejudices: An experimental study of confirmatory bias in the peer review system. *Cognitive Therapy and Research, 1*, 161–175.

Manning, N. P. (Ed.). (1985). *Social problems and welfare ideology*. Aldershot, UK: Gower.

Manojlovich, M., Saint, S., Forman, J., Fletcher, C. E., Keith, R., & Krein, S. (2011). Developing and testing a tool to measure nurse/physician communication in the intensive care unit. *Journal of Patient Safety, 7*, 80–84.

Mansfield, P. R. (2003). Healthy skepticism's new ad; AdWatch: Understanding drug promotion. *Medical Journal of Australia, 179*, 644–645.

Marchand, R. (1986). *Advertising the American dream: Making way for modernity, 1920–1940*. Berkeley, CA: University of California Press.

Margo, C. E. (2005). A pilot study in ophthalmology of inter-rater reliability in classifying diagnostic errors: An under-investigated area of medical error. *Quality and Safety of Health Care, 12*, 416–420.

Margolin, L. (1997). *Under the cover of kindness: The invention of social work*. Charlottesville, VA: University of Virginia Press.

Marlatt, G. A., & Gordon, J. R. (Eds.). (1985). *Relapse prevention: Maintenance strategies in the treatment of addiction*. New York, NY: Guilford.

Marris, P. (1996). *The politics of uncertainty: Attachment in private public life*. New York, NY: Routledge.

Martinic, M., & Leigh, B. (2004). *Reasonable risk: Alcohol in perspective*. New York, NY: Routledge.

Maslach, C., Schaufeli, W., & Leiter, M. P. (2001). Job burnout. *Annual Review of Psychology, 52*, 397–422.

Masson, J. M. (1984). *The assault on truth: Freud's suppression of the seduction theory*. New York, NY: Farrar, Straus & Giroux.

Masson, J. M. (1988). *Against therapy: Emotional tyranny and the myth of psychological healing*. New York, NY: Atheneum.

Matthews, G. (2001). Levels of transaction: A cognitive science framework for operator stress. In P. A. Hancock & P. A. Desmond (Eds.), *Stress, workload, and fatigue* (pp. 5–33). Mahwah, NJ: Erlbaum.

Mazzoni, G. A. L., Loftus, E. F., Seitz, A., & Lynn, S. J. (1999). Changing beliefs and memories through dream interpretation. *Applied Cognitive Psychology, 13*(2), 125–144.

McCabe, D. P., & Castel, A. D. (2008). Seeing is believing: The effect of brain images on judgments of scientific reasoning. *Cognition, 107*, 343–352.

McCann, J. T., Shindler, K. L., & Hammond, T. R. (2003). The science and pseudoscience of expert testimony. In S. O. Lillienfeld, S. J. Lynn, & J. M. Lohr (Eds.), *Science and pseudoscience in clinical psychology* (pp. 77–108). New York, NY: Guilford.

McCloskey, M. (1983). Intuitive physics. *Scientific American, 248*, 122–130.

McCord, J. (2003). Cures that harm: Unanticipated outcomes of crime prevention programs. *The ANNALS of the American Academy of Political and Social Science, 587*, 16–30.

McCormick, J. (1996). Health scares are bad for your health. In D. M. Warburton & N. Sherwood (Eds.), *Pleasure and quality of life* (pp. 189–199). New York, NY: John Wiley & Sons.

McCoy, R. (2000). *Quack! Tales of medical fraud from the museum of questionable medical devices*. Santa Monica, CA: Santa Monica Press.

McDaniel, P. A. (2003). *Shrinking violets and caspar milquetoasts*. New York, NY: New York University Press.

McDowell, B. (2000). *Ethics and excuses: The crisis in professional responsibility*. Westport, CT: Quorum Books.

McFall, R. M. (1991). Manifesto for a science of clinical psychology. *Clinical Psychologist, 44*, 75–88.

McFall, R. M. (2006). Doctoral training in clinical psychology. *Annual Review of Clinical Psychology, 2*, 21–49.

McGimsey, J. F., Greene, B. F., & Lutzker, J. R. (1995). Competence in aspects of behavioral treatment and consultation: Implications for service delivery and graduate training. *Journal of Applied Behavioral Analysis, 28*, 301–315.

McGovern, M. P., Newman, F. L, & Kopta, S. M. (1986). Metatheoretical assumptions and psychotherapy orientation: Clinician attributions of patients' problem causality and responsibility for treatment outcome. *Journal of Consulting and Clinical Psychology, 54*, 476–481.

McIntyre, N., & Popper, K. (1983). The critical attitude in medicine: The need for a new ethics. *British Medical Journal, 287*, 1919–1923.

McKnight, L., Stetson, P., Bakken, S., Curran, C., & Cimino, J. (2002). Perceived information needs and communication difficulties of inpatient physicians and nurses. *Journal of the American Medical Informatics Association, 9*(6 Suppl 1), S64–S69.

McLellan, D. (1986). *Ideology: Concepts in social thought*. Minneapolis, MN: University of Minnesota Press.

McNeil, B. J., Pauker, S. G., Sox, H. C., Jr., & Tversky, A. (1982). On the elicitation of preferences for alternative therapies. *New England Journal of Medicine, 306*, 1259–1262.

McReynolds, P. (1989). Diagnosis and clinical assessment: Current status and major issues. In M. R. Rosenzweig & L. W. Porter (Eds.), *Annual Review of Psychology, 40*, 83–108.

Medawar, P. (1979). A bouquet of fallacies from medicine and medical science with a sideways glance at mathematics and logic. In R. Duncan & M. Weston-Smith (Eds.), *The encyclopedia of delusions: A critical scrutiny of current beliefs and conventions* (pp. 97–105). New York, NY: Simon & Schuster.

Medawar, P. B. (1984). *Pluto's republic*. Oxford, UK: Oxford University Press.

Medication Errors Injure 1.5 Million People and Cost Billions Annually (http://www8.nationalacademies.org/onpinews/newsitem.aspx?RecordID=11623). The National Academic of Science. 2006. Retrieved 2006.

Meehl, P. E. (1954). *Clinical versus statistical prediction: A theoretical analysis and a review of the evidence*. Minneapolis, MN: University of Minnesota Press.

Meehl, P. E. (1973). Why I do not attend case conferences. In P. E. Meehl (Ed.), *Psychodiagnosis: Selected papers* (pp. 225–304). Minneapolis, MN: University of Minnesota Press.

Meichenbaum, D. (2008). Core tasks of psychotherapy/counseling: What "expert" therapists do. Presentation at the 12th Annual Melissa Institute Conference May. Downloaded March 3, 2012.

Meier, B. (2004, July 21). Some professional groups demand public listing of all test outcomes. *New York Times*, C-1.

Meier, B. (2011, June 26). In medicine, new isn't always improved. *New York Times*, Sunday Business, 1/7.

Meier, B., & Wilson, D. (2011, June 29). Spine experts repudiate Medtronic studies. *New York Times*, B1.

Mercer, J. R. (1973). *Labeling the mentally retarded*. Berkeley, CA: University of California Press.

Merrell, K., & Walker, H. M. (2004). Deconstructing a definition: Social maladjustment versus emotional disturbance and moving the EBD field forward. *Psychology in the Schools, 41*, 899–910.

Messing, J. T. (2011). The social control of family violence. *Journal of Women and Social Work, 26*(2), 154–168.

Michael, M., Boyce, W. T., & Wilcox, A. J. (1984). *Biomedical bestiary: An epidemiologic guide to flaws and fallacies in the medical literature*. Boston, MA: Little, Brown.

Michalos, A. C. (1971). *Improving your reasoning*. Englewood Cliffs, NJ: Prentice Hall.

Michiels, B., Thomas, I., Royen, P. V., & Coenen, S. (2011). Clinical prediction rules combining signs, symptoms and epidemiological context to distinguish influenza from influenza-like illnesses in primary care. A cross sectional study. *BMC Family Practice, 12*, 4, 1–4, 11. www.biomedcentral.com/1471-2296/12/4

Midanik, L. T. (2006). *Biomedicalization of alcohol studies: Ideological shifts and institutional challenges*. New Brunswick, NJ: Aldine/Transaction.

Milgram, S. (1963). Behavioral study of obedience. *Journal of Abnormal and Social Psychology, 67*, 371–378.

Mill, J. S. (1911). *A system of logic. Book 3: Of induction*. Chapter 5: Of the law of universal causation, 211–242.

Miller, A. G., Gillen, B., Schenker, C., & Radlove, S. (1973). Perception of obedience to authority. *Proceedings of the 81st Annual Convention of the American Psychological Association, 8*, 127–128.

Miller, D. (1994). *Critical rationalism: A restatement and defense*. Chicago: Open Court.

Miller, D. J., & Hersen, M. (1992). *Research fraud in the behavioral and biomedical sciences*. New York, NY: John Wiley & Sons.

Miller, S. D., Duncan, B. L., Brown, J., Sorrell, R., & Chalk, M. B. (2006). Using formal client feedback to improve retention and outcome: Making ongoing real-time assessment feasible. *Journal of Brief Therapy, 5*, 5–22.

Mills, C. W. (1959). *The sociological imagination*. New York, NY: Grove Press.

Mirowsky, J., & Ross, C. E. (2003). *Social causes of psychological distress* (2nd ed.). New York, NY: Aldine de Gruyter.

Mischel, W. (1968). *Personality and assessment*. New York, NY: John Wiley & Sons.

Mischel, W. (1973). Toward a cognitive social learning reconceptualization of personality. *Psychological Review, 80*, 252–283.

Mischel, W. (2004). Toward an integrative science of the person. *Annual Review of Psychology, 55*, 1–22.

Mischel, W., Shoda, Y., & Mendoza-Denton, R. (2002). Situation-behavior profiles as a locus of consistency in personality. *Current Directions in Psychological Science, 11*, 50–54.

Miser, W. F. (1999). Critical appraisal of the literature. *Journal of the American Board of Family Practice, 12*, 315–333.

Miser, W. F. (2000a). Applying a meta-analysis to daily clinical practice. In J. P. Geyman, R. A. Deyo, & S. D. Ramsey (Eds.), *Evidence-based clinical practice: Concepts and approaches* (pp. 57–64). Boston, MA: Butterworth-Heinemann.

Miser, W. F. (2000b). Critical appraisal of the literature: How to assess an article and still enjoy life. In J. P. Geyman, R. A. Deyo, & S. D. Ramsey (Eds.), *Evidence-based clinical practice: Concepts and approaches* (pp. 41–56). Boston: Butterworth-Heinemann.

Moncrieff, J. (2008). *The myth of the chemical cure: A critique of psychiatric drug treatment*. New York, NY: Palgrave.

Moncrieff, J., & Leo, J. (2010). A systematic review of the effects of antipsychotic drugs on brain volume. *Psychological Medicine, 20*, 1–14.

Mooney, H. (2011). Three out of 12 hospitals fail to meet essential standards of care of older people, finds watchdog. *BMJ 342*:d3346.

Moore, K. D. (1986). *Inductive arguments: A field guide*. Dubuque, IA: Kendall/Hunt.

Moran, G. (1998). *Silencing scientists and scholars in other fields: Power, paradigm controls, peer review and scholarly communication*. Greenwich, CT: Ablex.

Morgan, R. F. (Ed.). (1983). *The iatrogenics handbook*. Toronto, Canada: IPI Publications.

Morgan, T. (1982). *Churchill: Young man in a hurry 1874–1915*. New York, NY: Simon & Schuster.

Morrissey, J., & Monahan, J. (1999). *Coercion in mental health services: International perspectives*. Stamford, CT: JAI Press.

Moynihan, R. (2009). News: Court hears how drug giant Merck tired to "neutralize" and "discredit" doctors critical of Vioxx. *BMJ, 338*:b1432.

Moynihan, R. (2011). It's time to rebuild the evidence base. *BMJ, 342*:d3004.

Moynihan, R., & Cassels, A. (2005). *Selling sickness: How the world's biggest pharmaceutical companies are turning us all into patients*. New York, NY: Nation Books.

Moynihan, R., Heath, I., Henry, D., & Gøtzsche, P. C. (2002). Selling sickness: The pharmaceutical industry and disease mongering. *BMJ, 324*, 886–891.

Moynihan, R., & Mintzes, B. (2010). *Sex, lies and pharmaceuticals: How drug companies plan to profit from female sexual dysfunction*. Vancouver, Canada: Greystone Books.

Munro, E. (1996). Avoidable and unavoidable mistakes in child protection work. *British Journal of Social Work, 26*, 793–808.

Munro, E. (2004). A simpler way to understand the results of risk assessment instruments. *Children and Youth Services Review, 26*, 873–883.

Munro, E. (2011). *The Munro Review of Child Protection: Final report: A child centered system*. London, UK: Department of Education, May.

Munz, P. (1985). *Our knowledge of the growth of knowledge: Popper or Wittgenstein*. London, UK: Routledge & Kegan Paul.

Munz, P. (1992). What's postmodern, anyway? *Philosophy and Literature, 16*, 333–353.

Mussweiler, T., Strack, F., & Pfeiffer, T. (2000). Overcoming the inevitable anchoring effect: Considering the opposite compensates for selective accessibility. *Personality and Social Psychology Bulletin, 26*, 1142–1150.

Nadler, R. T., Rabi, R. R., & Minda, J. P. (2010). Better mood and better performance: Learning rule-described categories is enhanced by positive mood. *Psychological Science, 21*, 1770–1776.

Naftulin, D. H., Ware, J. E., & Donnelly, F. A. (1973). The Doctor Fox lecture: A paradigm of educational seduction. *Journal of Medical Education, 48*, 630–635.

Nagourney, E. (2008, January 8). Aging: Mental health overlooked in care of elderly patients. *New York Times*.

Najavits, L. M., & Strupp, H. H. (1994). Differences in the effectiveness of psycho-dynamic therapists: A process-outcome study. *Psychotherapy, 31*, 114–123.

Natale, J. A. (1988). Are you open to suggestion? *Psychology Today, 22*, 28–30.

Nathan, P. E., & Gorman, J. M. (2007). *A guide to treatments that work* (3rd ed.). New York, NY: Oxford University Press.

National Association of Social Workers. (2008). *NASW code of ethics.* Washington, DC: AuthorNational Institute on Mental Health Strategic Plan. www.nimh.nih.gov/about/strategic-planning-reports. Downloaded 6/30/2011.

National Science Foundation. (2002). Science and technology: Public attitudes and public understanding.

Nay, W. R. (1979). *Multimethod clinical assessment.* New York, NY: Gardner.

Naylor, R. (2002). *Medication errors: Lessons for education and health care.* Abingdon, UK: Radcliffe Medical Press.

Nelson, T. D. (Ed.). (2009). *Handbook of prejudice, stereotyping, and discrimination.* New York, NY: Psychology Press.

Nemeth, C. J., & Goncalo, J. A. (2005). Influence and persuasion in small groups. In T. C. Brock & M. C. Green (Eds.), *Persuasion: Psychological insights and perspectives* (2nd ed., pp. 171–194). Thousand Oaks, CA: Sage.

Nettler, G. (1970). *Explanations.* New York, NY: McGraw-Hill.

Nettleton, S., & Bunton, R. (1995). Sociological critiques of health promotion. In R. Bunton, S. Nettleton, & R. Burrows (Eds.), *The sociology of health promotion: Critical analysis of consumption, lifestyle and risk* (pp. 41–59). New York, NY: Routledge.

Neuringer, A. (1981). Self-experimentation. *Behaviorism, 9*, 79–94.

Newman, M. and the Campbell Collaboration Systematic Review Group on the Effectiveness of Problem-Based Learning. A pilot systematic review and meta-analysis. *ERIC-ED 476146.*

New report opens old debate about the nature of mental illness. (2005, July/August). *The National Psychologist, 23.*

Nickerson, R. (1998). Confirmation bias: A ubiquitous phenomena in many guises. *Review of General Psychology, 2*, 175–220.

Nickerson, R. S. (1985). Reasoning. In R. F. Dillon & R. J. Sternberg (Eds.), *Cognition and instruction.* Orlando, FL: Academic Press.

Nickerson, R. S. (1986a). Reasoning. In R. F. Dillon & R. J. Sternberg (Eds.), *Cognition and instruction* (pp. 343–374). Orlando, FL: Academic Press.

Nickerson, R. S. (1986b). *Reflections on reasoning.* Hillsdale, NJ: Erlbaum.

Nickerson, R. S. (1987). Why teach thinking? In J. B. Baron & R. J. Sternberg (Eds.), *Teaching thinking skills: Theory and practice* (pp. 27–37). New York, NY: W.H. Freeman.

Nickerson, R. S. (1988–1989). On improving thinking through instruction. In E. Z. Rothkopf (Ed.), *Review of research in education* (pp. 3–57). Washington, DC: American Educational Research Association.

Nickerson, R. S., Perkins, D. N., & Smith, E. E. (1985). *The teaching of thinking.* Hillsdale, NJ: Erlbaum.

Nisbett, R. E. (2003). *The geography of thought: How Asians and Westerners think differently . . . and why.* New York, NY: Free Press.

Nisbett, R. E., Borgida, E., Crandall, R., & Reed, H. (1976). Popular induction: Information is not necessarily informative. In J. S. Carroll & J. W. Payne (Eds.), *Cognition and social behavior* (pp. 113–134). Hillsdale, NJ: Erlbaum.

Nisbett, R. E., & Ross, L. (1980). *Human inference: Strategies and shortcomings of social judgement.* Englewood Cliffs, NJ: Prentice Hall.

Norcross, J. C. (Ed.). (2011). *Psychotherapy relationships that work: Evidence-based responsiveness* (2nd ed.). New York, NY: Oxford University Press.

Norcross, J. C., Beutler, L. E., & Levant, R. F. (Eds.). (2006). *Evidence-based practices in mental health: Debate and dialogue on the fundamental questions.* Washington, DC: American Psychological Association.

Norcross, J. C., Krebs, P. M., & Prochaska, J. O. (2011). Stages of change. In J. C. Norcross (Ed.). (2011). *Psychotherapy relationships that work: Evidence-based responsiveness* (2nd ed., pp. 301–315). New York, NY: Oxford University Press.

Norcross, J. C., & Lambert, M. J. (2011). Evidence-based therapy relationships. In J. Norcross (Ed.), *Psychotherapy relationships that work: Evidence-based responsiveness* (2nd ed., pp. 3–21). New York, NY: Oxford University Press.

Norman, G. (2009). Dual processing and diagnostic errors. *Adv Health Sci Educ Theory Pract,* Supplement, September 14, Supplement 1:37–49. Epub 2009. August 11.

Nosek, B., Banaji, M., & Greenwald, T. (2002). Harvesting implicit group attitudes and beliefs from a demonstration website. *Group Dynamics: Theory, Research and Practice, 6,* 101–115.

Nugus, P., Greenfield, D., Travaglia, J., Westbrook, J., & Braithwaite, J. (2010). How and where clinicians exercise power: Interprofessional relations in health care. *Social Science & Medicine, 71,* 898–909.

Nye, M. J. (1980). N-rays: An episode in the history and psychology of science. *Historical Studies in the Physical Sciences, 11,* 125–156.

Oakley, A. (1976). *Women's work: The housewife, past and present.* New York, NY: Vintage.

O'Conner, A. M. (2001). Using patient decision aids to promote evidence-based decision making. *ACP Journal Club, 135*(1), A11–12.

O'Connor, A. M., Bennett, C. I., Stacey, D., Barry, M., Col, N. F., Eden, K. B., et al. (2009). Decision aids for people facing health treatment or screening decisions. *Cochrane Database of Systematic Reviews, 3,* CD001431.

O'Connor, A. M., Wennberg, J. E., Legare, F., Llewellyn-Thomas, H. A., Moulton, B.W., Sepucha, K. R., et al. (2007). Toward the "tipping point": Decision aids and informed patient choice. *Health Affairs, 26,* 716–725.

O'Donohue, W., & Szymanski, J. (1994). How to win friends and not influence clients: Popular but problematic ideas that impair treatment decisions. *Behavior Therapist, 178*(2), 29–33.

Ofshe, R., & Watters, E. (1994). *Making monsters: False memories, psychotherapy, and sexual hysteria.* New York, NY: Scribners.

O'Hagan, P. E. (2003). Fraudulent misrepresentation and eating disorder. *International Journal of Law and Psychiatry, 26,* 713–717.

Olds, D., Henderson, C. R., Jr., Cole, R., Eckenrode, J., Kitzman, H., Luckey, D., et al. (1998). Long-term effects of nurse home visitation on children's criminal and anti-social behavior: 15-year follow-up of a randomized controlled trial. *Journal of the American Medical Association, 280,* 1238–1444.

Orasanu, J., & Connolly, T. (1993). The reinvention of decision making. In G. Klein, J. Orasanu, R. Calderwood, & C. E. Zsambok (Eds.), *Decision making in action: Models and methods* (pp. 3–20). Norwood, NJ: Ablex.

Oreskes, N., & Conway, E. M. (2010). *Merchants of doubt: How a handful of scientists obscured the truth on issues from tobacco smoke to global warming.* New York, NY: Bloomsbury Press.

Ortiz de Montellano, B. (1992). Magic melanin: Spreading scientific illiteracy among minorities, Part II. *The Skeptical Inquirer, 16,* 162–166.

Orwell, G. (1946/1958). Politics and the English language. In S. Orwell & I. Angus (Eds.), *The collected essays, journalism and letters of George Orwell: Vol. 4. In front of your nose, 1945–1950* (pp. 127–140). London, UK: Secker & Warburg.

Oskamp, S. (1965). Overconfidence in case-study judgments. *Journal of Consulting Psychology, 29,* 261–265.

Øvretveit, J. (1995). *Purchasing for health: A multi-disciplinary introduction to the theory and practice of health purchasing.* Philadelphia, PA: Open University Press.

Oxman, A. D., & Flottorp, S. (1998). An overview of strategies to promote implementation of evidence based health care. In C. Silagy & A. Haines (Eds.), *Evidence based practice in primary care* (pp. 91–109). London, UK: BMJ Books.

Oxman, A. D., & Guyatt, G. H. (1993). The science of reviewing research. In K. S. Warren & F. Mosteller (Eds.), *Doing more good than harm: The evaluation of health care interventions* (pp. 125–133). New York, NY: New York Academy of Sciences.

Oxman, A. D., Glasziou, P., & Williams, Jr. J. W. (2008). What should clinicians do when faced with conflicting recommendations? *BMJ, 337:* a2530.

Oxman, A. D., Thomson, M. A., Davis, D. A., & Haynes, R. B. (1995). No magic bullets: A systematic review of 102 trials of interventions to improve clinical practice. *Canadian Medical Association Journal, 153,* 1423–1431.

Paling, J. (2006). *Helping patients understand risks: 7 simple strategies for successful communication*. Gainesville, FL: Risk Communication Institute.

Parkes, J., Hyde, C., Deeks, J., & Milne, R. (2004). Teaching critical appraisal skills in health care settings (Cochrane Review). In *Cochrane Library*, Issue 3. Chichester, UK: John Wiley & Sons.

Parry, V. (2003). The art of branding a condition. *Medical Marketing and Media, 38*, 43–49.

Parsons, T. (1951). *The social system*. Glenco, IL: Free Press.

Pashler, H., McDaniel, M., Rohrer, D., & Bjork, R. (2008). Learning styles: Concepts and evidence. *Psychological Science in the Public Interest, 9*, 105–119.

Patai, D., & Koertge, N. (2003). *Professing feminism: Education and indoctrination in women's studies* (New ed.). Lanham, MD: Lexington Books.

Paul, R. W. (1987). Critical thinking and the critical person. In D. N. Perkins, J. Lochhead, & J. Bishop (Eds.), *Thinking: The second international conference* (pp. 373–404). Hillsdale, NJ: Erlbaum.

Paul, R. W. (1992). *Critical thinking: What every person needs to survive in a rapidly changing world* (2nd ed.). Foundation for Critical Thinking. www.criticalthinking.org

Paul, R. W. (1993). *Critical thinking: What every person needs to survive in a rapidly changing world* (3rd ed.). Foundation for Critical Thinking. www.criticalthinking.org

Paul, R. W., & Elder, L. (2004). *Critical thinking: Tools for taking charge of your professional and personal life*. Upper Saddle River, NJ: Prentice Hall.

Paul, R. W., Elder, L., & Bartell, T. (1997, March). *California teacher preparation for instruction in critical thinking: Research findings and policy recommendations*. Sacramento, CA: California Commission on Teacher Credentialing.

Paulos, J. A. (1988). *Innumeracy: Mathematical illiteracy and its consequences*. New York, NY: Vintage.

Pawson, R., Boaz, A., Grayson, L., Long, A., & Barnes, C. (2003). *Types and quality of knowledge in social care*. London, UK: Care Institute for Excellence.

Payer, L. (1992). *Disease mongers: How doctors, drug companies, and insurers are making you feel sick*. New York, NY: John Wiley & Sons.

Payne, J. W., & Bettman, J. R. (2005). Walking with the scarecrow: The information processing approach to decision research. In D. J. Koehler & N. Harvey (Eds.), *Blackwell handbook of judgment and decision making* (pp. 110–132). Malden, MA: Blackwell.

Pear, R. (2004, April 26). US finds fault in all 50 states' child welfare programs, and penalties may follow. *New York Times*, A27.

Peele, S. (1999). *Diseasing of America: How we allowed recovery zealots and the treatment industry to convince us we are out of control*. San Francisco, CA: Jossey-Bass.

Pekkala, E., & Merinder, L. (2004). Psychoeducation for schizophrenia (Cochrane Review). In *Cochrane Library*, Issue 4. Chichester, UK: John Wiley & Sons.

Penston, J. (2010). *Stats.com: How we've been fooled by statistics-based research in medicine*. UK: London Press.

Pepper, C. (1984). *Quackery: A $10 billion scandal. Subcommmittee on health and long-term care of the Select Committee on Aging. U.S. House of Representatives. No. 98-435*. Washington, DC: U.S. Government Printing House.

Pepper, S. (1981). Problems in the quantification of frequency experiences. In D. Fiske (Ed.), *New directions for methodology of social and behavioral science: No. 9. Problems with language imprecision* (pp. 25–42). San Francisco, CA: Jossey-Bass.

Perkins, D. N. (1985). General cognitive skills, why not? In S. F. Chipman, J. W. Segal, & R. Glaser (Eds.), *Thinking and learning skills: Vol. 2. Research and open questions* (pp. 339–364). Hillsdale, NJ: Erlbaum.

Perkins, D. N. (1987). Thinking frames: An integrative perspective on teaching cognitive skills. In J. B. Baron & R. J. Sternberg (Eds.), *Teaching thinking skills: Theory and practice*. New York, NY: W.H. Freeman.

Perkins, D. N. (1988). Creativity and the quest for mechanism. In R. J. Sternberg & E. E. Smith (Eds.), *The psychology of human thought* (pp. 309–336). Cambridge, UK: Cambridge University Press.

Perkins, D. (1992). *Smart schools: From training memories to educating minds*. New York, NY: Free Press.

Perkins, D. (1995). *Outsmarting IQ: The emerging science of learnable intelligence*. New York, NY: Free Press.

Perkins, D. N. (2002). The engine of folly. In R. J. Sternberg (Ed.), *Why smart people can be so stupid* (pp. 64–85). New Haven, CT: Yale University Press.

Perkins, D. N., Allen, R., & Hafner, J. (1983). Difficulties in everyday reasoning. In W. Maxwell (Ed.), *Thinking*. Philadelphia, PA: Franklin Institute Press.

Perkinson, H. J. (1993). *Teachers without goals, students without purposes*. New York, NY: McGraw-Hill.

Petrosino, A., Turpin-Petrosino, C., & Buehler, J. (2003). Scared straight and other juvenile awareness programs for preventing juvenile delinquency: A systematic review of the randomized experimental evidence. *The ANNALS of the American Academy of Political and Social Science, 589*, 41–62.

Petrosino, A., Turpin-Petrosino, C., & Finckenauer, J. O. (2000). Well-meaning programs can have harmful effects! Lessons from experiments of programs such as Scared Straight. *Crime & Delinquency, 46*, 354–379.

Petryna, A., Lakoff, A., & Kleinman, A. (Eds.). (2006). *Global pharmaceuticals: Ethics, markets, practices*. Durham, NC: Duke University Press.

Petty, R. E., & Cacioppo, J. T. (1986). The elaboration likelihood model of persuasion. In L. Berkowitz (Ed.), *Advances in experimental social psychology* (Vol. 19, pp. 124–206). Orlando, FL: Academic Press.

Petty, R. E., Cacioppo, J. T., Strathman, A. J., & Priester, J. R. (2005). To think or not to think: Exploring two routes to persuasion. In T. C. Brock & M. C. Green (Eds.), *Persuasion: Psychological insights and perspectives* (2nd ed., pp. 81–116). Thousand Oaks, CA: Sage.

Pewsner, D., Pattaglia, M., Minder, C., Marx, A., Bucher, H. C., & Egger, M. (2004). Ruling a diagnosis in or out with "SpPIn" and "SnNOut": A note of caution. *BMJ, 329*, 209–213.

Pfohl, S. J. (1978). *Predicting dangerousness: The social construction of psychiatric reality.* Lexington, MA: Heath.

Phillips, D. C. (1987). *Philosophy, science and social inquiry: Contemporary methodological controversies in social science and related applied fields of research.* New York, NY: Pergamon Press.

Phillips, D. C. (1990). Postpositivistic science: Myths and realities. In E. G. Guba (Ed.), *The paradigm dialog* (pp. 31–45). Thousand Oaks, CA: Sage.

Phillips, D. C. (1992). *The social scientist's bestiary: A guide to fabled threats to, and defenses of, naturalistic social science.* New York, NY: Pergamon.

Phillips, J. K., Klein, G., & Sieck, W. R. (2005). Expertise in judgment and decision making: A case for training intuitive decision skills. In D. J. Koehler & N. Harvey (Eds.), *Blackwell handbook of judgment and decision making* (pp. 297–315). Malden, MA: Blackwell.

Pilpel, R. H. (1976). *Churchill in America.* New York, NY: Harcourt Brace Jovanovich.

Plato. (1954/1993). *The last days of Socrates* (H. Tredennick & H. Tarrant, Trans.). New York, NY: Penguin.

Plomin, R. (2011). Commentary: Why are children in the same family so different? Non-shared environment three decades later. *International Journal of Epidemiology, 40*, 582–592.

Plous, S., & Zimbardo, P. G. (1986). Attributional biases among clinicians: A comparison of psychoanalysts and behavior therapists. *Journal of Clinical and Consulting Psychology, 54*, 568–570.

Pollack, A. (2009, August 6). Quick tests for the flu found often inaccurate. *New York Times.*

Pope, K. S., & Vasquez, M. J. T. (2011). *Ethics in psychotherapy and counseling: A practical guide* (4th ed.). Hoboken, NJ: John Wiley & Sons.

Popper, K. R. (1957/1983). The aim of science. In D. Miller (Ed.), *A pocket Popper* (pp. 162–170). London, UK: Fontana Press.

Popper, K. R. (1959). *The logic of scientific discovery.* London, UK: Hutchinson.

Popper, K. R. (1963/1972). *Conjectures and refutations: The growth of scientific knowledge* (4th ed.). London, UK: Routledge & Kegan Paul.

Popper, K. R. (1992). *In search of a better world: Lectures and essays from thirty years.* London, UK: Routledge & Kegan Paul.

Popper, K. R. (1994). *The myth of the framework: In defense of science and rationality.* M. A. Notturno (Ed.). New York, NY: Routledge.

Popper, K. R. (1998). *The world of Parmenides: Essays on the pre-Socratic enlightenment.* New York, NY: Routledge.

Porter, N., & Geis, F. (1981). Women and nonverbal leadership cues: When seeing is not believing. In C. Mayo & N. M. Henley (Eds.), *Gender and nonverbal behavior* (pp. 39–61). New York, NY: Springer-Verlag.

Porter, R. (2002). *Quacks: Fakers & charlatans in English medicine.* Charleston, SC: Tempus.

Pottick, K. L., Wakefield, J. C., Kirk, S. A., & Tian, X. (2003). Influence of social workers' characteristics on the perception of mental disorder in youths. *Social Service Review, 77*, 431–454.

Pratkanis, A. R. (2007). *The science of social influence: Advances and future progress.* New York, NY: Psychology Press.

Pratkanis, A. R., & Aronson, E. (2001). *Age of propaganda: The everyday use and abuse of persuasion* (Rev. ed.). New York, NY: W.H. Freeman.

Premack, D. (1965). *Reinforcement therapy.* In D. Levine (Ed.), *Nebraska symposium on motivation* (pp. 23–180). Lincoln, NE: University of Nebraska Press.

President's New Freedom Commission on Mental Health. (2005). Retrieved September 9, 2005, from www.mentalhealthcommission.gov

Prilleltensky, I., Prilleltensky, O., & Voorhees, C. (2008). Psychopolitical validity in the helping professions: applications to research, interventions, case conceptualization, and therapy. In C. I. Cohen & S. Timimi (Eds.), *Liberatory psychiatry: Philosophy, politics, and mental health* (pp. 105–130). New York, NY: Cambridge University Press.

Proctor, R. N., & Schriebinger, L. (Eds.) (2008). *Agnatology: The making and unmaking of ignorance.* Palo Alto, CA: Stanford University Press.

Pronin, E., Kruger, J., Savitsky, K., & Ross, L. (2001). You don't know me, but I know you: The illusion of asymmetric insight. *Journal of Personality and Social Psychology, 81*, 36.

Pronin, E., Puccio, C., & Ross, L. (2002). Understanding misunderstanding: Social psychological perspectives. In T. Gilovich, D. Griffin, & D. Kahneman (Eds.), *Heuristics and biases: The psychology of intuitive judgment* (pp. 636–665). New York, NY: Columbia University Press.

Pronin, E., & Ross, L. (1999). *Two views of romantic break-ups: Biased perceptions of the clarity of intimate communication.* Unpublished manuscript, Stanford University.

Prounis, C. (2004). The art of advertorial. *Pharmaceutical Executive, 24*(5), 152–164.

Pryor, J. B., & Kriss, M. (1977). The cognitive dynamics of salience in the attribution process. *Journal of Personality and Social Psychology, 35*, 49–55.

Pryor, K. (1984). *Don't shoot the dog.* New York, NY: Bantam.

Psychological Clinical Science Accreditation System (PCSAS). http://pscas.org

Pyszczynski, T., & Greenberg, J. (1987). Toward an integration of cognitive and motivational perspectives on social inference: A biased hypothesis-testing model. In L. Berkowitz (Ed.), *Advances in experimental social psychology* (Vol. 20, pp. 297–340). Orlando, FL: Academic Press.

Quinsey, V. L., Harris, G. T., Rice, M. E., & Cormier, C. A. (2006). *Violent offenders: Appraising and managing risk* (2nd ed.). Washington, DC: American Psychological Association.

Raghunathan, R., & Pham, M. T. (1999). All negative moods are not created equal: Motivational influences of anxiety and sadness on decision making. *Organizational Behavior and Human Decision Performance, 79*, 56–77.

Rank, H. (1982). *The pitch.* Park Forest, IL: Counter-propaganda Press.

Rank, H. (1984). *The peptalk: How to analyze political language.* Park Forest, IL: Counter-Propaganda Press.

Ravitch, D. (2003). *The language police: How pressure groups restrict what students learn.* New York, NY: Alfred A. Knopf.

Reason, J. (1997). *Managing the risks of organizational accidents.* Brookfield, VT: Ashgate.

Reason, J. (2001). Understanding adverse events: The human factor. In C. Vincent (Ed.), *Clinical risk management: Enhancing patient safety* (2nd ed., pp. 9–30). London, UK: BMJ Books.

Regan, D. T., & Totten, J. (1975). Empathy and attribution: Turning observers into actors. *Journal of Personality and Social Psychology, 32*, 850–856.

Regehr, G., Freeman, R., Robb, A., Missiha, N., & Heisey, R. (1999). OSCE performance evaluations made by standardized patients: Comparing checklist and global ratings scores. *Academic Medicine, 74*, S135–S137.

Reid, J. B., Patterson, G. R., & Snyder, J. (Eds.). (2002). *Antisocial behavior in children and adolescents: A developmental analysis and model for intervention.* Washington, DC: American Psychological Association.

Reiman, J. (2004). *The rich get richer and the poor get prison* (7th ed.). Boston, MA: Allyn & Bacon.

Renaud, H., & Estess, F. (1961). Life history interviews with one hundred normal American males: "Pathogenicity" of childhood. *American Journal of Orthopsychiatry, 31*, 796–802.

Renstrom, L., Andersson, B., & Marton, F. (1990). Students' conceptions of matter. *Journal of Educational Psychology, 82*, 555–569.

Renstrom, L., Andersson, B., & Marton, F. (1990). Students' conceptions of matter. *Journal of Educational Psychology, 82*, 555–569.

Rhoads, S. E. (2004). *Taking sex differences seriously.* San Francisco, CA: Encounter Books.

Richard, D. C., & Lauterbach, D. (2004). Computers in the training and practice of behavioral assessment. In S. N. Haynes & E. M. Heibey (Eds.), *Comprehensive handbook of psychological assessment: Vol. 3. Behavioral assessment* (pp. 222–245). Hoboken, NJ: John Wiley & Sons.

Richman-Hirsch, W. L. (2001). Post-training interventions to enhance transfer: The moderating effects of work environments. *Human Resource Development Quarterly, 12*, 105–120.

Robbins, L. C. (1963). The accuracy of parental recall of aspects of child development and child-rearing practices. *Journal of Abnormal and Social Psychology, 66*, 216–270.

Roberts, B. W., & DelVecchio, W. S. (2000). The rank-order consistency of personality traits from childhood to old age: A quantitative review of longitudinal studies. *Psychological Bulletin, 126*, 325.

Roberts, I., Kramer, M. S., & Suissa, S. (1996). Does home visiting prevent childhood injury? A systematic review of randomized controlled trials. *BMJ, 312*, 29–33.

Roberts, L., Ahmed, I., & Hall, S. (2004). Intersessionary prayer for the alleviation of ill health. Cochrane Review. *The Cochrane Library*, Issue 3. Chichester, UK: John Wiley & Sons.

Roediger, H. L., & Bergman, E. T. (1998). The controversy over recovered memories. *Psychology, Public Policy, & Law, 4*, 1091–1109.

Roese, N. J., & Olson, J. M. (Eds.). (1995). *What might have been: The social psychology of counterfactual thinking.* Mahwah, NJ: Erlbaum.

Rogowski, S. (2010). *Social work: The rise and fall of a profession?* Bristol, UK: Policy Press.

Rokeach, M. (1960). *The open and closed mind.* New York, NY: Basic Books.

Rook, K. S. (1984). The negative side of social interaction: Impact on psychological well being. *Journal of Personality and Social Psychology, 46*, 1097–1108.

Rose, D., Fleischmann, P., Wykes, T., Leese, M., & Bindman, J. (2003). Patients' perspectives on electro-convulsive therapy: Systematic review. *BMJ, 326*, 1363–1367.

Rose, S. C., Bisson, J., Churchill, R., & Wessely, S. (2002). Psychological debriefing for preventing post traumatic stress disorder (PTSD). (Review.) In *Cochrane Library*, Issue 1. Chichester, UK: John Wiley & Sons.

Roseman, M., Milette, K., Bero, L. A., Coyne, J. C., Lexchin, J., Turner, E. H., & Thombs, B. D. (2011). Reporting of conflicts of interest in meta-analyses of trials of pharmacological treatments. *Journal of American Medical Association, 305*, 1008–1017.

Rosen, A., & Proctor, E. K. (2002). Standards for evidence-based social work practice. In A. R. Roberts & G. J. Greene (Eds.), *The social workers' desk reference* (pp. 743–747). New York: Oxford University Press.

Rosen, A., Proctor, E. K., Morrow-Howell, N., & Staudt, M. (1995). Rationales for practice decisions: Variations in knowledge use by decision task and social work service. *Research on Social Work Practice, 15,* 501–523.

Rosen, G. M. (1981). Guidelines for the review of do-it-yourself treatment books. *Contemporary Psychology, 26,* 189–191.

Rosenau, P. M. (1992). *Post-modernism and the social sciences: Insights, inroads, and intrusions.* Princeton, NJ: Princeton University Press.

Rosenbaum, P. R. (2002). *Observational studies (Springer series in statistics)* (2nd ed.). New York, NY: Springer-Verlag.

Rosenhan, D. L. (1973). On being sane in insane places. *Science, 179,* 250–258.

Rosenthal, A. M. (1964). *Thirty-eight witnesses.* New York, NY: McGraw-Hill.

Rosenthal, R. (1994). On being one's own study: Experimenter effects in behavioral research—30 years later. In W. R. Shadish & S. Fuller (Eds.), *The social psychology of science* (pp. 214–229). New York, NY: Guilford.

Rosenthal, R., & Jacobson, L. (1992). *Pygmalian in the classroom: Teacher expectations and pupils' intellectual development.* New York, NY: Irvington.

Rosenthal, T. (1994). Science and ethics in conducting, analyzing, and reporting psychological research. *Psychological Science, 5,* 127–134.

Rosenthal, T. (2001). *Workshop on meta-analysis.* Berkeley, CA: University of California.

Ross, L., Amabile, T., & Steinmetz, J. (1977). Social roles, social control and biases in social perception processes. *Journal of Personality and Social Psychology, 35,* 485–494.

Ross, L., Greene, D., & House, P. (1977). The false consensus phenomenon: An attributional bias in self-perception and social perception processes. *Journal of Experimental Social Psychology, 13,* 279–301.

Ross, L., & Lepper, M. R. (1980). The perseverance of beliefs: Empirical and normative considerations. In R. A. Schweder (Ed.), *New directions for methodology of social and behavioral science: No. 4. Fallible judgment in behavioral research* (pp. 17–36). San Francisco, CA: Jossey-Bass.

Ross, L., Lepper, M. R., & Hubbard, J. (1975). Perseverance in self perception and social perception: Biased attributional processes in the debriefing paradigm. *Journal of Personality and Social Psychology, 32,* 880–892.

Ross, L., & Ward, A. (1996). Naïve realism in everyday life: Implications for social conflict and misunderstanding. In T. Brown, E. Reed, & E. Turiel (Eds.), *Values and knowledge* (pp. 103–135). Hillsdale, NJ: Erlbaum.

Rossi, P. H., Lipsey, M. W., & Freeman, H. E. (2003). *Evaluation: A systematic approach* (7th ed.). Thousand Oaks, CA: Sage.

Rubin, A., & Parrish, D. (2007). Problematic phrases in the conclusions of published outcome studies: Implications for evidence-based practice. *Research on Social Work Practice, 17,* 334–347.

Ryan, W. (1976). *Blaming the victim* (Rev. ed.). New York, NY: Vantage.

Rycroft, C. (1973). *A critical dictionary of psychoanalysis.* Totowa, NJ: Littlefield, Adams.

Rzepnicki, T. L., & Johnson, P. R. (2005). Examining decision errors in child protection: A new application of root cause analysis. *Children and Youth Services Review, 27,* 393–407.

Sackett, D. L. (1979). Bias in analytic research. *Journal of Chronic Disease, 32,* 51–63.

Sackett, D. L. (2002). The arrogance of preventive medicine. *Canadian Medical Association Journal, 167,* 363–364.

Sackett, D. L., & Oxman, A. D. (2003). Harlot pie: amalgamation of the world's two oldest professions. *BMJ, 327,* 1442–1445.

Sackett, D. L., Richardson, W. S., Rosenberg, W., & Haynes, R. B. (1997). *Evidence-based medicine: How to practice and teach EBM.* New York, NY: Churchill Livingstone.

Sackett, D. L., Rosenberg, W. M. C., Gray, J. A. M., Haynes, R. B., & Richardson, W. S. (1996). Evidence-based medicine: What it is and what it isn't. *BMJ, 312,* 71–72.

Sackett, D. L., Straus, S. E., Richardson, W. S., Rosenberg, W., & Haynes, R. B. (2000). *Evidence-based medicine: How to practice and teach EBM* (2nd ed.). New York, NY: Churchill Livingstone.

Sagan, C. (1987). The burden of skepticism. *The Skeptical Inquirer, 12,* 38–74.

Sagan, C. (1990). Why we need to understand science. *The Skeptical Inquirer, 14,* 263–269.

Sagan, C. (1995). The fine art of baloney detection. In *The demon-haunted world: Science as a candle in the dark.* New York, NY: Random House.

Salas, E., & Klein, G. (Eds.). (2001). *Linking expertise and naturalistic decision making.* Mahwah, NJ: Erlbaum.

Sally Clark freed after appeal court quashes her convictions. (2003). *News, BMJ, 326,* 304.

Salovey, P., & Turk, D. C. (1988). Some effects of mood on clinicians' memory. In D. C. Turk & P. Salovey (Eds.), *Reasoning, inference and judgement in clinical psychology* (pp. 107–123). New York, NY: Free Press.

Sameroff, A. J., Lewis, M., & Miller, S. M. (Eds.). (2000). *Handbook of developmental psychopathology* (2nd ed.). Dordrecht, Netherlands: Kluwer Academic.

Sampson, E. E. (1977). Psychology and the American ideal. *Journal of Personality and Social Psychology, 35,* 767–782.

Sanford, A. J. (1985). *Cognition and cognitive psychology.* Hove, East Sussex, UK: Erlbaum.

Sarnoff, S. K. (2001). *Sanctified snake oil: The effect of junk science on public policy.* Westport, CT: Praeger.

Schacter, D. L. (1999). The seven sins of memory: Insights from psychology and cognitive neuroscience. *American Psychologist, 54*(3), 182–203.

Scheff, T. J. (1984a). *Being mentally ill: A sociological theory* (2nd ed.). New York, NY: Aldine.

Scheff, T. J. (1984b). *Labeling madness* (2nd ed.). Englewood Cliffs, NJ: Prentice Hall.

Schlenker, B. R. (2003). Self-presentation. In M. R. Leary & J. P. Tangney (Eds.), *Handbook of self and identity* (pp. 492–518). New York, NY: Guilford.

Schnaitter, R. (1986). Behavior as a function of inner states and outer circumstances. In T. Thompson & M. D. Zeiler (Eds.), *Analysis and integration of behavioral units* (pp. 247–274). Hillsdale, NJ: Erlbaum.

Schneider, D. J. (2004). *The psychology of stereotyping*. New York, NY: Guilford.

Schnelle, J. F. (1974). A brief report on invalidity of parent evaluations of behavior change. *Journal of Applied Behavior Analysis, 7*, 341–343.

Schoenfeld, A. H. (1982). Measures of problem-solving performance and of problem-solving instruction. *Journal for Research on Mathematics Education, 13*, 31–49.

Schon, D. (1990). *Educating the reflective practitioner* (New ed.). San Francisco, CA: Jossey-Bass.

Schopenhauer, A. (1942). The art of controversy. In A. Schopenhauer, *The essays of Arthur Schopenhauer* (T. B. Saunders, Trans.). New York, NY: John Wiley & Sons.

Schrank, J. (2011). The language of advertising claims. home.olemiss.edu, downloaded March 14, 2011.

Schraw, G., & Dennison, R. S. (1994). Assessing metacognitive awareness. *Contemporary Educational Psychology, 19*, 460–475.

Schultz, T. (Ed.). (1989). *The fringes of reason: A whole earth catalog*. New York, NY: Harmony Books.

Schulz, K. F., Altman, D. G., Moher, D. for the CONSORT Group. (2010). CONSORT 2010 statement: Updated guidelines for reporting parallel group randomised trials. *BMJ, 340*, 698–702.

Schulz, K. F., Chalmers, I., Hayes, R. J., & Altman, D. G. (1995). Empirical evidence of bias. Dimensions of methodological quality associated with estimates of treatment effects in controlled clinical trials. *Journal of the American Medical Association, 273*(5), 408–412.

Schwartz, I. M. (1989). *(In)justice for juveniles: Rethinking the best interests of the child.* Lexington, MA: Lexington.

Schwartz, L. M., & Woloshin, S. (2011). The drug facts box: Making informed decisions about prescription drugs possible. In G. Gigerenzer & J. A. M. Gray (Eds.), *Better doctors, better patients, better decisions: Envisioning health care 2020* (pp. 233–242). Cambridge, MA: MIT Press.

Schwartz, L. M., Woloshin, S., & Welch, H. G. (2007). The drug facts box: Providing consumers with simple tabular data on drug benefit and harm. *Medical Decision Making, 5,* 655–662.

Schwartz, N. (2002). Feelings as information: Moods influence judgments and processing strategies. In T. Gilovich, D. Griffin, & D. Kahneman (Eds.), *Heuristics and biases: The psychology of intuitive judgment* (pp. 534–547). New York, NY: Cambridge University Press.

Science and Engineering Indicators: 2010. National Science Foundation, National Center for Science and Engineering Statistics. http://www.nsf.gov/statistics

Scott, S., Knapp, M., Henderson, J., & Maughan, B. (2001). Financial cost of social exclusion: Follow-up study of anti-social children into adulthood. *BMJ, 323,* 191–194.

Scott, T., Stanford, N., & Thompson, D. R. (2004). Killing me softly: Myth in pharmaceutical advertising. *BMJ, 329,* 1484–1487.

Scriven, M. (1976). *Reasoning.* New York, NY: McGraw-Hill.

Scull, A. (2005). *Madhouse: A tragic tale of megalomania and modern medicine.* New Haven, CT: Yale University Press.

Secker-Walker, J., & Taylor-Adams, S. (2001). Clinical incident reporting. In C. Vincent (Ed.), *Clinical risk management: Enhancing patient safety* (2nd ed., pp. 419–438). London: BMJ.

Sedgwick, P. (1982). *Psycho politics.* New York: Harper & Row.

Seech, Z. (1993). *Open minds and everyday reasoning.* Belmont, CA: Wadsworth Publishing Co.

Segal, D. L., & Hersen, M. (2010). *Diagnostic interviewing* (4th ed.). SpringerLink (Online service). eBook. Boston, MA: Springer Science & Business Media LLC.

Segal, S. P., Bola, J. R., & Watson, M. A. (1996). Race, quality of care, and antipsychotic prescribing practices in psychiatric emergency services. *Psychiatric Services, 47,* 282–286.

Self-test advertisement for professional liability insurance. (1987, April). *NASW News, 32*(4), 17.

Semin, G. R., & Manstead, A. S. R. (1983). *The accountability of conduct: A social psychological analysis.* Orlando, FL: Academic Press.

Shadish, W. R., Cook, T. D., & Campbell, D. T. (2002). *Experimental and quasi-experimental designs for generalized causal inference.* Boston, MA: Houghton Mifflin.

Shaffer, V. A., & Hulsey, L. (2009). Are patient decision aids effective? Insight from revisiting the debate between correspondence and coherence theories of judgment. *Judgment and Decision Making, 4,* 141–146.

Shanks, D. R. (2005). Judging covariation and causation. In D. J. Koehler & N. Harvey (Eds.), *Blackwell handbook of judgment and decision making* (pp. 220–239). Malden, MA: Blackwell.

Shanteau, J. (1992). How much information does an expert use? Is it relevant? *Acta Psychologica, 81*, 75–86.

Sharpe, V. A., & Faden, A. I. (1998). *Medical harm: Historical, conceptual, and ethical dimensions of iatrogenic illness*. New York, NY: Cambridge University Press.

Sheldon, B., & Chilvers, R. (2000). *Evidence-based social care: A study of prospects and problems*. Lyme Regis, UK: Russell House.

Sheldon, T. A., Guyatt, G. H., & Haines, A. (1998). Getting research findings into practice: When to act on the evidence. *BMJ, 317*, 139–142.

Sherden, W. A. (1998). *The fortune sellers: The big business of buying and selling predictions*. New York, NY: John Wiley & Sons.

Sherman, L. W., Farrington, D. P., Welsh, B. C., & MacKenzie, D. L. (Eds.). (2002). *Evidence-based crime prevention*. London, UK: Routledge.

Shermer, M. (1997). *Why people believe weird things: Pseudoscience, superstition, and other confusions of our time*. New York, NY: W.H. Freeman.

Shorter, E., & Tyrer, P. (2003). Separation of anxiety and depressive disorders: Blind alley in psychopharmacology and classification of disease. *BMJ, 327*, 158–160.

Shweder, R. A. (1977). Likeness and likelihood in everyday thought: Magical thinking in judgments about personality. *Current Anthropology, 18*, 637–658.

Shweder, R. A., & Miller, J. G. (1985). The social construction of the person: How is it possible? In K. J. Gergen & K. E. Davis (Eds.), *The social construction of the person* (pp. 41–72). New York, NY: Springer-Verlag.

Silverman, K. (1986). *Benjamin Franklin: The autobiography and other writings*. New York, NY: Penguin.

Silverman, W. A. (1980). *Retrolental fibroplasia: A modern parable*. New York, NY: Grune & Stratton.

Simon, H. (1955). A behavioral model of rational choice. *Quarterly Journal of Economics, 69*, 99–118.

Simon, H. (1982). *Models of bounded rationality*. Cambridge, MA: MIT Press.

Simon, H. A. (1983). *Reason in human affairs*. Oxford, UK: Basil Blackwell.

Simon, H. A. (1990). Alternative visions of rationality. In P. K. Moser (Ed.), *Rationality in action: Contemporary approaches* (pp. 189–204). New York, NY: Cambridge University Press.

Sinclair, J. C., Cook, R. J., Guyatt, G. H., Pauker, S. G., & Cook, D. J. (2001). When should an effective treatment be used? Deviation of the threshold number needed to treat and the minimum event rate for treatment. *Journal of Clinical Epidemiology, 54*(3), 253–262.

Sinclair, W. J. (1909). *Semmelweis, his life and his doctrine: A chapter in the history of medicine*. Manchester University Press, UK.

Singer, B. D. (1978). Assessing social errors. *Journal of Social Policy, 9*, 27–34.

Singh, I. (2002). Bad boys, good mothers, and the "miracle" of Ritalin. *Science in Context, 15*, 577–603.

Singh, I. (2004). Doing their jobs: Mothering with Ritalin in a culture of mother blame. *Social Science & Medicine, 59*, 1193–1205.

Skinner, B. F. (1974). *About behaviorism*. New York, NY: Knopf.

Skrabanek, P. (1990). Reductionist fallacies in the theory and treatment of mental disorders. *International Journal of Mental Health, 19*, 6–18.

Skrabanek, P., & McCormick, J. (1998). *Follies and fallacies in medicine* (3rd ed.). Whithorn, Scotland, UK: Tarragon Press.

Slovic, P., Finucane, M., Peters, E., & MacGregor, D. G. (2002). The affect heuristic. In T. Gilovich & D. Griffin (Eds.), *Heuristics and biases: The psychology of intuitive judgment* (pp. 397–420). New York, NY: Cambridge University Press.

Slovic, P., Fischhoff, B., & Lichtenstein, S. (1976). Cognitive processes and societal risk taking. In J. S. Carroll & J. W. Payne (Eds.), *Cognitive and social behavior* (pp. 165–184). Hillsdale, NJ: Erlbaum.

Slovic, P., Fischhoff, B., & Lichtenstein, S. (1982a). Facts versus fears: Understanding perceived risk. In D. Kahneman, P. Slovic, & A. Tversky (Eds.), *Judgment under uncertainty: Heuristics and biases*. New York, NY: Cambridge University Press.

Slovic, P., Fischhoff, B., & Lichtenstein, S. (1982b). Response mode, framing, and information-processing effects in risk assessment. In R. M. Hogarth (Ed.), *New directions for methodology of social and behavioral science: No. 11. Question framing and response consistency* (pp. 21–36). San Francisco, CA: Jossey-Bass.

Slovic, P., Kunreuther, H., & White, G. F. (1974). Decision processes, rationality, and adjustment to natural hazards. In G. F. White (Ed.), *Natural hazards: Local, national, and global* (pp. 187–205). Oxford, UK: Oxford University Press.

Smedslund, J. (1963). The concept of correlation in adults. *Scandinavian Journal of Psychology, 4*, 165–173.

Smith, C. R., & Hunsaker, D. M. (1972). *The bases of argument: Ideas in conflict*. Indianapolis, IN: Bobbs-Merrill.

Smith, R. (2003). Do patients need to read research? *BMJ, 326*, 1307.

Smith, R. (2005). Investigating the previous studies of a fraudulent author. *BMJ, 331*, 288–291.

Smith, R. S. W. (2011). The chasm between evidence and practice: Extent, causes, and remedies. In G. Gigerenzer & J. A. M. Gray (Eds.), *Better doctors, better patients, better decisions: Envisioning health care 2020* (pp. 265–280). Cambridge, MA: MIT Press.

Smith, T. B., Rodriguez, M. D., & Bernal, G. (2011). Culture. In J. C. Norcross (Ed.), *Psychotherapy relationships that work: Evidence-based responsiveness* (2nd ed., pp. 316–335). New York, NY: Oxford University Press.

Smits, P. B. A., Verbeek, J. H. A., & de Buisonjé, C. D. (2002). Problem based learning in continuing medical education: A review of controlled evaluation studies. *BMJ*, *324*, 153–156.

Snyder, C. R., & Clair, M. S. (1977). Does insecurity breed acceptance? Effects of trait and situational insecurity on acceptance of positive and negative diagnostic feedback. *Journal of Counseling and Clinical Psychology*, *45*, 843–850.

Snyder, C. F., Wu, A. W., Miller, R. S., Jensen, R. E., Bantug, E. T., & Wolff, A. C. (2011). The role of informatics in promoting patient-centered care. *Cancer*, *17*, 211–218.

Snyder, C. R., Higgins, R. L., & Stucky, R. J. (1983). *Excuses: Masquerades in search of grace*. New York, NY: John Wiley & Sons.

Snyder, C. R., Shenkel, R. J., & Schmidt, A. (1976). Effects of role perspective and client psychiatric history on locus of problem. *Journal of Consulting and Clinical Psychology*, *44*, 467–472.

Snyder, M., & Swann, W. B. (1978). Behavioral confirmation in social interaction: From social perception to social reality. *Journal of Experimental Social Psychology*, *14*, 148–162.

Snyder, M., Tanke, E. D., & Berscheid, E. (1977). Social perception and interpersonal behavior: On the self-fulfilling nature of social stereotypes. *Journal of Personality and Social Psychology*, *35*, 656–666.

Snyder, M., & Thomsen, C. J. (1988). Interactions between therapists and clients: Hypothesis testing and behavioral confirmation. In D. C. Turk & P. Salovey (Eds.), *Reasoning, inference, and judgement in clinical psychology* (pp. 124–152). New York, NY: Free Press.

Snyder, R. E. (1966). Mammography: Contributions and limitations in the management of cancer of the breast. *Clinical Obstetrics and Gynecology*, *9*, 207–220.

Soares, H. P., Daniels, S., Kumar, A., Clarke, M., Scott, C., Swann, S., & Djulbegovic, B. (2004). Bad reporting does not mean bad methods for randomized trials: Observational study of randomized controlled trials performed by the Radiation Therapy Oncology Group. *BMJ*, *328*, 22–24.

Sobell, M. B., & Sobell, L. C. (1982). Controlled drinking: A concept coming of age. In K. R. Blankstein & J. Polivy (Eds.), *Self-control and self-modification of emotional behavior* (pp. 143–162). New York, NY: Plenum.

Sokal, A. D. (1998). What the social text affair does and does not prove. In N. Koertge (Ed.), *A house built on sand: Exposing postmodernist myths about science* (pp. 9–22). New York, NY: Oxford University Press.

Soman, D. (2005). Framing, loss aversion, and mental accounting. In D. J. Koehler & N. Harvey (Eds.), *Blackwell handbook of judgment and decision making* (pp. 379–398). Malden, MA: Blackwell.

Sontag, S. (1991). *Illness as a metaphor and AIDS and its metaphors*. London, UK: Penguin.

Sparrow, M. (2000). *License to steal: How fraud bleeds America's health care system.* Boulder, CO: Westview Press.

Spock, B. (1945). *Baby and child care.* New York, NY: Pocket Books.

Staats, A. W., & Staats, C. K. (1963). *Complex human behavior: A systematic extension of learning principles.* New York, NY: Holt, Rinehart & Winston.

Stanovich, K. E. (1992). *How to think straight about psychology* (3rd ed.). New York, NY: HarperCollins.

Stanovich, K. E. (1998). *How to think straight about psychology* (5th ed.). New York, NY: Longman.

Stanovich, K. E., & West, R. F. (2002). Individual differences in reasoning: Implications for the rationality debate? In T. Gilovich, D. Griffin, & D. Kahneman (Eds.), *Heuristics and biases: The psychology of intuitive judgment* (pp. 421–440). New York, NY: Cambridge University Press.

Starcevic, V. (2002). Opportunistic rediscovery of mental disorders by the pharmaceutical industry. *Psychotherapy and Psychosomatics, 71,* 305–310.

Stein, T. J. & Gambrill, E. D. (1977). Facilitating decision making in foster care: The Alameda Project. *Social Service Review, 51,* 502–513.

Sternberg, R. J. (1987). Teaching intelligence: The application of cognitive psychology to the improvement of intellectual skills. In J. B. Baron & R. J. Sternberg (Eds.), *Teaching thinking skills: Theory and practice* (pp. 182–218). New York, NY: W.H. Freeman.

Sternberg, R. J., & Kagan, J. (1986). *Intelligence applied: Understanding and increasing your intellectual skills.* San Diego, CA: Harcourt Brace Jovanovich.

Sternberg, R. J., & Wagner, R. K. (Eds.). (1986). *Practical intelligence: Nature and origins of competence in the everyday world.* Cambridge, UK: Cambridge University Press.

Sterne, J. A., Egger, M., & Smith, G. D. (2001). Investigating and dealing with publication and other biases. In M. Egger, G. D. Smith, & D. G. Altman. (Eds.), *Systematic Reviews in Healthcare: Meta-analysis in Context* (2nd Ed.). London, UK: BMJ Books.

Steurer, J., Fischer, J. E., Bachmann, L. M., Koller, M., & ter Riet, G. (2002). Communicating accuracy of tests to general practitioners: A controlled study. *BMJ, 324,* 824–826.

Stivers, R. (2001). *Technology as magic: The triumph of the irrational.* New York, NY: Continuum.

Stoetz, D., Karger, H. J., & Carrilio, T. (2010). *A dream deferred: How social work education lost its way and what can be done.* New Brunswick, NJ: Transaction.

Stone, A. A., Turkkan, J. S., Bachrach, C. A., Jobe, J. B., Kurtzman, H. S., & Cain, V. S. (Eds.). (1999). *The science of self-report: Implications for research and practice.* Mahwah, NJ: Erlbaum.

Stone, G. C. (1979). Patient compliance and the role of the expert. *Journal of Social Issues, 35,* 34–59.

Storms, M. (1973). Video-tape and attribution process: Reversing actors' and observers' points are viewed. *Journal of Personality and Social Psychology, 27,* 165–174.

Straus, S. E., & McAlister, D. C. (2000). Evidence-based medicine: A commentary on common criticisms. *Canadian Medical Journal, 163,* 837–841.

Straus, S. E., Richardson, W. S., Glasziou, P., & Haynes, R. B. (2005). *Evidence-based medicine: How to practice and teach EBM* (3rd Ed.). New York, NY: Churchill-Livingstone.

Strohman, R. C. (2003). Genetic determination as a failing paradigm in biology and medicine: Implications for health and wellness. *Journal of Social Work Education, 39,* 169–191.

Strong, P. M. (1979). *The ceremonial order of the clinic.* London, UK: Routledge & Kegan Paul.

Strupp, H. (1976). The nature of the therapeutic influence and its basic ingredients. In A. Burton (Ed.), *What makes behavior change possible* (pp. 96–112). New York, NY: Brunner/Mazel.

Strupp, H. H., & Anderson, T. (1997). On the limitations of therapy manuals. *Clinical Psychology: Science and Practice, 4,* 76–82.

Strupp, H. H., & Hadley, S. W. (1979). Specific versus nonspecific factors in psychotherapy: A controlled study of outcome. *Archives of General Psychiatry, 36,* 1125–1136.

Sue, D. W., & Sue, D. (1990). *Counseling the culturally different: Theory and practice* (2nd ed.). New York, NY: Wiley-Interscience.

Sue, D. W., & Sue, D. (2002). *Counseling the culturally different: Theory and practice* (4th ed.). New York, NY: Wiley-Interscience.

Suedfeld, P., & Tetlock, P. E. (2001). Cognitive styles. In A. Tesser & N. Schwartz (Eds.), *Blackwell international handbook of social psychology: Intra-individual processes* (Vol. 1, pp. 284–304). London, UK: Blackwell.

Summerfield, D. (2001). The invention of post-traumatic stress disorder and the social usefulness of a psychiatric category. *BMJ, 322,* 95–98.

Surakka, I., Pirkola, S., Suvisaari, J., Lonnqvist, J., Peltonen, V., Ripatti, S., & Hovatta, I. (2010). Childhood adversities are associated with shorter telomere length at adult age both in individuals with an anxiety disorder and controls. *PLoS ONE, 5:*e10826.

Swann, W. B., Jr., & Guiliano, T. (1987). Confirmatory search strategies in social interaction: How, when, why, and with what consequences. *Journal of Social and Clinical Psychology, 5,* 511–524.

Swartz, R. J., & Perkins, D. N. (1990). *Teaching thinking: Issues and approaches.* Pacific Grove, CA: Critical Thinking Press and Software.

Sweet, M. (2011). Doctor who complained to regulator about weight loss product is sued for libel. *BMJ, 342*:d3728.

Szasz, T. S. (1961). *The myth of mental illness: Foundations of a theory of personal conduct.* New York, NY: Harper & Row.

Szasz, T. S. (1970). *The manufacture of madness: A comparative study of the Inquisition and the mental health movement.* New York, NY: Harper & Row.

Szasz, T. S. (1987). *Insanity: The idea and its consequences.* New York, NY: John Wiley & Sons.

Szasz, T. S. (1994). *Cruel compassion: Psychiatric control of society's unwanted.* New York, NY: John Wiley & Sons.

Szasz, T. S. (2001). *Pharmacracy: Medicine and politics in America.* Westport, CT: Praeger.

Szasz, T. S. (2003). *Liberation by oppression: A comparative study of slavery and psychiatry.* New Brunswick, NJ: Transaction Press.

Tallent, N. (1988). *Psychological report writing* (3rd ed.). Englewood Cliffs, NJ: Prentice Hall. (See also 4th edition, 1993.)

Tallis, R. (2011). *Aping mankind: Neuromania, Darwinitis and the misrepresentation of humanity.* Durham, UK: Acumen Publishing.

Tanne, J. H. (2010). U.S. drug companies paid $15 bn in fines for criminal and civil violations over the last five years. *BMJ, 341*:c7360.

Tarn, D. M., Heritage, J., Paternita, D. A., Hays, R. D., Kravitz, R. L., & Wenger, N. S. (2006). Physician communication when prescribing new medications. *Archives of Internal Medicine, 166*, 1855–1862.

Tavris, C. (1989). Anger: *The misunderstood emotion.* New York, NY: Simon & Schuster.

Tavris, C. (1992). *The mismeasure of women.* New York, NY: Simon & Schuster.

Tavris, C. (2001). *Psychobabble & biobunk: Using psychology to think critically about issues in the news* (2nd ed.). Upper Saddle River, NJ: Prentice Hall.

Tavris, C. (2003, February 28). Mind games: Psychological warfare between therapists and scientists. *Chronicle of Higher Education,* B7–B9.

Taylor, E., & Rutter, M. (2002). Classification. Conceptual issues and substantive findings. In M. Rutter & E. Taylor (Eds.), *Child and adolescent psychiatry* (4th ed., pp. 3–17). Malden, MA: Blackwell.

Taylor, S. E., & Fiske, S. T. (1975). Point of view and perceptions of causality. *Journal of Personality and Social Psychology, 32*, 439–445.

Teasdale, J. D., & Fogarty, S. J. (1979). Differential effects of induced mood on retrieval of pleasant and unpleasant events from episodic memory. *Journal of Abnormal Psychology, 88*, 248–257.

Teigen, K. H., & Brun, W. (2003a). Verbal expressions of uncertainty and probability. In D. Hardman & L. Macchi (Eds.), *Thinking: Psychological perspectives on reasoning, judgment and decision making* (pp. 125–145). New York, NY: John Wiley & Sons.

Teigen, K. H., & Brun, W. (2003b). Verbal probabilities: A question of frame? *Journal of Behavioral Decision Making, 16,* 53–72.

Temerlin, M. K. (1968). Suggestion effects in psychiatric diagnosis. *Journal of Nervous and Mental Disease, 147,* 349–357.

Terry, D. R. (1973). Structure of argument in debate. In D. R. Terry (Ed.), *Modern debate case techniques* (pp. 95–101). Skokie, IL: National Textbook.

Tesh, S. N. (1988). *Hidden arguments of political ideology and disease prevention policy.* New Brunswick, NJ: Rutgers University Press.

Tetlock, P. E. (2003). Correspondence and coherence: Indicators of good judgment in world politics. In D. Hardman & L. Macchi (Eds.), *Thinking: Psychological perspectives on reasoning, judgment and decision making* (pp. 233–250). New York, NY: John Wiley & Sons.

Tetlock, P. (2005). *Expert political judgment: How good is it? How can we know?* Princeton, NJ: Princeton University Press.

Thompson, J. B. (1987). Language and ideology. *Sociological Review, 35,* 517–536.

Thompson, C., Cullum, N., McCaughan, D., Sheldon, T., & Raynor, P. (2004). Nurses, information use, and clinical decision making: The real world potential for evidence-based decisions in nursing. *Evidence Based Nursing, 7,* 68–72.

Thomson O'Brien, M. A., Freemantle, N., Oxman, A. D., Wolf, F., Davis, D. A., & Herrin, J. (2003). Continuing education meetings and workshops: Effects on professional practice and health care outcomes (Cochrane Review). In *Cochrane Library,* Issue 3. Chichester, U.K.: John Wiley & Sons.

Thorngate, W., & Plouffe, L. (1987). The consumption of methodological psychological knowledge. In H. J. Stam, T. B. Rogers, & K. G. Gergen (Eds.), *The analysis of psychological theory: Methodological perspectives* (pp. 61–92). New York, NY: Hemisphere.

Thornley, B., & Adams, C. (1998). Content and quality of 2000 controlled trials in schizophrenia over 50 years. *BMJ, 317,* 1181–1184.

Thornton, H., Edwards, A., & Baum, M. (2003). Women need better information about routine mammography. *BMJ, 327,* 101–103.

Thouless, R. H. (1974). *Straight and crooked thinking: Thirty-eight dishonest tricks of debate.* London, UK: Pan Books.

Thyer, B. A. (2005). The misfortunes of behavioral social work: Misprized, misread, and misconstrued. In S. A. Kirk (Ed.), *Mental health in the social environment: Critical perspectives* (pp. 330–343). New York, NY: Columbia University Press.

Thyer, B. A., & Pignotti, M. (2010). Science and pseudoscience in developmental disabilities: Guidelines for social workers. *Journal of Social Work in Disability & Rehabilitation, 9,* 110–129.

Thyer, B. A., & Pignotti, M. (in press). *Pseudoscience in social work.* New York, NY: Oxford University Press.

Timimi, S. (2002). *Pathological child psychiatry and the medicalization of childhood*. London, UK: Brunner-Routledge.

Timimi, S. (2008). Children's mental health and the global market: An ecological analysis. In C. I. Cohen & S. Timimi (Eds.), *Liberatory psychiatry: Philosophy, politics and mental health* (pp. 163–182). Cambridge, MA: Cambridge University Press.

Timimi, S., & Taylor, E. (2004). ADHD is best understood as a cultural construct. *British Journal of Psychiatry, 184*, 8–9.

Todd, J. T., & Morris, E. K. (1983). Misconception and miseducation: Presentations of radical behaviorism in psychology textbooks. *The Behavior Analyst, 6*, 153–160.

Tooley, J. (1994). Demon, drugs and holy wars: Canadian drug policy as symbolic action. Thesis submitted to the Department of Anthropology, Carleton University.

Toulmin, S. E. (1958/2003). *The uses of argument*. Cambridge, UK: Cambridge University Press.

Toulmin, S. E., Rieke, R., & Janik, A. (1979). *An introduction to reasoning*. New York, NY: Macmillan.

Tousignant, M., & DesMarchais, J. E. (2002). Accuracy of student self-assessment ability compared to their own performance in a problem-based learning medical program: A correlation study. *Advances in Health Sciences Education, 7*, 19–27.

Transparency International. www.transparency.org

Trotter, W. (1916). *Instincts of the herd in peace and war*. London, UK: T.F. Unwin.

Truax, C. (1966). Reinforcement and nonreinforcement in Rogerian psychotherapy. *Journal of Abnormal Psychology, 71*, 1–9.

Truzzi, M. (1976). Sherlock Holmes: Applied social psychologist. In W. B. Sanders (Ed.), *The sociologist as detective: An introduction to research methods* (2nd ed., pp. 50–86). New York, NY: Praeger.

Tuchman, B. W. (1984). *The march of folly: From Troy to Vietnam*. New York, NY: Ballantine.

Tuchman, B. (1989). In Bill Moyers' *A world of ideas: Conversations with thoughtful men and women about American life today and the ideas shaping our future*. New York, NY: Doubleday.

Tuffs, A. (2004). Only 6% of drug advertising material is supported by evidence. *BMJ, 328*, 485.

Tufte, E. R. (1983). *The visual display of quantitative information*. Cheshire, CT: Graphics Press.

Tufte, E. R. (1990). *Envisioning information*. Cheshire, CT: Graphics Press.

Tufte, E. R. (2006). *Beautiful evidence*. Cheshire, CT: Graphics Press.

Turk, D. C., & Salovey, P. (1986). Clinical information processing: Bias inoculation. In R. Ingram (Ed.), *Information processing approaches to psychopathology and clinical psychology* (pp. 306–324). Orlando, FL: Academic Press.

Tversky, A., & Kahneman, D. (1971). Belief in the law of small numbers. *Psychological Bulletin, 76,* 105–110.

Tversky, A., & Kahneman, D. (1973). Availability: A heuristic for judging frequency and probability. *Cognitive Psychology, 5,* 207–232.

Tversky, A., & Kahneman, D. (1974). Judgment under uncertainty: Heuristics and biases. *Science, 185,* 1124–1131.

Tversky, A., & Kahneman, D. (1981). The framing of decisions and the psychology of choice. *Science, 211,* 453–458.

Tversky, A., & Kahneman, D. (1983). Extensional versus intuitive reasoning: The conjunction fallacy in probability judgment. *Psychological Review, 90,* 293–315.

Tweed, R. G., & Lehman, D. R. (2002). Learning considered within a cultural context: Confucian and Socratic approaches. *American Psychologist, 57,* 89–99.

Tyrka, A. R., Price, L. H., Kao, H. T., Porton, B., & Marsella, S. A. (2010). Childhood maltreatment and telomere shortening: Preliminary support for an effect of early stress on cellular aging. *Biological Psychiatry, 67,* 531–534.

U.S. Department of Health and Human Services. (1999). Mental health: A report of the surgeon general. Rockville, MD: U.S. Department of Health and Human Services Substance Abuse and Mental Health Service Administration, Center for Mental Health Services, National Institutes of Health, National Institute of Mental Health.

Valenstein, E. S. (1986). *Great and desperate cures: The rise and decline of psychosurgery and other medical treatments for mental illness.* New York, NY: Basic Books.

Valins, S., & Nisbett, R. E. (1972). Attributional processes in the development and treatment of emotional disorders. In E. E. Jones, D. E. Kanouse, H. H. Kelley, R. E. Nisbett, S. Vallins, & B. Weiner (Eds.), *Attribution: Perceiving the causes of behavior* (pp. 137–150). Morristown, NJ: General Learning Press.

Verhave, T., & Van Hoorn, W. (1984). The temperalization of the self. In K. J. Gergen & M. M. Gergen (Eds.), *Historical social psychology* (pp. 325–346). Hillsdale, NJ: Erlbaum.

Vincent, C., & Taylor-Adams, S. (2001). The investigation and analysis of clinical incidents. In C. Vincent (Ed.), *Clinical risk management: Enhancing patient safety* (2nd ed., pp. 439–460). London, UK: BMJ.

Voermans, N. C., Snijders, A. H., Shoon, Y., & Bloem, B. R. (2007). Review. Why old people fall (and how to stop them). *Practical Neurobiology, 7,* 158–171.

Volpe, R. J., DiPerna, J. C., Hintze, J. M., & Shapiro, E. C. (2005). Observing students in classroom settings. A review of seven coding systems. *School Psychology Review, 34,* 454–474.

Vrij, A., Granhag, P. A., & Porter, S. (2010). Pitfalls and opportunities in nonverbal and verbal lie detection. *Psychological Science in the Public Interest, 11,* 89–121.

Vul, E., Harris, C., Winkielman, P., & Pashler, H. (2009). Puzzlingly high correlations in MRI studies of emotion, personality and social cognition. *Perspectives on Psychological Science, 4,* 274–290.

Vyse, S. (2005). Where do fads come from? In J. W. Jacobson, R. N. Foxx, & J. Mulick (Eds.), *Controversial therapies for developmental disabilities: Fad, fashion, and science in professional practice* (pp. 3–18). Mahwah, NJ: Erlbaum.

Wacquant, L. (2009). *Punishing the poor: The neoliberal government in social insecurity.* Durham, NC: Duke University Press.

Wade, T. C., & Baker, T. B. (1977). Opinions and use of psychological tests: A survey of clinical psychologists. *American Psychologist, 32,* 874–882.

Wahler, R. G. (1980). The insular mother: Her problems in parent child treatment. *Journal of Applied Behavior Analysis, 13,* 207–219.

Wainer, H. (1976). Estimating coefficients in linear models: It don't make no nevermind. *Psychological Bulletin, 83,* 213–217.

Waitzkin, H. (1991). *The politics of medical encounters: How patients and doctors deal with social problems.* New Haven, CT: Yale University Press.

Walton, D. (1992). *The place of emotion in argument.* University Park, PA: Pennsylvania State University Press.

Walton, D. (2008a). *Informal logic: A pragmatic approach* (2nd ed.). New York, NY: Cambridge University Press.

Walton, D. (2008b). *Witness testimony in evidence: Argumentation, artificial intelligence, and law.* New York, NY: Cambridge University Press.

Walton, D. N. (1992). *Slippery slope arguments.* Oxford, UK: Clarenden Press.

Walton, D. N. (1995). *A pragmatic theory of fallacy.* Tuscaloosa, AL: University of Alabama Press.

Walton, D. N. (1997a). *Appeal to pity: Argumentum ad misericordiam.* Boston, MA: Kluwer Academic.

Walton, D. N. (1997b). *Appeal to expert opinion: Arguments from authority.* University Park, PA: Pennsylvania State University Press

Wampold, B. E. (2001). *The great psychotherapy debate: Models, methods, and findings.* Mahwah, NJ: Erlbaum.

Wampold, B. E. (2006). The psychotherapist. In J. C. Norcross, L. E. Beutler, & R. F. Levant (Eds.), *Evidence-based practices in mental health: Debate and dialogue on the fundamental questions* (pp. 200–208). Washington, DC: American Psychological Association.

Wampold, B. E. (2010). The research evidence for the common factors models: A historically situated perspective. In B. M. Duncan, S. D. Miller, M. A. Hubble, & B. E. Wampold (Eds.), *The heart and soul of therapy* (2nd ed.) (pp. 49–82). Washington, DC: American Psychological Association.

Wampold, B. E., Imel, Z. E., & Miller, S. D. (2009). Barriers to the dissemination of empirically supported treatment: Matching messages to the evidence. *Behavior Therapist, 32*, 144–145.

Ward, M., Gruppen, L., & Regehr, G. (2002). Measuring self-assessment: Current state of the art. *Advances in Health Sciences Education, 7*, 63–80.

Watson, A. C., & Eack, S. M. (2011). Oppression and stigma and their effects. In N. R. Heller & A. Gitterman (Eds.), *Mental health and social problems: A social work perspective* (pp. 21–43). New York, NY: Routledge.

Watson, D. (2005). *Death sentences: How clichés, weasel words and management speak are strangling public language.* New York: Gotham.

Watson, D. L., & Tharp, R. G. (2007). *Self-directed behavior: Self-modification for personal adjustment* (8th ed.). Monterey, CA: Brooks/Cole.

Watson, T. S., & Steege, M. W. (2003). *Conducting school-based functional behavioral assessments.* New York, NY: Guilford.

Webster, Y. O. (1992). *The racialization of America.* New York, NY: St. Martin's Press.

Webster, Y. O. (1997). *Against the multicultural agenda: A critical thinking alternative.* Westport, CT: Praeger.

Webster's New World Dictionary (3rd ed.). (1988). New York, NY: Simon & Schuster.

Wegwarth, O., & Gigerenzer, G. (2011). Statistical illiteracy in doctors. In G. Gigerenzer & J. A. M. Gray (Eds.), *Better doctors, better patients, better decisions: Envisioning health care 2020* (pp. 137–151). Cambridge, MA: MIT Press.

Weinstein, C. E., & Rogers, B. T. (1985). Comprehension monitoring as a learning strategy. In G. d'Ydewalle (Ed.), *Cognition, information processing, and motivation* (pp. 619–629). New York, NY: Elsevier.

Weisberg, R. (1986). *Creativity, genius and other myths.* New York, NY: W.H. Freeman.

Weisburd, D., Lum, C. M., & Yang, S.-M. (2003). When can we conclude that treatments or programs "don't work"? *The ANNALS of the American Academy of Political and Social Science, 587*, 31–48.

Weiser, B. (2011, August 24). In New Jersey, rules are changed on witness ID. *New York Times.*

Weiss, J., & Brown, P. (1977). *Self-insight error in the explanation of mood.* Unpublished manuscript, Harvard University.

Weisz, J., Suwanlert, S., Chaiyasit, W., & Walter, B. R. (1987). Over- and undercontrolled referral problems among children and adolescents from Thailand and the United States: The *wat* and *wai* of cultural differences. *Journal of Consulting and Clinical Psychology, 55*, 719–726.

Welch, H. G. (2004). *Should I be tested for cancer? Maybe not and here's why.* Berkeley, CA: University of California Press.

Welch, H. G., Schwartz, L., & Woloshin, S. (2011). *Overdiagnosed: Making people sick in the pursuit of health*. Boston, MA: Beacon Press.

Wells, G. L., & Lindsay, R. C. L. (1983). How do people infer the accuracy of eyewitness memory? Studies of performance and a metamemory analysis. In S. M. A. Lloyd-Bostock & B. R. Clifford (Eds.), *Evaluating witness evidence: Recent psychological research and new perspectives* (pp. 41–56). New York, NY: John Wiley & Sons.

Wells, G. L., Lindsay, R. C. L., & Ferguson, T. J. (1979). Accuracy, confidence, and juror perceptions in eyewitness identification. *Journal of Applied Psychology, 64*, 440–448.

Wennberg, J. E. (2002). Unwarranted variations in healthcare delivery: Implications for academic medical centers. *BMJ, 325*, 961–964.

Westermeyer, J. (1987). Cultural factors in clinical assessment. *Journal of Consulting and Clinical Psychology, 55*, 471–478.

When drug companies hide data. (2004, June 6). *The New York Times*, 12.

Whitehead, A. (1929). *The aims of education and other essays*. New York, NY: Dutton.

Whitfield, C. F., & Xie, S. X. (2002). Correlation of problem-based learning facilitators scores with student performance on written exams. *Advances in Health Sciences Education, 7*, 41–51.

Whitman, R. M., Kramer, M., & Baldridge, B. (1963). Which dreams does the patient tell? *Archives of General Psychiatry, 8*, 277–282.

Whitree v. New York State, 290 N.Y. 5. 2d 486 (Ct. Claims 1968).

Whittaker, R. (2002). *Mad in America*. Cambridge, MA: Perseus.

Whittaker, R. (2010). *Anatomy of an epidemic: Magic bullets, psychiatric drugs, and the astonishing rise of mental illness in America*. New York, NY: Crown.

Wilkes, M. S., & Hoffman, J. R. (2001). An innovative approach to educating medical students about pharmaceutical promotion. *Academic Medicine, 76*, 1271–1277.

Wilkins, L. T., Gottfredson, D. M., Robison, J. O., & Sadowsky, A. (1973). *Information selection and use in parole decision-making (Supp. Rep. 5)*. Davis, CA: National Council on Crime and Delinquency Research Center.

Willens, D., Cripps, R, Wilson, A., Wolff, K., & Rothman, R. (2011). Interdisciplinary team care for diabetic patients by primary care physicians, advanced practice nurses and clinical pharmacists. *Clinical Diabetes, 29*, 60–68.

Wills, T. A. (1978). Perceptions of clients by professional helpers. *Psychological Bulletin, 85*, 968–1000.

Wills, T. A. (1982). Nonspecific factors in helping relationships. In T. A. Wills (Ed.), *Basic processes in helping relationships* (pp. 381–404). Orlando, FL: Academic Press.

Wilmshurst, P. (2011). Editorial. The regulation of medical devices. *BMJ, 342:d2822*.

Wilson, J. A. (2001). Pseudoscientific beliefs among college students. *Reports of the National Center for Science Education, 21*, 9–36.

Wilson, J. M. G., & Jungner, G. (1968). *Principles and practice of screening for disease*. WHO Public Health Papers No. 34. Geneva, Switzerland: World Health Organization.

Witte, C. L., Witte, M. H., & Kerwin, A. (1994). Suspended judgment: Ignorance and the process of learning and discovery in medicine. *Controlled Clinical Trials, 15*, 1–4.

Wolf, F. M. (2000). Summarizing evidence for clinical use. In J. P. Geyman, R. A. Deyo, & S. D. Ramsey (Eds.), *Evidence-based clinical practice: Concepts and approaches* (pp. 133–143). Boston, MA: Butterworth-Heineman.

Woll, S. (2002). *Everyday thinking: Memory, reasoning and judgment in the real world*. Mahwah, NJ: Erlbaum.

Woloshin, S. & Schwartz, L. M. (2011, July 4). Think inside the box. *The New York Times*.

Woloshin, S., Schwartz, L. M., & Welch, G. (2008). *Know your chances: Understanding health statistics*. Berkeley, CA: University of California Press.

Woltmann, E. M., Wilkniss, S. M., Teachout, A., McHugo, G. J., & Drake, R. E. (2011). Trial of an electronic decision support system to facilitate shared decision making in community mental health. *Psychiatric Services, 62*, 54–60.

Wood, D. F. (2003). Clinical review: ABC of learning and teaching in medicine; Problem based learning. *BMJ, 326*, 328–330.

Woods, D. D., & Cook, R. I. (1999). Perspectives on human error: Hindsight biases and local rationality. In F. T. Durso, R. S. Nickerson, R. W. Schzaneveldt, S. T. Dumais, D. S. Lindsay, & M. T. Chi (Eds.), *Handbook of applied cognition* (pp. 141–171). New York, NY: John Wiley & Sons.

Woodward, K. L. (2004, May 28). A political sacrament. *The New York Times*, Sect. A, 21.

Woolf, S. H., Kuzel, A. J., Dovey, S. M., & Phillips, R. L. (2004). A string of mistakes: The importance of cascade analysis in describing, counting, and preventing medical errors. *Annals of Family Medicine, 2*, 317–326.

Worthman, C. M., Plotsky, P. M., Schlecter, D. S., & Cummings, C. A. (2010). *Emotive experience: The interaction of caregiving, culture and developmental psychobiology*. New York, NY: Cambridge University Press.

Wosinka, W., Cialdini, R. B., Barrett, D. W., & Reykowski, J. (Eds.). (2001). *The practice of social influence in multiple cultures*. Mahwah, NJ: Erlbaum.

Wright, R. H. (2005). The myth of continuing education: A look at some intended and (maybe) unintended consequences. In R. H. Wright & N. A. Cummings (Eds.), *Destructive trends in mental health: A well-intentioned path to harm* (pp. 143–151). New York, NY: Routledge.

Wright, A., Sittig, D. F., Ash, J. S., Feblowitz, J., Meltzer, S., McMullen, C., et al. (2011). Development and evaluation of a comprehensive clinical decision support taxonomy: comparison of front-end tools in commercial and internally developed electronic health record systems. *Journal of American Medical Association* doi:10.1136/amiajnl-2011-000133.

Wright, R. H., & Cummings, N. A. (Eds.). (2005). *Destructive trends in mental health: The well-intentioned path to harm.* New York, NY: Routledge.

Wu, A. W., Cavanaugh, T. A., McPhee, S. J., & Micco, G. P. (1997). To tell the truth: Ethical and practical issues in disclosing medical mistakes to patients. *Journal of General Internal Medicine, 12,* 770–775.

Wu, A. W., Folkman, S., McPhee, S. J., & Lo, B. (2003). Do house officers learn from their mistakes? *Quality and Safety in Health Care, 12,* 221–226.

Ying, Y. (2002). The conception of depression in Chinese Americans. In K. S. Kurasaki, S. Okazaki, & S. Stanley (Eds.), *Asian American mental health: Assessment theories and methods* (pp. 173–183). New York, NY: Kluwer Academic/Plenum Publishers.

Young, J. H. (1992). *American health quackery.* Princeton, NJ: Princeton University Press.

Zarocostas, J. (2007). Community care could prevent deaths of thousands of severely malnourished children. *BMJ, 334*:1239 (16 June).

Zegiob, L., Arnold, S., & Forehand, R. (1975). An examination of observer effects in parent-child interaction. *Child Development, 46,* 509–512.

Zhang, J., Patel, V. L., Johnson, T. R., & Shortliffe, E. H. (2004). A cognitive taxonomy of medical errors. *Journal of Biomedical Informatics, 37,* 193–204.

Zilbergeld, B. (1983). *The shrinking of America: Myths of psychological change.* Boston, MA: Little, Brown.

Zimbardo, P. (2007). *The Lucifer effect: Understanding how good people turn evil.* New York, NY: Random House.

Zsambok, C. E., & Klein, G. (Eds.). (1997). *Naturalistic decision making.* Mahwah, NJ: Erlbaum.

About the Author

Eileen Gambrill is the Hutto Patterson Professor of Child and Family Studies in the School of Social Welfare at the University of California at Berkeley. She received her BA degree from the University of Pennsylvania, her MSW degree from Bryn Mawr School of Social Work and Social Research, and her PhD degree from the University of Michigan in Social Work and Psychology. She has been a visiting scholar at the University of Oxford and Tel Aviv University and received a Benjamin Meeker Fellowship from the University of Bristol in 1999. She has won two Pro Humanitate Awards from the North American Resource Center for Child Welfare, one in 2001 and another in 2004. Her areas of interest include professional decision making, ethics, and the integration of research and practice in the helping professions. Books include *Social Work Practice: A Critical Thinker's Guide* (3rd ed.; 2012), *Critical Thinking for Helping Professionals—A skills-based workbook* (3rd ed.; with Len Gibbs, 2009), and *Propaganda in the Helping Professions* (2012).

Gambrill served as Editor-in-Chief of *Social Work Research and Abstracts* from 1984 to 1988, and as Editor-in-Chief of the *Journal of Social Work Education* from 2000 to 2003. She was elected by Division 25 members to serve on the Council of Representatives of the American Psychological Association from 2003 to 2005 and elected to the Board of Directors of the Council on Social Work Education from 2000 to 2002. She is a licensed psychologist in the state of California.

Author Index

Subject Index